The Life of Goethe

Frontispiece Goethe. Oil portrait by J. K. Stieler, 1828 (Neue Pinakothek, Munich).

The Life of
GOETHE

A Critical Biography

John R. Williams

First published 1998

Reprinted 2000

Blackwell Publishers Ltd
108 Cowley Road
Oxford OX4 1JF
UK

Blackwell Publishers Inc.
350 Main Street
Malden, Massachusetts 02148
USA

British Library Cataloguing in Publication Data

A CIP catalogue record for this book is available from the British Library.

Library of Congress Cataloging-in-Publication Data

Williams, John R., 1940–
The life of Goethe: a critical biography / John R. Williams.
p. cm. — (Blackwell critical biographies; 10)
Includes bibkiographical references and index.
ISBN 0–631–16376–X (alk. paper)
1. Goethe, Johann Wolfgang von, 1749–1832. 2. Authors, German – 18th
century – Biography. 3. Authors, German – 19th century – Biography.
I. Title. II. Series.
PT2049.W55 1998
831'6—dc21
   [B]   97-32840
                                                        CIP

Typeset in 10 on 11 pt Baskerville
By Best-set Typesetter Ltd., Hong Kong
Printed in Great Britain by T.J. International, Padstow, Cornwall

This book is printed on acid-free paper

Er Cof Annwyl
am
Llewelyn Williams 1901–1995
Mary Williams née Davies 1902–1996

Contents

List of Plates

The author and publishers are grateful to the following for permission to reproduce plates:

Stiftung Weimarer Klassik, Weimar: nos 5, 6, 9, 10, 13–17, 19, 23, 33. Photos: Sigrid Geske.
Goethe-Museum Düsseldorf Anton-und-Katharina-Kippenberg-Stiftung: nos 2, 3, 11, 12, 20, 24, 25, 27, 28, 31, 32, 35. Photos: Walter Klein.
Goethe-Museum Frankfurt Freies Deutsches Hochstift: nos 1, 4, 7, 8, 18, 21, 22, 26, 30. Photos: Ursula Edelmann.
Hamburger Theatersammlung, University of Hamburg: no. 29.
Department of Rare Books and Special Collections, Princeton University Library: no. 34.
Bayerische Staatsgemäldesammlungen, Munich: Frontispiece.

Preface

By a 'critical biography' I have understood a substantial critical account of a writer's creative works set in the context of his life and times. Of the two main approaches proposed by the series editor, I have chosen to present the narrative of Goethe's life before proceeding to a critical discussion of his works, rather than to merge critical discussion within a continuous biographical narrative. This is by no means in order to isolate biography from criticism, nor is it to suggest that a writer's life and works are separate, or even distinguishable, but in order to establish a firm biographical and historical base from which to proceed to an informed critical discussion. Indeed, I hope the account of Goethe's life and works in this volume will make it clear that his creative works follow a distinct biographical profile, while also demonstrating that the imaginative works can never be adequately accounted for in terms of biography alone.

The broad lines of Goethe's life, both private and public, can be discerned above all in his poetry, where literary influences, personal experience and imaginative originality combine to produce an astonishingly varied but coherent corpus of lyrical work. While his major dramas have exemplary status, they are also unmistakably the product of a writer who moved from youthful radicalism to a formal neo-classicism, from the specifically historical to a 'typological', allegorical and symbolic mode of expression; they also remain the work of the man who moved from the patrician class of a civic and urban environment in Frankfurt am Main to become a minister of state and leading eminence of the small but peculiarly distinguished court of the Duchy of Weimar. His minor dramas, libretti and occasional theatrical writings are even more clearly the product of his environment and his obligations; beyond this, some of them record his efforts to come to terms with the political issues of his day, in particular with the profound upheaval of the French Revolution and his country's experience of its historical aftermath. His narrative work, too, whether at its most classicizing and stylized in *Hermann und Dorothea*, or at its most allusive, fragmented and 'modern' in *Wilhelm Meisters Wanderjahre*, bears the stamp of his life and times. Conversely and paradoxically, his autobiographical work is an imaginative elaboration of personal experience into an almost fictional genre of 'poetry and truth'. To the biographical and critical sections of this book I have added a chapter on Goethe's science, an activity that also meshes with his personal and professional biography, and without which no study of Goethe is complete – even if this was done at the expense of an extended discussion of his aesthetic theory and his writings on art and literature.

This volume owes a great intellectual debt to many different sources in many different ways. It does not aim to match the comprehensive study of Goethe by Nicholas Boyle in scope, the shorter studies by F. J. Lamport and T. J. Reed in concision and synthesis, or the Goethe scholarship of E. M. Wilkinson in originality of insight; it seeks to introduce and explain Goethe's life and creative work to the student of literature, and to an English-speaking public with varying degrees of familiarity with German, in as accessible a form as possible. The discussion of Goethe's work proceeds generically and, with certain exceptions, chronologically within the generic categories. Such an arrangement, after the opening account of Goethe's life, involves some necessary overlapping but, it is hoped, not too much reiteration. This structure is designed to draw attention to Goethe's achievements in the various literary genres, as well as to help the reader or student who might otherwise approach the daunting corpus of Goethe's creative writing with some apprehension. As I have indicated in chapter two, the selection of poems chosen for particular critical attention is based on Erich Trunz's anthology in the *Hamburger Ausgabe*, which is likely to remain in print as a separate volume for some time; I am grateful to the Verlag C. H. Beck of Munich for their agreement to this.

All quotes in German have been translated into English. Where prose translations have been given, literal accuracy has been sought; with verse translations, including the translations of titles and first lines, word-for-word rendering has been given secondary consideration to fidelity of metre, rhythm, rhyme and diction, in an attempt to give readers who have little German some sense of Goethe's poetic expression. All translations in the text are my own; readers without German are also referred to the section of the bibliography listing Goethe's works in translation.

I have to acknowledge many specific debts of gratitude. To the Directors and staff of the Goethe Museums and Archives in Düsseldorf, Frankfurt and Weimar, especially for their help in compiling the illustrations and for permission to publish them; to the staff of St Andrews University Library; to Tony Butler and Bob Crawford for scientific advice, and to Barry Nisbet specifically for guidance on aspects of Goethe's meteorology; to Frank and Nanna Lamport for hilarity, and for help with Danish perplexities; to John Sullivan for help with Slavonic details; to the series editor, Claude Rawson, and quite especially to my commissioning editor Andrew McNeillie, for their generous patience and warm encouragement. To my wife Elizabeth, as always, I owe the greatest debt of all.

John R. Williams
St Andrews, January 1998

1

The Life

The Age of Goethe – or the *Goethezeit*, to use a term much derided because of its centralization of, and around, Goethe – is an arbitrary period useful principally to biographers and bibliographers; and yet its continued use indicates how comprehensively the period was, or is perceived to have been, dominated by one man and his literary achievement. Goethe's life is remarkable not only for its productive output in both quality and quantity, in terms of his original and comprehensive contribution to literature and other disciplines, but also in the historical era it spans. Born into the middle of the eighteenth century, into a Germany of late feudal absolutism, a Germany fragmented into the myriad constituent states of the Holy Roman Empire of the German Nation, into the last century of the Reich that did, in one form or another, just, last a thousand years, he died at a time when Germany, or the German Confederation, was beginning to coalesce into a modern nation state. Politically, his life spanned the Seven Years War and the consolidation of Prussian hegemony under Frederick the Great, the War of American Independence and its European counterpart, the French Revolution; the Napoleonic convulsions of Europe that followed; the subsequent – and consequent – collapse of the Western German Empire in 1806, and the tentative re-emergence of Prussian dominance that began from that nadir. He witnessed the restoration of neo-feudal monarchy in France, and in Germany the re-establishment of a system of modified absolutism after the Congress of Vienna – modified because the princes of the Confederation were in thrall to Metternich's foreign policy. At the end of his life he experienced, vicariously but vividly and with great alarm, the July Revolution in Paris, when he feared above all, as he put it, 'a reprise of the tragedy of 1790'.[1]

Goethe's experience of the 'tragedy' of the French Revolution was not first-hand, either; but he did share the appalling privations and miseries of a military campaign of the day to witness the aftermath of revolution in north-eastern France when he accompanied the invading counter-revolutionary forces of the Austro-Prussian coalition army in 1792 as far as Valmy, and he watched at dangerously close quarters the cannonade that turned the tide of foreign intervention in the French Revolution. Indeed, he even claimed to diagnose in that German defeat the emergence of 'a new epoch in world history' – and he did in fact say something to that effect, at least, at the time, even if his classic formulation actually dates from rather later.[2] For much of his subsequent life Goethe struggled to come to terms with the most momentous political upheaval of his age, acknowledging the causes of the Revolution without ever being fully able to accept its effects. And yet the common perception of Goethe as the 'lackey of princes', as a political quietist or reactionary who would by his own admission rather countenance an injustice than tolerate disorder, is a partial caricature. He was more than aware of the corruption, frivolity and irresponsibility of a decadent *ancien régime*; he was more than aware of, and worked assiduously to promote, the duties and obligations of the ruling class – and his relations with his own ruler, Karl August of Sachsen-Weimar-Eisenach, were often strained as a result. Even his notorious dictum on injustice and disorder is quite misleading out of its context; indeed, there is a striking irony in the incident, which took place in the vicious aftermath of the Siege of Mainz in 1793. The revolutionary régime in Mainz, briefly sustained by French military forces and by some German Jacobins, capitulated under honourable terms and was expelled under a royal guarantee of safe conduct; but a number of revolutionary sympathizers were left to the mercy of the Mainz counter-revolutionaries. Goethe intervened, with some pomposity but also with some personal courage, as one wretch was about to be lynched – because, as he pronounced to a friend, he preferred to sanction an injustice rather than tolerate disorder, because the rule of law was paramount over mob rule or acts of arbitrary revenge, whatever his own repugnance for the revolutionary fellow-travellers of Mainz.

Goethe's life spanned profound changes in the social order. While historical change was less spectacularly convulsive than in neighbouring France, he saw the profound shift from social, political and intellectual immaturity, even impotence, on the part of the educated German middle classes, as absolutism gave way to something resembling constitutional rule; he saw the educational reforms of Wilhelm von Humboldt and the administrative reforms of Karl Freiherr vom Stein (and he knew both men closely); he saw the legal reforms that sprang from the abolition of the *Reichskammergericht*, the supreme court of the Holy Roman Empire – which Goethe himself served briefly in Wetzlar in 1772. He was born into a Germany whose primitive agricultural and manufacturing infrastructure was dominated respectively by the vested interests of landowners and trade guilds; he witnessed, and took an informed interest in, the agricultural revolution and the beginnings of industrial revolution. By the end of his life, steam power had been introduced into industry, and even steam locomotion on rivers, canals and railways; he knew of Robert Owen's experiments in model industrial communities, and he discussed speculatively the building of canals in Suez, in Panama and between the Rhine and the Danube.

Goethe's life began in the early stages of the German Enlightenment, the age of Voltaire and Frederick the Great; it continued through the development of German Idealist philosophy, the age of Kant, Hegel and Schopenhauer, and it ended shortly before the emergence of Marxist thought, some fifteen years before the *Communist Manifesto*. His literary career began in the era of Gallic neo-classicism under the absolute authority of Gottsched (whom he visited as a student in Leipzig); he experienced, and contributed centrally to, the German pre-romantic *Sturm und Drang*, to German Classicism and Romanticism; and it ended at the point where the radical visionary writer Georg Büchner was studying anatomy in Strasbourg, and shortly after he moved to Paris. He lived through, and also contributed crucially to, the emergence of the German language and German literature from a position of neglect and even contempt, when the King of Prussia himself could dismiss his own tongue as uncouth and barbarous, to a status of parity among European cultures as the language of 'a people of poets and thinkers'.[3]

Outwardly, Goethe's career charts a rising social curve from the status of a moder-ately prominent and prosperous *Bürger* family of Frankfurt am Main to the minor nobility of the small duchy of Sachsen-Weimar, with the title of von Goethe and the status of Privy Councillor and Minister of State. But while he accepted, and perhaps sought, social position, his career was scarcely that of a social *arriviste* or courtier. For all the odium heaped on him by contemporary and subsequent tendentious ideologies, for all the perception of him as an establishment reaction-ary who had betrayed his youthful radicalism, for all that he observed courtly protocols and etiquettes with studied punctiliousness, for all that he willingly joined the careful dance of aristocratic society, whether at the Weimar court or relaxing in the teeming gossip of the Bohemian spas, for all that his relations with the ruling house of Weimar were conducted with often exaggerated tact and decorum – for all that, he displayed a frequently stubborn, even perverse sense of social independ-ence. As a *Bürger*, however famous, talented or charismatic, he was never fully integrated into the court circles of Weimar, even after his title of nobility in 1782. While a bosom friend of the young Duke, a favourite and confidant of the ruler and his wife, he was forever conscious that Karl August was his ruler and his patron, his source of income and preferment, for himself and for some close friends; and yet he did not flinch from disagreement, even from confrontation, with his ruler on social and political issues – or, famously, in 1817, when he resigned his position as Director of the Court Theatre in Weimar, ostensibly over the trivial issue of animals on stage, in fact because of growing differences and tensions on artistic and administrative policy. His programme of mildly radical social and political reforms during the 1780s foundered on the Duke's military ambitions, whereupon Goethe abruptly quit Weimar for Italy – though not before he had carefully assured his financial position. But anyone who craved acceptance by court circles would scarcely, as Goethe did immediately after his return from Italy, take as his mistress the socially quite unsuitable Christiane Vulpius – who, while no plebian as is often assumed, but from a literate if impoverished family, was not to become his wife until some eighteen years later.

The raw young writer who arrived in Weimar from the more relaxed artistic and intellectual circles of Strasbourg, Darmstadt and Wetzlar was ill at ease, in a socially precarious and financially insecure position. His initial wildness, encour-aged by his patron and fed by his sensational literary reputation, was tamed and refined under the decorous, if also constricting and possessive, tutelage of

Charlotte von Stein, whose position in the court was unassailable. And if Goethe in these early years in Weimar rid himself with some brusqueness of earlier, less tractable companions such as the unhappy poet Lenz, who evidently breached the rules of etiquette in an obscure but outrageous way – his brutality towards such unwelcome ghosts from the past has also been tendentiously exaggerated, diverting attention from his many acts of generosity towards fellow writers and artists in terms of cash, advice, encouragement or recommendation. Cold, aloof and unapproachable as Goethe seemed to many importunate or diffident individuals, his outward defences were those of a man himself not wholly secure, not wholly in sympathy with his own age, a man whose sublime or 'Olympian' indifference and detachment masked an often agonized struggle to achieve a balance between extremes of behaviour or opinion, a struggle to maintain what he expressly called his poetic duty to preserve an open-minded impartiality or serenity in the face of apparently irreconcilable doctrines.[4]

Goethe's status, not just his status for posterity, but his own self-esteem and the esteem of his contemporaries, rests not on his personal behaviour or his social advancement, but on his achievement in the republic of letters: on his achievement principally as a poet, secondarily as a man of immense intellectual versatility and prodigious intellectual energy, of an eclecticism and productivity that is almost unbelievable to a less leisured and more specialized age, and which was quite exceptional even for his own time. And for all his outward conformism in matters of behaviour or etiquette, Goethe was not a man to kowtow to the establishment, whether political, religious or intellectual. His critical stance towards the Berlin court of Friedrich Wilhelm II or even, occasionally, his own prince, his notorious scepticism towards the liberation of Germany from Napoleonic rule, his often savagely scathing attitudes towards the orthodox church, Catholic or Protestant, bear this out – as does his obsessive and ultimately wrong-headed, but for all that fearless and sustained campaign against Newtonian physics and against the established scientific orthodoxy of his day.

The received image of Goethe today, in its more negative aspects, is very much a reactive function of the uncritical adulation of Goethe as an official cultural exemplar for successive generations in Germany, of his ideological elevation as a national monument, exploited, sanitized, bowdlerized or otherwise distorted. More even-handed assessments of Goethe's works and personality, many of recent origin, have drawn attention to the more impulsively generous, fallibly human and even ribald elements of his self and his writing alongside the sometimes disturbingly pompous, frigid or brutal persona, and have revealed an often contradictory and perverse, but always complex and subtle man of his age.

EARLY YEARS: FRANKFURT AND LEIPZIG 1749–70

The city of Frankfurt am Main in which Goethe was born and raised was in the mid-eighteenth century a prosperous merchant and banking town of some 36,000 inhabitants. Predominantly Lutheran, with substantial Catholic and Calvinist minorities and a small Jewish ghetto, it was fiercely conscious of its quasi-republican status as a Free Imperial City of the Holy Roman Empire – sprawling, ramshackle and even abstract though that institution had by now become. Certain freedoms and privileges attached to its status, which was given symbolic legitimation by the tradition that any future Emperor, before his imperial coronation in Aachen, was crowned as German (or, formally, as 'Roman') King in the cathedral at Frankfurt: Goethe's autobiography gives a lengthy account of the formal election and coronation of Joseph II in 1764, when the fourteen-year-old witnessed the pomp and ceremony of these elaborate proceedings.[5] Closely associated with these events in Goethe's recollection is a curious and still opaque minor scandal involving the so-called 'Frankfurt Gretchen', with whom the young boy spent an innocent night when he forgot his house-keys. This friendship or infatuation led him into raffish company; he was even officially interrogated on his involvement with a group suspected of criminal activities. Though the affair was without serious consequences to himself, Goethe saw fit to report his experiences at some length when he came to write his life story very much later; it evidently left its mark emotionally, even if the identity of 'Gretchen' – a resonant name for Goethe – is obscure. Indeed, it is not clear that that was her true name; it is thought possible, not that she inspired the name of the heroine of *Faust* Part One, but rather that Goethe retrospectively gave the name of his fictitious heroine to the girl in Frankfurt.

Goethe was the issue of two prosperous but not especially distinguished families, established and respected, though neither had been in Frankfurt for more than a century: the Goethes were originally from Thuringia, the Textors from Franconia – the latter claiming descent from the sixteenth-century painter Lukas Cranach. The wealth of the Goethes (or, a generation back, the Göthes) was based on trade; the Textors were lawyers. Johann Caspar Goethe had also studied law, and at the age of thirty-two had used his wealth and some influence to purchase the title of Imperial Councillor (*Kaiserlicher Rat*), a scarcely more than honorific office that brought prestige but no specific professional occupation. He had completed his education by means of a Grand Tour to Austria, Italy, Paris and the Netherlands, and had amassed a considerable collection of books and paintings. His written and oral accounts of his travels made a profound impression on his son, and no doubt implanted in his young mind the dream of southern landscape and architecture that was to haunt him until he finally realized that dream himself in his late thirties.

Although Goethe was, in a much-quoted little verse jingle,[6] to attribute to his father his sense of the proper seriousness of living, and to his mother his imaginative and creative gifts, Johann Caspar Goethe was a man of leisure, a *rentier* rather than a hard-working careerist. The poet's mother Katharina Elisabeth was the lively-minded daughter of the *Schultheiß* (the senior professional civic administrator who presided with the two *Bürgermeister* elected from the 'benches' of the city council) Johann Wolfgang Textor; Goethe pays fond tribute to this even-tempered old gentleman after whom he was named, in whose well-tended garden the Goethe children spent happy times, and who was credited with (or claimed for himself) the gift of second sight – especially where his own promotions and preferments were concerned. The marriage of Goethe's parents was celebrated on 20 August 1748; on 29 August 1749 Johann Wolfgang was the firstborn. A sister, Cornelia, followed little more than a year later; she was to be her brother's close companion and *confidante* in a fiercely interdependent sibling relationship – though more intensely so on her side – and after a brief and unhappy marriage was to die at the age of twenty-seven. Of the other four children only one survived infancy, to die aged six. Family mortality was, even for the time, high – a mortality of which the poet, for all his affirmative and fundamentally positive spiritual outlook, was keenly aware: only one of his own five children survived infancy, and he himself was to survive that son by two years.

We are led to believe by Goethe's own account that his childhood and boy-hood in Frankfurt were, if not idyllically, then certainly more than usually happy times; and even allowing for retrospective nostalgia or conscious image-building, there is no reason to doubt that, while he suffered his share of childhood illness and trauma, this was broadly true. He was mostly, at this stage at least, on good terms with his father, and always enjoyed a fond relationship with an indulgent, unaffectedly cheerful and outgoing, if at times unconventional and even eccentric, mother. Though a precociously gifted youngster, he was no infant prodigy in the manner of Mozart, who was even then being paraded around Europe by his father; in August 1763 Goethe heard a concert by the seven-year-old in Frankfurt. The gift of a puppet-theatre from his grandmother set Goethe to dragoon his friends into a less than ideal audience – though it is unlikely that it played such a crucial role in his imaginative development as that of his fictional hero Wilhelm Meister. We are also told that the Lisbon earthquake delivered a severe shock to his religious sensibilities at the age of seven, to his perception of the deity as creator and preserver – but here again, it is not easy to sort retrospective wisdom from immediate experience.[7] Certainly, the imagery he uses to describe the 'explosion' of Lisbon, its effect on distant wells and springs, is part of the imagery of his old age; Voltaire may also have helped to colour his memory of the event.

The Seven Years War left its mark on the Goethe household; the Prussian sympathies of his father – or, more precisely, his admiration for Frederick the Great – led not only to tensions with the Textor family, but more dramatically to a brusque confrontation with the French officer, François de Théas, Comte de Thoranc, who had been billeted on the Goethes after the occupation of Frankfurt by French troops in 1759. But for the younger Goethe, French occupation and the presence of a cultured and amiable Frenchman in the house meant an expansion of linguistic and cultural horizons: in the French theatre of the garrison, he was introduced to the classical repertoire of Molière (of which he followed little) and, more memorably, to the formal alexandrines of *tragédie classique*, as well as the popular plays of Marivaux, Destouches and Nivelle de la Chaussée. Tuition in drawing and music supplemented his routine studies; his early education was in any case undertaken by private tutors who provided more specialized instruction after his father had taught the fundamentals. He had a good knowledge of Latin, French and Italian, some knowledge of Greek and Hebrew and, by the age of sixteen, sufficient command of English to attempt a less than perfect but still commendable poem, 'A Song over the Unconfidence towards Myself'. The young

Goethe's precocity was nourished by the indulgence of the more distinguished friends of his father who frequented the house: Johann Daniel von Olenschlager, the *Bürgermeister* of Frankfurt, who published a commentary to the Golden Bull of Charles IV, encouraged his historical and theatrical interests. He read widely; one of the most influential texts of his boyhood was Klopstock's vast religious epic *Der Messias* (The Messiah), and he was familiar with Homer, Tasso, the classical French dramatists and, oddly but subsequently of some influence on his poetic imagination and imagery, the Arabian Nights Tales. The Bible was of course required reading for the son of a moderately devout Lutheran household; Goethe's familiarity with the biblical texts was extensive well before Herder encouraged him to read them not as holy scripture, but as an ethnic and poetic epic of the ancient world.

At his father's insistence rather than according to his own plans or desires, Goethe was sent at the age of sixteen to study law at Leipzig University in 1765. Here he found a city quite unlike Frankfurt in architecture, language, fashion and political administration: courtly, self-regarding and self-consciously smart, setting the social, cultural and educational standards, in thrall to the canon of French neo-classicism. Johann Christoph Gottsched, the awesome pundit of German letters, who exercised despotic control over literary fashion via a network of influence, patronage, weekly magazines, theatres and publishing houses, also dictated through his own lectures and treatises the pre-eminence of neo-classical models. The theatre, above all the theatre of seventeenth-century France, was the benchmark for a renascent German literature: plays should be in alexandrines, Racinian or Cornelian in structure – if not actually translated from the French, they should aspire to give the impression that they had been. Gottsched's was a serious, high-minded and dogmatic programme – a prescriptive and indeed derivative one, too, in which frivolities like opera, ribald farce or bombastic *Haupt- und Staatsaktionen* (grand-guignol dramas of conspiracies and treachery) were banned from the stage, and in which a stern didactic moral purpose was prescribed, for the instruction both of princes and of the respectable and increasingly prosperous middle class, whose economic and literary influence was rapidly making itself felt in its voracious appetite for reading material (novels, moral weeklies, fables, narrative and descriptive poems, treatises) and for theatrical entertainment.

Goethe left in his autobiography *Dichtung und Wahrheit* (Poetry and Truth) a brief but hilarious account of a visit to Gottsched with his future brother-in-law Schlosser.[8] Admitted prematurely to the presence owing to a misunderstanding with the servant, they surprised the great man with his huge bald head uncovered. As the servant handed him his full-bottomed wig, the professor calmly and skilfully clapped on his headpiece with one hand while he cuffed his valet soundly with the other – a scene straight out of the harlequinades the old man so roundly condemned in public performance – whereupon the patriarch dispatiated with great gravity and at great length upon literary matters.

In Leipzig Goethe caroused as a freshman (or *Fuchs*), studied little enough law, frequented the theatre, studied drawing seriously with Adam Friedrich Oeser, who had taught Winckelmann himself, and cultivated intense and varied friendships with the gregarious and almost violent affability that was to become the youthful Goethe's salient and most discussed (or deplored) characteristic. His relations with Oeser's daughter Friederike were warm, but proper; those with his landlord's daughter, Kätchen Schönkopf, probably innocent, but still intense and fraught with jealousies and tiffs. A close friend was the talented calligrapher Ernst Wolfgang Behrisch, a literary dandy and acerbic observer of the social and literary scene to whom Goethe wrote three gloomy odes that express an intensity of personal and introspective emotion unusual in his poetry at this time. Oddly, though he had enthused over a performance of *Minna von Barnhelm* (which had particular emotional and political significance for the Saxon audience in Leipzig these few years after the Seven Years War), when Lessing himself visited the town for some four weeks, Goethe made no effort to meet him. It is possible that this was due to Lessing's perceived attack on Winckelmann in his *Laokoon* – Winckelmann was murdered that same year in Trieste just as Oeser and his pupils, Goethe included, were excitedly preparing to welcome him in Leipzig; but Goethe did, in *Dichtung und Wahrheit*, warmly attest the revelation of Lessing's writings on art as well as his impact as a dramatist.

In the same account, Goethe also associates the death of Winckelmann with concern for his own state of health to the point where he, too, feared for his life. To be sure, the circumstances were less sensational than those of Trieste: chest pains, aggravated by a fall from his horse and not improved by an ill-advised diet or by drastically primitive Rousseauistic notions of treatment, culminated in a lung haemorrhage at the end of July 1768. The cause of the illness, which was grave enough to require a convalescence of some eighteen months in Frankfurt, is obscure. Goethe himself hints that it may have been in part psychic in origin – he speaks of a long-established depressive or 'hypochondriac' temperament, of extreme mood swings among the hectic student life of Leipzig; the most plausible physical explanation would be a tubercular infection. At all events, after a month of treatment and nursing he left Leipzig on 28 August, to his own great relief but to his father's dismay, to recover at home in Frankfurt.

Almost three years of desultory study at Leipzig had advanced Goethe's legal qualifications hardly at all. His literary output was also meagre – a light comedy and some collections of verse; he had burned much of his juvenile writing in a crisis of inadequacy in October 1767. Leipzig generally was an unproductive period for Goethe, a blind alley in personal and creative terms, a false start that seemed to end fittingly with his illness and his flight back to Frankfurt. To be sure, he grew up during these three years, and educated himself in a way he could not have done in his home town; but it seems that he found the fashionable and self-regarding ethos of 'little Paris' constricting and unappealing in the long run. His own adolescent insecurities and mood swings no doubt contributed to a less than fulfilling period in his life, and in retrospect he was dismissive or satirical about the formative influences of Leipzig and about his uncertain apprenticeship there to contemporary German culture.

Convalescence at home in Frankfurt was slow and uneven, a period of profound introversion and self-questioning. Relations with his father were, understandably enough, tense, those with his sister almost unhealthily close – at least for her emotional well-being. His mother had developed a close bond with Susanna von Klettenberg, who belonged to a quasi-Moravian sectarian group, and whose pietistic leanings drew on the cult of introspective mysticism fed by occult, neo-Platonic and hermetic traditions. This weird conflation of alchemy, mysticism and pious devotion Fräulein von Klettenberg gently pressed onto her spiritually receptive, indeed vulnerable young pupil; it was during this shadowy period of Goethe's life, when thoughts of death were never very far away, that he indulged most seriously in the tradition of what he called 'mystical–cabbalistic chemistry'.

It is impossible to say how far Goethe ever accepted the literal truth of such extravagant and arcane doctrines, of Nostradamus, Paracelsus or Agrippa von Nettesheim, of Böhme or Van Helmont or Welling; but he seems at the time to have been at least highly receptive to them in both practical and theoretical terms. As he put it, Fräulein von Klettenberg had 'inoculated' him with the disease of alternative science and medicine – which to be sure was even then still close enough to much conventional science: the physician treating Goethe practised a holistic medicine, prescribed alchemical preparations dispensed (illegally) by himself, and passed on to interested patients 'certain mystical chemical and alchemical books'.[9] Like Newton, his later scientific *bête noire*, Goethe retained a lifelong interest in the lore and mystery of alchemy, and remained alive to its poetic and philosophical symbolism – even if, as with the Greek mythology he later adopted as the basis of his aesthetic credo, he was always conscious of such systems as a source of poetic rather than of literal truth. And for all his later profound suspicion of pietistic introspection, he was to leave an affectionate, though by no means uncritical, tribute to the companion of his convalescence in the 'Bekenntnisse einer schönen Seele' (Confessions of a Noble Soul) of *Wilhelm Meisters Lehrjahre*, and possibly also in the eccentric and enigmatic figure of Makarie in the *Wanderjahre* (see below, pp. 224–5 and 243–4).

No doubt it was the passage of time, rest and devoted nursing, as much as the spiritual ministrations of Fräulein von Klettenberg or the concoctions of his physician, that enabled Goethe to emerge from the physical, emotional or psychic traumas of 1768–9; and this experience no doubt also informed much of his subsequent literary symbolism of recovery, recuperation and renewal, of the therapeutic power of sleep, time and natural metamorphosis – motifs that recur memorably in his later writings. And it was with a sense of liberation and of emergence from the cocoon of the family and of Frankfurt that Goethe set out to complete his legal studies, not entirely willingly – he would have preferred Göttingen – but at least with his father's blessing, in Strasbourg at the end of March 1770.

STRASBOURG 1770–1

If Leipzig had been a German, indeed a Saxon city, which fashionably aped French manners and culture, Strasbourg was a hybrid town in quite the reverse way. Politically and administratively French, it was in character quintessentially German, quaintly medieval rather than elegantly baroque, centred on the towering Gothic cathedral which at first repelled, then gradually captivated Goethe's imagination. To the young Goethe, schooled in the neo-classical doctrines of harmonious proportion and simple architectural symmetry, the Strasbourg Minster, with its extravagant decoration, ogival arches and soaring vaulting, its forest of pinnacles and buttresses, its lopsided western elevation with only one of the towers completed, confronted him as an alien, barbarous form, a fascination and a challenge to his education and his sensibilities. Returning again and again to view the 'monstrous' building at all times of day and night, climbing the ramshackle steps and ladders to the highest accessible pinnacle, he conquered both his acute fear of heights and his cultural prejudices in a disciplined effort of will. The result was a rhapsodic essay in which he (outrageously) hailed the Gothic style as the 'German' architectural form *per se*, and in which he gleefully derided the prevailing neo-classical style as derivative, feeble and foreign. Long before the Gothic Revival, indeed many years before the revival of medievalism in the Romantic rediscovery of the German past, his essay *Von deutscher Baukunst* (On German Architecture) is an erratic forerunner, in the spirit of the 1770s, of these later developments, an uncritical and breathless polemic in the fiercely anti-Latin spirit of the *Sturm und Drang* which was included as such in Herder's cultural manifesto *Von deutscher Art und Kunst* (On German Character and Art). It is a panegyric to the supposed 'architect' of the Strasbourg Minster, Erwin von Steinbach, the master-mason whose genius, for Goethe, had been to raise a *natural* monument to the glory of God, a monument whose parts stood in relation to the whole as the leaves and branches of a tree, and which by analogy echoed the immensely diverse but organically harmonious wholeness of nature.

But it was through personal contacts that Goethe's time in Strasbourg was to become the seminal and revelatory experience that so spectacularly unleashed his talents and his personality. His law studies were pursued dutifully but without commitment, and his enthusiasms were reserved for the Minster, for the Alsatian landscape, and for intense exchanges of ideas, for the cultural and literary stimulation that he found in company altogether more congenial than anything in Leipzig: Johann Heinrich Jung-Stilling, Heinrich Leopold Wagner, Jakob Michael Reinhold Lenz – and Johann Gottfried Herder, the abrasive and demanding mentor who was to be the Socratic midwife to Goethe's early genius, as he was to the spectacular, if short-lived, creative renewal of national German literature that was to be labelled sensationally and fortuitously by subsequent historians as *Sturm und Drang*: Storm and Stress.

Herder's presence in Strasbourg was itself fortuitous: he arrived there for the treatment of a painful eye infection in September 1770, six months later than Goethe, after a long journey by sea from Riga to Nantes – a voyage vividly presented as a cultural odyssey in his *Journal meiner Reise im Jahr 1769* (Journal of my Journey in 1769). He had already achieved a considerable reputation as a preacher and literary critic; he had studied at Königsberg, where Kant taught, and was a friend and correspondent of the obscurely sibylline scourge of rationalism, the legendary 'Magus of the North', Johann Georg Hamann. This, and his seniority of five years, put him from the start in the position of tutor, indeed of taskmaster, to the young Goethe – a tutelage Goethe was to outgrow, and a relationship that was to become increasingly soured over the years, but one that Goethe always acknowledged as crucial to his emergence as a poet, indeed as a man.

For Herder's gospel was stimulatingly subversive; against prevailing neo-classical and Gallic doctrines, he led Goethe away from the tyranny of Gottsched more radically than even Lessing could have done, inspiring enthusiasms for German cultural exemplars, for the era of the German Reformation, for the virile language of Luther, for the (perceived) rough-hewn and robust art of Dürer and of Hans Sachs; for the vigorous, if anarchic, feudalism of sixteenth-century Germany, for the legendary chivalry of the reign of Maximilian I, for Justus Möser's patriotic celebration of late feudal legal, social and economic systems, of *Faustrecht* and of an imagined freedom under the loose but sacred commonwealth of the Holy Roman Empire. It was a fanciful and idealized vision of the German past; but it was a vision of a national past that was to give German writers and intellectuals a sense of atavistic pride and a source of native material that was not derived vicariously from an alien Gallic and courtly tradition. National renewal was also sought, poetically and linguistically, in folk song and folk tales – the native genius of the German people expressed anonymously and spontaneously by the unlettered *Volk*. To be sure, Herder's enthusiasms were not narrowly chauvinistic: while he had Goethe scouring the Alsatian countryside for folk songs from the mouths of toothless peasants, his own vision was eclectic, international and anthropological. His collection of folk songs is entitled the *Stimmen der Völker in Liedern* (Voices of the Peoples in Songs), his perception of natural, unaffected 'folk' culture extended to Lappland and Denmark, England and Scotland, even to American Indian cultures; his notion of folk epic embraced the tradition of oral transmission from the Old Testament to Homer to the Norse sagas to Macpherson's Ossianic fragments of Gaelic poetry.

Paradoxically enough, Herder's chief champion in his war on Gallic influences in German culture was another foreigner: Shakespeare. Sensing a Germanic affinity with the English bard that he missed with Latin civilizations, Herder proclaimed Shakespeare the poet of unvarnished nature, the 'interpreter of nature in all her tongues'.[10] It was this fanciful but infectious enthusiasm, carried to the point of incoherence in parts of his own delirious essay on Shakespeare, that Herder communicated to a Goethe whose previous knowledge of the English playwright had been limited to some of Dodd's *Beauties of Shakespeare*. And Goethe's equally delirious reception of Shakespeare is attested in his breathless speech *Zum Schäkespears Tag* (On Shakespeare's Anniversary) of 1771 – an uncritical rhapsody written in Frankfurt, but echoing the momentous revelations of the Strasbourg years.

The other significant personal encounter in Strasbourg was Goethe's most serious love affair hitherto. It is impossible to distinguish fact from fiction or legend, sexual reality from wish fulfilment, in Goethe's brief, intense and subsequently outrageously mythologized relationship with Friederike Brion, the evidently attractive and unaffected pastor's daughter from Sesenheim. His own retrospective account in *Dichtung und Wahrheit* appears to draw on his own poems of the time, on literary models like *The Vicar of Wakefield*, on his own self-compensating imagination, and perhaps also on an uneasy conscience, as much as on sober or accurate recollection, in order to construct a charming rural idyll around the Brion family. His own infectious energy and his much-attested personal charisma helped to create a series of lively domestic and rural episodes during his frequent visits to the village, where he found a surrogate family as well as a refuge from the intense intellectualism of his Strasbourg circle. The legend of Friederike is further veiled in layers of romantic speculation and sensationalism: the unhappy and deranged poet Lenz is supposed to have courted the girl abandoned by Goethe in a grotesque or pathetic attempt at *imitatio*. Goethe undoubtedly did abandon Friederike, but under what circumstances and for what motives, is unclear. There evidently was great affection on both sides, but what degree of intimacy or of personal commitment there was, is also uncertain. One of the poems most closely associated with Friederike, 'Heidenröslein', suggests very vividly a process of seduction, of defloration and betrayal; but this is *Dichtung*, not *Wahrheit*.

It would appear that Goethe's overriding personal imperative at this time, indeed for many years to come, was an unwillingness to settle, even a fear of sexual and emotional commitment, allied to a considerable ruthlessness in pursuing his destiny, however obscurely perceived, that drove him to ride roughshod over his own highly volatile feelings – and over those of others. It was not so much that he was reluctant to introduce a charming but countrified child of the manse to his sophisticated circle in Strasbourg, or to his family in Frankfurt, but rather that at the age of twenty-two he shied away from any permanent commitment as a check to his still immature plans for a career of which he was as yet quite uncertain, for a personal development or destiny that had scarcely begun: a not unreasonable existential position, but one that was bound to clash with anything more than a passing flirtation. The episode left its emotional mark on Goethe clearly enough, not only in its literary precipitation in poems, correspondence and perhaps even in the Gretchen tragedy of *Faust*, or in the Friederike legend carefully written into his autobiography, but also in the fact that it was not until eight years after his break with her (communicated abruptly and not wholly creditably by letter) that he revisited the parsonage in Sesenheim in a belated effort at reconciliation and perhaps penance: Friederike had suffered a severe illness as a result of their breach, and she was never to marry. The friendly and hospitable welcome he received in September 1779 might have exorcised a ghost for him; but it would scarcely have helped her to come to terms with her feelings.

Goethe completed his studies in Strasbourg without great distinction. His dissertation *De legislatoribus* was rejected by the university, but he was allowed to graduate as a Licenciate in Law by defending a series of legal theses or *positiones juris* – a not particularly rigorous examination, but one that conferred the right to the title of *Doctor juris*, satisfied his father's expectations and qualified him to practise the law, briefly, in Frankfurt and Wetzlar. It was with a considerable accumulation of emotional, intellectual and academic experience that Goethe returned to his native city in August 1771 after his brief but seminal period of scarcely seventeen months in Strasbourg.

FRANKFURT AND WETZLAR 1771–5

In Frankfurt Goethe almost immediately began to practise as an advocate, though at least as much time was devoted to literary activities: translations from Ossian (he sent his version of the *Songs of Selma*, with less than perfect tact, to Friederike Brion), the euphoric speech commemorating Shakespeare and, in six hectic weeks, the first version of the dramatized chronicle of Gottfried von Berlichingen – which apparently prompted from Herder the acerbic comment that Shakespeare 'had quite ruined him'. The public execution of the infanticide Susanna Margaretha Brandt took place that winter; some of Goethe's family were professionally involved in the case, which is generally thought to have provided the basic scenario of the Gretchen episode in *Faust*, which Goethe was by now planning, if not already writing down. But his sphere of activity was not restricted to Frankfurt; he had been introduced by his future brother-in-law Schlosser to Johann Heinrich Merck, a civil servant in Darmstadt and a literary journalist whose temper was at least as critical and sardonic as that of his two previous mentors, Behrisch and Herder, and all three exercised an almost Mephistophelian critical control over Goethe's bounding enthusiasms as well as his writings.

It was also Merck who introduced Goethe to the fashionable circle of cultivated *âmes sensibles* or *Empfindsame* at the court of Hessen-Darmstadt, and he became an occasional adoptive member of the 'Darmstadt Circle' orchestrated by the egregiously sentimental figure of Franz Michael Leuchsenring. Herder's fiancée Caroline Flachsland was a member of the group, along with other ladies of the court with whimsical aliases: Psyche, Lila, Urania. No doubt Goethe, dubbed 'der Wanderer' because he was given to tramping on foot between Frankfurt and Darmstadt in all weathers (the poem 'Wandrers Sturmlied' was composed at this time), drew copiously on his experiences among this emotionally demonstrative and lachrymose circle for his satires on the cult of sensibility – and Merck was surely the model for the sarcastic Merkulo of *Der Triumph der Empfindsamkeit* (The Triumph of Sensibility); at the same time, he was flattered enough to go along with the extravagant manners and the language of superheated emotionalism in the literary charades played by the courtly ladies of Darmstadt, even if he was soon to explode the illusory pretensions of the cult of feeling in his sensational novel *Werther*.

In May 1772 Goethe registered with the Supreme Imperial Court (*Reichskammergericht*) in Wetzlar, a small medieval town north of Frankfurt, home to 'the greatest institute for procrastination in Europe', where a backlog of unresolved cases had clogged a legal system of already byzantine complexity. Once again, the law took a back seat as Goethe surrounded himself with literary cronies, play-acting with adopted names (here he was 'Götz') and literary conceits. But this facetious and indeed fatuous way of life was to be interrupted by a starkly tragic incident which, combined with Goethe's own intimate and fraught relationship with a betrothed couple, provided the broad lines for the novel that was to make his international reputation. Goethe did indeed meet Charlotte Buff at a ball on 9 June; he was already on friendly terms with her fiancé Johann Christian Kestner. She was indeed the motherless oldest sister of eleven siblings at the age of eighteen. Goethe's increasingly embarrassing attentions to Charlotte were abruptly terminated at Kestner's insistence; yet even after his sudden departure from Wetzlar in September, good relations were maintained by correspondence, in spite of his frequent and irritating professions of adoration for Kestner's fiancée.

But the incident that struck Goethe with incalculable emotional force was outwardly unrelated to his unrequited and sentimental attachment to Charlotte Buff, except by merest coincidence. In October 1772 Karl Wilhelm Jerusalem, an acquaintance of Goethe's from Leipzig whom he had met again in Wetzlar, shot himself with a pistol borrowed from Kestner; and it was Kestner who, in a detailed report of the event to Goethe on 2 November, alluded to Jerusalem's problems at court and to his illicit passion for the wife of a court official – indeed, Goethe himself had evidently remarked to Charlotte, on meeting Jerusalem by chance, that the young man appeared to be in love. These two experiences, infused with the hectic emotionalism of the cult of *Empfindsamkeit*, were to form the raw material of *Die Leiden des jungen Werthers* (The Sufferings of Young Werther); and the close and grisly overlapping of biographical fact and imaginative fiction was to plague Goethe for the rest of his life – not to mention the lives of Charlotte Buff and her husband, whose marriage ended with his death in 1800.

By a further unkind irony, Goethe's abrupt departure from Wetzlar for Frankfurt in September 1772 led him to the household of Sophie von La Roche, an acquaintance from the Darmstadt Circle now celebrated as the author of a sentimental novel, *Geschichte des Fräuleins von Sternheim* (Story of the Life of Lady von Sternheim), published the previous year. Here he was captivated by another young woman already spoken for: Maximiliane, an engaging daughter of the house, might also have left her mark on Goethe's novel in the dark eyes of the fictive Lotte. She was engaged to the Frankfurt merchant Peter Brentano; the marriage of the future parents of the poet Clemens Brentano took place not long after that of Charlotte Buff and Kestner – and immediately before Goethe began work on the first version of *Werther*.

The years spent in Frankfurt between 1773 and 1775 were uneasy and frustrating years for Goethe in private terms, as he worked sporadically and without enthusiasm as a lawyer, oppressed by his native city and profoundly uncertain as to his future. And yet this subdued period of his life was spectacularly productive in literary terms. A revised *Götz von Berlichingen* was published anonymously in 1773, and under Goethe's name in 1774. It was premièred in Berlin in April that year (the original version was never published in Goethe's lifetime); the essay on German architecture appeared in Herder's *Von deutscher Art und Kunst* in 1773; *Clavigo* was written in 1774; and the same year Goethe burst spectacularly onto the national and international scene with the novel *Werther*.

The monotony of his social existence was broken by a new acquaintance in June 1774, when the Zürich pastor Johann Caspar Lavater visited Frankfurt. Lavater was not only a pietistic religious 'enthusiast' whose mysticism tended to the visionary, but also a keen advocate of the pseudo-science of physiognomy – a cult that enjoyed such prestige and popularity that at one period servants would not be employed until their characters had been assessed and approved on physiognomic criteria. Goethe's relations with Lavater were to be uneven, to say the least, over the years; for the moment, he found the pastor's infectious, if naive, enthusiasm stimulating, and with the pedagogue Johann Bernhard Basedow they set out in July for a journey on the Rhine and the Lahn, a trio of intense and garrulous spirits whose talk ranged bewilderingly over physiognomy, Spinoza, educational reform, religion and heaven knows what else. Though he was scarcely the silent partner in these eclectic discussions, Goethe's own satirical sketch of his two earnest companions is recorded in the poem 'Diner zu Koblenz' (Luncheon at Coblenz), where he characterizes the two 'prophets' dispatiating right and left, with the hedonistic *Weltkind* – himself – happily guzzling his food between them.

September 1774 brought another prophet to Frankfurt: Klopstock, no less, honoured the Goethes with a visit to the family house, where he stayed for two nights – an event important enough to warrant mention in the press, for the fifty-year-old bard was at the height of his literary career. Goethe's father was by now becoming impressed by his son's growing reputation; his mother, justifiably proud, delighted in receiving guests and in turn beguiled them with her unaffected and lively welcome – as she was to continue to do for any friends of her son to the end of her life. Goethe accompanied Klopstock to Darmstadt; it is thought that the ode 'An Schwager Kronos' (To Father Time) was composed in the coach on his return journey. His conversation with the great man centred apparently not around literature, religion, genius, or the high vocation of the poet, as one might have expected, but around ice-skating. Goethe had long been a devotee of the sublime sport to which Klopstock had written three odes celebrating the dangers and the exhilaration of skating, the Hermes-like gift of effortless motion on winged feet; Goethe's own literary exploitation of this gift is found not only in the symbolic poem 'Eis-Lebens-Lied' (Life Song on the Ice) but also, more memorably, in the eerie scene on the ice in the novella *Der Mann von fünfzig Jahren* (The Man of Fifty).

A truly momentous encounter in 1774, however, was to set the course of Goethe's life. In December the future Duke of Sachsen-Weimar, Karl August, was in Frankfurt on his way from Paris. Karl Ludwig von Knebel, who as tutor to the Prince's younger brother was in the party, introduced himself to Goethe, and thus began a friendship that was to last the whole of Goethe's life: Knebel, who survived Goethe by two years, was one of the few in Goethe's later years who were still on the familiar terms of the *du* pronoun with the poet. A brief introduction was arranged with the Princes Karl August and Konstantin, as a result of which Goethe was invited to join them during their stay at the court in Mainz. Whether Goethe cultivated the Weimar court at this time because he was flattered by their attentions, whether he saw an opportunity to make his peace with Wieland, who

was already a member of the *Musenhof* ('Court of the Muses') around the Duchess
Anna Amalia, and whom he had mercilessly lampooned in his sketch *Götter, Helden
und Wieland* (Gods, Heroes and Wieland), or whether he was already considering
the patronage of an eminent ruler as a career move, is uncertain. At all events, he
cannot have been unaware that the difficulties, indeed the impossibility of earning
an independent living as a writer at the time made such an option attractive
enough: after all, Klopstock and Lessing themselves had been forced to accept
patronage, in Copenhagen and Brunswick respectively.

Two further relationships were established during the winter of 1774–5. On 26
January Goethe began a correspondence with a woman who had been writing
anonymous fan mail to the author of *Werther*. His correspondent turned out to be
Auguste Gräfin zu Stolberg-Stolberg, the older sister of Christian and Friedrich
Leopold Stolberg, with whom Goethe was also soon to become friendly. This
extraordinary exchange of increasingly intimate and affectionate letters and verses
was to continue until 1782; the two correspondents never met, but Goethe
confided to his 'dear stranger' considerably more of his private feelings and
ambitions than he ever did to the woman who briefly became his fiancée, Anna
Elisabeth ('Lili') Schönemann.

The details of Goethe's brief, passionate but uneasy affair with Lili
Schönemann are not easy to follow, since much contemporary evidence was lost
or destroyed; but we can infer that Goethe, as he later attested, was emotionally
deeply committed, even if he projected himself as a clumsy outsider ill at ease
in the energetic social whirl into which his relationship with Lili plunged him.
He found much of the hectic socializing tiresome, and relations with her family
were strained, especially with her graceless brothers who had their own plans
for their sister's future. The affair was conducted in the party-go-round of
Frankfurt society, and also at the idyllic country house of Lili's uncle d'Orville
in Offenbach, which was more to Goethe's taste. But it seems that he was
aware from an early stage that it had no future, that he was living a game or an
illusion of love. Once again, his almost panic fear of permanent commitment
to a single person, place or profession seems to have blighted their relationship,
on his part at least; and within only three weeks of his betrothal to Lili in
April 1775 (the only time Goethe was ever formally engaged to be married) an
opportunity for escape, or at least for temporary absence, offered itself. The
Stolbergs, brothers of his vicarious correspondent 'Gustchen', called on the
author of *Werther* in May, and in this aristocratic but raffishly boisterous company
(the Stolbergs insisted they should all wear 'Werther costume' and behave as
'naturally' – or as noisily – as possible) Goethe seized the chance to distance
himself for some three months from his Frankfurt entanglement on a journey to
Switzerland.

In Karlsruhe he again encountered the future Duke of Weimar, who had
himself just become engaged to Princess Luise of Hessen-Darmstadt, and in
Emmendingen he had a sobering reunion with his beloved sister Cornelia, who
was suffering a troublesome and unwanted pregnancy, homesick and miserable in
her marriage. It appears that she implored her brother not to marry Lili, possibly
as a result of her own disenchantment, possibly for deeper reasons to do with her

own sibling feelings. In Zürich he was welcomed by Lavater, who in turn introduced him to the aged Johann Jakob Bodmer, who with his friend and colleague Breitinger had earlier done much to introduce English literature to the German public and had opened up more imaginative literary perspectives than Gottsched's prescriptive neo-classicism. Excursions by boat on Lake Zürich, and the heady inspiration of Klopstock's rhapsodic odes, prompted a version of the emotionally ambivalent poem 'Auf dem See' (On the Lake); strenuous tramps among the sublime Swiss landscape, which was even then assuming exemplary significance for the scenic enthusiasms of a pre-Romantic generation, led Goethe to the summit of the St Gotthard Pass where, he claims in his autobiography, he devised an equally ambivalent poem on the heart-shaped locket that still bound him to Lili.[11] Having glimpsed for the first time the borders of Italy, he resisted his companion's invitation to continue south and, no doubt with severely conflicting feelings, turned back towards Germany. Although he called at Strasbourg on his way to and from Switzerland, renewing his acquaintance with the Minster and old companions like Lenz (and where, by an eerie chance, he was shown a silhouette portrait of a lady of the Weimar court named Charlotte von Stein), he avoided Sesenheim: his final encounter with Friederike Brion was not to be until his second Swiss journey some four years later.

The return to Frankfurt resolved nothing in his confused relations with Lili – a confusion created almost entirely by his own unsettled and volatile state of mind as he convinced himself that he stood at a crossroads in his life, as he sensed that an important, if not momentous decision was imminent. And indeed it was: Karl August, again in Frankfurt on his way to his bride in Karlsruhe, had again pressed him to come to Weimar. The engagement to Lili was emotionally terminated in September. The degree of stress Goethe was placed under (or placed himself under) in his agonizing over the future was no doubt retrospectively dramatized by him in his autobiography – which, significantly enough, concludes with his departure for Weimar: these pages portentously invoke his 'daemonic' (*dämonisch*) sense of an irresistible personal destiny, but the pressures should not therefore be underrated. Logistic confusions heightened the drama of indecision and delay: Karl August and his new wife the Duchess Luise, calling yet again in Frankfurt, assured him that a coach would be sent to bring him to Weimar. The coach was delayed, and Goethe's suspense became intolerable; his father, convinced that the whole thing was a cruel deception on the part of a whimsical and possibly vicious court, encouraged his son to set out at last on his Grand Tour of Italy – and indeed Goethe did set out for Heidelberg on the first leg of that journey. Even here, however, chance and design coincided; for Goethe also calculated that his transport to Weimar, if it existed, would call in Heidelberg between Karlsruhe and Frankfurt. It turned out not quite to be so: in the early hours of the morning of 3 November he was awakened by the courier's horn, bringing a message from Frankfurt – the Weimar-bound coach had bypassed Heidelberg, and now he was summoned back to Frankfurt. He hurled himself into the mail coach, declaiming, if we are to believe the account with which *Dichtung und Wahrheit* ends,[12] Egmont's frantic image of the 'sun-steeds of time' harnessed to the chariot of destiny and careering headlong into an unknowable future.

THE EARLY WEIMAR YEARS 1775–86

The Duchy of Sachsen-Weimar of little over 100,000 subjects was one of several particularist states fragmented from the Electorate of Saxony by the complex processes of inheritance. Weimar itself incorporated the Ducal residence, its ancillary palaces and administrative buildings, and an unkempt and backward walled town of some 6,000 inhabitants. After the civic dignity and cosmopolitan traffic of Frankfurt, which Goethe had latterly found so confining, the effect was that of a village dominated by an absolutist court that had itself fallen on hard times. Even the official residence of the ruling family was in ruins; the palace, with its theatre and chapel, had burned down in 1774 and was not to be rebuilt for another fifteen years. Yet even in 1775 this modest court showed traces of the pretensions that were to transform it for the next hundred years and beyond into the cultural showpiece of Germany: as Goethe was to put it (not entirely seriously), its destiny was as that of 'Bethlehem in Juda, small and great'.[13]

The Dowager Duchess Anna Amalia, with whom Goethe was to form a respectful but close, on her part almost maternal bond, had been Regent since the death of her husband in 1758, keeping the state going in a precarious political and financial situation, but managing also to establish a lively cultural tradition, building the tiny court theatre and herself cultivating a moderate talent for music and painting. Her most significant appointment was to secure Christoph Martin Wieland as tutor to her sons in 1772 – and his reputation as an enlightened man of letters and translator of Shakespeare played some part in attracting Goethe to the Duchess's *Musenhof*. Wieland was no Voltaire, and Weimar was not Berlin; Karl August, though related by both blood and marriage to Frederick the Great, did not share that monarch's softer interests, but only his love of soldiering – his other passions being hunting and wenching. But the Duke of Weimar was wise, or shrewd, enough to appreciate Goethe as a celebrated and charismatic member of his entourage and as a prestigious addition to his mother's *salons*.

The relationship between Goethe and Karl August was to involve many differences, even tensions; but the Duke, a canny judge of men even then, just eighteen years old, was to play his part, largely by patronage and more often than not under Goethe's guidance, in the spectacular rise in prestige of his small state, and behind Goethe's many careful and tactful expressions of homage to his patron can be detected genuine affection and even genuine respect – for all his not infrequent private expressions of disapproval. In the formal context of the court, where rigid etiquette, snobbery and prejudice often called the tune, Goethe was introduced to a new and (in both senses) intriguing form of existence; for all his status as friend and intimate of the Duke, he observed the strictly orchestrated rituals of a court presided over by the prim and inhibited young Duchess – whom he adored. As a *Bürger*, Goethe was not permitted to dine at the Ducal table at official functions until he became von Goethe in 1782; outside the courtly regime, however, he and the young Duke ran wild as Goethe played up to his public and literary image as a rumbustious *Stürmer und Dränger*, rampaging through town and countryside with noisy pranks and drunken escapades, plaguing the citizenry to the point where Klopstock himself, who even in Hamburg had heard lurid reports of the scandalous goings-on, was moved to write a kindly, if pompous, reprimand reminding Goethe of his obligations as a rising young literary genius. It was a letter in the spirit of that of Graf Oliva to the young Egmont, and Goethe's reaction was that of Egmont; 'genius' in any case meant something different to the *Sturm und Drang* generation from Klopstock's bardic loftiness.

Further complications in Goethe's delicate and still insecure position *vis-à-vis* the court arrived in the form of past friends and literary allies: Lenz and Klinger were drawn to Weimar in the hope of preferment through the good offices of their old companion. The volatile Lenz, especially, behaved outrageously, and Goethe was obliged to engineer the brusque departure of his embarrassing friend. It is not true, however, that Goethe systematically 'dropped' his earlier friends during these early Weimar years, or pulled up the ladder to patronage that he himself had climbed: in February 1776 he helped Herder to an excellent position as the senior churchman in Weimar, effectively as chaplain to the court. Goethe has been accused from many sides of ruthless self-interest in his treatment of former friends; and the charge is not without some truth. Equally, there is much evidence of uncommon generosity, in financial and emotional terms, to his less fortunate contemporaries: gifts of money to struggling writers like Klinger, Müller and Bürger, a solicitous concern for the depressive Plessing (see below, pp. 21 and 66–7), and, most striking of all, his almost fatherly protection and education of an extremely troublesome young orphan, Peter in Baumgarten, whom he adopted as his ward in 1777 after the boy's original guardian was killed in the War of American Independence. In this last case, Goethe was emulating the charity of his own father who had for twenty-five years fostered a deranged and occasionally violent law graduate, Dr Clauer, in the family house in Frankfurt.

Of all the new friends Goethe made at this uneasy time of profound transition in his existence – and he had soon made enemies enough in the enclosed and jealously gossipy ambit of the court – two were of critical importance, one male and one female. Wieland, a generous-minded man who bore no grudges for the lampoons Goethe had directed at him, welcomed the raw young genius without a trace of envy or rivalry, and did much to defend and justify his wilder behaviour. Freifrau Charlotte von Stein, wife of the Duke's equerry, was a staid, motherly figure of thirty-three when Goethe arrived in Weimar, older than her years both physically and emotionally, but by all accounts a warm, sympathetic and companionable, if somewhat serious-minded and occasionally depressive woman. No great beauty and certainly no *femme fatale*, this emotionally enigmatic personality was to be Goethe's intimate confidante, sister, governess, surrogate wife and muse for the next twelve years or so, exercising a subsequently no doubt exaggerated and idealized, but incalculable didactic influence on his social and emotional development. Almost certainly entirely platonic, this love affair, for this is what it amounted to in all but a physical sense, was conducted in the most passionate terms: by notes and letters, private trysts and almost violently confessional unburdenings on Goethe's part – and on her side with all the coquettish possessiveness and proprietorial jealousy of a full-blooded sexual liaison. Sensuality, however, seems not to have been a factor in Goethe's social education under her tutelage: it was Charlotte von Stein who tamed the callow and refractory young *Genie*, who educated him in the decorum of the court, provided the sympathetic ear into which he poured his most private frustrations and insecurities and who, at least on the evidence of the intense and urgent poems addressed to 'Lida', held him as if spellbound to the charmed circle of Weimar.

To be sure, the relationship was ambivalent from the start, a twilight one between a woman unfulfilled by an unsatisfactory marriage and exhausted by constant childbearing and an emotionally volatile, perhaps sexually in-experienced but virile young man, between a sober, even prissy governess and her boisterous, over-imaginative charge. And over the first decade of Goethe's life in Weimar, tensions were in any case building up as the poet agonized characteristically over his personal destiny, torn between the confinement of the gilded cage of Weimar and his obscure but urgent sense of a wider world of activity, conscious of the discrepancy between the literary productivity of the early 1770s and the relatively meagre output of the early Weimar years. For Goethe's energies over this decade, immense as they were, were devoted to *not* completing major projects: *Egmont, Iphigenie, Tasso, Faust*, the Wilhelm Meister novel. It was even rumoured that the young genius of *Götz* and *Werther* had burned himself out, had opted for the life of a courtier, or had become the *maître des plaisirs* to the Weimar court.

There was a degree of truth in this impression. Goethe had not ceased to plan, even to write, major works, but the real productivity of the early Weimar period lay in less ambitious projects: a steady output of enthralling, if often introverted and ambivalent poetry, the poems to Lida, powerful ballads like 'Erlkönig', intensely lyrical songs like those of Mignon, the existential poems, and much occasional verse. Above all, however, his creative and organizational talents were expended quite extravagantly on more mundane but still demanding tasks: on playlets, *Singspiele*, masquerades, on the theatricals devised and presented for Anna Amalia's *Liebhabertheater* (amateur court theatre), on entertainments and spectacles laid on by the court for itself. Even more demanding were the official burdens he assumed; in June 1776 Karl August boldly, and not without opposition from the court, appointed Goethe to a junior but well-paid position in his administration – that of *Legationsrat* – and he was to become a full member of the Privy Council (*Geheimrat*) in 1779.

These were no honorific titles or sinecures; Goethe was expected to take on responsibilities, and this he did more than most. In the course of this first decade he was centrally involved in the administration of the mines and forests of the Duchy – though well-forested, the insuperable problems of transport allowed no very profitable trade in timber, and the silver and copper mines of Ilmenau were never to become remotely worthwhile, for all the considerable energies Goethe invested in his duties. He was active in the exchequer, attempting to rationalize the chaotic finances of the state, in the reorganization of the tiny standing army of Weimar and in the recruitment of conscripts for Karl August's war games; he proposed reforms in agriculture, industry and poor relief; and he was sent on diplomatic missions to the courts of the Thuringian princes, even to the court of Frederick the Great in Berlin. These duties were exhausting, and what was worse, ultimately frustrating: Goethe's reforms failed to engage the Duke's full support or enthusiasm, and by the end of a decade in Weimar Goethe was ready enough to quit these responsibilities, as he was ready to leave Weimar for a host of other reasons. By 1786 Karl August, too, had his mind on more glorious business than the everyday administration of his own state: he began negotiations to enlist in the wider sphere of Prussian military adventurism under his brother-in-law, the new King Friedrich Wilhelm II.

In April 1776 Goethe, who had been living in various rented premises, was gifted a modest but picturesque cottage outside the town: the now famous *Gartenhaus*, a centre of pilgrimage for visitors to Weimar, set idyllically in the Ilm Park, itself largely created by Goethe. The water-meadows of the River Ilm were then, of course, altogether more remote and unkempt than now; this was an invaluable bolt-hole for the poet, an opportunity to escape and reflect, to entertain informally and to indulge his developing interest in botany and horticulture. Many of his intimate letters to Frau von Stein and Auguste von Stolberg confirm his delight in the surroundings, his habit of bathing in the Ilm at dawn or by moonlight, or skating on the frozen river. But even this secluded retreat was visited by a tragedy that haunted Goethe: in January 1778 a young lady of the court, Christel von Laßberg, drowned herself in his beloved river after being jilted by her fiancé. A copy of *Werther* was found with her body, and in an act of grief and penance Goethe laboured with his own hands to carve a memorial to her out of the rock. In a letter to Charlotte von Stein he writes darkly of the power that water exerts over the mind, the enticing melancholy of stars and moon reflected in the river.[14] It was around this time that the first version of the elegiac poem 'An den Mond' (To the Moon) was written – though whether with reference to the tragedy or not, is unknowable. The previous year, in June 1777, Goethe had also lost his sister Cornelia, to whom he had been very close until her brief and unhappy marriage separated them. Never one to dwell on or make a great show of bereavement, Goethe was nevertheless deeply marked by the loss of his one surviving sibling – the first in a series of private losses that were to leave him, in domestic terms, increasingly isolated.

Apart from business tours and diplomatic missions, Goethe undertook two private journeys in this first Weimar decade; this was his way of escaping pressures and taking stock, which was to culminate spectacularly in his sudden departure for Italy in 1786. In November 1777 he set out in appalling weather for the Harz Mountains, with three principal objectives: to inspect in an official capacity the thriving silver mines of the Harz in the interest of his efforts to revive the mines in Ilmenau; to visit a depressive young man, Victor Leberecht Plessing, who had appealed to the author of *Werther* for emotional and spiritual counsel; and to climb the Brocken, the highest mountain of northern Germany – which was also by folkloric tradition a haunted mountain, the scene of the annual Walpurgis Night satanic revels. Goethe's own dramatization of his visit to the 'Devil's Altar' at the summit suggests that he sought, at least half-seriously, some symbolic omen or augury of his destiny, and a stock-taking of his personal, official and creative situation in Weimar; the result was the Delphic hymn 'Harzreise im Winter'

(Winter Journey to the Harz), which ends with the poet offering his profound thanks on the snowbound peak. His ascent of the Brocken in such conditions was adventurous, even foolhardy, enough: it took all his insistent urging to persuade the local forester to set out with him from the *Torfhaus* hut, and indeed it is probable that this was the first recorded winter ascent of the mountain, the summit of which they reached shortly after one o'clock on the afternoon of 10 December.

A second, more protracted escape from official pressures was undertaken in the autumn of 1779: a second journey to Switzerland of four months, this time not with the boisterous Stolbergs, but in the almost equally distracting company of Karl August. They called in Frankfurt, to the great delight of Goethe's mother, who by now had developed a lively correspondence with the Dowager Anna Amalia following her visit to the Goethe's house the previous year, and via Heidelberg reached Strasbourg. On 25 September Goethe called at Sesenheim for his first and last meeting with Friederike since August 1771; the very next day he visited Lili Schönemann, now von Türckheim and a young mother, and the following day he stood at the grave of his sister Cornelia: an extraordinary and concentrated retrospect of his past emotional life. Basel, Thun, Berne, Lausanne and Chamonix brought renewed acquaintance with the grandiose scenery of the Alps, still in the public mind more a spectacle of fearful awe than an accessible playground: Mont Blanc was not to be climbed until 1786 by Paccard and Balmat, and the following year by H. B. de Saussure, whom Goethe met in Geneva and consulted on his route through the passes. By 13 November he was again at the St Gotthard hospice in very severe weather, and again he turned his back on Italy with the obscure notion that he was still not ready for that revelation. On the return journey he stayed with Lavater in Zürich, who was still respected as the mentor of his early *Sturm und Drang* days – though Goethe was subsequently to deride the naive gullibility the pastor betrayed in his mystical and extravagant enthusiasms, and to break off relations with him after abruptly declaring that he, Goethe, was a convinced non-Christian.

Over the next four years or so, Goethe's life in Weimar was more integrated and more settled than the initial years. He threw himself willingly enough into his official duties and his obligations to entertain and divert the court, and began to develop a serious interest in natural science, partly stimulated by his work as minister of mines and forests: mineralogy, botany and comparative anatomy. In 1782 he appeared to have reached the summit of integration into the world of Weimar: he was elevated to the nobility, entrusted with serious diplomatic missions, and moved into a fine house on the *Frauenplan* – the house forever after associated with Goethe, and still standing as the National Goethe Museum. If his literary reputation at this time was at a low ebb, he was nevertheless working sporadically but at times intensively on major projects, even if it was to require pressures and stimuli from other directions to force these projects to completion – notably from the publisher Göschen, who was preparing an edition of his works. Goethe's 'discovery' of the intermaxillary bone in 1784 was announced with great excitement, even if its reception by the scientific community was to disappoint him (see below, p. 266).

And yet at the very point when Goethe seemed most securely bound to Weimar, his restlessness and dissatisfactions began to surface. Increasingly overwhelmed by official duties and frustrated by the lack of progress of his reforms, uneasy about his inability to complete his major literary works, disappointed at Karl August's waning interest in the welfare of his subjects and the proper governance of the Duchy, alarmed at the Duke's growing infatuation with his military career, chafing under his unfulfilling but demanding relationship with Charlotte von Stein, and no doubt experiencing the malaise of someone who had apparently achieved a number of goals, only to discover new ones beckoning: many pressures began to focus around a renewed urge to escape. Mignon's song 'Kennst du das Land' of 1784, written though it was for a specific narrative context, must also have articulated his own need for an environment that would provide creative freedom and a release from present stress, a need that became increasingly associated with escape from the gloomy north to an imagined – and imaginary – southern idyll.

Goethe's disenchantment with Weimar reached a critical point in 1786, when he finally resolved to emulate the most remarkable feature of his father's unremarkable life, and perhaps also posthumously to fulfil his father's wishes (Johann Caspar had died in 1782; Goethe had last seen him in 1779). At least three times he had tantalized himself with the prospect of Italy; twice he had turned back from its very borders. Cultural factors were just as urgently involved as a sense of emotional or political entanglement and frustration. He had for some time, as he reported after his escape, not been able to read a Latin text or glimpse any image of Italy; his growing obsession with classical and neo-classical art, architecture and literature had become a sickness from which only first-hand experience, only the presence and the very sight of Italy could cure him.[15] The critical need for a total break, for rejuvenation and release, the casting-off of an old and constricting skin, for a fundamental and radical reappraisal of his talents, his career, his emotional self – in short, of his destiny: this was how Goethe, at least in retrospect but also no doubt in prospect, viewed his carefully guarded secret project in the period leading up to September 1786.

Goethe had already got to know the fashionable spa town of Karlsbad (Karlovy Vary) in 1785, an elegant aristocratic playground that offered a stimulating combination of therapeutic leisure and intensive socializing. He was also flattered at his reception by the beau monde of the spas, where he was lionized and could extend his sphere of acquaintance and influence in both social and intellectual circles: visits to the Bohemian resorts of Karlsbad, Teplitz (Teplice), Eger (Cheb) and later Marienbad (Marianske Lazne) were to become a regular feature of his subsequent life, to the savage indignation of his more radical critics. For the moment, Karlsbad was to be the springboard for his escape from the confinement of Weimar; and after a period of intensive preparation, financial and cultural, he left for Karlsbad on 24 July to join Karl August, Herder and Frau von Stein. On 3 September, having written to all three explaining that he was leaving for a protracted leave of absence, but telling none of them of his actual destination, he left for Italy. Only his servant, Philipp Seidel, was told of his real plan: to live in Rome as a painter under the name of Jean Philippe Möller.

ITALY 1786–8

It was no accident that Goethe chose to live as an artist among the colony of German-speaking painters resident in Rome: Tischbein, Angelika Kauffmann, Johann Heinrich Meyer, Lips, Trippel, Schütz and Bury (and, later, Philipp Hackert). For at this point in his life, when so many of his literary projects lay uncompleted, Goethe was still unsure whether he should not take up painting as his major artistic activity. It was the visual and plastic arts, as much as classical literature or history, that brought him to Italy: not only the light, forms and colours of the Mediterranean scene, but Claude Lorrain and Palladio, Tiepolo and Michelangelo, the remains of Rome and the splendours of the Renaissance. It was, however, also in Italy that Goethe realized his own inadequacies as a visual artist, and by his return to Germany he had effectively abandoned any great ambitions in that direction.

Initially, it was the sheer childish excitement of illicit adventure, the over-whelmingly exotic novelty of landscape, vegetation and lifestyle that caught Goethe's enthusiasm as he hurried southwards over the Brenner Pass (even the most impatient traveller could then scarcely expect to cover more than forty-five miles in a twelve-hour day). He took cheerfully in his stride the extreme discom-forts of eighteenth-century travel, primitive inns, and even an awkward incident at Malcesine, on the border between Austrian and Venetian territories, where he narrowly escaped arrest as an Imperial spy – because he was busily sketching a fortress. This clandestine journey under a carefully guarded anonymity was in fact being followed with suspicion by the Venetian authorities, and for a time Goethe's mail was even being intercepted. By way of Trento and Verona, Vicenza and Padua he pressed on to Venice, marvelling at churches and Palladian villas, at domes and colonnades, symmetry and proportion. The erstwhile exuberant young champion of the 'German' Gothic style of Strasbourg Cathedral had left all such barbarities behind him in the gloomy north: in Assisi, for example, he passed by the 'Babylonian' churches of St Francis and their exquisite early frescoes 'with aversion', and spent much of his time admiring and sketching the late Roman front of the small temple of Santa Maria sopra Minerva – a complete reversal of today's cultural tastes and values, but understandable enough as this was the first unruined ancient building Goethe had ever seen.

In Venice he tolerated the stench of the canals to delight in the permanent open air carnival of entertainment, the *lazzi* and the street markets, the ceremo-nial processions and pomp of the republican powers, even the to him obscurantist liturgies of the Church. The Byzantine magnificence of St Mark's left him indif-ferent; all was oriented to the Renaissance – and to Rome. He visited Ferrara briefly (ignoring Ravenna completely), Bologna and Florence – where, again in striking contrast to the modern-day tourist, he spent little more than three hours: these were only distractions, staging-posts on his course to Rome. On 29 October Goethe finally arrived in the 'world's capital', and instantly set about making himself at home, anonymous, or at least under his *nom d'artiste*, among the frater-nity of painters. To be sure, his fame and status eased the way; for some time he had been instrumental in supporting the promising young Tischbein, and he very quickly identified himself to the painter as Goethe – a name that also gave him immediate entrée to the German artistic community. Tischbein procured him a sparse but adequate lodging in the *Corso*, and Goethe soon settled in to what, at least in retrospect, was to be the happiest and most fulfilling time of his whole life.

For the four months of his first spell in Rome, until February 1787, Goethe's life was as full as it ever had been, with sightseeing, excursions, sketching, reading, writing, and absorbing the teeming public scene of a city where even in winter life seemed to be lived outdoors. And yet for all his euphoria at his release, for all his almost desperate assurances to himself and others that he felt reborn, rejuvenated and totally happy in Rome, his first stay was relatively brief; the news that Vesuvius was becoming active aroused his artistic and geological interests, and on 22 February he set out with Tischbein to explore the *mezzogiorno*, leaving the noisy and, at this stage, tiresome Roman Carnival behind him. Not that Goethe had tired of Rome already; but at this point he did not anticipate that he would be in Italy for more than some six months, both because of his financial situation and because the Duke had not sanctioned any longer absence.

In Naples Goethe, now travelling *in propria persona*, having shed his unsuccessful incognito, was received in Neapolitan society – notably by Sir William Hamilton, who had commissioned Tischbein to make drawings from his collection of ancient vases, and whose voluptuous young mistress Emma Hart, subsequently his wife and later still Nelson's mistress, sensationally recreated Greek statues with her 'attitudes' as tableaux vivants, which Goethe was privileged to witness. He was also able to delight in his first close encounter with the seashore and coastal scenery, which in these regions was more striking than the Lido of Venice or the Roman shoreline. He made three ascents of Vesuvius, getting close enough to the new crater by dodging the regular eruptions of stones and ash, and was happy enough to escape uninjured. Excavations had been under way at Herculaneum and Pompeii for half a century, and these were duly visited; but the most impressive revelation for Goethe was his first exposure to Greek architecture at Paestum. As he confessed in his account of the Italian Journey, his eyes and his aesthetic senses had been schooled in altogether more refined and graceful architectural forms; confronted with the squat massivity of these archaic columns, he was overwhelmed, not to say oppressed – but he very quickly 'pulled himself together', and was soon able to appreciate these alien and forbidding temples in their historical perspective.[16]

Goethe had visited Paestum in the company of a young artist, Christoph Heinrich Kniep, whom Tischbein had recommended to him both as a companion-guide and as a visual amanuensis who would compile a dossier of sketches as a record of his journey. And it was with Kniep but without Tischbein that Goethe sailed for Sicily in March 1787, suffering badly from seasickness but still finding time to work on *Tasso* and take lessons in watercolours from his companion. Sicily in spring was a new and even more exotic dimension to Goethe's experience; here he felt as close to ancient Greece as he ever would, wandering like a terrestrial Ulysses through the gardens of the island – gardens where, he suggests more than half-seriously, he might at last fulfil an old whim by discovering the prototype of all plant forms, his vision of the *Urpflanze* (see below, pp. 265–6). The tour of Sicily took him anti-clockwise around the island: Palermo, Segesta, Agrigento, Caltanissetta, Catania – with an arduous ascent of Monte Rosso, an outlier of Etna, which was then active – and via Taormina to Messina, where the devastation of the earthquake of 1783 was still spectacularly evident. The return sea journey to Naples in mid-May was more than eventful: the ship, incompetently crewed, threatened to drift onto the rocks off Capri, and Goethe found himself compelled to calm the panicking passengers by exhorting them – to prayer. He himself, again grievously afflicted by seasickness, retired below decks to await the outcome calmly; and indeed the ship finally moved on a breath of wind slowly into the safety of the Gulf.

One of Goethe's strangest encounters in Sicily was a visit he engineered in Palermo to the family of Giuseppe Balsamo alias Cagliostro, the by now notorious charlatan whose influence on the credulous and ambitious Cardinal de Rohan had led, directly or indirectly, to the sensational 'necklace scandal' at the court of Marie Antoinette in 1785. From as early as 1781 Goethe had followed the fraudulent activities of Cagliostro with fascinated disapproval, and had been profoundly disturbed by the affair, which he – at least with hindsight – saw as the beginning of the end for the French monarchy, as the very symbol and symptom of the frivolity and decadence of government that led ineluctably to the Revolution. Purporting to be an English businessman, Mr Wilton, he contrived an introduction to the family, which had remained indigent while their outrageous kinsman promoted himself and his frauds in some of the highest courts in Europe. This was also an interest that Goethe was to exploit in literary terms: his satirical drama *Der Groß-Cophta* (The Great Copt), and some of the exploits of Mephistopheles in *Faust* Part Two, were to take their inspiration from the tactics and the personality of the self-styled 'Count Cagliostro' (see below, pp. 167–70).

Goethe was seriously interested in Cagliostro as an extreme example of the political influence of Freemasonry and other secret societies of the time, Rosicrucians and Illuminati, towards which his attitude was characteristically ambivalent. Like many leading spirits of the day – Lessing, Mozart, Herder – he was attracted to the humanitarian and utopian ideology, the lofty ideals of the brotherhood of man, enshrined in these more or less secularized religions of the eighteenth century; like many of them, he too was wary of the esoteric ritual, the potential for fraudulent manipulation and exploitation of human credulity, greed or ambition, that also attended these ostensibly enlightened but clandestine organizations. He was also suspicious of their vulnerability to political infiltration, and indeed in the aftermath of the French Revolution the Order of Illuminati became, in some politically paranoid circles in Germany, highly suspect as a vehicle for the spread of republican, even revolutionary programmes: 'Illuminatus' was commonly regarded as synonymous with 'Jacobin'.

Goethe, to his credit, did not share in this crude conspiracy theory; but he was aware that the secret and highly organized structures of Freemasonry could be abused. It may have been mere curiosity that led him to join the Weimar 'Anna Amalia Lodge' of Freemasons in 1780; at all events, his membership, and his rapid advancement through the degrees, gave him an initiate's insight into Masonic lore, both positive and negative, which he drew on for his devastating satire on the mysteries in *Der Groß-Cophta* and for some of the structures and activities of the quasi-Masonic organizations in the Wilhelm Meister novels. Moreover, he was also inducted, along with Karl August, into the Weimar Order of Illuminati in February 1783, under the lodge name of 'Abaris'. By this time, however, he had seen enough of Freemasonry to be highly sceptical, if not down-right suspicious, of its means and ends; indeed, it has been controversially suggested that both he and the Duke maintained their membership precisely because it allowed them to police any actually or potentially subversive tendencies within the Order.[17] But Goethe's active participation in the secret societies was short-lived: by 1785 he had ceased to attend, and in 1789 he supported Karl August's prohibition of the foundation of a lodge in Jena. The necklace scandal of 1785 confirmed many of his doubts, especially concerning Cagliostro; and his bizarre visit to the Balsamo family in April 1787 was by way of a postscript to his Masonic involvement, even if it testified to the continuing fascination exercised by the fraudulent Count.[18]

After a further three weeks in Naples Goethe returned to Rome on 6 June to begin the most substantial and significant part of his Italian experience: a second period of ten months in the city. This was an unplanned but eagerly welcomed bonus; Karl August, who by now had left Weimar to take up his commission in the Prussian army, readily gave him permission to stay on until the following year, and Goethe, relaxing into the prospect of a longer spell in Rome, now busied himself with a routine of writing, sketching, modelling, study (including, in the best Renaissance tradition, classes on perspective and anatomy) – and, equally intensively, with an obscure but evidently full and intimate sexual relationship with a young widow. This woman, of whom little is known, was to be celebrated as the indulgent and accommodating 'Faustine' of the *Roman Elegies*. For although this frank and joyous cycle of erotic poetry was clearly informed by his subsequent partnership with Christiane Vulpius, it is also no doubt a fairly accurate reflection of his affair with his Roman mistress, whom he characterizes fondly as loving and faithful, but without specific expectations – doubly reassuring to the still rather cautiously amorous German visitor who feared venereal disease as much as he feared permanent emotional commitment: in a Delphic but revealing aside in the *Italienische Reise* (Italian Journey) dealing with this stage in his life, he lets fall the vague reference to a personal oath by which he had undertaken not to be diverted from his principal aim in life 'by relationships of that kind'.[19]

Much speculation has been devoted to Goethe's sexual experience, to the point where it has seriously been suggested (it must be said, more on inference from his imaginative and poetic work than on any credible biographical evidence) that he was sexually inexperienced until his Roman adventure of 1787; indeed, his inno-cence of full sexual consummation until then has been attributed to a psycho-sexual neurosis involving *ejaculatio praecox*.[20] Nothing is knowable, given Goethe's own reticence, and that of the age, on such matters; on the evidence of some of his coarser writings, he had a more than average command of sexual vocabulary and anatomy, and it is quite possible that he had had experience of some rough wooing, if only in the early days of his escapades with the young Karl August, who was notoriously and indisputably the father of some of his subjects in more senses than one. The extent of Goethe's intimacy with Friederike Brion, Lili Schönemann or Charlotte von Stein is quite unknowable, though these affairs are generally accepted as chaste: the poet who would become celebrated, even my-thologized, as Germany's love-poet *par excellence* had the gift of supreme articula-tion of the emotions of love rather than the reputation of a Don Juan. Whatever the case, it can be safely assumed, for all the dearth of information about the identity of 'Faustine', that in Rome Goethe enjoyed, among all his other emanci-pating experiences, the total liberation of uninhibited sexual pleasure.

In February 1788 Goethe once again witnessed the Roman Carnival, but this time not as the tiresome and noisy distraction of the previous year; it was no doubt thanks to his more relaxed and integrated situation that he was able to observe, enjoy and write down a detailed account of the modern Saturnalia as a licensed festival staged by the people for the people, in which conventional social differ-ences were briefly suspended in a mood of tolerant celebration – though, as he remarked caustically, the Young Pretender Charles Edward Stuart, then living out the drunken twilight of his life in Rome as the Duke of Albany, incongruously masqueraded his royal pretensions by appearing frequently and ostentatiously in the *Corso* during the Carnival. No doubt Goethe was more of an observer than an active player in the Carnival; for all his fond remarks on the noisy outdoor life of Italy, he retained a fastidious distance from the crowd. But he was a sharp and informed observer, and the Roman Carnival, supplemented by his reading of descriptions of Florentine carnival processions, of classical and Renaissance *trionfi*, informed his own domestic productions of masquerades and pageants in Weimar, as well as the lavish symbolic *Mummenschanz* of the first act of *Faust* Part Two.

Once Easter had come and gone, with Goethe witnessing the musical liturgies at St Peter's with keen but detached interest, departure was imminent. It was not an easy break, even if he subsequently dramatized it by declaring he had not enjoyed a day's unalloyed happiness since he crossed the Ponte Molle out of Rome.[21] A moving passage in his retrospective account describes his emotional farewell to the city during a moonlit walk from the *Corso* to the Coliseum, identifying himself with the Ovid of the *Tristia ex Ponte* recalling the last night before his exile from the beloved city:

> Cum subit illius tristissima noctis imago,
>   Quae mihi supremum tempus in Urbe fuit;
> Cum repeto noctem, qua tot mihi cara reliqui;
>   Labitur ex oculis nunc quoque gutta meis . . .

> Wandelt von jener Nacht mir das traurige Bild vor die Seele,
>   Welche die letzte für mich ward in der römischen Stadt,
> Wiederhol ich die Nacht, wo des Teuren so viel mir zurückblieb,
>   Gleitet vom Auge mir noch jetzt eine Träne herab . . .

> When to my mind I recall that sorrowful night of departure
>   That was to be my last night in the city of Rome,

As I relive that time when I left so much that I cherished,
Tears that I cannot restrain flow even now from my eyes.[22]

In the company of his friend and musical collaborator Kayser, who was returning to Zürich, Goethe left Rome on 23 April 1788; after a rather more extended stay in Florence than he had allowed himself in his earlier rush to Rome, he returned via Milan and Lake Como, arriving in Weimar on 18 June.

The actual literary output of Goethe's Italian sabbatical was not immediately impressive: the revision of *Iphigenie* and *Egmont*, some progress on *Tasso*, two scenes for *Faust* ('Hexenküche' and 'Wald und Höhle'), plus one or two minor works and poems. He had sketched or painted more than 1,000 items in Italy – landscapes, urban scenes, anatomical and botanical studies, statuary – and yet Italy was the watershed of his career as a visual artist. He never ceased to draw or paint; but his Italian education had turned him into a committed and informed student of art rather than a serious practising artist. Clearly, his Italian experience had also furnished him with a lifetime's wealth of impressions and images that would be released and imaginatively exploited for years to come; it had also, paradoxically, reconciled him to his northern environment in Weimar, for all his frequent professions of nostalgia and alienation on his return. It had given him the will and energy to devote himself single-mindedly to the completion of his major literary projects (with the exception of *Faust*): by 1789 the eight-volume edition of his works had been published by Göschen – the summation of his life's literary output till then. At the same time, and in part as a result of his observations in Italy, he saw his future development more in terms of natural philosophy, of botany, anatomy and optics, than of purely literary or aesthetic activities.

WEIMAR AFTER ITALY; VENICE 1790; FRENCH CAMPAIGNS 1792–3

One of Goethe's first steps on returning to Weimar was to rid himself ruthlessly of the burden of official duties that had threatened to overwhelm him before his flight to Italy. He retained his titles as Minister of State and Privy Councillor, but active responsibility only for the Ilmenau mining commission, which continued to be a demanding and ultimately fruitless task for many years. Certainly, he was in the course of time to accumulate a huge range of official and informal commitments as his reputation and involvement in affairs, his sphere of influence and acquaintance, increased; but for the time being he held himself apart from specific affairs of state. His social relations were, moreover, considerably affected by his startling, indeed scandalous, defiance of convention when he set up his household with Christiane Vulpius, his twenty-three-year-old mistress who became his wife only in 1806. The wooing was brief: in early July 1788, not a month after his return from Italy, he was approached near his *Gartenhaus* by the personable and buxom figure of Christiane with a plea to help her brother August to a position.

The Vulpius family was indigent, but by no means as humble as is often presented. It is true that Christiane worked part-time in a small manufactory producing artificial flowers, set up as a charity for respectable families fallen on hard times; it is true that she was imperfectly educated, though not illiterate; that she subsequently effaced herself within Goethe's household, referring to him in public as the 'Herr Geheimrat' and retiring behind the scenes when visitors were received. But the Vulpius's forebears were professional people, clerks, lawyers and clergymen; her brother was a university graduate, and was to become a popular writer in his day. Goethe responded to her request honestly and conscientiously: he was to write many letters on her brother's behalf, pull many strings and disburse substantial sums. The sister he took as his mistress, fifteen years his junior, but already past the conventional age for marriage at the time; in his mood following the return from Italy, bereft and isolated, unsettled and even miserable, he found in Christiane an undemanding, unsophisticated and devoted companion with whom he could recreate and extend the erotic liberation of his Roman experience – and the *Roman Elegies*, begun during that winter of 1788/9, were inspired equally by profound nostalgia and by present fulfilment.

Needless to say, this unorthodox cohabitation caused affront in many Weimar circles, and Goethe's always less than complete integration into the coteries of the court was further loosened. For all the licence grudgingly allowed to fame and genius, he had declared his independence from convention, though not from patronage: he was careful always to retain the favour of the ruling family, and they, at least in the persons of the Dowager Anna Amalia and the Duke himself, were not unduly disturbed by such a breach of respectability. To one person in particular, however, this was the final straw: Frau von Stein, whose demands on her protégé had become increasingly querulous before his flight to Italy, and who had reacted with some petulance to his sudden and unannounced departure, in spite of his regular letters of conciliation to her, greeted him icily enough on their first reunion even before she knew of this new liaison so different from her own. Once it became public knowledge, her estrangement from Goethe was complete; and the publication of the *Roman Elegies*, though some five years after their break, surely affected her very much more deeply and more disturbingly than her simply prudish public disapproval suggested.

That same autumn of 1788, a momentous relationship began unpromisingly: Goethe's uncomfortable reunion with Frau von Stein was immediately followed by his first meeting on 7 September with Schiller, who was to spend that winter in Weimar. First reactions were mutually wary, even hostile; Goethe perceived the younger man as the callow and fire-eating radical of *Die Räuber* (The Robbers) – a phase he himself (and indeed also Schiller by now) had left far behind him. Schiller in turn saw Goethe primarily as a charismatic rival, enjoying an extravagant fame and favour of which he himself was deprived. Nevertheless, Goethe was partly instrumental in helping the struggling young historian to an academic position, albeit an initially ill-paid one, at the University of Jena in 1789, and the following year Schiller was able to marry and settle there, close enough to Weimar but not too uncomfortably close to the man who, he still felt, in many respects 'stood in his way'.[23]

Memories of Italy continued to haunt and unsettle Goethe; for all that he could now tap out his hexameters on Christiane's bare back, he was still withdrawn, at times misanthropic. It may be that this mood of recurrent, even quasi-depressive dissatisfaction and isolation was the basis for the attitude of resignation or renunciation (*Entsagung*) that he was to develop and refine into an existential stance in his later fiction. When the opportunity came for a second visit to Italy, he took it readily enough, but it was, as he must have expected, doomed to be disappointing, or worse, after the revelation of his first journey: it is as if he needed finally to exorcise the Italian demon and recommit himself to his destiny in Northern Europe. The signs were unpropitious from the start; he would not be travelling incognito on an exhilarating and almost illicit adventure into an unknown and yet half-familiar world, but retracing his steps in company – the purpose of this journey was to meet up with the Dowager Duchess, who had travelled to Rome accompanied by Herder and guided by Goethe's advice on her itinerary. In the event, he did not join his friends in Rome, but prevaricated until March 1790: the previous year had brought a variety of distractions. He had finally, in June, broken off relations with Frau von Stein with some acrimony (expressed, as so much of their passionately platonic affair had been, in letter form); he had forced himself to finish *Torquato Tasso*, and with it complete the edition of his works for Göschen; and his son August had been born on Christmas Day – the first and sole surviving child of five born to Christiane. Moreover, a huge shadow had fallen over absolutist Germany, though even the short-term consequences were as yet not fully appreciated: the storming of the Bastille on 14 July had set in train the political upheaval, the 'earthquake' or 'volcano', as Goethe subsequently termed it, of the French Revolution.

Nevertheless, he set out for Venice in March 1790, only to spend a cold, wet and desultory April waiting for Anna Amalia, passing the time with visits to museums, reflections on the Revolution, observations of religious ceremonies, of Venetian mores and street life – much of which found its expression in the often mordant and sardonic detachment of the *Venetian Epigrams*. It was not the Italy he had left, he wrote; his own circumstances had altered drastically, and he could no longer delude himself that he was a free spirit, uncommitted either personally or artistically. Grown away from his youth and his youthful aesthetic, sensing that a younger generation was challenging for the literary initiative, his 'destiny' no longer offered the infinite variety of options it had seemed to only four years ago; and his departure from Venice on 22 May had none of the elegiac intensity of his farewell to Rome. The ghost of Italy had been laid; it was the beginning of his coming to terms with the loss of his southern idyll, even if he was never to abandon his retrospective memory of Arcadia.

The 1790s marked a profound shift in Goethe's personal and artistic development. The public reception of his works was less than rapturous; those who expected sensation, more strong red meat from the celebrated author of *Götz* or *Werther*, were disappointed. The cool neo-classicism of *Iphigenie* and *Tasso* seemed to indicate that Goethe had outgrown his youthful radicalism and adapted to a more conformist official culture – and his eagerly awaited *Faust* had appeared only in truncated and fragmentary form. The French Revolution profoundly unsettled the assumptions of absolute rule, enlightened or unenlightened, in the German territories, as revolt developed into regicide and political terror; Goethe, for all his apolitical poetic instincts, was to find himself distracted and preoccupied by this European convulsion – and he was to come closer to first-hand experience of it than he had ever imagined. And while it is scarcely true to say that he turned away from his literary calling – the 1790s were to see, among other things, the completion of *Wilhelm Meisters Lehrjahre*, the final resumption of work on *Faust* Part One, as well as the 'revolution dramas', the ballads and epics – it is true enough that in this decade he wrote relatively little lyric poetry, and that his energies were also channelled in other directions: towards science on the one hand, and towards neo-classical aesthetics on the other.

Botany and anatomy, the morphology and 'metamorphosis' of plants and animals, continued to occupy him. But 1790 also saw the beginnings of the most bizarre crusade of Goethe's life: his protracted and obsessive battle to refute Newton's colour theory, his doomed attempt to take on virtually single-handed (albeit later with some not entirely helpful support from the young Schopenhauer) the whole establishment of professional science. The episode frequently cited to explain his sudden obsession with Newton is memorable, but – like the story of Newton himself and the apple – it anecdotally over-simplifies and obscures Goethe's serious interest in and knowledge of contemporary science. He had borrowed some optical instruments from a Jena physicist, Christian Wilhelm Büttner, which had lain for some time unused in a drawer. Early in 1790 Büttner requested the return of his apparatus; and as Goethe was on the point of packing it, he picked up a prism in order to observe the well-known Newtonian phenomenon of the refraction of white light into the colours of the spectrum. Squinting casually through the prism at his windows, this is of course what Goethe did *not* see: the classic projection of the spectrum is obtained only under carefully arranged conditions in a darkened room. But this failure to demonstrate Newton's optical theory became for Goethe a demonstration of the failure of the theory itself; and it marked the beginning of a lifelong devotion to the cause of disproving that theory (see below, pp. 260–4). It was a futile cause, but one to which Goethe was, over the next twenty years or so until his *Farbenlehre* (Theory of Colours) was finally published in 1810, and indeed well beyond that, to devote as much time as, and to attach rather more importance than, to any of his literary work – not excluding *Faust*.

In the course of the 1790s Goethe slowly reintegrated himself into official life in Weimar, though less hectically and time-consumingly than in his first decade. In 1791 he became director of the re-established Court Theatre, a demanding and largely administrative position that he exercised with often severe authority, involving himself in every aspect of commercial and artistic activity (including pedantic rules for actors in deportment and the speaking of dramatic verse); he held this position until 1817, when a combination of intrigue and a bitter controversy about the use of performing dogs on stage, which strongly offended Goethe's sensibilities, forced his resignation. The theatrical repertoire, largely determined by Goethe, was very mixed; while he and Schiller saw it as an opportunity to educate the Weimar public in their common programme of classical aesthetics, he was also careful to meet popular tastes. Goethe had in any case no great interest in adapting his own plays for stage performance – he left this to others, including

Schiller on occasion; and though performances of their own dramas were presented, notably the première of the *Wallenstein* trilogy in 1798–9 (the rebuilt theatre had opened with *Wallensteins Lager* in October 1798), the diet of Shakespeare, Calderón and Mozart (plus one or two disastrous performances of indigestible and recondite dramas by the Schlegel brothers, during one of which Goethe intervened publicly to admonish the audience for sniggering) was well-leavened with comedies by Goldoni and with popular domestic pieces by fashionable playwrights like Iffland and Kotzebue – the remarks of the Theatre Director in the prelude to *Faust* are based on first-hand experience of the theatre from both sides of the footlights.

His reintegration in Weimar was to be interrupted by two journeys in 1792 and 1793 during which Goethe, in a sense, went to war – as a privileged non-combatant, to be sure, but nevertheless sharing much of the extreme discomfort, danger and illness of an eighteenth-century military campaign. In 1788 Karl August had entered Prussian military service; Goethe had visited him on manoeuvres in Silesia in July 1790, and in August 1792 he was again bidden to join his ruler for the French Campaign. The Duke was given a command in the Austro-Prussian allied armies who, under the Duke of Brunswick, were expected to terminate the process of revolution by marching triumphantly into Paris, taking in their train a host of royalist riff-raff, aristocratic French émigrés who had fled France and had energetically fomented counter-revolution from the safety of the Rhineland. This the coalition army failed signally to do; indeed, its intervention precipitated the September massacres of 1792, and arguably sealed the fate of Louis XVI four months later.[24]

Goethe again reluctantly left Christiane and their infant son in Weimar, and after calling at Frankfurt to see his mother for the first time in thirteen years, he joined Karl August at Longwy on 27 August. In appalling weather, the huge and unwieldy army of more than 80,000 overran Longwy and Verdun by weight of numbers (and, it must be said, by the hasty capitulation of the fearful citizens), and began the advance on Paris. At Valmy on 20 September the coalition forces met the citizens' army – by no means the undisciplined rabble they had been led to expect, but a highly motivated and well-led force under Dumouriez; after a thunderous and protracted exchange of artillery, which Goethe observed at perilously close quarters, the coalition army was stopped in its tracks, and no further advance was made. Yet this inconclusive, if noisy and chaotic battle, in which casualties were minimal on both sides, was indeed, as it turned out, a turning-point in history: the Revolution, at least for the time being, was saved, and the coalition armies, divided and dispirited, began a long and miserable withdrawal in the course of which dysentery and typhus wiped out almost half their troops. Goethe's famous judgement, a French version of which still adorns the monument at Valmy – 'Von hier und heute geht eine neue Epoche der Weltgeschichte aus, und ihr könnt sagen, ihr seid dabeigewesen' (From here and now begins a new epoch in world history, and you can say you were there) – was almost certainly not pronounced in so many words at the time, but formulated some thirty years later with the benefit of considerable hindsight when he wrote up his account of the campaign; but it is true that he wrote something like it in letters to his friends Knebel and Voigt in September and October 1792. For the rest, Goethe also devoted himself during this fascinating but thoroughly uncomfortable campaign (he too contracted dysentery on the retreat from Valmy) largely to the *Farbenlehre,* his work on colour theory.

Back in Weimar in December, it was not long before Goethe was again called away to the wars by Karl August. After the turning-point at Valmy, the revolutionary armies under General Custine had counterattacked the German territories by invading the Rhineland: by October 1792 Speyer, Coblenz, Mainz and even, briefly, Frankfurt were occupied by the French, who envisaged a free revolutionary republic on the left bank of the river – this is the historical setting of the *Unterhaltungen deutscher Ausgewanderten* (Conversations of German Emigrants) and of *Hermann und Dorothea.* The Prussian forces soon liberated most towns, which contained few citizens with Jacobin sympathies; only in Mainz was the indigenous support for the Revolution powerful enough to declare a republic in March 1793, albeit one sustained by French military force, indeed virtually annexed by France. Georg Forster, a leading German Jacobin and noted traveller, was one of several influential and eloquent Francophile revolutionaries in Mainz; he was sent to Paris before the siege as a deputy for the 'Republic of the Rhine', only to die there in penury in 1794 – though not, like many of his fellow Jacobins, under the guillotine.

The Rhenish Republic of Mainz was short-lived; in April 1793 the forces of the revived coalition began a blockade, in June the town was heavily bombarded, and capitulated in July. An honourable truce was agreed; the revolutionary forces withdrew under a royal guarantee of safe conduct, but the Mainz mob threatened to lynch some of the less heavily protected Jacobin sympathizers. It was at this point that Goethe, no friend of the Revolution and still less of German fellow-travellers, intervened notoriously to affirm the rule of law against all his own anti-revolutionary instincts. Once again, he managed somehow to devote himself to his writing in less than ideal conditions: to *Reineke Fuchs* (Reynard the Fox) and, inevitably, to colour theory.

WEIMAR IN THE 1790s; SCHILLER AND WEIMAR CLASSICISM

Returning thankfully to Weimar, Goethe resumed his interrupted domestic life, as well as his long-since interrupted novel *Wilhelm Meisters Lehrjahre.* But he was now also beginning a period of serious scientific work, in which he was much aided by the professoriate of Jena University: it was a feature of Goethe's intellectual eclecticism that in spite of his often rugged independence of thought he was able to call on leading specialists in almost any field for discussion and guidance, the more so as his own reputation and stature grew. In 1794 he was instrumental in the appointment to a chair in Jena of Johann Gottlieb Fichte, a turbulent philosopher from whom Goethe hoped to learn much, since Fichte purported to reconcile the esoteric abstractions of speculative philosophy with Goethe's own robust notion of common sense. In this Goethe was to be disappointed; and in any case Fichte was dismissed from his chair in 1799. Goethe's role in the affair is opaque, since he destroyed all correspondence relating to the controversy; he may have made genuine attempts at reconciliation, but he has also been indicted as a prime mover in Fichte's dismissal. Whatever the truth, he had found little profit in the relationship, largely because of his own bafflement with, and distrust of, abstract thought.

More rewarding, though by no means perfectly harmonious, was his burgeoning friendship with Schiller, also in Jena since 1789. Their relationship had begun coolly, due equally to Goethe's aloofness and to Schiller's almost resentful sense of rivalry; and indeed it was an attraction of opposites rather than of like minds, united in a common cause of classical idealism and a high-minded mission to educate the German public. Schiller's speculative intellect, his struggle with Kantian thought, did not match Goethe's almost naive sense of realism; Schiller's more rigorous theoretical preoccupations constantly crossed Goethe's more pragmatic instincts and the poetic impulse that led his imagination into less systematic ventures. Paradoxically, their personal behaviour differed in quite the reverse way: Goethe's strictly regulated and disciplined routines were quite foreign to Schiller's more hectic and chaotic way of life, and the fastidious Goethe was repelled by his friend's personal habits, his smoking, snuff-taking and coffee-drinking, his eccentric dependence on the smell of rotting apples for stimulation – even by his sickly constitution.

Goethe had disapproved of *Die Räuber*, Schiller's immature and rebellious first drama, which had led to the dubious distinction, to Schiller's own great embarrassment, of his nomination as an honorary citizen of the French Revolution; Schiller had in turn written a respectful but critical review of *Egmont* which, for all its perceptiveness, had demonstrated the great conceptual gulf between them, as well as certain imaginative limitations on Schiller's part. They disagreed fundamentally, but frequently productively, on a whole range of issues. Schiller deeply offended Goethe by insisting that his beloved *Urpflanze* – which Goethe had only just failed to discover in Sicily – was a fine concept, but in the end an idea, not a reality; and Goethe was also irritated by Schiller's strictures on the more irrational and poetic dimensions of *Wilhelm Meisters Lehrjahre* and *Faust*. In spite of all this, Goethe listened carefully to his friend's views, and more often than not responded to them in some degree; indeed, it is possible that *Faust* Part One would not have been completed without Schiller's combative and challenging encouragements. Their friendship was founded on mutual respect, on a fruitful dialectic of often divergent intellects and sensibilities; if Goethe at times found Schiller's strictures tiresome, he also affirmed that they understood each other and made common cause even in those areas where they disagreed. Their common mission was a devotion to the cause of a classical culture in Germany and to a concerted and sustained assault on what they perceived as mediocrity in thought, art and literature – though it must be said that in the course of their decade of campaigning they lavished praise on much that was second-rate and ignored great talent; there is some truth in Heine's later jibe that to have been praised by Goethe was the true stamp of a writer's mediocrity.[25]

Schiller's single-minded antagonism towards the younger Romantic generation was, however, only uneasily shared by Goethe, whose own ambivalence was

qualified by the esteem in which he was held by many of the Romantic school –
for all his occasional magisterial disapproval of what he perceived as their religious
or 'neo-Catholic' sentimentality. But Schiller also flattered Goethe's self-esteem in
a more like-minded way by hailing him as the great 'naive' or unreflective genius,
on a level with Shakespeare and the ancient Greeks. For both Goethe and
Schiller, ancient Greece represented, in an extravagantly idealized perception, the
highest cultural, political and intellectual achievement of civilization; Goethe's
early proto-Romantic enthusiasms for the Gothic, for the folk-traditions of
Germany, for popular superstitions and folk religion, for the historicism of
Herder's early teachings – which the Romantic generation was to rediscover and
rehabilitate in a more systematic and scholarly way over the next two decades –
were entirely superseded by his and Schiller's notion of an exemplary neo-Greek
ideal of classicism and humanity. It is astonishing that it was precisely during his
collaboration with Schiller that Goethe was able, both in spite of and because of
Schiller's criticisms, to complete his work on what he now called his 'witch's
product', his 'nordic phantoms': *Faust* Part One.

Goethe's and Schiller's collaboration was conducted through a prolific and
regular correspondence as much as through their personal contact, as they
exchanged views on art, history and ideas, on dramatic and aesthetic theory, on
epic and ballad, as they co-operated in all manner of literary journalism, notably
in Schiller's *Die Horen* (The Horae) and *Der Musenalmanach* (Almanac of the Muses),
and prescribed cultural standards far and wide; their high-minded and combative
polemics raised hackles on all sides. In particular, their joint collections of sharp
satires, *Xenia* and epigrams, fired savagely and often indiscriminately at men of
high distinction and low mediocrity, at erstwhile allies and friends as well as
perceived enemies, spread fear and offence throughout the literary world:
Weimar Classicism, which has been worshipped by subsequent generations as the
peak of modern German cultural achievement (and which has also inevitably
suffered revisionist judgement as an élitist, apolitical and pompous sham), was
perceived even at the time by many as a baleful combination of lofty idealism and
peevish arrogance.

Goethe's visits to Karlsbad, Jena, Dresden, Leipzig and Göttingen during the
1790s and beyond extended his sphere of acquaintance; more significantly, visitors began to make their pilgrimages to Weimar. Wilhelm and Alexander von
Humboldt, Fichte, Johann Heinrich Voß, Hölderlin's somewhat fraught visit in
November 1794, the dramatist and impresario Iffland, the Schlegel brothers from
Jena, Jean Paul Richter, Schelling, Hegel, Tieck, Novalis, Sophie von La Roche,
the physicist Johann Wilhelm Ritter, the geologist Abraham Werner – these are
only some of the more prominent of a host of German and foreign visitors to
Weimar who sought out Goethe, whether admiring or disapproving, agreeing
or disagreeing, attracted or repelled. He could be charming and forthcoming or
brusque and intimidating, often quite unpredictably and whimsically. He quar-
relled violently with Herder, his former mentor who had benefited from Goethe's
influence in Weimar, in 1795, and only much later were they uneasily reconciled.
On his third journey to Switzerland in 1797, when he, Christiane and August saw

his mother in Frankfurt for the last time before her death in 1808, Lavater, who had suffered from Goethe's and Schiller's public polemics and was to be even more roughly handled, made a point of avoiding Goethe – as Goethe had avoided him the previous year in Jena. In October he visited the St Gotthard Pass for the third time; it was also during this journey that Goethe planned an epic poem around the figure of Wilhelm Tell – but it was eventually Schiller who used the material for his drama. A third journey to Italy, planned in 1795 and again in 1796, was abandoned, and the Swiss journey substituted. In July 1797 Goethe again, for reasons of his own, destroyed a great number of documents, as he had done much earlier in Leipzig: all the letters to him from Lili Schönemann, and most of those from Charlotte von Stein went into the fire along with other correspondence.

The decade of 'Weimar Classicism' saw Goethe at the peak of his intellectual activity. Not only his intense collaboration with Schiller, but also his scientific studies, occupied much of his life. His own creative literary output during this period, which can be nominally dated from 1794 to 1805, was not exactly neglected, but was scarcely prolific. It is true that he completed the two major projects whose origins lay many years back in the past: *Wilhelm Meisters Lehrjahre* was finished in 1796, and the first part of *Faust* in 1806 after a protracted revision of very nearly ten years, and ironically enough only after Schiller's death. But otherwise, different demands on his time and energy meant that this was not the most productive phase in purely literary terms: *Alexis und Dora*, *Hermann und Dorothea*, the major ballads of the 1797 'Balladenjahr', and a steady but not vast output of lyric poetry. Several projects were begun but left unfinished: the epic *Achilleis*, the sequel to Mozart's *Magic Flute*, and *Die natürliche Tochter* (The Natural Daughter) – although this last drama was completed in five acts, and indeed was performed in Weimar in 1803, the planned trilogy was never seriously resumed. Goethe's scientific studies, his devotion to classical aesthetics, the satirical *Xenia*, his theatrical activities, his translation of Benvenuto Cellini's autobiography, his exercises in classical prosody, above all his preoccupation with colour theory and his campaign to discredit Newton – all this seems to have distracted him from original literary work, while it was precisely during this period that Schiller, in a hectic and consuming blaze of creative effort, and in defiance of increasing ill-health, was producing his major dramas.

Goethe too was troubled by illness and occasional depressive withdrawal: in 1801 and 1805 he suffered severe illnesses, indeed in Vienna his death was actually announced in 1801. In December 1802 Christiane bore a daughter who survived only three days – the fourth child lost in infancy, and the last. The deaths of contemporaries and former associates cannot have left Goethe unaffected: his brother-in-law Schlosser in 1799, Corona Schröter in 1802, Herder in 1803 and, most heavily, Schiller in 1805. Goethe was himself in very poor health in the first months of that year; he had, as he wrote to Zelter, feared for his own life – and instead he had lost a friend, and with him half of his own existence.[26] Schiller died on 9 May; Goethe was only told the following day, and kept to himself for several days. Not until August did he publicly express himself, with the moving stanzas of his Epilogue to Schiller's poem 'Das Lied von der Glocke'; both works were performed at the commemoration in the Bad Lauchstädt theatre on 10 August.

THE ERA OF NAPOLEON; PERSONAL AND LITERARY RELATIONS
1805–13

In 1806 momentous historical events brusquely intruded on Goethe's Weimar. On 6 August the news reached him of the formal dissolution of the Holy Roman Empire; by October war had come to Jena and Auerstedt, and Prussia suffered its greatest humiliation at the hands of Napoleon. This in itself was of no very great concern to Goethe, who had little time for either the Prussian state or for its ruler Friedrich Wilhelm III, even though his own Duke held general rank in the Prussian army; indeed, Goethe's high regard for Napoleon, which came near to hero-worship, his perception of the Emperor as a 'daemonic' man of destiny who had saved France from the worst excesses of the Revolution, rendered Goethe's political and national sentiments during the French occupation of Germany ambivalent, if not confused. What agitated Goethe most urgently at this time was the chaotic disorder in the aftermath of the Prussian defeat: arson, skirmishing and pillaging threatened life and property in Weimar. One report has it that French troops forced a way into Goethe's house, whereupon Christiane boldly confronted them and declared that 'a friend of Napoleon' lived here. Whatever the truth of the anecdote – Goethe had not yet met the Emperor, but was in another sense a 'friend' – the house was spared, and it was perhaps partly as an act of gratitude, as well as in order to legitimize his domestic situation in such troubled times, that Goethe made Christiane his wife on 19 October; their sixteen-year-old son August was one of the witnesses.

On a wider scale, the ruling house of Sachsen-Weimar was also imperilled. Napoleon himself occupied the Residence, minded to wipe the Duchy, whose ruler had taken refuge in Prussian territory, from the map. It was the Duchess Luise who, in a resolute and dignified face-to-face encounter with the Emperor, defended her husband and her state, invoking on his behalf the imperative of national duty, as well as the cultural status of Weimar; and in December the Duchy reluctantly became a member state of the Rhine Confederation, allied with the French but retaining its sovereignty at the cost of severe financial reparations. Oddly, Goethe did not attend the initial audience of the Weimar Privy Council with Napoleon, perhaps because the Duke was also absent; he was to meet the Prometheus of modern European politics only two years later, at the congress convoked by Napoleon and Tsar Alexander at Erfurt. Exactly what passed between the two at this meeting on 2 October, during which the Emperor characteristically continued to busy himself with affairs of state, is unclear, since Goethe remained reticent about the details. Napoleon evidently made a mildly critical remark about *Werther*, which he knew well; he is supposed to have told Goethe he would find much material for his work in Paris; and he expressed his esteem with the cryptic words 'Vous êtes un homme!' (or, by one account, 'Voilà un homme!'). Goethe was also gratified to note that the Emperor concluded some of his expressions of opinion with the question: 'Qu'en dit monsieur Göt?'.[27]

Goethe's judgement of Napoleon was largely apolitical. He had only praise for the man who had led France out of anarchy, and he was not so committed to the almost mythical idea of the Holy Roman Empire to see its passing as a major disaster. He saw the inevitability of the eventual fall of Napoleon, the liberation of Germany from a foreign invader, and he was aware of the hubris of Napoleonic ambition: towards the end of his life he conceded to Eckermann that Napoleon was a man 'who had trampled underfoot the lives and happiness of millions'.[28] But he was also unable to share unreservedly the enthusiasm of his contemporaries for the defeat of Napoleon at Leipzig in 1813; for the rest of his life he took pride in the Légion d'Honneur presented to him in 1808, after two further meetings with the Emperor – and it is reported that in December 1812, as he passed through Weimar on his flight from Russia to Paris, Napoleon had his personal greetings conveyed to Goethe through his ambassador in Erfurt. Goethe was clearly flattered by the Emperor's attention, however brief and even summary their exchanges; it was evidently also the aura of power and destiny, his personal charisma, that captivated Goethe's keen sense of real and symbolic political authority.

Goethe was honoured, too, by his literary colleagues; the first volume of the Romantic collection of German folk songs, *Des Knaben Wunderhorn*, published in 1805 from Heidelberg by Brentano and Arnim, was fulsomely dedicated to 'His Excellency the Privy Councillor von Goethe' in recognition of his fostering of folk songs and ballads more than three decades earlier. He had always enjoyed the admiration of the younger Romantic generation in spite of his alliance with Schiller, whose hostility had prevented the development of any warm personal or literary relationships, and in spite of occasional rivalries and tensions between the neo-Catholic tendencies of the Romantic School and the declared neo-paganism of the Weimar philhellenes. With Heinrich von Kleist, however, Goethe could not have any easy rapport; Kleist was too ambitious, and Goethe too suspicious of the young writer's neurotic or 'hypochondriac' insecurities, for anything but a strained hostility between them. Goethe's brusque rejection of *Penthesilea*, which Kleist had offered him with resentful but intense expectations, as well as his less than successful adaptation of *Der zerbrochne Krug* (The Broken Pitcher) at the Weimar theatre, drove them bitterly apart: Kleist was convinced that Goethe had deliberately distorted, even sabotaged, his comedy.

On a more personal level, death and love visited Goethe in the years following 1805. The Dowager Duchess Anna Amalia, the spirited and open-minded patroness of the Weimar *Musenhof* who had done as much as anyone to create the relatively tolerant artistic ambience of the small Duchy and to foster its emergence as the cultural Mecca of Germany, died in 1807; Goethe's mother, who had herself developed a warm friendship and a lively correspondence with the Duchess, died the following year. Herder, Schiller, Anna Amalia and his mother: Goethe was being regularly reminded of mortality. Yet the man in his fifties – the novella of that title, subsequently included in *Wilhelm Meisters Wanderjahre*, was conceived in 1803 – was still susceptible to the sexual attraction of women less than half his age; and in spite of the formalization of his marriage to Christiane, he was still famous, or charismatic, or virile enough to be an object of their attentions. He had little time for the persistent attentions of the voluble and importunate Madame de Staël in 1804; but an even more insistent and intrusive woman was allowed to lionize him not long afterwards. Bettina, daughter of Maximiliane von La Roche, who herself had captivated Goethe briefly in 1772, granddaughter of Sophie von La Roche, younger sister of the poet Clemens Brentano and future wife of his collaborator Achim von Arnim: this well-connected and over-imaginative young woman had already busily, indeed obsessively, compiled a dossier of anecdotes and recollections of Goethe from his mother in Frankfurt. In 1807 she threw herself at the poet on her arrival in Weimar in a hectic combination of puppy-love and hero-worship, and for the next four years devoted herself to the cultivation of an almost certainly sexually innocent, but nevertheless often embarrassingly intimate and ultimately tiresome friendship with the great man, a relationship that formed the basis of the imaginative brew of half-truths and fantasies published by her in 1835 as *Goethes Briefwechsel mit einem Kinde* (Goethe's Correspondence with a Child), in which Bettina projects herself as Goethe's intimate confidante and muse.

More serious were Goethe's less involuntary relationships with two equally young women in 1807–8: the eighteen-year-old Wilhelmine ('Minna') Herzlieb, adoptive daughter of a Jena publisher, and the only slightly older Silvie von Ziegesar, whose father owned a baronial estate near Jena where Goethe was a frequent visitor, and who was often in his company in Karlsbad during the summer of 1808. No details are known about either relationship; sexually innocent they may well have been, but both women were to receive poems and correspondence that indicated a passionate, if sublimated, bond of affection that found its literary expression in the sonnet cycle of 1807/8 and, more obscurely encoded, in the tragic emotional complexities and confusions of the novel *Die Wahlverwandtschaften* (Elective Affinities) of 1808/9.

It would be a false process of biographical reductionism to draw from the bleak vision of *Die Wahlverwandtschaften* any direct inferences about either Goethe's emotional and psychological state of mind or his existential attitudes at this time. His own somewhat Delphic comment on the relation of the novel to his own life was that it contained nothing that he had not experienced, but nothing just how he had experienced it ('kein Strich . . . , der nicht erlebt, aber kein Strich so, wie er erlebt worden').[29] But there is evidence enough that as he approached sixty, Goethe was conscious of waning physical and literary energies, of his strong, even tough, mental resilience being sapped by the weight of accumulated experience. In spite of the throng of visitors who trekked to pay homage to the Sage of Weimar, the Sage himself was often withdrawn, isolated, resigned. The formalized, even pedantic routine and the innate caution that had always structured and disciplined even his more chaotic phases now became second nature; his diffident tendency to withdraw from social obligations was becoming an often seemingly brusque defence against unwanted attentions. He was less inclined to mince words, in conversation or correspondence, and often seemed indifferent to the public or even the personal effect of his more negative or sarcastic judgements. It seems that Goethe had by now assumed the weary scepticism of middle age as he described it in his scheme of the three ages of man in his *Maxims and Reflections*:[30] the passionate and affective idealism of youthful *Dumpfheit* (an untranslatable term literally meaning torpidity or inarticulacy, but to the *Sturm und Drang* Goethe a more positive quality of intuitive instinct) had been superseded by the weariness of doubt informed by the sullen weight of experience, and he had not yet achieved the conciliatory mysticism that is the privilege of old age. Nevertheless, several remarks from this time indicate that he felt he was approaching the final stages of his life, indeed, that he had already reached the point where he perceived himself in a 'historical' perspective – and he was customarily referred to by his younger contemporaries as 'the old gentleman'.

It was such promptings that impelled him in 1809 to begin drawing plans for the autobiographical accounts of his life that occupied him at intervals from 1811 to the year before his death: *Dichtung und Wahrheit*, the *Italienische Reise*, the Swiss Journeys of 1779 and 1797, the French Campaign and the Siege of Mainz, and the Rhineland Journeys of 1814 and 1815. His few close friends, Zelter, Knebel, Heinrich Meyer, were his only real confidants or intimates, and to them he confessed his often depressive sense of isolation and struggle. The cliché of Goethe as the serene Olympian, untroubled by doubt or self-questioning, as the intellectually, socially and emotionally secure Jove of Weimar, is based on a superficial and even hostile perception of his public persona. His relations with the younger generation, with his contemporaries, with Weimar society, even with his friend and patron Karl August, were not harmonious, for all the surface formality and exaggerated homage of his official addresses, and for all the exaggerated respect Goethe himself was accorded as Germany's foremost writer. He was feared and resented as much as he was loved and respected, and he disguised his most intimate doubts and insecurities behind an often intimidating mask of personal inscrutability – or within the complex imaginative structures of his poetic writing, in which existential tensions and polarities of pain and joy, stress and peace of mind, grief and affirmation, are dialectically balanced and, more often than not, purged and resolved in a cathartic process of aesthetic shaping.

A major factor in Goethe's sense of alienation and disillusion as he entered his sixties was the reception of his *Farbenlehre* by the scientific establishment. In 1810, after the mountain had laboured long and painfully, he presented his theory of colours in two volumes to the public; but although his complex and elaborate experiments and theories aroused some interest among practising artists and among those concerned with the subjective psychology of colour perception, although he was also in 1814 to find in the young Arthur Schopenhauer an initially enthusiastic and gratifying disciple, this *magnum opus* to which he attached so much significance was received, at best with patronizing politeness, at worst with complete indifference, by the scholars of physics and mathematics whose approval and applause Goethe most craved. He failed to topple the abstract edifice of Newtonian optics with his own holistic creed of sense perception – unsurprisingly, since within the scientific and epistemological context of the age, Newton was demonstrably and irrefutably right. But his blank rejection by the 'guild' of scientific orthodoxy was a check to his ambitions that Goethe could never reconcile himself to, and he continued, stubbornly and literally until his dying day, to pursue the mirage of his own accessible and, as he saw it, realistic and non-abstract doctrine of colour perception (see below, pp. 260–4).

In the years following Schiller's death the single-minded Hellenism of Goethe's classical preoccupations began to lose its impetus; while he never abandoned his Graecophile instincts, he was becoming less radically hostile towards medieval, in particular towards German, pre-Renaissance art and literature. No doubt his more relaxed relations with the Romantic generation were a significant factor. While he deplored the conversion to Rome of Friedrich Schlegel in 1808, and abhorred the overwrought religiosity of Zacharias Werner, who converted in 1811, his relations with the Romantics became more positive: Achim von Arnim, Clemens Brentano, Jakob and Wilhelm Grimm were hospitably received in Weimar, he found common ground with the artist Philipp Otto Runge on colour theory, and even took a distant interest in the work of Caspar David Friedrich. At the same time he began to revive, in a more systematic and informed way than under Herder's tutelage forty years previously, his interest in the Germanic sagas, the *Nibelungenlied* and the *Edda*, in Middle High German poetry, and to discuss the 'nordic' inheritance with the leading scholars of the day. While remaining unrepentantly an 'old heathen', he was becoming more sympathetic (or less unsympathetic) to the Romantic revival of interest in German medievalism that gained impetus under the Napoleonic occupation of the German territories, and which was indeed a symptom of the growing national consciousness of the need to liberate Germany both culturally and politically from France; while Goethe scarcely shared, indeed was highly sceptical of, such nationalist aspirations, he was inevitably caught up in its tendencies. His first meeting with Sulpiz Boisserée in May 1811, after an exchange of correspondence, was seminal; this Rhineland compatriot devoted his life to the study and the revival of interest in medieval art and Gothic architecture in Germany; he and his brother Melchior were to be among the prime movers in the campaign to complete the building of Cologne Cathedral, and their remarkable collection of early German and Flemish paintings, housed at that time in their Heidelberg residence, ultimately came to form the core of the *Alte Pinakothek* gallery in Munich. By slow degrees in the course of a warm and lasting friendship, Boisserée succeeded in educating an initially reluctant Goethe to a renewed, albeit cautious, appreciation of Christian medieval art – even if he never alienated him from his 'pagan' classical sympathies.

GERMAN LIBERATION; JOURNEYS TO THE RHINELAND 1814–15

In 1813 the groundswell of national consciousness, towards which Goethe took a notoriously ambivalent stance, reached its high tide in the Wars of Liberation. Napoleon's disastrous Russian campaign of 1812 was followed by his decisive defeat by Prussia, Austria and Russia in the so-called *Völkerschlacht* (Battle of the Nations) at Leipzig in October the following year. Sachsen-Weimar, technically allied with the French as a member-state of the Rhine Confederation, was in an equivocal political position: it was not until 1814 that Karl August was able to join the Prussian pursuit of Napoleon. Once again war, and the detested chaos it brought, had come to the neighbourhood of Weimar; and Goethe was uncomfortably torn between his ineradicable respect for the Emperor and his own ethnic and cultural loyalties, between his abhorrence of political and social upheaval and his recognition of the inevitability of his hero's nemesis. In the summer of 1813 he fled to the neutral (and peaceful) ground of Teplitz; though he returned to Weimar in August, he kept luggage packed and ready in case a speedy departure should be necessary.

After the victory at Leipzig, Wilhelm von Humboldt wrote to his wife that Goethe was still unimpressed by the liberation of Germany: he was complaining that the remedy was worse than the illness, and was not convinced that Germany yet had the political maturity to use its freedom to its best advantage.[31] Such somewhat lofty judgements are characteristic of Goethe's innate conservatism or gradualism; and yet for all his scepticism at the time, he later recognized and acknowledged the benefits of peace, of the settlement of the Congress of Vienna, even of the European Restoration and the political quietism of Metternich's post-Congress Europe in the German Confederation. His tendency to affirm the status quo, his abhorrence and fear of violent or even radical change, were profoundly rooted in his nature, intellectually and temperamentally, and in his scientific and political principles – as far as Goethe's principles could be called political at all. More strictly, his instincts were apolitical – which to those more committed to a political agenda appeared reactionary; to Goethe himself, an apolitical or non-partisan overview corresponded to a fundamental need, as he put it in the *Campagne in Frankreich* (Campaign in France), to preserve his integrity and independence as a poet, to rise above factionalism and to maintain an ironic mediation between warring parties.[32] This was not, Goethe insisted, a comfortable alternative or an evasion of commitment, for in all important issues, he points out, those who take sides have the advantage of those who do not: ironic or poetic impartiality is not an easy option.

It was also characteristic of Goethe that he should choose to escape the vexations and upheavals of the European struggle by a flight of the imagination, by what he called, in the poem of that title, his *hejira* ('Hegire'): in poetic terms, a flight eastwards to the exotic culture of fourteenth-century Persian poetry, in real terms a flight westwards to his native Rhineland. In June 1814 he read with increasing enthusiasm the *Divan-i-Hafiz* in the recent translation of Joseph von Hammer-Purgstall; in July that year, and again in May 1815, he set out for the Rhine and Main areas, for Hanau, Frankfurt, Wiesbaden, Bingen, Darmstadt and Heidelberg (and, in 1815, also Bonn and Cologne). In Heidelberg he was exposed to Boisserée's collection of early masters, and to his host's medieval enthusiasms; he also cultivated the academic luminaries of the university, where his son August had studied in 1808/9. He discussed ancient Greece with Johann Heinrich Voß, church music with the law professor Anton Thibaut, Arabic language and culture with the theologian Heinrich Paulus, mythology, anatomy and chemistry with other scholars. The whole journey was for Goethe a stimulating and rejuvenating experience, involving both the new and the familiar in landscape, culture and personal acquaintance; not, perhaps, as momentous a watershed in his life as the Italian journey, but certainly an Indian summer of emotional and creative renewal.

His first meeting with Marianne Jung, on 4 August in Wiesbaden, was unremarkable. The thirty-year-old former actress and singer, of some literary and musical talent, had been the ward of a wealthy Frankfurt banker, Johann Jakob von Willemer, since she was sixteen. On 27 September 1814 the twice-widowed fifty-four-year-old Willemer took her as his wife – coincidentally but intriguingly, very soon after her meeting with the sixty-five-year-old Goethe, and only three weeks before the three came together again at Willemer's small country house outside Frankfurt to witness the celebrations of the first anniversary of Napoleon's defeat at Leipzig. This second meeting was altogether more significant, at least in retrospect, for the two protagonists in a remarkable emotional and literary partnership. It marked the beginning of an allusive, elliptical, playful and yet profoundly serious and passionate relationship over the next twelve months as Goethe and Marianne played out the roles of the legendary lovers of the *West-östliche Divan* (East-West Divan), Hatem and Suleika, exchanging mutual gifts of oriental knick-knacks, playing exotic charades, corresponding in a private code based on the pages of Hammer-Purgstall's Hafiz translation, holding intense private trysts in the grounds of the romantically ruined castle in Heidelberg, and collaborating almost competitively on the poems of Goethe's own *Divan*: to this day it is not clear just how much of the collection is Marianne's own verse.

But it was not until the following year that literary partnership ripened into friendship, and friendship into a briefly passionate encounter. Returning to Weimar in October 1814, Goethe worked steadily during that winter on his orientalizing project while the future political constitution of Europe was being shaped in Vienna; also during this winter, Goethe's wife Christiane fell seriously ill. In May 1815 he again left Weimar for the Rhineland, where the news of Waterloo reached him in Wiesbaden. In July he met Freiherr vom Stein, the architect of the new Prussian state, and only in mid-August resumed contact with the Willemers. In Frankfurt, and more especially in Heidelberg that September, the brief love affair between Hatem/Goethe and Suleika/Marianne was enacted on an intense literary and emotional, though probably not a physical level, finding its emblematic expression in poems like 'Gingo biloba' (Ginkgo Biloba), 'An vollen Büschelzweigen' (In thickly clustered bunches) and, retrospectively, in the urgent and eloquent sensuality of 'Vollmondnacht' (Night of Full Moon). On 7 October Goethe left Heidelberg in a state of near-distraction. His oriental studies and poems for the *West-östliche Divan* continued for several years, but he was never to see Marianne, or visit the Rhineland, again. In July 1816 he set out for Baden-Baden, and no doubt also for Frankfurt and Heidelberg, but his coach overturned shortly after leaving Weimar, and this omen, as he saw it, led him to return home and to break off all contact with Marianne, in spite of her pleas – and indeed in spite of Willemer's extraordinary proposition that the poet should join him and his wife in a *ménage à trois* in Frankfurt. Their correspondence resumed in 1819, and continued until shortly before Goethe's death, when he returned all her letters together with a poignantly elegiac poem.

Goethe had suffered a more orthodox loss before the aborted third journey to the Rhineland: on 6 June 1816 his wife died after a protracted and distressing infection of the kidneys. For all Goethe's more or less innocent philanderings, for all the intellectual and social gulf separating them, for all her lack of public graces, and for all the over-indulgence in food and drink that quickly disfigured her robust physical charms, they appear to have shared a devoted and interdependent domestic existence. Malicious gossip suggested that she died unattended by her husband or her son; other reports have him kneeling pathetically by her dead body, vainly imploring her not to leave him. Certainly, Goethe's own written reactions and some eyewitness accounts indicate a desperately bereft and lonely widower. At the end of the same year, Goethe's inadequate and lethargic son August married the talented and lively, indeed over-lively, Ottilie von Pogwisch, who assumed the domestic responsibilities of his late mother. This unhappy marriage, while it provided Goethe with three grandchildren on whom he lavished affection, brought him little other comfort in his old age; with Ottilie his relations were affectionate, but the son could come to terms neither with his father's fame nor with his powerful and no doubt overwhelming personality. The frequent and audible marital strife fuelled by August's drinking drove Goethe to find refuge in his study – or in wine also; and August's sadly burdened and undistinguished existence ended with his sudden and premature death in Rome in 1830, where he was buried in a setting familiar to his father, indeed where Goethe had remarked some forty-five years earlier that it would be a fitting place to rest: in the Protestant cemetery near the Pyramid of Cestius that he had evoked in his seventh Roman Elegy.

Goethe was to experience one last and violent emotional spasm in his old age. In 1821 he made his first visit to Marienbad, recently developed as a spa town to rival his more usual Bohemian resorts of Karlsbad and Teplitz. Initially, it was his geological interests that had attracted him to Marienbad; but already in his first summer there he had developed an affection for, and had in turn been indulged by, the seventeen-year-old Ulrike von Levetzow, oldest daughter of a young widow who was herself in Marienbad more for sentimental reasons than for reasons of health. The following summer Goethe was again in Marienbad, staying in the same house as Frau von Levetzow and her daughters; and a serious illness in the early months of 1823 gave him the pretext for a third summer visit to the spa. In July he was Ulrike's constant companion on walks and at tea-parties, even, despite an age difference of fifty-five years, at balls. It is believed that a formal proposal of marriage was made, and that the Grand Duke (as he had been since the Congress of Vienna) Karl August himself acted as intermediary in these bizarre and tragi-comic negotiations. But all symptoms of passion appear to have emanated from the would-be fiancé; Ulrike herself, who lived unmarried until 1899, always forcibly denied any emotional commitment in an adult sense. The Levetzows anxiously decamped to Karlsbad, only to be pursued by the besotted *Geheimrat,* where his birthday was celebrated in their company. He left Karlsbad on 10 September for a Weimar seething with scandalized gossip and an anxious household; but by his arrival the following week the desperate trauma of the separation had already been sublimated into the formal stanzas of the most unequivocally and viscerally tragic lyrical expression of his poetic *oeuvre*: the 'Marienbad Elegy' that forms the central section of the *Trilogy of Passion*.

A Productive Old Age

The Marienbad affair was Goethe's final experience of emotional rejuvenescence, a last exercise in 'renewed puberty' on the part of the consciously ageing poet who had always affirmed the dynamic invigoration of constant psychic change and metamorphosis, of dying and becoming, of spiritual renascence. Now he exercised the other, more stoical aspect of his personality and buckled down to a regime of resigned acceptance and the punishing discipline of hard work as he willed himself to use productively the time left to him. He never visited the Bohemian spas again, and his last decade was devoted to three principal literary tasks: the preparation of his collected works, the *Ausgabe letzter Hand*, for publication by Cotta, the completion of *Wilhelm Meisters Wanderjahre* and of *Faust* Part Two – and otherwise to the final touches to *Dichtung und Wahrheit* and to a miscellany of scientific writings on geology, meteorology and comparative anatomy. Most remarkable of all, some of his most compelling and limpid lyric poetry was written during this last decade, as individual poems, as lyrical diptych, in cyclic form, or incorporated into the second part of *Faust*: the inscrutable 'Der Bräutigam' (The Bridegroom), the *Chinesisch-deutsche Jahres- und Tageszeiten* (Sino-German Seasons and Hours), the two Dornburg poems, the chorus of elves in the opening scene of *Faust* Part Two, and Faust's Arcadian vision in Act III.

Goethe's old age, distinguished in the public sphere by honours, fame and an ever-growing circle of admiring – and often importunate – visitors, acquaintances and correspondents, was in domestic terms, in spite of his continuing good relations with his daughter-in-law, not conventionally happy; and he was sustained by the company and fellowship of a very few close friends, Hofrat Heinrich Meyer, Kanzler Friedrich von Müller, Zelter, Knebel, and by various interlocutors: Riemer, Coudray, Soret, Eckermann and his secretary Johann August Friedrich John. His relations with his lifelong friend, ruler and patron Karl August remained warm, but the easy intimacy of youth had long since given way to a more formal relationship in which Goethe punctiliously observed the stiff etiquettes and formulas of court discourse: his letters to the Grand Duke are exemplary in their adherence to the protocols of address. His relationship with the Duke's long-suffering and occasionally depressive wife, the Duchess Luise, were always close, indeed had earlier been almost passionately so, and latterly a deep mutual respect developed between them.

For all his domestic vexations and recurrent periods of ill-health, however, it would be wrong to imagine Goethe's last years as miserable. A stream of visitors from all parts of Europe crowded to the house on the *Frauenplan*, and were for the most part hospitably received; the diaries indicate a vast range of reading, encounters and discussions; his correspondence was prodigious. His passion for collecting, a great characteristic of the age, was also indulged: drawings, etchings, statuary and bas-relief, coins, manuscripts, geological and botanical specimens were stored and catalogued with pedantic care. The crowded minutiae of Goethe's remarkably active last decade were recorded, more or less accurately, by his companion and literary executor Johann Peter Eckermann, who drew on his own and others' experiences to compile a substantial record of Goethe's daily round and of his views on a huge range of subjects.

What strikes the reader of the vast documentation pertaining to Goethe's last decade is above all that his eclectic and almost obsessive intellectual curiosity was undiminished as artists, musicians, writers, politicians, scholars, scientists, notables and aristocrats flocked to Weimar. With Alexander von Humboldt he discussed the explorer's travels, his own botanical studies and the geological theories that had long preoccupied him; with Wilhelm von Humboldt he discussed current affairs, philosophy and his own works, and with Felix Mendelssohn he discoursed on music. He received Grillparzer, Varnhagen von Ense and his wife Rahel, Prince Pückler-Muskau, Hegel, Freiherr vom Stein, Graf Brühl, Paganini, Thackeray, Prussian, Bavarian and Russian royalty. He corresponded with Walter Scott and Thomas Carlyle, he read the *Edinburgh Review* and the leading French journals. His respect for Byron, a blend of fascination and concern, of literary admiration and moral deprecation, was reciprocated: Byron dedicated two dramas to Goethe, and Goethe paid his own generous tributes to the maverick poet – 'the greatest talent of the century' – in poems, conversations, in a memoir, and, most movingly of all, in the third act of *Faust* Part Two.[33]

In 1832 he was sent drawings of the *Casa di Goethe* in Pompeii. His reading ranged from Plutarch to *Tristram Shandy*, from Calderón to Manzoni, Francis Bacon to Robert Burns, Walter Scott to Victor Hugo, Balzac to Chinese novels – while he remained indifferent to much of modern German literature. His feeling that the future lay with what he termed 'world literature' (*Weltliteratur*) rather than with national literatures was based on a somewhat diffuse notion of global literary communication that would break down national cultural barriers.

With the *Bürgermeister* of Bremen he discussed harbour construction and trade routes to Brazil; with Eckermann he talked of everything under the sun. His attitude towards a new era of trade and communications, to the beginnings of the Industrial Revolution, was a characteristic mixture of informed interest and cautious reserve. He talked of the future construction of canals in Suez and Panama, or between the Rhine and the Danube, anticipating (rather over-optimistically) their completion within fifty years of his death. He was instructed on the workings of the steam-engine, took note of steam navigation, and a month before his death received from some English admirers a brochure on the Liverpool to Manchester Railway; he had earlier been sent a model of Stephenson's 'Rocket'. He knew of the iron foundries of Coalbrookdale and of eastern France, and was informed on Robert Owen's New Lanark settlement. Much of *Wilhelm Meisters Wanderjahre* is devoted to an exhaustive survey of the Swiss cotton industry, its dependence on and vulnerability to the world market, as well as references to the optical telegraph, to mining technology and to the 'monitor system' of teaching developed by contemporary Scottish and English pedagogues. At the same time, he was more than sensitive to the potential confusions and dilemmas of scientific and technological progress; while he could scarcely anticipate the social and political problems that were to accompany industrial revolution – class struggle, the creation of a proletariat, profit and exploitation – he was fearful of the results of the mechanization of labour, of the threat to traditional manufacturing practice and social patterns, wary of fiscal reform, and altogether bewildered by what he confessed were, for him, 'confusing doctrines for confused dealings' in the 'absurd and confused times' of his old age.[34]

For all his huge circle of acquaintances and contacts, social, political, intellectual or artistic, Goethe evidently felt often detached and even isolated during these last years. His vision became, according to his own formulaic definition of the stages of life (see above, p. 41 and below, p. 122), a mystical one – a vision expressed not only in some late poems but also in conversations and correspondence with close friends. To Zelter in particular, he voiced a gnomic expression of his later outlook in which he professed an affinity with the quietistic fatalism of Islam – as he put it, a sense of profound acceptance, a detached but serene perception that rose above present vexations, but which also transfigured the real into a comprehensive symbolic meaningfulness:

> Unconditional submission to the inscrutable will of God, viewing with serenity the ever-circling and spiralling recurrence of the earth's restless bustle, love, affection, suspended between two worlds, all that is real refined, dissolving into symbol.

'What more', he asks wryly, 'could Grandpapa wish for?'.[35]

It was also to Zelter that he confided some of his most private thoughts on death and survival beyond death, as he sought to comfort his friend on the death of his son in 1827:

> Let us continue our efforts until . . . , summoned by the world-spirit, we return to the ether! May the eternal being then not deny us new activities analogous to those in which we have already proved ourselves. If he then in his fatherly love also grants us memory to recall a sense of what is right and good, such as we have willed and achieved in this life, then surely we should all the sooner be integrated into the mechanism of the universe. The entelechic monad must survive only in unremitting activity; if this becomes its second nature, it will not be idle through all eternity. Forgive these abstruse thoughts! But we have ever strayed into such regions, and sought to communicate in such terms, in those cases where reason is inadequate, yet where we do not wish unreason to prevail.[36]

Such occasional mystical utterances do not of course comprise or comprehend the whole of the aged Goethe's much-celebrated wisdom. As he grew older, he tended to refine and concentrate his experience and thought into reflective maxims and aphorisms, into epigram and sententious verse, into his imaginative writing, his poetry, and not least into his scientific studies. While no orthodox Christian believer, indeed an often savagely satirical debunker of religious ritual and Christian doctrines, of the Trinity, of redemption and the Eucharist, he did not hesitate to invoke God, the or a deity, an eternal being or spirit, the divine and other such numinous concepts in order to express his most personal beliefs. In *Faust* Part Two he formulated a quasi-Platonic conception of the relationship between real and ideal that relativizes reality as a reflection, a simile or symbol of the ideal, but which does not therefore devalue or ironize (as did the Romantic doctrine of transcendentalism) the beauty or meaning of what he called the 'richly gifted world' (*reichbegabte Welt*). 'All that is transient / Is but a likeness' (*Alles Vergängliche / Ist nur ein Gleichnis*): the lines of the final *Chorus mysticus* stand as a thematic motto over the complex symbolic diversity of *Faust* Part Two. We are, as Prometheus says in *Pandora* (line 598), destined to perceive not the light, but that which is illuminated: not absolute truth, but truth mediated through its symbolic reflection. For Goethe, however, the stubborn realist who could never favour abstraction or transcendentalism over the evidence of his own senses, for whom the perceived world was paramount, this mediated or metaphorical perception was sufficient:

> Und deines Geistes höchster Feuerflug
> Hat schon am Gleichnis, hat am Bild genug.[37]

> The highest fiery flight of human mind
> In likeness, image is enough defined.

Goethe's scientific work, for all its shortcomings, was itself based on a quest for the wholeness and integrity of 'God-Nature', for a unifying law or principle that would contain and explain the bewildering diversity of forms and species in nature. His own cabinets of specimens, the botanical, zoological and geological collections of the professional scientists, and his own close observation of forms, were daily evidence of the protean profusion of nature. But Goethe was enough a child of his own age to hold almost desperately to the belief in a coherent order and unity in creation; he was heir to the neo-Platonic doctrine of the Chain of Being, of a continuous but graduated hierarchy of forms in which humanity had its place – a tradition that was already under pressure in Goethe's day, and which would before long be swept away by a doctrine that also sought to impose unity and coherence, but in a very different perspective: that of evolution in *time* (see below, pp. 266–8).

In 1825 three jubilees were celebrated in Weimar: on 3 September the fiftieth anniversary of Karl August's accession, on 3 October the golden wedding of the ruling couple, and on 7 November the anniversary of Goethe's arrival in the Duchy to whose cultural prestige he had contributed so enormously. The Grand Duke paid him fulsome tribute in a personal dispatch and in a specially struck commemorative medal, and Goethe received the public homage of the civic authorities, of the academic establishment of Jena University and of the Weimar intelligentsia. More sombre landmarks in his career were to follow: in September 1826 Schiller's bones were taken from the public vault in order to be reburied in the mausoleum of the Dukes of Weimar. Goethe was shown the skull, which was taken to his own house for cleaning, and during the night of 25/26 September he composed the memorial in *terza rima* that celebrates the creative fire once housed within the dry shell of this 'mysterious vessel'. In December the following year Schiller's remains were laid to rest in the *Fürstengruft* – where, it was understood, Goethe would also be buried. In 1827 Frau von Stein died aged eighty-four; their bitter estrangement after 1789 had slowly been mended, Goethe had sent her frequent presents, and she had shown kindnesses towards his son, no doubt remembering how close Goethe had been to her own son Fritz – but she had never brought herself to treat his wife with anything more than distant condescension. She gave instructions that her funeral cortège should not pass Goethe's house, knowing how averse he was to public obsequies and displays of mourning, whether because he abhorred ritual as such or because he was profoundly fearful of any *memento mori*.

In 1828 Karl August died on his way back to Weimar from Berlin; Goethe, to the outrage of many in Weimar, absented himself from the funeral ceremonies, retiring to Dornburg for some two months – a gesture variously interpreted as one of profound grief, as emotional evasion, or as an abdication of public obligation. Since he had given up his summer visits to the Bohemian spa towns, the idyllic setting of Dornburg on a cliff above the River Saale, with its picturesque Renaissance and Rococo palaces, had been a preferred refuge for Goethe; in a small grace and favour apartment here he frequently spent his time reclusively, devoting himself to his botanical and geological studies – and, on this occasion, also writing two of his last and most delicate lyric poems, hymnic celebrations of the sky by night and by day that resume the profound acceptance and affirmation of a lifetime's experience (see below, pp. 130–1).

In January 1829 *Faust* Part One was given its first performance in Germany at the Court Theatre in Brunswick. It had been performed two months earlier in Paris; the following May Hector Berlioz sent Goethe the score of his 'Eight Scenes from *Faust*', accompanied by a fulsome letter of homage – to which Goethe, on the basis of Zelter's judgement of the music, did not reply. Further performances of *Faust* followed in Germany, and in August 1829 it was presented in Weimar. For reasons of his own, Goethe did not attend the performance, though it appears that he had some part in the rehearsals; no doubt the youthful emotional confusions of the first part now seemed more distant than ever to the poet who was struggling to complete his final task – the writing of *Faust* Part Two.

Goethe's cool indifference to the homage and the music of Berlioz was characteristic enough of his reception of modern Romantic composers: in 1825 Franz Schubert had sent him his settings of three poems by Goethe, and had also received no reply. In his understanding and appreciation of music, Goethe has commonly been perceived, at worst as an ignoramus, at best as an inexpert dilettante. It is true that he had little practical musical talent – though he did, in 1807, organize a series of house concerts in which he sang along with the bass voices, and in 1818 he was given some instruction on the pianoforte. But he was an enthusiastic and appreciative listener; he had heard the young Mozart play, and in later years Beethoven, Hummel, Maria Szymanovska and Mendelssohn were to play for him, as was the gifted concert pianist Clara Wieck, future wife of Robert Schumann, in 1831. Goethe had first met Zelter's pupil Mendelssohn as a twelve-year-old prodigy, and developed a warm and respectful relationship with the young musician, who taught him much about music and in 1825 dedicated his B minor piano quartet to Goethe. Goethe was very well informed on the history of Italian church music, and revered Bach, Handel and Mozart; his remark that to listen to Bach's music was to hear the harmony of creation such as God himself might have heard just before he made the world is perhaps fanciful, but these are not the words of someone who is unreceptive to music.[38] He staged many performances of Mozart's *Singspiele* and operas in Weimar, remarked that Mozart would have been the ideal composer for parts of *Faust* Part Two, and indeed set out to write a sequel to *The Magic Flute* – though in this he was no doubt drawn as much by the extravagant symbolism of Schikaneder's fairytale libretto as by Mozart's music. He knew and admired Beethoven, who in turn expressed his great esteem for Goethe – not least through his incidental music to *Egmont*. But Goethe was ill at ease with both Beethoven's abrasive social manners and the power of his music, which he found unsettling and overwhelming: his reaction to the opening section of the Fifth Symphony was to remark that it was as if the roof were falling in. Goethe's musical tastes were decidedly conservative, though the charge that he preferred mediocrity to excellence is not entirely just; certainly, he appeared to rely heavily on the judgement and advice of close friends like Zelter who, while not without talent (his simple setting of 'Der König in Thule' is hauntingly appropriate), was equally conservative in his compositions and his tastes.

In 1830 Goethe was once more to be profoundly challenged, indeed shaken, by the intrusion of international affairs: in July that year the political quietism of post-Congress Restoration Europe was disturbed by the abdication of Charles X in Paris, by the July Revolution and the accession of the 'Citizen King' Louis-Philippe. Goethe had taken a keen and informed interest in French affairs for some time, albeit with growing apprehension; he had read the French journals voraciously, in spite of his profound misgivings towards the assertive freedom of the French press and towards its increasingly republican tendencies. This led him to suspend all such reading in the summer of 1830, while at the same time keeping a wary eye on events in Paris, and to devote his energies and attentions to his literary and scientific work, to *Faust* and to a celebrated scientific dispute in the Parisian *Académie des sciences* between Baron Georges Léopold Cuvier and Etienne Geoffroy Saint-Hilaire concerning the principles of comparative anatomy.

Frédéric Soret, who was collaborating with Goethe on a French translation of the poem 'Metamorphose der Pflanzen', tells an amusing story that has become accepted as a typical example of Goethe's total indifference to politics. Visiting Goethe just as the news of the Revolution reached Weimar in early August, he was greeted with the words: 'Well, what do you think of this great news? Everything is in turmoil, it has been brought out into the open at last, the volcano has erupted!' It was some time before Soret realized that Goethe was talking, not of the Revolution, but of the scientific feud at the *Académie*. It is a fine anecdote, but not one that reflects the whole truth. Goethe's reaction to the July Revolution was one of profound anxiety – in the event, indeed, an over-reaction; what haunted him at this stage of his life was the spectre of that other revolution in Paris. Above all, as he reiterated in letters to his friends about what he termed the 'Parisian earthquake', he feared 'a reprise of the tragedy of 1790'; and what is more, he feared that, as the effects of the Lisbon earthquake were noticed in the remotest wells and lakes, so too the effects of this 'western explosion' might spread beyond the frontiers of France – as they had threatened to do, and as they had indeed done, in the 1790s.[39]

In the event, the European order, and the German Confederation in particular, were for the time being not imperilled, and Goethe could resume his literary and scientific work. On 10 November he received the news of his son's death in Rome; he had been corresponding with him regularly and following his itinerary closely. Later that month he suffered a haemorrhage which he attributed to the shock of bereavement, but soon resumed work on his writing. *Faust* was finally completed in July 1831; the manuscript was sealed for posthumous publication (though it was later to be reopened for minor alterations), and Goethe pronounced that he could regard the days remaining to him purely as a gift, a bonus as it were. In August he spent his last birthday quietly in Ilmenau with his two grandsons; there he recalled his considerable efforts to revive the silver and copper mines, which had come to nothing, and his attempts to relieve the privations of the miners, the weavers, the foresters and charcoal-burners of the region, reflecting almost enviously on their stoical, if deprived, existences – and he read once again, poignantly, the closing words of the laconic poem he had scratched on the wall of a wooden cabin on the slopes of the Kickelhahn more than fifty years earlier: 'Warte nur, balde / Ruhest du auch' (Wait though, shortly / You will rest too).

On 16 March 1832 Goethe's last illness set in with the painful and distressing symptoms of heart disease. His doctor noted the distorted and livid features that expressed great suffering and a dread of impending death; others palliated the unlovely reality with less clinical observations. But death came peacefully enough on the morning of 22 March as he was nursed by his daughter-in-law Ottilie. His last words are supposed to have been 'More light' (*Mehr Licht*), which may have been an instruction to open the window-shutters to let in the spring sunshine, an indication that his sight was failing, or, as is often believed, a final symbolic invocation. *Se non è vero, è ben trovato.* He was buried in the *Fürstengruft*, where he and Schiller lie side by side in large but simple oak coffins. From 1954 to 1994 the two coffins, placed prominently in the east vault, dominated the scene; in the obscurity of the side vaults lay, in some disorder, the more extravagant sarcophagi of the temporal rulers of the Duchy of Sachsen-Weimar-Eisenach. This politically symbolic arrangement was 'corrected' in the restoration of 1993/4, when the two *Dichterfürsten* were restored to their original, more modest, positions.

2

The Lyric Poet

For all his wide and varied achievements in other fields of literary and intellectual activity, there can be little doubt that Goethe's outstanding gift was as a lyric poet. He seems to have recognized this himself in spite of the fact that it was probably only during or after his journey to Italy that he finally and reluctantly acknowledged that his talents as a painter were unlikely to achieve more than a degree of accomplishment, and despite his stubborn and over-ambitious conviction that his scientific work would be more distinguished and have more lasting value than his literary achievement. Goethe's often seemingly simple and effortless mastery of poetic language, his creative control over sounds, images, diction, rhythms and versification informs, intensifies and vitalizes much of his literary work, including his letters and his scientific writings, his prose novels and novellas, his satires and epigrams; but it is in the lyrical power of his dramatic writing, pre-eminently in *Faust*, and in his lyric poetry as such that his quasi-magical gift of poetic expression is most strikingly evident.

Any theoretical or essential definition of the lyric poet or of lyric poetry as a genre is fraught with historical and methodological, even ideological problems, and none will be attempted here.[1] The narrowest understanding of lyric poetry as song would exclude huge areas of what is conventionally or editorially accepted within the lyrical canon, while the widest application of the term, say, to Goethe's poetry – or even to what Goethe himself subsumed under the heading *Lyrisches* – would include such a broad range of poetic utterance as to lose any useful meaning for purposes of definition.[2] In addition, in seeking to define Goethe's lyric poetry *qua* lyric poetry, the very notion of what is or is not, should or should not be, can or cannot be lyrical, is (at least in the German literary tradition, and at least for a long time after Goethe) conditioned and characterized by Goethe's own exemplary achievement, and by the achievement of subsequent generations for whom he was, for better or for worse, the touchstone of poetic expression.

Two further difficult and probably unanswerable questions raised all too frequently about Goethe's lyric poetry concern on the one hand the relationship between personal experience and imaginative expression, between first-hand 'truth' and vicarious 'fiction', and on the other hand the relationship between spontaneity and rhetoric, between the uncensored outpouring of compulsive articulation and the controlled discipline of organized aesthetic form. Critical positions have been taken up on these matters with regard to Goethe, often with some violence, and have no doubt contributed to a productive scholarly dialectic; indeed, any fifty-fifty equivocation on these questions runs the risk of appearing as uncommitted diffidence or even as middle-of-the-road banality. But it can scarcely escape any informed reader that Goethe's lyrical *oeuvre* meshes with his emotional, intellectual and even his professional career in a clearly recognizable biographical profile, while it also imaginatively elaborates and extends personal experience far beyond its biographical origins. Equally, it must be acknowledged that Goethe's verse is not solely the result of compulsive spontaneity, that he is no song-bird warbling his wood-notes wild; and yet the seemingly effortless and artless effect of much of his poetry is scarcely the sole product of rhetorical calculation or of dispassionate linguistic discipline and control. In any case, the degree of perceived or intended spontaneity or rhetoric will vary according to the purpose or nature of the individual poem, to the programmatic or stylistic phases of a poet's development, and to a host of other factors.

Stephen Spender has characterized Goethe's poetry as 'a heightening of spontaneous eloquence by the addition of poetic form';[3] and while the term 'addition' might sound over-mechanical or even culinary for what is surely a more subtle fusion or symbiosis, this is as succinct a judgement as any. Although Goethe himself occasionally encouraged the notion that his poems were written in a state of creative trance, he also reminds the reader in some of his own poetry that the poetic gift is the fusion between the compulsive expression of chaotic emotion and the sovereignty of formal verbal organization, expressed in the sonnet 'Natur und Kunst' (Nature and Art) as the harmonizing of free nature and organized control whereby mastery manifests itself in the discipline of craftsmanship, or in the poem 'Dauer im Wechsel' (Permanence in Change) as the fusion of substance and form that gives permanence to the mutability of human experience by means of poetic expression.

A final question to be addressed before turning to a critical study of Goethe's lyric poetry is the 'editorial' problem posed by the sheer volume of his poetic output. Unlike many lyric poets, Goethe lived to a high age, and continued to write lyric poetry well into his old age; and many students are daunted by this vast corpus of poems. As indicated in the preface, the selection of poems dealt with here is based on Erich Trunz's selection in Volume One of the *Hamburger Ausgabe* – though necessarily, reference will also be made outside that volume from time to time: to the poems of the *West-östliche Divan* in Volume Two of the *Hamburger Ausgabe* (and of course in all standard editions of Goethe's works), to certain apocryphal poems like 'Das Tagebuch' (The Diary), the suppressed Roman Elegies, and various epigrams or verses not included in Trunz's selection. These can be found easily enough in complete editions like the *Frankfurter Ausgabe*, and are marked with an asterisk (*) for convenience. Trunz's selection is arranged in thematic or generic sections in broadly chronological sequence; but the strict order of composition is frequently overridden by the thematic grouping. The selection studied here follows Trunz's ordering in the main, though not every poem will be given full attention; at all times the dates given are those of first composition or revision, as nearly as can be established, not of publication except where stated.

EARLY VERSE; LEIPZIG ROCOCO

Goethe's juvenile poetic output displays, if nothing else, a precocious confidence in the use of rhymed and unrhymed verse forms. A New Year's greeting to his grandparents at age seven is in remarkably accomplished alexandrines, probably not his own unaided work; an occasionally hilarious poem in English, 'A Song over the Unconfidence towards Myself'*, and other poems in English and French, show a reasonable command of a foreign literary idiom at the age of sixteen; a verse letter to his mother a year later, 'Obgleich kein Gruß' (Although no greeting), for all its ponderous imagery of the rock of affection washed over by the torrent of life, shows him experimenting with the flexibility of blank verse; and an early poem on Christ's harrowing of hell dramatically exploits the rhetoric of Baroque devotional verse and of Protestant theology. But Goethe's career as an original or significant lyric poet is conventionally dated to those poems he wrote in Leipzig, or subsequently in Frankfurt, during his early student days, which were collected in manuscript form into three albums – the volume *Annette* (1767); three poems of the same year addressed to his friend Behrisch; and a collection of songs, *Lieder mit Melodien* (Songs with Melodies), later expanded and published without Goethe's name as *Neue Lieder in Melodien gesetzt* by B. T. Breitkopf in 1769. These are the so-called *Leipziger Lieder* that survived Goethe's wholesale burning of his writings in October 1767.

Whether or not the 'Annette' of the title of the first volume derives from Anna Katharina ('Kätchen') Schönkopf, the partner of Goethe's tortured adolescent flirtation in Leipzig, it is unlikely that these coy sexual romps were inspired by his or Kätchen's behaviour; this is the prevailing literary idiom commonly (and often disparagingly) labelled 'Anacreontic'. Not only are the poems heavily indebted to earlier or contemporary German poets such as Hagedorn, Wieland, Gleim, Weiße, Zachariae or Ramler; some are expressly cited as translations from Italian or French (one explicitly from 'Herr von Voltaire'). Most revolve around erotic adventures, aided or frustrated by a rococo Cupid or Amor, between lovers with neo-classical names – Ziblis, Damoete, Chimene, Amino – in Arcadian settings. The principal emotions are those of triumph in the case of a successful, despair in the case of an unsuccessful seduction. This is the emotional idiom and style of eighteenth-century literary rococo, of gallantry and dalliance: witty, elegant, erotic, cynical – not the pre-Romantic worship of love as a primal force that is more usually associated with the young Goethe. Nature is here a bucolic backdrop for seduction strategies, with convenient groves, rushes or mossy bowers – not the awesome creative or destructive landscape that Goethe was soon to evoke. It is too easy to dismiss this idiom as trivial or prurient (though Goethe was later to charge

Wieland with those failings); there is much in the *Buch Annette* that reminds us that
the stuff of late eighteenth-century poetry is not only that of visceral emotional
responses or Promethean titanism, but also that of social behaviour, wit and
badinage, irony and entertainment. It is the idiom in which Goethe exercised his
early derivative poetic skills, the foil against which the dynamism of his *Sturm und
Drang* poetry is all the more sensational. The *Annette* collection was elegantly
transcribed by Behrisch, with appropriate rococo vignettes, but was never published during Goethe's lifetime; indeed, it was only discovered in 1894 among the
papers left by Luise von Göchhausen – a less spectacular find than that of the
Urfaust, but still an important addition to Goethe's lyrical corpus.

    Already in *Annette*, Goethe had composed an elegy on the death of Behrisch's
brother that stands out from the Anacreontic verses surrounding it, containing
some mildly subversive rhetoric on the tyranny of princes. It was to Behrisch
himself, who as the result of a malicious slander was dismissed from his position
as tutor to the Graf von Lindenau and who, to Goethe's dismay, left Leipzig in
October 1767, that the 'Three Odes to my Friend' were addressed. The three
poems express Goethe's (and presumably Behrisch's) bitterness with savage empathy as he advises his friend to trust no one, confide in no one, and to cauterize his
feelings for fear of renewed betrayal and disappointment. Sententious as much of
the misanthropic rhetoric might be, this style is also far removed from the facetious and arch expression of the rococo lyrics; it is a classicizing ode form of
unrhymed quatrains in free rhythms which, while no doubt derived from
Klopstock, occasionally takes on a lapidary simplicity that recalls Brecht's deceptively prosaic verse style:

> Verpflanze den schönen Baum,
> Gärtner, er jammert mich.
> Baum, danke dem Gärtner,
> Der dich verpflanzt!

> Transplant the fine tree,
> Gardener, I pity it.
> Tree, thank the gardener
> Who transplants you!

    The intensity of bitterness in these three odes, vicarious and rhetorical though
it may be, is the first sounding of a rare but strikingly empathetic articulation of
depressive melancholy or misanthropy in Goethe's poetry, anticipating the
powerful empathy with the depressive Plessing that is incorporated into the later
poem 'Harzreise im Winter' (see below, pp. 66–7):

> Ach, wer heilet die Schmerzen
> Des, dem Balsam zu Gift ward?
> Der sich Menschenhaß
> Aus der Fülle der Liebe trank.
> Erst verachtet, nun ein Verächter,
> Zehrt er heimlich auf

Seinen eignen Wert
In ungnügender Selbstsucht.

Ah, but who heals the pain
Of him for whom balm turned to poison?
Who from abundance of love
Drank his misanthropic hate.
First despised, now despising,
Secretly he consumes
His own worth,
Unfulfilled and self-absorbed.

To be sure, the lines on Plessing warn explicitly of the dangers of self-absorbed misanthropy, whereas the odes to Behrisch exhort the wronged man to adopt the carapace of emotional indifference; but the odes are the first imaginative treatment of a rare but distinct dark strain in Goethe's otherwise notably life-affirming poetic work. The third ode also anticipates a motif that will recur in Goethe's works with more or less tragic overtones – parting or separation:

Tod ist Trennung,
Dreifacher Tod
Trennung ohne Hoffnung
Wiederzusehn.

Separation is death,
Threefold death
Parting without hope of
Meeting again.

Some fifty-seven years later Goethe was to express with similar laconic force the 'death' of parting in his retrospective ode to Werther: 'Scheiden ist der Tod!' (Parting is death!).

The first poem of the *Neue Lieder*, by contrast, 'Neujahrslied'* (New Year's Song), is in Anacreontic style, advising those afflicted by misery or misanthropy to drown their sorrows in wine; others reiterate the standard themes of transience, *carpe diem*, dalliance, erotic fulfilment and frustration in an allegorizing and often wryly sententious manner. A poem like 'Unbeständigkeit' (Inconstancy, later slightly revised as 'Wechsel', Change) is a playful celebration of variety and inconstancy in love which, while it has none of the lyrical profundity of Goethe's later meditation on transience, 'Dauer im Wechsel', with which it has some imagery in common, shows an early mastery of dactylic rhythms.

Two other poems from the *Neue Lieder* are frequently singled out as marking the beginnings of Goethe's self-emancipation from the prevailing fashion, and are cited as perceived examples of a more powerful, urgent or 'true' emotional response to landscape and nature that heralds his future lyrical development: 'Die Nacht' (Night, revised as 'Die schöne Nacht', The Beautiful Night) and 'An den Mond' (To the Moon, revised as 'An Luna', To Luna – either to avoid confusion with the early Weimar poem 'An den Mond', or to match the invocation of the classical deity in the reworked final stanza). They are both accomplished poems; whether they are indeed more original, less affectedly rococo, whether they betray a more intense emotional response than the other Leipzig poems is an issue that raises a host of aesthetic and poetological questions. Certainly, 'Die Nacht' continues the neo-classical allegorizing of the rococo idiom: not Amor, but Luna and Zephyr accompany the poet's soulful progress through the 'sweet night' as he leaves the hut where his beloved dwells. But for all its emotional exuberance, for all that this is the first in a long line of memorable poems by Goethe in which the moon or moonlight feature in various symbolic or allegorical functions, the emotional tension is broken by the characteristic witty or ruefully facetious concluding *Pointe* of the rococo style:

> Und doch wollt' ich, Himmel, dir
> Tausend deiner Nächte lassen,
> Gäb' mein Mädchen Eine mir.

> And yet, heaven, I'd leave to thee
> Nights like this a thousandfold
> If my love gave one to me.

The emotional 'alienation effect' is even more striking in 'An Luna', which opens with a misty, sentimental apostrophe to the moon as an image of mournful tenderness ('Zärtlichkeit in Trauer'). Possible Ossianic associations, certainly reminiscences of the eighteenth-century tradition of lyrical melancholy inspired, as Goethe tells us in his autobiography,[4] by the English elegiac poets Thomson, Young and Gray, evoke the *frisson* of night thoughts on death and immortality; but this sombre introspection is confined to the opening stanza. By the second stanza, the 'cavalier' imagines himself beside the moon, peering through the window of his beloved's room, gazing on her 'rounded limbs'; but this erotic fantasy is in turn broken by a mock admonition to the voyeuristic lover – or to the moon. It is notable that in revising this poem for the 1815 edition of his works, Goethe removed the facetious *Pointe* of the final four lines, and sustains the vicarious eroticism by means of a conceit on the myth of Endymion and Luna.

THE SESENHEIM POEMS

For all the rhythmic and verbal virtuosity of the early Leipzig or Frankfurt poetry, it is as the poet of the so-called 'Sesenheim Songs' that Goethe's first truly original contribution to German lyric poetry is acknowledged. Goethe himself is at least in part responsible for this perception, having left in his autobiography a retrospective account of the emotional, literary and intellectual liberation he experienced in Strasbourg. Under the seminal and stimulating influence of his cultural mentor Herder, Goethe responded to what he and his teacher perceived as the unvarnished naturalness and spontaneity of popular poetry, which they championed against the formal and derivative traditions dominating German literature, whether drama or poetry. Natural genius, original, unaffected, creative and overwhelming: these were the qualities attributed to Shakespeare, to the Homeric epics and the Norse sagas, to folk song and to the robust language of Reformation Germany in a polemical defiance of prevailing tastes and norms, whether rationalistic and rococo in the lyric, or Gallic and classicizing in the drama. Freshness, immediacy, emotional exuberance, a response to the natural landscape as a living force, creative or destructive, idyllic or sinister – this was the effect that was sought and perceived as solely valid.

Whether this effect was in fact achieved by effervescent spontaneity or by painstaking effort is, as we have argued above, unknowable and scarcely relevant. But we might do well to remind ourselves that for example 'Willkommen und Abschied' (Greeting and Parting), the poem that exemplifies as much as any other the pell-mell exuberance associated with Goethe's *Sturm und Drang* poetry, the poem that seems to raise spontaneous impetuosity of action and feeling to an aesthetic principle, whose second line expresses the essence of spontaneity: 'Es war getan fast eh' gedacht' (Before I'd thought it, it was done) – that this version of that line is in fact the product of a much later revision for the 1789 edition of the poems. The original 1771 version of this line read, rather more conventionally and less 'spontaneously': 'Und fort, wild wie ein Held zur Schlacht' (Away, as a hero wild to war). The poetic effect of spontaneity is often the result of careful revision.

By no means all the Sesenheim poems celebrate the great outdoors of preRomantic landscape poetry; some of them read like an extension of the earlier verse, and much of the imagery revolves around roses, ribbons, the beloved asleep in her chamber. 'Kleine Blumen, kleine Blätter' (Small Flowers, Small Leaves – in revised form entitled 'Mit einem gemalten Band', With a Painted Ribbon) appears still beholden to elegant conceits and rococo imagery of allegorized Cupids and Zephyrs, though some critics claim to detect signs of a transition to a more dynamic lyrical and emotional commitment here. But it is the two poems probably also dating from the spring or summer of 1771 that are held to mark the true origins of Goethe's lyrical originality. 'Willkommen und Abschied' records in balladesque style a wild gallop through the nocturnal landscape to the beloved in Sesenheim – and in *Dichtung und Wahrheit* Goethe takes care to confirm the impression of an impulsive, unpremeditated headlong rush to join his sweetheart, matching his recollection to the poem in an amalgam of 'poetry' and 'truth'. The landscape is sinister, threatening, even demonic, and the personified and animated nature imagery is justly renowned and cherished by Goethe's readers: evening cradles the earth, oaks loom like mythical giants, the moon looks down mournfully (or, in the first version, 'sleepily'), and darkness peers from the bushes with a hundred black eyes. This spooky backdrop, however, is not without a certain contrived staginess; it is a scenic succession of threatening shapes and forms vividly evoked by a galloping rhythm and perceived as if glimpsed at full pelt from horseback. But it is a dark foil that is easily dispelled by the rider's fiery exuberance of spirit; this nocturnal stage-set has little of the panic terror of 'Erlkönig', and its meretricious horrors are quickly forgotten in the roseate glow of affection that greets him on his arrival, in the exchange of reciprocal glances. The final stanza resolves into the sweet sorrow of parting and an exuberant statement of faith in ecstatic mutual love. It is difficult to read the concluding lines of the final version of this poem without a biographical gloss: the persona of the lyric poem leaves his tearful sweetheart as Goethe might have left Friederike Brion for the last time in August 1771 – and indeed as Goethe was also to describe it in *Dichtung und Wahrheit*.[5] But not only the probable dating of the first version to the spring of that year militates against any overtly biographical reading: in this first version, it is she, not he, who leaves ('Du gingst, ich stund und sah zur Erden': You went, I stood with downcast eyes). Goethe was to articulate his guilt feelings *vis-à-vis* Friederike more powerfully and subtly in other parts of his dramatic works.

'Maifest' (May Fair, later entitled 'Mailied', May Song) is a poem devoted entirely and ecstatically to joy, sunlight, vernal growth, birdsong and love; the boldly emphatic, occasionally dactylic stresses of its short two-beat lines articulate Goethe's most unreservedly exuberant responses to landscape. The mood is set by the incomparable opening:

> Wie herrlich leuchtet
> Mir die Natur!
>
> How gloriously nature
> Shines for me!

and it continues in a series of apostrophes, exclamations and similies in which emotional spontaneity is identified with the compulsive urge of birdsong, an extravagant but highly expressive articulation of an unproblematic pathetic fallacy in which nature mirrors and mimics human responses as they mirror nature in perfect reciprocity. Even a note of reflective literary self-consciousness as the poet reminds his sweetheart that it is she who is the impetus for his 'new songs and dances' does not break the flow of a poem that for all its formal punctuation seems designed syntactically to be read, as it were, in one breath.

'Ein zärtlich-jugendlicher Kummer' (A tender-youthful sense of sorrow), written in Frankfurt in 1772 well after Goethe's return from Strasbourg, is a more subdued and conscious meditation, in rhymed madrigal verses of varying length, on the theme of hope in the barrenness of winter. It quietly juxtaposes a sombre mood of personal desolation with the stirring of nature at the end of winter, the physical and emotional burgeoning of a young pubescent girl, and the gardener's hopeful spring sowing of seed.

STURM UND DRANG: THE ODES AND HYMNS

While most of the Sesenheim poems, for all their occasional exuberant dynamism, did not stray very far from conventional lyrical themes and images – love, flowers, landscape, the seasons – or, with the exception of 'Mailied', from conventional metrical forms, it was in the so-called *Sturm und Drang* odes or hymns that Goethe's originality and mastery of poetic language emerged most strikingly. These expressive and often verbally experimental works are more characteristically the poetry of the *Geniezeit* – the period when a young and impatient generation of literary talents asserted itself against prevailing fashion in the name of a Promethean creativity that joyfully trampled on literary rules and conventions and claimed a freedom of form and style that produced, in the dramatic genre *Götz von Berlichingen*, in the narrative *Die Leiden des jungen Werthers* (The Sufferings of Young Werther), and in the lyric a series of extended poems on larger-than-life figures and themes: Mohammed, Prometheus, Ganymede, creative genius, nature, time and destiny. While not uninfluenced by Klopstock's free rhythms, Goethe's *Sturm und Drang* odes extend rhythmic freedom on the model of the prevailing understanding of Pindaric odes, which at the time were perceived (and printed), in a fruitful misunderstanding of Pindar's strict strophic and metrical forms, as free verse. Goethe's poems are also, in contradistinction to Klopstock's theological fervour, and for all their own vatic religiosity, secularized, or at least non-Christian or pagan, in content and inspiration.

The most strikingly chaotic expression of these heroic or titanic personae adopted by Goethe is in a poem he himself characterized as 'half-nonsense': 'Wandrers Sturmlied' (Traveller's Song to the Storm, 1772), a dithyrambic ode that celebrates the frenzy of poetic genius, the fiery glow of the creative mind as it defies the raging elements – though the *Genius* invoked in the opening stanza of the poem is not, apparently, human genius, but the tutelary spirit of inspiration the poet-genius calls on to be his guide through the storm. While a fundamentally serious poem, it is also a humorous and facetious conceit that presents the poet as a bedraggled traveller struggling through hailstorms, rain and mud towards the refuge of his hut. His voice rises above the gale like the lark's song; inspiration will lift him on wings of fire as he skims across the sea of mud like the Pythian Apollo winging his way over the receding floodwaters to slay the Python. The incongruous double perspective translates the traveller's discomfort as he battles with storms and atrocious roads into lofty themes of classical myth – the pinions with which his guardian spirit will protect him are woollen wings to keep him snug; the 'son of water and earth' is the mud through which he flounders; 'Jupiter Pluvius', who nourishes the Castalian Spring from which the Muses drink, is the rain. The fire of inspiration, the gift of the Muses, is to the poet as the life-giving warmth of the sun to the world – or, in an alternative perspective, as the prospect of a blazing hearth and the warming glow of wine, the gift of Bacchus, is to the peasant as he trudges homewards. In a cryptic passage of jumbled imagery the poet urges his inspiration to match the warmth of the sun, to 'glow towards Phoebus Apollo', lest his jealous rays should waste themselves on the evergreen energy of the cedar, which requires neither light nor heat to flourish:

> Kalt wird sonst
> Sein Fürstenblick
> Über dich vorübergleiten,
> Neidgetroffen
> Auf der Zeder Kraft verweilen,

Die zu grünen
Sein nicht harrt.

Coldly else
His imperious gaze
Will pass you by,
Envy-smitten
Linger on the cedar's strength
Which to grow green
Waits not for him.

The poet finally identifies his lyrical model: not the idyllic Anacreon nor the sybaritic Theocritus, but Pindar, who sang the thrills and perils of the chariot race, is the appropriate bard to invoke in his hymn to the 'storm-breathing deity', Jupiter the rain-bringer. This ecstatic, jagged and inventive jumble of heroic classical allusion finally ends on the bathetic image of the poet gasping for just enough divine inspiration or energy to allow him to flounder breathlessly through the mud to the shelter of his hut.

This chaotic and stammering dithyramb contrasts with the free but controlled expression of 'Mahomets Gesang' (Song of Mohammed, 1772–3). Here, creative genius is also celebrated; but it is the genius of a great spiritual leader whose progress, and that of his word, is allegorized in the course of a river from its early infancy among rocks above the clouds, protected by benevolent spirits, through its exuberantly youthful cascades as it carries its sibling streams down to the valley in a precocious spirit of leadership. Goethe's own precocious command of verbal rhythms is displayed as he evokes the triumphant and majestic progress of the river through a desert landscape, bearing its tributaries with it as they in turn swell its course: these 'brother streams' are the followers of the Prophet who will perish as shallow independent waters if they are cut off from the mainstream of his doctrine, swallowed by the thirsty sand. He carries ships on his back ('cedar houses'), towns and countries spring up under his feet, as he bears his children 'in rolling triumph' to the waiting creator, the ocean. This poem, originally conceived as a hymnic dialogue between Ali and Fatima to be integrated into Goethe's drama *Mahomet*, now stands as an independent poem that exemplifies his *Sturm und Drang* virtuosity in poetic vocabulary and rhythm. Compound neologisms give the poem a new expressive dimension: *Felsenquell* (rock-spring), *Sternenblick* (star-gaze), *jünglingfrisch* (youth-fresh), *schlangewandelnd* (serpent-winding), *silberprangend* (silver-resplendent), *freudebrausend* (joy-foaming); repeated and accumulated word-patterns and a relentless syntax contrive with vivid mimetic effect to suggest the irresistible momentum of the river as it bears all along with it to the sea.

'An Schwager Kronos' (To Father Time, 1774) quite lacks the reverential tone of 'Mahomets Gesang'. It similarly chooses a central image to convey the course of a human life; but here the half-serious, half-facetious image is that of a wildly impatient traveller in a post-chaise urging his coachman Father Time to 'get a move on' (*Spude dich*) in an uninhibited burst of youthful arrogance. The first stanza is a striking example of Goethe's experimentation with the expressive power of language in a jumble of fractured but vivid syntax:

Ekles Schwindeln zögert
Mir vor die Stirne dein Haudern.
Frisch den holpernden
Stock Wurzeln Steine den Trott
Rasch in's Leben hinein!

Your slowcoach dilly-dallies
Sickening giddiness in my head.
Smartly the stumbling
Stick roots stones of the trot
Hurry on into life!

Bumping, jolting, dizzy with excited impatience, the traveller urges the coach headlong into life. Soon straining uphill again, the perspective from the summit gives him an intuition of the 'eternal spirit' as he surveys the infinite panorama;[6] but nothing, not even the temptations of the girl who offers him refreshment at a staging-post, can stem the impetuous rush through life. In a defiant conclusion, the coachman is ordered to drive the traveller headlong into hell before old age brings palsied limbs and toothless jaws: his 'foaming eyes' blinded by the setting sun and drunken with its last rays, he would reel dizzily into Orcus – where the mighty rulers of the underworld are expected to rise and greet the traveller dutifully, as the hospitable landlord of a coaching-inn should do. The central coaching metaphor is clear enough in broad terms, as an allegory of the reckless exuberance of youth; but the reader is not allowed to dwell on incoherent or half-obscure passages as the traveller hurtles towards his premature destination – or destiny. Onomatopoeia, neologism and spluttering syntax carry the rebellious defiance of the theme:

Sieh, die Sonne sinkt.
Eh' sie sinkt, eh' mich faßt
Greisen im Moore Nebelduft,
Entzahnte Kiefer schnattern
Und das schlockernde Gebein . . .

See, the sun sinks.
Before it sinks, before I'm caught
Greybeard in the moorland mist,
With slobbering toothless jaws
And aguequaking limbs . . .

The symbolic figure of Prometheus was derived from Shaftesbury and used by the *Sturm und Drang* generation as an emblem of creativity: not, that is, the wretched Titan in his perpetual agony, chained to a rock in the Caucasus and scavenged by birds of prey, but Prometheus in his defiant pomp, the archetypal rebel who formed men out of clay, breathed life into them and gave them fire stolen from Olympus. Goethe had no greater praise for Shakespeare than to associate him with the creativity of the Titan. Shakespeare, he proclaimed in his rhapsodic speech *On Shakespeare's Anniversary* in 1771, had 'vied with Prometheus, formed his beings in every feature after his, but in Colossal Greatness'.[7] Like 'Mahomets Gesang', the poem 'Prometheus' (1774) was originally part of a drama on the subject of the Titan's defiance, and indeed in the final edition of his works Goethe included the poem in the dramatic fragment; but it is almost invariably read as an independent poem – often, and more dubiously, in isolation from its corrective companion-piece 'Ganymed'. The drama was abandoned, though Goethe was to rework the figure of Prometheus in a quite different light in his later play *Pandora* (see below, pp. 137–8 and 180–2).

As it stands, 'Prometheus' is a defiant shout of titanic autonomy, a youthfully blasphemous insult to the gods, jeering and resentful, asserting the stubborn pride of an independent creative will. Zeus is contemptuously challenged to spend his thunderbolts fruitlessly on mountain tops and trees like a boy who slashes at thistles; those who timorously worship 'the slumberer above' are deluded children or beggars. All he, Prometheus, has achieved was by his own strength, his own courage, his own 'sacred glowing heart'; here he sits, creating a race of beings in *his* image, who will defy the immortals like him. A third-person account is inadequate to convey the mighty egotism of the poem, which is articulated in an insistent 'I' form, contemptuously dismissive of the 'du' Zeus or 'euch', the gods. Once again, startlingly inventive compounds and Goethe's virtuosity in the handling of free rhythms lend expressive force as the Titan spits and hammers out his bilious defiance, undismayed by the frustration of his 'budding boyhood morning dreams' (*Knabenmorgen-Blütenträume*). The heavy tonic stresses of the shifting rhythms underscore his scathing contempt for divine authority and his unconditional assertion of his own powers:

> Ich dich ehren? Wofür?
> Hast du die Schmerzen gelindert
> Je des Beladenen?
> Hast du die Tränen gestillet
> Je des Geängsteten?
> Hat nicht mich zum Manne geschmiedet
> Die allmächtige Zeit
> Und das ewige Schicksal,
> Meine Herrn und deine?

> I honour you? For what?
> Have you yet lightened the anguish
> Once, of the burdened?
> Have you stilled the tears
> Once, of the terrified?
> What was it that forged me to manhood
> But all-powerful time
> And eternal fate –
> My masters, and yours?

And yet for all Goethe's imaginative and empathetic expression of titanic defiance in this violent lyrical philippic, it would be wrong to cite the Prometheus poem as entirely or generally representative of his own existential stance during the so-called *Sturm und Drang* period. For all the absolute passion and commitment of expression, we cannot identify Goethe too exclusively with any single one of the series of personae by means of which he chose to represent a whole range of human responses and attitudes. His poems must often be read in tandem or in series, since he was given to writing related but complementary, at times apparently contradictory, companion-pieces to poems that cannot properly be read in isolation: 'Prometheus' and 'Ganymed', 'Grenzen der Menschheit' and 'Das Göttliche' (Limitations of Humanity and The Divine), 'Eins und Alles' and 'Vermächtnis' (One and All and Testament). While Lessing, rather to Goethe's dismay, might have voiced his approval of the 'Spinozan' intellectual independence of his Prometheus, Goethe himself countered the absolute self-assertion of the Titan with the absolute self-surrender of 'Ganymed', a poem probably written half a year earlier, though it is usually placed after 'Prometheus' by editors. Here the free rhythms, far from hurling defiance at Olympus, articulate a pantheistic ecstasy as the catamite of Zeus finds that his euphoric hymn to springtime evokes an answering response from the clouds above him. In an erotic delirium he is drawn, 'embracing and embraced' upwards to the bosom of the 'all-loving father', as the pederastic overtones of the Greek myth are obscured in an intensely emotional expression of quasi-Christian nature mysticism.

Two other poems from the corpus of early 'hymns' are less visceral and more programmatic; indeed they are not always to be found in this context: 'Der Wandrer' (The Traveller, 1772) was placed by Goethe under the heading *Kunst* (Art) in the *Ausgabe letzter Hand*. This verse dialogue centres on the dual motifs of 'wanderer' and 'hut', restlessness and security, freedom and domesticity, that recur in much of Goethe's early lyric poetry. A lone traveller is welcomed by a woman living a simple domestic idyll near the ruins of an ancient and overgrown temple, the stones of which have provided her with a modest home; and he leaves the peaceful scene with a growing consciousness of his own rootless existence and a future vision of just such a domestic refuge. Written in the year of his friendship with Johann Christian Kestner and Charlotte Buff, the poem contains some of the motifs and sentiments of the novel *Werther* written in the aftermath of that relationship, and was explicitly associated by Goethe in a letter to Kestner of 15 September 1773 with his own feelings towards Charlotte. The aesthetic musings of the traveller are derived from Winckelmann's idealized classicism, and the visual scene very probably from a source in neo-classical painting; but the 'patriarchal' associations of the woman drawing water from the spring have biblical and Homeric references that link the poem with the novel, and the traveller's idealization of the humble domestic scene is similar to Werther's sentimentalized (and, as it subsequently turns out, illusory) perception of the domestic idyll of his beloved *Wahlheim*, his 'chosen home'.

'Seefahrt' (Sea Journey) is included by Trunz among the *Sturm und Drang* hymns, partly on stylistic grounds, partly because its theme is that of the poet venturing on a voyage into the unknown, facing the perils of the high seas and trusting in his 'gods' to protect and direct him. Written in 1776, however, a year after his arrival in Weimar, the poem has clearer biographical overtones than the earlier odes which symbolically articulated more general existential attitudes. The subject is presented as a ship's passenger, perhaps a merchant, first waiting for a favourable wind, then leaving his friends to witness the departure of his ship. At this point, the perspective changes from first person to third, to that of the friends ashore, as the ship is driven by storms: the passenger becomes helmsman, facing the alternatives of survival or shipwreck with confident faith in the powers that protect and guide him. Goethe was much given, especially at this period in his life, to invoking his destiny, his 'stars' or guiding powers, in poems and correspondence; and indeed he had used similar nautical imagery that year in letters to his friends to explain and justify his momentous decision to leave his native Rhineland for an uncertain future in Weimar.

The 'Harzreise im Winter' (Winter Journey to the Harz), written in December 1777, dates from well beyond the *Sturm und Drang* odes and, as Goethe pointed out in his later commentary to the poem, it has clear biographical reference to the early years of his first decade in Weimar.[8] But its rhapsodic style, its free rhythms and its cryptic invocations of various deities and tutelary powers, its theme of a journey through a symbolic landscape and its sporadic and shifting construction, all relate it to the earlier odes, and to 'Wandrers Sturmlied' in particular. The occasion for the poem was Goethe's journey to the Harz in November and December, with its threefold purpose of inspecting the Clausthal mines and foundries, calling on the depressive Plessing, and climbing the Brocken. He had also been expected to meet up with Duke Karl August and his entourage, who were hunting the forests around Eisenach; but this he did only after he had achieved his main objectives, after he had communed with the mysterious mountain in his quest for self-discovery, for a sign or omen that might offer some augury or guidance to his destiny.

The poem into which Goethe encoded the symbolic significance of his journey was not written in a single burst; but its sporadic structure is evidently contrived to suggest the disparate thoughts and emotions on the stations of a pilgrim's progress towards his goal. It is a meditation on human destiny by a poet who is himself still unsure of his own destiny, as he rehearses the different directions in which an individual life may run: the misanthropic withdrawal of the unfortunate Plessing, the suicide of Werther, the self-indulgence of the wealthy, the companionable fellowship of the hunting-party, the solitary pilgrimage of the poet. In the opening lines of 'Wandrers Sturmlied', Goethe had invoked the poet's voice in the image of the lark singing against the storm; here it is the bird of prey that is invoked as it soars to spy out its quarry. Much discussion has centred on this image, on whether *Geier* is to be understood generically or loosely as any bird of prey – in which case it might stand emblematically for the wide perspective of poetic vision; or alternatively, it might be taken literally as a vulture, in a reference to the ancient practice of augury by studying the viscera or the flight of birds – an allusion that reinforces the notion of divination, the seeking of auspices and signs that is implicit in the poet's solitary mission to the ominous mountain.[9]

Happiness and misery are human destinies prescribed by the gods: the fortunate run with the flow of life, the unfortunate resist its course, even if death is still bitter to them. Two of the impulses for Goethe's actual journey to the Harz – the tormented Plessing and the Duke's hunting-party – are juxtaposed here as two contrasting destinies. As he acknowledged in his own commentary, he is debating within himself the existential extremes he had personally experienced hitherto: the apparently effortless life of the child of fortune, pampered by fate and enjoying the favour of a prince, and the dark night of the soul he had explored in his novel *Werther*, and which had blighted the life of the young Plessing. The 'Father of Love' is implored to comfort the depressive and, in a shift of perspective, to bless the hunters who avenge the depredations of the game among the peasants' crops.

But the central figure of the poem is the lone poet as he battles on to the top of the Brocken, where he offers up his thanks on the snowbound summit to the love that has sustained him through his journey. And indeed, Goethe's *Harzreise* of 1777 is nowhere more vividly narrated and described than in the stream of affectionate letters addressed to Frau von Stein, who was the absent muse of his existential pilgrimage. The final lines of the poem celebrate the inscrutable mountain from which, as Goethe imagines with poetic rather than geologically informed vision, the seams of precious metals emanate to supply the mines of the neighbouring valleys, furnishing 'the kingdoms of the world and the glory of them'. On 10 December, the day he climbed the mountain, Goethe confides to Frau von Stein that this was indeed the true purpose of his whole journey. He also cryptically hints at its symbolic importance to him; but just how or why it was of such portent remains obscure. Whether it was the physical challenge (which was evidently a factor) that impelled him, whether it was his quest for guidance, whether this guidance concerned his own destiny in Weimar or elsewhere, whether or not any clear omen or portent was granted him on the summit, remains as mysterious as the mountain itself and the enigmatic poem it inspired.

ART AND ARTISTS

Erich Trunz has gathered together a group of poems designated as Goethe's *Künstlergedichte*, poems that also confront the problematic nature of genius and creativity, but with little of the extravagant or rhapsodic tensions of the *Sturm und Drang* odes. The artists of these *Künstlergedichte* are not vatic or titanic figures exploring existential or symbolic attitudes, but more modest painters or sculptors working in their studios or workshops, coping with the more mundane problems of a creative existence. This is not the dithyrambic poet of 'Wandrers Sturmlied' seeking inspiration from the raging elements or the lone traveller searching for omens on the Brocken; these poems are more practical in character, epigrammatic, parabolic or allegorical, often humorous and satirical. Certainly, creativity is celebrated in 'An Kenner und Liebhaber' (To Experts and Amateurs), or 'Lied eines physiognomischen Zeichners' (Song of a Physiognomic Artist); but there are also lampoons directed at the utilitarian perceptions of the commercial artist ('Ein Gleichnis': A Simile), at the sterility of the carping critic ('Anekdote unsrer Tage': Anecdote for Our Time, 'Da hatt' ich einen Kerl zu Gast': I had a fellow as my guest), or at the complacency of the philistine ('Der Adler und die Taube': The

Eagle and the Dove). On the other hand, the loftier pretensions of artistic idealism are also mocked in some of these poems, rather as the sententious poet of the 'Vorspiel auf dem Theater' (Prelude on the Stage) in *Faust* is mocked: in 'Des Künstlers Erdewallen' (The Artist's Lot on Earth), the portrait-painter is given some down-to-earth and wryly sensible advice by his Muse on the conflicting demands of his artistic integrity and the need to earn his daily bread. In 'Künstlers Apotheose' (The Artist's Apotheosis) the artist posthumously bemoans the fact that his genius, and with it the commercial value of his work, are only recognized by posterity: he might have benefited from the rewards of this recognition during his lifetime. In these genre poems, Goethe is humorously exploring the *Künstler-problematik* that was to be taken up later by Romantic writers, but which was already an issue for artists a generation earlier: the problems of private patronage and public approval, of artistic independence and commercial or critical success, the agony of the artist and the *malheur d'être poète* that arose from a profound shift in the conception of the status and the nature of creative genius in the second half of the eighteenth century.

EARLY BALLADS

Throughout his creative career as a poet, Goethe returned time and again to the ballad – a term notoriously difficult to define, and one covering a wide range of poetic form and expression. Indeed, Goethe himself wrote in 1821 that the ballad mysteriously combines all three literary genres, lyric, epic and dramatic, as it were embryonically: 'wie in einem lebendigen Ur-Ei zusammen' (together as in a living primal egg).[10] Goethe's own ballad output can be categorized broadly into three phases: the early ballads, written under the influence of Herder and his program-matic essay 'Über Ossian und die Lieder alter Völker' (On Ossian and the Songs of Ancient Peoples) that opened the *Sturm und Drang* manifesto *Von deutscher Art und Kunst*; the more sophisticated early Weimar ballads; and the later 'classical' ballads that include the ballads of the so-called *Balladenjahr* of 1797, when he and Schiller discussed, corresponded on and wrote a series of lengthy ballads that are very much more elaborate and didactic than the simple quasi-folk ballads of the 1770s.

It was Herder who in Strasbourg had directed Goethe's attention to the oral tradition of folk song and ballad, to what he perceived as the unaffected and spontaneous primitivism of unlettered and unsophisticated nations, to the origins of song in the rhythms of daily work, to the narrative legends and myths of bards and minstrels, to the simple expression of untutored peoples before 'art came and extinguished nature'.[11] To be sure, Herder himself was indebted to printed sources, to sixteenth and seventeenth-century collections (or fabrications) of 'folk song', to Percy's *Reliques of Ancient English Poetry* and to Macpherson's *Poems of Ossian*; to be sure, no very scholarly distinctions were drawn between Germanic and Celtic traditions, and no very systematic definitions were sought of the elusive terms folk song or ballad, whether those of North American Indians, of Lapps or

Norsemen, of the Scottish Borders or of Alsatian peasants. All were deemed to share the common hallmark of freshness and spontaneity, or the narrative and structural incoherence resulting from what Herder defined as the *aerugo*, the patina or weathering that accumulated over generations of oral transmission.[12] It was Goethe who was largely responsible for infusing into the modern German literary tradition the idiom of folk song, an idiom that was continued by other generations, by Gottfried August Bürger, and most notably by the Romantic collectors of folk tales and folk song; it is no accident that the best-known and most influential corpus of German folk song, *Des Knaben Wunderhorn*, was dedicated by its editors (and part-authors) Arnim and Brentano to 'His Excellency the Privy Councillor von Goethe'.

'Heidenröslein' (Little Rose on the Heath), presumably based, at least in its essentials, on a traditional form heard and copied by Goethe in Alsace in 1771, but also possibly from a printed source, was itself included by Herder in his manifesto, unattributed and quoted from memory.[13] He praises the 'child's voice', the refrain and the informal elision of articles and syllables – which Goethe may well have undertaken at his prompting; and yet for all its skilfully artless simplicity of language and diction, the poem has an erotic dimension that may well owe as much to Goethe's own experience as to perceived folk song traditions: it is often associated with his callously abrupt abandonment of Friederike Brion. Of course there is no evidence to suggest that Goethe deflowered Friederike as the wild lad 'broke' the rose in the poem; but the allegory is clearly enough one of seduction, betrayal and guilt. The later ballad 'Das Veilchen' (The Violet, 1773–4) also strives for the effect of folk song in its allegorized theme and its metrical, if not literal, refrain; but the violet's unrequited love for the young shepherdess is reminiscent of rococo and Anacreontic lyrical conventions, and is expressed in less robust terms than the frankly physical sexual encounter between the boy and the rose on the heath.

The romantic legendary ballad of 'Der König von Thule' (The King of Thule) was evidently written during Goethe's Rhineland journey with Lavater and Basedow in the summer of 1774. It is well known for its dramatic setting as the ballad sung by Gretchen in the *Urfaust* (and later, in its revised version, in *Faust* Part One); indeed, so perfectly does this song fit into the psychology of the dramatic action that it is scarcely believable that Goethe wrote it independently of its context in the play. Taken in isolation, it is the story of the fidelity of the king of a mythical northern country to the memory of his mistress, symbolized in the golden goblet she bequeathed to him on her deathbed – an erotic image doubtless derived from the Song of Songs, and one that Goethe was to use with (for the twentieth-century reader, at least) sensationally sexual implications in a later poem, 'Der Becher'* (The Goblet). But in its context in the action of *Faust*, the poem assumes a whole new dimension as Gretchen innocently hums to herself the 'old' song of the fidelity of a king to his low-born mistress; it is here the unconscious or half-conscious musing of a young girl on the possibility of such fidelity in such a relationship just after she has been accosted by a 'gentleman' on the street – a relationship as yet only conceivable to her in the objectified projection of an archaic myth or fairy-tale.

'Hoch auf dem alten Turne' (High on the ancient tower), written during the same Rhine journey of 1774, is a similarly antiquarian romantic ballad evoking the spirit of the heroic past, the rugged individuality of a free knight such as Götz von Berlichingen. 'Der untreue Knabe' (The Faithless Lad), a horror-story in ballad form from the same year, has distinct affinities with Bürger's 'Lenore', also written in 1774, which came to represent the quintessential *Sturm und Drang* ballad narrating a ghostly ride through the night to the grave. This theme of the wild night ride Goethe had already used in the Sesenheim poem 'Willkommen und Abschied'; he was to exploit it dramatically in 'Erlkönig', and it was to feature in some of the contributions to *Des Knaben Wunderhorn*. In 'Der untreue Knabe' the theme of seduction and betrayal, in the odd versification of the seven-line Lutheran stanza, leads to a wild gallop and a dramatically macabre conclusion as the young man is about to face the corpse of the woman he betrayed. 'Vor Gericht' (Before the Court, *c*.1776) treats a related theme that became almost a stock-in-trade of *Sturm und Drang* domestic tragedy, and which was also a contentious issue of the day: the story of the unmarried mother, frequently coupled with the attendant crime of infanticide. H. L. Wagner's *Die Kindermörderin* (The Infanticide) and Goethe's own *Urfaust* are the two best-known literary treatments of the theme; although there is no indication of infanticide as such in the ballad 'Vor Gericht', it still has affinities with those two dramas, and indeed with the historical case of the Frankfurt infanticide Susanna Margaretha Brandt in 1771. It expresses the forthright and defiant stance of a young unmarried mother in the face of the legal, social and religious pressures brought to bear on her, pressures also graphically illustrated by Goethe in the *Urfaust* scene 'Am Brunnen' (At the Well), and which contributed more often than not to subsequent ostracism, distraction and even infanticide.

The Lament of the Wife of Asan Aga (1774–5), included by Trunz among the early ballads, is not an original composition of Goethe's at all, but his adaptation of the translation of a Serbo-Croat folk legend from Dalmatia; a tale of tribal vendetta and Islamic marriage customs, it was included by Herder in the first volume of his eclectic collection, the *Volkslieder* (Folk Songs) of 1778.

OCCASIONAL POETRY 1770–75

It is not surprising that a poet like Goethe, to whom writing in prose or verse came, or at least appeared to come, as naturally as eating or drinking, and who was for so much of his life the semi-official poet to the Weimar court, should have left a large corpus of occasional verse, dedications and encomia, addressed to individuals among his wide circle of acquaintances. It was also customary in eighteenth-century Germany, indeed it has continued so to the present day, to write dedicatory poems in albums or letters as tributes of affection or gratitude. Trunz gives a selection of Goethe's occasional poems from the 1770s, some of which are of literary or biographical interest. 'Pilgers Morgenlied' (Pilgrim's Morning Song, 1772), addressed to Luise von Ziegler ('Lila'), one of the

Darmstadt Circle of fashionably sentimental spirits at the court of the Landgravine of Hessen-Darmstadt, has somewhat etiolated echoes of 'Wandrers Sturmlied' and 'Ganymed'. The verses from letters to J. C. Kestner and Charlotte Buff evoke the chaotic domestic idyll and some of the emotional tension of *Werther*, harmlessly enough; but the verses appended as motto to the second edition of the novel in 1775, 'Jeder Jüngling sehnt sich, so zu lieben' (Every young man longs to love like this) issue a stern warning to the reader not to emulate the fictive hero. It is a measure of Goethe's alarm at the sensational reception of his novel that he should issue this stern moral injunction, which is not very far removed in spirit, though quite different in tone and style, from Pastor Goeze's pompous philippic against the subversive novel. The 'Bundeslied' (Song of Fellowship) of 1775, written for the marriage of an Offenbach pastor, is still, in its later version, part of the corpus of *Burschenlieder* bellowed out at fraternity gatherings at some German universities – in spite of the fact that Goethe himself was never associated with any form of *Verbindung* as a student. The best-known of these occasional poems is a vignette in *Knittelvers* from the Rhineland journey of 1774, 'Zwischen Lavater und Basedow' (Between Lavater and Basedow, more usually entitled 'Diner zu Koblenz', Luncheon at Coblenz), in which Goethe carefully fosters his own image as the carefree and hedonistic *Weltkind* who devours his food with youthful gusto while the 'prophets' Lavater and Basedow prose away on theological and pedagogic matters on either side of him.

POEMS TO LILI SCHÖNEMANN

The poems written to Lili Schönemann in 1775 do not have the adolescent exuberance of some of the Sesenheim poems associated with Friederike Brion, nor do they display the introverted intensity of his early Weimar poetry to Frau von Stein. While they self-evidently express the affection, even the adoration, of the moody and restless twenty-five-year-old for his charming and sociable young fiancée, they also agonize about the degree of fulfilment and commitment on his part and betray, not only with the benefit of hindsight, the uncertainty and unease in their relationship – whether this was due to Goethe's own existential uncertainties at the time, to his temperamental inability to commit himself finally to one person, one place or one career, or to his uncomfortable ambivalence towards the social obligations in which his betrothal involved him. 'Neue Liebe, neues Leben' (New Love, New Life) conveys the discomfort of his estrangement within the charmed circle, of being held by the 'magic thread' that binds him to a capricious but adored woman. 'An Belinden' (To Belinda), for all its intense expression of irresistible attraction, equivocates between moonlit solitude and dreams of love on the one hand, and the public duty of attendance in brightly lit salons in the company of 'intolerable faces' around the gaming-tables on the other. In 'Lilis Park' (Lili's Park) he casts himself as the uncouth bear who has been tamed and charmed into Lili's 'menagerie'; fettered to her by a silken thread, ensnared in a lace shawl, his feral instincts lead him to escape – not to a free habitat, but only across manicured lawns past artfully constructed cascades to a corner of the garden, and always ready to run to her feet at her call.

The poems to Lili in her own social milieu may well express Goethe's own often fraught and ambivalent feelings; they may perhaps only voice the conventional rhetoric of the lover's complaint. But two short poems stand out, if only because they treat the affective problems of the relationship in a more oblique and symbolic way than the others. 'Ich saug' an meiner Nabelschnur' (I suckle through my navel-cord, later revised and entitled 'Auf dem See', On the Lake) was written by, or in part even on, Lake Zürich during Goethe's journey to Switzerland in the early summer of 1775, in response both to the immediate landscape and to the literary stimulus of Klopstock's lengthily rhapsodic ode to the same lake. The exuberant image with which the poem opens is striking, if confused: the poet draws nourishment from nature both umbilically as a child in the womb, and simultaneously by suckling at her breast. And indeed, this was modified in the revised version into a less vivid but more consistent metaphor. The poem expresses in emphatic iambic rhythms the immediate and physical rapport with nature that had been absent in the other poems associated with Lili Schönemann; the steady beat of oars pulls the boat towards the horizon – or the future – as if only now, in the freedom of the grandiose Swiss scenery, can the poet's vision free itself and move forwards. But even here, towering mountains block the onward perspective; and in the second stanza the forward momentum of the poem is halted by a drastic change of mood and metre. Four trochaic lines force the gaze downward and inward into the waters of the lake, as 'golden dreams' of his other existence surge up and intrude on the idyll, creating a pause in the steady rhythm of the oar-beat. And though this introspective and retrospective dream is quickly banished, the third section of the poem has lost the uncomplicated exuberance of the first stanza. The lake sparkles in the morning sunlight, mists obscure the distant peaks, a wind springs up around the bay, and the dactylic metres suggest renewed forward movement; but the final image of the poem is one of reflection, as the fruit around the shore is mirrored in the surface of the lake, in the very depths from which dreams of the past had surfaced to disturb the idyll. The poem ends poised between past, present and future: the reflected fruit is ripening, but not yet ripe, and maturity is only implied as a possible future state.

Maturity is also the theme of 'Im Herbst 1775' (Autumn 1775, later entitled 'Herbstgefühl', Autumn Mood). While the poem has no explicit reference to Goethe's relationship with Lili Schönemann, it is more than tempting in view of its date of composition – shortly after the formal ending of his betrothal and shortly before his departure for Weimar – to associate it with a decisive period of his life, an ending and a beginning. It is a densely textured poem which, while it lacks the formal ode form of Hölderlin's poetry, comes close to his compact and formal verbal articulation in its measured free rhythms and its steady tempo; it is as if the poem aims in its very density to mimic the image of grapes thickly clustered in bunches, swelling to maturity in the brooding warmth of the sun and the magical coolness of moonlight. In the final lines, an affective dimension is invoked: the vine is watered by the tears of love, by an emotional fullness that corresponds to the swelling fruit on the vine. Whether or not we relate these two outstanding poems of 1775 to Goethe's relationship with his fiancée, or to the other critical imponderables of his life in that year, both poems convey a sense of existential brooding, of doubt and uncertainty, of urgent self-questioning and meditation on the passage of time and the processes of maturity.

The emotional scars left by his betrothal are attested in Goethe's last poems to his former fiancée that date from his first twelve months in Weimar: 'Holde Lili, warst so lang' (Dearest Lili, for so long), 'An ein goldenes Herz' (To a Gold Locket), and 'Im holden Tal' (In lovely valley). The second of these, which, Goethe seems to suggest in *Dichtung und Wahrheit*, was written in June 1775 at the summit of the St Gotthard Pass,[14] is more probably dated to the winter of 1775/6 in Weimar. All three are addressed to her memory, and articulate the emotional cost of breaking with her – in particular in the image of the bird that has escaped its captivity but still trails the thread that bound it to its cage. The images of captivity and release, confinement and freedom that recur in these poems to her seem to be more than mere rhetorical figures, and hint at the severe emotional crisis of his engagement and disengagement – for she was indeed the only woman to whom Goethe was ever formally betrothed; it is even widely believed that when, towards the end of his life, Goethe wrote his enigmatic poem 'Der Bräutigam' (The Bridegroom, see below, pp. 128–9), the elegiac recollection of a distant state of betrothal from the perspective of old age is, at least in part, informed by his memories of the uneasy, troubled and yet 'golden' times of his love for Lili Schönemann.

EARLY WEIMAR OCCASIONAL POEMS

The occasional poems that Trunz includes from the early Weimar years do not and cannot give a very full impression either of the frantic public and political, social and artistic activity of this period, or of the large number of minor occasional works that constituted Goethe's literary output. These poems show only the public and published image that he wished to convey, especially of his relationship with and his feelings towards his friend and patron Karl August of Weimar. Nevertheless, the poem 'Ilmenau' (1783) is an important poetic document that reveals much about Goethe's perception of his own position in Weimar and about his relations with Karl August, who was at that time, as Goethe recalled to Eckermann in 1828 a few months after the death of his patron,[15] a young man whose impulsive, unbridled and yet generous temperament caused as much pain and anxiety to himself as to those around him. The poem, written in free stanzas of *Madrigalvers* (iambic lines of varying length), falls into three sections which shift from the present to the past of some six or seven years earlier. In the opening section, the poet casts himself as a lone wanderer losing his way among the idyllic hills and forests of Ilmenau – a place of refuge for Goethe as well as the scene of his efforts to restore the fortunes of the Duchy of Weimar by the recommissioning of the silver and copper mines there. He stumbles across a hunting-party encamped in the forest, where he recognizes his erstwhile companions: Knebel, Seckendorff, Karl August asleep in a rough shelter – and, standing guard over the young Duke, his own ghostly *doppelgänger*. The central section is a hypnotic monologue spoken by the past poet to his present self, a rueful account of his own situation and that of his young patron. 'Cast up' in Weimar from a foreign shore and held in thrall by friendship, the ghost of the younger Goethe tells of his 'Promethean' poetic mission, the youthful ideals he brought with him, only to see them blunted and frustrated by the compromises and formalities of court life: the poetic fire he brought is not pure flame, his poetic destiny has not been fulfilled. His master, still immature in spite of his responsibilities as a ruler, is still in the 'larval' stage of his development, his metamorphosis still in the inscrutable future; and the poet himself is caught in the toils of an oppressive and ambivalent dream, anxious about the present and uncertain of the future.

At this point (line 156) the interiorized monologue is brusquely broken by a return to the present as the poet exploits the occasion (in fact, Karl August's twenty-sixth birthday, 3 September 1783) to address an exhortation to the Duke and banish the anxious vision of the past. Karl August is urged to shed the immaturity of his youth and to assume his duties as ruler of his people, to harness the industry of the weavers of Apolda and the miners of Ilmenau and to create prosperity in the land. Goethe here touches on some of the reforms he himself urged on the Duke – many of which did not, in the event, bear fruit, but were sown on barren ground like the seed of the sower invoked in the final stanza. For all the promise and optimism of the final section, however, the poem is memorable less for its official exhortations than for the poetically compelling central section in which Goethe confronts both his own and Karl August's destiny in an intense and ambivalent meditation.

'Auf Miedings Tod' (On the Death of Mieding, 1782) is a more conventional occasional poem that gives a glimpse of another aspect of Goethe's duties during the early Weimar years: a tribute to the cabinet-maker to the Weimar court who, as stage carpenter to the amateur *Liebhabertheater*, was the practical guiding spirit of the whole venture. It is a tribute to his conscientious and unpretentious craftsmanship, allied with uncertain health and an unpredictable temperament, and also to the efforts of a small but energetic group of enthusiasts who kept the Weimar stage alive between 1774, when the Court Theatre was burnt down, until 1783, when a professional troupe was established. For all its irony and mock rhetoric, it is an affectionate tribute to Mieding, giving a vivid genre picture of the frantic activity involved in the court theatricals – and also paying a diplomatic tribute to the group's most distinguished performer, the professional singer and actress Corona Schröter, who played Iphigenie to Goethe's Orest in a performance of the prose version of the play on 6 April 1779 (lines 165–6). The poem also touches lightly on Goethe's own role in Weimar as he offers in lines 39–46 an ironic mock apologia for the small provincial corner of Germany that had become the object of so much esteem – and so much lip-pursing disapproval – beyond its borders. Like Bethlehem in Juda, the small town had become not the least among the cities of Germany: this is the poet's tribute to his own part in establishing the occasionally equivocal public reputation of the Weimar *Musenhof*.

Early Weimar Lyric Poetry

The introspective, uneasy and ambivalent state of mind so compellingly evoked in the central section of 'Ilmenau' is characteristic of much of Goethe's lyric poetry of the early Weimar years; it is also consistent with his personal development after his arrival in Weimar. If for a time he was expected to, and indeed did, live up to his *Sturm und Drang* image of wild and uncouth genius, or the passionate sentimentalism of Werther, these posings soon gave way to a growing sobriety of temperament and behaviour and to a steady accumulation of official responsibilities. And it would be difficult to discount the effect on both his personality and on his lyric poetry of the influence of Charlotte von Stein, the 'Lida' to whom much of this poetry is expressly or implicitly addressed. The early Weimer poems associated with her are subdued and even troubled, in a more profound sense than the youthful conflicts and tensions of the poems to Lili Schönemann; and they have little of the exuberant vitality of the Sesenheim poems or the early hymns and odes. But they convey compellingly the alluring spell cast by Weimar, its landscape and its people, and above all by the half-motherly, half-sisterly restraint and control exercised by Frau von Stein on the uncertainly maturing Goethe. If there was no physical intimacy, the language in which Goethe expressed their relationship in letters and poems was that of a passionate and intense love-affair with all its crises and despairs, joys and uncertainties: the poem 'Der Becher'* (The Goblet, 1781), for example, in which Amor invites the poet to drink nectar and balm from the lips of 'Lida', has sensual implications that recall the imagery of the Song of Songs – for all that its erotic connotations are overlaid with an element of rococo gallantry. There is also in these poems often an element of tension or conflict that reflects both his intimate emotional experience and his besetting existential doubts and confusions, expressed in terms of a profoundly ambivalent state of mind between extremes of homelessness and security, freedom and confinement, pain and joy, restlessness and peace.

'Jägers Nachtlied' (Night Song of the Hunter, 1775/6, revised as 'Jägers Abendlied', Evening Song of the Hunter) sets the tone of much of the poetry of this period. Its literary antecedents are to be found in the nocturnal poetry of *Empfindsamkeit*, in the moonlight meditation of Klopstock's 'Die frühen Gräber' (The Early Graves), and indeed in Goethe's own earlier nocturnal poems 'Die Nacht' and 'An Luna'; its central motif is the familiar figure of the *Wanderer*, here the huntsman who is caught between the restless drive of his troubled spirit and his yearning for peace, represented here, as in the later 'An den Mond' (To the Moon), by the steady and calming light of the moon. Many critics insist that the poem bears traces of Goethe's recent break with Lili Schönemann, while others point to 'An den Mond', which is unequivocally associated with Frau von Stein, as evidence that it belongs firmly among the 'Lida' poems; at all events, its theme and imagery relate it clearly enough to the other early Weimar nocturnal poetry of introversion, restlessness and peace.

Undoubtedly addressed to Frau von Stein is the haunting and compelling poem 'Warum gabst du uns die tiefen Blicke' (Why did you give us such profound perceptions), sent to her in a letter of April 1776; it is the most powerfully, if not most lucidly articulated statement of their spiritual relationship. In urgently chanted trochaic pentameters the poem insistently and repeatedly questions the fate that has given them alone such intimate and profound understanding of each other's feelings, why they alone seem to have the misfortune to know each other so closely. It is a strange complaint, which is only partly explained by the second stanza: the very depth and complexity of their mutual self-knowledge robs the lovers of the spontaneous affection that is based on illusion or half-knowledge. So many others, unburdened by such painfully clear perceptions, are able to react uninhibitedly to pain or joy; their dulled awareness, their very torpidity (*Dumpfheit*), their capacity for self-deception allows them to live their lives as an unpredictable adventure free from the pale cast of thought. And the poem suggests, startlingly, why the two must suffer this troubled intensity of vision: she was surely, in times long past, his sister or his wife.

That such a quaintly exotic religious notion as that of reincarnation should be invoked here is not as astonishing as it might seem. For even in the secularized theology of eighteenth-century deism, such unorthodox ideas were dabbled in at times: even Lessing, in his treatise on *Die Erziehung des Menschengeschlechts* (The Education of the Human Race), had eccentrically raised the question of metempsychosis in the course of his theological argument. And Goethe himself, in his occasional pronouncements on immortality, and in the later sections of *Wilhelm Meisters Wanderjahre*, speculated on the survival of the soul or 'entelechy' beyond death. In his poem to Frau von Stein he uses the notion (as he did in a letter to Wieland on the nature of his relationship with her)[16] as a poetic metaphor both to explain the uncanny, as it were pre-existing awareness that they have of each other, and to express his grateful tribute to the 'education' he received at her hands. In a striking, quasi-liturgical incantation of second-person verb forms he recalls the psychic therapy she brought him, how she read his most intimate thoughts and instincts, how she soothed his bruised spirit, guided his wildest urges and calmed his most turbulent feelings. All this is expressed in the *past* tense; it was thus in their previous incarnation, and yet it is also the expression of a present relationship. And in a series of uneasy paradoxes the final stanza returns to the lament of the opening lines: this state is only 'half blissful', it turns the brightest day to dusk and casts a shadow over the keenest joy – and yet the closing lines affirm the good fortune of this ambivalent and twilight state of being.

The other poems to Charlotte von Stein are less complex and problematic than this tortured expression of psychic malaise; but they often betray the tensions and ambiguities that afflicted their relationship, as well as Goethe's continuing uncertainty about his place in the narrow world of Weimar. 'Den Einzigen, Lida' (The Only One, Lida, 1781) projects her as a Madonna among clouds, glimpsed through the frantic bustle of everyday life as the 'eternal stars' are glimpsed through the elusive beams of the Northern Lights. This is a striking image probably, but not certainly, based on actual experience: Goethe did witness the aurora in Weimar in February 1817, and wrote a careful note of another display in January 1831 for his scientific studies.[17] He was also to use the imagery of stars and Northern Lights in a well-known later poem, 'Um Mitternacht' (At Midnight, 1818), where the stars similarly represent constant values, and the aurora transient or ephemeral ones – but it is not recorded whether he had actually experienced the phenomenon before 1781. The stars are also invoked as agents of fate in 'Gewiß, ich wäre schon so ferne, ferne' (For sure, I would have gone so far, so far, 1784), which acknowledges the hold she has on him, the magnetic pull that binds his life to hers; and yet it was to be only two years later that he would wrench himself from this apparently iron destiny and begin the process that severed their relationship irreparably.

Goethe moved into his *Gartenhaus* overlooking the water-meadows of the River Ilm in May 1776, and many of his poems, letters and sketches reflect and depict that landscape. The brief but evocative lines 'Und ich geh' meinen alten Gang' (And I go my wonted way, 1777) allude to his habit of bathing morning and evening in the Ilm; they also touch on a symbolic association that was already hinted at in 'Jägers Nachtlied', and which is more resonantly exploited both in some early sections of *Faust* and in the central early Weimar poem 'An den Mond', where the cool and steady light of the moon is a metaphor for a healing calm that allows care to be soothed away in a mystical process of natural therapy. In the shorter poem, it is the cares of daytime activity that are bathed away in the moonlight; in 'An den Mond' the moonlight, diffused through the mist over the river, floods the landscape with its mild light, soothing and releasing the spirit like the gaze of the loved woman. That this poem has an intimate and complex series of references to Goethe's relationship with Charlotte von Stein is attested by the fact that she herself later wrote a bitter parody of what she evidently regarded as 'her' poem when Goethe left for Italy: 'An den Mond nach meiner Manier' (To the Moon in my Fashion).[18]

Goethe's 'An den Mond' exists in two substantially different versions: the 'Füllest wieder 's liebe Tal' (You fill once more the lovely vale) of c.1777, and the revised version of some ten years later that begins 'Füllest wieder Busch und Tal' (Once more filling bush and vale). Much controversy has centred on the precise dating of Goethe's two versions and that of Frau von Stein, that is, on whether her parody was written before Goethe's revised version (in which case she must be credited with some of the changes he made in his revision), or whether her poem was not the 'bridge' between Goethe's two versions, but was based almost entirely on his second version. Few critics are prepared to accept that Frau von Stein's poem was an intermediate version, or to credit her with some of the changes made in his second version; but the impossibility of dating either one reliably rules out any certainty. Contention also surrounds the identity, or the gender, of the subject of Goethe's two versions: is the first version a love poem spoken by a male voice, and is the voice of the revised version that of the same male – or is it the voice of a woman who responds to the ardent lover of the first version with a cooler celebration of friendship or platonic love? Can the changes in Goethe's feelings for Frau von Stein before and after his Italian journey be read into the changes in his two versions? Finally, can the reference to a ghost haunting the banks of the river in the first version (or indeed to the river swollen with death in the fourth stanza) be related to the suicide of Christel von Laßberg, who drowned herself in the Ilm in January 1778? Again, the absence of reliable dating, even of the first version, precludes certainty.[19]

Goethe's first version reads as a love poem addressed by a male voice to a woman. It also appears to resume many of the sentiments of his poems to Frau von Stein: the calming and soothing influence attributed here to the light of the moon, holding the poet as if spellbound to the banks of the Ilm, or to the charmed circle of Weimar itself. The last two stanzas are then understandable as a response to her occasionally depressive moods of withdrawal; the male voice counsels and comforts the 'Liebste' of the second stanza, celebrating their spiritual companion-ship and the labyrinthine emotions that had been so ambivalently evoked in 'Warum gabst du uns die tiefen Blicke'. The second version, an altogether more complex poem, might be taken as the retrospective response of a female voice to the first version: 'Liebste' and 'Mann' are changed to 'Freund', a (male) lover or companion. Or it can be read as the voice of the male poet of the first version, elaborating and expanding the relatively straightforward love lyric into a complex emotional and spiritual crisis. The imagery of the central stanzas of the first version, of the river in winter and springtime, is incorporated into a heavily elegiac central section in which the river becomes a powerful symbol of transience and mutability. The figure held spellbound by the double image of the moon and the beloved becomes a lone introspective voice caught between past and present, joy and pain, meditating on the transience of love, laughter and fidelity. In the pivotal fifth stanza, an emotional crisis is articulated as the insistently repeated 'doch' expresses the despair of loss; but from this point the poem moves towards a resolution. The elegiac appeal to the river of the fourth stanza ('Fließe, fließe, lieber Fluß') modulates into a more resolute imperative ('Rausche, Fluß') as the river itself, the very metaphor of transience, becomes the source of the poet's song: by articulating his feelings, he can sublimate his sense of transience and loss through his poetry, through the therapy of self-expression. At this point the revised poem returns to the subdued but conciliatory coda that had concluded the first version: a relatively straightforward poem of landscape and love has become a subtle statement of crisis and resolution, and perhaps also a tribute to friendship and companionship.

Whether or not Goethe's two versions of the poem, and indeed Frau von Stein's parody, chart their own relationship – and her version surely does – the poem and its revision are characteristic of the mood of much of the early Weimar lyric poetry: a sense of uncertainty, an ambivalent twilight zone of uneasy accep-tance, a complex and introspective sense of integration and alienation, of content-ment and expectation. The same ambivalence is more explicitly articulated in the poem 'Einschränkung' (Confinement, the revised version of 'Dem Schicksal', To Fate, 1776), where the poet celebrates the narrow confines of the small world to which he is bound by a magic thread, but also confirms his awareness that fate still holds other possibilities for him, his intuition that fulfilment is still elusive. The revised version, written after Goethe's return to Weimar from Italy, is of course a retrospective characterization of his feelings before his escape from the pleasant but narrow restriction of his 'small world':

Was bleibt mir nun, als eingehüllt,
Von holder Lebenskraft erfüllt,
In stiller Gegenwart die Zukunft zu erhoffen!

Secluded here, I wait on destiny,
Replete with life's rich energy,
And in this quietude I hope for things to come!

EXISTENTIAL POETRY 1775–86

The poems grouped by Trunz under the heading of *Natur- und Weltanschauungslyrik* comprise a loose grouping of landscape or mood poems, literary tributes and set pieces that might best be described as existential poems dealing with broad themes of human life, ethics and mortality; the group concludes with the allegorical poem 'Zueignung' (Dedication) that Goethe chose to place as an introduction to his collected poems. Many are light occasional pieces: those on Hope and Care (1776) have none of the profound existential force of Hope as presented in weightier pieces such as 'Meine Göttin', the Orphic 'Urworte' or the drama *Pandora*, and Care has here none of the terrifying overtones of *Sorge* as the debilitating and corrosive power invoked in Faust's confrontation (*Faust*, lines 11424ff.). Nor does 'Eis-Lebens-Lied' (Life Song on the Ice, 1775/6) have any of the lofty rhetoric of Klopstock's odes to the recreation that he made popular among the German *literati* – including Goethe, who introduced it to the Weimar court. 'Dem Schicksal', as we have seen, is an almost programmatic statement of Goethe's own uncertainty of mind in the early years in Weimar; the direct biographical allusions of the first version, to Karl August and to the immature energies that are more explicitly described in the central section of 'Ilmenau', are modified in the revised version ('Einschränkung') to a more generalized (and more urgent) anticipation of future fulfilment.

The two literary tributes to Hans Sachs and to 'Johannes Secundus' (both 1776) commemorate not simply two sixteenth-century poets – the cobbler-poet of Nuremberg and the Dutch neo-Latinist Jan Everaerts; they also celebrate two cultural traditions to which Goethe owed much, the Reformation and the Renaissance. Hans Sachs, the *Meistersinger* of the German Reformation, is cast as the honest and unaffected craftsman whose inspiration draws on the unpretentious but colourful hurly-burly of the urban scene around him, on his knowledge of the folk-traditions of biblical and historical legend, and on the tradition of the popular printed tales of late medieval and Reformation Germany: Till Eulenspiegel, Fortunatus, Reineke Fuchs. Goethe's interest in the Reformation and its leading figures – Martin Luther, Albrecht Dürer and Hans Sachs – was kindled by Herder in Strasbourg, and this poem is Goethe's attempt to introduce that interest to his Weimar circle, to convey his enthusiasm for the quaint and, as he saw it, the honest and down-to-earth craftsmanship of Sachs's poetry, of Dürer's engravings and woodcuts, and of Luther's robust and virile language. Key words and concepts emphasize Goethe's (and Herder's) perception of the art and language of Reformation Germany: honesty, truth, simple piety and virtue, the solid skills of the industrious and conscientious craftsman. The verse is a pastiche of sixteenth-century German, quaintly archaic and cast in Goethe's own free adaptation of Hans Sachs's *Knittelvers*, the form he chose for his more robust early works such as *Pater Brey, Hanswursts Hochzeit* and, most memorably, the *Urfaust*. The poem to Johannes Secundus (later revised as 'Liebebedürfnis', Love's Need) is a tribute to the contemporaneous but quite distinct sixteenth-century German tradition, the neo-Latin poetry of the Northern European Renaissance. It is not a direct translation, but a pastiche, of Secundus's poetic cycle *Basia* (Kisses); and its mildly playful sensuality is closer to the earlier 'Anacreontic' poetry of Leipzig than to the interiorized emotional idiom of the early Weimar love poems. It is more questionable whether, as some commentators suggest, it also anticipates the open sensuality of the *Roman Elegies*.

Altogether more characteristic of Goethe's lyric poetry, and very much more familiar to his readers, are the two 'Wandrers Nachtlieder', which Trunz has prefaced with the intriguing quatrain 'Alles gaben Götter, die unendlichen' (All was given by the gods, the eternal ones) taken from one of Goethe's letters to Auguste von Stolberg, the confidante with whom he corresponded intimately and affectionately between 1775 and 1782, yet whom he never met. Like the brief poem 'Und ich geh' meinen alten Gang' from a letter to Frau von Stein, the quatrain is associated with Goethe's *Gartenhaus* by the River Ilm; in the letter to 'Gustchen' of 17 July 1777 Goethe describes how these lines came to him as he emerged from the river, where he had been swimming late into 'a glorious moonlit night'. Once again, the association of moonlight and water conveys a powerful symbolism of therapy, or spiritual healing and renewal – the renewal that Faust, for example, imagines in his vision of bathing in the moonlit dew as he seeks release from the dusty confines of his study (*Faust*, lines 386–97). The quatrain expresses a sense of profound thankfulness, an acceptance of the totality of experience as a gift of the powers that govern individual destinies. It anticipates the affirmation of Goethe's late lyric poems, but it is also characteristic of much of his early Weimar poetry in its pairing of affective opposites: joy and sorrow, pleasure and pain, possession and loss.

The pairing of emotional and existential polarities also runs through the 'Wandrers Nachtlied' (Traveller's Nocturne) that was included in a letter to Frau von Stein in 1776: the tension between the restless wanderer and his longing for peace, between 'double' misery and 'double' relief, between exhaustion and rest. The poem is in the form of a fervent supplication, a prayer for peace, the urgency of which is strikingly conveyed by the emphatic trochaic stresses on the initial syllables of each line and by the complex syntax that delays the statement of the grammatical subject until the penultimate line: three relative clauses dependent on 'du' in lines 1–4, an encapsulated relative clause ('der doppelt elend ist') in the third line, and two interjections in parenthesis (lines 5 and 6) precede the invocation of 'sweet peace'. The peace invoked here is of higher, perhaps divine, origin – the opening line echoes, but does not travesty, the opening of the German Lord's Prayer ('Vater unser, der du bist im Himmel'); and peace descends, is willed down, as it were, from above towards and into the heart of the lyrical persona.

This movement downwards and towards the subject is replicated in the companion-piece known as 'Wandrers Nachtlied II', or alternatively as 'Ein Gleiches' (Of a Kind) – though in this more cryptic and laconic poem, the ultimate origin of the quiet of evening is unidentified. Written, we are told, by Goethe one evening in September 1780 on the wall of a wooden hut on the slopes of the Kickelhahn, a hill near Ilmenau, and celebrated as one of the shortest and most resonantly evocative of all German lyric poems, it is the quintessential expression of the phenomenon of *Abendstille*, the hush that dusk brings to remote mountain regions: a hush that is evoked in a dense accumulation of assonantal and alliterative verbal effects that reach a provisional pause in the acoustic imagery of 'Hauch', intensified by the suggestion of the birds falling silent in the forest, and reaching its resolution in the subjective response of the last two lines. Although the movement is that of the previous poem, it is a movement not urgently willed but unsolicited, a process as natural and as unhurried as the onset of dusk itself: peace descends from the distant peaks to the tree tops to the birds to the human observer in a progression that moves through the chain of creation, mineral, vegetable, animal, human.

The acoustic and rhythmic density of this brief poem both invites and resists, demands and defies analysis. It is quite misleading to suggest, for example, that a predominance of long vowels contributes to the verbal articulation of rest or peace – of the thirty-eight syllables, short vowels outnumber long vowels or diphthongs by a ratio of almost 2:1. On the other hand, long vowels or diphthongs receive proportionately more metrical stress, and sounds are manipulated into assonantal patterns to acoustic and even mimetic effect. The rhythm is fundamentally a rocking dactylic cadence, at times subtly disguised or varied: the dactyl formed by the enjambment of the first two lines passes almost unnoticed, but in the fourth, fifth and sixth lines the dactyls become more pronounced. The last two lines are also dactylic; but in the final line the emphatic 'du' modifies the dactylic pattern.

The inscrutable simplicity and the dense brevity of this masterpiece of lyrical understatement has provoked the whole gamut of critical response, from awe-struck silence to savage parody.[20] It can be read as a hopelessly escapist or self-indulgent idyll, or as an expression of helpless resignation in the face of the human misery that Goethe encountered on his official travels around the Duchy of Weimar – the conditions touched on in the third stanza of the poem 'Ilmenau' written in this same landscape exactly three years later, and often urgently addressed in his correspondence at this time. It might represent his flight from the tensions and pressures of his life in Weimar, or the isolation of a human individual lost in the vast silence of nature that is a metaphor for the silence of death; or it might be simply the evocation of profound peace in the crepuscular hush of the natural landscape. In its evocation of profound peace or rest, it is characteristic of much of the early Weimar lyric poetry, even if the polarity of restlessness, the persona of the driven *Wanderer* that also haunts many of these poems, is at most implicit in the text itself.

It is a feature of Goethe's lyrical gift that he is able to adopt a huge range of emotional and intellectual perspectives in his poetry. Side by side with the profound empathy with natural landscape demonstrated in poems like 'An den Mond' or the second 'Wandrers Nachtlied', we also find among the early Weimar poems works that explore quite different areas: existential poems, conventionally labelled *Gedankenlyrik*, that explore our place in the universe and articulate questions about the scope and limits of human powers, human knowledge and human pretensions. Again, as in the earlier existential poetry of the *Sturm und Drang*, no single statement or stance can be finally identified as Goethe's own; a poem stressing the limitations of human powers is complemented and modified by one that celebrates the quasi-divine attributes of humankind.

The four major examples of early Weimar *Gedankenlyrik* are related less by theme or philosophy than by a verse form which, while it shows some variation in rhythmic pattern and diction, is common to them all. Less anarchic and less assertive than the rhapsodic or 'dithyrambic' style of the *Sturm und Drang* hymns, these poems use a short line of two or three stresses without rhyme or regular strophic structure – a form sufficiently flexible to articulate both lapidary statements of the human condition and the lyrical imagery in which Goethe often chooses to express his ideas.

The 'Gesang der Geister über den Wassern' (Song of the Spirits over the Waters), inspired by Goethe's visit to the Staubbach cascade during his second Swiss journey in October 1779, is a metaphorical statement of the relationship between fate and the soul, expressed as that between wind and water: fate modifies and affects human individuality as wind affects water. To be sure, this cryptic simile leaves many questions unanswered: not only wind, but also the accidents of landscape determine the nature of the river as it cascades down the cliff face. The journey of the soul is both cyclical and linear; it is analogous on the one hand to the eternal cycle of rainfall and evaporation, and on the other to the course of a river in its individual existence. As in 'Mahomets Gesang', the river moves from its infancy as a turbulent torrent, beginning as an undifferentiated pure column that dashes against the rocks in its path, atomizes as spray and falls in veils, foaming with youthful impatience in a flight of cascading steps to the plain below. Only when it meanders down the valley to form a lake can it reflect the heavens in its calm surface – as so often in Goethe's lyrical expression, the reflection of moon and stars in the surface of water suggests a reciprocal harmony between the human and the cosmic order; but this balance can be disturbed by the arbitrary action of fate on an individual existence.

'Meine Göttin' (My Goddess, 1780) is a hymn to fancy, to the gift of creative imagination, allegorized as the favoured daughter of Jove in her changing moods, as an idyllic vision of summer or in sombre and tragic mode. The poet's or artist's allegorical family is presented in whimsical terms: fancy as his young wife, hope as her older sister, and wisdom as her mother-in-law whose strictures are damaging to the free-ranging imaginative vision. Less solemn than its companion-pieces, the poem nevertheless touches on a theme that also concerns 'Das Göttliche': the spiritual and intellectual gifts that release us from the iron laws of bare existence.

Though written some two years apart, respectively *c.*1781 and 1783, the two poems 'Grenzen der Menschheit' (Limitations of Humanity) and 'Das Göttliche' (The Divine) are closely complementary; the latter reads as a more positive amplification or elaboration of the former. Both poems articulate a typical preoccupation of the late eighteenth century: the question of the scope and the limits of the autonomous human spirit or intellect. It is a question confronted by both Goethe and Lessing in their treatment of the figure who more than any other strained against human limitation: Faust. It is also the dilemma faced by Iphigenie in her struggle, not so much to assert her intellectual autonomy against the will of the gods, but rather to reconcile her own moral convictions with their apparent will. The first poem is a submissive acknowledgement of the numinous nature of the gods, the second a forthright assertion of the ethical sense that raises humanity above the animals and gives it quasi-divine authority.

It is with an expression of submission that 'Grenzen der Menschheit' opens, with the image of a patriarchal deity (whether of pagan classical or Judaeo-Christian origins is unclear) that commands absolute, if loving, awe: humans cannot and should not measure themselves against the gods. It is the piety of Iphigenie, mindful of the ever-present example of the fate of Tantalus, as she acknowledges the limits of human aspiration:

> Das sterbliche Geschlecht ist viel zu schwach,
> In ungewohnter Höhe nicht zu schwindeln.[21]
>
> This puny mortal race cannot look down
> Without confusion from such dizzy heights.

Humankind can vie neither with the gods, nor even with the natural phenomena within its ken; the strength of the oak or the tenacity of the vine dwarf our physical powers. The distinction between gods and humans is expressed in two metaphors. The gods exist beyond the eternal stream of time that flows by them, while our existence is contained within a ring; our own immortality consists only in the continuum of a successive chain of generations, in which each life is only a link. This, at least, is what Goethe appears to say in his *revised* version of the last stanza; in the earlier version it reads more confusingly, not as 'Reihen sich dauernd' (are perpetually linked), but as 'Reihen sie dauernd' (they perpetually link) – as if the very immortality of the gods themselves were dependent on the succeeding generations of humankind.[22]

The distinction drawn in 'Das Göttliche' is not, as in the previous poem, that between gods and humans, but between us and the 'creatures we know' – that is, the animals. We cannot know the gods, but we can imagine or have an intuition of them (*ahnen*); moreover, our own behaviour can teach us to believe in them as the arbiters of ethical principles, as the source of authority for our own values. All creatures are bound by the iron laws of mortality: chance, fortune, time itself. Goethe uses the words of Christ from Matthew 5. 45 in isolation from their context in the Sermon on the Mount, not to express the notion that all beings are creatures of God, but to indicate the moral indifference of 'unfeeling' nature: the sun shines on the evil and the good, rain and storms fall indifferently on all, fortune visits the innocent and the guilty. But this implacable indifference of existence is redeemed by human ethical and intellectual autonomy, by our ability to choose and judge, to reward and punish, to save and heal. We can give permanence to the transient, record and remember; we should strive to emulate the higher beings whom we project as exemplary, and honour the immortals *as if* they were exemplars of noble humanity. Once again, we are close to Iphigenie's assertion of the gods as ethical models of humane values as she struggles to preserve her beliefs against the baleful image projected in the 'Parzenlied' (Song of the Fates).[23]

This magisterial statement of the ethical sense that marks off humankind from the animals and constitutes its divinity can be related to the remarkable observation (a more accurate term, perhaps, than 'discovery', though that is how he excitedly announced it) made by Goethe the very year after the poem was written: of the intermaxillary bone. For what he saw as momentous in his observation was not simply his pride in a scientific 'first' (a disputed claim in any case – see below, p. 266), but its zoological and theological implications: that humans were anatomically related to the animals, that there was an overall unity of types that included humans, and that the distinction between humans and animals lay not in physical, but in ethical and intellectual attributes. Goethe's 'discovery' of the intermaxillary bone appeared to confirm the existential theology of 'Das Göttliche'.

'Zueignung' (Dedication, 1784) was originally written as a prologue to Goethe's projected epic poem *Die Geheimnisse* (The Mysteries); when this was abandoned, the poem was used as the opening dedication to the first volume of his collected works, the Göschen *Schriften* which appeared in 1787, and it has opened most subsequent editions of Goethe's poems. It is written in the stanzas of *ottava rima*, a form that Goethe generally reserved for solemn or elegiac themes: the fragment *Die Geheimnisse* itself, the dedicatory poem also entitled 'Zueignung' that prefaces *Faust*, and the 'Epilog zu Schillers "Glocke"' (Epilogue to Schiller's 'The Bell'). The declamatory style and the self-questioning dialogue of 'Zueignung' is not unlike that of 'Ilmenau'; but the regularity of the iambic pentameter, the rhetorical diction and the very structure of *ottava rima*, that of a discursive sestet of alternating rhymes plus a hendecasyllabic rhyming couplet that lends itself to sententious expression, make this poem altogether more formal and less intimate than the freer expression of the poem written in the previous year.

And yet the theme is not unrelated to 'Ilmenau': it concerns the uncertain self-questioning of the poet who has lost his way, who is aware of a mission unfulfilled, of youthful dreams and projects frustrated. In 'Ilmenau' he had regretted that the Promethean fire of creativity had turned to impure flame; here, confronted by the allegorical vision of his Muse in the guise of Truth, he invokes the biblical metaphor of the buried talent that he has left unexploited, and acknowledges his neglected duty. For all the generalized and sententious rhetoric of the poem, it is possible to discern a reference not only to early genius that has failed to fulfil its promise, but also to the many projects started but left unfinished in the relatively fallow years of the first decade in Weimar. The figure of Truth challenges him to justify himself to the world in terms that recall Antonio's challenge to Tasso as he urges the ravaged poet to take pride in his unique gifts, to recognize and assert his creative talent: 'Erkenne dich, leb' mit der Welt in Frieden!' (Avow yourself, live with the world in peace!). And she hands him the emblematic symbol of his creativity: the veil of poetry, 'woven from morning mist and bright sunlight', that mediates truth and makes it accessible, that both conceals and reveals the absolute and interprets it as metaphor or symbol. This is, albeit in terms of solemn and sententious allegory rather than of grandiose lyrical symbolism, an early statement of Faust's insight (*Faust*, lines 4704ff.) that we perceive the dazzling light of absolute truth only in mediated or reflected form, as the sun's light manifests itself through the refracted colours of the rainbow in the veil of spray thrown up by the waterfall.

EARLY WEIMAR BALLADS

The early Weimar ballads at once continue and refine the popular folk song idiom that Goethe had drawn on for his *Sturm und Drang* ballads. While the seeming artlessness of his early folk songs was no doubt carefully contrived in a sophisticated effort to convey a simple spontaneity, these ballads exploit poetic subtleties and virtuosities of rhythm, sound and verbal organization more consciously. To be sure, Goethe draws on popular traditions here too; but in 'Erlkönig' and 'Der Fischer' it is the dark folk superstitions of a natural landscape peopled by elemental spirits, the myths later exploited by the Romantic writers in their symbolic *Märchen*, of an ambivalent nature haunted by unpredictable and often baleful forces, personified as undines, kobolds, elves and woodland demons. 'Der Fischer' (The Angler, 1778) derives from the mythology of water sprites, nixies or undines who lure mortals to their destruction; but it also evokes with visual and acoustic subtlety the alluring attraction of water. If we are to believe a much later comment by Goethe to Eckermann, the poem expresses simply the enticing coolness of water that tempts us on warm summer days to bathe;[24] but he also showed his awareness of the more sinister attractive power of water over the imagination in a letter to Frau von Stein written in the same year as this poem, and immediately after the death of Christel von Laßberg in the Ilm. The sadness of such a tragedy, he wrote, has the same dangerously attractive appeal of water itself and the alluring reflection of stars in its surface.[25] It is this hypnotic attraction of water that the poem evokes as the fisherman is enticed by the nixie to join her in the cool depths of her magically reflected world beneath the waves, from which sun, moon and sky shine with doubled appeal. And yet this ballad is surely not unequivocally sinister or demonic; it does not have the starkly definitive and numbing tragedy of 'Erlkönig'. The fisherman is a half-willing victim of the nixie's seduction as he slips quietly into the 'transfigured blue' of her watery realm to share the well-being of the fishes; and the sinister aspect of the siren allure to which he succumbs is modified by the comic irony of nature taking her revenge as the fisherman, not the fish, is lured to his doom.

'Erlkönig' (1782) is a starkly different account of the brutal malevolence of a jealous and demonic nature visited on an innocent victim, of a quasi-pederastic assault on a child whose vision of a haunted landscape – the projection of a perhaps fevered, perhaps preternaturally acute, imagination – terrifies the boy into a fatal paroxysm. Two years before writing this most powerful of all demonic encounters, Goethe had written a whimsical letter to Frau von Stein together with the 'Gesang der Elfen' (Song of the Elves), which he claimed to have overheard while walking through the Ilm Park by moonlight. This song of spirits dancing among alder trees in the water-meadows has only the faintly uncanny magic of a dream; in the ballad of the 'Alder King', this ghostly dance has become a nightmare vision of brutal physical attack.

The overwhelming effect of 'Erlkönig' lies not only in its striking exploitation of combined narrative, lyrical and dramatic idioms, not only in the conflicting tensions of the four distinct voices that carry the story – the narrative voice that opens the ballad with a terse question and closes it with a brutally laconic statement, the calm rationalities of the father, the wheedling enticements of the demon, and the rising panic of the boy's voice as he fails to convince his father of the reality of his vision; it lies not only in the rhythmic and acoustic virtuosity of the poetic articulation. It also depends crucially on a fundamental ambiguity that Goethe has introduced into his version – an ambiguity that was absent from his source material. It is well known that Goethe's poem is based on Herder's free translation of a Danish ballad which Herder had entitled, not 'Elf-King's Daughter' but 'Alder King's Daughter' (*Erlkönigs Tochter*) – evidently confusing the Danish for 'elf' with 'alder'.[26] This intriguing mistranslation has caused some speculation; most probably Herder's ignorance of Danish was responsible for his rendering, but it has also been suggested that Herder might, wittingly or unwittingly, have imaginatively identified the malevolent sprite of his version with a woodland demon as the daughter of the Alder King. At all events, it is as the Erl King or Alder King, not as the Elf King, that Goethe's ballad, and Schubert's incomparable setting of it, is known.

But the striking difference in Herder's straightforwardly 'primitive' folk ballad, where Herr Oluf is struck dead on his wedding day for resisting the faery charms of the Erl King's daughter as he meets her in the woods, is that here we are invited, as a purportedly credulous folk audience, to accept the reality of the demon and of her revenge. Goethe's version, on the other hand, quite apart from its incomparably greater poetic subtlety and sophistication, rests on a crucial ambiguity of perception: the reader is quite uncertain whether the boy's vision is presented as reality within the conventions of popular superstition, whether, that is, we are asked willingly to suspend our disbelief in elemental demons – or whether we are invited to rationalize the child's vision in the father's terms as the ghostly effects of wind, light and shade on the nocturnal landscape. Is the demon a malevolent elemental spirit, or a projection of a sick child's febrile imagination? No answer is given to this double perspective, other than the brutal final reality of the child's death.

'Der Sänger' (The Minstrel, 1783) is a legendary ballad included in, and presumably written specifically for, *Wilhelm Meisters theatralische Sendung* (Wilhelm

Meister's Theatrical Mission, see below, pp. 217–22), where it is sung by the Minstrel (Harfenspieler), an enigmatic and tragic figure who appears in the novel as an unkempt and lonely itinerant haunted by an obsessive sense of atavistic guilt. For the most part, the songs he sings are dismal statements of suffering visited on helpless humanity by vengeful and malevolent gods. They express a bleak vision of existential isolation and misery which is quite unique in Goethe's lyrical *oeuvre*. Even the emotional anguish of the *Marienbad Elegy* is mitigated and relativized by its context within the *Trilogy of Passion*; and it is perhaps significant that Goethe chooses to express both the unmitigated suffering of the Minstrel's songs and the tragic nostalgia of Mignon's through their fictive personae in the novel, not within the corpus of his personal lyric poetry. The themes associated with the Harfenspieler, and the material of his songs, are a fearful intuition of guilt and retribution at the hands of implacable powers ('Wer nie sein Brot mit Tränen aß': Who never ate his bread with tears, 1783); a sense of utter existential isolation in which the loneliness of the grave seems preferable to life ('Wer sich der Einsamkeit ergibt': Who pledges himself to solitude, 1783); and a mendicant existence of homeless misery ('An die Türen will ich schleichen': Past the doorways I will creep, written later in 1795 for inclusion in *Wilhelm Meisters Lehrjahre*).[27]

'Der Sänger', however, is an exception to these songs of unrelieved angst; it is the first of the Harfenspieler's songs in the novel, a set-piece performance from his repertoire sung to entertain the company and to celebrate the honourable status of the bard. It projects a romantic and unproblematic image of the itinerant minstrel who sings as the birds sing, for whom song is its own reward, and who demands only the symbolic payment of the finest wine from a golden goblet. Within the context of the novel, the song is doubly ironic; for not only is this idealized vision of poetry and of the poet-minstrel sung by the tragic and wretched figure of the Harfenspieler, but it also reflects Wilhelm Meister's own earlier idealized perception of his very first vocation: that of the poet who is beholden to no one and who writes for himself alone.[28] This immature perception very soon gives way in the novel to an equally immature, and ultimately also illusory, commitment to the theatre.

The other enigmatic and tragic figure who impinges on Wilhelm Meister's career, and who also expresses herself in hauntingly lyrical verse, is Mignon, the waif whose songs articulate not the atavistic guilt of the Minstrel, but a harrowing nostalgia that remains inscrutably unspecific until the disclosure of their common fate after her death in the novel: she is the child of the Minstrel's innocently incestuous union with his sister, was abducted from her home in Italy at an early age, and was sold into a wretched existence with a travelling circus from which Wilhelm Meister released her. The nostalgia expressed in her intensely pathetic songs is, in the first instance, for her homeland ('Kennst du das Land, wo die Zitronen blühn': Do you know the land where the lemons bloom, *c.*1783), for her protector ('Nur wer die Sehnsucht kennt': Only those who know what longing is, 1785), and finally, in her last song, written later for the *Lehrjahre*, for death ('So laßt mich scheinen, bis ich werde': Let me appear thus till I become, 1796). A further song, 'Heiß mich nicht reden, heiß mich schweigen' (Bid me not speak, bid me be silent, *c.*1782) appears to indicate that she has some awareness of her true identity, which she cannot or will not reveal to her protector Wilhelm Meister.

Mignon's songs are fully understandable only from the context of the novel – where, to be sure, they are enigmatic enough. In particular, 'So laßt mich scheinen', with its references to her white gown, her angelic manifestation, her troubled androgynous personality, and the resolution of the vexations of gender in death, is closely related to the narrative situation. But her songs are also often enough cited as independent lyric poems, none more so than 'Kennst du das Land', which is the prototype for many Romantic and post-Romantic expressions of longing for an exotic dream of the south, specifically for Italy. In the context of the novel, it is the articulation of Mignon's vague childhood recollections of her homeland, of oranges and lemons, myrtle and bay trees, of a Palladian villa decorated with columns and marble statuary, and of her journey across the Alps: a childish, almost mythical vision of mules picking their way through mist, of torrents, vertiginous cliffs and dragons' lairs. But irrespective of its function within the novel, or of its exemplary significance for many generations of poets who reiterated the theme of 'Sehnsucht nach dem Süden' (Yearning for the South), it is also a poem written by Goethe only some three years before his own Italian journey; this emblematic and idealized landscape beyond the Alps is the imaginative and vicarious fulfilment of his own increasingly urgent commitment to the country he was shortly to experience at first hand. The poetry Goethe was to write after, and as a result of, that first-hand experience is strikingly different in style and mood from the diffuse and nostalgic landscape of Mignon's vision.

ROMAN ELEGIES

It is only to be expected that a watershed experience such as his Italian journey should have left its mark on the shape of Goethe's career as a lyric poet; but it is still surprising that there is so little nature or landscape poetry that reflects very clearly the visual or emotional impact of the Italian scene. To be sure, there is description enough of the southern and Mediterranean scenery in the letters and diaries from Italy, and subsequently in the *Italienische Reise* itself; there are innumerable sketches and watercolours of Italy by Goethe, Kniep and others; and there are occasional references to urban and suburban garden landscapes in the *Roman Elegies* and in 'Alexis und Dora'. But the vein of lyric poetry that Goethe had worked on into the 1780s seems to run out around the middle of that decade; the subdued and ambivalent tensions of the early Weimar years that produced the often intense and introverted poems of these years are missing from the post-Italian lyric poetry, and for a considerable time Goethe ceased to write in that particular emotional genre.

This is by no means to say that Goethe ceased to write lyric poetry during or after the Italian journey: the *Roman Elegies* themselves, and the flood of epigrams, elegies, occasional poems, satires, ballads and sonnets bear witness to his continuing productivity in verse. But lyric poetry of the kind we associate with the younger Goethe, the subtle and often symbolic blending of emotion and nature, of 'inscape' and landscape, seems to run out in his mid-thirties; and it was not until the late poems of his old age that Goethe returned to a significant output of lyrical verse that has any clear continuity with the early Weimar poetry, that he once again blends landscape and emotion in a symbolic empathy. It is as if the experience of Italy, with all the personal, emotional, cultural and even actuarial significance it had for him as a watershed, removed the need or the desire to write poetry that explored such ambivalent, unfulfilled and twilight states of mind. Indeed, this appears to be expressed with programmatic emphasis in the seventh Roman Elegy, where he celebrates the sharp sunlit forms and colours of Italy and looks back with revulsion at the grey formlessness of the northern landscape that invites such introspective brooding:

> O wie fühl' ich in Rom mich so froh! gedenk' ich der Zeiten,
> Da mich ein graulicher Tag hinten im Norden umfing,
> Trübe der Himmel und schwer auf meine Scheitel sich senkte,
> Farb- und gestaltlos die Welt um den Ermatteten lag,
> Und ich über mein Ich, des unbefriedigten Geistes
> Düstre Wege zu spähn, still in Betrachtung versank.
> Nun umleuchtet der Glanz des helleren Äthers die Stirne;
> Phöbus rufet, der Gott, Formen und Farben hervor.
> Sternhell glänzet die Nacht, sie klingt von weichen Gesängen,
> Und mir leuchtet der Mond heller als nordischer Tag.

> Oh how happy I feel here in Rome, when I fall to recalling
> How in the north a grey dullness pervaded the sky!
> Heavy the sombre skies weighed down, oppressing my spirit,
> Colourless, formless the world seemed to my wearisome sight,
> How I, inwardly turning in restless dissatisfaction
> Gloomily searched my mind, lost in the shadows of thought.
> Now the radiance of clearer skies is above and around me;
> Phoebus the sun-god reveals colours and shapes that are new.
> Night is ablaze with stars, and softly the melodies echo;
> Here the moonlight shines brighter than northerly day.

The *Roman Elegies* were of course not written in Rome, though that is the fiction sustained throughout the cycle. They were composed between the autumn of 1788 and the spring of 1790, by which time not only the Italian experience, but also all contact with Charlotte von Stein, was behind him; he was free from the intolerable combination of physical abstinence and emotional dependence she had demanded of him, free from a companionship of souls which, however sublime and educative it may have been, however productive of enthralling lyric poetry, had imposed increasingly intolerable restraints on a poet already sufficiently burdened by other existential and professional frustrations. The sexual liberation Goethe had found among so many other freedoms in Rome was effortlessly continued in his partnership with Christiane Vulpius; the obscure figure of his Roman mistress merges with that of his Weimar mistress, Faustine with Christiane, as Goethe recreates his supreme experience in Rome from Weimar.

At the same time, the literary impulses that inform the cycle should not be overlooked. Rome was for Goethe the city of the poetic 'triumvirate' Catullus, Propertius and Tibullus, the city from which Ovid was also banished; and it is in the spirit of these mentors that he composes his own retrospective elegies. His *Erotica Romana* are elegiac in form rather than in mood, for it is only in the circumstances of their composition that they represent a lament for lost happiness. In 1815 Goethe prefaced the published version with a motto that indicates their personal elegiac dimension: 'Wie wir einst so glücklich waren! / Müssen's jetzt durch euch erfahren' (Memories of happy times / We must now seek in these lines). But intrinsically, the elegies are an affirmative and hedonistic celebration of the present here and now. The elegant formality of the elegiac couplet or distich (hexameter + pentameter), used with some prosodic freedom, allowed Goethe – as he, at least, saw it – to present racy (and, in the unpublished elegies, positively scabrous) material in a stylized classicizing idiom that was frank and yet inoffensive: a perception not shared by Frau von Stein and the more prudish elements at the Weimar court.

AMOR:ROMA is the palindrome that informs the cycle: Rome past and present, contemporary and historical (even the French Revolution figures briefly but distantly in the second elegy), actual and mythical, is the setting and the tutelary spirit of the poems, as the earnest cultural tourist is transformed into an acolyte of Amor's temple. 'Geborgen' – safe, protected, in hiding in the anonymity of Rome – the childlike excitement of the man who insisted on his incognito as the German painter 'Möller' long after his cover was blown, is conveyed in the opening poems; indeed, in his original version of the second elegy, Goethe curses his European reputation as the author of *Werther*, a reputation that persecutes him even in Italy and pursues him like the dismal ghost of his famous hero. The eroticism of the poems is underscored by mythological references to the 'heroic age' when gods and goddesses, mortals and immortals, fell into instant and impatient embrace; the chiastic symmetry of the classicizing pentameter is exploited to convey the rapid succession of desire and consummation:

> In der heroischen Zeit, da Götter und Göttinnen liebten,
>   Folgte Begierde dem Blick, folgte Genuß der Begier.

> In the heroic age of gods' and goddesses' embraces,
>   Passion soon followed a glance, pleasure soon followed desire.
>   (Elegy III)

The eclectic pantheon of Roman polytheistic religions is invoked in a manifesto of pagan sensuality, in the humorous and joyous equation of cultural and sexual experience. Only now does the lover truly understand the plastic forms of statuary, as his eye takes in the shape of his mistress's breast and his hand caresses her hips; the rhythms of the hexameter are tapped out on her bare back as she sleeps. Again, the very structure of the pentameter mimics the symbiosis of erotic and aesthetic sensation:

Und belehr' ich mich nicht, indem ich des lieblichen Busens
  Formen spähe, die Hand leite die Hüften hinab?
Dann versteh' ich den Marmor erst recht: ich denk' und vergleiche,
  Sehe mit fühlendem Aug', fühle mit sehender Hand.

Do I not improve my mind when softly caressing
  Rounded hips, when my gaze dwells on the shapes of the breast?
Now I can value the sculptor's art in the forms of the marble,
  Seeing with eyes that can feel, feeling with hands that can see.

(Elegy V)

The 'mists of the gloomy north' are dispelled in a land where the moon shines brighter than the northern sun, in a land of noisily swarming humanity, of busy 'southern fleas'. The elegies proceed in a series of situations and playful analogies from outdoors to indoors, day to night, from Olympus to the bedroom, the bedroom to the inn, from the inn to the vineyard and back to the lodgings where the lover impatiently urges the sun to set on the domes and monuments of the eternal city and hasten the darkness that will bring another night of love, when the northern barbarian will claim possession of a Roman body. The uniform rising and falling of the distichs belies the changing tones and moods of the verse as the poet mixes humour and passion, irony and erotic intensity, fun and dignity; finally, in the twentieth elegy, he casts himself as the servant of King Midas whose compulsion to communicate his 'fullness of heart' leads him to confide his erotic secrets, not to the reeds, but to hexameter and pentameter: 'Wie sie des Tags mich erfreut, wie sie des Nachts mich beglückt' (How she by day brings me joy, how she by night brings me bliss).

This is the cycle of twenty elegies as they were first published in Schiller's journal *Die Horen* in 1795; but there are two more elegies that Goethe withheld from publication, and a further two he had no intention of publishing. Most modern editions now print the four extra elegies, either as apocryphal or in a conjectural reconstruction of the order Goethe had, or might have had, in mind.[29] 'Mehr als ich ahndete schön, das Glück' (Happiness such as I never imagined) was evidently originally planned as the second of twenty-two, that is, between Elegies I and II of the standard canon, and 'Zwei gefährliche Schlangen' (Two most dangerous serpents) as the sixteenth between Elegies XIV and XV. The former now answers the questions posed in the opening elegy: when will the monuments of Rome speak to him, when will love animate the ancient stones? The answer is quickly supplied as his mistress slips off her simple woollen dress, and the pair worship their own deity to the rhythmic creaking of the bed in the joys of 'authentic, naked love'. 'Zwei gefährliche Schlangen' is a more explicit elaboration of a theme touched on discreetly in the canonical Elegy XVIII ('Eines ist mir verdrießlich': One thing is odious to me), where the poet congratulates himself, not without some complacency, on the fidelity of his mistress – secured, as he frankly admits in the second elegy, by gifts in cash and kind: not for him the youthful torment of suspected infidelity, but the security of possession. More important still than this, however, he confesses in Elegy XVIII, is that they can exchange 'safe kisses', free from the risk of venereal infection, the poison that lurks

among the roses of passion. The apocryphal 'Zwei gefährliche Schlangen' confronts the fear of syphilis more frankly, if still metaphorically, as the 'poisonous
slime' that pollutes Amor's life-giving dew. It is a modern affliction, the poet wryly
points out, unknown to the ancients: just imagine what ructions there would have
been on Olympus if the gandering Jupiter had infected his spouse! To be sure,
even latter-day pagans can have recourse to the gifts of the healing god; but if a
night with Venus means a lifetime with Mercury, the poet is content to remain
safely monogamous.

Goethe evidently felt unable to present such material in print: if even the
published elegies caused offence, how would these have been received? But there
are two further priapic elegies which he carefully consigned to his *Walpurgissack*
(Walpurgis sack), the private repository of highly risqué material that has only
relatively recently been given the dignity of uncensored publication. It has been
suggested that these two celebrations of the phallic deity Priapus, the 'god of the
garden', should stand monumentally as the first and last elegies in a cycle of
twenty-four.[30] But this is a hypothesis that would radically restructure the cycle;
and the ironically self-conscious conclusion of the canonical version in the twentieth elegy, where the cycle comes full circle as the poet confides his intimate
secrets to his elegiac couplets, is an appropriate end to a series of poems that had
indeed articulated a compulsive sexual and emotional confession. The two priapic
elegies can stand on their own, as it were, as examples of Goethe at his most
robustly and frankly ribald – albeit within the respected and established classical
tradition of literary *priapeia*. Priapus, who appears briefly and allusively in the
published Elegy XI, invoked in the final line as the son of Bacchus and Venus, is
in the first of these two suppressed elegies appointed guardian of the poet's garden
of erotic blooms ('Hier ist mein Garten bestellt': Here my garden's set out). He is
instructed to keep them for those who wish to enjoy them innocently, and only
meddling prudes and hypocrites shall fear his punishment: to be sodomized with
his virile 'stake'. In the second priapic elegy ('Hinten im Winkel des Gartens': Hid
at the end of the garden), the 'last of the gods' deplores his own cultural neglect.
He has become a rotting scarecrow whose mighty member has snapped under the
weight of the gourds whose tendrils cling to it; besmirched with filth from boys and
birds, he will soon be only a spongy mass of rotten wood. Only the artist, in paint
or in words, in ivory, bronze or marble, can preserve his pride; and for this service
the god will reward him with unflagging virility as he rehearses with his mistress
all the inventive configurations of sexual congress.

Venetian Epigrams

If the literary inspiration of the *Roman Elegies* had been the Latin love poets, that
of the *Venetian Epigrams* (1790–5) were the savage and often scurrilous satires of
Martial. The biographical context was also radically different from that which
had, in retrospect or in actuality, informed the *Elegies*. If Goethe did have any
hopes that he might revive or recreate his arcadian experience of two years

previously, he was soon disabused of the notion that it was possible to bathe in the same rejuvenating river twice, and it was with a very different image of Italy that he returned after a brief two months to his domestic establishment in Weimar, to which he was now all the more committed by the addition of his baby son August. Whereas the motto that prefaced the 1815 edition of the *Elegies* had evoked the lost happiness of his Roman experience, that prefacing the *Venetian Epigrams* strikes a wryly ironic note: 'Wie man Geld und Zeit vertan, / Zeigt das Büchlein lustig an' (How time and money wasted were / These verses cheerfully aver).

The awareness of the impossibility of recreating the novelty and excitement of his first journey, and the temporary and desultory nature of his second visit as an idle tourist in Venice as he waited for the Dowager Duchess, inform these epigrams; now he ruefully casts himself as the cultural sightseer, as the deluded pilgrim who searches for the scattered relics of his saviour (21, 'Emsig wallet der Pilger': Busily the pilgrim searches).[31] Now he no longer shrugs off the discomforts of travel as he had in his first headlong rush down the Trentino, no longer puts up with the improvised chaos of Latin life with the cheerful tolerance of a traveller to whom all is new and exciting; it is a painful progress south, beset by memories of those he has left behind in Weimar, and by the tiresome and rapacious attentions of ostlers, coachmen, untrustworthy servants, and customs officials (3, 'Immer halt ich die Liebste': Always I hold my dearest). This is Italy – but not the Italy he had left with such sharp regret (4, 'Das ist Italien, das ich verließ': That is the Italy that I left). His Faustine is now in Weimar, not here; and in a self-conscious parody of himself as the suspicious German tourist who more than half expects to be swindled, he bemoans the absence of the Teutonic virtues:

> Deutsche Redlichkeit suchst du in allen Winkeln vergebens;
>   Leben und Weben ist hier, aber nicht Ordnung und Zucht.

> Upright German honesty, wherever you look you won't find it;
>   Hustle and bustle is here, order and discipline not.
>   (Epigram 4)

Even the coffin-like gondolas rocking their way along the Grand Canal prompt lugubrious thoughts of life between the cradle and the grave (Epigram 8) – an association reprised by Gustav von Aschenbach in Thomas Mann's *Der Tod in Venedig* (Death in Venice).

The 103 published epigrams range over a vast spectrum of themes, of which two stand out: disenchantment with Italy, coupled with fond thoughts of the wife and child he left behind in Germany, and a fierce anti-Church and anti-clerical polemic that mocks the Passiontide ceremonies of the Venetian Church and betrays Goethe's aversion to Church ritual, and in particular to the gruesome instrument of torture on which the faith of the *Schwärmer* (religious 'enthusiast' or fanatic) centres. In one (79, 'Alles erklärt sich wohl': Surely all is explained), his repugnance to any dogmatic theory and to the crucifix is devastatingly brought together as the cross is implicitly compared to the bed of Procrustes, where the living flesh is violently forced to fit into an unnatural structure. Others strike out in all directions: a grateful tribute to Karl August (34b, 'Klein ist unter den Fürsten Germaniens': Small among the princes of Germany); the German language (29, 'Vieles hab ich versucht': Many talents I've tried); the French Revolution (53, 'Frankreichs traurig Geschick': France's sad destiny); Newtonian optics (78, 'Weiß hat Newton gemacht': Newton has made white). Vignettes from the teeming street life of Venice include several observations of the prostitutes (*Lazerten* or 'lizards') who flit across the streets and slip into the darkness of the coffee-houses (67–72); a whole group is devoted to the truly remarkable agility of a pretty young street acrobat, Bettina (36–47); and one even records the early introduction of the yo-yo into Europe (90, 'Welch ein lustiges Spiel!': What an amusing game!).

If some of the published epigrams are startlingly frank, even shocking, by eighteenth-century standards of public taste – one reviewer commented that Goethe had emptied a Venetian chamberpot over his readers – those unpublished by Goethe are capable of raising eyebrows even in the late twentieth century. The anti-clerical and anti-Christian polemic here becomes violently ribald: during the displaying of holy relics in St Mark's on Maundy Thursday, a hysterical girl shouts for the monstrance of the sacred 'part' of Christ, and is brutally advised by the poet to demand, not that of the crucified saviour, but one that will heal her more surely – that of the god from Lampsacus, namely Priapus ('Heraus mit dem Teile des Herrn!': Out with the part of the Lord!). The resurrection is a trick played by the disciples ('Offen steht das Grab!': Open stands the grave!); in others religious bigotry, Christian fanaticism and absurd ritual are compared unfavourably and scurrilously with the healthy sensuality of paganism. The lithe contortions of Bettina are even more sensationally and anatomically described here ('Was ich am meisten besorge': What concerns me the most) than in the published collection, where he had already advised her not to display her upturned legs to the sky for fear Jupiter might glimpse her charms, to the dismay of Ganymede (38, 'Kehre nicht, liebliches Kind': Do not turn your legs, lovely child). The 'base material' of the German language that he had deplored in one of the published epigrams (and which he had in an earlier phase celebrated as the plain and robust language of Luther) is here the butt of ribald etymological punning. *Schwanz*, the German for tail (and, vulgarly, for penis), is dismissed as 'something from behind' – not, the writer assures us, his style at all: how much nobler the Greek *phallos* sounds to a poet! ('Gib mir statt "Der Sch . . ." ein ander Wort, o Priapus!': Give me, rather than pr . . . another word, O Priapus!). An approving allusion to the pleasures of (heterosexual) sodomy should not be construed either as a contradiction of the previous sentiment, or as necessarily reflecting the poet's own tastes ('Knaben liebt ich wohl auch, doch lieber sind mir die Mädchen': Boys I might fancy too, but girls I like so much better); Goethe is here writing in the persona of Martial as much as *in propria persona*, and this epigram is very close in spirit to one of his models.[32]

The *Venetian Epigrams* have neither the cyclic coherence nor the joyful hedonism of the *Roman Elegies*, nor do they show the virtuosity in the use of the distich displayed in the *Elegies*; they are, as Goethe concedes in the introductory motto and in the final epigram of the published collection (103, 'Und so tändelt ich mir':

So I frittered away), a record of idle and frustrating days spent in 'Neptune's city'. But they are also a witty, satirical and often scabrous record of Goethe's observations on religion, sexuality, human mores and many other subjects. They reveal him as a caustic, perceptive and indeed compassionate observer of the human condition – an aspect of his personality that is often ignored or obscured behind the received image. Among the published epigrams is the song of a Venetian prostitute (No. 72), in which the economic foundation of conventional morality is underlined in a spirit not far removed from that of Büchner or Brecht:

> 'Wär ich ein häusliches Weib und hätte, was ich bedürfte,
>   Treu sein wollt ich und froh, herzen und küssen den Mann.'
> So sang, unter andern, gemeinen Liedern, ein Dirnchen
>   Mir in Venedig, und nie hört ich ein frömmer Gebet.

> 'If I were a housewife, and had all I ever could ask for,
>   Then I'd be loving and glad, and to my husband be true.'
> This was one of the songs a tart sang to me in Venice;
>   And a more pious prayer never before had I heard.

The much-abused 'lackey of princes', whose time in Venice was indeed spent waiting on the delays of a Dowager Duchess's progress through Italy, was not above a close empathy with 'Gaukler und Volk', with street-acrobats, whores and sinners.

IDYLLS AND ELEGIES

Goethe continued to write verse in classicizing metres in the 1790s: elegies, epistles, the *Weissagungen des Bakis* (Prophecies of Bakis), the *Vier Jahreszeiten* (Four Seasons), and the polemical *Xenien* written in collaboration with Schiller. Many of these works were destined for publication in Schiller's *Musenalmanach* or *Die Horen*, the periodicals that proclaimed the ideology of Weimar Classicism – indeed, as Goethe remarked many years later, much of his work during this period would not have been written if Schiller had not been short of manuscripts for his publications. Most of these works are in elegiac couplets; the *Epistles* and some other single poems, for example 'Metamorphose der Tiere' (Metamorphosis of Animals) are in the continuous 'epic' hexameter that Goethe also used for his major epics of this decade, *Reineke Fuchs, Hermann und Dorothea* and the unfinished *Achilleis*. After 1800 Goethe's use of epic hexameter virtually ceased, though his dramatic fragment *Pandora* of 1807–8 mixes iambic trimeter, choriambic ode forms and modern rhymed verse, and he was to return to the ancient dramatic forms of trimeter, tetrameter and choric ode some twenty-five years later when he resumed work on the Helen episode of the third act of *Faust* Part Two, an episode that symbolically, and indeed prosodically, charts and celebrates the modern Western assimilation of the cultural heritage of classical Hellenism. While Goethe manifestly acquired a high degree of flexible mastery in classicizing metres, a mastery that is at its most impressive in his earlier efforts like the *Roman Elegies*, he became increasingly uneasy under the tyranny, not so much of the distich form as such, but rather of the scholarly strictures of the contemporary experts whose guidance and correction he earnestly sought – notably Johann Heinrich Voß and August Wilhelm Schlegel. But he finally grew weary of the prosodists of the 'Strict Observance', as he put it (a term denoting the rigorous dogmas of certain Masonic lodges), and he effectively abandoned his efforts to reconcile expressive freedom with metrical purism – though not before he had made his own considerable creative contribution to German classical metres.

'Alexis und Dora' (1796) also underwent considerable prosodic revision under Schlegel's guidance; no doubt the second version is metrically more correct, but it may reasonably be questioned whether it is rhythmically or syntactically more felicitous.[33] The poem is consciously classicizing not only in metre, but also in style, rhetoric and genre. Much discussion has centred on whether it is an idyll, an elegy or a combination of both genres – it was published in Schiller's *Musenalmanach* for 1797 with the subtitle 'Idylle', and referred to as such in their correspondence; but Goethe also later talked of 'this elegy'. If we take as broad working definitions that of the idyll as the present description of an ideally harmonious or happy state, and that of the elegy as a lament for a past or lost state of happiness, we should remember that the idyll is also traditionally threatened: for death, we are told, was also present even in Arcadia.

The basic situation of the poem is clearly elegiac; it opens with the ship bearing Alexis inexorably away from his agonizingly brief encounter with Dora, and from line 10 (or arguably from line 12 – the transition between third person narrative and first person voice is fluid to the point of obscurity) the whole poem, with the exception of the poet's 'riddle' in lines 25–30, and his *envoi* in the last four lines, consists of Alexis's elegiac recapitulation of his lost idyll and the events leading to and from it. The brief central idyll of lines 76–102 is encapsulated within Alexis's recollection, which is in turn framed by the poet's introduction and conclusion. But even the idyllic core of the poem is threatened by the tensions of time, by the frantic calls of the sailors and the imminent departure of the ship (lines 57–9, 75, 103–4); and Alexis's retrospective reverie is drastically broken by his lapse into suspicion, jealousy and despair. The pace of the poem shifts constantly as the focus moves from the ship moving inexorably out to sea, to a series of flashbacks detailing the early, casual acquaintance of the lovers, punctuated by the urgency of departure, until time is briefly suspended in their climactic encounter in the garden. The highly charged erotic emblems of this encounter – the garden gate standing open, the heavy roundness of the orange, the supple plasticity of the fig, and the musky scent of the myrtle (identified by Albrecht Schöne as the key to the poet's 'riddle')[34] are the very factors that provoke the subsequent outburst of suspicion and jealousy that retrospectively sours the idyll, as Alexis calls down destruction on the ship bearing him away. The profound irony of this problematic poem is that Alexis must curse the mercantile mission that was both the means of bringing the lovers together and the cause of their separation, of both the creation and the destruction of their idyll.

'Euphrosyne' (1798) is also a product of the aesthetics of Weimar Classicism; it is the classicizing counterpart to Goethe's earlier tribute to the arts of the stage manager Mieding. While the earlier poem was affectionately humorous and ironic in its mock-heroic style, 'Euphrosyne' is solemnly formal in rhetoric and diction; where Mieding's epitaph evoked the smell of greasepaint and size, the clattering machinery of eighteenth-century stagecraft, the make-believe world of costume and scenery, lighting and sound-effects, this elegiac *Nachruf* draws on the classical imagery of mortality. A traveller in the mountains is visited by the apparition of a woman, a spirit on her journey to Hades under the direction of Hermes Psychopompos, the guide of the dead. The ghost is that of Christiane Becker or Neumann, a young actress whom Goethe had coached and directed in the Weimar Court Theatre, and who had died while he was away in Switzerland in 1797. One of her last parts was that of Euphrosyne, one of the three Graces; but the role recalled here is that of Prince Arthur in Shakespeare's *King John*, in which Goethe had directed her and in which she had feigned the death that is now reality. As in 'Alexis und Dora', the elegy is structured by encapsulation: the monologue of the dead woman (lines 23–140) is framed by the poet's descriptive narrative, but within her monologue she also quotes (lines 63–96) the poet's own tribute to her when she was alive. She appeals to him to save her from the anonymity that awaits her as a formless shade in Hades by commemorating her in verse, in a striking parallel to the concluding episode of the third act of *Faust* Part Two. There, the chorus of Trojan women will not follow their mistress Helen to the underworld; they are anonymous figures who cannot survive in history or legend, in literature or art, but only by assimilation as elemental spirits into the cycles of 'ever-living nature'. The plea of Euphrosyne is for the posthumous identity that only the Muses can give her: celebrated by the poet, she will share the immortality of Penelope, Euadne, Antigone and Polyxena.

The invocation of classical models is the very theme of 'Hermann und Dorothea' (1796), a poem originally planned as an introduction to and apologia for the epic of the same title; it was withdrawn on Schiller's advice, no doubt because its polemical tone made it an unsuitably provocative preface to the more moderate irony of his domestic epic poem. Here Goethe squares up to his critics – who were indeed at this time legion. His unconventional household, his lofty withdrawal into high-minded classicism, his literary volte-face from the earlier radicalism of the *Sturm und Drang*, his assumption of the duties and privileges of a Weimar Privy Councillor, his and Schiller's polemical campaign of *Xenien* against their detractors, the raciness of the *Roman Elegies* and the *Venetian Epigrams* – all this and more had earned Goethe many and powerful enemies in all quarters. Propertius and Martial, Homer himself (or, more strictly, the 'Homerides', the Homeric poets – for it had recently been proposed by Friedrich August Wolf that the *Odyssey* and the *Iliad* were the products of collective authorship) are enlisted in defence of his classicizing efforts, as is the German translator and poet Johann Heinrich Voß, whose own rural idyll in hexameter, *Luise*, had appeared in 1795. If the *Elegies* and *Epigrams* had caused offence among an undiscerning public, Goethe no doubt feared a similarly uninformed reception for his modern epic in which a homely contemporary German scene was to be touched with ironic Homeric grandeur.

DE RERUM NATURA

It is unsurprising that the themes of Goethe's classicizing poetry during the 1790s should be those of love, Rome, even of modern Venice, as elegy, epigram, or epitaph. Even the polemical *Xenien*, directed at contemporary figures and institutions, are in the tradition of Martial or Juvenal. It might initially seem odd that he should also use the forms of classical elegy or epistle to convey his scientific observations in the distichs of 'Die Metamorphose der Pflanzen' (The Metamorphosis of Plants, 1798) or the epic hexameter of 'Metamorphose der Tiere' (Metamorphosis of Animals, *c*.1799). But Goethe's holistic worldview saw no radical break between literary and scientific expression, between humankind and nature; already in 'Das Göttliche' (The Divine) his existential thinking was informed by his anatomical studies and expressed in lyrical form, and later poems like 'Howards Ehrengedächtnis' (In Honour of Howard) or the *Gott und Welt* (God and World) collection are poetic statements of his scientific convictions. Here too, the model is a classical one: Lucretius. Around 1798–9 Goethe had considered writing a comprehensive work on natural philosophy, and took a great interest in the work of his close friend Karl Ludwig von Knebel, who was at the time engaged in translating Lucretius's *De rerum natura*; and it was at Knebel's suggestion that Goethe adopted hexameters for the second of his 'metamorphosis' poems – the opening lines of which, moreover, appear to presuppose a previous body of didactic material. Had he persevered with this grand design, earlier geological and anatomical studies, as well as later meteorological, botanical and zoological studies, might have been versified and included; whether this modern Lucretian project would have included the *Farbenlehre* is more doubtful. In the event, it is probable that he did no more than toy with the idea, and abandoned it around 1800 – at the same time as he gave up writing classical hexameters, having lost patience with the pedantic strictures of the metrical purists (though he continued to write in elegiac couplets for a number of years). Only the 'Metamorphose der Tiere' remains as a vestigial trace of his great plan.

'Die Metamorphose der Pflanzen', addressed, it is generally understood, to Christiane Vulpius, is a poetic statement, part didactic poem, part love lyric, of Goethe's botanical ideas as he expressed them in his treatise of 1790 *Versuch, die Metamorphose der Pflanzen zu erklären* (Attempt to Explain the Metamorphosis of Plants) (see below, pp. 264ff.). It sets out to explain the bewildering variety and multiplicity of forms and species by reference to a single principle of development and structure, that of metamorphosis. 'Stufenweise', by steps, the plant develops from the seed by a process of expansion and contraction; the seed contains within it the pattern – we would say the genetic code – of its future shape. The seed is the greatest form of contraction, the alpha and omega that ensures the continuity of the chain of generations and guarantees the survival of the species. By a progression through alternating steps – cotyledons, stem, leaves – the plant develops into more complex forms, sepals and petals, calyx and reproductive organs, until the circle is closed by the setting of new seeds. Thus reduced to a prototypical pattern, the mysterious hieroglyphs of nature can be deciphered and the inscrutable law can be discerned in the jumbled diversity of forms.

Similarly, all animal forms, however bizarre their metamorphosed structures may be, bear the mark of the primal form, the skeletal structure. The 'limitless gifts' of nature allow each creature to exploit its environment to satisfy its needs: mouth and limbs determine food and habitat, which in turn affect the physical form. Each creature is, as it were, sufficient unto itself, perfectly formed for its own existence; each is a variation of a primal archetype, but adapted to its needs. There is no divine purpose, no teleological plan, in the diversity of zoological forms; but nature herself is infinitely inventive within the limits of her own laws. For no creature can overdevelop in one direction without a compensating under-development in another, and by a law of 'compensation' the economy of forms is preserved: no animal can bear both horns and a full complement of teeth. The law of nature is a balance between the arbitrary and the necessary, between the power to develop and the need to limit, between freedom and restraint. As Goethe put it elsewhere (and as Darwin was later to put it in not dissimilar terms),[35] for all its diversity, nature works within a strict rubric or 'budget': it will never incur debt or become bankrupt. The final line of the poem is a paradigmatic expression both of Goethe's scientific method and of his classical convictions – steady, clear-sighted perception, *Schauen*, will reveal what no amount of speculative enthusiasm, *Schwärmen*, can convey; certainty is accessible to informed and painstaking observation, not abstract conjecture.

CLASSICAL SATIRE

The remaining poems in classical metres selected by Trunz are classified under the rubrics of 'Mixed Epigrams' and 'Xenien'. Some of the first group date from before 1786 – for Goethe practised distichs well before his Italian journey. They are sententious and lapidary dedications or inscriptions – indeed, the first two, 'Einsamkeit' (Solitude) and 'Erwählter Fels' (Chosen Rock), both 1782, were designed to be chiselled in stone and set up in the Ilm Park or in the garden of Goethe's *Gartenhaus*; others were written for personal albums or *Stammbücher*. The second group is a selection of the *Xenien* written by Goethe in close collaboration with Schiller in 1795–6. Martial had written a number of brief epigrams or *Xenia*, vignettes in verse, not of a satirical character, which were presented to friends and guests as hospitable gifts. In 1795 Goethe proposed to Schiller that they should adopt this genre as a means of riposte to the literary attacks mounted against them, and specifically against *Die Horen*, the programmatic classicizing monthly periodical edited by Schiller. Most of these *Xenien* were published anonymously in Schiller's annual *Musenalmanach* for 1797, which appeared in September of the previous year; and public interest in these frequently polemical and occasionally

vitriolic epigrams was enormous, creating amusement, resentment and curiosity
in varying proportions. Goethe was to write a vast number of *Xenien*, which are
conventionally divided into 'zahme' (tame, gentle) and 'scharfe' (sharp) *Xenien*; the
former are in a variety of verse forms, the latter in distichs – but the distinction
between them in degrees of savagery is not hard and fast.

In so far as they attacked perceived mediocrity or banality, and in so far as they
counter-attacked critics of *Die Horen*, the classicizing *Xenien* were an important
element in Goethe's and Schiller's educative classical mission to the Germans; but
they were hardly designed to win hearts and minds. Many old scores were settled,
and many new ones compiled; some of the antagonisms created were to last for
years, even beyond Schiller's death, for all Goethe's subsequent efforts to make
peace with their erstwhile victims. The targets were not chosen with any great
discrimination; the distinguished and the mediocre, the famous and the obscure,
the gifted and the untalented were peppered by the volleys from Weimar. Literary
luminaries like Klopstock; former friends and allies like Lavater or the Stolberg
brothers; the high-priest of the waning *Aufklärung* circle in Berlin and writer of
indefatigably pedantic travelogues, Friedrich Nicolai; scholars and linguists like
Campe and Adelung; popular dramatists like Iffland and Kotzebue; the Jacobins
Georg Forster and Johann Friedrich Reichardt (who had set many of Goethe's
works to music); even Wieland, though leniently treated, was not excluded. The
leading theorist of the early Romantic movement, Friedrich Schlegel, was among
Schiller's *bêtes noires*; and a whole host of undistinguished scribblers, pedants and
journeyman literati were honoured with unwonted prominence by these polemics. Goethe's and, by now, 'Citizen' Schiller's antipathy to the French Revolution (for Schiller, to his subsequent embarrassment, had been created an honorary
citizen of revolutionary France on his reputation as the author of *Die Räuber*)
finds expression here, as does Goethe's sustained and bitter confrontation with
Newtonian optics.

Most of these polemical distichs are now of limited specialist interest, written
as they are in an archaic form that limps even by its own standards (they were in
turn attacked for their slipshod prosody), and directed as many of them are at
such esoteric topical issues that they can only be read with the help of detailed
editorial notes. Some serve to decipher or to gloss the more cryptic allusions in the
Walpurgisnachtstraum (Walpurgis Night's Dream) of *Faust* Part One – where Goethe
eccentrically deposited some of his spare material from the *Xenien*. Some again are
worth noting on their own merits: Goethe's elegant tribute to his metrical mentor
Voß, with its erudite reference to the golden chain of Zeus (35, 'Hängen auch alle
Schmierer und Reimer': Though all the scribblers and rhymsters cling to you)[36] –
for not all these *Xenien* are satirical; the sheer insolence of the jibe at Nicolai's
literary and philosophical punditry (53, 'Querkopf! schreiet ergrimmt': Wrong-
headed! angrily shouts); Goethe's exasperated bafflement at Fichte's epistemology
of Self and Non-Self (158, 'Was nicht Ich ist': What is not Self); Schiller's terse
parodies of various philosophical systems, in particular his struggle to reconcile
himself to Kant's categorical imperative (93, 'Gerne dien' ich den Freunden':
Gladly I serve my friends); or, finally, Goethe's witty persiflage of teleological
systems:

*Welche Verehrung verdient der Weltenschöpfer, der gnädig,
Als er den Korkbaum schuf, gleich auch die Stöpsel erfand!

Praise and honour our gracious creator, for when he created
Cork trees, he also devised bottle and stopper as well!

LYRIC POETRY 1786–1813

The poems grouped by Trunz under the rubric *Lyrisches* form a broad and heterogeneous collection of lyric poetry written between the Italian journey and the *West-östliche Divan*. None of them are from the section entitled *Lyrisches* in the *Ausgabe letzter Hand*; the majority are from the *Lieder* or *Gesellige Lieder*, though some are from *Vermischte Gedichte*, *Epigrammatisch* and *Gott und Welt*.

'Amor als Landschaftsmaler' (Cupid as Landscape Painter), written in Italy in 1787, is close to the *Künstlergedichte* of the 1770s (see above, pp. 67–8); indeed, it was placed by Goethe under the rubric *Kunst* between 'Künstlers Morgenlied' and 'Künstlers Abendlied'. Trunz places it as a companion-piece to another Italian poem of the same date, 'Cupido, loser, eigensinniger Knabe!' (Cupid, wanton, wilful boy!), no doubt because of a certain thematic affinity. If in the final stanza of the first poem Goethe appears to hark back to the erotic *Schlußpointe* of the Anacreontic style, both poems also have motifs in common with the *Roman Elegies*: Amor or Cupid as the rogue who by turns educates, inspires and distracts the poet or artist. The disruptive dactylic rhythms of the second poem recapitulate the theme of the thirteenth Elegy: Amor at once gives the poet the material for his songs, and robs him of the time and discipline required to shape his art.

The following two poems were written in 1788 – but in Weimar, not in Italy, shortly after Goethe set up his household with Christiane Vulpius. 'Der Besuch' (The Visit) also has some affinity with the image of the sleeping woman in the thirteenth Elegy, but in a domestic context shorn of classical associations; 'Morgenklagen' (Morning Lament) of the same year, with its celebration of night as the time for love, its deprecation of the daytime and the impatient counting of the hours of absence, is also reminiscent of Elegies XIV, XV and XVII. These two poems are, as it were, the 'German' counterpart of the *Roman Elegies*; if the *Elegies* had been, at least in part, the expression in classicizing form of Goethe's relationship with Christiane in an imagined or recollected Roman setting, these are their domestic equivalents in the less exotic setting of Weimar. 'Frech und froh' (Bold and Cheerful), written about the same time, is also a celebration of sensual, physical love in the spirit of the *Roman Elegies*, as an antidote to the futile pangs of unrequited desire.

The 'Coptic Song' of 1787 was written for the *Singspiel* entitled *Die Mystifizierten* (The Mystified), a project that was not completed, though the idea was reworked into the satirical drama *Der Groß-Cophta* (The Great Copt, see below, pp. 167–70). The song forms part of the instruction given by the sinister Count Rostro to a young Knight in the course of his initiation into the (fraudulent) mysteries of his Masonic 'Egyptian Lodge'. In the context of the play, it represents the cynical manipulation by the thinly disguised Cagliostro figure of a gullible initiate; the ruthless message of the song is mendaciously presented as part of the temptations and tests he must submit to during his induction into the higher mysteries of the Count's pseudo-Masonic order.

'Meeresstille' and 'Glückliche Fahrt' (Calm Sea and Safe Voyage, *c*.1795) are companion mood-poems which exploit changing metres to mimetic effect in a similar manner to the earlier poem 'Auf dem See'. The first conveys the flat calm of the sea in regular four-beat trochaics, and the alternation of feminine and masculine endings emphatically marks off every second line; the second uses more dactylic rhythms to convey the release of the becalmed ship by a freshening breeze. Whether it is a recollection of Goethe's own experience off the Gulf of Naples in May 1787 is uncertain: imagery of mist dispersing and skies clearing is a frequent motif of hope and fulfilment in the symbolic landscape of his nature lyrics. 'Nähe des Geliebten' (Presence of the Beloved, 1795) is also an exercise in rhythmic patterns, though here the metre is not Goethe's, but a reworking of a poem by Friederike Brun which came to his attention in a setting by his close friend and trusted adviser in musical matters, Zelter. It is close to the original model in form and imagery as well as metre, but Goethe's version lacks the explicit reference to separation through death in Brun's final (fifth) stanza. Thematically, it also has affinities with 'Gegenwart' (Presence) and the later *Divan* poem 'In tausend Formen' (In a thousand forms), which also invoke a series of images associated with a loved person; metrically, it is unique in Goethe's poetic *oeuvre*, with its striking alternation of five and two-beat iambics with respectively rising (feminine) and falling (masculine) final cadences. It is a litany of reiterated responses that invoke a series of paired contrasts: the reflection of sun and moon in water, the traveller by day and by night, sound and silence, distance and proximity. The imagery of sun and stars in the final stanza anticipates that of the later poem that also articulates, albeit in a more complex pattern, themes of recollection, separation and hope of reunion: 'Der Bräutigam'.

'Der Musensohn' (Child of the Muses, *c*.1799) presents the persona of the itinerant musician and other motifs – the linden tree, the dance, exile and longing – that were to become a stock-in-trade of German Romantic lyric poetry. The free but homeless vagabond figure here has none of the legendary charisma of the Minstrel of 'Der Sänger', nor any of the existential self-questioning of the vatic genius figures of the earlier *Sturm und Drang* hymns like 'Wandrers Sturmlied' or 'Harzreise im Winter': the persona of the wandering minstrel is unproblematic, and his existence idyllic. 'An die Günstigen' (To the Well-inclined, 1799), expressing a similarly unproblematic lyrical credo, was written as the introductory poem to Goethe's collection of *Lieder* in the Cotta edition of his works in 1800. 'In goldnen Frühlingssonnenstunden' (In golden hours of sunny spring, *c*.1800) relates to the composition of *Faust* Part One, the dream or vision confidently embarked on in his youth that cost him such strenuous effort to resume in mid-life.

In the two sonnets written around 1800, the emphasis is on poetry or art as craft, as duty, discipline and containment. The fundamental metaphor of these poems is craftsmanship – in the first, the skills of the joiner, in the second, the discipline, industry and mastery of the skilled trades. If Goethe's early lyrical work was characterized by freedom of form and expression, by exuberant spontaneity (or at least the fiction of it), the self-imposed discipline of the sonnet is here wryly acknowledged as the bed of Procrustes to which the creative urge must adapt itself. For all his protestation that he is ill at ease within the constraints of this severe form, for all that he now, as he ruefully puts it, must join and glue rather than shape his work from the whole block, Goethe here strives programmatically to make necessity a virtue. The free impulses of nature and the formal discipline of art are only apparently at odds; inchoate emotion and intellectual control, anarchic freedom of spirit and the constraints of law, can be harmonized and reconciled in the prescribed measures of the sonnet, and only the ability to operate freely within imposed limitation shows the master's hand: only the law can make us truly free. It has been suggested that line 6 of 'Das Sonett' (The Sonnet) and lines 10–11 of 'Natur und Kunst' (Nature and Art) can be understood as a caustic rebuff from the classical Olympian of Weimar to the restless transcendentalism of the early Romantic ideologists of Jena. This is by no means clear; and if it is so, it is ironic that it was precisely August Wilhelm Schlegel and the Romantic poets who revived interest in the Petrarchan sonnet, and Schlegel who actually corresponded with Goethe on the subject at some length in 1800. Nor did Goethe's professed unease with the constricting severity of the sonnet form prevent him writing, in 1807–8, a whole cycle of love poems in that form (see below, pp. 108–11).

The lyric poetry written between the *Roman Elegies* and the *West-östliche Divan* is, by Goethe's standards, relatively unremarkable. One poem stands out, however, as a profound lyrical meditation on mutability and continuity, flux and permanence, the ephemeral and the lasting: 'Dauer im Wechsel' (Permanence in Change, 1803). What begins as an elegiac statement of transience in nature modulates into an affirmation of the creative triumph over the flux of time as an overwhelming sense of change and decay turns into a celebration of the human gift of articulating, and therefore overcoming, that transience. The notion that had been allusively and cryptically implied in the early Weimar poem 'An den Mond' – that the river, the very emblem of transience, can itself become the subject of the poet's song – is here extended to the whole natural landscape, to the passage of the seasons, to the human frame itself. That we ourselves are caught up in the same constant process of decay and regeneration as the rest of nature is an idea Goethe found vividly illustrated in a neurological study by Johann Christian Reil, a medical specialist of Halle University. In 1803 Reil wrote that without a consciousness of the continuity of our personality, we would be like ephemera or mayflies; the old man imagines he is the same person he was as a child, whereas in fact the human organism progressively changes its substance, recreating what it has destroyed, so that 'no atom remains of what we were eighty years before'.[37] *Panta rhei*, all is flux; the Heraclitan axiom that we never bathe in the same river twice and the Horatian *carpe diem* are invoked in a series of statements in which imagery, rhythm and syntax combine to evoke a rapid succession of momentary states. Blossoms scattered by the winds of spring, leaves soon to be stripped by autumn storms, fruits ripening while others are already in seed, the landscape changing from day to day, we ourselves, our bodies, perceptions and emotions, our physical, moral and existential identity – all is caught up in an inexorable process of mutability. But counter to this sense of the headlong rush of time as a succession of fleeting moments, the second stanza already hints at the continuum, the 'chain' of perpetuation and survival in nature that Goethe had described in 'Die Metamorphose der Pflanzen' (lines 59–62). Change and decay are the very condition of permanence and continuity, of 'Dauer im Wechsel'; fruit and seed, ending and beginning, constitute the overlapping dynamics of existence. The gnomic statement that opens the final stanza, that beginning and end should merge into one, suggests not a repetitive circular process, but a cycle of dynamic renewal; caught as we are in the rapid succession of linear time, our perception of continuity can be given shape and form in art or poetry. The creative mind can give coherence to fragmented and ephemeral experience, can give form to inchoate feeling and defy mutability.

'Weltseele' (World Soul, *c.*1802) is a mystical cosmic vision based on a bizarre conflation of Leibnitz's monadology and Schelling's identity theory, presented in terms of a creation myth. If spirit and universe are identical, then the cosmos can be imagined as spiritual, even as 'spirit-infested': individual monads or 'entelechies' (for Goethe a term roughly synonymous with soul or personality) are conceived as indwelling in cosmic space, as scattered points of light, as wandering stars or comets, animating the new worlds that coalesce from nebulous chaos into solid shape. In time, organic life emerges from the barren ocean, and the process of creation will begin over again as it did in the first paradise. Such speculative mysticism is mercifully rare in Goethe's work, and it is by no means clear how seriously we are meant to take this imaginative extravaganza – it was after all written as an occasional poem to be read before a gathering of Goethe's *Mittwochskränzchen*, a coterie of *beaux esprits* who held regular meetings for convivial and cultivated entertainment; it may even be a private joke, an ironic persiflage of Schelling's ideas. But Goethe's rare speculative remarks on such metaphysical matters do indicate that he had some serious conception of a monadology or theory of survival beyond death, as attested in a conversation with Johann Daniel Falk of 25 January 1813, and in a letter to Zelter of 19 March 1827 (see above, p. 48). He was also to return to the idea of the identity of self and universe in some later poems, and most strikingly in the extraordinary figure of Makarie in *Wilhelm Meisters Wanderjahre*, who, we are told, leads a dual existence, in microcosmic terms as a model of human benevolence and charity, and in macrocosmic terms in a mystical existence at the remote edges of the solar system.

The lyrical section of Goethe's classical period closes with a loose assortment of love and nature poetry. 'Die glücklichen Gatten' (The Happy Couple, 1802) celebrates what the earlier dialogue poem 'Der Wanderer' had presented as wish-fulfilment: a domestic idyll of security and integrity where the sacraments of marriage and baptism mark the continuity of the generations of family life. The poem may well be an idealized projection of Goethe's own often less than idyllic domesticity; the recollection of the procreative energy of the young married couple in the fourth stanza is less explicit than, but similar to the (also retrospective) account of sexual imperatives in the erotic poem 'Das Tagebuch'* (The Diary, 1810), where the traveller also recalls the ubiquity of his love-making and the role of Eros in the domestic scene. This poem, unpublished during Goethe's lifetime and consigned to the private *Walpurgissack* in which he kept his more explicit erotic or scabrous writings, is a ruefully ironic tribute to the principle of marital sexual fidelity. Narrated in a mock-sententious form of *ottava rima*, the poem relates how a traveller returning home to his wife is detained by an accident in an inn, where the chambermaid offers herself to him with innocent frankness. To his comic fury and shame, the traveller's 'master part' fails to rise to the occasion, and the girl's innocence is preserved; only by recollecting the scenes of his wife's embraces, in the bridal bed or in fields of corn, can the 'master' be recalled to his task – by which time the opportunity has passed and adultery has been averted as duty and love reassert their rights.

Whatever the biographical relevance of these two poems, the mock-naive allegory of 'Gefunden' (Found by Chance, 1813) is generally thought to be a tribute to the woman Goethe had 'transplanted' to his own house in 1788: it was sent to Christiane dated 26 August 1813 in evident commemoration of their twenty-five years together. 'Mailied' (May Song, *c.*1810) and 'Schweizerlied' (Swiss Song, date uncertain) are examples of Goethe's continuing interest in song forms and popular poetry; the more sophisticated 'Gegenwart' (Presence, 1812) appears to draw on the imagery of the Song of Songs – sun, moon, garden, roses, lilies. It has the same association as the biblical poem of the unspecified 'du' (thou) with the perceived phenomena of the natural world, though there is some blurring of the association; the identity of 'du' and 'Sonne' (thou and sun) appears to be separate in the first stanza, but becomes merged in the latter half of the poem. This could be a result of its composition: like 'Nähe des Geliebten', it was written to an existing melody, extemporized by Goethe to the metrical and strophic form of a text by Hermann Ueltzen, but otherwise bearing little resemblance to its model.

OCCASIONAL POETRY 1800–15

The few occasional poems included by Trunz from the years 1800–15 serve to show Goethe's extraordinary scope of style and manner even within this particular genre; these poems range from the solemnly formal *ottava rima* of the 'Epilog zu Schillers "Glocke"' (Epilogue to Schiller's "The Bell") to the *Knittelvers* of the charming verses sent with an album of landscape drawings to Princess Caroline of Weimar in 1807, from the encomium to Napoleon's wife Marie Louise of 1812, also in *ottava rima* and expressing Goethe's tribute to Napoleon as the leader who led France out of revolutionary chaos, and on whom all hopes of a European peace are centred, to the rumbustious drinking song 'Ergo bibamus!' (And so let us drink!, 1810) which is still among those bellowed out by German *Burschenschafter* at their beery fraternity gatherings.

The tribute to Schiller was first delivered after a dramatized performance of his poem 'Das Lied von der Glocke' (The Song of the Bell) on 10 August 1805, three months after the poet's death; it was extended and revised for a second performance on the fifth anniversary of his death, and again for the tenth anniversary on

10 May 1815. Schiller's ballad had counterpointed an account of the skilled process of casting a bell with human individual and historical destinies; as the casting is completed and the bell is hung high in the church steeple, the final lines invoke the message of peace that the new bell shall ring out. Goethe's poem takes the final couplet as its starting point for a reference to the brief period of peace in Germany between Napoleon's effective termination of the French Revolution in 1799 and the outbreak of the continental wars in 1805 – which was also the period between Schiller's completion of 'Das Lied von der Glocke' and his own death. The historical ironies were only intensified by the performance in May 1815 – two months after Napoleon's escape from Elba, and only some five weeks before Waterloo. The first stanza also refers to 'Die Huldigung der Künste' (Homage to the Arts), a festival drama written by Schiller shortly before his death to celebrate the marriage of the Crown Prince of Weimar to Maria Pavlovna, the sister of Tsar Nicholas I; the irony of the events informs the pathos of the opening stanzas of Goethe's poem in the juxtaposition of peace, marriage and homage to the arts with the tolling of the bell for Schiller's death. After this solemn opening, the mood of the tribute becomes elegiac but affirmative, an affectionate celebration in the stately cadences of *ottava rima* of Schiller's difficult life: his deprived childhood, his early radicalism, his constant struggle against ill-health, his eccentric working habits, his historical studies, his commitment to the theatre, his high idealism. In the final image of the departing comet, Goethe expresses his own awed appreciation of his literary and polemical companion-in-arms, of the man who had encouraged and irritated, stimulated and exasperated him in a productive tension that powered one of the most remarkably symbiotic and fruitful literary partnerships ever known.

LATER BALLADS

Among the products of Goethe's and Schiller's literary collaboration are the 'classical' ballads of the *Balladenjahr* of 1797; in the course of that year the two friends corresponded on the ballad genre and competed in composing ballads, producing 'Der Schatzgräber' (The Treasure-seeker), 'Legende' (Legend), 'Der Zauberlehrling' (The Sorcerer's Apprentice), 'Die Braut von Korinth' (The Bride of Corinth) and 'Der Gott und die Bajadere' (The God and the Bayadère) and, on Schiller's part, 'Der Taucher' (The Diver), 'Der Handschuh' (The Glove), 'Der Ring des Polykrates' (The Ring of Polycrates), 'Die Kraniche des Ibykus' (The Cranes of Ibycus) and others. All were published in Schiller's *Musenalmanach* for 1798. To talk of 'classical' ballads might seem a contradiction in terms; for while Goethe was quite aware of theories linking the Homeric epics with ancient oral traditions of narrative poetry and story-telling, the ballad is more readily associated with Goethe's *Sturm und Drang* interest in primitive poetic forms, or with the later Romantic enthusiasm for popular poetry, than with literary classicism. Indeed, Goethe remarked that it was his and Schiller's preoccupation with the ballad that had helped to redirect his attention to the strictly non-classical theme of Faust at a time when quite different literary models claimed his attention.[38] The broad difference between Goethe's ballads of 1797 and his earlier efforts is in the markedly didactic and sententious nature of these longer poems; he is no longer concerned to recreate the unsophisticated diction or the popular fables of his earlier ballads, but rather, no doubt under Schiller's influence, to place his poetic imagination in the service of a conceptual or ethical idea – as Schiller had indeed also urged him to do with his *Faust* drama. The differences between the two poets, however, are still discernible in their ballads: Schiller's, for all their romantic or legendary settings, remain largely within the human sphere of ethical or moral choice, while Goethe's draw more on the supernatural traditions of apparitions, magic and popular belief.

And yet Goethe's ballads are of such diversity of form and theme that definition or categorization are almost impossible. They comprise narratives from past or recent history ('Die Braut von Korinth', 'Johanna Sebus'); from legend, fairy-tale or folk superstition ('Der getreue Eckart': Faithful Eckart, 'Der Rattenfänger'*: The Pied Piper, 'Der Fischer': The Angler); they might deal with an allegorized story of unhappy love ('Heidenröslein') or with the stark death of a child ('Erlkönig'); they might be humorous ('Der Zauberlehrling', 'Die wandelnde Glocke': The Walking Bell), sentimental ('Kennst du das Land') or horrific ('Der Totentanz': Danse Macabre). They might be presented as monologue ('Vor Gericht'), as historic narrative ('Der König in Thule') or as the dramatic orchestration of four voices ('Erlkönig'); they might be based on religious legend, on episodes from the story of Christ ('Legende') or of the apostles ('Groß ist die Diana der Epheser': Great is Diana of Ephesus). They may not be in narrative form at all, but presented as affective statement – 'Kennst du das Land' and 'Vor Gericht' both strain any essentialist definition of the ballad, but are firmly included among Goethe's balladry. The familiar criterion of the refrain, of reiteration or recapitulation derived from the conditions of public oral recitation, and which, as Goethe thought, give the ballad its decisively lyrical character, is by no means a common feature; only 'Heidenröslein', 'Das Veilchen', 'Ballade' and 'Kennst du das Land' have literal refrains – though three of the 1797 ballads have more sophisticated and striking 'metrical' refrains ('Die Braut von Korinth', 'Der Gott und die Bajadere', and 'Der Zauberlehrling').

'Der Schatzgräber' is a rueful self-admonition by Goethe adapted from a distinctive ballad tradition of treasure-seekers. In May 1797 he bought a ticket in the Hamburg lottery in the hope of winning a large cash prize and a substantial property in Silesia – a deluded venture that supplies the message of the poem; the motif of a child offering a shining bowl as an emblem of courage to leave his dubious searchings and face the demands and rewards of daily toil he found in an illustrated edition of Petrarch. The 'Legende vom Hufeisen' (Legend of the Horseshoe), in the idiom of Hans Sachs, is a similarly humorous admonition in the style of a homespun parable or fable.

'Die Braut von Korinth' is a bizarre cultural hybrid, a legend from a late classical source onto which is grafted a theme that is more closely associated with modern Romantic, indeed Christian traditions, namely vampirism: a dead woman rises from the grave to claim the fiancé pledged to her under a pagan rite, a promise on which her mother reneged after her conversion to Christianity. Goethe exploits the eroticism inherent in the vampire legend, and associates it with the free sensuality of paganism in a compelling narrative that proclaims the life-enhancing values of a polytheistic culture against the life-denying bigotry and fanaticism of monotheistic Christianity – the poem caused widespread offence on both counts. Equally controversial was the Indian legend of 'Der Gott und die Bajadere', the story of a temple prostitute tempted and redeemed by the god Shiva – even though its message of hope and comfort for the repentant sinner is at least as characteristic of the Christian ethic as of any Hindu creed. 'Der Zauberlehrling' is derived from a classical source in Lucian's *Philopseudes* (Lover of Lies), a humorous caution against meddling with forces beyond one's control. But it seems reasonable to believe that Goethe's interest in the ballad form lay as much in the art of story-telling as in any didactic message: in the ghostly tale of the revenant who demands posthumously the erotic rights denied her in life, in the rough wooing by which the god tests the bayadère, or in the sheer hilarity of the story of the sorcerer's apprentice. Each of these three ballads is also an exercise in rhythmic virtuosity; the trochaic metre basic to all three is strikingly varied – by the shortened fifth and sixth lines in each stanza of 'Die Braut von Korinth', by the dactylic refrains of 'Der Gott und die Bajadere', and by the variations in the length of the trochaic line in 'Der Zauberlehrling'.

The remaining ballads in this section show that Goethe regularly returned to the genre after the *Balladenjahr* of 1797. They are all anecdotal narratives dealing with a striking or noteworthy event, whether real or fantastic, from legend or recorded history, from past or present: the Count's bizarre dream of the dwarves' wedding in 'Hochzeitlied' (Wedding Song, 1802), the bogus incident of telekinesis in 'Wirkung in die Ferne' (Distant Influence, 1808), the heroism of Johanna Sebus (1809), the Thuringian fairy-tale of 'Der getreue Eckart' (1813), the gothic *danse macabre* of 'Der Totentanz' (1813), the household fable of 'Die wandelnde Glocke' (1813), the revelation of identity in 'Ballade' (1813). The narrative structure ranges from the simple linear narrative of 'Der Totentanz' or 'Die wandelnde Glocke' to the encapsulated narratives of 'Hochzeitlied' or 'Ballade' (a source-poem for the latter, 'The Beggar's Daughter of Bednall Green' from Percy's *Reliques*, has a similar encapsulated structure), to the fragmented dialogue of 'Johanna Sebus' – which is also distinguished by the modulated refrain that opens each stanza. If Goethe defined the *Novelle* axiomatically (and somewhat gno-mically) as 'eine sich ereignete, unerhörte Begebenheit' (an extraordinary, yet authentic happening), he also suggested that in the ballad the narrator or 'singer' is similarly dealing with a significant or suggestive (*prägnant*) topic;[39] he can begin in lyrical, epic or dramatic mode, can vary the forms at will, can hasten or retard his narrative. A selective collection of ballads, he concluded, might demonstrate the whole potential range of poetics *in embryo*.

SONNETS 1807–8

It has puzzled most commentators that Goethe, who so eloquently expressed his unease with the formal constraints of the sonnet form in the two sonnets of *c.*1800, should only a few years later turn his hand to a whole cycle of seventeen such poems, the very themes of which alternate between the record of a somewhat detached love affair and self-referential observations on the sonnet as a poetic vehicle for emotional expression. The biographical impulses informing the content and form of the cycle are respectively personal and literary. In the winter of 1807/8 Goethe was a frequent guest in the house of the publisher Carl Frommann, with whose foster-daughter Wilhelmine ('Minna') Herzlieb he had a warm and close relationship that may have been more than just a make-believe flirtation with an eighteen-year-old; what is certain is that her name is plainly alluded to in the ninth line of the tenth sonnet, and more cryptically as the solution to the 'charade' of the final sonnet. It is, however, generally thought that Minna Herzlieb was not the only personal stimulus for the cycle; in Karlsbad in the summer of 1808 Goethe also met Silvie von Ziegesar, who worshipped the indulgent poet some thirty-five years her senior – and who is usually associated with the beginnings of Goethe's work on *Die Wahlverwandtschaften*, the novel which charts the daemonic eruption of uncontrolled passion between older and younger generations. Too little is known about both relationships to identify the female partner of the sonnets unequivocally with either; and there is further evidence that some motifs and allusions in the sonnets are derived from Goethe's correspondence with Bettina Brentano, the daughter of Maximiliane von La Roche.

But it was literary influences that determined the use of the sonnet form. In 1807, Zacharias Werner's readings of his own sonnets in Jena and Weimar had stimulated an interest, indeed a craze, for the form already fostered by August Wilhelm Schlegel; and Goethe found himself drawn into competing with the younger generation of early Romantic poets in this neo-classical genre for which Petrarch was the exemplary model. It was, as Goethe explained in his biographical notes (*Annalen*) for that year, the first time since Schiller's death that he had found both human company and a literary activity that promised to fill the gap left by the loss of his friend and collaborator; and while neither the literary nor the emotional partnerships proved to last much beyond 1808, the sonnets are a curiously erratic memorial to the experiences of that year in their poetic form, in theme, and in the self-conscious 'Romantic' irony with which Goethe reflects on the structural demands of the sonnet in the sonnet.

The sense of a new beginning is articulated in the portentously symbolic opening poem of the cycle, 'Mächtiges Überraschen' (Momentous Intervention), in which the familiar Goethean image of the river in its course to the sea indicates an existential metaphor. The initial imagery is, as it were, the negative obverse of that of the 'Gesang der Geister': the impetuous momentum of the current allows no calm reflection of the cosmic order as it surges onwards and downwards. But here the river is not destined to continue its natural progress to the ocean; a violent landslide represents the irruption of a 'daemonic' force that checks the impetus of the current. The outcome of this violent clash between static rock and dynamic current, however, is a constructive one: the synthesis between the collision of opposites is the lake that reflects the stars in a new reciprocity, a harmonious balance – a motif that recalls similar imagery of reflection in other metaphorical contexts ('Gesang der Geister', lines 25–7; *Tasso*, lines 3442–5; *Faust*, lines 4642–9). At the same time, the imagery of calm reflection in the sonnet also recapitulates the notion of a synthesis of opposites that was associated with the sonnet form itself in the two sonnets of 1800: the harmonization of nature and art, of passion and form, of freedom and limitation.

The remaining poems of the cycle chart the effects and consequences of the irruption of unexpected passion. Goethe's original conception of the cycle, which he showed to Zelter in 1808, was a sequence of six poems in the order (though with slightly differing titles): 'Mächtiges Überraschen', 'Freundliches Begegnen' (Friendly Encounter), 'Wachstum' (Growing up), 'Kurz und gut' (In a Word), 'Reisezehrung' (Provisions for a Journey), 'Abschied' (Farewell). This initial cycle is the relatively straightforward account of an affair, charting an unexpected meeting, affection and courtship, renunciation and separation; but even in this early form the cycle has an element of self-reflective irony as the lover-poet in 'Kurz und gut' takes the reader through the process of writing his poems. In the tenth sonnet of the extended cycle, 'Sie kann nicht enden' (She cannot close), the playful irony of the lovers' correspondence is elaborated further into the fantasy of the female persona that she *might* send her lover, in lieu of a letter, a blank sheet of paper – on which he then *could* write the words of love that she *would* read with such delight. Already in the *Roman Elegies* (notably in the fifth and twentieth elegies) Goethe had played self-consciously with references to his dual role as lover and poet, as he confided his erotic 'Roman' experience, his 'fullness of heart', to the alternating rhythms of hexameter and pentameter; so also in the sonnets he will convey his feelings 'in fond and loving, sadly cheerful tones' ('Kurz und gut'). But in the final sonnet sequence the relationship is less straightforward, for the lovers are aware of discrepancies of generation and status; she perceives him both as a lover and as a public monument in marble ('Das Mädchen spricht': The Girl Speaks). The eleventh sonnet ('Nemesis') returns to the ironic treatment of love and art: for all his aloof detachment, for all his resistance to the plague of love or to the craze for elaborately rhymed verses, he must succumb to both – sonnet-writing and passion.

Sonnets XIV and XV return insistently to the problem of poetic expression; to the charge that 'the heart's fullness' cannot be painstakingly articulated within the constraints of rhymed octaves, sestets and tercets, to the mocking suggestion that sonnet-writing is tantamount to the labour of Sisyphus, the lovers reply defiantly that passion will melt the most refractory material. When in Sonnet XV the female voice doubts that true feeling can be adequately conveyed through the artifice of elaborately wrought and fashioned lines, the poet replies with an assurance that all his skill and art is not proof against the volatile and elemental force of passion: however carefully the most experienced sapper may dig his mines and place his charges, he too can be the victim of his own explosive arts. There is a note of ironic scepticism here towards the notion often attributed to Goethe, and most portentously expressed in the final scene of *Tasso*, that the poetic articulation of emotion can alleviate the pain of emotional anguish by a cathartic process of unburdening or self-confession. As Goethe was to imply with a degree of sarcasm in the opening poem of the *Trilogie der Leidenschaft*, addressing his erstwhile hero

Werther, the poet may sing affectingly of the pain of separation, but his suffering is not therefore any the less real.

The Sonnets I–XV were published as a cycle in the 1815 edition of Goethe's works; but two further sonnets were withheld and only included in the *Ausgabe letzter Hand* in 1827. They celebrate the two figures that stand as the twin creative impulses of the collection, Petrarch and Wilhelmine Herzlieb: the reference in 'Epoche' to Advent of the year 1807 is a clear enough allusion to the time Goethe's acquaintance with Minna developed into a more adult affair, and the solution to the charade of the seventeenth sonnet is clearly a pun on her name – 'Herz' and 'Liebe' (Heart and Love). And yet it is not clear that these two sonnets were withheld simply out of consideration for her identity, for she is unequivocally identified in the ninth line of 'Sie kann nicht enden' – and in any case she survived well beyond 1827 in an unhappy marriage until her death in 1865.

DER WEST-ÖSTLICHE DIVAN (EAST-WEST DIVAN)

In its self-reflective irony, its counterpoint of passion and detachment, of unaffected feeling and self-conscious speculation, in its intimate and playful dialogue between the personae of two lovers, the sonnet cycle anticipates in many ways the major cycle of poems that Goethe wrote some six years later, the *West-östliche Divan* – and in particular the *Buch Suleika* (Book of Suleika) of that collection. Here again, personal and literary impulses combined to produce an erratic and unique cycle of poetry, an initially experimental nonce creation that quickly grew into an extended *Divan* or collection of orientalizing verse that is both a reflection of Goethe's emotional experience and an exotic exercise in cultural empathy. To be sure, this was by no means Goethe's first acquaintance with mid-eastern or Semitic cultures. Herder had stimulated his interest in the Old Testament, and in particular for the poetry of the Psalms and the Song of Songs; his knowledge of the Koran dated from the 1770s, and he had an almost lifelong affection for the Arabian Nights Tales; he showed an early fascination with the life of Mohammed and the Bedouin poetry of the Moallakat; and in January 1814 he was a fascinated observer at Islamic prayers held for the troops of the Bashkir Host serving with the Russian armies, which took place in the hall of the Protestant School in Weimar. But Goethe's first encounter with the Sufi poets of the Persian tradition was in June 1814, when he first read Joseph von Hammer-Purgstall's 1812 translation of the *Divan-i-Hafiz*; characteristically, he rapidly absorbed much of the available scholarship on Turkish, Arabic and Persian literature, acquiring an expertise that allowed him to conduct an informed debate with the leading Arabists of his day and to produce the scholarly but somewhat rebarbative *Noten und Abhandlungen zu besserem Verständnis des West-östlichen Divans* (Notes and Essays for a Better Understanding of the East-West Divan).

Three principal stimuli inform this remarkable product of yet another of the poet's 'renewed puberties': Hammer-Purgstall's translation of Hafiz, the journeys of 1814 and 1815 to his native Rhineland, and the emotional and cultural experiences stemming from these journeys – notably, a renewed enthusiasm for Rhenish architecture and for the paintings of pre-Renaissance German and Flemish masters, and his literary and personal relationship with the gifted Marianne von Willemer. The emotional bond between Goethe and Marianne, who saw each other only sporadically and briefly during his summer visits to the Rhineland, was close, but by all accounts within the bounds of propriety; but their sublimated literary relationship was intense, passionate and outspoken. Not only did they correspond intimately and privately in encoded letters (see 'Geheimschrift': Secret Message) based on an edition of Hammer-Purgstall's translation (a correspondence that ceased, abruptly and significantly, in 1815, only to resume four years later); not only are they projected as the lovers Hatem and Suleika in the most substantial *Nameh* (Book) of the *Divan*; but Goethe also paid Marianne the supreme and unique compliment of incorporating her own verses, often only minimally recast, into the collection itself, notably in the poems to East and West Wind in the *Buch Suleika* – though the exact extent of her authorship in the *Divan* is not clearly established. The poem 'Gingo biloba' takes the ginkgo leaf not only as a general emblem of unity in duality, but also as an elegant and affectionate tribute to Marianne's contribution to the cycle.

Most but by no means all the *Divan* poems were written between June 1814 and October 1815 – the period that spans Goethe's two journeys to the Rhineland; it should also be remembered that several poems were written well before Goethe met Marianne von Willemer. Further poems were added to the collection in 1818 for its publication the following year, and more were incorporated as late as 1827 without disrupting its relatively loose structure, arranged on the model of the Sufi collections into books: The Book of the Minstrel, of Hafiz, of Love, of Aphorisms, of Discontent, of Timur (Tamburlaine), of Suleika, of the Inn, of Parables, of the Parsee, of Paradise. The books, and the poems within them, while not entirely random or arbitrary in sequence, are characterized more by sheer variety than by structure or genre. The formal and metrical scope is vast, but only very occasionally does Goethe attempt to mimic oriental or specifically Persian forms; the *Ghazal*, with its reiteration of a word or phrase in varying grammatical contexts, is only formally attempted in 'Höchste Gunst' (Highest Favour), in 'Sie haben wegen der Trunkenheit' (They have charged us with drunkenness) and, more flexibly and imaginatively, in 'In tausend Formen' (In thousand forms). By no means all the poems display any oriental or exotic colouring; indeed, some are occasional poems *à clef*, exclusively and cryptically concerned with contemporary German personalities and specific local affairs ('Den Gruß des Unbekannten': Honour the stranger's greeting, 'Frage nicht, durch welche Pforte': Do not ask through which gate), with German customs ('Das Leben ist ein Gänsespiel': Life is a game that children play). 'Höchste Gunst', though it is surrounded by orientalizing poems, is a clear enough tribute to Karl August and his wife Luise; in 'Geheimstes' (Most Secret) Goethe disingenuously upbraids the hunters for clues (*Anekdotenjäger*) who seek specific references in a poem that in fact ironically alludes to a reported request from the Empress of Austria that she should *not* be referred to in any of his works.

The verse forms of the *Divan* veer drastically from the liturgical rise and fall of the iambic pentameter of 'In tausend Formen' to laconic and prosaic unrhymed free verse ('Schlechter Trost': Poor Comfort), to the *Knittelvers* of the dialogues in the *Buch des Paradieses*, where even the complaisant houris of the Muslim paradise speak in the verse of Hans Sachs to flatter a German guest. Rhymes are occasionally used with the facetious incongruity of Heine ('Dreistigkeit': Boldness), and the whispered gnomic wisdom of 'Selige Sehnsucht' (Sublime Yearning) stands side-by-side with the most startling neologisms: *Kriegestunder* ('Zwiespalt': Conflict) or *Schlechtnis* ('Beiname': Epithet). In another poem ('Keinen Reimer wird man finden': No rhymster can be found), Goethe facetiously juxtaposes *Mäusedreck* and *Koriander* (mouse droppings and coriander). While many poems are virtually literal translations from the Koran or from the Sufi poets, others are more loosely adapted: the intense sensuality of 'Vollmondnacht' (Night of Full Moon) and the equally intense and erotic mysticism of 'Selige Sehnsucht' are close to their Persian models without being pastiche copies. Many of the poems require some biographical glossing: the lovers' emblematic image of sun and crescent moon ('Die Sonne kommt!': The sun approaches!, or 'Abglanz': Reflection) plays on an amulet bought by Marianne in Frankfurt and presented to Goethe as the purported gift of a Turkish merchant; on the other hand, the light imagery of many poems is also close to that of the Sufi poets ('Nachklang': Dying Echo). The emblematic character of many of the *Divan* poems (the moth and the flame of 'Selige Sehnsucht', the ripening chestnuts of 'An vollen Büschelzweigen', the ginkgo leaf of 'Ginkgo biloba') is consistent with the imagery of Goethe's Persian sources; but it is also not irrelevant to know that the chestnuts and ginkgos are almost certainly those of the terraced gardens of the castle in Heidelberg, as Goethe playfully mirrors Eastern and Western traditions and images.

It is unclear how far Goethe exploited the ambivalence of Sufi imagery, whether for example wine and sexual love (for Suleika or for the epicene potboy Saki of the *Schenkenbuch*) are used as mystical metaphors for spiritual rapture or religious fervour, or whether he uses them unequivocally as romantic motifs in the style of FitzGerald's liberal translation of Omar Khayyám. Goethe was certainly aware of the ambiguity of Persian and Arabic literary imagery – in a public notice announcing his collection on 24 February 1816,[40] he points out that while many of his poems allow a sensual interpretation, many can also, as in the eastern tradition, be understood spiritually; at the same time, the poem 'Offenbar Geheimnis' (Open Secret) also mocks the over-earnest scholarly exegesis of religious or mystical allegory in Hafiz's poetry. A poem like 'Selige Sehnsucht' uses the procreative urge in the service of a mystical symbolism of spiritual death and rebirth; one like 'Vollmondnacht', on the other hand, is surely a poem of frankly exotic sensuality.

The most overtly oriental colouring of the collection lies in the frequent use of names or Koranic references (Hatem and Suleika, Behramgur and Dilaram, Hafiz and Ferdusi, Medschnun and Leila, Dschemil and Boteinah, Wamik and Asra, Mufti, Vizier, Sultan) – though Phoebus, Cupid and Mars also figure, as do Christian allusions; in features of the landscape (cypresses, canals, oases and desert sands; in shawl, musk, amber, turban, Bulbul the nightingale and Hudhud the hoopoe); in topographical references (the Transoxus, Bokhara, Samarkand); and in the evocation of Eastern riches, of ointments and perfumes ('Nur wenig ist's': It is but little that I ask). And yet the collection remains self-consciously aware of its 'East–Western' character: the Rhine is thinly disguised as the Euphrates; when the 'new dervishes' are lampooned for their exegeses of the Koran, it is Western theologians that Goethe has in mind ('Sonst, wenn man den heiligen Koran zitierte': Once, when quoting from the Holy Koran); the poppies in the fields around Erfurt are perceived as the roses of Shiraz magically translated to the Thuringian landscape ('Liebliches': Vision of Loveliness); Tamburlaine's final disastrous winter campaign in northern China is assimilated to Napoleon's winter retreat from Moscow ('Der Winter und Timur': Winter and Timur).

The predominant tone of the *Divan* is a mood of easy bantering, an ironic, relaxed, at times deliberately careless expression of playful or whimsical ideas – the playfulness that allows the poet to write *Hatem* when the rhyme demands *Goethe* ('Locken, haltet mich gefangen': Tresses, hold me captive). The poem 'Hegire' (Hejira), the opening declaration of his own flight (literally westwards to the Rhineland, imaginatively eastwards to the land of Hafiz) sets the keynote of the collection: escape, a journey in the mind to drink at the well of Chizer, of eternal youth. The notion of effortless poetic composition, the sense of release from the formal disciplines of Western literary convention, whether ancient distich or modern sonnet, is emblematically illustrated in 'Lied und Gebilde' (Song and Figure): the severe plasticity of Greek statuary cedes to the magical power of the poet to dip into the waters of the Euphrates and hold the liquid element between his hands as a perfect sphere – an image Goethe derived not from Middle Eastern sources, but from the Hindu myth that he later exploited in the *Paria* trilogy.

But the dark foil to the joyous escapism of the *Divan*, unobtrusive though it is, cannot be ignored. Already in the very first lines of the collection, the political and historical realities of its context are invoked: the turbulent years of the German Wars of Liberation, of the Battle of Leipzig, of Napoleon's defeat and return. Goethe reports in his *Annalen* how the news of Waterloo reached him in Wiesbaden during his second Rhineland journey – first it was reported as lost, then, correctly and to general rejoicing, as won. Goethe's own immense admiration for Napoleon made him ambivalent towards the defeat of his hero and the liberation of Germany; his horror of the chaos and terror of war, however, was unequivocal. The European wars are only cryptically and occasionally touched on in the *Divan* ('Hegire', 'Liebliches', 'Zwiespalt', 'Hab' ich euch denn je geraten?', 'Der Winter und Timur'); but in 'Timur spricht' (Timur speaks), some of Goethe's respect for Napoleon as a 'daemonic' force of history might be detected in Timur's defiant riposte: If Allah had destined me to be a worm, as a worm he would have made me.

The *Divan* is generally considered to mark a decisive stage in Goethe's development as a lyric poet, specifically to mark his emergence from the severe and programmatic phase of Weimar Classicism, and a step towards the freer lyrical expression of his late poetry. For his part, the poet chose to stress the unique or nonce nature of the collection: in 1827 he remarked to Eckermann that he no longer felt any affinity with the passionate and exotic poems of the *Divan*, they had ceased to live in his mind and had been left by the wayside like a cast snake's skin. The *Divan*, for all its ostensible escapism, was the specific product of the experiences of 1814 and 1815 (even if he continued to add to the collection for many years afterwards); as he wrote in the press notice of 24 February 1816, he presents himself as a traveller to an exotic land, as a stranger who nevertheless absorbs and empathizes with its culture, its people, customs and beliefs to the extent that he might almost be taken for a Muslim. In the *Buch Suleika* above all, he leaves a record of the 'sigh, the spirit of a passion which, like a vintage wine harvest, will not readily be repeated.'[41] The *Divan* is by no means a literal record of Goethe's emotional or physical relationship with Marianne von Willemer; it is the lyrical harvest of a brief encounter in a geographical and cultural context in which he was uniquely at home and from which he was also, in both time and space, far removed: the Rhineland.

APHORISMS AND SATIRES

The verse aphorisms, proverbs, maxims, satires and *aperçus* categorized by Trunz under the heading *Sprüche* are compiled from various sources from the last two decades of Goethe's life. Some were published in editions of his collected works under the titles *Sprichwörtlich* (Proverbs) or *Zahme Xenien* (that is, the 'gentle' polemics as distinct from the 'sharp' *Xenia* in distichs produced with Schiller in the 1790s); others are taken from the corpus of unpublished material. Many of these *obiter dicta* are revealing as supplementary glosses to Goethe's late work and thought, to his scientific and existential wisdom, though not all should be read as his final word on a particular topic. Some are mutually contradictory, as many proverbs or maxims are; some involve a complementary dialectic, while others reflect his immediate, often satirical, response to events or ideas. Many are often quoted as axiomatic, without reference to context, to the poet's changing ideas and attitudes, or to the possibility that Goethe is at times creating a carefully censored public persona. Nevertheless, *toutes proportions gardées*, it can be assumed that the gap between self and persona is here rather narrower than in much of the so-called 'confessional' verse.

The *Sprüche* touch on philosophical and existential questions, on our relationship to nature, to the cosmos and the world around us (Nos 1–5);[42] on the physical world, the origins of life in water (6–12), and on archetypal phenomena (in Goethe's term, *Urphänomene*) like magnetism and the principle of polarity (13–16). Others explore the human condition, our image of ourselves, humanity in relation to perceived or projected divine powers, to the stages of life, to past and future. One striking example, 'Nachts, wann gute Geister schweifen' (When by night good spirits roam, 31–2) expresses in one stanza a profoundly mystical dream of nearness to God, a disembodied sense of eternity and infinite space, in the characteristic imagery of Goethe's late lyric poetry – night, moonlight and starlight; but it follows this solemn vision with a stanza of ironic bathos that ruefully recalls the reader to the daily round of mundane sobriety. Many *Sprüche* are self-characterizations (99–125), including the much-quoted quatrain 'Vom Vater hab' ich die Statur' (From Father comes my upright bearing, 99), in which he claims to have inherited his stature and self-discipline from his father, his temperament and imagination from his mother – which is no doubt true; but these lines are more often than not isolated from the context of the whole portrait with its self-ironizing conclusion.

Goethe uses some of his favourite analogies for personal development and metamorphosis in these self-portraits: the cast-off snake's skin (119), or the transformation from grub to pupa to imago (125). He lampoons his *bêtes noires*, the menagerie of pedants, philistines, critics, populist revolutionaries and egalitarians, Jacobins and *sans-culottes* (161ff.). He flaunts his prejudices openly: his disapproval of the press – which he himself read assiduously – and of press freedom (170–2), his impatience with theological dogmatics (176ff.). Of particular historical interest are the satires in which he reveals his ambivalent views on the liberation of Germany from the spectre of Napoleon and the restoration of much of the old European order after the Congress of Vienna – views that are consistent with the attitudes discernible from the allegorical action of the fourth act of *Faust* Part Two. He could never fully endorse or approve the fall of his hero Napoleon (158), for all his recognition of its inevitability; No. 160 sums up his notorious scepticism towards the 'liberation' of Germany – a liberation that also involved some loss of civic freedom for the citizens of the restored German Confederation. In particular, the fable of the angels who fight valiantly for justice against the powers of darkness (169) is a clear expression of Goethe's misgivings towards the European allies who encompassed the defeat of Napoleon; the angels are forced to adopt devils' tactics for their cause, just as in *Faust* Part Two the Emperor can only defeat his rival, the Napoleonic *Gegenkaiser* (rival emperor) with the help of Mephistopheles and his black arts, and finds himself compromised by his compact with the powers of hell.

Goethe's conservative, but resolutely apolitical stance towards the confusions of contemporary political history is revealed in two tendencies. On the one hand, there is a utopian perception of North America in the celebrated 'Amerika, du hast es besser' (America, you are more favoured, 173), where the New World is perceived as a continent free from the historical debris of ancient national rivalries, of 'geological' (metaphorically for historical and political) controversies, free from romantic nostalgia for an idealized past of bogus chivalry and feuding dynasties (this from the author of *Götz von Berlichingen*!). On the other hand, Goethe's civic ideal appears as a form of resigned withdrawal in the face of present confusion, a homely but faintly despairing quietism that recalls Voltaire's *Candide*: cultivate your garden, or, as Goethe has it: 'Ein jeder kehre vor seiner Tür' (Let everyone keep his threshold swept, 95 and 174). This spirit of quietistic and private isolationism has contributed to the perception of Goethe by nineteenth and twentieth-century radicals as at best a passive conservative, or at worst an active reactionary; it is more generously construed as a realistic recognition of the incorrigible perversity of human political affairs and an assertion of the individual's right to do his civic duty with all the conscientious decency that he is allowed. His scathing judgement on human delusions and ambitions is expressed in a manner worthy of La Fontaine in the parable of the frogs who would sing like nightingales (186); and his conclusion is given in the following aphorism – keep your own counsel:

> Bei solchem Lied und Reigen
> Das Beste – ruhn und schweigen.

> In such a clamour we'd best seek
> Counsel silently to keep.

Yet it would be misleading and misguided, to say the least, to leave these *Sprüche* with the impression that Goethe's stance can be finally or adequately character-ized as a resigned withdrawal into quietistic isolation. For above all in his epigrams and apophthegms, in his mild and his sharp *Xenia*, Goethe is more often than not out to provoke and stimulate, to lampoon complacency and pretension, to shock and offend with all the weapons of ribaldry, satire and wit. The conservative defender of the status quo could also adopt the persona of the incorrigible iconoclast who did not mince his words when it came to expressing his deepest and most fiercely held opinions – or prejudices.

LATE OCCASIONAL POETRY

Of the occasional poems from the last two decades of Goethe's life, most are of little more than biographical interest: encomia to Karl August and his family, or to friends and visitors, verses for Masonic ceremonies (even though Goethe had withdrawn his membership of the Weimar Lodge in 1812), for anniversaries and memorial services. Some stand out by virtue of language or metre: the quiet idylls that celebrate Goethe's native landscape of the Rhine and Main, or the formal stanzas of *ottava rima* in the tribute to his Weimar friend and administrative colleague Christian Gottlob von Voigt. The two tributes to Lord Byron, the first written shortly before Byron's death in 1824, the second a posthumous *Nachruf*, are addressed to the philhellene and poet for whom Goethe had a quite special regard that was the literary equivalent of his admiration for Napoleon. Byron was, he argued to Kanzler von Müller in extravagant terms, the 'greatest talent of the century' who, had he lived, would have become for Greece a second Solon or Lycurgus;[43] and in the figure of Euphorion, the issue of Faust and Helen in *Faust* Part Two, he allegorized Byron as the very paradigm of modern poetry, as the synthesis of modern and classical literary traditions. The iconoclastic Goethe is also seen in some of these poems, the anti-clericalist whose disapproval of the Church of Rome stopped just short of bigotry: 'Parabel' (Parable, 1813) is an affectionate recollection of his Protestant upbringing in Frankfurt that modulates finally into a sharp jibe at the aesthetic neo-Catholicism of the Romantic genera-tion. Not that Goethe was a particularly devout Lutheran; his poem on the third centenary of the Reformation in 1817 ('Dreihundert Jahre hat sich schon': Now for some three hundred years) is less a celebration of the Lutheran Church than of Luther as a rebel with whom Goethe identifies himself: just as Luther fought the wiles of the priests, so Goethe protests against Romantic neo-Catholicism or struggles with the Newtonian 'guild' of professional science in his *Farbenlehre*. The final poems of Trunz's selection also show that Goethe could be crudely brutal in his treatment of lesser talents who crossed him: Kotzebue, Merkel, Menzel, and even the widow of a Cologne cleric who misguidedly presumed to seek Goethe's religious conversion ('An Frau K. in C.': To Frau Krafft in Cologne, 1830).

The most substantial single item in this section is the grandiose trilogy devoted to the English meteorologist Luke Howard, whose essay of 1803, *On the Modifications of Clouds*, had been brought to Goethe's notice in 1815. Goethe was so impressed with Howard's studies and terminology, and found that they corresponded so closely to his own observations, that he wrote between 1820 and 1822 a series of meteorological notes and the poems celebrating Howard's contribution to science (see below, pp. 271–3). Moreover, Goethe also perceived a metaphorical significance in the metamorphoses of cloud formations that was to inform his literary symbolism: the upward modification of cloud is expressed as an ascending spiritual urge towards redemption (*Erlösung*).

The opening poem of the trilogy ('Atmosphäre': Atmosphere) celebrates Howard's achievement in the identification and naming of cloud forms, while the closing stanzas ('Wohl zu merken': Nota bene) stress the result of the dialectic created between analysis and synthesis, separation and combination. Howard had described the *modifications* of cloud forms; but in a perception incompatible with modern meteorology, Goethe understood the vertical *metamorphoses* of one form into another as the dynamic principle he sought to detect in all natural processes. This is the principle described and celebrated in the central section of the trilogy, 'Howards Ehrengedächtnis' (In Honour of Howard).

The apparently arbitrary and whimsical metamorphosis of clouds, evoked here as the Hindu deity Camarupa, the 'Wearer of Shapes at Will', as Goethe puts it in his own commentary to the poem,[44] is ordered on the one hand by the human imagination, by the will to discern shape and pattern in chaotic formlessness as the mind perceives animal or human figures in the clouds, and on the other hand by the analytical vision of the scientific mind that gives formal classification to inchoate shapes and processes. Myth, imagination and science work to define the undefinable, to see order and form in the most evanescent and mutable products of nature, clouds. Thus water vapour, rising from ponds, lakes or oceans, presents itself to the eye as a ghostly and diffuse stratus or carpet of mist; this mist rises to an intermediate altitude as layered cloud, obscuring the sky. Here, Goethe sees the further metamorphosis of cloud in terms of a struggle between higher and lower regions: if stratus rises, it will gather or consolidate (*sich ballen*) into the splendid castellated forms of cumulus towering into the higher atmosphere. At this point, drier or moister conditions will determine whether cumulus will modify into the even higher, thinner form of cirrus, or into the thundercloud formation of rain-bearing nimbus; and here Goethe invests Howard's cloud categories with his own symbolic construction. The dynamics of cloud modification, the struggle between higher and lower atmosphere, between dry and moist, is given a spiritual analogy: the upward urge of the spirit towards redemption ('Erlösung ist ein himmlisch leichter Zwang': Redemption is a gentle heavenward urge), and the downward pull of earthly activity, of human political and social reality ('Der Erde tätig-leidendes Geschick': Our active destiny of earthly woe). It is entirely characteristic of Goethe that he should express his enthusiastic acknowledgement of a fellow-scientist's achievement in existential or spiritual terms, in terms of the twin souls in Faust's breast that pull respectively upwards to an intimation of transcendence and downwards to the physical limitations of earth – the duality that also informs poems on the human condition such as 'Grenzen der Menschheit' and 'Das Göttliche'. Clouds and mist, falling, rising or dispersing, had long been a potent feature of Goethe's lyrical symbolism; and in the final scene of *Faust*, the upward progress of Faust's soul towards 'higher spheres' is expressed as a process analogous to the upward modification of cloud in the stanza 'Cirrus' of the poem to Howard. Howard's achievement, as Goethe characterizes it in the final section of the trilogy, is to have given the human spirit, the painter and the poet, an analytical and scientific basis on which, by means of imaginative synthesis, the causality and coherence of the perceived world can be understood: the disparate, the inchoate, the ephemeral and the apparently unstable can be grasped, intuited, and shaped by the 'living gifts' of the creative imagination.

LATE EXISTENTIAL POEMS

The late poems grouped by Trunz under the heading *Die weltanschaulichen Gedichte* (which we might understand as 'existential' poetry) were mostly arranged by Goethe himself under the rubric *Gott und Welt* (God and World). Goethe's heading is helpful, since these poems are lyrical statements of a life's thought and experience, of scientific and philosophical convictions concerning the perceived world and the laws, principles and forces that impinge on and determine human existence. If it seems surprising that Goethe, a convinced 'non-Christian', even an 'old heathen', as he characterized himself, should so frequently invoke a deity, even *the* Deity, in these poems, this is only consistent with a lifelong habit of using God or gods to denote a power or powers that govern human, terrestrial and cosmic existence, but which do not have any necessarily specific historical or theological reference.

The Greek titles given to some of these poems are daunting, but explicable: *Prooemion* (stanzas 1–2 1816, stanzas 3–4 *c.*1812) is a prefatory poem; *Parabase*, *Epirrhema* and *Antepirrhema* (1818–20) are terms from classical Greek drama denoting choric interjections into the mimetic action. Goethe placed these three poems respectively before, between and after his two morphological poems 'Die Metamorphose der Pflanzen' and 'Metamorphose der Tiere'. 'Prooemion' borrows the style of liturgy to invoke a self-created, eternally creating power that is essentially unknowable, albeit called by any number of names: *Erdgeist* (Earth Spirit), *Weltseele* (World Soul), God-Nature, Pan, Allah, Jehova. The world we know is an emanation of that creative principle, of which the world is therefore a likeness; we know creation only as a mediated simile or likeness of that principle, as a reflection of the divine. And yet, as the poem emphatically states, this simile or reflected image is wholly sufficient for our highest perceptions or our boldest speculations. The symbolism is that of the opening scene of *Faust* Part Two: while Faust cannot grasp truth in its absolute form, he can perceive it in its coloured reflection, in the sunlight mediated as a rainbow in the flying spray of the waterfall. If this wisdom is accepted, the poem suggests, then the world through which we move is decked out and furnished for our delight; Goethe's existential poetry is a lyrical and sensuous, as much as a cognitive, expression of his sense of awed joy in creation. He exploits the etymology of the word *kosmos* as ornament or decoration: Lynkeus describes creation in *Faust* (line 11297) as 'die ewige Zier' (the eternal adornment). And in these poems Goethe returns time and again to the same idea: 'Und wo du wandelst, schmückt sich Weg und Ort' ('Prooemion': And where you walk, all places are adorned); 'Zum Erstaunen bin ich da' ('Parabase': To wonder at it I am here). In his last major poem, 'Vermächtnis' (Testament), he speaks of the laws that preserve 'die lebend'gen Schätze, / Aus welchen sich das All geschmückt' (the living treasures / That adorn the universe), and of his delight in the 'Auen reichbegabter Welt' (the meadows of the richly gifted world) revealed to us if our understanding is alert to the perception of our senses.

The God of these poems is not the secularized rationalization of a first principle, not the supreme architect or the 'great clockmaker' of eighteenth-century deism, nor is it the fervently emotional inner voice of Pietism or the Judaeo-Christian Jehova throned in splendour; it is a quasi-Spinozan God in Nature and Nature as God, immanent in the perceived world around us or, more mystically, the *Weltseele* in the universal whole. This God-Nature is conceived and described in apparently (but only apparently) paradoxical pairings of opposites; as 'Parabase' has it, the eternal oneness in nature manifests itself as great in small, small in great, near and far, change and permanence, formation and transformation. Flux and stasis, being and becoming, essence and appearance, inner and outer, kernel and husk, singularity and multiplicity, creation and destruction, *Zettel und Einschlag* (warp and weft): these are not oppositions for Goethe, but necessary conditions of wholeness. 'Antepirrhema' reiterates almost verbatim the words written some fifty years earlier with which Mephistopheles seeks to convey to the young student the incalculable complexities of the human mind (*Faust*, lines 1922ff.): on the loom of nature are strung the eternal warps onto which the master-weaver threads the creative weft in an infinite complexity of combinations and patterns. God not as architect or watchmaker, but as master-weaver: the essential difference is that the Goethean metaphor suggests not a finished edifice or mechanism, but a dynamic continuum of creative effort and renewal, analogous to the activity of the *Erdgeist* of the earliest draft of *Faust* (lines 508–9) who weaves the living garment of the deity on the whirring loom of time.

Not all the late existential poems are concerned with Goethe's conception of God-Nature. 'Urworte. Orphisch' (Words of Orphic Wisdom, 1817) adapts a contemporary knowledge of pre-classical Greek religious mysteries to formulate an account of the forces governing individual and collective human destinies in five gnomic stanzas of *ottava rima*. *Daimon* is the innate individuality, the unchanging and unique stamp of selfhood with which we are born, our 'horoscopic' destiny, as Goethe puts it (metaphorically!) in his own commentary to the poem;[45] it is the indestructible core of our being over which we have no control – today we might speak of our genetic makeup. *Tyche*, fate *qua* chance, modifies this intransigent identity as nurture acts on nature: upbringing, education, cultural and social environment condition our unique selves in a dialectic interaction. *Eros* – not only sensual love, but all forms of affective attachment – is governed by both *Daimon* and *Tyche*, by self and chance; it gives scope for error and confusion, but finally bonds individual destinies to each other in families, tribes or nations through which the individual is contracted to the social whole. Now the dialectic process of the poem narrows to *Anangke*, the necessary duties, laws and conventions of organized peoples; the individual urge of free will is curbed by moral, legal and social obligation, by *Sollen* rather than *Wollen*. The final stanza invokes a mystical notion of hope, *Elpis*, in a further dialectical qualification that modifies the constricting force of *Anangke*; the Goethean imagery of cloud, mist and veil suggests a release from the iron laws of necessity into a state of grace as the spirit liberates itself from temporal constraints and transcends present confusion.

The trilogy *Paria* (Pariah, 1821–3) is a metaphysical ballad or legend close in spirit, and indeed also in its source, to the Hindu legend of 'Der Gott und die Bajadere', which is in fact referred to in the third stanza of the opening poem, the Pariah's Prayer; both tales are derived from Pierre Sonnerat's account of a journey to India, which Goethe had known for some thirty years before the trilogy was written. The striking motif of the brahminee's purity manifested in her ability to gather water between her hands in a liquid sphere was also known to Goethe from this source, and he had already used it in the *West-östliche Divan* in order to represent the imaginative power of the poet to give pure shape to thought or experience ('Lied und Gebilde'). Here it serves to signal the innocent guilt of the brahmin's wife, whose sexuality is aroused by a fleeting reflected image of male beauty in the sacred Ganges. Whether the image is that of the god Brahma, or whether it is the woman's perception of divinely created human form, is unclear; what is clear is that the temptation is understood by both brahminee and pariah as willed and ordained by Brahma as an exemplum of compassion. The grotesque hybrid of a high-caste head grafted onto the body of an untouchable is a physical symbol of the duality of the human condition, of the twin souls within Faust's breast, of the tension between spirituality and physicality, the ideal and the real; but in this exemplary legend it is not the expression of despair, but an emblem of conciliation and compassion. Although it has been argued that the spirit of both this and the earlier Hindu legend of the bayadère is more Christian than Hindu, both tales appear to be accepted by Goethe as authentically sourced in Sonnerat; equally, it is notable that he chose from his source two legends that are entirely consistent with a Western Christian and humanitarian ethos.

God-Nature is the central device of the poem, untitled by Goethe, known as 'On the Contemplation of Schiller's Skull' ('Bei Betrachtung von Schillers Schädel'), or as 'Schillers Reliquien'. In 1826 Schiller's bones were exhumed for reburial in the Weimar *Fürstengruft*, and the skull was taken to Goethe's house for cleaning; in the poem, the fiction of the charnel-house is used as the context for a meditation on common mortality and exceptional genius, on transient physical existence and lasting creative achievement. It is written in *terza rima*, the fluid but

constant verse form used on only one other occasion by Goethe (in *Faust*, lines
4679–727); here it is the appropriate form for the articulation of the paradox of
God-Nature that makes the flesh ephemeral and the spirit substantial:

> Wie sie das Feste läßt zu Geist verrinnen,
> Wie sie das Geisterzeugte fest bewahre.

> How it resolves the substance into spirit
> And what is born of spirit can sustain.

To each stage of human life, Goethe wrote in one of his *Maxims and Reflections*
('Jedem Alter des Menschen . . .'),[46] a particular existential philosophy corresponds. The naive realism of childhood gives way to the stormy idealism of youth;
after the scepticism of manhood comes the mysticism of old age. The wisdom of
age is to perceive how so much seems to depend on chance or accident, how the
irrational can prevail and the rational can fail, how fortune and misfortune can
balance out – and to accept these contradictions and acquiesce in the will of Him
who is, was and always will be. He also summed up this serene acquiescence of old
age in his eloquent confession to Zelter as an 'unconditional submission to the
inscrutable will of God' (see above, p. 48). It is this profound and grateful
acceptance that informs the mystical religiosity of much of Goethe's late lyric
poetry: the disembodied mysticism of 'Nachts, wann gute Geister schweifen' or
the profound peace of 'Wenn im Unendlichen dasselbe' (When in the infinite
heavens recurring, date unknown, published 1827). The constant wheeling of the
heavens, the infinite complexity and the vast energies of the cosmic order, the
stresses and conflicts of human existence, are all subsumed under a profound
affirmation of harmony and peace in God: 'ewige Ruh in Gott dem Herrn'. A
similar expression of thankfulness for the splendour of creation is found in the
poem based on the emblematic figure of a winged genius poised above the world,
gesturing with one hand to the heavens and with the other towards earth
('Schwebender Genius über der Erdkugel': Genius poised above the Globe, 1826).
What is above and what is beneath, the infinite blue of the sky and the colourful
variety of the world around us, the landscape by day and the skyscape by night:
all is celebrated in a hymn to the human spirit that can perceive and respond to
the splendour of creation. A cryptic quatrain written much earlier ('Wär nicht das
Auge sonnenhaft': Our eyes, were they not like the sun, *c.*1805) adapts a mystical
perception of Plotinus that it is only through the divine element in us that we can
respond to divine creativity itself:

> Läg' nicht in uns des Gottes eigne Kraft,
> Wie könnt' uns Göttliches entzücken?

> If God's own power were not within us,
> How could His godlike works delight us?

If the wisdom of Goethe's late poetry expresses itself most typically in a
dialectic of polarities and paradoxes, this is nowhere more strikingly illustrated

than in the two poems 'Eins und alles' (One and All, 1821) and 'Vermächtnis' (Testament, 1829). The connection between the two is closer than the dates might suggest; for in 1828 a scientific congress in Berlin had chosen the last two lines of 'Eins und alles' as a banner headline for the meeting. Goethe objected to the way this selectively quoted paradox, which took no account of the preceding line 'Das Ewige regt sich fort in allen' (The eternal impulse moves in all), appeared to give undue stress to non-being (*Nichts*); and he riposted in 'Vermächtnis' by reiterating and emphasizing the continuity of being (*Sein*) that the earlier poem had also affirmed through the eternal process of creation and destruction, re-creation and transformation.

'Eins und alles' opens with the speculative monadology of the earlier poem 'Weltseele', where the will of the individual self or entelechy is assumed into a universal consciousness analogous to the cosmic order: the 'world-soul' that gives the individual an intuition of the divine creative principle. The self gladly gives up its turbulent identity to be assimilated into the collective consciousness of the world-soul; and yet this passive assimilation is followed by the imperative to renew its activity, even its struggles (*Ringen*), in its new existence – once again, Goethe's remarks on the entelechy and its survival in his letter to Zelter come to mind (see above, p. 48). The title of the poem invokes the Spinozan *hen kai pan*, the inseparability of one and all, of God and universe; the eternal creative principle works dynamically through perpetual change, what is created is re-created, what is formed is transformed, stasis is illusory, destruction is a condition of survival as the universe regenerates itself in the process of cosmic renewal.

'Vermächtnis' develops these awesome cosmic principles into a statement of the continuity and coherence of existence at the level of human experience and perception: the microcosm is an analogy of the macrocosm, to the Copernican cosmic order corresponds a human moral order in which the senses, the conscience and the intellect give coherence and structure to our lives. No doubt Goethe has in mind here Kant's existential dictum on the twin realities that relate directly to our existential consciousness: 'der bestirnte Himmel über mir und das moralische Gesetz in mir' (the starry heavens above me and the moral law within me);[47] the poem is a similar celebration of awed reverence for the laws that govern and define our existence. This insight into the historical and moral coherence of existence is the testament, the inheritance of the past that allows us to make sense of the present and to anticipate the future; but the poem is also Goethe's own philosophical testament in its affirmation of truth as fruitful and productive, and above all in its joyful celebration of the 'treasures' of the cosmos and of the 'richly gifted world' that our senses reveal to us.

LATE LYRIC POEMS

Among the poems of Goethe's old age are some of his most remarkable lyrical statements. It might be expected that a mind of such subtlety and complexity, and a life of such vast experience, should produce maxims or epigrams, Delphic wisdom in verse, or that someone of Goethe's literary reputation and public status should be required to produce a mass of occasional verses and personal encomia. What is less expected is that he should also compose a series of limpid lyrical poems that combine the expressive freshness and integrity of his early verse with the complex and sophisticated emotional responses of some of the early Weimar poetry. What characterizes the finest of these late lyric poems is a seemingly effortless fusion of perception and emotion, of observation and symbolism, the dense but lucid articulation of profound insights by means of simple images. But they are images that have the resonance, and in some cases the specific metaphorical associations, of years of figurative expression: central and fundamental Goethean imagery of sun and moonlight, day and night, light and darkness, cloud and mist, the weather and the seasons, the hours of the day and months of the year.

What also characterizes many of these late poems is their fundamentally affirmative tone. They are poems of grateful and positive acceptance of what life has brought and may yet bring, not from any simplistic Panglossian mentality, but in a spirit of affirmation in spite of suffering, separation, loss or death; many are poems of light and darkness, or of light dispelling darkness. To be sure, the 'Marienbader Elegie' stands out among these poems, and indeed in Goethe's lyrical *oeuvre*, as a visceral shout of desolation; but even this grief is poetically sublimated in a spirit of conciliation, at least within the context of the whole trilogy. Among the poetry of Goethe's old age should also be included the lyrical set-pieces he integrated into the second part of *Faust*: the four vigils of the night sung by a spirit chorus to the spiritually devastated Faust in the opening scene (lines 4634–65), the evocation of a Virgilian Golden Age as Faust describes the Arcadia in which his nuptials with Helen will take place (lines 9526–61), or the verses of Lynkeus as he surveys the 'eternal adornment' of the created world (lines 11288–303) – even if these lines are set in a brutally ironic dramatic context.

Poems such as 'Frühling übers Jahr' (Lasting Spring, 1816), 'März' (March, 1817), 'Blick um Blick' (Look for Look, *c.*1815), or 'Immer und überall' (Ever and Everywhere, 1820) indicate that Goethe never lost the ability or the will to write unsophisticated love or nature poetry. But 'Um Mitternacht' (At Midnight, 1818), to which he provided substantial glosses and which he described as a *Lebenslied*, a poem of particular emotional and existential significance for him,[48] is one of the most striking of these late poems. Three stages of life, childhood, youth and age, corresponding to three of the stages outlined in his *Maxims and Reflections* (see above, p. 122) are symbolized in progressively more intense light imagery experienced at the same moment of midnight, which also forms the mantra-like refrain binding the three disparate phases of existence. The boy perceives the stars with childish delight as undifferentiated points of light; the young man, torn by emotional imperatives, experiences the night sky as conflict, that between the permanent order of the stellar constellations and the elusive ephemerality of the *aurora borealis*; until then at last (the syntax of the second and third stanzas forms an unorthodox sequence of subordinate temporal clauses, not the only example in these late poems) the steady vision of old age is represented in the clear light of the full moon, as the mind encompasses past and future in an instant of mystical revelation at the same moment of midnight. The rhythmic and syntactical articulation of the poem is highly sophisticated, its synchronization of past and present is subtle, and its ultimate insight is inscrutable; but its vocabulary and imagery are utterly lucid.

'Zwischen beiden Welten' (Between Two Worlds, 1820) is a retrospective tribute to two of the lodestars of Goethe's early years, 'Lida' (Charlotte von Stein) and 'Wilhelm' (Shakespeare); it is possible that the first six lines actually date from the years of the poems to Lida. 'St Nepomuks Vorabend' (St John of Nepomuk's Eve, 1820) records impressions of the festival of lights in the Bohemian spa town of Karlsbad in celebration of the Czech priest who was martyred by drowning for refusing to break the seal of the confessional; the lights floated on the river replicate the legend that the saint's body was surrounded by reflected stars signifying that his soul had entered heaven. 'Wandersegen' (Traveller's Blessing, 1821), written as an introductory poem to the first version of *Wilhelm Meisters Wanderjahre*, is a further metamorphosis of the pilgrim or traveller motif in Goethe's poetry: not here the wild vatic figure of the early *Wanderer* poems, but the grave and introspective journeyman who treads his way cautiously and piously. 'Wilhelm Tischbeins Idyllen' (Wilhelm Tischbein's Idylls) were the response to a request in 1821 by Goethe's early friend and guide in Rome, now repatriated to Germany, to provide texts to a series of idyllic landscapes in which classical motifs are placed in romantic settings: overgrown ruins, ideal vistas, oaks, nymphs and sylphs, and Chiron the centaur as teacher of Achilles.

'Äolsharfen' (Aeolian Harps, 1822) is the first of a series of passionate love lyrics that culminate in the 'Marienbader Elegie' of 1823; for all the lack of clear biographical reference, there is no reason not to associate the poem with Ulrike von Levetzow. The striking central image is the Aeolian or wind harp, an instrument of symbolic fascination to German Romantic and post-Romantic writers, for whom it represented the very voice of the wind resonating to a natural harmony. The relationship is that of two lovers who are separated but attuned in intuitive harmony, a dialogue of grief that resolves itself in the image of the rainbow, of Iris the mediatrix and symbol of hope. The collection of short verses to Ulrike von Levetzow, from 1823 or the previous year, are less heavily coded, but retain a playful element reminiscent of the sonnets or of the Hatem/Suleika verses of the *West-östliche Divan*. They give little warning of the agonized desolation of loss to come as Goethe gently mocks himself and his meteorological studies – and perhaps also his earnest pedagogical disquisitions on the subject to Ulrike; but the pathos of the last poem that laments her absence among the warm springs of Karlsbad ('Am heißen Quell') throws a shadow forwards to the elegy that records their final parting.

The *Trilogy of Passion* is a remarkable composition, in the first instance because it is a composite rather than an organic trilogy: the three parts are arranged in the reverse order of their composition. The third section, 'Aussöhnung' (Reconciliation), is an occasional poem written before the central section, and before the experience that prompted that section, as a tribute to the musical talent of the Polish pianist Maria Szymanovska, whom Goethe met, heard and befriended in Marienbad in August 1823. The common motif of passion and suffering is evidently fortuitous, and the reasonable inference is that Goethe appended this poem to the central elegy in order to mitigate or balance aesthetically, if not emotionally, the tragic bleakness of the central elegy. 'An Werther' (To Werther) is also an occasional poem in the sense that Goethe was prompted to exhume the memory of his youthful hero by the request of the publisher Weygand in 1824 for a dedicatory preface to an edition of the novel celebrating the fiftieth anniversary of its first appearance. The central elegy was written in September 1823.

The 'Elegie' is remarkable in another sense, in that it is in itself the most starkly and unequivocally tragic of all Goethe's 'confessional' lyric poetry. It has become a commonplace among critics to perceive Goethe as a writer who avoided tragic confrontations or conclusions in his work – a perception fostered by Goethe himself, who pronounced that he was by nature 'conciliatory'.[49] Yet there is in Goethe's whole *oeuvre*, lyric, dramatic and narrative, a saturnine tragic thread, even a psychopathology that cannot be ignored, for all the overwhelmingly affirmative nature of most of his writing: the self-destructive solipsism of Werther or Tasso, the madness of Orest, the brutal death of the child in 'Erlkönig', the life-destroying nostalgia of Mignon, the Harfenspieler's implacable vision of guilt and retribution, the destructive impact of passion on rational free-will in *Die Wahlverwandtschaften*. It is notable that in Goethe's lyrical work, the tragic vision and fate of Mignon and the Harfenspieler are articulated through distinct personae, through characters who are also distanced by being placed in the narrative and fictive context of the novel in which they appear; only in the 'Marienbader Elegie' is there the articulation of such tragic experience in the direct first person mode. To be sure, this does not mean that the 'Elegie' should be read as a literal biographical record of Goethe's anguish at his separation from Ulrike von Levetzow; no literary artefact, if only because it is the articulation of possibly experienced emotion by means of careful and sophisticated aesthetic fashioning, can represent at first hand the actual psychological or emotional record of such suffering. Nevertheless, all the circumstances of the poem's composition – in September 1823 on the journey back to Weimar after the final parting from Ulrike in Karlsbad – indicate that it is as immediate an expression of personal anguish as any such lengthy and formal poem can be. The relativization of the pathos of the 'Elegie' by means of the two poems that frame it does not alter this; but the opening poem 'An Werther' introduces (retrospectively, as it were, in order of composition) two further perspectives on the tragic dimension of the 'Elegie'.

On the one hand, 'An Werther' emphasizes the pathos of parting, of final separation. In Werther's case, of course, this final parting was death; but there is an ambiguity in the phrase 'Scheiden ist der Tod!' For Werther, it meant just that; but time and again, with reference to *Tasso* above all, Goethe insisted that the basic motif of all tragic situations was parting, the loss of or separation from a situation of happiness or a loved person.[50] In every great separation there is the seed of madness – whether it is the physical death of Werther, the spiritual death Goethe experienced when he left Rome, or the emotional death on parting from Ulrike von Levetzow. On the other hand, 'An Werther' also touches on Goethe's own response to tragic experience: the frequently invoked ability to sublimate or purge personal suffering by means of poetic articulation. A more disabused age might take a more sceptical attitude towards the notion that profound emotional distress or personal tragedy can be purged by the therapy of aesthetic expression; and it might also be noted that there is no direct record in artistic form of Goethe's reaction to the deaths of his sister, his mother, his wife or his son (other than the monodrama *Proserpina*, which may have been a memorial to Cornelia and a bitter allegory of her unhappy marriage).

Goethe himself certainly contributed to this notion of the cathartic power of literary expression by hinting that if he had not written the novel, then he too might have perished like Werther; he also suggested with some irritation that in view of the novel's sensational reception, it might have been better if he had in the event blown his brains out. But the tone of rueful bitterness in 'An Werther' reads more like an ironic parody of the theory of catharsis. Lines 9–10 articulate the desolate admission that by his death, Werther had lost little; lines 11–12 are a bitter travesty of the celebration of life and the world that we find elsewhere in Goethe's late poetry:

> Des Menschen Leben *scheint* ein herrlich Los:
> Der Tag wie lieblich, so die Nacht wie groß! (my emphasis)

> How enviable the lot of man might seem:
> The day so lovely, and the night serene!

Our paradisal joy in the 'richly gifted world' is vitiated by the bitter experience of tragic passion, and the last four lines of the poem again appear to mock the notion that suffering is alleviated by poetic expression: 'Wie klingt es rührend, wenn der Dichter singt' (It sounds so moving when the poet sings). The final couplet, paraphrasing the words of Tasso, the 'gesteigerte Werther',[51] might invoke the therapy of articulation; but the context also reminds us that the moving pathos of the poet is rooted in real suffering. Nevertheless, Tasso's lines stand almost word for word as a motto over the central Elegy: 'An Werther' is verbally and thematically integrated with the 'Elegie' in a way 'Aussöhnung' is not, and it may be that the opening poem is, as its date of composition suggests, a truer conclusion to the 'Elegie' than the poem that actually concludes it.

The formal contrast between the 'Elegie' and 'An Werther' is striking. Where the opening poem was an intimate confiding of the poet in his hero, spoken in informally structured stanzas, the central poem has the high pathos of rhetoric couched in regular six-line stanzas that are close to the structure of *ottava rima*. But for all its rhetorical diction and structure, its complex shifts between present and past, for all its elaborate figures and allusions (the banishment from Paradise, the cloud-imagery of the seventh stanza, the lofty metaphors of lines 55, 71–2, 85–8, the biblical invocation of lines 73–4), for all the rhetoric of the penultimate stanza with its gesture of turning away from the world that is reminiscent of *Empfindsamkeit* at its most self-dramatizing – for all that, the 'Elegie' contains some of the most direct expressions of bleak and inconsolable suffering in all Goethe's lyrical work:

Was hilft es mir, so hohe Weisheit lernen! (line 108)
Da bleibt kein Rat als grenzenlose Tränen (114)
Allein dem Geist fehlt's am Entschluß und Willen (120)
Wie könnte dies geringstem Troste frommen (125)
Mir ist das All, ich bin mir selbst verloren (133)
Sie trennen mich, und richten mich zu Grunde (138)

What use is such high wisdom now to me! . . .
No comfort now remains but endless tears . . .
And yet my spirit lacks resolve and will . . .
How can I take the slightest comfort here . . .
The world is lost to me, I to myself . . .
And as they separate us, they destroy me.

The beloved woman whose presence had been so movingly evoked in stanzas 2 and 3, whose absence had been mitigated by recollection and reassurance in the retrospective central section of stanzas 7–15, whose own voice had comforted him in stanzas 16–17, has by the end of the poem assumed the fatal ambivalence of Pandora: 'So reich an Gütern, reicher an Gefahr' (So rich in gifts, in perils richer still). Such visceral anguish and despair can scarcely be purged or sublimated by the eloquent hymn to the soothing power of music that is attached as the concluding section of the trilogy.

It may be that the true coda to the 'Marienbader Elegie', and to the emotional experience that inspired it, is to be found neither in 'Aussöhnung' nor in 'An Werther', but in the elusive and intense ambiguities of 'Der Bräutigam' (The Bridegroom), a poem written in 1824 or 1825, at all events not long after the *Trilogie der Leidenschaft*, and one on which Goethe made no recorded comment. This is not to say that the 'bridegroom' of the enigmatic title is to be understood as a wish-fulfilment of the aged Goethe's hopes of engagement to Ulrike von Levetzow; the German term *Bräutigam* has in any case two meanings, that of fiancé and of bridegroom, and it is not used unequivocally as the former here. The tradition of the bridegroom (as opposed to the fiancé) being admitted over the threshold of the bridal chamber seems to be alluded to in the last stanza, and some critics have detected a reference (albeit a very cryptic one) to biblical and doctrinal metaphors of Christ as bridegroom in the poem. Moreover, the poem has been associated not only with Ulrike von Levetzow, but also variously with Frau von Stein, with Goethe's wife Christiane and with Lili Schönemann, the only woman who was in a formal sense engaged to Goethe.

It may be, as more cautious critics have claimed, that distant memories of Lili Schönemann and recent memories of Marienbad coalesce in this mysterious poem that appears to articulate the thoughts of an ageing man looking back from the present moment of midnight (in the last stanza) to a moment of midnight from the distant past (evoked in the first stanza). From this recollection flow memories of togetherness and separation, of dreaming and waking, of absence and toil through the heat of the day and of reunion and rest in the cool of the evening, of parting at sunset and hope of meeting again the following day. From the present perspective of the final stanza the erstwhile bridegroom, prompted by a mystical perception of starlight, projects his thoughts across space to the 'threshold' where she lies, and across time to a future reunion beyond that threshold: what was once the threshold of the bridal chamber has now become the threshold of death. The complex temporal structure of this poem, its enigmatic references and ambiguities, its subtle rhythms and antitheses, allow no clear understanding of its processes; there is still no clear consensus about the timespan of the poem – whether the midnight of the last stanza is separated from the midnight recalled in the first stanza by only twenty-four hours or by a whole lifetime, whether a whole lifetime is symbolically concentrated into twenty-four hours. Whatever the reading, the final line unequivocally articulates a characteristically Goethean affirmation of life whatever it may bring; the tragic experience of parting that was so viscerally and despairingly voiced in the 'Marienbader Elegie' is here sublimated into an affirmation that marks a coming to terms with despair and loss. The emotional and existential equipoise achieved in this poem is confirmed by the chiastic balance between the fourth and final lines: to the despairing question 'Was ist es mir, so viel er bringen mag?' (What's it to me, whatever it may bring?) comes the answering affirmation 'Wie es auch sei das Leben es ist gut' (Whatever it may bring us, life is good).

The cycle *Chinesisch-deutsche Jahres- und Tageszeiten* (Sino-German Seasons and Hours) of 1827 is in part the product, though scarcely as obviously or as intensively as in the *West-östliche Divan*, of Goethe's interest in Eastern cultural sources, in this case a brief acquaintance with Chinese literature in English and French translations, and with novels rather than with verse – though he did adapt six Chinese poems from translations, also in 1827. It is not clear how many or which motifs and stylistic devices Goethe drew from Chinese sources, literary or visual. Lilies, roses, birds, the peacock, lovers trysting in an ornamental garden, willow leaves dancing on moonlit water, the eremitical seclusion of the Confucian sage, his gifts of laconic wisdom to his disciples, the opening invocation of a Mandarin's escape from professional and political burdens into idyllic seclusion (the equivalent, in less specific terms, of 'Hegire' in the *Divan*): these motifs are lightly drawn hints at Goethe's exotic sources. The visual delicacy and decorative simplicity of these poems also corresponds to our perception of the style of far-eastern lyrical or pictorial expression. Nowhere is this more striking than in 'Dämmrung senkte sich von oben' (Twilight from above descending), a poem which sustains a visual perception of landscape throughout, evoking the fall of darkness and the emergence of moonlight in a series of delicately brushed images: dusk, evening star, mists, dark lake, the glow of approaching moonlight, and willow branches dipping into moonlit water. Even the subjective response to this nocturnal landscape – the coolness of the moonlit scene – is registered visually through the eye. And yet the motifs and rhythms of these poems are essentially Goethean, familiar from other contexts: roses and lilies, mist or cloud dissolving before the sun, moonlight and starlight reflected in water. 'Dämmrung senkte sich von oben' has the same metre, and much of the same imagery, as the elves' chorus in the opening scene of *Faust*

Part Two (lines 4634–65); and 'Ziehn die Schafe von der Wiese' (When the sheep have left the pastures) is a metaphorical expression of hope and promise in the dispersal of mist and cloud, a frequent and resonant image in Goethe's lyrical language.

The seemingly effortless and artless limpidity of the 'Chinese' cycle is fused with a more powerful, though still subtle, symbolism in the two Dornburg poems of 1828: 'Dem aufgehenden Vollmonde' (To the Full Moon Rising) and 'Früh, wenn Tal, Gebirg und Garten' (When garden, hill and valley early). In July 1828 Goethe withdrew to Dornburg for two months after the death of Karl August, devoting himself intensively to his scientific studies, but also, as he wrote to Eckermann, drinking in the glory of the night sky and the sunrise, and communing with the vines covering the terraced gardens. He had also, he added, been writing some poems again which were 'not bad'.[52] The two Dornburg poems, written respectively on or around 25 August and 8 September, were evidently written as companion-pieces, one nocturnal, the other diurnal. They share much the same metre, a similar internal and external structure, they both even feature the same adverbial genitive construction in exactly the same place in the tenth line ('Reiner Bahn' / 'Reiner Brust': With pure path / With pure heart). And yet they are strikingly distinct, complementary and reciprocal in their differences: the more deliberate cadences of the nocturnal poem, which stop the rhythm at the end of alternate (even) lines with a masculine ending, differ substantially from the continuous flow of the diurnal poem, which runs in unbroken (if obscure) syntax throughout the three stanzas in a series of feminine endings. The structure of 'Früh, wenn Tal, Gebirg und Garten' is also reinforced by dynamic verbs and verb forms, by present participles and by the clause structure. To be sure, the subordinate clauses that comprise the first ten lines and qualify the main clause of the last two lines are not unambiguous; but it might reasonably be taken that the *wenn* clauses of the first two stanzas are temporal (when), while the inversion of subject and verb in the ninth line is a conditional construction (if you then give thanks . . .).

The first poem is an emotional dialogue between self and moon in a subdued minor key; there is a distant echo of a motif in the *Divan* poem 'Vollmondnacht', where the separated lovers had promised to greet each other by the full moon – and indeed Goethe sent a copy of the Dornburg poem to Marianne von Willemer in October 1828 with an implicit reference to the *Divan* poem, which she immediately detected. The second poem is in major key; it is a sharp visual perception of forms and colours in a landscape and skyscape in which the sun is the central symbolic image. Both poems describe the emergence of light from obscurity – in the first the moon emerges from clouds to be greeted with a triumphant affirmation of love in spite of separation; in the second, early morning mist and cloud are dispersed by sun and east wind, giving the promise of a clear day and, at the end, a sunset in which the setting sun will gild the whole horizon. Hope or promise fulfilled is the theme of both poems; but in both there is an important qualification. The affirmation of the moonlit night is qualified by an acknowledgement of the pain of separation; the glory of the setting sun is conditional on an appropriate attitude of thankfulness. In the second poem Goethe's meteorological interests, his careful observations of wind-direction, cloud formations and barometric pressure, are allied with his metaphorical perceptions of the times of day, which might well here stand for the phases of life. This poem characterizes the best of Goethe's late lyric poetry: the gift of expressing in the simplest images, but with a complex subtlety of rhythm, sound and syntax, a serene vision that responds to and affirms the natural world and individual existence in an unforced synthesis of perception and emotion, of empirical observation and symbolic vision.

3

The Dramatist

EARLY DRAMA; *GÖTZ VON BERLICHINGEN*

From an early stage Goethe saw his literary career as much as that of a dramatist as that of a lyric poet. In *Dichtung und Wahrheit* he records his childish delight in a puppet-theatre of his grandmother's, and his efforts to learn French from the plays performed by the garrison theatre in Frankfurt; it is then not surprising that his earliest surviving dramatic efforts were in the French tradition, or at least in the Gallicizing idiom of Gottsched or Gellert. Of his first play *Balsazar* (Belshazzar, 1765) only fragments remain in the form of two speeches in alexandrines, treated very much in the style of Gottsched – though he planned even then, as he confided to his sister Cornelia, to write the fifth act not in the French style but in the metre used by 'the Briton' (Shakespeare): iambic pentameter.[1] The first complete play to survive is a brief pastoral comedy, also in alexandrines, that presents the mutual infidelities and reconciliations of rococo shepherds and shepherdesses, *Die Laune des Verliebten* (The Lover's Whim) of 1767–8, a dramatic equivalent of the early poems of the *Buch Annette*, and a work which, as Goethe remembered in his autobiography, was written from direct personal experience as an attempt to come to terms with his jealously fraught flirtation with Kätchen Schönkopf in Leipzig.[2]

Die Mitschuldigen (Partners in Guilt), first written in 1769 but heavily revised later in the same year and again in the early 1780s, is a comedy of misunderstandings set in a socially more realistic but still theatrically conventional milieu (an inn) which uses the stock stage devices, plot, situations and characters of neo-classical comedy: vice pitted against virtue, virtue rewarded, misunderstandings, *dialogues des sourds*, on-stage eavesdropping, the figures of the aristocratic libertine, the inquisitive innkeeper, the dissolute husband and the severely tested but virtuous wife. The title, the dénouement (confusion and misunderstanding dispelled, vice confounded and virtue vindicated, mutual forgiveness) and the language (again alexandrines) indicate Goethe's debt to Gottsched's programmatic theatrical reforms that tamed and harnessed the traditions of the improvised comic theatre through its refinement in French neo-classicism and the 'Saxon Comedy' into a genre of virtuous and enlightened moral realism. But Goethe was also to claim much later in his autobiography that this burlesque and apparently innocuous comedy also reflected his insight into the vicious and even sinister currents he had detected beneath the respectable surface of family life in Frankfurt.[3]

Goethe's drama did not remain very long under the spell of Gottsched or the French neo-classical theatre, any more than his poetry remained within the conventions of the *Buch Annette*, and his next completed drama was sensationally different in every way from that tradition. It is difficult to exaggerate the profound and far-reaching change in Goethe's literary perceptions and productions as the result of little more than sixteen months in Strasbourg; and before the end of 1771 *Götz von Berlichingen* sprang, as it were, fully armed from the head of Shakespeare. This early dramatic product of what was then not yet known as the *Sturm und Drang*, of a radically creative phase of German literature in which a younger generation believed it was throwing off the shackles of an establishment culture, cannot be exclusively credited to Herder's influence – whose reaction to the first draft was at best tolerantly, at worst devastatingly critical, according to whether we take the evidence of Goethe's answering letter of July 1772 or his later account of its reception in *Dichtung und Wahrheit*.[4] But it was Herder who stimulated Goethe's imagination in a spectacular way, who directed his interests and enthusiasms away from neo-classical formalities towards German cultural traditions, and in particular towards the vivid period of German history at the crossroads between the Middle Ages and the modern era, in short towards the Reformation. It was Herder who referred Goethe to the essay by Justus Möser on the medieval–chivalric code of feud or vendetta, *Über das Faustrecht* (literally, On the Right of the Fist), which in turn led him to other and older documents on the legal and constitutional history of the Holy Roman Empire at a time when it was in danger of collapsing under its inherent political tensions and contradictions – as indeed it again appeared to be doing in the latter half of the eighteenth century. Goethe's reading also included the memoirs of an imperial knight whose life spanned the reigns of two Emperors (Maximilian I and Charles V), the age of the Reformation and the Peasants' Revolts, the age in which the robust independence and purportedly chivalric code of the free knights clashed, often violently, with the rising power of the urban merchant classes on the one hand and with the territorial magnates of particularism on the other: a struggle in which a politically and territorially enfeebled Emperor, the 'last of the knights' Maximilian, could intervene only ineffectually, for all his efforts to proclaim a series of edicts promulgating an end to feuding and territorial battles, which culminated in the *Ewiger Landfriede* (Decree of Perpetual Peace) of 1495.

Whether Goethe wished to hold up to his own century the mirror of the Reformation period, whether he wished to champion a fancied and fanciful Golden Age of integrity, independence and originality as a foil to the perceived decadence and derivative timidity of his own political and literary scene; whether he saw in the self-seeking tyranny of sixteenth-century Princes, Prince-Bishops and Landgraves a parallel to the absolutism of his own times; whether he wished to banish French neo-classical dramatic models in the name of Shakespeare and to provide German literature, thus paradoxically, with a 'native' theme and style that would help to throw off the burden of Racine and Corneille: it was also Herder who, in his at times incoherently enthusiastic Shakespeare essay in *Von deutscher Art und Kunst*, urged the young Goethe to set up a monument to Shakespeare 'from *our* age of chivalry'.[5] It was also Herder who reacted to the first draft of Goethe's response to this call with the acerbic comment: 'Shakespeare has quite ruined you'.

This first version was the *Geschichte Gottfriedens von Berlichingen mit der eisernen Hand. Dramatisiert* (History of Gottfried von Berlichingen Ironhand. Dramatized). It was written in prose, with some intercalated songs, in six weeks during November and December 1771: Shakespearian blank verse was almost unknown in German literature at that time, and all but one of Wieland's Shakespeare translations had been in prose. The literary standard to which this drama owed its inspiration was raised 'with great ceremony' by Goethe and a few friends in Frankfurt on the previous 14 October, when Shakespeare's name day (St William's day) had been celebrated with an excited speech proclaiming his Shakespearian credo. To be sure, in the name of 'nature' Goethe out-Shakespeared Shakespeare, and used the temporal and spatial freedom of the English stage to create a chronicle play in which time and place are extravagantly relativized in both theatrical and historical terms: Swabia merges with Franconia, Maximilian's reign is extended to take in the Peasants' War, Götz's own life is drastically foreshortened, the Prince-Bishop of Bamberg is turned from a tolerant humanist scholar into a scheming and unscrupulous prelate, and the robber-baron Gottfried von Berlichingen into a paragon of conservative feudal values of loyalty, honesty and courage against the enfeebled decadence of his erstwhile friend turned sentimental courtier, Adelbert von Weislingen. Into this heady brew of romantic and fanciful historicism Goethe also introduced the bewitching fairy-tale figure of Adelheid von Walldorf, Götz's adversary and his true equal in status (though they never meet face-to-face in the play), as heroic in her criminal ambitions as Götz in his integrity; the two of them are living exemplars of Goethe's dictum in his Shakespeare speech that 'that which we call evil is only the obverse of good'.[6] The official of the *Fehme*, the secret court that represents an almost supernatural agency of justice and retribution, who is sent to execute her, narrowly fails to fall for her seductive spell, and can only exclaim as he carries out his grim commission: 'God, you made her so beautiful, and yet could not make her good!'[7]

For all that his hero is an exemplar of honesty who robs fat Cologne or Nuremberg merchants and rights injustices done to poor craftsmen, who bloodies the noses of ambitious land barons and champions freedom in the absolute and uncritical tones of the *Sturm und Drang* generation, Goethe does not present Götz in unproblematic terms. To be sure, Götz's enemies are mendacious, timid, unscrupulous or demoniacally evil; to be sure, he is misrepresented to Maximilian by Weislingen, and subsequently tricked into an honourable surrender only to be captured in a treacherous ambush; to be sure, his wife, his betrayed sister, his companions and above all his young squire Georg, are upright, loyal and self-proclaimed free individuals on whose side, as he tells the perfidious Weislingen, are light and right. But the freedom to which they – and he – pretend is an increasingly unreal freedom, undermined by forces and strategies with which they cannot cope. The discrepancy between the unreal power of the Emperor, to whom Götz claims sole allegiance, and the *realpolitik* of the princes is so wide that such survivals of feudal loyalty are illusory; the *Faustrecht*, the right to declare and wage feud in order to right a real or imagined wrong, was by Götz's time an anachronism, a recipe for anarchy in an already fragmented Empire, and a right that had in any case been curtailed by a series of *Landfrieden*.

Götz's position becomes progressively less tenable in the course of the play; even if Maximilian is able to indulge his personal affection for Götz and Selbitz, he cannot resist the power of his princes, and is in any case too preoccupied with external politics, with the threat of the advancing Turks. If Götz can still, in the third act, invoke his sole loyalty and obligation to God and the Emperor while at the same time dismissing the authority of Weislingen's imperial task force by roaring that its captain can lick his arse, he becomes unable to hold to this fiction as the play, and with it the historical tide, moves on. Götz's rescue by Franz von Sickingen from imperial arrest at Heilbronn is by force of arms, not by constitutional right, and his subsequent alliance with the peasants – who are presented here not as an exploited underclass defending itself against the brutal depredations of territorial self-interest, but as a murderous rabble – finally puts him beyond the pale even of his own shaky and atavistic feudal code; for he joins them not so much in order to check their murderous anarchy, but because he is fretting under the enforced idleness of his house arrest, his *Urfehde* or undertaking to keep the peace.

Götz dies in despair, isolated from his allies, from his own age and indeed from his own values – as even his loyal wife Elisabeth has to acknowledge. The individual freedom to which he had pretended has clashed with the inexorable course of the whole, and for all the pathos of his end he is a noble anachronism stranded by history. For all his deep and passionate sympathy with his hero, for all the venality of Götz's enemies, Goethe is not blind to the fact that Götz's vision of freedom is untenable in changed times, however dismal the vision of these new times may be. His Emperor Maximilian, self-styled 'last of the knights', is dead; his friend and ally Sickingen has gone on to pursue other personal and political ambitions; his surrogate son Georg is dead, and his own son, a feeble, bookish personality (a somewhat unkind invention of Goethe's) is in a monastery; only his wife and the faithful Lerse remain to witness his end. There is even (no doubt unintentionally) something faintly comical about the pair of warrior-knights Berlichingen and Selbitz fighting their futile rearguard action against history: Götz with one hand, Selbitz with one leg, defending bravely but hopelessly the tattered standard of their code, their freedom – but freedom to do what? Perhaps the essential freedom embodied in the play is less a political freedom than a cultural one: the literary liberation from the shackles of the French classical theatre.

None of this could alter the powerful appeal of the play to Goethe's contemporaries; indeed, it still retains a special place in the affections of the German public, and not only thanks to Götz's ribald riposte to the imperial forces in Act III. To writers of the time like Lenz and Bürger, Hamann and Claudius, Eschenburg and Möser (though not to Lessing), to the countless imitators of the *Ritterdrama* style of chronicle play, indeed to Walter Scott, who translated it in 1799, the effect was overwhelming; and this was no doubt due equally to the theme and to its treatment. The robust archaising prose and the broad historical canvas (though the Reformation itself is nowhere explicit, the youngish figure of Martin Luther appears, thinly disguised, in Act I, and the introduction of Roman law into the German Empire is satirized in the figure of Olearius), the bewildering military actions, the genre scenes, the larger-than-life figures, the supernatural or quasi-supernatural elements, the spell of Adelheid's evil beauty – all this, organized into a restlessly shifting, but by no means wholly unstructured kaleidoscope of scene changes and swift leaps across some thirty years of turbulent history, forced Shakespeare and the supposed Shakespearian dramaturgy onto the attention of the educated German public. While Wieland, Herder, Lessing and Eschenburg may have contributed much to a serious knowledge and understanding of Shakespeare in Germany, while the definitive German version of Shakespeare may have been provided only in the early nineteenth century by August Wilhelm Schlegel and his collaborators, it was *Götz von Berlichingen* that provided the impetus for a national fascination with Shakespeare that continues in Germany to the present day.

In his revision of the 'dramatized history' of Götz into the *Schauspiel* version of 1773, Goethe made some substantial changes, though he did not go very far to reduce the apparently chaotic jumble of scene changes in the original. These are indeed many, but they scarcely render the play unperformable, as was thought at the time; they are no more unstageable than many Shakespearian battle scenes, and certainly not beyond an adequate theatre. A scene from the Imperial Diet at Augsburg at the beginning of the third act was omitted, in which the Archbishop of Mainz delivers an impassioned but deeply ambiguous speech to the princes, enjoining them to support Maximilian against the Turks even if by doing so (as he carefully reminds them) they will abandon their own lands to the internal anarchy of the Empire; all that remains of this scene is Weislingen's treacherous lobbying of the Emperor for permission to proceed against Berlichingen and Selbitz. The most substantial changes over the earlier version involve the fifth act, where Goethe felt that the baleful beauty of Adelheid (whose activities were indeed in the first version more explicitly associated with witchcraft) had threatened to usurp the main interest: not only had Weislingen and his squire Franz fallen under her spell, but also a young gypsy, Götz's ally Sickingen and the agent of the *Fehmgericht* sent to execute her. In the final version she destroys only Weislingen and Franz – though she also appears to have (unfulfilled) designs on the future Emperor Charles V. Goethe also added at the end of the second act a brief genre scene where Götz presides patriarchally over a peasant wedding. This scene is not simply a 'colour' episode; it continues the theme of the introduction of Roman law into the German territories (historically, a process long since completed) that had been satirized earlier in the owlish figure of Öhlmann/Olearius. Here, the traditional system of case law administered quickly and cheaply by local rulers or magistrates, backed up by appeals to the imperial visitations, is favourably contrasted to the lengthy and expensive administration of a complex new legal code manipulated by rapacious lawyers like the 'damned swarthy Italian Sapupi' – not only a chauvinistic jibe at an alien system, but also the anagram of a well-known but unloved Wetzlar lawyer of Goethe's day, Papius.

STURM UND DRANG: THE GENIEZEIT

In the period between the first and second versions of *Götz*, Goethe had explored other dramatic possibilities for treating historical or mythological figures of 'colossal' Shakespearean dimensions: Julius Caesar, Socrates, Mohammed, Prometheus. Of the first two, only jottings survive; of the *Mahomet* project only fragments of dialogue and two poems – a Koranic hymn to the Creator spoken by the Prophet, and a lyrical dialogue between the Prophet's daughter Fatima and her husband Ali to the achievements of Mohammed, which entered the corpus of Goethe's lyric poetry as 'Mahomets Gesang'. It seems that Goethe was drawn to the story of Mohammed at least in part to correct a prevailing perception of the Prophet that was largely the result of Voltaire's drama of 1741, in which the Prophet is presented as a charlatan, and his mesmeric hold on his followers as deception; Goethe's response to this was to cast him as a charismatic leader who proclaims a single universal God against the polytheistic idolatry of his time – in terms of the pantheistic enthusiasms of the *Sturm und Drang*.

But it was Prometheus who caught the young Goethe's imagination as the emblem of his rebellious generation. As an archetype of independent creativity and self-reliance, Prometheus is invoked in many ways throughout Goethe's works; but again, little survives of this early project other than a series of dialogues, and a monologue by Prometheus in his workshop as he moulds and shapes his creatures, a titanic shout of defiance at the authority of Zeus, indeed at authority as such. It is not certain that Prometheus's monologue, familiar as the ode published among the other *Sturm und Drang* hymns of the time (see above, p. 64), was intended to be an integral part of the *Prometheus* drama – for the fragment of the drama that has survived appears to be a dramatic representation of the ideas and attitudes expressed in the ode, and the fragment contains verbatim several lines from the ode itself. Prometheus defies Zeus through his messenger Mercury, ignoring the pleas of his pious brother Epimetheus. He is helped in his task of creating humankind by Minerva, daughter of Zeus (and it is she, not Prometheus, who knows the means of bringing to life the statues he has formed from clay). Prometheus is cast as the loving father of his new race, teaching them to build their primitive huts, healing them and instructing his 'daughter' Pandora on the human condition of joy, pain and mortality.

It remains unclear how Goethe's *Prometheus* drama was to develop – whether the Titan was to meet his mythical fate bound to the rock, or whether his revolt was to be pardoned; for Zeus's judgement in the fragment is inconclusive. It may be that while Prometheus's arrogant defiance was to be punished, his creatures would be allowed to survive under the stern authority of the Olympian Zeus.

Goethe was to return to the Prometheus myth in his (also uncompleted) later drama *Pandora*, though here the subject was to be treated in a very different way. But a reminiscence in Book 15 of *Dichtung und Wahrheit* indicates that Goethe did not forget his youthful archetype of rebellion; indeed in 1820, the year after Metternich's Karlsbad Decrees, issued to curb national and liberal movements in the universities, he remarked wryly to Zelter that his early Prometheus ode should not be republished for fear it might be adopted by 'our revolutionary youth' as a gospel of protest.[8] *Tempora mutantur, nos et mutamur in illis.*

The *Prometheus* fragment and the Ali–Fatima dialogue known as 'Mahomets Gesang' were written in the free rhythms of Goethe's *Sturm und Drang* hymns, derived partly from Klopstock's experiments with free verse, but also from the contemporary understanding of Pindaric odes which were perceived and printed, erroneously, as unmetred verse. These free rhythms are in contrast both to the prose idiom of *Götz von Berlichingen* and to the sixteenth-century style with which Goethe experimented in a series of brief farces written in or around 1773, namely *Knittelvers*. Two of these pieces also draw on the late medieval and Reformation traditions of *Schembartlaufen* and *Fastnachtspiel*, Shrovetide entertainments staged in southern German towns and associated for Goethe above all with Hans Sachs, in whose homely style he perceived the thriving popular culture of the Reformation. It was from this culture, and from the robust narratives of the early era of the printing-press, that Goethe derived the essentially popular inspiration for the first beginnings of his work on *Faust*; but while the early scenes of the *Urfaust* were taking shape, he also composed a number of short sketches in *Knittelvers*, of which the most substantial is *Das Jahrmarktsfest zu Plundersweilern. Ein Schönbartsspiel* (Plundersweilern Market Fair. A Carnival Masquerade). From an early stage Goethe was attracted to the forms of carnival revue, pageant or masquerade, whether in their popular public forms as street art and fairground entertainment, or in more lavish and sophisticated Renaissance or Baroque form as courtly spectacle and festival; these were forms that would also appear as intercalations in some of his major works, notably in *Faust*, either as naturalistic genre scenes or in increasingly complex allegorical elaboration.

In *Das Jahrmarktsfest zu Plundersweilern* (1773, published 1774; revised version 1778) Goethe himself figures as the 'Doctor' – one of the names by which he was known to his Darmstadt Circle – rubbing shoulders with a fairground throng of barkers, hawkers crying their wares, citizens, gypsies and street entertainers. These carnival junketings are the framework for an 'official' entertainment, a tragedy in alexandrines (though in the first version in *Knittelvers*) based on the biblical story of Esther and Ahasuerus, which is an absurd burlesque of Gottschedian drama – ostensibly a decorous and edifying performance, in fact, as the 'Doctor' sardonically remarks, a boring piece of sententiousness from which all vulgarity of language or behaviour has been removed. It is the revenge of Hanswurst on Gottsched for his formal banishment from the respectable German stage, a send-up of official culture not unlike the performance of *Pyramus and Thisbe* by Shakespeare's rude mechanicals.

The *Fastnachtsspiel vom Pater Brey* (Father Gruel. A Shrovetide Play, early 1773, published 1774) is a more directly personal satire by Goethe. If the Tartuffe-like figure of Mordechai in the Esther–Ahasuerus burlesque had been a veiled attack on Franz Michael Leuchsenring, Goethe was even more specifically savage in this short piece. Leuchsenring, a soapy pietist whom Goethe knew as part of the Darmstadt *Empfindsamkeit* circle, where he held the position of *Hofmeister* (private tutor) to the young Prince of Hessen-Darmstadt, was suspected of paying his attentions to Caroline Flachsland during the absence of her fiancé Herder, court-ing her with his sentimental religiosity. In the farce, the *Teufelspfaff* (devil's priest) Pater Brey is unmasked by a trick in which Leonora's fiancé, Captain Balandrino, returns disguised as a rich and elderly aristocrat who puts the treacherous parson to work to convert his pigs to a godly life. To be sure, Herder was an unlikely Balandrino, and the dubious innuendoes behind this less than hilarious piece of horseplay severely embarrassed Goethe's friend and erstwhile mentor; as a result, and not for the last time, relations between them became strained, for all Goethe's disclaimers that the piece was no more than a satire on hypocritical religiosity.

Also written in 1773, despite its heading giving 1770 as the date (this was added in the first publication of 1817), and also in *Knittelvers*, is *Satyros oder der vergötterte Waldteufel* (Satyros or The Wood-Devil Deified), another farce lampooning the figure of the *faux dévot*, which is derived directly from Hans Sachs's version of an Aesop fable of a hermit and a satyr. Many of Goethe's contemporaries have been cited as the model for the satyr who, taken in by a generous but naive hermit, quickly establishes a cult of nature-worship among the gullible populace; but it is likely that Goethe was satirizing not any individual, but rather certain cultural and intellectual fads – notably, the cult of a natural and asocial idyll, sentimentalized in the figure of the credulous hermit and vulgarized in the lecherous and amoral satyr who exploits such gullibility in order to set himself up as the high priest of a religion of unbridled lust. It may be that two sides of derived Rousseauism are being lampooned here: the unworldly withdrawal from urban corruption on the one hand, and the uncontrolled libidinism of false prophets of mystical pantheism or exalted *Empfindsamkeit* on the other. But at times the satyr also appears to come close to parodying Goethe's own *Sturm und Drang* 'Genius' figures, Prometheus or Faust; his hilarious version of the cosmogony seems stylistically to travesty Ganymed's pantheistic ecstasy ('Umfangend umfangen': Embracing, embraced) when he instructs his disciples in his gobbledegook version of creation, of how the 'Urding' (the Primal Thing) was born of the 'Unding' (the Non-Thing), how the elements coalesced 'Alldurchdringend, alldurchdrungen' (All-penetrating, all-penetrated) to form 'Das all und ein und ewig Ding, / Immer verändert, immer beständig!' (The eternal one and universal Thing, / Ever varied, ever constant). The satyr is finally exposed as, like Tartuffe, he attempts to ravish the wife of one of his disciples under the cover of religious ritual.

In these early uninhibited *Sturm und Drang* sketches Goethe is experimenting, often wildly, with forms, figures and ideas, just as he did more seriously in his contemporary hymns and odes; the *Concerto dramatico* (1773), for example, is an innovative exercise in the expressive musical effects of speech, a verbal orchestra of tempi and movements written to entertain his Darmstadt friends. While it was unpublished during Goethe's lifetime, indeed did not appear in print until 1869, it has some affinities with the later literary–musical experiments of the Romantic writers, with Tieck's *Die verkehrte Welt* (The Topsy-Turvy World) or E. T. A. Hoffmann's *Kreisleriana*. The prose farce *Götter, Helden und Wieland* (Gods, Heroes and Wieland, 1773, published 1774) is a mischievous persiflage of Wieland's sentimentalized recasting of classical myth, specifically in his *Singspiel* of 1773 entitled *Alceste*. The young Goethe of the *Sturm und Drang*, for whom the figures of classical mythology loomed and glittered like the 'colossal' characters of Shakespeare, perceived in Wieland's treatment a rococo enfeeblement of their poetic and symbolic stature. Wieland, summoned in his nightwear to Hades to answer for his literary travesties of Euripides, is abused in turn by the great tragedian (who is himself not entirely free of authorial vanity), by Mercury for the journalistic excesses of his magazine *Teutscher Merkur* (The German Mercury), by Admetus, Alcestis, and finally by Hercules, a rumbustious hooligan who objects violently to Wieland's portrayal of him as 'a moderately virtuous, well-formed man of average size'. To this Goethe has Wieland, whose *Singspiel* was composed and performed for the Weimar court at the instigation of Duchess Anna Amalia, protest with unwitting irony (for within two years Goethe himself was to join him, indeed to be warmly welcomed by him, in the Duchess's *Musenhof*) that he is after all writing for a public whose expectations are altogether different from that of Euripides.

All this exuberant irreverence contributed greatly to the public image of an immensely talented but iconoclastic young writer whose gregariousness and infectious charm did not always succeed in smoothing the feathers of those who suffered from his irrepressible lampoons. His relationship with Herder remained fraught, that with Wieland cool until the older man's civility and tolerance cemented a friendship of mutual (or almost mutual) respect; Lessing remained wary of his gifted young rival, and openly dismissive of the Frankfurt–Wetzlar–Darmstadt *Geniekult*. Goethe's almost adolescent delight in ripping away a facade of respectability or pomposity is shown at its most exuberant in the Rabelaisian fragment *Hanswursts Hochzeit* (Jack Pudding's Wedding), a ribald Germanic version of Harlequin's Wedding, written shortly after his novel *Werther* in 1774–5. The sketch concerns the desperate (and vain) efforts of Hanswurst's guardian Kilian Brustfleck to make his pupil socially presentable – a less radical, but equally futile, parallel to Gottsched's efforts to banish the shameless clown and his antics from the German stage. Hanswurst concedes that he must do his duty to feed his wedding guests, but insists on his own right to pleasure his Ursel in the hay; he agrees that a fervent sentimental discourse in the manner of Werther is appropriate to his wooing – but only as a preliminary to the real business of shafting her like the crack of doom. It is to be regretted that this unpublished fragment stopped short of the wedding-feast of Hanswurst, leaving only a hilariously ribald guest-list worthy of Rabelais himself.

CLAVIGO and *STELLA*; *DER TRIUMPH DER EMPFINDSAMKEIT*

Those satirical sketches from 1773–4 that were published at all appeared in relatively small circulation (though *Götter, Helden und Wieland*, published with some *schadenfreude* by J. M. R. Lenz, went through four editions in 1774). Goethe's first drama of any length since *Götz von Berlichingen* was the prose play *Clavigo*, written, it seems, in little more than a week in May 1774, shortly after his intensive work on *Werther*. After the colourful action and lively characterization of *Götz*, the reception of *Clavigo* was less than enthusiastic, for all its highly charged emotionalism and its occasional affinity with the earlier drama: the emotional lability of Clavigo echoes that of Weislingen, and both, as Goethe later claimed in *Dichtung und Wahrheit*, were literary confessions of his own guilt *vis-à-vis* Friederike Brion.[9] But the play's often overwrought rhetoric and its melodramatic elements seem inappropriate to the story of private family revenge in the domestic milieu of *bürgerliches Trauerspiel* (domestic tragedy). Goethe took the broad lines of his drama from an episode in the memoirs of the French playwright Beaumarchais which had appeared in Paris earlier that same year. Beaumarchais himself had sought and obtained satisfaction for the betrayal of his sister by the Spanish writer José Clavijo y Fajardo in 1764; but whereas Beaumarchais had in fact been content with a written confession that had ruined Clavijo's position at the Spanish court, Goethe adds the Iago-like figure of Carlos whose intrigues and manipulations of his weak friend result in Clavigo's dying at the hands of Beaumarchais beside, indeed over, the corpse of Marie Beaumarchais. What is remarkable in this is that Goethe was adapting – and radically changing – the story of two protagonists who were still alive, Clavijo and Beaumarchais; indeed the latter even saw, and disapproved of, Goethe's play in Augsburg in 1774.

Clavigo is a dramatic hero by default; purportedly a literary genius, he appears as an ambitious, possibly talented but deeply insecure writer who is anxious to consolidate his status at the Spanish court, even – as his unscrupulous *alter ego* Carlos urges – to rise to the heights of fame and position. If he is a *Sturm und Drang* figure, he has none of the titanism or charisma of Goethe's mythical or legendary figures, and all the emotional fickleness of Weislingen, the sentimental courtier who functioned as a dual foil to the larger figures who loomed above him: Götz and Adelheid. Clavigo vacillates between his ambitions and his purported love for Marie, between a glittering public reputation and banal domestic happiness, between the cynicism of his friend Carlos and the implacable demands of her brother Beaumarchais, with his own conscience in third place. He is neither a Faust nor an Egmont, nor even a Werther, and certainly not a writer of real stature like Tasso, but a second-rate Weislingen, elevated from Weislingen's secondary dramatic function and stripped of his romantic historical context, caught in the toils of a saga of family honour. Much (too much) of the literature on the play has been preoccupied with the identification of biographical models for the characters: Goethe and Friederike Brion, Goethe and his sister Cornelia, Goethe and his make-believe relationships with the Darmstadt Circle, Goethe and Charlotte Kestner. The marginal and undeveloped figure of Buenco, a shadowy prototype of Brackenburg in *Egmont*, has been associated with J. M. R. Lenz and his sad wooing of Friederike in Goethe's footsteps. But the figures of the play are too labile and ambivalent to support any sure biographical parallels; the work conveys the impression of a potentially interesting experiment in psychological conflicts, suggested in the sexual tensions between Clavigo, Carlos and Marie, but one written hurriedly and without total conviction on Goethe's part. The figure of Marie Beaumarchais is enigmatic and elusive – a pale prototype of the Princess Leonore d'Este in *Tasso*; and the dénouement over her corpse, derived, as Goethe revealed, from folk-ballad motifs, touches on sentimental melodrama. *Clavigo* is of interest largely by virtue of its unfavourable comparison with the truly experimental and innovative drama Goethe was planning and writing during the years 1770–5, in which he would combine personal emotional experience, historical and literary sources, a driven hero and his diabolical companion, a tragically betrayed heroine, *bürgerliches Trauerspiel* and folk-ballad motifs in an altogether more compelling and poetic way, namely, in the early fragmentary scenario of the *Urfaust*.

Stella, 'A Play for Lovers', was written in the first four months of 1775, coinciding precisely with the early stages of Goethe's love-affair with Lili Schönemann; and inevitably this awkwardly constructed drama has been read as a sublimated reflection of that fraught and problematic relationship, of Goethe's emotional ambivalence, of his fear of total personal commitment or domestic confinement, of his need to keep his existential and emotional options open. But the theme of an emotionally labile and irresolute man unable to choose between competing female attractions dates back well before 1775, and Fernando is another figure in the mould of Weislingen. To be sure, he is not torn between a saintly sister figure and a demonic temptress, but between the wife (and daughter) he has abandoned and the very model of an *Empfindsamkeit* heroine, Stella, whom he has also abandoned in her turn; Stella now devotes herself to public good works and to a private sentimental cult of death and moonlight as she communes with her stillborn child in the language of Klopstock and Ossian among the leafy bowers of her garden. When the four protagonists are brought together by means of an engineered coincidence, Fernando is utterly incapable of choosing between his clear-sighted wife and his vulnerable mistress; indeed, it is made unclear whether his earlier abandonment of Stella was prompted by a resolve to return to his legal wife and family, or by the diffuse and innately restless temperament of a self-indulgent egotist. The emotional impasse is resolved with startling abruptness by the eminently practical suggestion of his wife Cäcilie, who cites the legendary precedent of a crusading knight who had returned from the Holy Land with an exotic mistress whom his wife accepts as an equal partner in a *ménage à trois* – a solution which immediately appeals to the gratified Fernando as well as, rather less credibly, to the distraught Stella.

This contrived drama was published in 1776, and Goethe, with what might seem less than perfect tact, sent a copy of the first edition to Lili Schönemann, accompanied by the moving poem 'Im holden Tal, auf schneebedeckten Höhen'. Her reaction is not recorded, but the daring if clumsily integrated dénouement caused outrage in less tolerant quarters: for Pastor Johann Melchior Goeze of Hamburg it was yet another blasphemy from the pen of the author of *Werther*. It was perhaps in order to pre-empt such strictures that in 1806 Goethe rewrote the final passages for performance in Weimar: without any great effort at preparation or motivation, this version substitutes for Cäcilie's solution the simultaneous deaths, by poison and bullet respectively, of Stella and Fernando. Both versions were published in the collected works: the original *Schauspiel für Liebende* in 1787, the tragic version in 1816. While there is little evidence of an association in Goethe's mind, and for all the differences in scale, genre and subtlety, it is worth noting that the broad lines of *Stella* do anticipate in some respects the figures and situations of *Die Wahlverwandtschaften* (Elective Affinities): an emotionally volatile married man who leaves his practical and level-headed wife and a sensitively vulnerable younger woman to follow the fortunes of war, and who returns to an uneasy companionship with both, to an impossible situation that can only be resolved by the death of two of the protagonists.

In October 1776 Goethe wrote a brief one-act drama that also deals with an emotional triangle, but one with a rather more intriguing, and very possibly a more intimate personal dimension. In *Die Geschwister* (The Siblings) the merchant Wilhelm lives with Marianne as brother and sister, the children of the widowed Charlotte who had died when Marianne was an infant. Only Wilhelm knows that Marianne is not in fact his sister: Charlotte had been his benefactress, and would have become his wife but for her early death. Marianne, however, knows with emotional certainty that she is uniquely devoted to her brother. Only when a forceful suitor presses Marianne to marry him is Wilhelm compelled to reveal the truth of their relationship; but Marianne has already declared her inability to leave her 'brother' for a husband, and the play ends with an embrace that marks the transition (if such it is) from sibling affection and dependence to sexual love. Even so, Marianne's final words ('Wilhelm, it cannot be true') articulate the enigmatic ambivalence of the happy ending as she struggles to grasp the profound emotional shift she is experiencing. This playlet has been associated with Goethe's uneasily platonic relationship with Frau von Stein, hovering between a fulfilled brother–sister affection and a frustrated or sublimated sexual one; rather more likely is the suggestion that it is a discreet adumbration of Goethe's feelings for his sister Cornelia, unhappily married to J. G. Schlosser since 1773, who was to die shortly after the birth of a child in 1777. The fact that Goethe was careful not to distribute the play widely has led many to conclude that it is a testament of intimately personal feelings; and yet if it was a conscious expression of quasi-incestuous promptings, it seems odd that he should have sent it to Frankfurt to be read by his mother, his father and by Cornelia herself, or that he should have put on a performance in the Weimar amateur theatre with himself in the role of Wilhelm.

A more overt and moving tribute to his sister is generally seen in the prose monodrama he wrote some time during the year following Cornelia's death, *Proserpina*. This long monologue is the lament of Ceres' daughter Proserpine, abducted by Pluto and condemned to share his throne and his bed in Hades: the analogy to Cornelia's unhappy marriage, or at least to Goethe's perception of it, is there to be drawn. In the course of her desperate recital she picks and eats the pomegranate seeds that bind her to the underworld, and the monodrama ends with the triumphant chorus of the Fates who hail their reluctant queen. There is no reference to the subsequent remission of her fate, to her seasonal release from Hades for six months of each year – only a bitter tirade against the odious embraces of her detested husband. But once again, if this is such profoundly personal material for Goethe, his subsequent treatment of the monodrama is cavalier, not to say bizarre. For it was interpolated, in an only slightly revised form in free verse, into a literary satire he wrote in 1778–9, *Der Triumph der Empfindsamkeit* (The Triumph of Sensibility), a half-serious, half-whimsical comedy that lampoons the modish cult of sensibility, and which appears to mark Goethe's final reckoning with the literary tradition that had informed his sensational novel *Werther*, much of his early poetry, and dramas like *Stella*. To be sure, in both *Werther* and *Stella*, excessive emotional solipsism had been treated problematically, if not exactly satirically; here, it is the vicarious and synthetic dimension of fashionable sentimentality that is hilariously ridiculed.

Andrason, the 'humoristic' king of a fanciful country, is forced to consult an oracle on his domestic problems: his *précieuse* wife is besotted with a young prince, Oronaro, an exquisitely delicate *Empfindsamkeit* swain. Hypersensitive as he is, Oronaro's constitution is not robust enough to withstand the rigours of outdoor nature, where the discomforts of weather, midges and dew interfere with his rhapsodic communings; instead, he carries with him an elaborate theatrical scenery that provides him with a suitably ersatz landscape of leafy bowers, cascades, moonlight and nightingales, in which he can devote himself to his vicarious emotionalism and to the worship of his ideal woman – who takes the form of Mandandane, Andrason's wife. It turns out, however, that the Mandandane on whom he lavishes his affection is not the flesh and blood wife (though she believes herself to be his muse), but a dummy stuffed with sawdust – and with a small library of sentimental literature that includes Johann Martin Miller's *Siegwart*, a maudlin bestseller of 1776, Rousseau's *La Nouvelle Héloïse*, Goethe's *Werther*, and (in a manuscript version of the play) *Stella*. Forced to choose between the real Mandandane and her patchwork double, the Prince unerringly chooses the ersatz version, and all have learned their lesson – not least the emotionally overwrought Mandandane.

For all its elegance and lightness of touch, the play contains some robust parody and satire: not only on its central target, *Empfindsamkeit* and its weepy excesses, but also on Klopstock's poetry of death and moonlight, on fashionable literary forms, and on the craze for park landscapes in the English style. Under the supervision of an English Lord and his Lady, Hades (the setting for the monologue of Proserpine/Mandandane) has become 'nature improved': Pluto's gloomy realm has been remodelled with the help of Sisyphus and his fellow Titans into a new Elysian Fields, an eclectically picturesque park with every conceivable accessory – *temples d'amour*, pagodas, minarets, kiosks, grottos, bathhouses, *points de vue*. Even Cerberus's dog-kennel has been transformed into a Gothick chapel. There are also Weimar in-jokes; one of the Prince's army of servants is 'Directeur de la nature', the title affectionately given to the court cabinet-maker and stage manager Mieding, and there is some ironic play with theatrical illusion when Andrason (played by Goethe at the Weimar première in January 1778) remarks that the actors are in fact only playing themselves.

Biographical speculation has surrounded the play: it reflects the outrageous behaviour of J. M. R. Lenz at the Weimar court that so embarrassed Goethe, or the marital problems of Karl August and his wife, or – in the Proserpine monodrama – Goethe's grief at his sister's death. But if this monologue was in fact originally written as a threnody for Cornelia, it seems astonishing that Goethe should then harness it to the service of his satirical comedy, thus relativizing its pathos into bathetic farce; for in its context in *Der Triumph der Empfindsamkeit* the monodrama is declaimed by the histrionic Mandandane, and her final words execrating her 'husband' Pluto are overheard by her husband Andrason, who is confused and dismayed by what he takes to be a diatribe against himself. It is altogether more reassuring to see both the play itself and the interpolated mono-drama not as testimonies of personal relationships, but as the satirizing of fashionable literary pretensions in which Goethe is liberating himself, perhaps not without some degree of rueful or nostalgic self-parody, from his own involvement with the *Empfindsamkeit* tradition, and quite particularly from its more tiresome and extravagant enthusiasts.

Goethe's free version of Aristophanes' *The Birds* (*Die Vögel*, 1780) adapts the social and political satire of his model to the German literary scene – though there are also incidental political allusions to the emblematic eagles of Prussia and the Holy Roman Empire, to the labyrinthine customs and excise laws of the German territories, and to the enfeeblement of the 'gods', presumably a reference to the impotence of imperial institutions. Treufreund and Hoffegut, the German equivalents of Aristophanes' protagonists, appear in burlesque as Scapin and Pierrot, respectively the resourceful servant and the clown, purporting to be men of letters who are looking for an alternative country where their idle pursuits will be richly rewarded by a gullible public. The pompous and voracious Owl (a critic) and the vacuous Parrot (a reader) will have nothing to do with them; but Treufreund finds a more credulous following among the other birds, to whom he promises a Cloud Cuckoo Land of their own: under his leadership they will establish a kingdom of the air from which they will exploit both gods and humans. The satire is double-edged; not only critics and readers, not only the gullible feathered public, but also the two charlatan 'authors' are derided. For although Goethe never completed a planned second act, it might be inferred that Treufreund and Hoffegut were to satisfy their appetites in the new utopia by exploiting (or simply by eating) their subjects, who are explicitly compared by Scapin/Treufreund to the innocent savages who, as travellers have reported, can be most easily deceived by a show of honesty and friendship.

It seems that for all his and Schiller's later efforts to establish a republic of letters in Weimar and Germany in the 1790s, Goethe was at this stage around 1780, when both *Empfindsamkeit* and *Sturm und Drang* seemed to be losing impetus or were degenerating into derivative and modish literary crazes, profoundly sceptical towards any notions of a renewal of German literature in that direction. His 1781 sequel to the earlier Plundersweilern vanity fair, *Das Neueste von Plundersweilern* (The Latest from Plundersweilern), continues the *Knittelvers* lampoon in a parade of political and literary satire: the Landgrave of Hessen's shameful selling-off of his superfluous subjects to the English as cannon-fodder in the American colonies, literary coffee-houses, and the avid but undiscriminating reading public. Pirate publishers (at whose hands Goethe suffered much) ply their trade as whores, editors and critics beaver away in their literary sweatshops. An author (Goethe) stumbles along with the corpse of Werther on his back, a pistol in his hand; the private moonlight introspection of *Empfindsamkeit* has become a public fashion; the poets of the Göttingen *Hainbund* worship their ageing idol Klopstock. Wieland and his *Teutscher Merkur*, *Götz von Berlichingen* and the *Ritterdrama* craze it spawned are represented; the *Sturm und Drang* reaction against the neo-classical theatre has now become the noisy new orthodoxy, the theatrical unity of place has been banished for a stage that takes the spectator on a world tour from London to China – Hanswurst's revenge on Gottsched is complete. All these motley figures and fashions are treated with good-humoured and fairly decorous satire (it was narrated by Goethe as the commentary to a painting by Georg Melchior Kraus at a performance before the Dowager Duchess Anna Amalia and the court at Christmas 1781); but the satire still suggests that Goethe no longer identified himself with, and certainly had ceased to see himself at the leading edge of, the literary hurly-burly of the 1770s.

SINGSPIELE AND LIBRETTI

Notably in the 1770s and 1780s, Goethe devised a series of *Schauspiele mit Gesang* (Plays with Song) or, as he later termed them, *Singspiele*. This genre of light opera had been fostered in Germany by Christian Felix Weisse and by Wieland, whose *Alceste* had prompted Goethe's lampoon *Götter, Helden und Wieland* of 1773; by the end of the same year Goethe had begun his own first contribution to the genre, *Erwin und Elmire*, a less pretentious subject than Wieland's, and one which Goethe no doubt felt was more appropriate to the form. Goethe's *Singspiele* generally observe the convention whereby the songs are linked by spoken vernacular dialogue rather than the Italian tradition of recitative; but the revised versions of *Erwin und Elmire* and *Claudine von Villa Bella*, for example, which were done in Italy in 1787, are entirely versified in the manner of *opera buffa* or *opera seria*. While Goethe is not noted for any great expertise or critical perception in musical matters, he displayed a serious interest in and appreciation of the lyric theatre, and encouraged musicians personally known to him – Seckendorff, Kayser, Reichardt – to co-operate in his musical dramas; moreover, he acknowledged and respected the primacy of the composer in this collaboration. It was not simply the artistic achievement of Mozart's *The Abduction from the Seraglio* and his later *Magic Flute* that enhanced the status of this genre for Goethe; he had already long since developed a keen interest in the various forms of theatrical entertainment even before his quasi-official position as *maître des plaisirs* at the Weimar *Musenhof* impelled him to produce a long and imaginative series of operettas, masques, pageants, revues and *trionfi* for all kinds of occasions. While these pieces are of distinctly uneven literary substance or significance, they testify to Goethe's enduring interest in and commitment to live theatre, to music and dance, mime and spectacle, décor and costume, which was given ample opportunity for expression in the amateur *Liebhabertheater* of the early years in Weimar as well as later during his long spell as director of the re-established Weimar Court Theatre. His early apprenticeship to theatrical spectacle informs his more serious drama: music and choreography, mime and allegory are not unimportant elements in *Egmont* and, most notably, in the second part of *Faust*, where a whole range of theatrical spectacle, carnival and triumphal revue, operatic *Singspiel* and allegorical masque carries large sections of the work.

Erwin und Elmire, largely completed in 1774, is based on the romance of Edwin and Angelina in the eighth chapter of Goldsmith's *The Vicar of Wakefield*. Elmire, whose modish education has endowed her with the lofty emotional sensibilities of *Empfindsamkeit*, is at odds with the world because she is bereft of her lover Erwin, who has disappeared as a result of her treatment of him. She is also at odds with her mother Olimpia, whose practical but less than sympathetic advice offends Elmire's Rousseauistic fancies: 'I assure you, if the poet's vision of paradise could be found out there in the wide world, we would not have shut ourselves up in the towns.' An older friend of more delicate sympathies advises Elmire to consult a sage hermit about her troubles – a hermit who, since he is in fact the reclusive Erwin, is more than ready to renounce his isolated idyll for a domestic existence with Elmire on being assured of her love. Without the stark tragedy of *Werther* or the caustic satire of *Der Triumph der Empfindsamkeit*, this slight operetta treats the sentimental cult with kindly and ambivalent indulgence: the lovers, once they are reunited in more socially conventional bliss, will be able to revisit the solitary hut and vicariously enjoy in short spells the natural paradise of the poets' imaginings.

Claudine von Villa Bella (Claudina of Villa Bella, 1774–5) is a more substantial piece; though fundamentally unserious, it sets a respectable bourgeois family against the figure of the noble rebel Crugantino (Rugantino in the revised version of 1787, which was set to music by Reichardt in 1789). The motif of hostile brothers, here Pedro and Crugantino, is a theme common, indeed central to the rebellious ethos of the *Sturm und Drang*, reaching its most extreme expression in Schiller's *Die Räuber* of 1781. But Goethe's presentation of the conflict is very attenuated and entirely in keeping with the *Singspiel* tradition; Crugantino has none of the furiously destructive idealism of Karl Moor, Pedro none of the perverted malice of Franz, and the reconciliation of the estranged brothers requires no more than a noble renunciation on Crugantino's part, and Pedro's acknowledgement of his brother's delicate sensibilities. Crugantino's rebellion against domestic and social conformity is ultimately only a harmless sowing of wild oats, and it is quite out of character that he should threaten to use Claudine as a human shield in order to escape capture: the psychology of the rebel is explained by the cliché that even the most respectable person might have been a bit of a lad in his youth. Goethe clearly had high hopes for his operetta on the stage: he revised it radically in Italy in 1787, substituting blank verse recitative for the prose dialogue between the songs. But in spite of settings by Seidel, Reichardt, and even one by Schubert which has not survived, it had only a muted public success.

Lila (1776–7, revised substantially in 1778) has attracted more serious critical attention than most of Goethe's early libretti, if only because it has been reassessed in the light of modern theories of psychotherapy and psychodrama. Goethe described it to the director of the Berlin Opera, where it was performed twice in

1818, as 'a psychic cure in which madness is cured by madness'.[10] Lila suffers from a depressive melancholy (in the language of the day, 'hypochondria'), which has become dangerously acute because she has been informed in error of the death of her husband. He is in fact only wounded; but in her state of alienation she imagines that she has lost him because he is in thrall to ogres and demons. She is cured by the imaginative methods of the mysterious Dr Verazio, a magus-like figure who proposes that Lila should be allowed to act out her fantasies: her family and friends will co-operate in a choreographed masque that will enact her husband's liberation from the demonic forces. Through her own emotional or psychic identification with her role as liberator of her husband, Lila is able to accept the fact of his survival and is swiftly restored to her friends, her family and normality. While the device may in some ways anticipate modern psychothera-peutic practice, it should also be noted that it is based loosely on a literary source, a seventeenth-century drama by Jean de Rotrou, *L'Hypochondriaque*, and on the other hand that it was conceived in its early Weimar context as a didactic occasional piece, intended as a tactful exercise in personal counselling for Duke Karl August and his wife the Duchess Luise. The early years of their marriage, which coincided with Goethe's own first years in Weimar, were not untroubled; her new situation and surroundings, her husband's robust appetites and lifestyle, and her own depressive and introverted temperament caused ten-sions of which Goethe, as the intimate confidant of the Duke, was well aware, and his devotion to the enigmatic Duchess impelled him to intervene – with discretion, to be sure, but with some boldness, given his own less than secure position at the court.

Jery und Bätely (1779) is a bucolic playlet of no great distinction or interest, involving the tricking of a self-willed peasant girl into matrimony; but it seems to have been close to Goethe's heart, if only because it recalled for him the land-scapes and people encountered during his journey to Switzerland with Karl August in the last quarter of 1779. *Die Fischerin* (The Fishergirl, 1782) was written specifically for performance in the park at Tiefurt, the summer residence of the Dowager Duchess Anna Amalia; the whole production was evidently centred on the spectacle created by torchlight as the fishing community searches for the supposedly drowned fishergirl Dortchen. But this slight operetta is also distin-guished by the folk songs scattered through the text: it opens with Goethe's own recasting of Herder's translation from the Danish, 'Erlkönig', and includes several other songs adapted from Herder's *Volkslieder* volumes – another Danish ballad of a water-demon, an English riddle ballad, Wendish and Lithuanian folk songs.

In 1784, theatrical activity in Weimar was extended well beyond that of the amateur enthusiasms of the *Liebhabertheater* by the establishment of the repertory company of Giuseppe Bellomo, who staged a more sophisticated programme of entertainment in a modest but purpose-built theatre. Bellomo's productions fa-voured the Italianate *opera buffa* as well as recent German drama, and in 1785 Goethe wrote *Scherz, List und Rache* (Jest, Guile and Revenge) as a contribution to the repertoire, a libretto deriving from the *commedia dell'arte* and from Goldoni in which Scapin and Scapine cheat the gullible and miserly Doctor out of his precious ducats. Goethe went to immense trouble to accommodate his libretto to

Kayser's music and to coax a completed setting from the dilatory composer in Zürich; but for all his efforts, the work was not performed in Weimar – though later composers, including E. T. A. Hoffmann, were to write music to it. In any case, both this and a second libretto, *Die ungleichen Hausgenossen* (The Ill-matched Household), begun in 1785 but never completed, were soon overshadowed by the performance of Mozart's *Seraglio* in December 1785. Goethe, like so many others, soon overcame his initial resistance to the exotic extravagance of the *Seraglio*, visited three of the five performances, and remained forever impressed by the achievement of the *Singspiel* genre in the work, which seemed to dwarf his own efforts and those of others.

Mozart continued to fascinate Goethe; long after he had given up writing *Singspiele*, he instigated as director of the Court Theatre productions of *Don Giovanni* in 1792, in the following year *Le Nozze di Figaro* and in 1794 *Die Zauberflöte*. It was *The Magic Flute*, with its heady mixture of pantomime, sentiment, cosmic symbolism and Enlightenment ethics that captivated Goethe's interest to the extent that in 1795–6 he began work on a sequel to Schikaneder's libretto, *Der Zauberflöte zweiter Teil* (The Magic Flute, Part Two). Work on this project was protracted, but never more than sporadic, and it was never completed; it remains a matter for speculation whether this was because Schikaneder himself in 1798 wrote a sequel of his own, because Goethe believed he would not find a second Mozart to write the music, or because he was unable to create to his own satisfaction a coherent unity out of the bizarre thematic and symbolic *mischmasch* inherited from the inspired daftness of Schikaneder's original text. It is, however, noteworthy that Goethe was to develop at least one motif from his *Zauberflöte* fragment, as well as using the *Singspiel* form itself, in the operatic final scene of the third act of *Faust* Part Two: Euphorion is unmistakably the direct poetic descendant of the spirit child of Tamino and Pamina.

Goethe's sequel to the Mozart/Schikaneder opera concerns the plot by the forces of darkness, the Queen of the Night and Monostatos, to seize and perhaps also to destroy the child of Tamino and Pamina, who now rule as king and queen in the Realm of the Sun; the original Masonic brotherhood appears to have adopted a monarchic form, while also retaining its hieratic and didactic functions. Sarastro has abdicated his leadership in order to spend a year's pilgrimage in quest of the wisdom to be learned from the empathetic study of nature and of deprived humanity. Papageno and Papagena, still childless, are miraculously provided with huge eggs from which fledged children are hatched. The chthonic, Hecate-like powers of the Queen of the Night (who appears in an even more spectacular staging than in Mozart, accompanied by aurorae, comets, St Elmo's Fire and ball lightning) have enabled her creatures to seal the child into a golden casket, but not to remove it from the Kingdom of the Sun; Tamino and Pamina must once more submit to the ordeal by fire and water to release their son from his underground vault. The boy rises from his casket and escapes the clutches of his guards by transcending his confinement as a spirit being or *Genius*.

The fragmentary nature of the libretto, which contains elaborate directions for scenery, performance and musical effects, allows little certainty about the conclusion or the interpretation of the text. Goethe has taken over most of the main figures, the settings and the symbolism of the original *Zauberflöte*, but it remains unclear whether he intended some reconciliation between the forces of night and those of the sun, between superstition and reason, irrationalism and enlighten- ment (as one might have expected of him, and which would have restored the primal cosmic harmony already shattered in the Mozart/Schikaneder version) – or whether the baleful magic of the Queen of the Night was to be finally routed. It is also unclear just what function the spirit-child was to perform – whether he was to perish like Euphorion, or to be the agent of a restored order. The work remains an intriguing but inconclusive fragment; in its rudimentary form, and without a musical dimension, it is less than satisfactory, and it is largely the speculative links with the Euphorion episode of *Faust* Part Two (which, as Goethe wistfully remarked,[11] ideally required the musical genius of Mozart) that engage the critical attention. Nevertheless, Goethe evidently took his text seriously enough to try to negotiate its sale to the Vienna Court Theatre, and A. W. Iffland was interested in procuring it for Berlin; but Schikaneder's own sequel stood in the way. Perhaps the most sage judgement of all was that of the Viennese composer Wranitzky, who wrote tactfully to Goethe that the project must surely be ap- proached with extreme caution, given the respective artistic gulf between Schikaneder's and Goethe's literary talents on the one hand, and between his, Wranitzky's, and Mozart's musical talents on the other.[12]

Goethe was to sketch out two further operatic libretti, neither of which was completed in spite of the interest shown by Iffland and by the Berlin kapellmeister Bernhard Anselm Weber. *Der Löwenstuhl* (The Lion Throne), conceived as a play in 1803 and as an opera in 1813, is a dramatization of the theme of the ballad 'Herein, o du Guter! du Alter, herein!' The drama is notable for its use of verse forms that were later to be used in *Faust* Part Two: classicizing trimeter and 'Spanish' four-beat trochaics (Goethe had previously used iambic trimeter for the prototype version of Helen's first scene in Sparta in or around 1800). *Feradeddin und Kolaila* (1815–16) is a fairytale romance set in Persia that was prompted by Goethe's reading of oriental sources during the time of the *West-östliche Divan*. Neither libretto progressed much beyond the most sketchy fragments.

It is difficult to reach a proper critical judgement of Goethe's achievement in the field of musical drama. His *Singspiele* are rarely performed, and as he himself was well aware, a libretto on the printed page is a lifeless text, far more so than a dramatic text; moreover, his libretti were mostly scored by or written for less than distinguished composers. To be sure, it is a common belief that it is not the most outstanding texts, in poetic or dramatic terms, that make the most successful *Lieder, Singspiele* or operas – even if settings like Schubert's 'Erlkönig' and 'Gretchen am Spinnrade', Zelter's 'Der König in Thule' or Hugo Wolf's 'Kennst du das Land' challenge that assumption. Goethe's *Singspiele* belong consciously and by definition to light opera – even his *Zauberflöte* sequel, for all its Masonic solemnity and portentous symbolism. They are for the most part his early contri- butions to the cultural activities and entertainments of the Weimar *Musenhof*, and an aspect of his apprenticeship to live theatre, to all areas of the performing arts: production, recruitment, scenery, lighting, costume, acting techniques, finance, choreography and music, voice production and the delivery of verse. His activity

Plate 1 The Goethe family house in Frankfurt by F. W. Delkeskamp, 1824.

Plate 2 Goethe by G. F. Schmoll, 1774.

Plate 3 Goethe's sister Cornelia. Based on a drawing by her brother, c.1770.

Plate 4 Frankfurt from the east by J. S. Mund, *c*.1770.

Plate 5 The Parsonage at Sesenheim. Drawing by Goethe, 1770/1.

Plate 8 Charlotte Kestner, née Buff
by J. H. Schröder, 1782.

Plate 6 Goethe by G. O. May, *c.*1779.

Plate 7 Anna Elisabeth ('Lili') von
Türckheim, née Schönemann, *c.*1780.

Plate 9   Weimar from the east by G. M. Kraus, *c.*1800.

Plate 10   Goethe's *Gartenhaus* in the Ilm Park by G. M. Kraus, 1806.

Plate 12 Duke Karl August of Sachsen-Weimar.

Plate 11 Silhouette of Goethe, *c.*1782.

Plate 13 Goethe's house on the *Frauenplan* in Weimar by E. Lobe.

Plate 14 The Recruiting Centre. Drawing by Goethe, 1779.

Plate 15 Moon rising above a river (almost certainly the Ilm). Drawing by Goethe, *c*.1777.

Plate 16   Charlotte von Stein by G. Wolf. Believed to be based on a self-portrait.

Plate 17   Performance in Weimar of the prose version of *Iphigenie auf Tauris* (Act III, scene 1): Corona Schröter as Iphigenie, Goethe as Orest. By G. M. Kraus, 1779.

Plate 18 Goethe in his Roman lodgings. Drawing by J. H. W. Tischbein, 1787.

Plate 19 Goethe by Angelika Kauffmann, Rome, 1787.

Plate 20   The Temples at Paestum by C. H. Kniep, 1787.

Plate 21   Goethe rescues a horse by J. H. W. Tischbein, Italy, *c.*1787.
The incident is not recorded.

Plate 23   Christiane Vulpius. Drawing by Goethe, 1788.

Plate 22   Goethe by J. H. Lips, 1791.

Plate 24 'Passans cette terre est libre': a 'Tree of Liberty' in eastern France. Watercolour by Goethe, 1792.

Plate 25 The hot spring at Karlsbad by E. Gurk, early nineteenth century.

Plate 27 Manuscript of 'Ginkgo biloba' in Goethe's hand, with two pressed ginkgo leaves. Believed to have been sent to Marianne von Willemer. Dated 15 September 1815.

Plate 26 Marianne Jung, later von Willemer, by J. J. de Lose, 1809.

Plate 28   Christiane von Goethe, Goethe and August von Goethe
by K. J. Raabe, 1811.

Plate 29   Sketch by Goethe of cloud formations after Luke Howard, *c.*1821: Cirrhus
(*sic*), Cumulo Cirrhus, Cumulus, Strato Cumulus, Stratus.

Plate 30   Ulrike von Levetzow, *c.*1821.

Plate 31   Marienbad in the 1820s by Ludwig Graf Buquoy.

Plate 33 Goethe in his study with his secretary J. A. F. John,
by J. Schmeller, 1831.

CARL·AUGUST·BEI·GOETHE.

Plate 32 Karl August and Goethe in the house on the *Frauenplan*, by K.
A. Schwerdgeburth. An imaginative reconstruction, 1860.

Plate 34   Goethe by L. Sebbers, 1826.

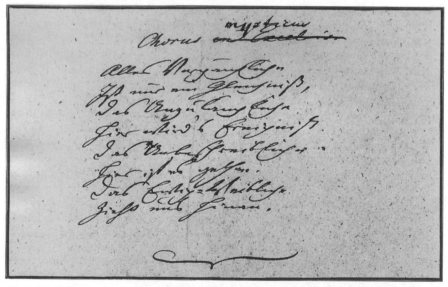

Plate 35   Manuscript in Goethe's hand of the final lines of *Faust* (Chorus mysticus, originally: Chorus in Excelsis).

as a leading light of the amateur *Liebhabertheater* and later as director of the Court Theatre demanded an intensive involvement in the theatre, in its artistic, practical and political dimensions; and while his directorship may have been that of a not always benevolent despotism, he brought an enormous range of culture and entertainment to Weimar, including much for which he had little personal enthusiasm or respect. The *Singspiele*, whatever their intrinsic literary quality or interest, are yet another dimension of Goethe's vast range of activities.

The Early Weimar Dramas: *Egmont*

It is customary to bracket the three major plays *Egmont*, *Iphigenie auf Tauris* and *Torquato Tasso* under the loose rubric of 'Early Weimar Dramas', because they were begun during his first decade in Weimar, or even as his early 'classical' dramas – whether in the sense that they are exemplary, or because they show distinct classicizing tendencies in form or subject-matter. This is not inappropriate in the case of *Iphigenie* or *Tasso*: they are written in unrhymed iambic pentameter, which is by no means a neo-classical metre, but an English form which nevertheless quickly displaced the alexandrine as the standard verse of the classical German theatre. They are neo-classical, Racinian in construction; and they treat respectively Greek and Renaissance subjects – for all that each play is also unmistakably the product of late eighteenth-century values, whether ethical or literary. *Egmont*, in conception the earliest of the three, is the least obviously classicizing play. It is perhaps trite to say that it bridges *Götz von Berlichingen* and the neo-classical dramas, or that it stands mid-way between Goethe's *Sturm und Drang* historicism and Weimar Classicism. But its conception does lie very close to the revised version of *Götz*; its inspiration is still distinctly Shakespearean; it is set in the same sixteenth-century historical context as *Götz* and the *Urfaust*, if a little later; and its hero is a charismatic personality, a man whose attraction for Goethe lay, as he put it, in his 'human and chivalrous stature'.[13] Its historicism, while occasionally freely handled, is less fanciful than that of *Götz*, but it still retains a powerful sense of local and cultural colour as the chronicle of a momentous period of change, if not in the history of Germany itself, then certainly in that of the Holy Roman Empire, indeed of modern Europe.

The classicizing features of *Egmont*, if indeed there are any, are less easily defined; it may be that they are more discerned than discernible, in the sense that its final completion was protracted into Goethe's 'classical' phase. For while its conception lies in the years before 1775, when he discussed the subject enthusiastically with his father in Frankfurt, while he made efforts to pick up the threads of writing in 1778 and again in 1781, it was not until his second period in Rome in 1787 that the play was finally completed, to appear the following year in the fifth volume of Goethe's *Schriften* published by Göschen. It is often thought that the tendency of the prose monologues to break into (fairly) regular passages of iambic pentameter indicates a classicizing element; but apart from the objection that there is nothing intrinsically classical about Shakespearean blank verse, it should be remembered that Goethe was at the time, even before his Italian journey, beginning to write in a rhythmic prose that could easily be modified into blank verse – the first version of *Iphigenie* was in such a style. Furthermore, it is uncertain whether Goethe thought of the rhythmic tendencies of some passages in *Egmont* as a classicizing feature, or whether he introduced iambic rhythms in order to dignify or enhance the pathos of certain situations. *Egmont* might be said to represent a more 'classical' conception than, say, *Götz* in the sense that the perspectives of the play are more balanced, less passionately partisan or romantic than those of *Götz*: in the figure of Alba, Goethe has given Egmont a more worthy and serious antagonist, and has given more balance to the political debate in the play, than he had in his earlier historical drama. Alba, for all that his political philosophy is based on a gloomy fanaticism, for all his repellent personality and the ruthlessness of his *realpolitik*, is a figure of altogether more commanding stature than the Bishop of Bamberg, less a figure of demonic wickedness than Adelheid von Walldorf, and not remotely comparable with Adelbert von Weislingen. If the political authority informing the earlier play was the genial, romantic but ineffectual figure of Maximilian, the reactive 'last of the knights', the authority brooding unseen over *Egmont* is the joyless, monastic and proactive figure of Philip II.

The stage in the struggle for the independence of the Netherlands that occupies Goethe is the very early stage at which the established provincial governors or *Stadhouder* still strove to reach a compromise with their Spanish masters. Egmont, who had fought the Spanish cause at St Quentin and Gravelines with conspicuous courage and loyalty, is himself as committed to the preservation of the colonial status quo as Philip or Alba; their radical divergence is on the question of the most effective means to do so. Anything but a revolutionary in this respect, Egmont is as conservative as Götz; the ideals of both lie in the past, at least a generation back, and it is the turbulently proactive reforms of Spain that Egmont resists, as Götz had resisted the centrifugal territorial ambitions of the particularist princes. Indeed, Egmont sees with a clarity of vision sanctioned by subsequent history that the means employed by the Spanish to subdue the provinces are precisely those that will most surely cost them their sovereignty: excessive taxation, the suppression of traditional rights and privileges, and the repression of the freedom of political and religious expression. It is odd but significant that the Reformation, which had been only implicit in *Götz von Berlichingen*, is also by no means the central issue in *Egmont*. We hear of the Calvinist iconoclasts, of the populist religious movement that alarms the Spanish authorities and supplies a pretext for their fanatical repression; we hear of the packing of Church positions with Spanish bishops. But Egmont is no Posa; he might treat the Protestant preachers intercepted by his men leniently, but he has no more sympathy for their new creed than he has for the rabble-rousing demagogery of Vansen – who, for all that he is presented unsympathetically by Goethe, represents the aspirations of the Netherlanders for independence more truly than Egmont himself. Indeed, Egmont's words to the citizens on freedom as he tells them to go peacefully about their business are disturbingly close in purport, though not in spirit, to Alba's scathing remarks to Egmont in the fourth act: 'What freedom do they want? What is the freedom of the freest? – To do what is right!'

Like the historical Egmont (and Hoorn, totally obliterated from this play), Goethe's Egmont is an adherent of the true faith – though this dimension is not unduly stressed; he is a Knight of the Golden Fleece – even if this honour was bestowed not by Philip, but by his predecessor Charles V; he was trained at the Spanish court and is, we may assume, as fluent in Spanish as he is in his native tongue. Unlike the historical Egmont, he is young, single and careless of his personal safety. It was a telling, if not wholly imaginative or sympathetic point made by Schiller in his acerbic review of the play that the historical Egmont, a man with heavy and costly family obligations, could not flee the country as William of Orange had been able to do without bringing himself and his family to ruin; instead, he was tragically forced to become one of the exemplary victims of Spanish pacification tactics. Goethe's hero, as Schiller argues with relentless if sanctimonious logic, has no such personal obligations; on the contrary, he has all the more obligation in his freedom of action to serve the cause of his people by adopting Oranien's politically more effective tactics – instead of which he prefers to sacrifice those obligations for the sake of his own lifestyle, and in particular for a few hours with his mistress.[14]

Schiller's strictures on the play, for all that he was generous in his praise of its theatrical colour and structure, and in particular his strictures on Goethe's presentation of his hero, have been echoed by the majority of critics;[15] only a few lone voices have questioned the orthodox judgement of Egmont as a brave, charismatic and vibrant personality, but as a politically and tactically naive, even fecklessly irresponsible leader of his people who rushes blindly and perversely towards his almost self-willed destruction. And indeed, the arguments are compelling. Egmont refuses to be warned – by the Regent Margaret of Parma, by his secretary, by Oranien; he falls headlong into Alba's trap, blindly trusting in his star and in his Order of the Golden Fleece, even in his sincerely professed loyalty to Philip, to protect him from Alba's ruthless manoeuvrings. Does he not compare himself, in two notorious extended metaphors, to a sleepwalker who is miraculously preserved from danger   provided he is not woken and alerted to that danger? Or to Phaeton, the charioteer of the 'sun-steeds of time', who can exercise only minimal control over his runaway team as they bear him inexorably to his fate? Does he not adopt the very worst possible tactics in his interview with Alba, antagonizing his adversary and simply presenting him with cast-iron evidence of his treasonable opinions? And is it not an act of fatuous self-delusion that, having thus uselessly thrown away his life and abdicated his political responsibilities, he should then proclaim that he is dying in the cause of the freedom of his people, for which he had lived and fought, and to which he now sacrifices himself?

There have been some attempts to answer Schiller's formidable case against Egmont's attitudes and behaviour, and the many subsequent elaborations of that case.[16] Even the apparent evidence in his two metaphors, on the face of it unequivocal proof of an almost solipsistic fatalism, has been subtly – perhaps oversubtly – reinterpreted. For the sleepwalker is, by popular belief at least, safe in his unawareness of peril; the charioteer of the steeds of time does retain a measure of control over the course of his destiny, even if it is indisputable that he cannot retard the onrush of time itself. Does not Egmont shy from Oranien's drastic measures, seeing in such a bellicose gesture of defiance a sure way to provoke Spain and unleash all the horrors of insurrection and civil war? Does he not eloquently and passionately, with total disregard of personal safety, argue a cogent and prudent case for the governance of his people in the very heart of the spider's web – an argument of which the crucial premise is not the political independence of the provinces, but precisely the perpetuation of Spanish authority, albeit in a more humane and tolerant form?

Some of these justifications for Egmont's behaviour have the whiff of special pleading, and do little to shake the 'Schillerian' case against him. But over and above the self-evidently more attractive and charismatic aspects of Egmont's character or conduct, as opposed to the equally self-evident cynicism and fanaticism of Alba's, it is still possible to construct a case for Egmont the politician – and not simply the somewhat patronizing case that he is a stout-hearted, if ultimately naive and inept, champion of ethnic or native rights. For all his conservatism, Egmont sees more clearly and with infinitely more foresight than Alba the means to ensure, not just the relative freedom and privileges of his people (values which, as Alba caustically and correctly remarks, the native governors have shared very unequally with their 'brothers'), but also, most crucially, the continuation of Spanish rule.

In order to underscore this point, Goethe has introduced into the play the unhistorical figure of Machiavell, secretary to the Regent Margarete herself (though the name may well be a bow to the political philosopher and author of *Il Principe*). For there is virtually nothing to choose between the enlightened arguments put forward by Machiavell in Act One (to which, it appears, Duke Karl August of Weimar took some exception) and those of Egmont in the play as a whole. To be sure, Machiavell's case, even to the relatively benevolent Margarete, verges on treason and, what is worse, on heresy; but Margarete, for all her enlightened instincts, is an insecure and irresolute regent, and a slave to her brother Philip and to the religious imperatives of Spain. Of course Egmont is wrong to dismiss Oranien's urgent warnings concerning his personal safety at the end of Act Two; but he is indisputably right in foreseeing the consequences of following Oranien's tactics of defiance. Most crucially of all, Egmont is indeed mistaken in his refusal to believe that Alba will take such a drastic and inflammatory measure as to execute the *Stadhouder*. But this incredulity is based not on naive trust, not so much on an illusory belief that his status, his charisma, his loyalty or the privilege of the Golden Fleece will protect him, not on a refusal to believe that Alba will commit an outrageous act of political murder; it is based rather on his inability to believe that Alba would commit such a political, indeed such a historical blunder. For if there ever were a sure way to provoke the uprising that would lead ineluctably to Spain's loss of the provinces, it would be just that: to pursue these tactics of absolute oppression to their absolute conclusion. That is what Alba did, and subsequent history showed Egmont's vision to be the more far-sighted.

It may be arguable, in historical terms, how far, how effectively or how directly the deaths of Egmont and Hoorn contributed to the struggle for Dutch independence; what is indisputable is that Goethe linked the death of his literary hero to that political development. The final allegorical tableau of the play, dismissed by Schiller as 'a somersault into the world of opera',[17] provides the crucial historical perspective: five years after Egmont's death in 1568, Alba had withdrawn from the Netherlands, and his successors were unable to resist the forces mustered by William the Silent (Oranien), who became Regent of the Netherlands. Eleven years after Egmont's death, William was reluctantly forced to accept the partition by which the northern provinces became effectively independent, and from these eventually emerged the modern nation state of Holland. By historical happenstance, just as Goethe was completing his play in 1787–9, the Austrian authorities to whom the Spanish provinces had meanwhile passed were introducing measures to curtail the traditional privileges and constitution of the southern provinces – measures that would ultimately lead to the struggle of those provinces for independence and, in 1830, to the emergence of the state of Belgium. The political lessons of *Egmont* have been repeated time and again during the decolonization processes of the present century – which is not to argue that Goethe was historically or politically prescient, nor that his Egmont is a consummate political strategist, but only that Goethe, while he may have over-simplified and over-personalized historical cause and effect, does not present a politically completely inept or an intransigently solipsistic hero.

Like so many of Goethe's dramas, *Egmont* displays an unconventionality, even a looseness of dramatic structure and development: the untidy retarding devices of the fifth act, where the rehabilitation of Egmont's morale is effected by the admiration and encouragement of Alba's son Ferdinand, or the set-piece dialogues between Margarete and Machiavell, Egmont and his secretary, Egmont and Oranien, Egmont and Alba, in which the debate proceeds antithetically but not dialectically, each voice stubbornly reiterating its own position against the others. And yet there is drama and theatre enough in the play. The confrontation between Egmont and Alba has a double dramatic irony: Egmont is doomed from the start, and his arguments only serve to confirm Alba's pretext to destroy him. The three distinct milieux – the political stage, the civic scene and the domestic sphere – are juxtaposed and linked by the explicit or implicit presence of the hero as the action moves between the three levels. The crowd scenes, no doubt derived in part from *Julius Caesar*, are, as Schiller conceded, a masterly presentation of a cross-section of citizenry in vivid genre scenes; and the retarded entry of Egmont in Act Two after the careful expositions of the first act, when he spectacularly quells the public unrest, is a *coup de théâtre*, supported by detailed stage-directions, that shows a mastery of dramatic timing.

In order to enhance the image of Egmont, his *attrativa*, his youthful sexuality and his informal closeness to his subjects, Goethe has created the charming figure of Klärchen, who has some of the characteristics and social origins of the *Urfaust* heroine Gretchen. But there are fundamental differences between the two women: Klärchen has none of the troubled conscience of Gretchen, she is less a victim of her own *bürgerlich* code. Klärchen is frankly and contentedly in a morganatic relationship with Egmont; she is openly his mistress, and accepts that situation with cheerful fatalism, even if it jeopardizes her chances of a respectable match with Brackenburg, who is a more developed version of the hapless Buenco in *Clavigo*. If it seems offensive (as it did to certain ladies in Weimar) that Egmont in prison, knowing that he and those associated with him are to be destroyed, cheerfully bequeaths to Ferdinand not only his horse but also his mistress, this is not so much a casual gesture of laddishness, but rather a frank and pragmatic assessment of their relationship and a recognition that she, too, will need a protector in the days to come. This gesture is, in the circumstances of the dramatic action, an ironically futile one, for Klärchen has already died by her own hand; but it does not demean the hero.

The theatricality and spectacle of *Egmont* distinguish it sharply from Goethe's two other early Weimar dramas, which use altogether more restrained gestic devices and stage effects. Klärchen's songs, Egmont's appearance in the regalia of the Golden Fleece, the colour and bustle of the earlier crowd scenes that give way to the sombre mood of the streets after Alba's arrival, the closing of Alba's trap and the dramatic arrest of Egmont at the end of Act Four, the guttering of the lamp as Klärchen dies, the music designated here and elsewhere – all this gives the play a compelling visual, aural and mimetic dimension. And yet many since Schiller have baulked at the spectacular final allegory in which Klärchen appears to descend as *dea ex machina* in an extravagant tableau of conciliation.

The first point to note here is that this tableau does not represent a very convincing example of Goethe's notorious 'avoidance of tragedy',[18] nor is Klärchen a *dea ex machina* at all. This is not a *salto mortale* into the world of eighteenth-century opera, where gods descend on clouds to impose a happy ending; Klärchen's appearance is a dream of Egmont's, not a divine or supernatural intervention into the dramatic action, and it does nothing to avert Egmont's execution. Moreover, this allegory is an important and integral part of the historical perspective of Goethe's drama of revolt in the Netherlands, both for Egmont and for the theatre audience. Egmont is convinced that his death is a significant step towards the freedom of his people, and his dream is a dramatic projection of that conviction: the emblems indicated to him by Klärchen are those of unity (the bundled arrows) and of freedom (the hat and staff). *Egmont* cannot be treated in classical or neo-classical terms as a drama whose effects are wholly contained within the unity of time. We are on the contrary invited, indeed compelled by the dramatist to look beyond the ending of the play, to consider the dialectical processes of history in which, as Goethe put it in 1813 as he looked back on his early historical drama in his autobiography,[19] that which is lovable perishes and that which is hateful triumphs; but from this emerges a third state that corresponds to the general will.

IPHIGENIE AUF TAURIS (IPHIGENIA ON TAURIS)

Goethe evidently conceived the plan of a drama on the subject of Iphigenia very soon after his arrival in Weimar, though it was not until 1779 that he began to work seriously on the first prose version of the play. The circumstances under which this first draft was written in February and March that year were incongruous, to say the least; he was frantically involved in his multifarious administrative duties for the Duchy of Weimar, and was discovered working on the manuscript of his lofty and humanitarian reworking of the ancient Tantalid story in the chaos of a military recruitment office. As he wrote to Frau von Stein on the jarring cultural dissonances between present economic realities and the remote classical *éloignement* of his subject: the King of Tauris must speak as if the stocking-weavers of Apolda were not starving.[20] This early version, in a rhythmic prose that is already more than half-way to blank verse, was performed with music by the Weimar amateur theatre in April 1779; a painting by Georg Melchior Kraus shows Corona Schröter in the title role with Goethe as Orest in the recognition scene. But it was only in Italy that the verse version was completed, principally during Goethe's first stay in Rome in November and December 1786.

There had been many neo-classical versions of the Iphigenia story, whether of the events in Aulis or Tauris, derived from Sophocles or Euripides. Goethe chose the Tauris episode, though he subsequently also planned a sequel to it, in which Iphigenia was to return to Delphi in fulfilment of the oracle's conditions for the expiation of the Tantalid curse.[21] Here, the disturbed Electra is waiting for her brother and Pylades to return with the statue of Diana; but she is misinformed by a Greek that he had seen the two led off to be sacrificed by the priestess of Diana on Tauris just before he himself had managed to escape. Iphigenia enters without her companions (and, of course, without the statue) and is identified to Electra by the Greek. Electra is about to strike down her own sister with the very axe with which Orestes had murdered Clytaemnestra (and Aegisthus murdered Agamemnon), when the appearance of Orestes and Pylades averts yet another bloody manifestation of the Tantalid curse. It is clear from this, and indeed from *Iphigenie auf Tauris* itself, that for all his reworking of the original story, for all that he averts impending catastrophe in both these versions, for all that his Greeks, and even his Taurians, might at times appear to be thinly disguised paragons of enlightened eighteenth-century ethical values – that Goethe was still mindful of the potentially barbarous behaviour of both men and their gods, of the savagery that is only precariously held in check by the restraints of civilization.

To be sure, Goethe does not share Kleist's bleak metaphysical vision of the fragility of existence, of the appalling tragic results of coincidence or human misunderstanding; but neither is it entirely true to suggest that he simply glossed over the arbitrary and barbaric substratum of human behaviour by elevating his Greeks to an unreal or Platonic ideality, or that he simply averted tragedy by recourse to a Panglossian optimism masquerading as a humanitarian ethic. It is true that he transformed the Greeks of his classical sources from cunning and resourceful schemers, pitting their intelligence against the slow-witted barbarians of Tauris, into figures of profound integrity and trust in the fundamental goodness of gods and of humankind – or at least that he did this in the figure of Iphigenie and, more strikingly, also in the figure of the civilized 'barbarian' Thoas. It is true that he resists the literal intervention of gods and goddesses on the stage to solve the tragic impasse in the manner of his Greek sources, and substitutes instead an intellectual *deus ex machina*, a play on words whereby the cured Orest is able to suggest an inspired reinterpretation of the ambiguities of the oracle. But for all that, this is no morally sanitized version of the Tantalid legend that Goethe presents. The vivid recital by Iphigenie in the third scene of Act One of the murderous bloodletting of her ancestors; the presence of her crazed and paranoid brother, who is hunted by the demons of matricidal guilt; the situation where, it seems, she herself must perform the final (or possibly not even the final) savage working-out of the Tantalid curse as she is ordered to sacrifice the brother just restored to her so providentially; the intolerable pressures on her as her adaman-tine faith in divine benevolence cracks, and from her dormant memory an atavis-tic horror-vision of implacable and vengeful deities wells up to full consciousness in the 'Parzenlied' (Song of the Fates) – these knife-edge crises, eventually resolved though they may be, indicate that this is not a play in which 'real evil', as at least one critic has put it, has no part.[22] And if Goethe is to be charged here with the avoidance of tragedy, this is no more and no less than he found in his sources, where protective deities looked after their own and intervened directly into hu-man affairs.

It is also frequently asserted that in modernizing his Greek sources, by demon-strating that the gods are little more than projections of the ethical values of German Idealism, by substituting human integrity for divine intervention, Goethe has demythologized his story and constructed an entirely anthropocentric moral and metaphysical system. This is surely also to over-simplify the case. Iphigenie's apparently indestructible faith in divine benevolence, her conviction that the will of the gods is consonant with that of human conscience (which is itself a notion not unknown to Goethe's Greek sources), quite apart from the fact that it is not unshakable, quite apart from the fact that she is forced under intense moral and emotional stress to gamble crucially on that faith as she declares the truth to the unpredictable Thoas – Iphigenie's faith is founded on the incontrovertible evidence of her own experience. Her conviction of divine benevolence derives absolutely from her own rescue from the altar at Aulis by unequivocal divine intervention – by the clouds of Diana that transported her to Tauris; the fact that Goethe sees fit to record this as a reported incident from before the action of the play does not alter its reality for her. Iphigenie does not measure herself against the gods – that was the original sin of Tantalus for which her family still suffers appallingly, and which she believes, even at the end of the play, only she can expiate; but she does demand the sanction of the gods for her every action. It is to the gods – specifically, to Apollo and Diana – that she turns in despair for the cure of her brother, and it is the gods that she finally challenges to reveal their goodness as she struggles with her dilemma.

Nor is the Tantalid curse itself secularized in rationalist Enlightenment fashion into a form of moral allegory; to Thoas's sceptical jibe that her ancestors' behav-iour might have been a result of their own inherent wickedness rather than of the guilt of Tantalus, she replies that it was Zeus himself who forged the 'brazen band' about their heads (lines 327ff.). The curse is more than real to Iphigenie, more than a family legend to explain inherited evil; it is manifest to her here and now, in her brother's fate and her own. Her whole behaviour in the play is motivated not simply by her urgent personal desire to return home to the land she has 'sought with her soul' for so many years, not only to preserve herself and her countrymen without recourse to deceit, but crucially to retain her priestly purity and integrity, which alone will allow her to return to Greece, to consecrate the family threshold, expunge her mother's blood and lift the curse. And the only means to this end is the faithful fulfilment of the oracle's command.

A comparison with the treatment of religious supernaturalism by Lessing in his almost contemporaneous *Nathan der Weise* (Nathan the Wise) is instructive. When Nathan's daughter Recha insists on attributing her rescue from a fire to the agency of an angel, Nathan almost brutally demolishes the young girl's superstitious impulses and condemns them as the promptings of pride and vanity. Goethe, on the other hand, retains the religious structures of his mythical and literary sources: the clouds of Diana, the ambiguities of the oracle, the human sacrifices offered until recently to the Taurian Diana, Orest's persecution by the Furies, Iphigenie's conviction of her sacrosanct mission to purge the Tantalid curse, the curse itself, and her absolute faith in both the existence and the benevolence of the gods. The specific dramatic manifestation of the curse, Orest's madness, as opposed to its epic manifestation across the generations of the Tantalid family, is cured in terms of the religious system of the play; while Orest's cure can be secularized as a form of confessional therapy or psychic catharsis, Goethe is careful to preserve the mythical integrity of his drama, and Orest's cure is effected both by the prayers of the priestess of Diana and by the psychodrama of his vision of the reconciliations and the resolutions of secular horrors in the underworld. When Iphigenie's faith in goodness is shaken, it is not human wickedness she invokes, but the ancient vision of vengeful gods in the 'Parzenlied'; when she decides to put truth to the test, she does not simply appeal to human mercy or generosity, but challenges the gods to manifest their truthfulness, and truth itself, through her.

To be sure, the truth and integrity, the humane benevolence that Iphigenie ascribes to her gods are nothing like the partisan and all-too-human quarrels and rivalries of the Greek gods of Goethe's classical sources; these are indeed the values of eighteenth-century Enlightenment, of Weimar Classicism and German Idealism. To be sure, Goethe exploits the religious system of Greek mythology and the literary material of Greek culture in terms of modern ethics; but he does so without destroying or reductively secularizing the poetic truth of that religious system. The conflict in *Iphigenie auf Tauris* is not presented as that between superstition and rationalism, between a superseded religion and an autonomous human ethic, but rather as a historical transition between a primitive and barbarous religious system on the one hand, and one based on civilized and humane values on the other. In this sense, Iphigenie's deities are indeed exemplars of the highest human and humane values; but they are for her not simply ideal projections of those values – they are also the source and the ultimate arbiters of those values. This is why the whole drama turns crucially on her conviction that the will of the gods and the promptings of her heart and conscience are one and the same: for Iphigenie, God is not dead.

The play has been seen as a statement of the primacy of human will, as the expression of a secular moral and intellectual autonomy against the unquestioning acceptance of inherited values and authority – as it were, the dramatic articulation of Kant's motto of Enlightenment that hails the coming of age of humanity: 'Sapere aude! Habe Mut, dich deines Verstandes zu bedienen' (Dare to know! Have the courage to use your understanding).[23] It might even be read, somewhat cynically, in its urgent search for the sanction and approval of the authority of absolute powers, as a justification of enlightened or benevolent despotism. But it is entirely characteristic of Goethe that he should use a religious or mythical system in a subtly ambivalent way. Without believing in or demanding any belief in the gods of his play, he nevertheless contrives to exploit the poetic or moral truth of that system without its wholesale secularization, without reducing it to an allegorical ethical fable; he is able to exploit the resonance and the drama of a superseded religious system while refashioning it in terms of modern ethical values – and indeed in this he may be rather closer to his Greek dramatic sources than is often believed.

While Goethe may have succeeded in integrating the Greek religious framework of his source material with modern ethics, in demonstrating the transition of a religious system from barbarism to civilization, it is less certain that he has succeeded in creating an integral dramatic action in the play. It is often noted, not without some justification, that the play loses much of its dramatic impetus after Act Three; it has even been suggested that the original occasion for the first prose version (the provision of a *Festspiel* to commemorate the first 'churching' of the Duchess Luise after the birth of a daughter in February 1779) obliged Goethe to avert the tragic outcome demanded by the action. This is hardly convincing; after all, the fortunate outcome of the action in Tauris for the Greeks was provided in Goethe's sources, even if he was unwilling to use the physical intervention of a deity as those sources had done.

And yet there is a dramatic unevenness between the first three and the last two acts. The horrific recital of the crimes of the Tantalids by Iphigenie in Act One, the situation in Act Two where she must listen to the atrocious sequel to those crimes as it afflicted her own family, the prospect in Act Three that she must apparently sacrifice her own brother in the latest manifestation of the curse on her family, the crisis of Orest's madness and its cure – all this is not, as Schiller described the play, 'astonishingly modern and un-Greek',[24] but authentically in the spirit of a relentless Greek tragic action and of the raw material of the Tantalid myth. Subsequently, in the course of the last two acts, the conflict becomes less sensational as it is interiorized into Iphigenie's moral dilemma and her crisis of faith; it is here that the play becomes 'modern and un-Greek' – for the Iphigenia of Euripides had no such scruples in deceiving the barbarian Thoas. Goethe might have resolved the intractable dilemma in a more modern way by having Orest kill Thoas in single combat – as at least one modern dramatist had done, and as seems a distinct possibility at one stage in Goethe's version; but this would clearly have violated the play's ethical system. Goethe cuts the tragic knot not by secularizing or demythologizing his Greek material, but by remaining within the religious framework of his sources and substituting for the original *deus ex machina*, the intervention of Pallas Athene to rescue the Greeks, Orest's inspired re-interpretation of the oracle's words that at once preserves the integrity of the religious assumptions of the play and its humanitarian ethic.

TORQUATO TASSO

Torquato Tasso, like *Egmont* and *Iphigenie auf Tauris*, was conceived well before Goethe's Italian journey; but it was only taken up again in Italy and completed in Weimar after his return. The first reports of work on the play, a version of the first two acts in rhythmic prose, date from 1780–1. This *Urtasso* fragment has not survived, though many more or less speculative attempts have been made to reconstruct it. It was not until 1787, under adverse circumstances, that Goethe resumed work on the play: plagued by seasickness, he planned the final version 'in the belly of the whale' – below decks on the ship taking him from Naples to Sicily. He worked on it in Rome the following year, but the final writing-out was done substantially during the first half of 1789 in Weimar, and it appeared in the Göschen *Schriften* in 1790.

Very much more 'modern and un-Greek' than *Iphigenie*, the play is set not in the ancient world, but in late Renaissance Italy, appropriately enough for a drama whose hero is a creative artist rather than a man of public affairs or of action – even if the play revolves precisely around the tension between private and public, literary and political activity, and touches on the ideal symbiosis of poet and hero. It is also clearly enough a reflection of Goethe's own private and public experience at the cultured court of Weimar; while it is otiose to draw simple biographical equations between Duke Alfons and Karl August, between the two Leonores and Duchess Luise and Frau von Stein, or between Goethe and Tasso or Antonio, Goethe nevertheless testified to the profoundly personal relevance of the play, affirming that it was 'Bein von meinem Bein und Fleisch von meinem Fleisch' (Bone of my bone and flesh of my flesh).[25]

The play addresses on the one hand the dilemma of artistic patronage, a problem very much of Goethe's day, the relationship between an artist and his patron, the conflicting demands of intellectual or artistic freedom and personal or financial security, the discrepancy between art as the vehicle of courtly prestige or *Repräsentation* and a more Romantic, even demonic, perception of art as autonomous creativity; on the other hand, it no doubt also reflects Goethe's own hectic and burdensome early Weimar years in which he frantically tried to combine his major literary projects (of which so many remained uncompleted during these years) with his obligations as *maître des plaisirs* to the Weimar court and with his executive duties in the Duchy. It may well also record Goethe's personal confrontation of the problem of the very value and validity of the poetic existence, even of poetry itself; Tasso's profound insecurity and sense of inadequacy represents not only the neurotic perfectionism of the artistic sensibility, not only the driven and unstable personality and destiny of the historical Tasso, but also an uneasy questioning of the justification of art and poetry and an ambivalent perception of the conflicting demands of art and life. *Tasso* is one of the first major German literary works to confront the problematic nature of art itself, one of the first *Künstlertragödien* that were to preoccupy the Romantic generation, from Wackenroder to Hoffmann and beyond. Novalis wrote his *Heinrich von Ofterdingen* expressly as a polemical corrective to *Wilhelm Meisters Lehrjahre*, to what he perceived as the 'economic' philistinism and the snobbery of Goethe's novel, in which poetic or romantic values were sacrificed to what he called 'artistic atheism' (see below, pp. 227–8); but he might have detected in *Torquato Tasso*, too, the undercurrent of unease *vis-à-vis* the solipsism of art for art's sake that now seems to us a distant but distinct forerunner of the awareness of the bad conscience and *mauvaise foi* of the artistic existence and temperament that later assumed such problematic dimensions in the work of Thomas Mann. Goethe's Tasso is an early but powerful articulation in the German literary tradition of a very modern agony, the *malheur d'être poète*; and while that specifically Romantic or post-Romantic perception may have been foreign to most Renaissance artists and poets, Goethe found in the story of Torquato Tasso, 'whose whole life was spent wandering hither and thither',[26] the historical figure who seemed to correspond most closely to that image.

The discrepancy between art and life, or 'die Disproportion des Talents mit dem Leben', as Caroline Herder reports Goethe's statement of the meaning of the play,[27] is indeed the broad conflict of *Tasso*. But this conflict is not only exteriorized as that between the respective roles and functions of Tasso and Antonio, in the rivalry between two men who, as Leonore Sanvitale shrewdly remarks, are enemies because nature did not make them into one person; more crucially, the conflict is interiorized as the intolerable struggle of Tasso with himself. It is the conflict between his paralysing sense of inadequacy and his proud conviction of his talent, between social withdrawal and gregariousness, between his restless migratory urge and his need for a protected, even pampered, existence, between the insecurity that craves the acclamation of his literary peers and his fierce creative independence, between the solitude of his imagination and the rich pageantry of the brilliant Ferrara court, between his role as an asexual castrato, as a nightingale set upon a golden bough to sing, and his own sexuality, between his detached observation of the world and his longing for active involvement, between his compulsive creative urge and the unstable psychology that seems inseparable from that urge. In a fascinatingly complex and, it must be said, occasionally confusing dramatic construction, Goethe integrated this tense interior conflict with other strands of dramatic interest: the courtly intrigues and jealousies of Leonore Sanvitale and Antonio, the earnest but uncomprehending demands of a benevolent but autocratic patron/father figure, Duke Alfons, and a disastrously misinterpreted relationship with a psychologically elusive and emotionally enigmatic muse/mistress figure, the Princess Leonore d'Este.

Much critical ingenuity has been spent on taking sides for and against Tasso or Antonio. In particular, the consistency or integrity of the character of Antonio has been debated: why does Antonio appear to change his behaviour radically in the play, from the avowedly jealous and provocative antagonist of the first two acts to the man of scrupulous integrity in Act Three who refuses to co-operate in Leonore Sanvitale's selfish intrigues, again to the ambivalent courtier of Act Four who, while pretending to act in Tasso's best interests, is in fact (at least in the paranoid perceptions of the poet) seeking to oust him from the court, and finally to the steadfast rock to whom the poet clings as his mind threatens to disintegrate? These questions were answered, or at least met, positivistically by earlier critics by suggesting that Antonio's role was based by Goethe on two different historical figures from Pierantonio Serassi's life of Tasso – Giambattista Pigna and Antonio Montecatino, successive secretaries to the Duke of Ferrara. In more integral readings of the text, it has been suggested that Antonio's behaviour towards Tasso changes in the course of the play from his initial scornful dismissiveness (and jealousy) to a more responsible and sympathetic attitude – though whether this is a genuinely altruistic shift, or one simulated in order to maintain himself in the Duke's favour, is a further unclarity. When Antonio recites a satirical catalogue of Tasso's childish and petulant behaviour to Alfons in Act Five, is he treacherously undermining Tasso's position, or is he using all his diplomatic skills to persuade the Duke to let Tasso leave Ferrara – and this against his own better judgement, since he has already tried to convince Tasso that it would be in his, Tasso's, own best interests to stay in that protected environment? Is he manoeuvring to ensure that the original of Tasso's manuscript remains in the hands of the Duke of Ferrara, and does he in fact wish to get rid of Tasso, only refusing to co-operate with Leonore Sanvitale (as Tasso's own suspicions suggest) because he cannot afford to appear to be conspiring to remove his rival? How genuine or how lasting is the gesture of friendship and support offered by him to Tasso after the poet's catastrophic attempt to embrace the Princess? Can the dreamer and the man of practical affairs ever be reconciled in present reality (whether sixteenth-century Italy or eighteenth-century Weimar) – or is this only possible in an imagined mythical Golden Age, or in Elysium?

If there is anything like a present critical consensus, it is generally pro-Antonio: in *Tasso*, Goethe has presented the tragedy or the pathology of the poetic temperament, as he had presented the pathology of the melancholic or *empfindsam* temperament in Werther. If Goethe knew and experienced the anguish of the creative personality, he also possessed the robust psychology of the *Bürger*; he was too aware of the imperatives of duty and obligation to indulge the darker or more hysterical sides of that personality. Conscious of the need to balance imagination and discipline, artistic sensibility and the craft of writing, of the excesses of an exclusive aestheticism on the one hand and of philistinism, however culturally pretentious, on the other (for Antonio's praise of Ariosto shows him as a man of education, for all that his praise may be calculated to provoke Tasso): this is Goethe's characteristically unpartisan, or ambivalent, stance. There are, however, those who would defend Tasso: he is the victim of wagging tongues, of spiteful court intrigues and a ruthless power-broker struggling for influence or, in the case of Leonore Sanvitale, for literary immortality, albeit as reflected glory. Tasso is destroyed by the conflicting demands made on him by uncomprehending or malicious people, by the dissonance between his imaginative ideals and the implacable realities of a claustrophobic court life.

And indeed it must be conceded that Tasso's unfortunate house-arrest, which he takes in drastic terms as a disgrace and a humiliating rejection, leads to his absence and isolation for more than a whole act of the play, during which time he is indeed intrigued against – but during which time his psychic wound also festers, his imagination poisons itself and he is led to the verge of a paranoid abyss. It is also true that his behaviour in the quarrel scene with Antonio, while it may be naive and impulsive, is remarkably restrained in the face of intolerable provocation, and only snaps when he is contemptuously accused of physical cowardice by Antonio. It is *perhaps* true that he misconstrues Alfons's motives for wishing to keep possession of the manuscript of his masterpiece, *Gerusalemme liberata* (Jerusalem Delivered); and most critically of all, it is surely the case that the Princess is culpable, at best of an incautious, and at worst of an irresponsible emotional ambivalence towards him. But for all Goethe's profound sympathy, indeed his empathy with the unhappy poet, it is also the case that Tasso's absolutist and hysterical temperament, whether it stems from inherent instability or from the hypersensitivity of the artistic psyche, must play havoc both with court etiquette and with his relations to those around him.

It is not a question of attributing degrees of blame to the respective protagonists; Goethe explores in this play the conflicts and tensions of his own personality and his own experience, his own commitment to art and to social and political realities. To identify Goethe with the unstable and hysterical poet he found in his historical sources and transmuted into the persona of his play would be as absurd as to identify him with the devastatingly sardonic and self-controlled courtier Antonio; Goethe was as aware of the dangerous solipsism of the one as he was of the imaginative limitations of the other. *Torquato Tasso* is frequently described as the tragedy of the poet (or the tragedy of The Poet). But it is the tragedy of a specific poet who is not Goethe, but Goethe's imaginative re-creation of the historical poet who, while he was undoubtedly intrigued against, would (among other instances of distinctly unbalanced behaviour) accuse the Inquisition of wilfully imperilling his immortal soul by refusing to declare him a heretic; who suffered from fits and delusions; who attacked a servant with a knife; who wandered the length of Italy until he finally returned to Ferrara, only to persist in biting the hand that fed him until a long-suffering and repeatedly slandered patron was finally forced to imprison him, in less than intolerable conditions for the age, in the hospital of St Anna in Ferrara – which Goethe visited on his way to Rome, doubting that the miserable cell he was shown was indeed the authentic 'prison' of Tasso.[28]

The several tensions that remain unresolved at the end of the play, which are so vividly expressed in the confused and shifting metaphors of Tasso's final speech – of rock and wave, ship and wave, sun and moon, calm and storm, of disintegrating ship, and finally of shipwrecked mariner clinging to the very rock on which he foundered (or was about to founder, or was meant to founder – the ambiguities of this conclusion are reflected in the multitude of its interpretations): these unresolved tensions suggest not so much that such conflicts are inherently incapable of resolution, but rather that they still remained unresolved in the mind and the imagination of the author. To be sure, Goethe does in the final scene of the play sound a note, if not of resolution, then at least of the hope of survival or resolution: not only in the possible (but only possible) reconciliation of Tasso and Antonio, of wave and rock, but also in the notion of literary expression as catharsis – the suggestion that the poet is gifted to articulate, and thereby perhaps to relieve, his suffering. This is a notion that Goethe touched on at times in his work and in his personal pronouncements; he may indeed have believed that in writing *Werther*, for example, he had saved himself from his hero's fate. But he was also capable, in the poem 'An Werther', of sarcastically parodying the glib assumption that the poet might relieve his suffering by the eloquence of his song. Moreover, what seems to comfort and reassure Tasso in his penultimate speech is not so much the therapeutic power of poetic articulation, but rather Antonio's reminder of his exceptional talent: what he *is*.

The poet, or his poetic talent, may indeed survive; but the play is still concerned with the dangerous ambivalence of that talent. One of Tasso's most intense and passionate speeches is where he expresses in a telling metaphor the compulsive urge of poetic creation (lines 3079–91): the poet creates as the silkworm creates its thread, spinning itself into a pupa, a tomb from which it is uncertain whether it will emerge as *imago*. *Torquato Tasso* is not only Goethe's reckoning with the conflicting claims of art and life; it is also a play in which he confronts the potentially destructive power of the creative imagination and of poetic talent. The morbidity or the pathology of art and the artist, the pitfalls of high talent tragically allied to an unstable temperament or to outrageous fortune, which Goethe knew vicariously from his reading of Tasso's life, and at firsthand from the career of his erstwhile friend and literary colleague J. M. R. Lenz, and of which he surely had some direct personal experience, is a spectre that Goethe also attempted to exorcise in the two figures he introduced into, and finally banished from, his novel *Wilhelm Meisters Lehrjahre* – the first version of which has its origins in the same period of his life as *Tasso*. In the figures of Mignon and the Harfenspieler, the tragic dissonance of art and life, the morbidity and rootless vagabond existence of a certain kind of artistic temperament, the association of genius and madness, of art and death, are hauntingly and pathetically embodied. It was this morbid and Romantic perception of art that Goethe turned his back on as he became increasingly preoccupied with what he was later aphoristically to call the 'healthy' dimension of classicism.[29]

Tasso is a highly interiorized play, so much so that Goethe feared that it might not be successful or suitable as a stage play. Yet it is no mere *Lesedrama*, for all its verbal and structural density. The subtle dynamics of the five voices pitched against each other produce the tense relationships of a musical quintet; the *sententiae* pronounced by the dramatis personae (a feature of Euripidean drama noted and imitated by neo-classical dramatists) give the dialogue its lapidary character, expressing the collision of divergent and contradictory perceptions. Appropriately enough in a play that concerns the problematic nature of poetry and the poetic existence, it is an eloquently figured text containing passages of dense lyricism, voiced not only by the poet Tasso, but by the other figures of this highly cultivated cast in the *hortus inclusus* of Belriguardo: Leonore Sanvitale's evocation of spring in the first scene of the play, or Antonio's encomium to Ariosto in the fourth. Most notable of all are Tasso's set-piece elaborations: his vision of the Golden Age (which draws on a passage from Tasso's own pastoral drama *Aminta*) and of Elysium reflected in the 'magic mirror' of a well are compelling reminders that the protagonist is the outstandingly gifted poet of his generation – while at the same time they also suggest the incompatibility of his dangerously narcissistic imaginative ideal with the realities, suspicions, intrigues and jealousies of an all too human courtly environment. Tasso's monologues in Acts Four and Five demonstrate the destructive dimensions of his overwrought sensibilities, as he spins himself into a web of paranoid self-delusion, releasing the monsters and demons that swarm from the darkest corners of his mind. His increasingly hysterical perceptions of court hostility on the one hand, and of the Princess's feelings for him on the other, are elaborated into two extraordinary passages in which he projects himself beyond the present into deranged fantasies of himself as a wild-eyed pilgrim to his childhood home in Sorrento, or as a gardener tending the lemon trees of Consandoli. Finally, the drastic metaphorical shifts of his final speech, while they may be the poetic articulation of his anguish, are also the expression of a mind on the verge of disintegration.

The gesture with which the play ends, with Tasso clinging to his ambivalent friend as his patron and his muse abandon him, is the last in a series of powerful, if restrained examples of gestic symbolism that run through the play. The first scene opens with the crowning of the busts of Virgil and Ariosto respectively with laurel and floral wreaths, a conventional enough game that assumes altogether less playful dimensions when Tasso reacts passionately to his own crowning with the laurels from the head of Virgil. Tasso's drawing of his sword is more than an act of rash temper; it is a gesture that shatters the decorous code of behaviour that rules the court, and leads to a disgrace that forces him to give up not only his sword, but also the laurel wreath that had assumed such significance for him. His embrace of the Princess is shocking not only because it violates court etiquette even more drastically than his naked sword, not only because it sensationally breaks down the barrier between imagination and reality, between Tasso's poetic sublimation of his feelings and his sexuality, but also because it is a passionately physical gesture that erupts into a hitherto highly verbalized action. The laurel wreath also finally assumes the attributes of a victim, of a sacrificial animal decked with garlands and fillets for the altar.

Torquato Tasso opens with a piece of whimsical mummery which, while it might primarily be a reference to the pastoral poetry of the historical Tasso, also recalls irresistibly the make-believe bucolic fancies of a court much closer in time to Goethe, of Marie Antoinette and her ladies as milkmaids in the *Petit Hameau* of Versailles or at Rambouillet. This is not to suggest that the prescient shadow of revolution falls across the play; it was already completed very shortly after the fall of the Bastille, and few in Germany immediately appreciated the full implications or anticipated the full consequences of 14 July 1789. But Goethe's next drama was to be the first in a series of plays that address, even if they do not fully confront, the causes and the effects of the French Revolution.

REVOLUTION DRAMAS

Goethe's hostility to the French Revolution, indeed his fear and horror of all kinds of civil unrest, anarchy or war, is well enough known, even notorious; and he has been singled out for much abuse as a result of his consistent and implacable inability or refusal to come to terms with the greatest, or at least the most spectacular event in the political history of his age. Even his own claim to 'poetic impartiality' (which some would call ambivalence) did not allow him to acknowledge very much more than the historical necessity of the Revolution – and that only in France. He was on occasion forced to concede the creative forces, both political and cultural, thrown up by the Revolution, which he frequently compared to a cataclysm of nature, to an earthquake, a volcano, or a plague. But he was by instinct, temperament and conviction a gradualist, an evolutionist, at times a reformist, in his political attitudes, just as he was in the geological doctrines he often used as analogies or metaphors for political and historical processes; and he was traumatized and alienated – as indeed were many of his contemporaries who, unlike Goethe, had initially harboured revolutionary or 'Jacobin' sympathies – by the murderous developments of the *Terreur*. It is true that he believed, as he protested to Eckermann later in his life, defending himself against the common perception of him as 'a friend of the status quo' (*ein Freund des Bestehenden*), that the French Revolution, indeed all revolutions, were the fault not of the people, but of bad or weak government;[30] at the same time he was careful to distinguish between *Volk* (the people) and *Pöbel* (the mob).

But neither did Goethe have any time for the querulous and pampered émigrés, the French aristocrats who accompanied the Duke of Brunswick's forces into France, hoping for an effortless ride to their former way of life on the backs of the counter-revolutionary allies; for he was convinced that it was the feckless and frivolous irresponsibility of the French monarchy and aristocracy that had unleashed the Revolution in the first place. And the very symbol and symptom of that irresponsibility was, for Goethe, the incident upon which the first of his 'Revolution dramas', *Der Groß-Cophta* (The Great Copt), is clearly based: the diamond necklace scandal of 1785. To be sure, when Goethe began to write the first version of this play, he had no idea that the scandal would assume, at least in his eyes, such momentous significance in European history. For it was in Italy in 1787 that he first conceived the plan of a work – in the form of *opera buffa* – on the subject of Cagliostro and the *Halsbandaffäre*; and it was in Sicily that same year that he actually visited Cagliostro's impoverished family, to whom he was later to donate the publisher's fee for the play in which he lampooned the fraudulence of their outrageous relative (see above, pp. 26–7).

The first draft, *Die Mystifizierten* (The Mystified), remained unfinished – though the surviving fragments indicate that it was to proceed along very similar lines to the completed play *Der Groß-Cophta*; and in August 1787 he spelt out to his composer Kayser the transparent parallels between the historical protagonists of the necklace scandal and his own characters.[31] But it was not until 1791 that he abandoned the plan for an operatic form and wrote the prose comedy; for in the meantime events had spectacularly confirmed to him all his profound suspicions towards Cagliostro, indeed he had come in retrospect to see the scandal of 1785 as a prophetic omen of the Revolution itself – the 'sombre portent' that found its 'most hideous fulfilment' in the Revolution, as he was to put it much later. The scandal had, he claimed, undermined the state, destroyed public respect for the Queen and the dignity of the monarchy; as he also put it to Kanzler von Müller in 1831, quoting the judgement of the historian Niebuhr, the madness of the French court had broken the talisman that held the demon of revolution in check.[32]

It is still unclear even today just how directly 'Count' Cagliostro was involved in the scandal of 1785; what is clear is that Goethe's interest in, and suspicion of, Cagliostro dated from some time before this. As early as 1781 he had expressed his profound unease about the notorious 'magician' to his credulous friend Lavater; he had described the infiltration of the most prestigious courts of Europe by such charlatans as the undermining of the political and moral order of the time – for Cagliostro was only one of several more or less fraudulent *Wunderapostel* who had captured the imagination of gullible persons in high political and social positions. Cagliostro, with his purported magical gifts, spirit séances, miracle cures and sensational displays of prophecy, with the Masonic mysteries of his 'Egyptian rites' and his hypnotic charisma, had enthralled court circles from St Petersburg to Warsaw, from Mitau to Strasbourg, and even to Paris.

In particular, he had captivated the gullible and vain Prince-Bishop of Strasbourg, the Cardinal Louis René de Rohan, who was desperate to re-establish himself in the favour of Queen Marie Antoinette. But de Rohan, and Cagliostro himself, became the victims of an even more devious and unscrupulous operator, the adventuress Comtesse Jeanne (Valois) de la Motte, whose title (by marriage) and claim to descent (by blood) from the royal house of Valois were, to say the least, suspect. By means of forged letters purporting to be in the Queen's hand and a farcical piece of mummery in the royal gardens at Versailles, in which de Rohan was duped into believing that he had been granted a secret meeting with the Queen herself (in fact, a prostitute, Nicolette Leguay, alias 'Oliva'), Jeanne de la Motte was able to trick de Rohan into making the first payment on an extravagantly expensive necklace which the Queen was believed to covet; the Queen herself was to supply the balance. The necklace was delivered to de Rohan and purloined by Jeanne de la Motte and her husband, who actually managed to smuggle some of the stones to London; but when the balance failed to materialize the court jewellers Boehmer and Bassenge reported the matter to the King. As a result de Rohan, Cagliostro and Jeanne de la Motte were arrested; the Countess was sentenced to a brutal flogging and branding, but de Rohan and Cagliostro were acquitted by the French Parliament – to the great delight of the Paris crowd, who had adopted them as heroes. However, the King meted out his own summary justice by banishing de Rohan and Cagliostro; and this overruling of a popular acquittal, as much as the mud that stuck from the scandal itself, contributed to the serious undermining of the prestige of the royal family. After further adventures in London and Italy, Cagliostro was tried and sentenced by the Holy Office in Rome in 1791, and died miserably in an Italian prison in 1795.

For Goethe, at any rate, the affair was a significant precursor of the Revolution, indeed a direct contributory factor. In this view he no doubt overcentralized the scandal, and in particular demonized the figure of Cagliostro, whose exact role in the affair is obscure. But it was in *Der Groß-Cophta* that Goethe recorded both his own outrage at the scandal and his severe judgement on Cagliostro, on charlatan obscurantism in general, and on the cynicism, corruption and gullibility in high places that had, as he put it, contributed to the collapse of 'the finest throne in the world'.[33] Goethe was no uninformed or paranoid outsider, no 'conspiracy theorist' in his suspicions of Freemasonry, Rosicrucianism or other secret societies; he had himself been inducted as a master in the Masonic Lodge 'Anna Amalia zu den drei Rosen' in 1782, and was also involved in the Weimar Order of Illuminati. But whether in spite of or because of his inside knowledge of such ritualistic cabals, whether because of their obscurantist mysteries or because he perceived them as potential cells for covert Jacobinist or subversive activity, he quickly became very wary of all kinds of Masonic influences, and quite especially he developed a fascinated aversion to the figure who for him personified the baleful manipulation of credulous minds by charlatans: Cagliostro.

Der Groß-Cophta is an intriguing mix of identifiable allegory and deviation from the historical model. The events, and most of the main characters, follow the broad lines of the necklace scandal – or at least of Goethe's perception of it. 'Graf Rostro di Rostro impudente' is clearly Cagliostro; the *Domherr* (Canon) a somewhat simplified provincial version of the Cardinal de Rohan. The Marquise plays the exact role of the Comtesse de la Motte, and the Marquis that of her husband; even the court jewellers are represented in the second scene of Act Three. The historical role of Nicolette Leguay, the milliner/prostitute, is transferred to the niece of the Marquise, who is involved on the one hand in a sentimental relationship with the unhistorical figure of the Chevalier (*Ritter*) Greville, and on the other hand in an altogether less sentimental affair with the lecherous Marquis. The figure of the Ritter Greville is used by Goethe not only as an agent to expose the fraud and trickery of both Graf Rostro and the Marquise; it also introduces an emotional conflict in which both the 'innocent' niece and the 'virtuous' Ritter play ambivalent roles. For the niece is not sexually innocent, though she is morally virtuous – she is dismayed at the deception she is forced into by her treacherous aunt and guardian; the Ritter is both sexually and intellectually naive (he too is in thrall to the charismatic spell of the bogus 'Great Copt') – but he is impelled to sacrifice his claims on the niece when he exposes both the fraudulence of Graf Rostro and the criminality of the Marquise, evidently at least in part for reasons of personal ambition and preferment.

What is interesting in Goethe's *drame à clef* is that he appears to separate the roles of Rostro/Cagliostro and the Marquise/Comtesse de le Motte – thus perhaps reflecting the uncertainty surrounding the extent of Cagliostro's actual involvement in the historical scandal. For while Graf Rostro is duping the *Domherr* (and indeed the *Ritter*) as Cagliostro did the Cardinal de Rohan, he himself is being duped and manipulated by the Marquise; there is no indication that the Graf is implicated in the necklace fraud, only in the absurd and bogus mumbo-jumbo of his 'Egyptian' rites and observances – albeit also to his own profit. Goethe is, as it were, killing two historical birds with one stone, and he distinguishes clearly enough between the criminal financial fraud of the Marquise on the one hand and Graf Rostro's intellectual fraud – the captivation of credulous minds by 'magic' – on the other. Indeed, Goethe gives us a telling insight into the powerful hold exercised by Cagliostro over those such as de Rohan who might have been expected to see through him: it is precisely the Marquise, herself outstanding in duplicity, who acknowledges Graf Rostro's supreme skills as a master of manipulation in the second scene of Act Two.

But for all Goethe's careful historical parallels, for all his savage exposure of gullibility, fraudulence and criminality in high places, the play pulls its political punches. The setting of *Der Groß-Cophta* in a small state, of which the ruler and his daughter, the Princess, who do not even appear in the action, are mere provincialized versions of Louis XVI and Marie Antoinette, marginalizes its political impact. The foundations of 'the finest throne in the world' are not shaken, the dignity and authority of the rulers are not undermined, and there is no hint that any form of social or political unrest, let alone revolution, might ensue from *this* scandal. On the contrary, the just and benevolent authority of the ruler is confirmed as the whole affair is cleared up in a denouement that recalls the finale of Molière's *Tartuffe*: the criminals are caught red-handed, a charlatan is unmasked and a dupe is confronted with his own folly as the Swiss Guard intervenes to arrest all those concerned in the double fraud. Possibly for reasons to do with his own position in Weimar, Goethe has marginalized what was for him a momentous historical affair; the play cannot be read as an attack on the irresponsibility or frivolity of the ruling class, whether in France or in Germany, but only as a satirical exposure of the susceptibility of certain highly placed persons to criminality and fraud.

Der Bürgergeneral (The Citizen General) was written, so Goethe claimed, within eight days in April 1793, some two months before he witnessed the bombardment that was to end the short-lived 'Rhenish Republic' of Mainz, and three months after the execution of Louis XVI. Not that these world events impinge directly on this comic one-acter, subtitled *Zweite Fortsetzung der 'beiden Billets'* (Second Sequel to 'The Two Letters') and based on a German sequel to a French comedy, *Les Deux billets* by J. P. Claris de Florian. From the original Goethe took the peasant family and the hapless figure of the incompetent swindler, the barber Schnaps who, while he might be descended from the same comic tradition as the barber Figaro, has little of his celebrated cousin's quick-witted intelligence or guile. Nevertheless, the ninth scene, in which Schnaps very nearly succeeds in tricking the doltish father, Märten, into providing him with a tasty meal is a piece of comic writing that has some affinity with the stage business of the *commedia dell'arte*: as Schnaps explains to the gullible Märten, the separated soured milk is an allegory of class distinctions, which are to be stirred into equality as he stirs curds and whey, bread and sugar – the rich and the bourgeoisie, nobility and clergy – into a nourishing breakfast. Schnaps's greedy appetites remain unsatisfied, however, thanks to the resource of the peasant lovers Görge and Röse, just as his half-baked revolutionary ambitions are frustrated: the jumped-up provincial German Jacobin, the 'Citizen General', is quickly exposed as a clumsy opportunist.

The playlet is less a comment on events in France (or even in Mainz) than a contemptuous satire on small-time German revolutionaries, on those who, as Goethe put it later to Eckermann, strove to introduce into Germany by artificial means events which in France were the result of a great historical necessity.[34] While he acknowledged the causes of revolution in France, he was careful to insist that attempts to spread the 'fever' beyond the frontiers of France were absurd and dangerous. At the same time, he was keenly aware that the most potent defence against the infiltration of such ideas or such tactics into Germany lay not only in ceaseless vigilance, but also in the proper exercise by all classes of their duties and responsibilities: mutual tolerance, respect for the rights of their subjects by the rulers, timely reform to prevent the abuse of such rights, and a proper deference on the part of the lower orders. Justice, rather than liberty, and certainly not equality, was for Goethe the talisman that would hold the demon of revolution in check, at least in Germany. To be sure, such a thinly disguised apologia for enlightened absolutism, which Goethe strove not only to preach in his revolution dramas, but also to practise in his political and administrative duties in the Duchy of Weimar, earned for him well beyond his own lifetime a great deal of abuse as a reactionary defender of the status quo, or worse, as the lackey of princelings who affected an 'Olympian' indifference to political principles. But *Der Bürgergeneral* is not simply an expression of Goethe's fastidious contempt for bogus revolutionary hooliganism (or of his morbid fear of it). While the figure of the nobleman, who appears only at the very beginning and the very end of this short farce, may be an improbably idealized authority figure, it is notable that Goethe's satire is directed not only at the fraudulent Jacobin Schnaps, not only at the credulous peasant Märten, but also, in a brief but telling appearance, at the paranoid over-reaction of the empurpled magistrate who would have the pathetic Schnaps tortured, the militia mobilized and houses ransacked to deal with what wiser heads see as a storm in a teacup – and as an exemplary reminder of the duty of all to pre-empt any pretext for 'Jacobin' disaffection.

Goethe takes rather more serious issue with the potential causes of revolution in *Die Aufgeregten* (The Agitated), a play also written in 1793, but which remained fragmentary; it was only in 1816 as he prepared his collected works for publication that he supplied the prose narrative that outlines the missing third and fifth acts. While the details of the action of these two acts are sketchy (in Act Three, we are told, the aristocratic characters act out scenes from the revolutionary convention in Paris; in Act Five the class tensions are quickly dispelled by means of a comic denouement, and the play ends 'to the general satisfaction'), Goethe's political stance is clear enough from the completed sections. Once again, the would-be revolutionary figure is a surgeon-barber, the vainglorious and half-educated Breme 'von Bremenfeld', whose demagogery is allied with the educated subversion of the Magister, the tutor of the young Count, who is here lampooned as a malcontent intellectual whose Jacobinism is the result of his having been (quite properly) dismissed from his post. Against these ineffectual but potentially disruptive insurgents are ranged the (again idealized) figures of political and social authority. The Countess, who has read the French *philosophes*, and has recently returned from revolutionary Paris, where she has interpreted events with shrewd insight, echoes Egmont's sentiments to Alba when she explains to the equally enlightened *Hofrat* (Minister) that while human nature might be coerced or even humbled, it cannot and should not be oppressed or destroyed; she for her part is determined to do all in her power to prevent or to put right injustice – and thereby, of course, to remove all pretext for revolutionary disaffection – even at the risk of being libelled as a democrat.[35] In a neatly chiastic exchange of views, the ideal aristocrat confesses to liberal sympathies, while the equally ideal *Bürger*, the *Hofrat*, declares himself an enemy of envy-driven class hatred and an admirer of aristocratic excellence: a statement of Goethe's ideal symbiosis of enlightened aristocracy and responsible *Bürgertum* that anticipates the sociopolitical programme of the 'Society of the Tower' in *Wilhelm Meisters Lehrjahre*.

The barber Breme is presented as a deplorable figure, tiresome and self-important (though with a degree of redeeming comic absurdity), an opportunist riding the tiger of sedition with all the pompous rhetoric of German Jacobinism and his constant invocation of 'the first servant of the state', his hero Frederick the Great. But his grievance is genuine: a legal agreement between the ruling house and the tenantry has been ignored, the rights of the lower orders have been neglected. It then turns out that the apparent neglect of legal rights is no fault of the aristocracy but of a dishonest official, the *Amtmann*, who has concealed the document for his own purposes; he is forced to disgorge it in a scene of high farce when the tomboy daughter of the Countess threatens to blow off his head with her hunting-rifle. The play again reflects Goethe's conviction that timely reform, the correction of identifiable abuses and an enlightened imperative of duty or *noblesse oblige* on the part of the ruling classes would, if not in France then at least in Germany, hold Jacobinism in check – as indeed proved to be the case in some Rhineland states. It was this 'democratic' but authoritarian stance, as he remarked acerbically to Eckermann, that had led him to be maligned as an enemy of the people, while Schiller, who was in truth far more of an aristocrat than himself, had the good fortune to be regarded as their friend.[36]

While in his first revolution dramas Goethe sought to express his views through satire, comedy or farce, he made two attempts to confront contemporary history in terms of tragedy – in which, moreover, he situated his action not in Germany, but in revolutionary or pre-revolutionary France itself. *Das Mädchen von Oberkirch* (The Girl from Oberkirch, 1795–6) never progressed beyond two opening scenes and a very sketchy scenario for five acts from which little can be inferred; it was evidently intended to conflate the historical fate of the Duc d'Orléans ('Philippe égalité') with the anecdote of a young Alsatian peasant girl who was guillotined in Strasbourg for refusing to appear as the Goddess of Reason in a festival based on the Parisian *Fête de la liberté et de la raison* of November 1793. The surviving fragments suggest that some attention was to be drawn to the unpopularity of the émigré French aristocracy in Germany, and that the young aristocrat was to be exposed as an opportunist whose affection for the young woman was prompted by self-interest rather than love or any democratic instinct. But this attempt to set a personal tragedy in a revolutionary context was abandoned, and it was not until the turn of the century that Goethe was to attempt one final (and also unfinished) dramatic treatment of recent political history, also as tragedy – but as highly stylized, indeed sublimated neo-classical tragedy.

Die Natürliche Tochter (The Natural Daughter)

In 1799 Goethe read the extraordinary story of Princess Stéphanie-Louise de Bourbon Conti in her own *Mémoires historiques* published in the previous year,

'Year Six' of the revolutionary calendar; and this account of a young woman who was at once the victim of her own initiatives, of an accident of birth and of the most brutal abuse of arbitrary power, led him to write his last major literary attempt to come to terms with 'this most terrible of events',[37] the French Revolution. Not that this play, or indeed any of Goethe's other revolution dramas, directly confronts or depicts the Revolution itself; Goethe seemed unable or unwilling to bring himself to any form of historically naturalistic presentation of the Revolution, but only presented it in the most allusive or allegorical form – in the *Reise der Söhne Megaprazons* (see below, pp. 248–9), in the Seismos episode of the *Klassische Walpurgisnacht* in the second act of *Faust* Part Two, and in the bizarre charade of the *Convention* staged by the aristocratic characters of *Die Aufgeregten*, which is available to us only in a retrospective prose summary by Goethe. *Die natürliche Tochter* deals with events that took place well before 1789; it is, on an altogether more serious thematic and stylistic level than *Der Groß-Cophta*, an analysis of the causes and symptoms of revolution – though Goethe did at one stage plan to take the action of the projected trilogy of plays through the history of the Revolution itself. But this effort did not progress beyond the first, integral but abruptly concluded, five-act drama of *Die natürliche Tochter*, written between October 1801 and March 1803.

The *Mémoires* of Princess Stéphanie begin in 1773 in the reign of Louis XV. An illegitimate daughter of noble blood who was tutored by Rousseau himself, and whose father was involved in the political opposition of the *Parlements* to the King, she was promised that she would be formally granted her legitimate status by the King on condition that she did not publicly or prematurely reveal this undertaking. This she did, however; her mother, who feared exposure to scandal, and her legitimate half-brother, who was politically at odds with his father and who also feared the loss of his patrimony, conspired to abduct the 'princess' before her legitimation, with the connivance of her governess Madame Delorme. Her father was informed that she was dead, and she was forced into a *mariage blanc* with an unscrupulous lawyer; and by this *mésalliance* her claims to noble status were vitiated. She later managed to escape from her domestic humiliation and tried to revive her claim, but the outbreak of the Revolution frustrated her ambitions; in spite of her active intervention in the monarchist cause, she survived the Revolution and died in wretched circumstances in 1825.

Goethe transforms this historically relatively insignificant autobiography of a pretentious, albeit ill-used, minor figure into a portentously symbolic example of the most brutal abuse of power and intrigue by the political factions of the *ancien régime*. In doing so, he conflates events which took place in the 1770s with the more immediate pre-revolutionary situation of the 1780s. He elevates the character of his heroine from the ambitious Stéphanie, who is as much a victim of her own vanity and social aspirations as of the intrigues of her family, to the idealized, almost mythically typified, ethically and temperamentally 'Amazonian' figure of Eugenie who, for all that she indulges in a fatal hubris, is presented as an individual of exemplary aristocratic courage and humanity; and he transposes a squalid minor episode of domestic callousness into a paradigmatic indictment of the corruption and despotism of the *ancien régime*. His ironically named Eugenie

('well-born') is abducted not through the agency of her mother (for her legitimation becomes possible in Goethe's play only after her mother's death), but through
that of her half-brother, a shadowy figure of melodramatic evil who is politically
at odds with his (and Eugenie's) father. Her governess is not the unscrupulous
catspaw Madame Delorme, but an ambivalent and pitiable figure who reluctantly
connives in Eugenie's abduction because she is emotionally and sexually enslaved
by the ruthless Secretary who, while ostensibly in the service of Eugenie's father,
is conspiring with the son. The Secretary also holds in thrall a figure of equally
ruthless opportunism, the Abbé (*Weltgeistlicher*), who is prepared to testify falsely to
Eugenie's death in a riding accident to her father.

But the most radical change Goethe made over his source affects the action of
the last two acts of the play. For the illegal abduction of Stéphanie by the agents
of her mother and brother, he substitutes a motif that draws into this brutal
intrigue the whole constitutional machinery of the *ancien régime*. Not only is
Eugenie's fate to be a particularly outrageous one – she is to be banished to the
'fever islands' of the French Caribbean colonies; but this banishment is also
decreed by a royal *lettre de cachet*, a warrant that carries absolute and incontrovertible authority and bypasses all legal processes – the sinister 'talisman' of absolute
power. To be sure, it is unclear from the play whether this awful document is
authentic or forged; either way, it is a central symbol of the hopeless corruption of
the rule of law, and it serves to block off any hope Eugenie has of protection from
the representatives of legal, civil or religious authority. Just as historically improb-
able is Goethe's use of a stratagem by which Eugenie can escape the apparently
irreversible force of the *lettre de cachet*: by consenting to marriage with the bourgeois
(and, in Goethe's version, not unworthy) figure of the lawyer (*Gerichtsrat*), she can
place herself beyond the reach even of this royal decree. On this uneasy double
note of salvation and renunciation, Goethe's play ends: salvation through a
marriage which, while it is idealized as a bulwark of private bourgeois human
rights and values against public corruption and the official abuse of power, is a
contrived *mésalliance* and a desperate stratagem, unconsummated, loveless and
opportunistic; renunciation because the heroine must thereby abandon not only
all pretensions to her legitimation as a princess of royal blood, but also all claim
to personal happiness and fulfilment.

This is the individual tragedy behind which looms the impending catastrophe
of the Revolution, the great *Naturnotwendigkeit* (natural necessity) that Goethe
described in a letter to Schiller as the irresistible confluence of streams and
torrents merging and swelling into a mighty flood, and which he puts into the
mouth of a monk in the closing stages of his play as an apocalyptic vision of
imminent universal destruction.[38] Goethe titles his drama a tragedy; it is unclear
whether this indicates that his heroine was eventually to perish, perhaps in the
Revolution itself in a subsequent part of the planned trilogy, or whether it
indicates the tragic choice forced upon her as a result of her own impatient guilt
and of her innocent involvement in an outrageous conspiracy. The symbolic
references with which the play teems seem designed to emphasize the parallels
between the ineluctable political processes driving a modern European nation
towards catastrophe and the tragic inevitability of the ancient myths. Eugenie is

associated with Icarus as she urges her horse to breakneck leaps, and with Phaeton's disastrous adventure by the *Gerichtsrat*; her impatiently premature opening of the chest of clothes in which she is to appear before the King for her ceremony of legitimation is associated with the opening of Pandora's box – for she has been expressly and urgently warned not to open the chest or to divulge to anyone the secret of her forthcoming acceptance at court. These clothes are also described as the lethal wedding-dress of Creusa; the apple of the Garden of Eden and the apple of Eris that became the prize of the Judgement of Paris are invoked both to indicate Eugenie's tragic guilt and to cast her as the undeserving victim of a power-struggle which, like those of the warring Olympian gods, takes place above her head and quite beyond her control. She acquiesces in her disproportionately savage destiny because she has herself contributed to it; but she achieves a bitterly tragic form of individual freedom which removes her from the arbitrary abuse of power in a grotesquely unsatisfactory and unfree marriage.

Die natürliche Tochter is not only a fragmentary play, it is also generally perceived as a flawed one. It is fragmentary in the sense that Goethe failed to complete his planned trilogy, or even the single-drama sequel he subsequently envisaged; it is also fragmentary in that once again he stopped short of a full literary representation of the historical watershed that preoccupied him so long – and, as he conceded, so fruitlessly. The Revolution itself is here only anticipated, albeit in sensational terms, and in both cases, oddly enough, by clerics – by the dishonest Abbé (lines 1657–68) and by the disillusioned monk (lines 2783–808); the play concerns itself overwhelmingly with the constitutional rottenness to which Goethe attributed the cataclysm that followed. Heavily stylized as it is in language, form and characterization, it has been attacked by many on artistic grounds. Schiller and Fichte were enthusiastic, and Herder is reported to have admired it, while adding that it was too refined for current public taste; but Herder also replied with characteristic acerbity, when his opinion was sought by Goethe, that 'he preferred his "Natural Daughter" to his natural son' – which finally ended an already severely strained friendship.[39]

Though classicizing in form and construction, the unities of time and place are perforce sacrificed; more seriously, the action lacks the taut development and concise construction of neo-classical drama as the scene shifts from one context to the other in an arbitrary fashion without much regard to internal dramatic coherence, and Eugenie appears as a puppet manipulated by obscure political forces. The first two acts concern her position before her abduction; the abduction plan is hastily adumbrated in the second act, together with her 'original sin', the premature opening of the chest. A disproportionate time is devoted in Act Three to the Duke's extended lament at his daughter's supposed death; and the last two acts deal at length with her eleventh-hour struggle to avoid deportation. It is unclear whether the *lettre de cachet* is authentic or forged, and some confusion remains in the reader's or spectator's mind whether, or how far, Eugenie is to be perceived as the victim of her own hubris rather than of sinister political machinations: as she herself pleads in bewilderment, how is it that so minor a transgression should be so cruelly punished? The language is highly formal, rhetorical and sententious without the flexibility or lyricism of *Iphigenie* or *Tasso*, the device of stichomythia is tediously overused, and the schematizing, even abstraction of the characters, where the good are unreally good and the bad melodramatically evil, put the play beyond the sympathy of many.

The severe stylization robs the play of much historical coloration, even of intrinsic historical interest, except as a record of Goethe's attempts to come to terms with history. The political figures are typified into little more than allegories of a power-struggle – Eugenie is the only named character, the rest being designated by status – and there is only scant information on the precise implications of the struggle, since its principal figures scarcely appear on stage. Perhaps these objections would be less significant had Goethe gone on to complete his planned continuation of the story of Eugenie; as it is, the play suffers from the uneasy discrepancy between the anecdotal and private material he found in his source and the 'typological' representative dimensions with which he sought to invest the story of a figure who was at most a minor actress on the historical fringe of pre-revolutionary France.

OCCASIONAL DRAMA, FESTIVAL PLAYS AND MASQUERADES

Die natürliche Tochter, unfinished, allusive and inconclusive as it was, marked Goethe's final attempt to exorcise in literary terms the historical trauma of the French Revolution, the significance of which he fully recognized, the causes of which he acknowledged, but the effects of which he could never bring himself to accept. It was only in the second part of *Faust*, completed in the last years of his life, in his encyclopedic final literary testament, that he succeeded in relativizing the Revolution by integrating it into a retrospective – and indeed prospective – historical profile of his own age; and even this he was able to do only allusively and allegorically, by adumbrating in a highly literary, abstract and symbolic pattern the antecedents and the consequences of what he had himself termed 'a new epoch in the history of the world'.

The major dramatic task preoccupying Goethe between 1797 and 1806 was the huge effort of will required to complete the first part of *Faust*, the project of his youth that he had worked on sporadically since the early 1770s, and which, he must have known by now, was destined to be a major, if not the major work of his life – even if he persuaded himself at times that this distinction belonged to his *Farbenlehre*. At all events, it was during these years devoted to the completion of *Faust* Part One that he realized his Faust project would eventually be continued into a second part, even if he could have had no very clear idea of just how, or how much later in his life, that second part would be resumed. Part One itself was not finished until 1806 – ironically enough, in the year following the death of Schiller, who had urged its completion. The Faust-drama will be considered integrally towards the end of this chapter.

Apart from the massive task of finishing *Faust* Part One, between *Die natürliche Tochter* and his resumption of work on Part Two in 1825, Goethe completed no major dramatic work other than his allegorical celebration of the defeat of

Napoleon, *Des Epimenides Erwachen*; the dramatic project that seemed to mean most to him in literary and existential terms during these years, *Pandora*, remained unfinished. For the rest, the last thirty years or so of Goethe's life produced only a string of occasional works: *Singspiele*, *Festspiele*, masquerades, *trionfi*, prologues and epilogues for the inauguration or reinauguration of theatres in Weimar, Lauchstädt, Leipzig, Halle, Berlin. This aspect of Goethe's literary activity is scarcely central to his *oeuvre*, but it should not be overlooked; it is a reflection of his intense personal involvement in live theatre in all its practical and aesthetic dimensions, and of his inventive sense of theatricality, of illusion and mimesis, allegory and masks, mime and choreography, music and song. And in these more or less elaborate court spectacles we can see the prototypes and antecedents of some of the spectacular theatrical set-pieces that he was to incorporate significantly into the *Gesamtkunstwerk* of *Faust* Part Two: the masquerade of Act One, the marine *trionfo* that concludes Act Two, and the operatic Euphorion episode of Act Three. Goethe's development of a highly stylized, allegorical and symbolic stage-craft in these occasional pieces is to some extent the extension and elaboration of the classicizing tendencies of earlier dramas, of *Iphigenie*, *Tasso* and *Die natürliche Tochter*; it may also be in part his effort to perpetuate, whether from personal conviction or courtly duty, pre-revolutionary aesthetic and theatrical values into the post-revolutionary period. It is equally the inheritance of the years of high classicism in Weimar, during which he and Schiller campaigned – with mixed success – against what they perceived as the banality of dramatic 'naturalism', that is, against the decadence of the earlier vigorous tradition of domestic realism in the theatre, of *bürgerliches Trauerspiel* (domestic tragedy) into the sentimental and lachrymose *Familiengemälde* (scenes of family life) of popular dramatists like Iffland and Kotzebue.

Paläophron und Neoterpe, a *Festspiel* of 1800 written in fulsome homage to the Dowager Duchess Anna Amalia, the founder and benevolent patroness of the Weimar cultural scene, is dedicated to her as a monument to the tradition she established. It is written for the most part in classicizing iambic trimeters, the metre in which that same year Goethe was drafting the earliest version of the Helen episode that was to reappear some twenty-five years later in Act Three of the second part of *Faust*; it uses theatrical masks in the perceived tradition of the Greek and Roman theatre, and represents in highly stylized and allegorical form the *querelle des anciens et des modernes*, the rivalry between classicizing traditionalism and innovative modernity – an issue that seemed particularly apposite to the turn of the century, even if the theme is lightly handled. Paläophron and Neoterpe, age and youth, the old and the new, are accompanied by their respective attributes, Griesgram and Haberecht (Grumpy and Opinionated), Gelbschnabel and Naseweis (Greenhorn and Knowall); they are finally reconciled when they dismiss their tiresome companions.

Was wir bringen (What We Offer) of 1802 is a similarly occasional piece of allegory written as a *Singspiel* to celebrate the opening of a new theatre in Lauchstädt, where the Weimar Court Theatre (itself re-established in 1791 under Goethe's supervision) held its summer performances. It is a burlesque that mixes figures from the popular stage with those of classical allegory: a peasant couple, at odds over the refurbishment of their ramshackle cottage (the old theatre at Lauchstädt was indeed a rustic affair) are visited, like Philemon and Baucis, by Mercury, who promises the magical transformation of their rude hut into a temple of high art. To be sure, this means the loss of a certain charming primitivism personified by the Rousseauistic Nymph, to the advantage of Phone (opera) and Pathos (tragedy); it also involves some persiflage of Father Märten and Mother Marthe as figures from Iffland's and Kotzebue's plays. The aesthetic reconciliation is pronounced by the romantically nostalgic Nymph, who recites Goethe's sonnet 'Natur und Kunst' to celebrate the higher union of real and ideal, nature and art, mimesis and symbolism in the neo-classical theatre – or, more precisely, in the neo-classical opera: *Was wir bringen* was acted as a prologue to a performance of Mozart's *La Clemenza di Tito* at Lauchstädt.

Among Goethe's most consistent contributions to the entertainment of the Weimar court was a series of *Maskenzüge, Aufzüge* and *trionfi*, of allegorical revues, masquerades and processions. From the earliest celebrations of the birthdays of Duchess Luise from 1776 to the elaborate masquerade for Maria Fedorovna in 1818, these more or less lavish court spectacles for various occasions were a regular feature of his output. As Goethe himself reminds us in a preamble to the published version of *Paläophron und Neoterpe*,[40] the printed scenario can give only a pale image of these performances: costume, décor, music, choreography and setting – indoors or outdoors – were the essence of such pageantry, which continued a long historical tradition of public and semi-public allegorical spectacle. Goethe knew of the Alexandrian triumphs described in minute detail by Athenaeus; he knew the pictorial representations of triumphs by Renaissance artists like Mantegna and Dürer; and he had read accounts of Florentine *trionfi*. He knew of the elaborate Baroque court festivals of the seventeenth and eighteenth centuries, and allegorical, often didactic, processions and festivals were a popular public art form throughout the eighteenth century, even into the era of the Revolution and of Napoleon in France. The most decisive experience of this kind of public spectacle for Goethe was the Roman Carnival, which he observed with barely concealed irritation in February 1787, but with absorbed fascination the following year as a popular *Volksfest* in which society held up a mirror to itself, distorting and caricaturing, carousing and commenting in the tradition of the Roman Saturnalia.[41]

To be sure, there is little of the street-theatre pantomime or the robust vulgarity of the Roman Carnival in Goethe's official masquerades, staged as they were for decorous and formal occasions of state, with members of the Weimar court and their children appearing in the often elaborately costumed roles. The great majority, not all of which have survived, were performed on and for the birthday of Duchess Luise on 30 January; the text of the dedicatory poem or prologue would be printed on silk ribbons and presented to Her Highness by one of the masks. Goethe was not always an enthusiastic contributor to these literary and theatrical chores demanded of him at Weimar – nor, by all accounts, was Karl August a keen participant. But Goethe's growing devotion to the Duchess, and no doubt his awareness of the need to keep her good will, ensured a regular output of such entertainments.

The themes and figures of the masquerades are fanciful and allegorical, mythical and historical: in 1781 a procession of Lapplanders and an Allegory of Winter with figures representing sleep, night, dreams and the various indoor activities of wintertime, followed by a procession of masked characters from the *commedia dell'arte*; in 1782 a pantomime or *comédie-ballet* with sorcerers, gnomes and nymphs, and a Carnival of the Four Ages in which the Golden Age was played by the Dowager Anna Amalia and the Age of Silver by the Duchess Luise; in 1784 a Dance of the Planets with zodiacal and astronomical figures. In the *Maskenzug* for 30 January 1798 to celebrate simultaneously the Duchess's birthday and the Peace of Campo Formio, a text of rather ponderous *ottava rima* was enlivened by choreographed contributions from various ladies of the court masquerading as Victory, Peace, Art and Agriculture; Abundance was represented by the mountainous wife of Chamberlain von Werthern. The birthday masquerade of 1802 allegorizes the literary genres united in homage to the Duchess; that of 1806 celebrates the Peace of Preßburg in the shadow of the threat of renewed hostilities between France and Prussia; elemental and planetary symbolism formed the basis of that of 1809. For 30 January 1810, Goethe staged an elaborate literary masque entitled *Die romantische Poesie* (Romantic Poetry) – not a celebration of the modern literary movement as such, but rather of the world of medieval culture that the Romantic writers and scholars had rediscovered and revived, in part at least as an assertion of German national consciousness at a time of political humiliation: the *Maskenzug* commemorates the legendary thirteenth-century *Sängerkrieg*, the literary tournament that took place in the Wartburg of Eisenach, which itself lay within the territorial borders of Sachsen-Weimar. *Minnesang* and *Nibelungenlied*, medieval love poetry, romances and sagas are invoked in a tribute acknowledging the richness and fascination of medieval literary traditions: the recognition by the 'Old Heathen', the pagan classicist, of the 'nordic' or 'gothic' heritage of German culture.

The most elaborate of all the Weimar masquerades is that composed and directed by Goethe for the visit to Weimar in December 1818 of Maria Fedorovna, Dowager Empress of Russia and mother of Princess Maria Pavlovna, the wife of Karl August's son and heir Karl Friedrich. According to Goethe, it required some six weeks of uninterrupted work – as long as it had taken him to write the first version of *Götz von Berlichingen*. Almost 150 people were involved, and the surviving cast-list includes some well-known names; Goethe himself played Mephistopheles. The revue combines due homage to the distinguished visitor with a celebration of Weimar culture, of the *Musenhof* established by the late Anna Amalia, of the achievements of Wieland, Herder, Schiller and Goethe himself; it also mingles political references with the literary material – to the Revolution, the Napoleonic Wars and German liberation, to the re-establishment of peace and unity in the European Restoration – albeit in official, public and politically quite uncontroversial terms. Also of some interest, finally, is the ceremony scripted by Goethe for the opening of a salt mine at Stotternheim near Erfurt in 1828, in which geological and technical advances in the mining industry are allegorically celebrated. Goethe had long since been officially and knowledgeably involved in the mining activities of the Duchy of Weimar, few of which were entirely successful or profitable. Here, he hails the techniques that allow the reliable detection of mineral wealth and its extraction from the chthonic powers that traditionally guard it – the gnomes who also appear as miners in the fiery spectacle of the *Flammengaukelspiel* that concludes the masquerade in the first act of *Faust* Part Two.

PANDORA AND EPIMENIDES

Pandora, a mythological *Festspiel*, was written in 1807–8 on commission for a Viennese literary periodical, *Prometheus*. It is unclear what prompted Goethe, other than this fortuitous commission, to return to the mythical material that had preoccupied him so centrally during his early creative career, and it seems that the project, for all his assertions that it meant so much to him, remained unfinished for equally fortuitous reasons: relations between the two editors of the journal had deteriorated so far that the completed first part of the play was withdrawn from publication. Further distractions, including the writing of *Die Wahlverwandtschaften*, prevented the completion of the second part, which was to deal with Pandora's return to the world.

Goethe's reformulation of the Pandora/Prometheus myth is radical. Prometheus is no longer the *Sturm und Drang* icon of creativity and defiant autonomy who taunts the Olympian gods and forms human creatures in his own image; Pandora is not the baleful, if alluring woman sent by Zeus to punish his rebellion, who unleashed all human ills onto the world to plague the creatures of Prometheus. These myths are superseded in Goethe's play, they lie in the past: if for Prometheus Pandora had represented a dire temptation devised by the gods as retribution, for his brother Epimetheus she was the highest gift bestowed on humanity, all-gifted and all-giving. Having loved Epimetheus she departed, leaving with him only one daughter, Epimeleia (Care); their other daughter, Elpore (Hope) had vanished with her mother. Epimetheus, bereft and consumed by nostalgic grief, passes his days in depressive mourning of his loss and in hopeful but ineffectual dreaming of her future return, while Prometheus rules with tyrannical authority over a race of enslaved humanity devoted to armed struggle and oppression: his smiths have become armourers, his shepherds warriors. In this state of fall, disharmony and violence are endemic; Epimeleia is violated by one of the shepherds, who is killed by her cousin and lover Phileros, the son of Prometheus. But she is in turn attacked by Phileros in a jealous rage; it seems that Pandora's daughter is both the heiress and the victim of her mother's destructive gifts. At this point an already heavily symbolic action moves into mythical abstraction: in penance for his attack on Epimeleia Phileros hurls himself into the sea, but is saved from self-destruction by an extraordinary process apparently orchestrated by Eos, the dawn, harbinger of Helios and herald of the gods' will. Fishermen surround him, dolphins carry him to shore, and as he emerges reborn from the waves he is surrounded by a Bacchic *thiasus* and fêted as a young Dionysus. Epimeleia, herself saved from the flames in which she was to perish as a victim of the warrior-shepherds' revenge, is reunited with him, and a new generation supersedes the dismal antagonism of their respective fathers. Eos leaves Prometheus with her cautionary *envoi*: Titans and humans may propose, but the gods dispose – their will be done.

The import of this thematically and linguistically dense and complex allegory is less than clear – quite apart from the fact that it remained fragmentary. In the schematically planned sequel entitled *Pandorens Wiederkunft* (Pandora's Return), the antagonism of the brothers, which had been temporarily suspended in their efforts to rescue their children, re-emerges; the second coming of Pandora overrules Prometheus, and the opening of her casket brings, not the ills and plagues of the traditional myth, but the gifts of art and science, to which Phileros and Epimeleia will devote themselves in a sacred priesthood. Pandora and Epimetheus take their place among the immortals, and *Elpore thraseia* (Bold or Confident Hope) pronounces the epilogue *ad spectatores*.

In the antagonistic duality of Prometheus and Epimetheus, Goethe has typified the tension between activism and inertia, between a ruthless will to power and enervating introversion, between progressive utilitarianism and utopian dreaming. The allegorical reference of this existential dichotomy, if there is one, is not immediately obvious. It can be, and has been, read in cultural terms as the tension between the progressive ethos of the Enlightenment, the technological optimism of the *philosophes* with their dictionary of *arts et métiers*, and the passive sentimentalism of Rousseauistic *Empfindsamkeit*. It might be seen prophetically in terms of a proto-Marxist doctrine of alienation, of the enslavement of labour and the exploitation of a workforce in the name of a ruthless 'Promethean' work ethic, the only present alternative to which is an existence of futile quasi-aristocratic inactivity and idleness. It has been deciphered more specifically as the historical confrontation between Napoleonic military aggression and the passivity of Prussia before and after the Battle of Jena: the play was written in the years immediately following the nadir of Prussian history in 1806.

The progression of the play, in its prehistory and its projected sequel, is structured on the pattern of the triadic myth that informs much of Romantic ideology, and which also underlies Schiller's aesthetic thinking: the loss of an original Arcadia, the state of fall that follows, and the final redemption and establishment, not of the original harmony and innocence, but of a new and perhaps higher state of reintegrated harmony. The invocation of Poussin to indicate the stage setting in the opening scene suggests a lost Arcadian idyll, a duality and disharmony that can only be redeemed by a drastic revision of values and behaviour. The elemental symbolism of fire and water, the ordeals from which Epimeleia and Phileros emerge respectively, indicate the restoration of violated nature, the reintegration of an elemental harmony of which the Arion myth, modulating into the epiphany of Dionysus, is the archetype. It is the harmony shattered by Prometheus's ruthless exploitation of the elements to forge weapons and machinery, anticipated by the reunion of Phileros and Epimeleia as lovers in a Dionysian festival, subsequently to be signalled by the second coming of Pandora, and finally realized by the lovers as priests of a higher culture that unites arts and science in a common human purpose. The abandoning of a perverted Prometheanism and the apotheosis of Pandora and Epimetheus leaves the future to this new generation under the aegis of *Elpore thraseia*, Hope not for a vanished and lamented dream, but as a symbol of energetic and productive confidence in a new era.

For all its portentous abstraction, *Pandora* is a remarkable, if allegorically obscure, mingling of ancient myth and modern reference; it is also notable in that it mixes classicizing metrical forms with modern rhymed verse in a way that anticipates Goethe's other (and rather more coherent) allegory of ancient and modern themes, the third act of *Faust* Part Two. In its wide range of prosodic and rhetorical styles, its admixture of iambic trimeter and choric ode forms with dactylic and trochaic rhymed verse; in its intercalation of passages of high lyricism (Epimeleia's elegy of lines 491–568, Eos's recital of Phileros's triumphal emergence from the sea in lines 997–1042), and of the aggressive chants of smiths, shepherds and warriors; in the allegorical abstraction of its *dramatis personae*; in its Dionysian symbolism, its use of the festive *trionfo*, of operatic and balletic chorus and choreography – in all these aspects, *Pandora* anticipates the form and idiom of the work in which Goethe also sought to integrate high classicism with issues and concerns that were essentially those of his own day. This fragmentary *Festspiel* is in many ways a prototype of the Helen episode of the second part of *Faust*.

Des Epimenides Erwachen (The Awakening of Epimenides) is also an allegorical *Festspiel*, but one whose political and historical reference is altogether less obscure than that of *Pandora*. Commissioned in May 1814 by the director of the Prussian Royal Theatre in Berlin, August Wilhelm Iffland, to celebrate the defeat of Napoleon, the rehabilitation of Prussian prestige and the establishment of peace in Europe, its composition and performance were beset by problems. The original intention to stage it for the triumphant entry into Berlin by King Friedrich Wilhelm III, Tsar Alexander and Emperor Franz was frustrated by a bizarre combination of factors. The dilatoriness of the composer Bernhard Anselm Weber, Friedrich Wilhelm's hostility to Goethe's authorship, and the sudden death of Iffland led to a series of delays, with the result that the pageant was not performed until 30 March 1815, a year after the surrender of Paris to the allies. But by then history had provided its own *coup de théâtre*: on 1 March Napoleon had escaped from Elba, and twenty days later was back in Paris – which effectively dampened the reception of *Epimenides*. By the time it was performed in Weimar in February 1816, with tactful textual emendations in honour of Grand Duke Karl August and his wife, the spectre of the Hundred Days had passed; but Goethe had already, in an epigram written in the autumn of 1814, unwittingly remarked (with reference to the tiresome delays in the Berlin performance) that his Epimenides will have woken too late – or too early.[42]

The legend of Epimenides is the classical archetype of the figure – in its modern manifestation, that of Rip van Winkle – who outsleeps his own time, and returns gifted with a unique clarity of vision to observe social or political changes from a detached, ironic or satirical perspective: Epimenides of Crete slept for fifty-seven years, and subsequently achieved the status of seer or prophet. The initial reaction to Goethe's presentation of his pageant as the awakening of a slumberer was that his hero represented Friedrich Wilhelm of Prussia and, by extension, the Prussian nation's early impotence in the face of the Napoleonic threat. This alarming interpretation, to which Iffland himself initially subscribed, was resisted strenuously by Goethe, who had no wish to jeopardize his already uneasy relationship with the Prussian monarch – who in any case appears rather more heroically in the play as the 'Prince of Youth' (*Jugendfürst*). It is certainly feasible to see the sleeping hero as Prussia itself, but the critical consensus is that Epimenides is a projection of Goethe's own perceptions of the turbulent period of German and European history up to 1814–15: had he not held himself aloof from political commitment between 1789 and 1815 in his Olympian classical isolation in Weimar, had he not held Napoleon in such high esteem, and had he not expressed profound reservations towards the liberation of Germany from Napoleon in 1813?

Even allowing for the frankly tendentious nature of this piece commissioned specifically to celebrate the defeat of 'his' Emperor, it is still astonishing that Goethe was able to adapt to such triumphalist and almost jingoistic material. If Epimenides is indeed supposed to be a figure of detached and unpartisan historical perspective, of the ironic ambivalence of the poet on which Goethe prided himself, there is little enough evidence of it in this one-sided celebration of the defeat of Napoleon; indeed, it is difficult not to see in the figure of Epimenides the personification of the spirit of Germany, of Prussian or of German resistance to Napoleonic ambition which finally roused itself to confront the tyrant in a spirit of liberty and unity. The final chorus of the pageant celebrates unequivocally this new national unity and the pride in nationhood it engendered:

> So rissen wir uns ringsherum
> Von fremden Banden los.
> Nun sind wir Deutsche wiederum,
> Nun sind wir wieder groß.

> And so on every side we tore
> The foreign bonds in twain.
> Now Germans we can be once more,
> Now we are great again.

And yet for all its disturbing nationalism, the play is also a vivid expression of Goethe's profound revulsion from war, from its barbarities and its chaotic disruption of social and political continuity, which he had witnessed at first hand in the campaigns of 1792 and 1793; if he detested social disorder, revolution and civil strife, how much more abhorrent was the wholesale organization and mechanization of those evils into full-scale modern European conflict. Indeed, in the light of the territorial scrambles of the Congress of Vienna, Goethe wrote the following lines, entitled *Epimenides' Awakening, final verse*, in which he urgently warns his own countrymen against the ambition and aggression that had undone Napoleon – lines that he did not, however, publish, but consigned to his personal papers:

> Verflucht sei, wer nach falschem Rat,
> Mit überfrechem Mut,
> Das was der Korse-Franke tat

Nun als ein Deutscher tut!
Er fühle spät, er fühle früh,
Es sei ein dauernd Recht;
Ihm geh es, trotz Gewalt und Müh,
Ihm und den Seinen schlecht!

A curse on those misguided, who
In arrogance are led
To seek as Germans now to do
That which the Corsican did!
For let them know at every hour
That right it will prevail;
For all their efforts and their power,
They and their kind shall fail!

Des Epimenides Erwachen is a nice demonstration of the dilemma of the 'official' man of letters, of the uncomfortable compromises forced on the *engagé* poet – whether he is committed to a stance of opposition or of conformity. The extravagant and fulsome style of Iffland's request for co-operation in the project gives an idea of the expectations invested in this tendentious piece of theatrical propaganda: since Luther's Reformation, writes Iffland, there can have been no more lofty undertaking than the recent liberation of Germany, than the national zeal with which Prussia, almost entirely by her own efforts (*sic*!) rose to honourable nationhood – and there could be no better pen to commemorate this historic apogee than that of the nation's most distinguished citizen.[43]

Goethe was not immune to flattery; but he must have been conscious of the ironies of this commission, which demanded that he should abandon his purported poetic impartiality for a political statement in which he was to celebrate the defeat of his hero Napoleon by a massive European military alliance, in which he was to rejoice in peace while hailing it as the achievement of a Prussian feat of arms, and in which he was to glorify a national unity that was founded on the ruins of the Holy Roman Empire. The dedicatory poem in *ottava rima* that prefaces the play points up the uncomfortable position of the poet as political apologist; it reformulates in its opening lines a maxim that was originally included in a poem of 1812 addressed to Napoleon's Empress Marie Louise, in which the poet expresses the conviction that a man whose ambition is universal must also have ambitions of peace. By 1816 this perception of Napoleon was perforce modified, if only for the purposes of the *Festspiel*, into the maxim that Napoleonic ambition was not a will to universal peace, but a will to universal power.

The allegorical action of *Des Epimenides Erwachen* is operatic and balletic, with an admixture of masquerade and *trionfo*. While the passive 'hero' sleeps, destructive forces are unleashed in the guise of demons. The Demons of War and Oppression devastate the land, but even more subversive are the Demons of Guile, of vested interests and opportunism: clerical, legal, diplomatic and political forces swarm in the wake of brutal militarism, manipulating and exploiting the consequences of disorder and chaos. Love and Faith are wooed and enslaved by the Demon of Oppression – under Napoleonic occupation, many in Germany were captivated, voluntarily or involuntarily, for political or apolitical reasons, by the charismatic spell of the conquering Bonaparte, among them Goethe himself; for many, indeed, he was, at least initially, less a foreign invader than an enlightened liberator who introduced legal, administrative and political reform into a moribund order.

Only Hope resists the blandishments of the Demon, frees her sisters and proclaims a new era of resistance and liberty: the combined forces of Russia, Austria, Britain and Sweden are gathering, and Epimenides finally emerges from the vault in which he has been sleeping into the ruins of the old order. Hope and the 'Prince of Youth' – possibly a conflation of Friedrich Wilhelm of Prussia and the young German student activists of the Wars of Liberation – call the (Prussian) people to arms in a spirit of new nationhood. They lead on a triumphal *défilé* of the allied nations, represented in the Weimar performance as the four allied commanders Blücher, Schwarzenberg, Wittgenstein and Wellington, and fulsome homage is paid to the respective rulers of Prussia, Austria and Russia (and, in the local performance, to Karl August and Duchess Luise). The burning of Moscow, the disaster of Napoleon's retreat from Russia, the battles of Leipzig and Waterloo and the second occupation of Paris are celebrated in the final apotheosis of the spirit of German (or at least of Prussian) unity, closing with a chorus in the cadences of a Lutheran hymn that is tantamount to a national anthem. *Des Epimenides Erwachen* is a classic instance of history being written by the victors, it is Goethe's public statement as the official poet of the German people, and as such it conceals his most private feelings and opinions on contemporary historical events more than it reveals them; indeed, it may well be that his own deepest sentiments at this time were altogether too complex and ambivalent to find expression in such a pageant of national celebration. Only some fifteen years later was he able to present these sentiments in more subtle and no doubt more accurate, albeit more cryptic form: in the heavily coded allegories of the fourth act of *Faust* Part Two.

FAUST

The summit of Goethe's dramatic achievement is undoubtedly the play that also represents the major single work of his creative *oeuvre*, *Faust*. And yet the terms drama, play, even dramatic poem are scarcely adequate to define generically a *Gesamtkunstwerk* that not only draws on a vast range of stage conventions and traditions, that not only reflects and demonstrates the great spectrum of Goethe's literary and intellectual activity, but which also represents his existential testament, his last (and indeed some of his first) thoughts on humanity, on human history and institutions, on the grandeurs and the follies of the human condition, its hopes and despairs, its values and its illusions, its scope and its limitations, its nobility and its criminality. It is unlikely, when his imagination was first captivated by the obscure and notorious figure of Dr Faust, whether in his childhood or again in his early youth, that Goethe remotely imagined that this ambivalent and fascinating, but historically quite insignificant figure would become the central focus of a work that would, for better or for worse, be perceived as both a major national German poem and a universal fable.

It is only to be expected that such a protracted and sporadic literary project written over the whole span of Goethe's creative career should reflect the changing cultural, philosophical and aesthetic preoccupations of its author, and that its thematic and formal diversity should raise intractable problems of unity and continuity. When Goethe was first prompted to literary treatment of the semi-legendary magus Faust who haunted the cultural fringes of Reformation Germany, it was no doubt the outrageous, even blasphemous, aspect that caught his imagination: the man supposed to have defied God and allied himself with the devil, to have put himself beyond the pale of social and religious conformity, was perceived as the specifically German, specifically sixteenth-century manifestation of the Promethean archetype, as the arrogant but fearless assertion of human individuality against human limitations, against accepted pieties and wisdoms. Goethe brought to Faust, the negative exemplum of Reformation demonology, both the intellectual autonomy of the German *Aufklärung* and the emotional self-assertion of the *Sturm und Drang*, both the restlessly enquiring scepticism of the human mind and the passionate assertion of existential freedom, creating in the process a myth of modern, post-Reformation, if not quite post-Christian, complexity and ambivalence.

THE *URFAUST*

The first dramatic treatment of the Faust figure by Goethe, the so-called *Urfaust* of *c*.1770–5, is a creative concoction of Goethe's cultural interests and enthusiasms of the time: the German Reformation, the secular and spiritual overlap of Middle Ages and Renaissance, the mingling currents of mysticism and thought, of alchemy and science, the popular idioms of folk song and ballad, of itinerant theatre, puppet play and *Fastnachtspiel*, of narrative chapbook and woodcut, of domestic drama – and Shakespeare. This early and fragmentary draft form of the first part of *Faust*, preserved quite accidentally and only discovered and published in 1887, gives a fascinating palimpsest of the final version of the first part, which was only completed in 1806 and not published until 1808; it is a glimpse into the raw and youthful *Sturm und Drang* material that was refined and partly obscured when the fifty-year-old Goethe forced himself to bring his story of Faust to a provisional conclusion.

The profound theological and existential dimensions of the completed Part One are scarcely touched on in the *Urfaust*, even implicitly; this is a story of human defiance and hubris, of a despairing scholar who turns from 'natural' magic to the black arts, who compacts with the devil and finds love. To be sure, the love he finds is not the casual lechery of the traditional Faust of the narrative legend, neither the succubus Helen of Troy nor the icon of classical beauty that transports Marlowe's Faustus; but nor is it, for all the domestic milieu of Gretchen and her family, conventional marital bliss. It is an ambivalent and precarious *mésalliance* between a renegade intellectual and an artless, though by no means wholly naive, young woman that is blighted from the beginning: symbolically by Faust's pact with hell, and psychologically and dramatically by his own dualism, by the struggle between his appetites and his conscience, by the discrepancy between his persona as young lover and his other self, the reckless intellectual and emotional adventurer. It is the well-worn eighteenth-century literary theme of sentimental novels and domestic drama (as well as a familiar social phenomenon of the time): the seduction and abandonment of a woman by a man of superior social or educational class, and her subsequent despair, distraction, infanticide and execution. If it is domestic tragedy, it is also domestic tragedy with supernatural dimensions, with the potential symbolic implications that arise from Faust's (in this early version, unstaged and inexplicit) pact with Mephistopheles. But whatever Faust's motives for entering into a pact with hell – and Goethe does not present them as wholly deplorable – it is his own, Faust's, instincts that initiate and precipitate the human tragedy of Gretchen; the devil merely encourages and expedites a catastrophe from which Faust cannot exculpate himself. Having encompassed the devastation of Gretchen and her family, Faust has no answer to Mephisto's terrible question when Faust seeks to shift the blame: 'Who was it that led her into destruction? I – or you?'

The power of the *Urfaust* fragment lies not only in the moral ambiguities of Faust's emotional and diabolical entanglement, but also crucially in the compelling poetic virtuosity of its apparently untidy and sporadic sequence of scenes. To be sure, the action veers and plunges drastically; Faust changes roles bewilderingly from frustrated scholar to browbeating intellectual to carousing magician to ardent young lover to self-hating betrayer and finally to the frantic and helpless witness of Gretchen's misery. The profound resonances of the opening scene where Faust conjures the visions of the Macrocosm and the Erdgeist give way to scenes of satire, farce, drunken pranks, sentimental courtship and finally to harrowing pathos. To be sure, the reader or spectator must imaginatively infer many links missing from the explicit stage action: the introduction of Mephistopheles and his pact with Faust, the deaths of Gretchen's mother and brother, her killing of the child and her death sentence for infanticide, and the action leaps from Faust's last assignation with her to the morning of her execution – a gap of at least one year. And yet this kaleidoscopic, flickering series of disparate encounters is held together by a vividness and verve of language and characterization, of movement and tempo, of lyrical intensity and dramatic concentration that can only partly be accounted for by the spell cast on Goethe by Shakespeare's seemingly chaotic dramatic construction, or by Herder's explication of the sporadic structure of orally transmitted folk traditions, of epics and ballads that leap and plunge from one peak of narrative to the other. For all its gaps and jolts, the *Urfaust* is held together by a vivid poetic unity that is paradoxically utterly diverse in its forms: the bumpy *Knittelvers* and flexible *Madrigalvers* that make up its basic idiom, folk song and prayer, free rhythms and prose, drinking songs and religious sequence.

Most of all, however, it is the sheer speed and dramatic economy that holds the

Urfaust together – an economy in which the lacunae of the story itself are a significant factor. After the (relatively) leisurely pace of the opening 'university' scenes and the interlude in Auerbach's Cellar, the tragedy of Gretchen, its inception, its crisis and its catastrophe, is acted out with an intensity that is only matched – if it is matched – by Büchner's similarly fragmentary drama *Woyzeck*. In this extreme form of dramatic concentration, the lyrical density of speeches and songs, of symbolic images and gestures, are of first importance as vehicles of the psychological action: Gretchen's folk song 'Der König in Thule' has a dramatic function similar to Ophelia's or Desdemona's songs; Faust's 'catechism' to Gretchen speaks volumes about the specious evasiveness of his protestations; Gretchen's passionate meditation at the spinning-wheel charts her frank emotional and physical responses; the scene between her and Lieschen at the well reveals a whole spectrum of religious and social bigotry; her prayer at the shrine of the Mother of Sorrows in the cadences of the *Stabat Mater* reveals the anguish of her mind poised between doubt and hope; the awesome and claustrophobic scene of her panic fear in the cathedral is underscored by organ music and the terrible imagery of the *Dies irae*; Faust's tirade of the cascading torrent that engulfs the peaceful alpine hut encapsulates all his ambivalence and self-hatred; and Gretchen's prison song adapted from a fairy-tale harrowingly conveys her distracted grief as she awaits her execution.

It was this extraordinary, indeed unique, mixture of clowning and mysticism, of vulgar farce and high pathos, of wit and solemnity, of rhetoric and artless expression, of poetry and prose, of evil and innocence, cynicism and idealism, criminality and sentiment, that later went to form the substance, though not the framework, of *Faust* Part One. This original inner core of Goethe's *Faust* drama was the product of the *Sturm und Drang* years, the years in Strasbourg and Frankfurt that also produced *Götz von Berlichingen*, a similarly kaleidoscopic, if very much less economically structured drama that draws on the same period of German history, albeit from a quite different perspective. Faust is here a figure of the *Sturm und Drang*; his one-sided debate with his assistant Wagner is, among other things, the assertion of impassioned feeling over arid rationalism, of mercurial genius over plodding endeavour. It is a nice matter of debate, however, how far Faust's impatient and restless dissatisfaction can be identified with that of Goethe himself, even at this early stage. The young Goethe is surely closer to Faust's Promethean defiance than to Wagner's submissive timidity; but Goethe has also qualified and relativized Faust's extravagant strivings with the cynical wit of Mephistopheles, who constantly provides the caustic antidote to Faustian self-delusion and self-deceit – and Goethe's devil has many of the best lines, if not the best tunes. This is a speculative problem; but the older Goethe, as he came to fill out and extend his Faust drama, created an increasingly ironic distance between himself and his hero. Moreover, the fact that this original Faust material lay unknown to the wider German public for so long (though Goethe did read from the manuscript to selected friends, who would convey their more or less garbled impressions to others) meant that there was no great literary response to this *Sturm und Drang* product – in contrast to *Götz von Berlichingen*, which spawned a plethora of *Ritterdramen*. Although it appeared in fragmentary form in 1790, the impetus of the

Sturm und Drang had by then spent itself; by the time *Faust* Part One appeared in its final form, heavily padded out and encapsulated within a metaphysical frame, that phase of German literature was a distant memory.

FAUST PART ONE

Among the many unfinished manuscripts taken by Goethe to Italy in 1786 was the *Urfaust* manuscript, or a version of it. It is generally thought that he wrote at least two additional scenes in Rome, 'Hexenküche' (Witch's Kitchen) and part of 'Wald und Höhle' (Forest and Cavern); and on his return he worked on an interim version that was published, to great public interest, in 1790. *Faust. Ein Fragment* (Faust. A Fragment) is tantalizingly unfinished; not only does it break off at the end of the cathedral scene with Gretchen's swoon, omitting the subsequent scenes already contained in the *Urfaust,* but it also still lacks the details of Faust's pact with Mephistopheles – only some 100 lines of dialogue between them after the apparent conclusion of a bargain were published. Some prosodic changes and cuts were made to certain scenes; otherwise, the only new material comprises the 'Hexenküche' and 'Wald und Höhle' scenes. The latter also incorporates some of the *Urfaust* material already written, and it is placed in a way that interrupts the dramatically swift and powerful succession of the three short scenes that follow each other in the *Urfaust*: 'Am Brunnen' (At the Well), 'Zwinger' (A Shrine) and 'Dom' (Cathedral). Why Goethe published his work in this unsatisfactory form is unclear – whether in response to public curiosity, whether because he doubted that he would ever finally complete it, or whether in order to fill out the volumes of the edition of his collected works for Göschen. At all events, it was a further seven years before he resumed work on the final phase of the composition of *Faust* Part One.

By this time, 1797, Goethe was approaching fifty. He had come a long way from the immature enthusiasms of his early youth, he was no longer the volatile and charismatic *Stürmer und Dränger* who had been able, however partially, to empathize with the extravagant aspirations of his Faust; he was a Privy Councillor of the Duchy of Weimar, returned from his Grand Tour of Italy, the sober student of natural philosophy, the paterfamilias who had experienced, both vicariously and at first hand in the French Campaign of 1792, the historic upheavals of the French Revolution and its aftermath, he was the author of *Iphigenie* and *Tasso*, of the domestic epic *Hermann und Dorothea* and of the monumental novel *Wilhelm Meisters Lehrjahre*. Above all he was, in collaboration with Schiller, the leading theorist and pundit of classical Weimar culture, worlds away from the 'barbarous', 'nordic', gothic extravagance of his Faust drama. And yet it was Schiller who urged him to complete this 'witches' product', as Goethe called it, and it was Schiller who advised him to contain the exuberantly imaginative material of the *Fragment* within a conceptual framework, within a ring or hoop that would bind the disparate material with a coherent informing idea. This posed a double problem for Goethe; not naturally given to abstract thought, he nevertheless acknowledged that some conceptual organization or superstructure was needed to raise the play from its original inchoate, if creatively vibrant form. In addition, he realized what an effort of will and imagination would be required to think himself back over almost thirty years, from his present plateau of high classicism and exemplary models to what he now considered frankly to be the product of an immature fascination with the bizarre and the fantastic. What is remarkable about the final version of *Faust* Part One is not only the inventive and unconventional way in which Goethe imposed his new material onto that of the two previous phases, but that he completed this first part of the work at all.

The ambivalent feelings with which Goethe approached this task are articulated in the *ottava rima* 'Zueignung' (Dedication) with which he prefaces *Faust*; the 'shadowy figures' addressed in his opening lines, whether they are taken as those of his own imaginative creation or as the earlier friends and companions of his youthful literary efforts, emerge from the 'haze and mist' of his creative past. This poem, and the two prefatory scenes Prelude on the Stage and Prologue in Heaven, form the conceptual framework that relativizes the human action of the whole story of Faust; for by now Goethe had decided that it was to be in two parts, even if the second one was uncertain of completion, and this framework is evidently designed to encapsulate both parts of the work. While the function of the Prologue in Heaven is clear enough – to provide a cosmic perception of Faust's career on earth *sub specie aeternitatis* – that of the theatrical prelude is less obvious; indeed, it has been suggested that it was composed for another occasion altogether, and subsequently (as was the 'Walpurgis Night's Dream') interpolated into *Faust*.

Certainly, the Prelude reads like some of Goethe's formal speeches or preludes written to inaugurate theatrical performances in and around Weimar, which as director of the Court Theatre he was expected to provide; but this comic–serious exchange between the three principals of an itinerant theatre also contrives to suggest the fiction that the play we are about to see is indeed the one discussed by the three figures: an impromptu, last-minute concoction devised by the respective advocates of commercial success, popular entertainment and high art. The voice of the poet–playwright cannot be identified as that of Goethe – the poet and his lofty pretensions are ironized at least as much as the anxious commercialism of the director or the sardonic pragmatism of the clown; the whole scene is informed by Goethe's own manifold theatrical duties and responsibilities in Weimar. The Prelude is also the author's apologia to his audience, his signal to the public to expect from the drama a whole gamut of theatrical experience, a bold mixture of themes and styles, of pathos and farce, of sentiment and spectacle – an expectation more than fulfilled in the second part of the work, even if at this stage Goethe had no very clear idea of how it would progress beyond Part One. The Prelude is also a factor in the structure of encapsulation that characterizes *Faust*, and this glimpse behind the scenes stresses the theatricality of the play: the following scene, for all its momentous metaphysical implications, represents a theatrical heaven that opens and closes as a piece of stage machinery – a feature that recurs in the penultimate scene of Part Two, where Mephistopheles is cast as the stage-manager of a theatrical hell that is wheeled onto the stage like the scenery of a medieval morality play. The story of Faust is in many ways, albeit on a grand scale, a morality play acted out in the great theatre of the world; and if the Prelude presented the stage as a world, the scene in Heaven presents the world as a stage.

It is on this world stage that the cosmic experiment involving Faust is to be acted out: in Part One on the narrow and circumscribed stage of a small German university town, and in Part Two on the wider scene of public affairs. In the course of an ironic exchange of verbal cut-and-thrust between God and devil, the criteria for an individual's salvation are laid down – but in terms that are, to say the least, opaque. For not only does the Lord appear in this scene to anticipate Faust's salvation, and to allow that effort and error are inseparable in human activity; he also calmly informs the devil that he is an active agent in that salvation – by constantly goading humankind into activity, by preventing man from falling into sloth, inertia, indolence and passivity, the devil works creatively in the divine scheme. Undeterred by this paradoxical role assigned to him, Mephistopheles challenges the Lord to a wager for Faust's soul; he appears confident enough that he can seduce Faust from his *Urquell*, his 'primal source', and drag him down the devil's path to perdition. These are the criteria laid down from the beginning for the theological experiment that is to be tested in the life of Faust. It is unlikely that Goethe at this stage had any clear idea of how, or in what terms, he was to resolve the complex issues raised here and later in the bargain concluded between Faust and Mephistopheles – though it is almost certain that he had already envisaged Faust's salvation in one form or another. At all events, the scene is set for the action on the world's stage; Goethe was to leave the final working out of Faust's end and the fate of his soul for another twenty-five years or more.

Goethe now set out to adapt the already existing material from the *Urfaust* and *Fragment* versions to this metaphysical framework. Quite remarkably, this involved very little change from the early versions, but it did require the considerable addition of new scenes which, while they formulate much more fully the relationship between Faust and Mephistopheles, do not affect the substance of the original draft, which survives in its main lines quite clearly into the final version: the scenes of Faust's despair, his invocation of magical visions, his emancipation from the arid world of scholarship, and his disastrous affair with Gretchen. The most substantial new material concerned the filling out of the 'great gap' in the action, the introduction of Mephistopheles to Faust and the concluding of a pact and bargain between them. Since Goethe wished at least to leave open the possibility of Faust's ultimate salvation, since he had indeed appeared to signal it in the Prologue in Heaven, it was clearly impossible to present the pact in terms of the traditional legal contract of the narrative or theatrical versions of the Faust legend: that the devil should serve Faust for a period of twenty-four years, and be entitled to his soul at the expiry of that term. Instead, Goethe substituted for the contract a confusing and ambiguous wager in which Faust challenges the devil to satisfy his desires: he bets Mephistopheles that the devil's arts cannot reduce him to a state of self-satisfied torpor. If Mephisto can so delude him or beguile him with pleasure as to make him wish to suspend time and bid the passing moment stay, if Faust should be so satisfied as to lay himself on a 'bed of indolence', then the devil can cast him in fetters, then he will gladly perish, then he will acknowledge that his time has come.

The terms of this obscure wager – which are, *nota bene*, Faust's terms, not those of Mephisto or the Lord – raise almost insoluble problems. For since the Lord has already made it clear to Mephistopheles himself that his very function in creation is to spur men out of sloth into activity, it appears prima facie that the devil is here accepting a wager or challenge that he cannot possibly win – that is, to reduce Faust to a bed of indolence; indeed, Mephisto himself appears already to have acknowledged his paradoxically positive role to Faust, when he introduced himself as 'a part of that power that always wills evil and always creates good' (lines 1335–6). There are certain factors that qualify this bizarre situation. First, Faust no-where alludes specifically to the fate of his soul or to the hereafter – indeed, he explicitly declares that 'das Drüben' (the Beyond) is of little concern to him; his terms appear only to refer to his own death, to the end of time for him, and to the devil's release from his obligations – though admittedly much depends here on the understanding of the phrase 'zugrunde gehn' (line 1702), whether we read it as 'perish' or 'be damned'. Second, even in the Prologue in Heaven, it appears that there is a possibility of perdition for Faust: that is, if the devil can lead him downwards on *his* path, then he might lead Faust into a morass of sin and guilt that would put him beyond the reach of redemption. And Mephistopheles realizes that with someone of Faust's insatiable appetites, this is a distinct possibility; as he gleefully anticipates in lines 1856–67, Faust's unbridled curiosity, his titanic insa-tiability is the very dynamo that will drive him to perdition. Third, and most crucially, the wager between Faust and Mephisto is not the only arrangement concluded between them, for the devil has been careful to stipulate his own terms for their relationship in lines 1656–9: that he will serve Faust assiduously on earth, provided that Faust will do the same for him in the hereafter. Since Faust is indifferent to any talk of the 'Drüben', the devil meets no opposition to his own terms.

It is idle to speculate whether it is the devil's terms, or Faust's, that are formally written into the 'blood-scribed document' that Mephistopheles carefully keeps for the rest of Faust's life, since no text is given; but it does appear that these are the terms and conditions on which the devil is operating, and we ignore Mephisto's pact, as opposed to Faust's wager, at our critical peril. It is reasonable to assume that Mephisto ignores the terms of Faust's sententiously rhetorical and very imprecise wager or challenge, content in the knowledge that in binding the devil to himself in a master–servant relationship, Faust has also bound himself to the devil; it is notable that at the end of the play Mephisto makes no mention of any wager with Faust, but invokes only his contract with him (lines 11612–13), and speaks only of 'the lofty soul that pledged itself to me' (line 11830). It might even be argued that Mephistopheles goes out of his way *not* to win his wager with Faust, indeed, that he actually contrives to lose his wager with Faust in order to win his much more important wager with the Lord; for far from trying to satisfy Faust's aspirations, he will contrive to destroy, to negate and to frustrate those aspirations, whether they concern Gretchen, Helen of Troy, or Faust's political, aesthetic, technical or sociological ambitions in the second part of the drama. In this respect, as in many others, Mephistopheles is part of a well-established tradition of popular comedy – that of the clever and resourceful servant who succeeds at once in furthering and in frustrating his master's wishes. And in doing so, he imagines, he will lead Faust down his path beyond the pale of salvation, and will have won his challenge or wager with the Lord. And indeed, in the final instance it is a close-run thing; Faust's salvation is secured not in terms of Faust's wager or of Mephisto's contract or pact, nor unequivocally in terms of the wager in Heaven – only by an act of subterfuge, by a hilarious stratagem of seduction, are the powers of Heaven able to snatch Faust's soul from the legions of hell.

In this way, albeit at the cost of some unclarity and even confusion, Goethe was able to integrate the existing material of the *Urfaust* and *Fragment* into his final conception. For now Faust's conjurations of the Macrocosm and the Earth Spirit are no longer isolated elements in Faust's desperate search for release from conventional scholarship and for mystical revelation; they also represent his abandoning of the *vita contemplativa* for the *vita activa*. In turning from abstract speculative thought to active engagement in the welter of human experience and the affairs of the world, Faust is already embarking on the programme that Mephisto has in mind for him: away from the 'barren heath' of speculation into the lush green pastures of life (lines 1830–3). From now on, Mephistopheles will be Faust's constant companion, mentor, servant, guide and incubus as Faust sets out on a journey of self-discovery that takes him from the confines of petty-bourgeois domesticity in Part One to the wider world of public affairs and European history in Part Two.

And so, after the brief transition from university to domestic milieu, from greybeard professor to ardent young lover, Faust embarks on his tragic affair with Gretchen, which proceeds very much as in the *Urfaust*; his own specious and uneasy duality, the falsity of his position and his awareness of the impossibility of the liaison contribute to its disastrous outcome just as effectively as the devil's presence does. What is remarkable about the tragedy of Gretchen is that Goethe has integrated a dimension of diabolism with a simple domestic tragedy – but he has done so without in any way detracting from or interfering with the human and emotional integrity of that tragedy; and this is an achievement that proved to be beyond the efforts of his contemporaries to tackle the theme of Faust, from Paul Weidmann to Lessing. To be sure, the dimension of diabolism is there, with all the paraphernalia of black magic: caskets of jewels, poison, witches' potions, magic horses, even the satanic interlude of a witches' sabbath on the Brocken. But these supernatural trappings do not affect the emotional realism of the tragedy of Gretchen – even if some of the interpolated episodes do at times interrupt and hold up the swift tempo of the original *Urfaust* action.

The most significant addition to the *Urfaust* and *Fragment* versions of the Gretchen episode in the final form of Part One is of course the Walpurgis Night and its puzzling sequel, the Walpurgis Night's Dream. Goethe evidently felt that even if the detailed sequence of Gretchen's fate after her desertion by Faust was not to be literally represented on stage, some material was required, if only to indicate the passage of time during which Faust was to be diverted from her terrible experiences as she bears his child, kills it in distraction and is tried and sentenced for infanticide. In order to fill this gap in time (one whole year – and even in the final version there is a fundamental, if ultimately unimportant chrono-logical incongruity), Goethe devised an episode that has only the most tenuous connection with the traditional Faust material, though it was a familiar and frequent element in the demonology of German folklore: Faust's visit to the annual satanic revels, the *Walpurgisnacht* of 30 April on the Blocksberg or Brocken mountain. This satanic episode was to be Goethe's valedictory working-out of the 'nordic' culture of the Faust material, his final reckoning with his 'witches' prod-uct', with the demonic trappings of the sixteenth-century legend of superstition and religious fanaticism, before he could turn to the Hellenic cultural tradition that was even then, around 1800, claiming his attention as the future sphere of activity for his Faust.

For his spectacular staging of Faust's visit to the Brocken, Goethe drew on all manner of sources in demonology and records of witchcraft; and indeed, for some 200 lines he does evoke a sensational vision of satanic revels as witches, warlocks, will o' the wisps and various creatures of darkness stream towards the summit of the haunted mountain to pay homage to Satan who, we are told, sits enthroned as Urian on the rocks known as the Devil's Altar. But the reader or spectator is not, any more than Faust, allowed a glimpse of this apotheosis of evil; instead, Faust is diverted – astonishingly, by Mephistopheles himself – from the summit to a quiet glade where an eccentric assembly of figures is gathered in a 'club'. Here we find not worshippers of Satan, but a group of survivors from the *ancien régime* bemoaning the way of the world and the loss of their former status – and, with them, Friedrich Nicolai, a superannuated rationalist with whom Goethe had some literary scores to settle, masquerading as the *Proktophantasmist*, the 'man with the haunted backside'. Although Faust and Mephisto cavort with two witches, the satanic impetus of the *Walpurgisnacht* has by now spent itself in satire and horse-play; even the vision of Gretchen, appearing to Faust with the stigma of her imminent execution, is dismissed as sorcery, as an apparition of the Gorgon Medusa, and fails to activate his memory or his conscience.

Immediately following these encounters is the final diminution of the satanism of the *Walpurgisnacht* into a whimsical masque entitled 'The Golden Wedding of Oberon and Titania', which is itself only the tenuous framework for a procession of bizarre and ludicrous figures across the stage, a pageant of contemporary figures and types ranging from the prominent to the obscure, who represent a series of satires or *Xenia* on topical tendencies and fashions in literature, philoso-phy and politics. In a dramatic *reductio ad absurdum*, this is the innermost core of the successive encapsulations of *Faust* Part One: a satirical revue, of nugatory interest to anyone but a contemporary of Goethe's, within a fey intermezzo within the grotesque revels of the *Walpurgisnacht*, which is itself an interlude in the tragedy of Gretchen, contained within the story of Faust that is in turn framed by the Prologue in Heaven and Prelude in the Theatre, and prefaced by the dedicatory poem. At this point, the action diminishes to a hushed silence as the insect orchestra fades in the light of dawn.

To many critics and commentators, readers and spectators, and to the over-whelming majority of stage directors, who almost invariably cut the scene outright, the *Walpurgisnachtstraum* represents a feeble and quite superfluous episode in the action of *Faust* Part One – even if most would agree that the drastic transition from this elfin silence to the brutal realism of the following prose scene from the *Urfaust* is an extraordinary *coup de théâtre*. For all the many ingenious and imaginative efforts to explain and justify the *Walpurgisnachtstraum* as an integral, even a central or core episode in the theatrical or aesthetic structure of the play, it is still perceived by most as an unnecessary and dispensable scene; and the fact that it was originally written by Goethe without any thought of including it in *Faust* is adduced to support this view. It has also been more plausibly suggested that Goethe only included this puzzling interlude because his original conception of the *Walpurgisnacht* (of which a substantial, if disjointed body of material survives as a discarded scenario) was simply too scabrous and sensational to publish at the time.[44] The scarcely satisfactory result is that the *Walpurgisnacht*, for all its powerful beginnings, fails to sustain its impetus and develops quickly into whimsy and satire before returning to the swift and brutal conclusion of the *Urfaust* material in the three final scenes.

Goethe recast the final prose scene of the *Urfaust* in verse in order, as he wrote to Schiller,[45] to mitigate the direct effect of such harrowing material. But if the final version is any less harrowing than the *Urfaust* scene, this is due less to the change from prose to verse as such than to the changes and extensions to the text: the revised version is less starkly economical than the original. Presumably for the same reason – in order to introduce a note of reconciliation into the brutal human tragedy of Gretchen – Goethe added the theatrical assurance of her salvation in the 'Voice from Above', answering Mephisto's 'Sie ist gerichtet!' (She is condemned) with 'Ist gerettet!' (Is saved). Essentially, however, *Faust* Part One ends as the *Urfaust* had ended, with the lone voice pathetically calling Faust's name from within the prison as he makes off with Mephistopheles. It ends leaving Faust in mid-career, still bound to his companion, while Gretchen accepts and awaits her secular judgement in the certain conviction that she will be redeemed. It would be another two decades before Goethe resumed work on the second part of *Faust*.

Faust Part Two

In or around 1800, even as he was struggling to complete the barbarous 'nordic' material of Part One, Goethe already planned, and even in part wrote out, an episode for its sequel. Returning to the old Reformation fable of Dr Faust, he had envisaged an encounter between the magician and Helen of Troy: not the satanic succubus provided by Mephistopheles in the legend to satisfy Faust's lechery, but Helen as the emblem of mythical, Homeric beauty, as the symbol of the highest achievements of Hellenic culture and civilization. It may even be that already at this stage, he imagined the union of Faust and Helen as the symbolic cultural union of Germanic or Western Europe with the Hellenic tradition, the union of ancient and modern, classical and romantic, pagan and Christian in a synthesis that for Goethe was supremely achieved in the Renaissance, but which succeeding centuries had failed to sustain. At all events, he did compose, before he abandoned work on his Faust project for so many years, an episode in the style of Attic tragedy enacting the return of Helen from the Trojan War to her palace in Sparta – an episode that corresponds almost exactly to the first 300 lines or so of the final version of Act Three of *Faust* Part Two (up to line 8802). But between 1800 and 1825 Goethe did little further work on this project, except to dictate in 1816 a scenario of how he imagined the second part. This is a fanciful romance in which the broad lines of the first three acts are discernible, together with one or two motifs from Act Four. While the setting is the Germany of Maximilian I, Helen is magically conjured from Hades within the fairytale medieval context of a castle whose owner is crusading in Palestine. The son of Faust and Helen strays beyond the limits of the enchanted castle, and is killed by 'a consecrated sword'. After the disappearance of Helen and her son, monks attack the castle, but with the help of Mephistopheles and his three henchmen Raufebold, Habebald and Haltefest, Faust avenges his son's death and wins great estates.[46]

The 1816 synopsis contains only some recognizable material from the final story of *Faust* Part Two; there is here moreover only the faintest trace that Faust and Helen, German and Greek, are meant to represent emblematically their respective cultures. In 1825, however, Goethe – whether at Eckermann's urging, or that of his publisher, or simply because it was now or never – began to work steadily and seriously on completing the second part. This he achieved, albeit in a sporadic and non-sequential progression, over the last seven years of his life. It may well have been the death of Byron at Missolonghi in April 1824 that prompted Goethe to take the 1800 Helen fragment as the starting-point for an episode which, as he later wrote to his friends,[47] spans 3,000 years of history from the fall of Troy to the capture of Missolonghi: the third act of *Faust* Part Two. This was published separately in 1827 as *Helena. Klassisch-romantische Phantasmagorie. Zwischenspiel zu Faust* (Helen. Classical–Romantic Phantasmagoria. Interlude to Faust). Between May 1827 and July 1831 he went on to complete the preceding and following acts of Part Two, which was published posthumously in 1832.

Faust Part Two is of course the continuation of, or the sequel to, *Faust* Part One; it is the extension of the story of Faust into the world of public affairs. The Faust of the early narrative versions of the legend had been taken on cosmic and terrestrial journeys, he had visited the Pope in Rome, the Holy Roman Emperor, or (in the puppet plays) the Duke of Parma; he had won battles for his patrons by conjuring phantom armies, and he had had a son, Justus Faustus, by Helen of Troy. Goethe's Faust is also introduced to the Imperial court, he also meets and consummates his union with Helen, who also bears him a son – though in the classical persona of Euphorion. He also wins an important battle for the Emperor by means of a phantom army conjured by Mephistopheles, and wins great estates – or at least the title to reclaim territory from the sea. Unlike the traditional Fausts, however, he is not torn to pieces by devils at the end of twenty-four years and consigned to hell; he dies, as Goethe indicated, at the age of 100, having renounced magic, and is assumed into Heaven.

Faust Part Two is the continuation of an individual's struggle to assert himself against confusion and despair, against the cynical nihilism of the spirit of negation who is his constant companion, it is the continuation of Faust's striving. But it is so different from Part One in scope, style, structure, characterization and genre that many have doubted whether there is any unity between the two parts, whether the second part can meaningfully be understood as related to the first; it has even been questioned whether the terms of the original wager between Faust and Mephistopheles are still valid, at least for all but the very last scenes of the play. And indeed, there are times in the second part when the wager seems to be in abeyance. At the highest moment of Faust's experience, his union with Helen, Mephisto could surely step in and claim that Faust has effectively bid the present moment stay – say, in lines 9380–1. Moreover, for much of the second part Mephisto appears to be playing not the role of the spirit of negation or denial, but to be positively and constructively furthering and aiding Faust's highest aspirations, above all in the Helen episode. But if we accept that Mephistopheles has no intention of meeting the conditions of *Faust's* wager, but rather that he is intent on dragging Faust down *his* path to perdition in terms of his wager with the Lord, then there is no great inconsistency here. Mephistopheles is still contracted to Faust as his servant, to fulfil his every whim and ambition; indeed, it is precisely by doing this that the devil is confident that Faust will involve himself in a sum of error and confusion that will put him beyond redemption, confident that Faust's ever more ambitious schemes and designs will end in failure and despair. What Mephisto cannot resist or alter, however, is that it is Faust's very dissatisfaction, his unremitting striving, that will in the end provide the necessary, if not the sufficient, condition for his salvation.

Nevertheless, the second part of *Faust* is radically, indeed bafflingly different from the first, and Goethe himself time and again stressed these differences. The second part, he claimed, was less fragmentary than the first; it engaged the mind more than the first part, it was designed to exercise the reader's intellect, indeed his learning and his education. The story was more conceptual, for all its imaginative or poetic dimensions. The first part dealt with the specific, the second tended towards the generic. The first part was 'almost entirely subjective', it concerned a constricted, more passionate individual; the second part was more objective, revealing a 'higher, wider, brighter, less passionate' world. The second part concerned human error just as the first had; but it was experienced in a 'nobler, worthier, higher sense' than the 'common' experience of the first part.[48]

It has been suggested that in spite of its external dramatic form – to be sure, an unconventional enough dramatic form – *Faust* Part Two is epic rather than dramatic in conception and structure. It is perfectly true that the first part was not exactly a generically orthodox drama, in structure, style or scope; but for all that, for all its originality and unconventionality, for all its symbolism, its lyricism and its sporadic structure, it belonged ultimately to what Goethe and Schiller called dramatic 'naturalism': it engaged the emotional involvement of the reader or spectator as the action proceeded relentlessly towards its conclusion.[49] In the second part the action is broader and more dispassionate, discursive and panoramic, as we witness Faust's involvement in national and indeed international affairs: affairs of state, politics and culture, wars and revolutions, commerce and civil engineering. The action of the second part is abstract rather than mimetic, allegorical rather than dramatic. The characters are less individualized by dramatic psychology or motivation; rather, they perform a series of representative roles or functions, appearing as types or even as masks, however elaborate or complex these types may be. Faust himself appears in a series of roles as court magus, as the Emperor's adviser and *maître des plaisirs*, as an actor in the dumb show of the Rape of Helen who steps out of his role, as a travelling philhellene, as a crusading Frankish knight, as the consort of Helen of Troy, again in the imperial service as chief of staff, as engineer and merchant prince, and finally as a utopian visionary. Mephistopheles, too, appears (at times quite literally) in a series of allegorical or symbolic masks: as court jester, as Cagliostro, as Zoilo-Thersites, as Avaritia, as Sheherezade, as Old Iniquity, as Phorcyas, as midwife to Faust's son and therefore to post-Renaissance culture, as Faust's military arm, as bailiff and factor of his estates, and finally in burlesque as the Satan of traditional Christian demonology.

The opening scene of *Faust* Part Two, a 'pleasant landscape' set in mountain scenery in which Faust is discovered lying restlessly in a flower-strewn meadow, is both a postscript to the tragic experience of Part One and a prelude to the wider or 'generic' world of Part Two. As Goethe indicated, the purpose of this scene was to heal and restore Faust's shattered spirit after the tragic horror of the first part – not by any process of exculpation, but by means of the gift of amoral nature, the therapeutic metamorphosis of sleep and oblivion.[50] Beneficent nature-spirits are instructed by Ariel – in a rather different role from that of the whimsical *Walpurgisnachtstraum* – to take Faust's spirit through a healing cycle of profound sleep and recuperation, represented in four intensely lyrical stanzas sung as the four vigils of the night: sleep as a process of nature, represented by twilight, by starlight and moonlight reflected in the still depths of a lake, by the shadowy promise of dawn and by Faust's emergence from the 'husk' of sleep into the sunrise of a new day.

The exuberance of Faust's response to the sunrise, however, is immediately checked, as his first act is an attempt to look directly into the sun – an immoderate, 'Faustian' gesture of hubris that dazzles him. And in an image of grandiose symbolism Goethe indicates the spirit in which the adventures of Part Two are to be experienced, the ethos of this new level of activity for Faust. He will seek truth not as direct spiritual revelation, but in the experience of life; and the symbolic emblem of this reflected or refracted perception of truth is the rainbow discerned in the flying spray of the mountain torrent as the sun's light forms an evanescent but stable play of colours. As Goethe expressed it more than once, pure light is an absolute, a primal phenomenon which, as a metaphor for pure truth or divinity, is beyond human perceptions. We are destined to perceive not light, but that which is illuminated, we perceive the effects of light on the physical world – that is, in the colours registered by the eye as light and dark overlap to form the intermediate, and accessible, zone of colour: Goethe's poetic symbolism is here, as so often, informed by his scientific thinking (see above, p. 49 and below, pp. 260–4).

Faust turns his back on the sun, and finds before him the 'changing permanence' of mediated truth: the myriad atomized phenomena of human experience which, as the final *Chorus mysticus* suggests, are an analogy or simile – a 'likeness' (*Gleichnis*) of absolute truth. The first and last scenes of *Faust* Part Two articulate a symbolic perception that defines and informs Faust's journey through the wider, more public and less individuated world in which he now moves and in which he plays a more dispassionate and representative role as a figure whose adventures and experiences reflect those of the age of Goethe himself: a symbolic summary of the political, intellectual, cultural, military and industrial history of the period known as the *Goethezeit*.

To suggest that *Faust* Part Two is an allegorical profile of the age of Goethe is not to suggest that it constitutes, as it were, an imaginative or allegorical biography of Goethe himself – if only because, as he observed, the third act spans 3,000 years from the fall of Troy to Missolonghi (whether to the death of Byron there in 1824 or to the capture of the town from the Turks in the Greek Wars of Independence in April 1826). *Faust* Part Two is, rather, an allegorical résumé, in admittedly fanciful and often fantastic form, of the historical and cultural experiences and preoccupations of Goethe and his age: from the *ancien régime* of absolutist pre-revolutionary eighteenth-century Europe, through the French Revolution and the Napoleonic occupation of the German territories, the demise of the Holy Roman Empire and the wars of liberation from Napoleon, through the political and cultural restoration of the Congress of Vienna to the burgeoning industrial, commercial and agricultural revolutions of post-Congress Europe in the German Confederation. It is also, in the second and third acts, a symbolic record not only of Goethe's own commitment to and fostering of classical culture in Weimar, but also of the Western European response to and absorption of classicism, adumbrating successive encounters between Western Europe and the Eastern Mediterranean, from the Germanic migrations to the medieval crusades, and from the Renaissance to the very years in which these acts were written. Over and above that – and here the continuity of the two parts of *Faust* must be emphasized – Part Two is also the continuation of the existential progress (though 'progress' not necessarily in a qualitative sense) of the flawed and ambivalent individual Faust, in his struggle to assert himself against confusion, delusion and despair and to resist the sterile nihilism of the spirit of denial who has been pitted against him.

The symbolic and allegorical structure of *Faust* Part Two is based on a historical double perspective that presents the issues and concerns of Goethe's day in an imaginative and poetic historical guise. In the imperial scenes of Act One we are plunged into a stylized and composite representation of a Renaissance or late medieval German court – actually identified in the 1816 synopsis as that of Maximilian I, but stylized beyond specific historical reference in the final version. Having infiltrated this court in the guise of a disturbingly well-informed jester, Mephistopheles then introduces Faust as a miracle worker or magus who will solve the financial, and therefore the political woes of an Empire on the very brink of collapse. In the course of an elaborate Italianate carnival masquerade, Faust (or, more strictly speaking, Mephistopheles) introduces an inflationary paper currency that appears, at least temporarily, to have solved all problems; but Faust's cryptic warnings to the hedonistic young Emperor to institute radical political and economic reforms go unheeded – with the result that, as we only discover in the fourth act, the Empire is threatened with total collapse. Behind this fanciful sixteenth-century historicism, however, is an allegorized commentary on the decadence and hedonism of the European *ancien régime* of the eighteenth century, on the frivolity and insecurity of the court of Louis XVI, perhaps also on Prussia and the absolutist powers of the Holy Roman Empire. There are also no doubt echoes of the reforms Goethe himself sought to introduce to the Duchy of Weimar in his first decade there; among the solutions proposed by Mephistopheles for the financial problems of the Empire is the exploitation of buried mineral deposits – possibly a rueful reflection by Goethe on his own energetic but ultimately fruitless involvement in the copper and silver mines of Ilmenau. Mephisto's role in these scenes, as court jester and malign manipulator of the body politic, is also a barely disguised allegory of Goethe's perception of the sinister influence of Cagliostro and his confrères in magic, in France and elsewhere in Europe; Faust's unheeded warnings of the irresponsible use of new-found wealth or credit, encoded into the spectacular mummery of the masquerade and the fiery conflagration or *Flammengaukelspiel* that concludes it, are a dire anticipation of political chaos and disorder – the political and social crucible of the French Revolution, unquestionably the most significant and traumatic historical turning-point of Goethe's lifetime.

And yet it is remarkable, even astonishing, that there is in *Faust* Part Two no direct enactment of the Revolution itself. There is, it is true, in the unlikely context of the Classical Walpurgis Night, which takes place in a fanciful and mythical Thessaly, a confused but discernible allegory of revolution in the so-called Seismos episode (lines 7519–675), in which the slaughter of the aristocratic herons by the aggressive pygmies represents clearly enough the class warfare of the Revolution; but this incident is peripheral, and does not impinge directly or significantly on the broader themes of the *Klassische Walpurgisnacht*. What we see in the political scenes of Part Two (that is, in the first and fourth acts) is the anticipation of a revolution in the European order, and the direct or indirect aftermath of that revolution: namely, the Napoleonic invasion and occupation of the German territories, the threat to the existence of the Holy Roman Empire and the collapse of that Empire, the eventual liberation of Germany, and finally the restoration of the old European order in the political settlements of the Congress of Vienna.

Between the imperial scenes of Acts One and Four, however, the symbolic action of the play moves far away from contemporary European politics to a cultural allegory that adumbrates not simply Goethe's own long and urgent preoccupation with classical culture, but the whole history of the response of Western European civilization to Hellenism and classicism: Faust's obsession with, his quest for and the consummation of his union with Helen of Troy. His first encounter with Helen at the Imperial court in Act One is accidental, arbitrary – and premature: he has been commanded at the whim of the Emperor to conjure the spirits of Paris and Helen – such a séance or conjuration was the stock-in-trade of eighteenth-century 'miracle workers', Rosicrucians and other more or less fraudulent tricksters. At this first spectral encounter with the phantom image of Homeric beauty, Faust is overwhelmed and besotted. His failure to distinguish between reality and the illusion he himself is helping to create causes him to step out of his role and attempt to intervene in the spirit séance; the result is an explosion that knocks him unconscious and paralyses his wits – as Mephisto caustically remarks (lines 6568–9), those who are thus smitten by classical beauty are not easily brought to their senses. If Faust is to encounter Helen as a cultural equal, he must undergo a lengthy quest, an educational apprenticeship – in short, a classical education: that is, the education that Western Europe itself was to undergo before the cultural apogee of the Renaissance, indeed the education that Goethe himself underwent before the summit of 'Weimar' classicism. And in order to chart Faust's education towards the Hellenic ideal Goethe devised the extraordinary myth of the Classical Walpurgis Night to represent Faust's experience of the archaic demonology of Greek religion and Greek culture that culminated in the flowering of the Hellenic Golden Age, whose cultural emblem and icon is the 'most unique figure' (the emphatic superlative is quite deliberate: *die einzigste Gestalt*), Helen of Troy.

To experience the prehistory of Hellenic culture, Faust and Mephistopheles must travel to the Plain of Pharsalus in Thessaly on the anniversary of the Battle of Pharsalus. On this journey they are accompanied, indeed guided, by a fantastic creature who is initially the product of Professor Wagner's crazed alchemist's dream (though Goethe indicated that Mephistopheles also had some hand in his creation): the Homunculus or *filius philosophorum*, the product of the creation of living matter *in vitro*. This irrepressible little 'chemical mannikin', intellectually precocious but physically precarious, an androgynous creature who cannot survive outside the confines of the glass phial in which he was created, is one of Goethe's most whimsical and imaginative creations. His presence in the second act raises many puzzling questions, of which two are pre-eminent: what does he represent, or what is his role and function in the action, and what, if any, is the relation of his function or activity to that of Faust? For when the travellers arrive in Greece, they split up and pursue their own adventures, which only overlap briefly: Faust sets out on his classical education, his quest for Helen, which leads him finally to Hades; Homunculus sets out to discover a means by which he can be released from the confines of his phial and become an independently viable organism, which leads him finally to his erotic and fiery 'marriage' with the ocean by smashing his glass on Galatea's scallop-shell chariot; Mephistopheles' more haphazard quest leads him to discover a new identity, which he finds in the ineffable ugliness of the Graiae or Phorcyades.

Most commentators accept the evidence of a reported remark by Goethe that Homunculus represents 'pure entelechy', pure intellect or spirit in a state of pre-existence, before it has become 'darkened' or 'confined' by physical or temporal existence; the term *Entelechie*, borrowed from Aristotle, appears to be used by Goethe as virtually synonymous with the Leibnitzian monad, or even with soul or spirit in a theological, though not in an orthodox Christian sense. This artificial creation, produced by 'crystallization' in Wagner's laboratory, is not a viable organism, for all his freakish intellectual gifts; in this sense, both he and Faust seek fulfilment in the *Klassische Walpurgisnacht*, however divergent their goals and their progress. Indeed, it has been persuasively argued that Faust and Homunculus pursue radically different ends in the episode:[51] Faust seeks a cultural emblem, the icon Helen, through the archaic prehistory of Hellenic culture and religion, an ideal that belongs to the world of art and the imagination, while Homunculus seeks a physical, indeed a biological identity, which he can only find in the elemental profusion of natural forms, beginning in the ocean, the fecund source of all life. And it may well be that Faust and Homunculus, and their respective goals, represent two areas of Goethe's own activity during a long period in his life: on the one hand his preoccupation with classical culture and aesthetics, and on the other hand his keen interest in the natural sciences, in the botanical, zoological, anatomical and other areas of natural philosophy, in nature in its protean variety of types, forms and species – in a word, what he called his 'Morphology' (see below, pp. 264–8).

Faust's quest in the *Klassische Walpurgisnacht* leads him through the monstrous wonderland of archaic myth, through the hands of successive mentors – chimaeras, gryphons, sphinxes – to the centaur Chiron, the archetypal pedagogue who had known and taught the figures of the Heroic Age of Greek myth like Achilles and the Argonauts, and who had once carried Helen on his back as he now carries Faust. This is the course of Faust's classical education, his preparation for his encounter with Helen, for the moment when he can appear as her equal, her lover and her consort: that is, when the 'barbarian' German, as representative of Western European civilization, can encounter and indeed take possession of the Hellenic ideal in a symbolic synthesis that will represent the cultural and historical apogee of the Renaissance. Faust descends, like Orpheus or Alcestis, into Hades to retrieve and revivify Helen by the absorption of the classical ideal into modern Western culture.

Homunculus pursues an even more bizarre series of adventures which also take him through a succession of mentors, away from the terrestrial upheavals of the Pharsalian Plain down the River Peneus to the shores of the Aegean. He is guided towards the sea by the natural philosopher Thales, whose scientific antagonist Anaxagoras is discredited and routed in a philosophical debate concerning the origins of organic and inorganic nature. These two comical savants indulge in an absurd *dialogue des sourds*, the one dogmatically defending the 'vulcanist' theory of the origins of rocks by igneous processes, the other insisting equally one-sidedly on the 'neptunist' doctrine that water was the source of all life (see below, pp. 268–71). To be sure, it appears that Homunculus is well-advised to seek his natural evolution in water, because the swarming creatures engendered by volcanic violence are summarily obliterated by a further cataclysm when a meteor falls from the moon to squash 'both friend and foe'. In terms of the political allegory that seems to inform this confused episode, this may well represent the decisive intervention of Napoleon as First Consul in 1799, which effectively terminated the revolutionary process in France,[52] and Homunculus is subsequently passed on by Thales to two crusty old marine demigods, Nereus and Proteus. Proteus, the very personification of natural metamorphosis, accompanies Homunculus to the sea, where at the climax of a tumultuous pageant of elemental marine creatures he consummates his marriage with nature and pours himself into the ocean to begin the infinitely long and slow process of development through the great chain of being. If this birth of Homunculus into a state of organic existence does have any relation to the story of Faust, it is surely that of a complementary mirror-image: Homunculus seeks a physical and biological goal, Faust a cultural and aesthetic ideal. Moreover, the metamorphosis of Homunculus into a physical existence is also the reverse process of the transfiguration mystery at the end of the drama when Faust's soul or 'entelechy' is released from its physical confines in a process of spiritual metamorphosis.

The adventures of Mephistopheles in the *Klassische Walpurgisnacht* are more haphazard and more burlesque than those of Faust or Homunculus. Initially disoriented and confused in the pagan demonology of Hellenism, by a cultural and religious system that appears to lack any modern sense of sin or shame, the devil of Christian theology gradually finds his way into this alien world. The final stage of Mephisto's quest leads him to the classical equivalent of negation: the sublime ugliness of the Phorcyades whose mask he now adopts. It is in this persona, as Phorkyas, that he will confront the sublime beauty of Helen in the following act; it is also a mask that transforms him into a cultural and historical hybrid of pagan and Christian, Hellenic and Germanic, classical and modern traditions. And just as Mephistopheles appears in this cross-cultural guise, so too Faust will in Act Three assume a persona that bridges two cultures: he will appear as a Frankish crusading knight who settles in the very homeland of the Greek Helen, in a medieval fortress in the heart of the Peloponnese.

As Goethe remarked, the pivotal third act of *Faust* Part Two covers, albeit in a highly sporadic, selective and symbolically concentrated scheme, the three millennia from the fall of Troy to Missolonghi. It charts in a fantastic, 'phantasmagoric' series of scenes the three stages in the historical metamorphoses of Hellenic culture and the Greek ideal from the perspective of Western European perceptions in the early nineteenth century. The first scene outside the Palace of Menelaus in Sparta is a revival of ancient Greece, a story from the Heroic Age, that of Helen's return from Troy, treated in the style and manner of fifth-century Athenian tragedy; it indicates the fate of Hellenic culture in the post-classical period, its historical transience and its survival only as a lost ideal, as a cultural Golden Age. The second scene, set in the medieval Morea, as the Peloponnese came to be known, represents the pre-Renaissance encounters between the barbarian West and Eastern Mediterranean culture, in the Germanic migrations and the medieval crusades; it culminates in the union of Faust and Helen in Arcadia as a symbolic representation of the Renaissance. The third scene reflects the post-Renaissance neo-classicism of the modern age, of seventeenth and eighteenth-century European culture, and also specifically Goethe's elegiac retrospective perception of his own classical achievement in Weimar, the passing of which he lived to see just as Faust sees Helen return to Hades at the end of the act.

In the first scene Helen appears speaking in the lofty style of Euripidean tragedy,[53] in unrhymed trimeters alternating with agitated trochaic tetrameter and the rhythmic choriambic responses of her chorus of Trojan women. Her return to her own palace is barred by the fearsome and repulsive figure of the hag Phorkyas/Mephistopheles, who undermines her existential security and challenges her very identity, confusing her as he recites the sensational legends that have accrued to her as the ambivalent emblem of female beauty. She is no longer an individual person, but a phantom ideal, the survival of a 'dead' culture, who can now only be revivified as an icon by being absorbed into and appropriated by succeeding cultures in the historical manifestations of the classical heritage. The threat issued by Phorkyas – that her husband Menelaus intends to sacrifice her as the *casus belli* of the Trojan conflict – is part of a strategy to drive Helen into the protection of the 'barbarian' invader Faust; it is also an indication that the Greek cultural heritage, left in the hands of Eastern European cultures (whether Hellenistic, Roman or Byzantine), has been abused and neglected. It is the barbarian West that will resurrect and revive the Hellenic ideal in the synthesis of pagan and Christian, classical and romantic, ancient and modern cultures.

Phorkyas/Mephistopheles functions in Act Three not only as the spirit of negation, of ugliness confronting beauty, or as the manipulator and orchestrator of Helen's encounter with Faust. She/he is also the demon or agent of historical change; it is she/he who drives Helen from ancient Sparta to the medieval Morea, from classical antiquity to the Middle Ages, from Hellenic to Gothic, from a pagan to a Christian era. It is Phorkyas/Mephistopheles who announces the threat of the Byzantine reconquest of the Peloponnese, driving Faust and Helen to the protection of a new Arcadia, the new Golden Age of the Renaissance; it is she/he who acts as midwife to the post-Renaissance era with the birth of Euphorion, the genius of modern European culture – and it is she/he who finally urges Faust to 'hold fast' to Helen's cloak and veil as demons threaten her with renewed oblivion.

In order to stage the encounter and eventual union of Faust and Helen, Goethe chose the historically specific and culturally symbolic meeting of north-west and south-east in the Fourth Crusade, when Frankish knights, diverted from the Holy Land to Constantinople and on to the Peloponnese, established their medieval fiefdoms among the Slavs and the Byzantine Greeks of the peninsula. It may even be that as a result of his wide reading on the history and topography of the Morea in 1825, Goethe had in mind the specific establishment of the short-lived Frankish settlement at Mistra, a Byzantine city built on a hill only some few miles from the site of classical Sparta – a city that subsequently, after its reconquest in 1259, became the intellectual and artistic centre of Byzantine culture, and as such played a seminal role in the New Learning of the emerging Renaissance. At all events, the Arcadian union of Faust and Helen celebrates the Renaissance in a lyrical panegyric to the Golden Age (lines 9526–61) in terms of the ideal *locus amoenus* of pastoral idyll, as Faust takes possession of the Hellenic ideal. The delicate wooing of the medieval German knight and the emblem of Hellenic beauty is also conducted in a cultural code: in the prosodic symbolism of the scene in which Faust instructs Helen in the 'modern' art of end-rhyme, as her unrhymed classical trimeter is usurped by rhyming couplets of iambic pentameter.

The Renaissance, as the ideal union of their respective cultures, cannot last as Helen and Faust move into the modern era. The severe formality of Hellenic tragedy in the opening scene in Sparta, which had become enmeshed with modern prosodic elements in the scene in Faust's medieval fortress, now modulates spectacularly into the modern idiom of operatic *Singspiel* as the action, and the cultural allegory, moves into the post-Renaissance era. The issue of their union, the son Euphorion, who becomes progressively associated with the unruly spirit of Byron for Goethe, the most representative poet of his own age, classical in his ideals but romantic in his self-destructive instincts – fails to sustain the ideal synthesis of the Renaissance. Like Icarus he soars too high, like Byron he leaves the confines of Arcadia to involve himself in a war of freedom, and soon lies dead at his parents' feet; this is Goethe's elegiac acknowledgement that the modern manifestations of the classical ideal, the metamorphoses of Helen in and through modern culture up to and including his own Weimar Classicism, have come and gone. And yet Faust's last act in this episode is to hold fast to the *exuviae* of Helen; her cloak and veil are the 'archeological' evidence, whether in plastic, literary or architectural form, of the Greek ideal – and this, as Phorkyas/Mephistopheles urgently tells him, is infinitely precious and should not be given up to oblivion. The act ends, however, not on this note of cultural loss as Helen joins her son in Hades, but in an extraordinary Dionysian festival of renewal and survival in the eternal cycles of elemental nature as the chorus of Trojan women are metamorphosed into dryads, oreads, naiads and Bacchantes.

Whether the Helen episode is perceived as triumph or as failure for Faust, as error, as temptation or as a positive stage in the dialectic of his continuing battle with Mephistophelean nihilism, it plays a major, indeed a pivotal part in Faust's adventures in the second part of the drama. In terms of the broad allegorical scheme of Part Two, it represents the classical experience and the commitment to the classical ideal not simply of Goethe himself, but of Western civilization, its achievements and its failures; and as such it is an integral part of Goethe's literary testament. In the following acts the symbolic focus of *Faust* Part Two moves away from cultural history to political and social history, as the action returns from south-eastern to north-western Europe, to the Europe of the nineteenth century with its wars, its uneasy peace settlements, and its new ethos of industrial, technological and commercial progress.

Act Four opens with a speech that is Faust's valediction to Helen, but which also looks further backwards and forwards across the play to his past relationship with Gretchen and to her future intercession on his behalf in the final scene. It also indicates his return from Greece to Germany, and the reversion of the action of the play from the cultural allegories of Acts Two and Three to the political allegories that had informed the first act. Helen's garments, dissolving into cloud, have lifted him and carried him to a high mountain range, presumably identifiable as the Alps, the geographical and cultural divide between northern and southern Europe; an unpublished sketch explains how the cloud divides and climbs 'half as Helen to the south-east, half as Gretchen to the north-west'.[54] The speech is spoken as iambic trimeter, in the classicizing idiom of Helen; the afterglow of Faust's classical experience still lingers, until the entry of Mephistopheles, cued by a bizarre and very striking stage-direction, marks the decisive shift of the dramatic and allegorical action to Germany. As Mephisto steps down from his seven-league boots, he expresses his satisfaction at the enormous strides he has made, geographically, culturally and historically, away from the alien and uncomfortable Hellenic world; and the metre at this point reverts to the form of *Madrigalvers* in which the greater part of *Faust* is written.

Faust's opening speech is one of several set-piece monologues in which he steps back from the dramatic action in order to take stock and appraise his position, his progress and his problems in the course of his career; as in 'Wald und Höhle', in 'Anmutige Gegend', in his 'confession' to Sorge and in his final speech, he is able, at least provisionally, to assess his situation without the distracting presence of Mephistopheles – who, to be sure, soon breaks in on Faust's solitary thoughts and impels him to further restless activity. The cloud symbolism that informs the structure of the speech is uniquely Goethean, an adaptation of Luke Howard's meteorological observations that had attracted Goethe's scientific and imaginative attention. Howard had classified cloud formations by altitude, and Goethe had followed his terminology: water vapour rises by evaporation, condensing respectively into stratus, cumulus and cirrus, becoming progressively thinner, lighter and, in terms of Goethe's symbolism, more spiritual as it climbs upwards towards the 'Father' (see above, pp. 118–19 and below, pp. 271–3). Here, Helen's form looms massively as castellated cumulus on the eastern horizon, reflecting the glory of his momentous encounter with Helen, while Gretchen's image rises as cirrus into the heavens. However, in this sequence a fourth form is implicit: nimbus, responding to the pull of earth, descends as heavy, rain-bearing cloud. The hidden implication here is that Faust will now return from his lofty vantage-point to the world of political reality, of wars and power-struggles; the years of Goethe's devotion to classical idealism in Weimar were also the years of revolution, invasion, counter-invasion and occupation in Western Europe. If Faust left the Empire at the end of Act One in a state of imminent collapse, he finds it in Act Four in that state of collapse; and it is to its restoration that he will, if only as a means to an end, devote himself in this act.

The political situation in which Faust finds himself in Act Four is a broad but discernible reflection of the political situation in Western Europe, specifically that of the Holy Roman Empire, between the French Revolution and the Congress of Vienna. The Empire has collapsed into anarchy, and is under threat from an invading usurper; a rival Emperor has challenged the authority and legitimacy of Faust's young Emperor – or 'our' Emperor, as a stage-direction (before line 10817) characterizes him. Behind the historical résumé of Mephistopheles in lines 10260–90 can be discerned the humiliation of the European powers Prussia, Austria and Russia, and the formal abolition of the old millennial Reich by Napoleon in 1806. Each of these powers had been forced to make its peace, individually or severally, with Napoleon; and many Germans, including Goethe, held the French Emperor in high regard, only occasionally tempered by fears of his ambitions of world conquest. Indeed, by no means all the princes of the Holy Roman Empire were even politically or militarily opposed to Napoleon; the years 1795 to 1813 saw a shifting pattern of alliances and desertions that fatally weakened European resistance to Napoleonic ambitions, and it was only in 1813 that the allied forces of Prussia, Austria and Russia delivered the fatal military blow in the Battle of Leipzig, known to Germans as the Battle of the Nations

(*Völkerschlacht*), which was to become a historical landmark in the cause of German liberation and, eventually, of German unification.

The battle fought and won by Faust on the legitimate Emperor's behalf with the help of Mephistopheles' demonic legions of elemental spirits is of course a motif derived from the old narratives of the Faust legend. In the context of the historical allegories of *Faust* Part Two, it represents the German Wars of Liberation from Napoleon, towards which Goethe preserved an attitude of sceptical reserve. He was also less than enthusiastic about the territorial squabbles and manoeuvrings of the Congress of Vienna, of which the final scene of this act is a barely disguised satirical parody, as the Emperor is forced to preside over the decentralization of his power into the hands of his electoral princes – and of the Church. To be sure, this scene is ostensibly based on the fourteenth-century Golden Bull of Charles IV, which Goethe knew well; as a boy in Frankfurt he had discussed the Bull with the constitutional scholar J. D. von Olenschlager, who had drawn his attention to its historically ironic opening words: 'Omne regnum in se divisum desolabitur; nam principes ejus facti sunt socii furum' (Every kingdom divided against itself will be brought to desolation; for its princes have become the companions of thieves).[55] The Golden Bull, devised to counter papal interference in the Empire and to establish an orderly procedure for royal and electoral succession, had also perpetuated, indeed confirmed particularism and checked the centralization of imperial power and authority. But the Congress of Vienna also perpetuated the divisions of the old Reich and frustrated the cause of German unity; and this faintly absurd scene of pomp and ceremony, written appropriately in the stilted and formal rhythms of neo-classical alexandrines, betrays Goethe's profound scepticism towards the European Restoration after the defeat of Napoleon.

To be sure, Goethe's reservations about the 'liberation' of Germany were based not so much on the reactionary and illiberal character of Metternich's post-Congress Europe, but rather on his ineradicable admiration for Napoleon, whose total defeat was the precondition of restoration. Nevertheless, from the perspective of 1831, when this act was written – the year after the July Revolution in Paris, which Goethe had watched from Weimar with growing alarm, and in which he had feared (unnecessarily, as it turned out) 'a reprise of the tragedy of 1790' – from this perspective, Goethe was able to affirm the stability and order of post-Restoration Europe and of the German Confederation. This did not, however, prevent him from including in his allegory of the German Wars of Liberation and of the Congress of Vienna an unmistakably satirical dimension. It was also no doubt his high regard for the French Emperor that led him to present the figure of his Anti-Emperor with such ambivalent reticence in the fourth act. This figure, who never appears on stage, is a shadowy but potent threat to the old Empire, but also a figure who, it is suggested (lines 10278–84), might present a constructive and creative alternative to the old order – one who might, as Napoleon indeed partially did, introduce an enlightened system of legal and administrative reforms into its obscure and archaic institutions. But this rival Emperor is finally defeated by dubious means and with the help of untrustworthy allies, and abruptly quits the historical scene. At this point Faust also leaves the service of absolutism and the restored powers of the old order; as a reward for his military services to the Emperor he has been granted the fiefs of the tidal territories which will allow him to embark on his last ambition: to reclaim new lands from the sea. And in order to stage Faust's final episode on earth, Goethe extends the historical allegory of his play further into the nineteenth century, beyond the Congress of Vienna into the new era of communications and trade, industry and technology, that began to develop in the stable, if politically quiescent, period of the German Confederation.

Faust appears in Act Five no longer as an officer of the Imperial General Staff, as the Emperor's military adviser; indeed it seems (though this is not explicit) that he has freed himself from any dependence on the neo-feudal absolutism of the restored old order. He is a man of the burgeoning industrial revolution, a merchant prince, civil engineer and colonizer, an entrepreneur whose trading practices are scarcely distinguishable from piracy, whose technology is miraculous but sinister, and whose expansionist schemes are carried out with ruthless energy and singlemindedness. This is indeed a profoundly ambivalent image of industrial and commercial revolution. Goethe appreciated and acknowledged the beginnings of the spectacular expansion of trade and finance, of engineering and communications, of technology and industry in the last two decades of his life; but his reaction was a characteristic mixture of acceptance and reservation, of affirmation and suspicion.

Just as Goethe's attitude to the new age was ambivalent, so too his 'hero' Faust is here, as ever, a fundamentally ambivalent individual; for the age of Faust is also the age of Goethe. Philemon and Baucis, who represent a centuries-old tradition of impoverished but stable rural and agrarian existence, whose idyllic hut is both a stark contrast to the palace of the merchant prince Faust and a tiresome impediment to his schemes, a constant reminder of the limitations of his powers and his territories, must be summarily removed. To be sure, Mephistopheles and his henchmen murderously exceed Faust's instructions; but this is the inevitable consequence that flows from his pact with the devil, it is a last instance of the criminality that has attended his career and which now compels him to confront the spectre of Care, who forces from him a secular confession, a retrospective review of his life and his activities in lines 11433–52. It is at this point (line 11423) that Faust resolves to renounce magic; it may also be at this point that the scope of his ambitions becomes less egotistic, more humanitarian and more philanthropic.

The origins of Faust's plans to conquer the sea, to impose order on chaos and to create stability from flux, lie in Act Four, where he reveals to Mephistopheles the titanic scope of his ambition (lines 10181–233). At this early stage, he makes no mention of establishing any community, there is no social or utopian dimension to his projects; he talks only of a mighty struggle with the elements, against the pointless and barren monotony of ebb and flow, and of the power and territory he might gain by controlling the tides. This vision is indeed a Faustian one, consistent with his earlier Prometheanism, with his imperious will to divine the secrets of nature and the macrocosm, or to vie with the heroes of Greek myth in the possession of Helen of Troy. After his crucial encounter with Care, however, after his rueful confession of lines 11433–52, in which he appears to renounce fruitless metaphysical speculation and acknowledges that the here and now offers more than adequate scope for his insatiable aspirations, there is a distinct shift in the nature of Faust's ambitions. To be sure, it is still his insatiable will, his dissatisfaction that drives him (lines 11451–2); but in his final speech there is an idealistic and utopian dimension, a concern with human needs, that was quite missing from his projects hitherto. Here (lines 11559–80) he is concerned not only with asserting himself against the elemental forces of nature, not only with power and territory, not only with the perpetuation of his name for generations to come, but also with the establishment of a free community on free soil, a community that will earn its freedom by unremitting daily struggle and co-operation. Indeed, Goethe made some very significant emendations to the manuscript of Faust's final speech, emendations that seem to indicate clearly enough that he wished to emphasize this shift in the quality of Faust's ambitions. His successive alterations to line 11580 read: 'To stand on land that is my own'; 'To stand on land that is truly my own'; 'To stand on land that is truly free'; 'To stand on free land with a free people' (*Auf freiem Grund mit freiem Volke stehn*).

Faust's final project on earth is indeed a characteristically hubristic undertaking, a colossal challenge; but it is an undertaking that renounces metaphysical speculation on what is beyond human understanding for the sake of a practical and ultimately, though not immediately, realizable ideal that still demands unremitting activity and effort – even if that activity may, as the Lord acknowledged, involve ever more error, confusion and even criminality. That is, it involves the kind of ceaseless striving that in the end, as we are told in the words of the angels bearing Faust's spirit (lines 11936–7), can render a man accessible to redemption. In the course of his final utopian project, in which philanthropy and vainglory, humanitarianism and hubris, sociological experiment and personal aggrandizement are inextricably confused, it also seems that Faust resolves to renounce Mephistopheles – or at least that he wishes to be free from recourse to magic in the achievement of his ambition: it is notable that in Faust's final scene, Mephistopheles must make his replies in asides, or *sotto voce*.

The fact that this vision of a free people is articulated by a man who has himself been unfree for most of his career, that this society is imagined by a man who has never felt himself part of a human social community, that this work ethic is formulated by a man who has always had recourse to magic rather than toil, is an irony that casts Faust and his works in an ambivalent light; but it does not therefore wholly invalidate that vision, nor does it mean that it is Mephistopheles' sterile nihilism that has the last word. Faust dies of old age and infirmity (Goethe noted that he would be '100 years old' at this point),[56] physically blinded but guided by an inner conviction; he dies because he has abjured magic, because he will not resort to supernatural solutions, because he wishes to stand alone before nature as a man armed with his own powers. In his final speech he articulates a provisional vision of a future ideal community, utopian perhaps, but not hopelessly out of line with contemporary developments; Goethe knew of such projects as Robert Owen's model industrial settlement at New Lanark, as well as other, more fanciful, social and industrial utopias. At this point, Faust is ready to die, he himself invokes the terms of his wager with Mephistopheles; he imagines, if only provisionally and conditionally, that he might be able to bid the passing moment stay, and he acknowledges the here and now as his 'highest moment'. As he foresaw, time now runs out for him, the secular clock stands still; but the fate of his soul, which had never been of any great concern to Faust, is left for a higher authority to determine.

Goethe's justification of Faust and of his activities, the credibility or acceptability of his redemption, is a matter of continuing contention. In particular, the debate on the validity of his final vision rumbles on today: is it a delusion of the physically and morally blinded Faust, not a celebration of, but a satire on certain utopian or proto-socialist programmes of the early nineteenth century? Leaving aside the political or theological assumptions that inform the judgements of many commentators, it seems clear enough that Goethe's justification of Faust is not determined by the real or illusory, lasting or ephemeral, humane or criminal, moral or immoral nature of his activities or achievements. It is indeed difficult, if not impossible, to accept at face value Goethe's reported characterization of Faust's progress as 'an ever higher and purer activity to the end';[57] but it is equally difficult to dismiss Faust's achievements as utter illusion, as deluded failure, for this would be to concur in the dismal nihilism of Mephistopheles. But neither is Faust redeemed, surely, by the very fact of his striving, by an amoral perception of all activity as positive, wherever it may lead – for all the Lord's assurance that error is inseparable from human striving; the words of the angels in lines 11936–7 suggest that unremitting striving is a necessary, but not a sufficient, condition of redemption. Goethe evidently felt that Faust's life, for all its error and confusion, was justifiable; he evidently also felt that such justification was beyond human judgements, beyond any secular balance-sheet of moral credit or debit. He was careful not to introduce at the end any tribunal in Heaven with the Lord or Christ presiding, as he seems to have intended at one stage;[58] the issues are too finely balanced for that. Instead, he depicted Faust's redemption in two final scenes of extraordinary contrast: the one a ribald and comic burlesque, the other a solemn mystery of transfiguration. Both scenes are informed by love, the merciful and forgiving force through which Faust's redemption is accomplished; but love, whether divine or profane, whether as *caritas*, *agape* or *eros*, or as a love that passes all understanding, is presented in radically different terms in the two scenes.

Mephistopheles summons the legions of hell to capture Faust's soul; but they are confronted by a host of angels who pelt them with roses – the ammunition, as it were, of intercession and divine love. The forces of darkness are routed by their own incompetence and by the hilarious discomfiture of their commander Mephistopheles, who is smitten by a pederastic lust for the seductively epicene angels, distracting him and allowing the powers of Heaven to snatch Faust's soul. This victory of Heaven may be a triumph of love over hate, of grace over malice; but it is also a form of theological sleight-of-hand, the victory of one kind of deceit over another.

Any such moral or theological dubieties are, however, quite absent from the final scene, which shows the transfiguration of Faust's soul (his 'immortal part' as the text has it, his 'entelechy' as a manuscript version has it).[59] Anchorites, Fathers of the early Church, bear witness to his upward ascent as he sheds the last integuments of earthly existence in a process of metamorphosis analogous to the *imago* shedding the wisps of the cocoon; angels buoy him up as he approaches the radiance of Heaven, and a chorus of penitents, among them one 'who was once called Gretchen', intercede for him, pleading for grace from the Virgin Mary enthroned in splendour. She points the way to 'higher spheres', and the final Mystic Chorus glosses and amplifies Faust's earlier perception that life on earth is a coloured reflection of absolute or divine truth as it adumbrates a reality that is no longer transient, no longer a simile or likeness, where the unattainable becomes actual and the ineffable is realized. Love and grace, the 'eternally feminine', draws Faust's spirit onwards and upwards in a mystical and continuing process of lightening and purification.

The extravagant mysticism of the final scene of *Faust* has offended the sensibilities of many commentators, not only because Goethe has thereby unequivocally justified Faust's questionable career, but also because he has used the doctrinal imagery and iconography of the Catholic Church, of medieval theology, of Dante and of the Counter-Reformation. He did so, as he carefully explained,[60] because he felt the need to give a firm delineation to his poetic intentions, and feared that he would lose himself in spiritual abstractions if he did not exploit the firmly established, and above all familiar, corpus of iconography and doctrine provided by the Christian Church. In the course of *Faust*, Goethe has drawn on the borrowed imagery of various systems – of alchemy, of classical and pre-classical myth, and of Judaeo-Christian religion; this is not to say that he subscribed in any literal sense to any of these systems. Faust is not saved by good works, nor is he justified by faith or grace alone. If there is any biblical or theological sanction for Goethe's justification of Faust's flawed humanity (and he did suggest that Faust's salvation was 'in accord' with our religious ideas – which is not to say that it is identical with them),[61] then it would seem to come close to the Mosaic and Pauline doctrine (Exodus 33. 19 and Romans 9. 15): 'I will have mercy on whom I will have mercy, and I will have compassion on whom I will have compassion'.

But Goethe also insisted that Faust's salvation is not a theme or idea that informs the whole work or each particular scene of the work;[62] indeed, for great stretches it appears to be of less than primary importance. *Faust* is an encyclopedic work of immense theatrical, poetic, structural, thematic, stylistic and metrical variety that cannot be reduced to any single idea, except that it is the life's work of an exceptionally talented and versatile poet. Goethe's Faust does not represent all humanity, he is not the allegorical cypher of Everyman; he represents an exceptional individual who shares, and rages against, human limitations. He does not represent Goethe; but he is a representative, at times emblematic figure of the age of Goethe, whose career has broad but distinct parallels to Goethe's first-hand and vicarious experience. He is neither an exemplary ideal figure nor an exemplary warning figure; Goethe has exploited the paradoxes and ambivalences in the figure and legend of Faust, which even the Lutheran authors of the early narrative versions, for all their strident orthodoxy, could not entirely suppress, and has used them as a principle that informs the whole work.

4

The Novelist: The Prose and Verse Narratives

DIE LEIDEN DES JUNGEN WERTHERS
(THE SUFFERINGS OF YOUNG WERTHER)

'Faust came into being with my Werther.'[1] The first version of Goethe's first novel, written in sustained creative concentration over four weeks in February and March 1774 and based freely on events from some two years earlier, was indeed concurrent with his more protracted work on the *Urfaust*; and there are many points of comparison between the dramatized story of the titanically dissatisfied magus and the narrative of the self-torturing, self-deluding and self-dramatizing young lover and failed diplomat. Both Faust and Werther assert the unconditional primacy of feeling, of inner emotional conviction and intuition, of the promptings of the heart – for all that both are sophisticated and educated minds. If the Faust of the *Urfaust* version exemplifies the more muscular mental assertiveness of the *Sturm und Drang* against the arid scholarship of established intellectual and theological orthodoxy, Werther exemplifies, or more accurately he travesties, the *Empfindsamkeit* tendency to centralize and universalize the sentimental impulse of emotional solipsism. He is driven by the behavioural manifestations of the cult of feeling: melancholy introspection, restless wanderings and reveries, escapist nature-mysticism, morbidity, pathological sensibility, and, for all his compulsive and no doubt sincere instinct to empathize with the material or spiritual misery of others, an accompanying inability to spare the deepest and most intimate feelings of those closest and dearest to him. Faust's emotional ruthlessness and egotism in his treatment of Gretchen is only the more brutal equivalent of Werther's misguided sentimental ruthlessness and egotism in his emotional devastation of Lotte.

Both Faust and Werther desperately strive to escape restriction – Faust the prison of his scholar's cell, the intellectual impasse of his academic career, and the limitations of the human condition, Werther the implacable demands and expectations of 'lamentable domestic circumstances' (*die fatalen bürgerlichen Verhältnisse*):

family, career, class, urban existence – even, paradoxically, binding emotional ties. For as Lotte recognizes with perceptive pathos, it is the very impossibility of possessing her that makes this desire so appealing to him; the more irrevocably she is bound to her fiancé and in due course to her husband, the more compulsively Werther pursues her, the more ruthlessly he undermines her peace of mind. His obsessive pursuit of an illicit and impossible passion diverts him from commitments which might involve responsibility, fulfilment, or a loss of his unique emotional status, a betrayal of his heart which, as he asserts in the characteristic language of sensibility, is his alone, to be cherished 'like a sick child'. Like Faust, Werther swings between contradictory extremes of behaviour. No sooner has Faust escaped the confines of his study than he is drawn to the narrow charmed circle of Gretchen's domesticity; no sooner has Werther left the confines of his home town than he accepts the restriction of a 'hut' or refuge – *Wahlheim*. Tearing himself away, he roams aimlessly from his professional post at court to his own home town, to the hunting lodge of Graf von C.; he toys with the idea of going to the wars, and is finally drawn back to Lotte's domestic scene; his restless 'pilgrimage' on earth ends in the ultimate confinement of the grave.

Both Faust and Werther are in these respects deplorable, negative, even cautionary figures, and both end their careers in harrowingly catastrophic circumstances – Faust, that is, in the context of the *Urfaust* and of Part One. And yet, paradoxically, both embody the most positive aspects of human aspiration, even of Goethe's own idealizing urges; it cannot be doubted that they rehearse many of their creator's most urgent personal concerns and convictions, whether intellectual or emotional. Faust's agonized self-questionings, his frustrations, his impatient dismissal of Wagner's earnest pedantry, the tortured ambivalence of his self-knowledge *vis-à-vis* Gretchen, invite the reader's sympathy and understanding, if not his approval, just as the impulsive generosity of Werther's nature does. But in both cases the integrity of the hero is undermined; the very wellspring of Werther's generosity of spirit, his unconditional impulse to follow the promptings of his heart, his adolescent tendency to universalize his own troubles, become the forces that destroy him, and very nearly destroy that which was most precious to him. With a relentless precision and symmetry that belies the hectic chaos of Werther's only apparently disordered correspondence, the author progressively demolishes Werther's fond illusions one after the other. His delight in the teeming creativity of nature turns into an appalled vision of a chain of destruction and death; his idealized vision of simple 'patriarchal' village life, sustained and encouraged as it is from the beginning by his relative wealth and status, by an illusory identification with a complaisant and possibly even venal peasantry, crumbles into a stark reality of inheritance squabbles. His 'Homeric' idyll distorts into a crazed 'Ossianic' landscape of atavistic violence; his 'Ganymedic' response to springtime renewal and the fulfilment of high summer follows the seasonal curve into a depressive autumnal sense of decline and wintry desolation. When the 'there' becomes the 'here', he longs again for a distant prospect; his delight in people or landscape degenerates into disturbingly negative existential images of nature as a lifeless lacquered picture, men and horses as peep-show objects, fellow humans as wooden marionettes, existence as a cage or a prison, himself as a galley-slave. The pious resolution to follow a diplomatic career is shattered by the most undiplomatic behaviour, the farmhand he had championed as a model of noble sentiment and selfless devotion is revealed as a jealous homicide; and he finally devastates the very object of his affections – for while Lotte evidently survives the catastrophe physically, she is just as evidently emotionally scarred for life.

The narrative structure of the novel itself progressively invites the reader's emotional detachment from the hero – though not before his sympathy is carefully elicited by the 'editor's' opening remarks and by the early letters. In contradistinction to the conventional epistolary novel of the eighteenth century, for the greater part of the novel the reader is supplied only with Werther's letters, not with any objective narrative or with the opinions and arguments of his correspondent Wilhelm, which can only be inferred from Werther's responses. But while this journal form may initially incline the reader to engage sympathetically with Werther, the reader is also put on his guard against the emotional self-indulgence of the diarist; and as the second part unfolds, the disintegration of Werther's enthusiasm into emotional solipsism and the illusory nature of his perceptions become all the more strikingly evident. His wild identifications with Christ, the universalizing of his own bruised sensibilities, the increasingly imperious assertion of his feelings, are more than adequately expressed in his own letters; but the narrative master-stroke is the introduction of the 'editor's' voice, hitherto confined to prologue and footnotes, after 17 December 1772. Based on the content and style of Kestner's report to Goethe of the death of Karl Wilhelm Jerusalem, the editor's sober report not only forms a telling foil to Werther's emotional turmoil; by intercalating his report with the text of Werther's last letters to Wilhelm and Lotte, the editor gives the reader important information about Lotte's distress, her emotional ambivalence, her relations with her husband, and the circumstances of Werther's death – information that ironically at once confirms the unreality of Werther's state of mind and re-engages the reader's appalled sympathy with the hero at the very point where his letters threatened to alienate it by their solipsistic and extravagant *radotage*. By thus manipulating the epistolary form, as much as by the inflammatory and sensational nature of Werther's own letters, Goethe created in the mind of his readership a series of ambivalent responses that precipitated an equally sensational reception for the novel, which very quickly became an international bestseller and provoked violently differing responses from the reading public, ranging from empurpled moral outrage to an enthusiastic *parti pris* for the hero that spawned a host of would-be Werthers following their role-model in speech, dress, behaviour and, reputedly, in mode of death.

It was the sensational success of *Werther* that made Goethe's name, in Germany and beyond – though he profited very little from it financially owing to an almost complete absence of copyright protection. Its success also generated both a prurient inquisitiveness as to its biographical sources and an aftermath that plagued Goethe long after its first publication in 1774. While he may have been gratified by its *succès de scandale*, while he may even have played up to the image of his fictive hero during the early years in Weimar, appearing frequently in 'Werther costume', Goethe very soon found it irksome to be clumsily identified with Werther, even to be tiresomely fêted as his creator; and it was in part to escape such notoriety that he insisted on a careful incognito during his early period in Italy. To be sure, Goethe could scarcely have been surprised that the public should very soon have unearthed his Wetzlar years, his relationship with Charlotte Buff and her fiancé Kestner (whose marriage he had been unable to bring himself to attend – and unlike Werther's, this had been a voluntary abstinence), or the fate of the wretched Jerusalem as Kestner had reported it to Goethe, as it were in the function of Goethe's *Herausgeber*. But Goethe, as well as the Kestners, was painfully embarrassed that the public should take almost literally the fiction he had imaginatively extrapolated from a relationship whose exact emotional parallels are, and will forever remain, unclear.

Goethe was as much disturbed by the critical reception of the novel as by its emotional aftermath; for while reports of the supposed Werther imitators who staged their own death-scenes may well be exaggerated, he was profoundly shaken by the incident that took place almost on his own doorstep, when Christiane von Laßberg drowned herself in the Ilm, reportedly clutching a copy of the novel, in January 1778. This incident, and other evidence of the destabilizing effect of the book on such as Plessing, for example, no doubt shocked Goethe more directly than its predictably hostile reception from the Church, from literary figures like Lessing (who protested at the travestied image of his friend Jerusalem), or from the *Aufklärung* pundit Friedrich Nicolai. After all, such as Nicolai could be counterattacked with their own weapons, as Goethe in fact did with 'Nicolai auf Werthers Grabe' (Nicolai on Werther's Grave), his devastatingly scatological riposte to Nicolai's satirical parody *Die Freuden des jungen Werthers* (The Joys of Young Werther). In this brief – and unpublished – poem, Goethe imagines Nicolai defecating on Werther's grave, and having thus relieved himself, concluding smugly:

> 'Der gute Mensch, er dauert mich,
> Wie hat er sich verdorben!
> Hätt er geschissen so wie ich,
> Er wäre nicht gestorben!'

> 'The poor young man! It makes me sigh,
> A life so misapplied;
> If he had shat as well as I
> He never would have died!'

Goethe became concerned to discourage both any close biographical identification and any imitative tendencies on the part of his readers. Already in the second (1775) edition of the novel, he prefaced the first and second parts respectively with the two strophes of the poem 'Jeder Jüngling sehnt sich, so zu lieben' (Every young man longs to love like this), the final lines of which implore the reader in the words of Werther's ghost: 'Be a man and do not follow me.' It is also probable that the revised version of the novel, published in 1786, was intended by Goethe to correct the public perception of Werther by subtly alienating the reader's sympathy and by relativizing the hero's behaviour, especially *vis-à-vis* the figure of Albert, who is supposedly more sympathetically portrayed in this version than in the first. This at least is what Goethe wrote to Kestner in 1783, assuring him that while Werther might have misunderstood his rival's behaviour and feelings, the reader would no longer be able to do so.[2] And yet it is not certain that, if this was indeed Goethe's intention, he wholly succeeded either in diminishing the reader's sympathies for Werther or in increasing those for Albert. Stylistically, the *Sturm und Drang* prose of Werther, with its elisions and its slipshod syntax, was tidied up; but the effect of this was to make Werther less wildly extravagant in his expression – which scarcely contributes to the reader's detachment from the hero. The episode of the farmhand who murdered his rival, completely new material in the 1786 version, does indeed point up Werther's naive assessment of 'simple folk' in a brutal way, and stresses his hysterical tendency to universalize individual or anecdotal suffering; but it also identifies Albert firmly as an implacable and emotionally indifferent supporter of the legal and social status quo.

Apart from this *Bauernbursche* episode, the most significant change over the first version is that the editor, who claims to have reconstructed his narrative from the reports of Lotte, Albert and other witnesses, and whose insights are plausibly limited by what they have been prepared to divulge to him, becomes very much better informed in the revised version, indeed, he becomes practically an omniscient narrator. He is able to read Lotte's secret thoughts and to expose her emotional ambivalence more fully than the first version had done. Werther, we are told, had become so dear to her that she could not imagine life without him; she wished he were her brother, or married to one of her friends – but then, the 'editor' adds slyly, she could think of none of her friends to whom she would willingly surrender him. Again, the editor spells out much more clearly than in the first version Lotte's inhibitions towards her husband, her fear of exposing her ambivalent feelings, and he even ventures to comment that if their relations had been more secure or confident, if their exchanges had been more open and candid, then perhaps 'our friend' might still have been saved. All this – and, most strikingly of all, the letter of 12 September 1772 added in the second version, where Lotte teases Werther coquettishly as she feeds breadcrumbs to her canary from her own lips – seems designed to present Lotte in a morally and emotionally more ambiguous light; but it scarcely exonerates Albert or alienates the reader's sympathy from Werther. Rather, it highlights the possibility that Werther's death might have been prevented, or at least postponed, at the point where he requests the loan of Albert's pistols, and where Lotte's inhibited silence and vacillation have disastrous consequences.

Nevertheless, it seems that by 1786, whether as a result of the unfortunate aftermath of the first version or of a waning of youthful feelings and enthusiasms, Goethe was no longer as able or as willing to elicit approval for his hero as he had been at the age of twenty-four. A similar process of detachment or relativization no doubt occurred in the case of Faust: the young Goethe was closer to the titanism of the *Urfaust* than the writer who, by an immense effort of will and imagination, set out to complete Part One in his late forties. The younger Goethe could empathize with the hero of his novel, for all that he could also distance himself from Werther's excessive solipsism and disturbed mind; precisely because he had indulged in such emotionalism, he was equipped to describe and exorcise such excesses. Indeed, he confessed that by writing the novel, he might well have saved himself from the same fate – even though he also wryly remarked, in the light of its public impact, that he would perhaps have done better to have blown his own brains out instead.[3]

Many years later, still plagued by the reception and the reputation of his novel, Goethe was reported by an English visitor, Henry Crabb Robinson, to have spoken of Ossian with contempt, and to have insisted that no one seemed to have noticed that while Werther is relatively sane his literary hero is Homer, and that he only turns to Ossian when his mind is unhinged.[4] And yet in 1771, only three years before they appeared in such a dramatic context in the novel, Goethe had translated some of the Songs of Selma for Friederike Brion; Werther's versions are a reworking of these passages. It seems probable that Goethe himself at that time shared the passionate response of Lotte and Werther to Macpherson's sentimental and rhapsodic 'translations'; and in a novel that teems with literary allusions and vicarious literary sensibilities – Goldsmith, Klopstock, Lavater, Rousseau, Homer, Ossian, the Bible – Ossian is only one of the more striking examples. Werther's enthusiasm for Ossian is not a cause, perhaps not even a symptom, of madness or morbidity; but it is the extreme expression of the sentimentality towards which Goethe felt a profound ambivalence, of the cult of feeling in which he had himself shared, and against the excesses of which he wrote in the novel a sympathetic, informed and heartfelt warning exemplum. *Die Leiden des jungen Werthers* touched a nerve for a whole generation in Germany, and summed up a whole range of social, professional and existential frustrations. Goethe's ambivalent warning, erupting as it did onto a public conditioned by novels that were immaculately prescriptive, in which clearly identifiable models of vice or virtue were tempted and tested, punished or rewarded, damned or redeemed, and from which the reader could effortlessly infer the right way, unsurprisingly provoked a response of emotional, moral and critical confusion from which the novel is not entirely free even today.

WILHELM MEISTERS THEATRALISCHE SENDUNG (WILHELM MEISTER'S THEATRICAL MISSION)

Goethe's major, though not necessarily his most admired, narrative project is the saga of Wilhelm Meister. It comprises three novels that might be regarded, if not quite as a formal trilogy, then at least as the charting of three distinct stages in the personal development of the central figure: his theatrical mission, his years of apprenticeship, and his journeyman's years or years of travel (*Wilhelm Meisters theatralische Sendung, Wilhelm Meisters Lehrjahre* and *Wilhelm Meisters Wanderjahre*).[5] To be sure, Goethe published only the last two novels as a more or less sequential story; for all their radical differences in style, structure and even genre, the *Wanderjahre* can be regarded as the sequel to the *Lehrjahre*. But in spite of all the common material shared by the *theatralische Sendung* and the *Lehrjahre*, the differences in conception and intention between them justify the common perception that the former is not just a first draft of the latter, but a work conceived on fundamentally different lines from the novel actually published by Goethe as *Wilhelm Meisters Lehrjahre*.

To be sure, the *Sendung* contains huge portions of narrative that were taken into the *Lehrjahre* with little essential emendation; and the *Sendung* does cover most of the events, features most of the characters, and follows a very similar structure to the first five books of the *Lehrjahre*. In this sense, it is the first draft version of the published *Lehrjahre*, a draft that was destroyed, like the *Urfaust*, by Goethe when he completed the revised version; and like the *Urfaust*, it was rediscovered – by Gustav Billeter in 1910 in the form of a copy made by Barbara Schultheß and her daughter in Zürich, whom Goethe had met on his first Swiss journey in 1775. And we cannot know how, or whether, at the time of writing the *theatralische Sendung* (between 1777 and 1785), Goethe intended to continue the narrative beyond the conclusion of this first version, that is, beyond Wilhelm's apparently firm and lasting commitment to a theatrical career with Serlo's company – which is, to all intents and purposes, a simulacrum of the Hamburg Theatre of Friedrich Ludwig Schröder. At all events, the subsequent *Lehrjahre* version, written between 1793 and 1796, takes an abrupt and radically different direction from that point; it uproots Wilhelm brusquely from his theatrical calling, and thereby relativizes his obsession with the stage as a blind alley, an immature infatuation and merely a first step in the wider progress of his education, of his social, political and cultural integration – in short, of his *Bildung*. The *theatralische Sendung* is not in any very meaningful sense a *Bildungsroman*, an example of that uniquely German and portentous narrative genre that emerged largely in the wake of *Wilhelm Meisters Lehrjahre*; it is the story of a young man's obsession with the stage, of an 'education' that begins and ends with the theatre. And while from the later perspective of the *Lehrjahre* this education is utterly relativized and indeed vitiated as an error, as a lamentable confusion of art and life, illusion and truth, theatre and reality (albeit as a fruitful and even necessary error according to the pedagogic doctrines of the 'Society of the Tower'), it is still by no means clear from the *Sendung* alone that the younger Goethe of the years 1777–85 regarded it as such – and certainly not with the same conviction as the older author of the *Lehrjahre*.

The *theatralische Sendung* is the story of Wilhelm Meister's dissatisfaction with the mercantile banality and the domestic circumstances of his middle-class milieu. His imaginative and creative gifts, at once precocious and immature, find expression in a childish, but already proprietorial fascination with domestic puppet-shows and amateur theatricals, in which the boy directs, writes and takes leading roles in plays that derive from the already derivative Baroque and neo-classical dramas of mid-eighteenth-century Germany. His stage-struck activities lead him into a passionate relationship with Mariane, a second-rate but good-hearted actress – a liaison that not only crosses the clear social line dividing the respectable *Bürger's* son from the vagabond and *bohémien* existence of travelling players, between the mercantile and the artistic, but also hastens his painful emotional maturity when he discovers that his now pregnant mistress is being kept by a wealthy rival. After a severe illness he leaves home, ostensibly on an errand to collect commercial debts for his father – in fact, on a protracted journey that allows him practically unlimited freedom to indulge his true passion, the theatre. To this end he becomes acquainted successively with the popular *Volkstheater*, amateur impromptus given by workers at a manufactory and at a miners' festival; with a travelling troupe of quarrelsome, venal and occasionally talented players under the direction of the formidable Madame de Retti; with the unpredictable and often humiliating experience of aristocratic patronage of the performing arts; and he finally ends up in H[amburg] as the financial 'angel' and principal actor of a professional theatre.

In the course of his theatrical career Wilhelm also touches peripherally on the social and cultural milieu that will, in the subsequent *Lehrjahre*, supersede the theatre and provide the context for his wider and, we must assume, infinitely more important 'education': the intellectual and social élite class of aristocrats and officers by which the *Bürger* Wilhelm will become as captivated in an upwardly mobile direction as he has hitherto been by his downward *mésalliance* with the theatre. He makes the acquaintance of a Count and Countess, of the cynical but well-disposed officer Jarno, of a mysterious traveller who crosses his path in various guises and dispenses oracular advice (subsequently revealed as the powerful and manipulative Abbé of the *Lehrjahre*), and, in a fleeting and dreamlike episode, of the charismatic Natalie who, in the very last pages of the completed *Lehrjahre*, almost becomes his wife. For she is, as it transpires very much later in the final version of the novel, the beautiful 'Amazon' who saved his life when his wandering band of troublesome players were set upon by robbers on their way to the theatrical Mecca of Hamburg.

But these prefigurations of the urbane aristocratic world in which Wilhelm is to become involved in the latter half of the *Lehrjahre* appear only peripherally and tangentially in the *theatralische Sendung*, which moves for the most part in the *demi-monde* of the theatre, indeed of the itinerant stage. And in many ways, the *Sendung* is a loosely allegorical account of the state of German theatre and drama in the second and third quarters of the eighteenth century, of its immaturity, its lack of tradition and resources, its hand-to-mouth existence and its dependence on aristocratic patronage, its domination by the academic and prescriptive punditry of Gottsched, and of the split between the robust and vigorous, if crude, native traditions of the popular stage and the ponderously derivative neo-classicism of the 'legitimate' theatre. Madame de Retti and her troupe are a thinly disguised portrait of Caroline Neuber and her players, Serlo is the fictive equivalent of Schröder, and Hamburg was of course the city that fathered the short-lived attempt to establish an independent National Theatre that foundered, to Lessing's despair and personal loss, in 1769. Wilhelm's enthusiastic and interminable diatribes on the purpose and mission of the theatre in his own country, his lectures on the cultural and didactic importance of the stage, on the role and status of the actor (which regularly reduce his listeners to stupefaction, even to sleep), his excited discovery of Shakespeare: all this reflects faithfully Goethe's first-hand and vicarious perception and experience of German theatre and drama in the early years of his life.

The principal figures of the *Sendung* are not those of the as yet mysterious and inscrutable brotherhood of the Society of the Tower who dominate the subsequent developments of the *Lehrjahre*, but the vivid and memorably characterized figures encountered by Wilhelm in the course of his theatrical career. It is one of the more attractive features of the *Sendung* material, as against the more solemn and portentous elaborations of the *Lehrjahre*, that Goethe presents, alongside the more tedious *longueurs* of Wilhelm's protracted discussions of his theatrical mission, a lively and relatively realistic narrative of his adventures across Germany: the folkloric festival at the beginning of Book Three, the petty rivalries and quarrels among the itinerant players that soon begin subtly to undermine Wilhelm's naive and idealistic notions of the theatre, the financial wheelings and dealings that make him indispensable to his fellow actors, the brutal disappointment at the shabby reception given to the company at the Count's castle, the officers who treat the actresses as fair game and the actors with patronizing contempt, the chaotic organization of the travelling company and the disastrous expedition in the course of which, for all their romantic notions of self-defence, they are attacked and robbed. Even more memorable is the cast of figures Wilhelm encounters on his mission: the apparently (but only apparently) feckless and treacherous Mariane; the opportunistic Melina and his resentful wife; the formidable but fallible Madame de Retti and her drunken lover; the amoral Philine; Friedrich and 'Laertes'; the extrovert Serlo and his tragically haunted sister Aurelie. These figures beguile and distract, exasperate and entertain the reader as they do Wilhelm in his struggle to keep his missionary career on course.

What gives the *theatralische Sendung* a quite different, original and intriguing dimension, however, is the introduction of two powerfully drawn figures who stand apart from both the aristocratic and the theatrical milieu. Although they are introduced naturalistically enough into the narrative, they are from the start surrounded by an aura of mystery and of tragic destiny that is alien to the relative realism of the novel, and they seize the imagination of both Wilhelm and the reader in a compelling, indeed mesmeric way: Mignon and the Minstrel (*Harfenspieler*). Mignon, in particular, is one of Goethe's most enigmatic and alluring creations, intruding exotically into the story like a creature from another world and, for a while, dominating Wilhelm's attention. Attached, indeed bonded as a slave to a visiting troupe of acrobats by whom she is cruelly treated, she is rescued by Wilhelm from this bondage, whereupon she becomes his utterly devoted companion and servant. In the circus she had been trained, animal-like, to perform her *Eiertanz* – a blindfold dance, stepping unerringly but mechanically and soullessly over a pattern of eggs arranged across the floor. It is not this accomplishment, however, that catches Wilhelm's attention, nor is it even, initially, the compelling song she sings, but the whole pathos of her enigmatic being: exotic, lonely, shy, waif-like, restless, alien and profoundly, inscrutably unhappy. Pre-pubescent and androgynous – even the narrator at first switches strikingly between masculine, feminine and neuter pronouns to describe her – she dresses as a boy, behaves in a restlessly tomboyish manner and speaks a strange mixture of Italian, French and broken German. Her whole demeanour expresses a visceral nostalgia and brittle pathos that she distils into three songs that are expressive of unmitigated suffering: 'Heiß mich nicht reden' (Bid me not speak), 'Kennst du das Land' (Do you know the land) and 'Nur wer die Sehnsucht kennt' (Only those who know what longing is).

Goethe's technique of intercalating lyrical poems or songs into the narrative of the *Sendung* is a feature that was to have a marked influence on subsequent Romantic novels; and Mignon herself is a quintessentially pre-Romantic figure. She has something of the enigmatic symbolic aura of the *Knabe Wagenlenker* (Boy Charioteer) or of Euphorion – though whereas these figures are entirely congruous within the allegorical idiom of *Faust* Part Two, Goethe is careful, within the narrative realism of the novel, to rationalize or adapt the poetic or symbolic overtones of Mignon's character and talents into the story. This he does by means of the fiction that her songs are either learned ('Heiß mich nicht reden', 'Nur wer die Sehnsucht kennt'), or alternatively that Wilhelm himself translated the original Italian text into German ('Kennst du das Land'). Despite this device, it is clear that these songs are indeed exquisite expressions of Mignon's profound and life-threatening nostalgia and suffering, articulations of her sense of existential insecurity and alienation. 'Kennst du das Land' is an expression of her aching nostalgia for the land of her birth, a vivid but distantly recollected vision of an Italian home and landscape – and of the Alps, the barrier that separates her from her lost childhood. Moreover, the refrain seems to be directed specifically at Wilhelm as Mignon's 'lord and master' (*Gebieter*); and intriguingly, in the later *Lehrjahre* version of the song, the refrain appears to prefigure even more strikingly Mignon's complex relationship with Wilhelm as it will develop in the course of the novel, although it is sung by her almost immediately after their first meeting: here, the refrain is addressed respectively to a lover (*Geliebter*), a protector (*Beschützer*) and a father (*Vater*).

The Harfenspieler, an itinerant minstrel introduced quite arbitrarily into the narrative of Wilhelm's theatrical adventures, is a tragic companion-figure to Mignon, a wild and unkempt figure with bardic beard and robe living a rootless mendicant existence. The first songs he sings to the carousing players are romantic and unproblematic, albeit moving, celebrations of the status and gifts of the wandering minstrel: 'Der Sänger' (The Minstrel) is cited as an example of his performance sung to the harp. But it soon becomes clear that the harpist's subsequent songs are harrowingly bitter and profoundly tragic articulations of his own experience, even if they are universalized as descriptions of the human condition. 'Wer nie sein Brot mit Tränen aß' (Who never ate his bread with tears), 'Wer sich der Einsamkeit ergibt' (Who pledges himself to solitude) and (in the *Lehrjahre*) 'An die Türen will ich schleichen' (Past the doorways I will creep) express in tragic counterpoint to Mignon's pathological nostalgia a devastating vision of existential desolation, of human life isolated and exposed to remorselessly vindictive and vengeful powers, of guilt arbitrarily visited on unwitting mortals, who are relentlessly pursued and punished in a pitilessly wretched existence.

These two devastated existences, then, are not so much assimilated into the narrative; rather, they accompany Wilhelm incongruously and, it seems at times, fatefully, on his theatrical career. They are outsiders even in this raffish and *bohémien* context – far more than Wilhelm himself, who is, for all his ambivalent efforts at integration, constantly aware, or more accurately is constantly made aware, of the social, cultural and intellectual gulf that separates him from his colleagues in the theatre. It may be that these two mysterious figures have been overcentralized, romanticized and even demonized by subsequent generations of commentators on the novel; they have been understood on the one hand as representing the sublimity of art or poetry, and on the other hand the misery of the artistic existence. But in the course of the novel they become more than simply part of Wilhelm's accumulated baggage, more than quaint, and occasionally troublesome, members of his extended family; they appear to constitute symbolic warning exempla of the more dangerous dimensions of the artistic temperament, pathological existences that exemplify, if not the *malheur d'être poète*, then at least the perils of a temperament that can only express itself poetically and tragically.

The songs sung by Mignon and the Harfenspieler are compelling and eloquent; but they are rooted in the most bitter suffering. The two figures are in this sense warnings to Wilhelm of the several pitfalls of his chosen career, of the rootless vagabond insecurity of the life that he embraces so uncritically and enthusiastically, of the discrepancy between his high cultural ideals for the theatre and the squalid and banal realities of the performing stage. Mignon in fact urgently and persistently pleads with him to quit the stage – though her advice, based as it is on her consuming obsession to return to Italy, is perhaps not as relevant or ominous as it might seem. But more broadly, her pleadings and her very fate appear to warn of the problems and dangers of the artistic or poetic temperament *per se*, of the tragic isolation, solipsism and dislocation of the artist that Goethe also portrayed so harrowingly in his drama *Torquato Tasso*. Within the context of the *theatralische Sendung* alone, these two figures are relatively incon-sequential; they form for a while part of the *ménage* with which, at the conclusion of the narrative, Wilhelm finally appears to settle down as a member of Serlo's theatre company in Hamburg: Serlo, Aurelie and her (putative) son, Mignon, the Harfenspieler, Philine. But their situation and their destinies remain unresolved within the *Sendung*, and they retain their aura of uncanny and inscrutable mystery. It was only with the extension of the narrative beyond this stage, in the subsequent denouement of the *Lehrjahre*, that Goethe was to resolve their problematic role in the novel.

WILHELM MEISTERS LEHRJAHRE (WILHELM MEISTER'S APPRENTICESHIP)

While the *Sendung* ends with Wilhelm, for the time being at least, firmly encamped with Serlo's company, the *Lehrjahre* allows no such respite for 'our friend', as the narrator calls him with ironic condescension; for in Book Five of the revised version his career and the novel itself make an abrupt shift of course, and Wilhelm's decision to remain with Serlo turns out to be only a temporary pause. He achieves the apogee of his theatrical career by appearing sensationally as Hamlet in his own enthusiastic and much-discussed adaptation of the play – a role with which he identifies himself totally, not least because the news of his own father's death reaches him shortly before the performance. What is more, this performance is haunted by yet another mysterious intervention into his obscure journey of self-discovery: the part of the ghost is dramatically filled at the last minute by an unknown stranger whose uncanny and more than convincing performance gives the whole production an urgent conviction for actors and audience alike. The mystery actor disappears as suddenly as he had appeared, leaving behind the veil that had obscured his features, and on which is written the warning: 'For the first and last time! Flee, young man! Flee!' Equally mysteriously, Wilhelm is visited by an anonymous female figure who makes passionate love to him and disappears before her identity is revealed. The strong suspicion is that this quasi-phantom lover is Mignon, whose behaviour towards her adoptive 'father' had already shown distinct, if oblique, sensual tendencies. Only much later in the novel is it revealed that his visitor was in fact the amoral Philine; but it is also revealed that Mignon had indeed intended to visit him that night, only to be forestalled by her sexually liberated rival, who thus unwittingly contributed decisively to the young creature's already life-threatening misery.

Soon afterwards, Wilhelm's disillusionment with the theatre, the tiresome squabbles of the company, and the death of Serlo's sister Aurelie lead him to quit the town, leaving behind him not only the theatrical milieu, but also the three figures to whom, by chance and by mysterious attraction, he had become attached: Mignon, the Harfenspieler and the child of Aurelie. And at this point the theatrical mission to which the first version of the novel had been dedicated becomes relativized as merely a provisional, indeed as a misguided, albeit necessary stage in Wilhelm's wider 'education'. For it turns out that his career hitherto has been observed, and to some extent manipulated, in an eccentric but ultimately benevolent and almost providential way, by a circle of cultivated and aristocratic figures who make up the quasi-Masonic Society of the Tower. The guiding spirit of the *Gesellschaft vom Turm* is the anonymous Abbé, the stranger who had already appeared incognito to Wilhelm on previous occasions, and whose pedagogic principles are based on the tenet that the individual must be allowed to fulfil his own destiny, to effect the full development of his talents and of his personality, by a process of learning through experience and error. It was under the aegis of this mysterious (and, it must be said, sententious and pretentious) fellowship that Wilhelm had been kept on the loose rein of his theatrical mission, whose specious but misguided confusions of art and life, of illusion and truth, are subsequently recognized as provisional steps in his immature but sincere quest for self-improvement.

This radical shift in the nature and direction of Wilhelm's progress puts the whole of his career in the *theatralische Sendung* into a quite different perspective. To be sure, the hero of the *Sendung*, with his naive artistic and theatrical illusions and ambitions, with his high-minded rejection of the mercantile ethos of his own culture (which had not prevented him from exploiting the resources of the family business to finance himself and others quite extravagantly in the course of his stage-struck career) had been consistently, if benevolently, ironized by his narrator; and the *Sendung*, with its clear, almost allegorical account of the state and the development of German drama and dramaturgy in the second and third quarters of the eighteenth century, had no doubt also adumbrated many of the author's own hopes and despairs concerning his native theatrical traditions. But in the *Lehrjahre* the theatrical dimension is more drastically relativized; and while the material taken over from the *Sendung* is in many ways structured less diffusely (the several *longueurs* of Wilhelm's interminable accounts of his childhood experiments with amateur theatricals, or his extended dramaturgical harangues delivered to an indifferent audience of professional players are greatly reduced), what the narrative of the *Lehrjahre* gains in tautness of construction, it loses in terms of colourful realism, as the story of Wilhelm's naive and infectious infatuation with the stage gives way to the altogether more portentous issue of his *Bildung*.

The shift of direction in the *Lehrjahre* is marked by an extraordinary hiatus in the narrative, by the interpolation of a long section (Book Six) entitled 'Confessions of a Beautiful (or a Noble) Soul' (*Bekenntnisse einer schönen Seele*). This comprises the life story of a vulnerable and introverted *Stiftsdame*, the member of a lay order of pietistic gentlewomen, whose minutely detailed account of her spiritual progress towards a life of contemplative and other-worldly mysticism is based on the life and personality of the family friend, Susanna von Klettenberg, who had counselled Goethe in the traditions of mystical pietism and hermetic thought in Frankfurt during his convalescence of the years 1768–70.

Goethe's predilection for introducing oblique, if not apparently irrelevant material into his works is well known; and it is not easy to justify this particular excursion from the narrative, even if it does very effectively mark the watershed of Wilhelm's career. To be sure, the spiritual biography of the *schöne Seele* is tenuously integrated into the novel in that the pious *Stiftsdame* is revealed as the aunt of Natalie, of the 'beautiful Amazon' who had intervened mysteriously and dramatically into the story by rescuing Wilhelm and his company after their ambush by bandits, who had stamped herself indelibly on Wilhelm's imagination and was to play a major role in the subsequent course of the novel – indeed, who is on the point of becoming his wife at the very end of the *Lehrjahre*. But this kinship is fortuitous and inconclusive, and any further thematic relevance of the aunt's confessions is ambiguous. For it is quite unclear whether the *schöne Seele* is presented as a negative or a positive exemplar of human behaviour, whether her life is to be judged as a model of selfless piety or as one of self-indulgent, even self-obsessed, neurotic introspection; her own niece Natalie, herself a paragon of practical and self-sacrificing altruism in the service of others, acknowledges her aunt's obsessive preoccupation with herself, her moral and religious fearfulness and her excessive sensibility. And the *schöne Seele* is indeed an unedifying example of neurotic *Empfindsamkeit*, whose introspective piety appears to be based on the keen awareness, and the violent suppression of, her own sensuality (including a pathological fear of venereal infection), on a complex pattern of self-disgust and self-pity alternating with a Pharisaic spiritual pride and self-righteousness. Her withdrawal from life and from social responsibility leads her to the *Herrnhuter*, the Moravian community of Graf Zinzendorf – to which community Wilhelm's erstwhile patron the Count is also drawn later in the novel, largely, we are led to believe, as the result of a bizarre jape in an earlier episode from Book Three, when the Count had discovered Wilhelm masquerading as himself, following which the

Count had become traumatized into a superstitious pietism, convinced that this confrontation with his own *doppelgänger* was a supernatural sign that he should devote himself to a spiritual mission.

Whatever our judgement of the *schöne Seele*, after her ambivalent hagiography the narrative resumes with Wilhelm's total break with the theatre and his assimilation into the social, cultural and ethical milieu of the *Gesellschaft vom Turm*, which operates from a castle that once belonged to the patriarch of an extended family that now comprises Lothario, his sisters Natalie and the Countess – and his madcap brother Friedrich, who had appeared sporadically in the *Sendung* as an eccentric member of the strolling players. With this family are also associated Lothario's two fiancées, Lydie and Therese, Jarno and the manipulative mentor of the Society, the Abbé – who, moreover, has a mysterious brother who may or may not have performed the role of the ghost in Wilhelm's production of *Hamlet*. It is within this ethos and in this strangely familiar milieu (for the castle contains many items from the art collection of his own grandfather) that Wilhelm's education will take its new departure; for he is presented, at the end of the penultimate book of the novel, with his *Lehrbrief* or certificate of apprenticeship, a sententious document that recites in a series of gnomic maxims the Abbé's pedagogical principles. After a portentously solemn quasi-Masonic ceremony and the presentation of the *Lehrbrief*, the Abbé pronounces that Wilhelm's years of apprenticeship to life are over: nature has pronounced him free.

For all the Masonic flummery of Wilhelm's rite of passage, this is a decisive moment in his career, for it coincides with a truly momentous biographical revelation: Felix, the adopted child of the deceased Aurelie, is none other than his own son, born to his first mistress, the actress Mariane, who had died some time before in the conviction that she had been callously abandoned by Wilhelm as a faithless woman, rather than as the result of a disastrous misunderstanding. By devoting himself to the upbringing of Felix, Wilhelm will learn to integrate himself into the human community and assume his full responsibilities as a citizen; he will fulfil himself in a higher sense than that of his mercantile and *bürgerlich* origins, and certainly in a more meaningful way than in his erroneously adopted career on the stage. The theatre, with its illusions and vanities, its rootless and anarchic confusions of art and life, is not the engine of personal or national renewal; art has a part to play in social and personal education, but it is subsumed under a wider and more selfless humanitarianism.

For all the presumptuous prescriptiveness of the *Turmgesellschaft*, for all the sententious and diffuse generalities of its didactic ethics, we are meant to believe that it is in this direction that Wilhelm's true destiny lies; and to this end, the final book of the *Lehrjahre* is devoted to the rapid but complex denouement of his confused education. The overriding concern is that he should marry; and after a complicated comedy of errors in which, as a result of Lothario's involved liaisons, he comes within a hair's breadth of an erroneous marriage to Lothario's Therese, he is finally betrothed (though he is not, it is revealed in the subsequent *Wanderjahre*, in the event married) to his true bride, his beautiful Amazon, the perfectly gifted and saintly Natalie. The novel ends with the celebrated analogy with which Wilhelm compares himself in his new-found happiness of integration and fulfilment to Saul the son of Kish, who went out to seek his father's asses and found a kingdom – a truly ambivalent note on which to end the novel, for it is unclear whether the reader is meant to reflect on Saul's subsequent, and quite disastrous, destiny as the ruler of Israel.

Even without inferring this dire note, however, the denouement of the novel is by no means unproblematic. For Wilhelm's new family had consisted not only of Felix, but also of the two tragic beings for which he had assumed responsibility, Mignon and the Minstrel. While their symbolic function in the *theatralische Sendung* might have been as warnings of the rootless insecurity, or even of the demonic perils of the artistic temperament, while they were at the very least inscrutably haunted creatures who expressed their misery in harrowingly beautiful lyrical form, there is no room for such problematic existences in the ethos of practical humanitarianism that characterizes the ultimate development of the *Lehrjahre*, however imprecisely defined that ethos may be. They are, therefore, somewhat brutally 'killed off' by Goethe in the course of the final book in an act of literary homicide that many critics and readers have since found it difficult to forgive. Wilhelm has in any case relinquished direct responsibility for their care; the Minstrel has been entrusted to a rural physician who undertakes, it appears for a time successfully, to cure the wretched man of his paranoid delusions and existential angst. Mignon for her part is given over to Natalie's tutelage, but for all her strenuous and kindly efforts, the child is doomed; her complex and intense relationship with Wilhelm, her pathological nostalgia for her unknown home, her existential fragility are inaccessible to any form of care or education, however enlightened or benevolent. Although she appears finally to have accepted her female gender, she articulates her hopeless suffering in one last song of intense pathos, 'So laßt mich scheinen, bis ich werde' (Let me appear thus till I become), in which she presages her imminent death and looks forward to an angelic existence of paradisal innocence where she will be released from the fretful burdens of growing up, of gender and of existential misery. She dies in Wilhelm's arms, and in the presence of Therese, Natalie and Felix, to his profound distress and self-reproach.

At this point, the tragic pathos of Mignon's death and the poetic mystery of her unhappy life are rationalized in a bizarre and abruptly fortuitous way. Her obsequies take place under the auspices of the *Turmgesellschaft*; her embalmed body is entombed in a secularized ceremony that verges perilously on tasteless and macabre kitsch; and the chance arrival of an Italian *Marchese* reveals a pitilessly rational, if also profoundly tragic, explanation of the mystery surrounding both Mignon and the Minstrel. He, it appears, is Augustin, the older brother of the *Marchese*, whose unwitting incest with his estranged sister Sperata had unhinged his already deeply susceptible mind; Mignon was the child of this innocent but disastrously illicit relationship, and she had been abducted from her foster-parents by travelling circus-folk and forced into the slavery from which Wilhelm had ransomed her. Sperata had died, distracted with grief, in the most pathetic and bizarre circumstances; Augustin escaped from the monastery in which he had been confined, to embark on the miserable itinerant existence from which Wilhelm had also rescued him. Scarcely has the *Marchese* departed after his lengthy and harrowing narrative than the Minstrel, after a short-lived and deceptive period of recovery from his condition, dies by his own hand, having very nearly fulfilled what he perceives as his tragic destiny by coming within a hair's breadth of inadvertently poisoning Felix with a flask of opium.

The 'happy ending' of the *Lehrjahre*, then, shows Wilhelm's integration into a stable, if not entirely lucidly or fully formulated, ethos of living – or, more accurately, it shows the completion of his apprenticeship to life and the point from which he can set out on his journeyman's progress to the status of *Meister*: his family name remains an irony of which he is fully conscious. But this happy ending is also shot through with ambiguities and darkened by the tragic fate of his two protégés. It is as if – and this is a critique frequently made against the *Lehrjahre* – Goethe had been so embarrassed by the poetic, romantic and irrational aura of the 'Italian' figures he had blithely introduced into the *theatralische Sendung* that he saw no alternative, in the solemnly pedagogic ethos of the *Turmgesellschaft* to which the new conception of the *Lehrjahre* addressed itself, but to rationalize and demythologize the aura of mystery surrounding Mignon and the Minstrel. Indeed, criticism of the *Lehrjahre*, long even before the chance discovery of the manuscript of the *Sendung*, has been radically split, on the one hand between those who applaud Wilhelm's (and therefore, it is thought, Goethe's) abandoning of his early immature enthusiasms, of the romantic vagabondage of his theatrical mission and the alluring but perilous siren songs of Mignon and the Minstrel for the enlightened and philanthropic humanitarianism of the *Turmgesellschaft* (and, it should be added, for the prospective integrity and stability of marriage and fatherhood), and on the other hand those who deplore Goethe's betrayal of the poetic irrationalisms of Wilhelm's early career for an élite ethos of cynical self-interest masquerading as enlightened humanity.

Schiller, characteristically, congratulated Goethe on his sensible resolution of the mysteries and irrationalisms of the earlier part of the novel; for him, the fate of Mignon and the Minstrel were entirely attributable to clerical superstition and obscurantism. Only from the womb of ignorance and superstition could such monstrous destinies emanate, he wrote to Goethe, commending him for demonstrating how they derived from the grotesque contortions of piety; for Augustin's upbringing, Schiller noted, exposed him to the barbarous and unnatural superstitions of a monkish training.[6] Other critics, among them Jean Paul Richter and Ludwig Börne, deplored Goethe's treatment of his Italian figures; for this school of opinion, the quality of the novel lay not in Wilhelm's conversion to the self-righteous ethic of the *Turmgesellschaft*, but in the poetic appeal of the original conception of the *Sendung*, in the colourful magical realism of Wilhelm's theatrical adventures and in the fascinating pageant of figures he encountered.[7]

One of the first critics to take issue with the 'unpoetic' development of Goethe's novel was Novalis – paradoxically, after initially expressing his overwhelming enthusiasm for the work. What Schiller praised is what Novalis so bitterly resented as the betrayal of the poetic or 'romantic' dimension: the book is a satire on poetry and religion, 'economic reality' is all that remains at the end. It is in truth a *Candide* directed against poetry, the romantic element, the element of wonder, is destroyed; 'artistic atheism' is the spirit of the novel.[8] Novalis derided Wilhelm's snobbery, his uncritical acceptance of the intellectual and cultural élitism of his self-appointed mentors, his 'pilgrimage to a title of nobility'; and Novalis then set out to write a corrective *Bildungsroman* in which poetry should assume its rightful function and purpose in the redemption of humanity: *Heinrich von Ofterdingen*.

The Romantic and post-Romantic critics of *Wilhelm Meisters Lehrjahre* can be, and have been, accused of overcentralizing, indeed of romanticizing, the poetic or irrational elements in the novel, and more especially the 'Italian' figures. Of all Goethe's contemporaries, it was Friedrich Schlegel, enthusiastically hailing the work as a literary revolution analogous to the effect of the French Revolution in politics and of Fichte's epistemology in philosophy, who held the most balanced view and had the acutest ear for its ironies. He gives the symbolic figures their full due; for him, Mignon and the Minstrel are 'the holy family of natural poetry, who lend romantic magic and music to the whole', and who are consumed by the hectic excesses of their own spiritual intensity.[9] But without unduly centralizing these figures, Schlegel also stresses the limitations of the *Turmgesellschaft* and its ethos – for even in the text of the novel, the Society is on occasion explicitly ironized, as when Jarno describes it as the relic of a youthful idea, when Wilhelm protests that its pious maxims are incapable of curing 'a wounded heart', or when he doubts whether he can ever achieve 'the harmonious development of his nature that his birth has denied him'.[10] Schlegel points out that the rationality of the brotherhood and its ethos is itself one-sided and inadequate, that the ideal *Bildung* predicated in the novel is a balanced synthesis of feeling and intellect, heart and head, art and life, of poetic imagination and prosaic responsibility. While he may have resented it deeply, Novalis was not inaccurate in identifying the prevalent 'economic' dimension of the *Lehrjahre*; even in the *theatralische Sendung*, it is only Wilhelm's fortuitous and unearned income from his father's debtors that sustains his indulgence in the theatre and his oddly assorted gallery of hangers-on. In the final version of the novel, it is his brother-in-law Werner who manages the family fortunes while Wilhelm spends generously but extravagantly; and it turns out that even the high-minded *Gesellschaft vom Turm* finances its philanthropic projects by means of shrewd financial dealings, indeed that it is actually negotiating through Werner with Wilhelm's own family business.

The *Lehrjahre* concludes on a quite open-ended note; it remains unclear just what Wilhelm intends to do with, indeed what he wants from, his future life – other than marriage to Natalie, which in the event is not to be. Whether he should travel Europe with the *Marchese*, whether he should go to the New World to which the *Turmgesellschaft* is beginning to turn its opportunistic attentions, to Russia with the Abbé, or whether he should remain in Germany, is unresolved. He has only just come into his 'kingdom', the business of life and living is ahead of him; his apprenticeship is complete, but he is only now embarking on his years as a journeyman.

DIE WAHLVERWANDTSCHAFTEN (ELECTIVE AFFINITIES)

Goethe's 'best book', as he once described it, contains nothing, he claimed, that had not been experienced by him, but also nothing just as it had been experienced.[11] This enigmatic and tantalizing remark is as characteristic of his own comments on the work as it is of the novel itself; indeed, it virtually reiterates the Delphic observation of the narrator on the veracity of the interpolated novella *Die wunderlichen Nachbarskinder* (The Odd Companions), that 'just about everything and nothing' in the short story told things 'as they were'.[12] The novel should be read at least three times, Goethe advised – quite possibly with some degree of ironic understatement; it will escape no one, he said, that it betrays a deep emotional gash, a 'passionate wound' that is reluctant to heal and grow over, a heart that is fearful of recuperation.[13]

Die Wahlverwandtschaften was originally planned in 1808 as a brief *Novelle* to be incorporated into *Wilhelm Meisters Wanderjahre*, on which work had begun in the previous year; and like *Der Mann von fünfzig Jahren* (The Man of Fifty), which eventually did appear in the *Wanderjahre*, it was to address the problem of emotional relationships across the generations – or, as Goethe is reported to have put it, to be a symbolic representation of social circumstances and of the conflicts they engender.[14] It very soon grew into a full-length novel which was completed by October 1809 – or at least into a novel whose extreme density and complexity belies its length of scarcely more than 100,000 words; to most readers it must appear very much longer.

The book's conception as a brief but dense and stylized narrative seems to be reflected in its style, its characterization and its structure. In the course of the first book, events and relationships develop very quickly, almost with the inexorable swiftness of the chemical reactions that constitute the title and the fundamental metaphor of the work, whereas after the departure of Eduard and the Hauptmann (Captain) at the end of Part One, the action assumes the calm tempo of the epic genre – as the narrator carefully suggests to the reader at the beginning of Part Two. In the absence of two of the principals, the relationships of the protagonists are held in suspension, and the pace of the novel is drastically slowed by a series of digressions and retardations: by the dispute over Charlotte's rearrangement of the churchyard, by the successive visits of the architect, Luciane and the assistant schoolmaster, of the English Lord and his companion, by the restoration of the chapel, by the tableaux vivants, by discursive discussions on pedagogics, religion, art or landscape, by Ottilie's journal and by the story of *Die wunderlichen Nachbarskinder*. For all that things happen during this part of the novel – the birth of the child, for example, whose long gestation is concurrent with these digressions – the flow of the narrative meanders until Eduard's return from the wars brusquely precipitates the denouement.

The novel has been described as experimental; and this epithet is appropriate in at least two senses. While it has some affinities, stylistic and in part even thematic, with Goethe's generically named *Novelle* and with *Wilhelm Meisters Wanderjahre*, it is like nothing Goethe had written before. The alien, stiffly formalized detachment of style and characterization has proved troublesome, even rebarbative, to many readers then and now; others than Wilhelm Grimm have found it tedious, pallid, frosty – even, as a recent English translator has put it, a chilling and in some ways a repellent book.[15] To some of Goethe's contemporaries, it was *Die Qualverwandtschaften*, a torture to read, a tiresome puzzle without any meaningful clues; to others it was 'the apotheosis of wicked lust',[16] a book that subverted marriage and celebrated adultery; to yet others a deeply moral and edifying treatise on the wages of sin. Ottilie has been canonized as a secular saint, a penitent whose renunciation and atonement makes her into a second Maria Aegyptiaca, writing a silent message to those who survive her; to others, she is a *femme fatale*, an emotional *demi-vierge*, even a vampire who freezes those around her and leaches the life from Eduard. To some she is exemplary, her nun-like devotion to her own vows, which she has broken as if in a trance, justifies her self-imposed martyrdom; to others, she is a depressive neurotic, hysterical and anorexic, manipulative and even (towards the egregious Luciane, as at least one of her diary entries indicates), spiteful and malevolent.

The quicksand of irony and contradiction on which the narrative appears to be constructed allows no certainty of perspective; Goethe himself contributes to the critical enigmas of the novel when he confesses that he 'cannot abide' Eduard, and yet finds him estimable because he loves unconditionally and absolutely.[17] Ottilie's most characteristic gesture is one of defensive refusal and denial; yet we are invited to detect in her journal or commonplace book (having been carefully warned by the infuriatingly tantalizing 'omniscient' narrator that not all her entries can be regarded as her own thoughts – which quickly becomes obvious anyway) a 'scarlet thread' of devotion and affection. Ottilie is at several points implicitly and explicitly associated with the Virgin Mary – not only in the tableau vivant of the crib that she enacts for the architect, but in a myriad ways by reference to iconographic traditions, to plane trees, as a figure immersed in a book or within a *hortus inclusus*, and most strikingly of all when she holds the dead child to her breasts in a bleak and bitter travesty of virgin mother and baby. At other times, she is obliquely depicted as Pandora, the gods' ambivalent 'gift' to humankind, from whose box emanated all the ills of the world, against which only hope is left as a bitter consolation. Constantly, it seems, the reader's perceptions are confused as the narrator subverts his own account by means of irony, ambiguity and contradiction, as the characters themselves stubbornly insist on mistaken interpretations and explanations, as they almost comically fall into fatal confusions and make false predictions, mistake signs and portents, read chance as fate and impulse as necessity. Charlotte suggests that the 'strange accident' of her pregnancy should be respected as an act of providence; and near the end of the novel we are solemnly told by the narrator that the shattered body of Nanny is held over Ottilie's corpse 'by chance or by some special providence', and immediately recovers from her fall. If the 'omniscient' narrator himself cannot distinguish between chance, fate and providence, how are the figures themselves – or the reader – to know?

The stance and the perspective of the narrator are at the root of the uncertainties of the novel, for this narrator is anything but omniscient; on the contrary, his equivocation time and again undermines the reader's confidence. Not only is the narrator by turns owlishly sententious, slyly perceptive, detached and involved, knowing and baffled; but the narrative voice also relates events as if they were anecdotal – not as the omniscient creator of the fiction, but as if it had been reported to him. In this respect, his voice is not dissimilar to the 'editor' of *Werther*, whose sober account of events as he had 'gathered' them from friends and survivors contrasts so powerfully with the overwrought rantings and transports of Werther's own voice. But there is no such drastic contrast of style in *Die Wahlverwandtschaften*; for if the narrator's voice is deliberate, sententious, evasive, remote and bland, the characters themselves (with the notable exceptions of Mittler and perhaps Luciane) also express themselves and address each other in a strikingly stilted, stylized and formal way.

In this sense, too, the novel is experimental, and not only because the title and theme concern a chemical analogy. The narrator's stance is that of a dispassionate observer of a chain-reaction of human behaviour; the figures themselves behave in a manner that suggests they are only half in control of their actions, if that. The house and estate are sealed off from the world outside, which only impinges, if at all, in the form of visitors, emissaries, letters, accounts and newspaper reports; the characters are contained in this oppressive milieu as if in a laboratory or chemical apparatus, into which various elements and combinations are introduced by the author *qua* chemist or *Scheidekünstler*. To be sure, Eduard goes off to the wars, the Captain leaves to advance his career, and returns as a Major; but these episodes are almost casually brushed over as irrelevant to the central experiment in human relationships that is being conducted within the house and estate, within this crucible in which emotions are smelted and alloyed. Even the single illustrative example of the chemical cross-combination described by the men to Charlotte seems to apply curiously aptly to the subsequent human relationships (for all that Eduard comprehensively misapplies the analogy): calcium carbonate mixed with sulphuric acid immediately forms, by elective affinity, 'a refractory gypsum' or calcium sulphate, while the carbon dioxide released by this process combines with water to form a dilute gaseous carbonic acid, which we know as a health-giving mineral water. Without taking the analogy too far, the reader might reasonably infer, in flat contradiction of Eduard's misinterpretation, that the gypsum corresponds to the emotional bonding of Eduard and Ottilie, for which 'refractory' is the precise term – an affinity or combination that is stubbornly irreversible – while the more 'delicate' combination of carbon dioxide and water is, like the bond between Charlotte and the Captain, altogether less intransigent.

Characteristically, however, the chemical analogy or metaphor for human behaviour is, if not vitiated, then severely modified. For the very term 'Wahlverwandtschaft', *elective* affinity, derived from the German translation of Torbern Bergman's *Disquisitio de attractionibus electivis*, uses, as Goethe acknowledged, an ethical notion to describe chemical reactions:[18] it is a human concept of choice transferred incongruously to inexorable natural processes – and as Charlotte rightly protests, human beings distinguish themselves in many ways from chemical substances. So in applying a chemical analogy to human affairs, Goethe appears to be committing the same solecism in reverse as the chemists do in describing their affinities, albeit metaphorically, as 'elective'. However, Goethe carefully explains his purpose in his anonymous announcement of the novel: the analogy or metaphor is that of the relationship between choice and necessity, free will and compulsion, between human rationality and what is today often called emotional or sexual 'chemistry', between the ethical imperatives of duty, fidelity and integrity on the one hand and the irresistible impulses of passion on the other. He felt all the more justified, he explains, in using the chemical analogy, since everywhere there is only one nature, and since even the apparently serene realm of rational freedom is shot through with traces of an obscure passionate necessity – which, he goes on to add Delphically, can only be expunged by a higher hand, and even then perhaps not in this life.[19]

The clash between free will and compulsion in the novel is similar to, though not identical with, Goethe's other articulations of the conflicting forces in human existence: in the poem 'Urworte. Orphisch', and in his formulation of what he termed *Das Dämonische* in the concluding chapter of *Dichtung und Wahrheit*. The poem moves dialectically between the inalienable personality (*Daimon*) and chance (*Tyche*), love (*Eros*) and necessity (*Anangke*) – with hope (*Elpis*) as a synthetic final release from the implacable clashes of these forces. In his autobiography, Goethe also describes a force in terms of his own metaphor of the 'daemonic' – an amoral, irresistible compulsion that rides roughshod through the 'moral world order' and plays havoc with human volition and ethical systems.[20] As he puts it, the strands of daemonic compulsion and human freedom are inextricably interwoven like *Zettel und Einschlag*, like the warp and weft of a textile fabric – or, we might conclude, like 'the traces of obscure passionate necessity' that run through 'the serene realm of rational freedom'.

We might be tempted to apply Goethe's notion of *Das Dämonische* to *Die Wahlverwandtschaften* – and many commentators have done so, for Eduard and Ottilie do indeed appear to be in the grip of an implacable amoral force that wreaks havoc with conscience, duty, fidelity and responsibility; Ottilie herself speaks explicitly of a malevolent *Dämon* that has taken control of her, wrenched her from her path and forced her to break her own laws. But whether we apply the chemical parallel or Goethe's image of a daemonic force in human existence, we are still dealing in metaphor and analogy, the literal application of which is of limited usefulness; for the inscrutability of *Die Wahlverwandtschaften* lies not in how far it can or cannot be explained in, say, chemical terms, but in the fundamental and inherent ironies and contradictions on which all attempts at objective or definitive interpretation of the novel founder.

Eduard predicts ABCD as Charlotte, himself, the Captain and Ottilie respectively; in this prediction he is proved disastrously wrong. He puts an irrational faith in the survival of the glass engraved with the initials E and O, in spite of knowing that they represent his own and the Captain's names, not his and Ottilie's: an absurd self-deception – and yet he later detects the substitute glass when his relationship with Ottilie, like the original glass, has been destroyed. The characters attempt to secure the lakes with dams and sluices – only for a young man to come within a hair's breadth of drowning. Ottilie is, by the Englishman's account, a skilled oarswoman – and yet her clumsiness on the lake causes the death of the child. After the child's death, Charlotte consents to a divorce – only to find that Ottilie has made this step impossible by her holy vow to renounce Eduard. The plane trees planted by Eduard are taken by him as a sign that he and Ottilie are destined for each other, for he planted them on the very day of her birth; but the same trees witness the appalling tragedy of the child's death that finally destroys the possibility of their union. Ottilie renounces Eduard; but they remain drawn irresistibly and mysteriously to each other by 'an almost magical attraction'. The characters toil and plan to make things safe, they provide life-saving equipment, landing-stages and boats, they create paths though woods and across rocks, but to no avail; and there is surely an analogy here for the fallibility, even the futility, of human moral and social bulwarks – marriage and family, convention and duty, education and reason – set up against the 'obscure passionate necessity' that smashes through those defences.

The characters contradict themselves again and again. Eduard cannot tolerate anyone seeing a text he is reading – until Ottilie arrives; and he ends up being dependent on her looking over his shoulder. Mittler is a zealous marriage counsellor who can do nothing for the marriage of Eduard and Charlotte, a do-gooder whose clumsy tactlessness precipitates two deaths. The Count and the Baroness are freethinking rationalists advocating marriage as a renewable five-year contract – until their own marriage becomes possible. The architect is a romantic idealist with notions of Gothic revival and of neo-Catholic religiosity; but his decoration of the chapel serves only to decorate Ottilie's final resting place with angelic figures whose resemblance to her betray his real obsession. Charlotte's attempts to 'democratize' death and prettify the churchyard are an ironic counterpoint to the shadow of death that pervades the whole work; for death is the fundamental motif of this novel, with its portentous attributes in gravestones, funerary chapel, water, asters and poplars (the trees of the underworld): death intrudes everywhere into this contrived and stagey Arcadian milieu. Most notoriously of all, the conclusion of the novel is profoundly ambiguous: Ottilie is revered as a saint, yet she has destroyed the lives of those around her, innocently or no. The cult that springs up after her death is a profoundly ironic episode; it has distinct similarities to the cult surrounding the death of Sperata described in Book Eight, Chapter Ten of *Wilhelm Meisters Lehrjahre* – and Goethe's aversion to such religious hysteria is well enough known. The final apotheosis of Eduard and Ottilie at the very end also shows Goethe at his most evasive: are we to accept this transcendental reconciliation at its face value, or is it a final bitter irony, a conciliatory arabesque arbitrarily tacked on to the end of a deeply tragic work?

The uncertainties created in the mind of the reader by the labyrinth of symbolic blind alleys and false trails, by the ambiguities and enigmas of the narrative and its inscrutable narrator, have destabilized and deconstructed the critical response to the novel. It has, above all in recent years, become a veritable honeypot for commentators who have expended prodigious amounts of intellectual energy on its exegesis, drawing on all manner of disciplines and cultures to explicate the text: astrology, alchemy, mythology, iconography, landscape gardening, lexical symbolism, numerology, and much else besides. Eduard, Charlotte, Otto form ECHO – which in turn relates to allusions to the myth of Narcissus and Echo at various points. Charlotte, Eduard, Mittler form CHEM – a significant acronym, even if Mittler signally fails to catalyse or restore the relationship between Charlotte and Eduard. OTT is the stem of the names of Eduard (one of whose names is Otto), Charlotte, the Captain, Ottilie – and the child. As an anagram, OTT becomes TOT (dead); as a palindrome, OTTO represents an ironically harmonious mirror-image. Ottilie is near enough to OTT-LILIE: lilies are symbols of purity, attributes of the Virgin Mary – and flowers of death. E-O are not only the initials of Eduard and Ottilie, or Eduard and Otto, but also of Eurydice and Orpheus – which relates neatly to the symbolism of Mittler as Hermes, ubiquitous messenger and Psychopomp, the conductor of souls to the underworld. The cryptic encodings of the novel have even been related, somewhat obscurely, to Mittler's win on the lottery: L-OTTO![21]

References and allusions have been discovered in the text to mathematical, mystical and alchemical ideals – the squaring of the circle, the Magnum Opus, the *hieros gamos* or chemical wedding, the Philosophers' Stone: the child of Eduard and Charlotte is perceived not only as a living example of double or 'crossed' elective affinity, but also in terms of the Homunculus, the product of the chemical wedding. The symmetry of Eduard's and Ottilie's headaches or migraines is that of complementary opposites, hinting at the perfection of the Platonic androgyne. Psychiatrically, the four main characters are diagnosed respectively as manic-depressive (Eduard), anorexic–hysterical (Ottilie), anally retentive (the Captain) and repressive (Charlotte). More plausibly, contemporary cultural preoccupations are demonstrated in the configuration of the estate; the formal seventeenth-century style of Eduard's father gives way to the carefully arranged informality of English landscape gardening, to an Arcadian vision of 'nature perfected' – while beyond this organized naturalness lurks a faunish, untamed, unmanaged and unpredictable landscape in which human will and ethical control are in abeyance.

The editor of the relevant volume of the recent *Frankfurter Ausgabe* of Goethe's works sees the whole novel as conceived under the aegis of Saturn, the planet of melancholy.[22] All four main figures are more or less 'saturnine' (depressive or melancholic) in temperament, and among the activities and attributes associated with Saturn are fruitful trees (and unfruitful ones); water, floods and drowning; earth and chthonic creatures; time; beggars; counting, measuring and surveying; orphans; landowners and travellers; millstones, gravestones and funerary monuments; monkeys; coal; asters and plane trees; and of course, lead – that is, the lead pottery glazes which cause Charlotte in the fourth chapter to worry about their toxicity (the verdigris on copper vessels, which is presumably therefore associated with Venus, remains unmentioned). Certainly, there is no lack of critical ingenuity and imagination invested in *Die Wahlverwandtschaften*; how far such extravagant exegesis contributes to an overall understanding or appreciation of the novel, or whether Goethe was aware of or intended the myriad submerged meanings in his own text, is uncertain. At the other extreme, that of critical sobriety, it has been argued that a work so inscrutable, so full of inconsistent and contradictory signs, portents and enigmatic ironies, is essentially resistant to lucid or unequivocal interpretation.[23]

Whether or not the main characters of the novel are clinically depressive, or 'hypochondriac' in the language of Goethe's time, they are certainly shown to be inadequate to cope with the pressures that build up against them. Indeed, it has often been remarked that they are all, more or less, dilettantes, amateurs, even bunglers, pottering about their estates, gardening, restoring, building, prettifying, music-making, entertaining, administrating, collecting, arranging – in short, filling their otherwise empty lives with busyness in lieu of business or of any wider public or political activity. They are typical of the leisured minor aristocracy of late eighteenth-century Germany and of the years before the Napoleonic occupation – though they can scarcely be said truthfully to be idle. It is clearly a novel about adultery – or rather, as Goethe put it, it concerns the words of Christ that 'whosoever looketh on a woman to lust after her hath committed adultery with her already in his heart'; as such, it may well be a broad comment on the social problems of marriage and divorce which Madame de Staël observed as 'a certain anarchy' afflicting German family life around 1800, or it may even be a direct allusion to the freethinking domestic morality of the Jena Romantics.

Condemned as an immoral attack on marriage and family, championed as a deeply moral treatise, the novel cannot plausibly be presented as either; it charts with chilling directness the sheer inadequacy of social institutions and human volition to cope with the emotional, social and moral anarchy of unbridled passion in an inappropriate situation. To be sure, Eduard is weak, stubborn, self-indulgent and self-deceiving; but he loves, as Goethe put it, unconditionally. To be sure, Ottilie is submissive, self-abnegating, even self-abasing, and has a highly developed sense of duty and obligation; but she too loves absolutely, and her moral conscience is in abeyance as a result. The virtual impossibility for the lovers to master or mitigate their feelings is conveyed by the chemical metaphor and by the quirky symptoms of compulsive sympathy they display – Eduard's unconscious self-betrayal when he describes Ottilie as 'a pleasing, entertaining girl' when she has scarcely opened her mouth; the mutual migraines; his tolerance of Ottilie looking over his shoulder; their easy adaptation to each other's deficiencies in music-making; and Ottilie's adoption of Eduard's handwriting. The final implausible, shocking, indeed grotesque symbol of the child's resemblance to the absent partners in the act of 'spiritual adultery' is only the most bizarre of these symptoms.

The inappropriateness of the present situation, or of passion in that situation, is underscored by the ironies of the novel: Charlotte had indeed intended to match Eduard and Ottilie, but was frustrated by his impatient impulse to revive the dead past. The Captain would indeed have made an appropriate match for Ottilie; but human beings are more unpredictably volatile than chemical elements. Divorce is indeed a feasible solution – until the conception of the child; with its death, that perspective reopens, only to be implacably closed off by Ottilie's renunciation. With or without regard to the ominous anagram TOT, death pervades the novel as the characters struggle to free themselves from the emotional labyrinth in which they have lost their way. The futility of this struggle is indeed related to the mythical archetype of the Fall, or of Pandora's Box, as they attempt to delude themselves that the ills released by the opening of the box can be returned to their original confinement, that a state of prelapsarian harmony can be restored. The word *Wahn*, delusion, recurs ominously as the protagonists, and more especially Charlotte, cling to the delusion 'that it is possible to return to an earlier, more circumscribed state of affairs, that forces violently unleashed could be brought under control' (I, 13), to the hope 'that a previous state of happiness might be restored' (II, 15), or to the illusion 'that everything was as it had been before' (II, 17). This is the state of affairs in the penultimate chapter of the novel – a fragile situation brought about fortuitously by the postponement of the Major's departure, a fraught, brief and illusory episode that very quickly and brutally ends when Mittler's characteristic bungling delivers the *coup de grâce* to Ottilie's will to live. And yet this knife-edge situation is, in retrospect, only a more explicit, more complex development of the brittle false idyll that pertained at the beginning of the novel, when Eduard and Charlotte were also attempting to reconstruct a precarious image of previously frustrated happiness.

Notwithstanding the bitter irony of the concluding paragraph, there is little relief in the course of this doom-laden story; and it may be that in writing the novel, for all its apparently calm detachment, for all the dispassionate perspective of its formal and sententious narrative restraint, Goethe was working out some saturnine strain in his own experience or his own personality, as he hinted that he had done with *Werther*. In the first decade of the nineteenth century, as he himself approached sixty, Goethe's personal and creative life had indeed passed through a sombre phase, with the death of Schiller in 1805, of Anna Amalia in 1807, and of his mother in 1808. He was beset by other vexations – by his ambivalent response to a younger generation of writers who professed to adulate him while challenging his most cherished doctrines; by the enormous creative effort to finish the first part of *Faust*; by the labours of his work on optics; by domestic difficulties compounded by occasional philanderings; by his permanently uneasy relationship with the Weimar court, and even difficulties with his friend, patron and ruler Karl August; and whatever emotional or spiritual crises he might have suffered in the sixth decade of his life. His drama *Pandora*, with which *Die Wahlverwandtschaften* has some thematic and symbolic affinities, had been abandoned; and Goethe himself attested that the novel betrayed the infliction of 'a deep passionate wound'. The precise nature and causes of this psychic wound will probably never be established; Goethe's meetings with Minna Herzlieb and Silvie von Ziegesar are close enough to the composition of the novel, but no clear parallels can be drawn between these brief affairs and the figures or events of the story. Goethe had, of course, become formally married only in 1806, and it is not surprising that his fiction should address issues of marriage and adultery. It has even been suggested that the humorous and *risqué* narrative poem 'Das Tagebuch' (see above, pp. 104–5), written less than a year after the completion of the novel, a poem that is a wry moral fable on the successful, if involuntary, resistance of sexual temptation and a return to conjugal fidelity, forms a robust antidote to the tragic dissonances of the novel,[24] – thus perhaps also confirming the therapeutic or cathartic effect of its composition.

Even within *Die Wahlverwandtschaften* itself, the interpolated story of *Die wunderlichen Nachbarskinder* might provide a foil to the tragic story that frames it, mitigating or even contradicting the pitiless bleakness of the novel. For water here is indeed a 'friendly element' that precipitates not catastrophe, but salvation; here, a compulsive 'elective affinity' is unproblematically demonstrated, here the protagonists act decisively, if histrionically, to seize their opportunity and make themselves masters of their destiny. This might well be the case if the novella were presented as a quite separate alternative to the sombre course of the novel; but it is not, since here too, enigmas and ambiguities cloud the issue. For we are led to believe that something broadly similar had decisively influenced the Captain's life – evidently some time before the events described in the novel, since it is alluded to already in the fourth chapter. But the inferences we might be meant to draw are confused, the signals and parallels are quite unclear – it is impossible to say with any certainty whether the Captain was the 'official' fiancé who loses his bride, or the erstwhile enemy who finally wins her by plunging into the river to save her. The textual clues – the Captain's efficiency, his lack of independent means and his dependence on patronage, his military career, his skill at swimming – suggest overwhelmingly that he is the latter; and yet if this is so, he appears to have subsequently lost the woman he had won so boldly. If he is supposed to be the 'official' fiancé of the novella, then this might be consistent with the emotionally passive, indeed inhibited, role he plays in the novel; but the narrator's equivocation clouds the issue entirely. Either way, the novella appears to represent only an imagined ideal, a possible alternative of fulfilment under quite different premisses from those of the novel; indeed, it is presented in remote and almost fairy-tale terms as a charmed idyll, as a betrothal realized in a rural wilderness quite removed from family and society – the sort of idyll that the figures of the main narrative strive, but conspicuously fail, to achieve. We are led to mistrust the happy ending of the novella, just as we are led to mistrust the specious 'happy ending' of the final sentence of the novel. As the Count remarks in a discussion on marriage and divorce in Chapter Ten of Part One, the happy endings of stage comedies are false: in real life the curtain goes up again on the marriage to reveal an altogether more problematic set of circumstances. *Die Wahlverwandtschaften* is indeed no drawing-room comedy; but it might reasonably be described as a drawing-room tragedy.

WILHELM MEISTERS WANDERJAHRE
(WILHELM MEISTER'S JOURNEYMAN'S YEARS)

There are indications that even as he completed *Wilhelm Meisters Lehrjahre* in 1796, Goethe had in mind a sequel to that novel – or at least that he left open the possibility of its continuation. Not only did the *Lehrjahre* itself contain several pointers to the future development of 'our young friend's' career, and not only did Goethe write to Schiller that any sequel would have to be 'dovetailed' with the previous novel;[25] the very metaphor upon which the work is predicated – that of the career structure of the craft guilds, the progress of skills from apprentice to journeyman to master – suggested such a development. Indeed, Wilhelm had already in the *Lehrjahre* changed his name from *Meister* to *Geselle*, master to journeyman; and there is even reason to believe that Goethe might have intended to continue the *Wanderjahre* into a third and final novel in which the hero would achieve his mastership. In the event, it was the *Wanderjahre* that closed the sequence; and, as with Goethe's other encyclopedic late work, *Faust*

Part Two, the writing of the final stage of the Wilhelm Meister novel was protracted, almost haphazard, and to say the least, unorthodox in structure and
composition.

A first version of the *Wanderjahre* was written sporadically during 1807, 1810
and 1820–1, and was published in 1821 under the title *Wilhelm Meisters Wanderjahre
oder Die Entsagenden. Erster Teil* (Wilhelm Meister's Journeyman's Years, or The
Renunciants. Part One); this is the version translated by Thomas Carlyle in 1827.
The implied second part was never even begun; instead, a heavily revised and
extended version of 'Part One' was written between 1825 and 1829, and was
published that year. The first version, no doubt under the influence of Goethe's
reading of the *Decamerone* in 1807, was originally conceived as a series of novellas
(of which *Die Wahlverwandtschaften* was to be one) contained within a broad framework narrative structured on Wilhelm's travels as a journeyman in the service of
the *Turmgesellschaft*, and described largely through his correspondence with
Natalie, to whom he had become engaged at the end of the *Lehrjahre*: she, Wilhelm
and his son Felix were to be the principal threads joining the two novels. The first
version of the *Wanderjahre* already contains much of the material found in the final
version, though neither in quite the same form nor in the same sequence as in the
revised version. To be sure, this first version is a sporadic, disrupted, heterogeneous narrative of many different perspectives, themes and registers, but this is
not because it is a preliminary 'roughed-out' version of the novel; on the contrary,
the final version is even more bewilderingly sporadic and multifaceted than its
predecessor.

The symbolic and narrative complexity of the *Wanderjahre* has split critics and
commentators as few other works have done; moreover, its early reception was
confused not only by Goethe's own two versions, but also by the malicious
publication, in the same year as his first version, of a bogus anonymous work
entitled *Wilhelm Meisters Wanderjahre* – a polemical critique of Goethe and his works
by a Lutheran pastor, J. F. W. Pustkuchen, which impertinently borrowed the title
of his latest novel. Even as perceptive and sensitive a reader as Hugo von
Hofmannsthal professed himself bemused by Goethe's novel, while admitting
wryly that it was quite possible that there was 'in all this' a far deeper meaning
than he was capable of grasping.[26] To recent deconstructionist critics, the
Wanderjahre has become the prototype of the self-referential text, a 'meta-text' –
and the intractable symbolism of the casket, on which so many scholars have
exercised their ingenuity in so many different ways, a symbol of the symbol, an
inscrutable and quintessential literary mystery.

Goethe was well aware of the encyclopedic, composite and symbolic nature of
his last novel. He claimed he had always intended it as an 'aggregate', a compila-
tion, a serial counterpoint of ideas, themes and symbols which might reflect and
complement, but which equally might contradict each other. At one point, the
narrator describes himself explicitly as 'der Sammler und Ordner dieser Papiere'
(the collector and arranger of these documents) – some of which he reveals to his
readers, while others are purportedly withheld for reasons of space or because of
their controversial nature. It is of course the continuation of the story of Wilhelm
Meister and of his 'education', his progress or development as an individual, his

integration into life, society, the fellowship of men and the world around him, sustained by the metaphor of his qualification through the grades of a skilled craft. But this education or training, it is implied, is still incomplete at the conclusion of the novel ('Ist fortzusetzen' – to be continued); and it would be extremely difficult to define, or even to describe, just what Wilhelm's final mastership consists in, other than in his maximum exposure to the widest possible variety of social and cultural experience.

Indeed, for long stretches of the novel Wilhelm himself recedes from the direct consciousness of the reader. He functions often as a passive observer, listener, writer or receiver of letters, and only a brief section of the work is devoted, in almost summary fashion, to his training for his specific skill or craft – that of a surgeon. The education and upbringing of his son Felix is another strand of experience that belongs to his full development as a human being; but Felix's education is left largely to the Delphic and often eccentric precepts of the teachers of the 'Pedagogic Province'. Wilhelm's relationship to Natalie is a further aspect of his personal welfare, his maturity as a 'citizen of the world' and a member of the human community; but he and Natalie remain separated throughout the novel, and they communicate only vicariously across vast distances in a relationship more spiritual and symbolic than physical and real. Instead, Wilhelm encounters a plethora of women, directly or indirectly, in reality or in fiction, with whom he maintains often ambiguous relationships. Hersilie, for example, is wooed excitedly and histrionically by Felix, and covertly by Wilhelm; she is too old for the son, and too young for the father. And if, by the conclusion of the narrative, Wilhelm might at last have found his *métier* (for it is his medical skills that allow him to restore the drowned Felix to life), the emphasis of the story of Wilhelm Meister appears to have been transferred to the next generation, as Wilhelm affirms the continuity of the human race in the perpetuation of the 'glorious image of God', continually reborn into an existence in which it is vulnerably exposed to hurt and harm. The *Lehrjahre* had ended with an Old Testament reference summing up Wilhelm's previous adventures: like Saul the son of Kish, he had set out to find his father's asses and had found a kingdom. In the *Wanderjahre*, Wilhelm's story ends on a note that recalls the affirmation of God the Father's love for Christ: 'This is my beloved son, in whom I am well pleased'.

The *theatralische Sendung* had charted Wilhelm's (and indeed the German nation's) immature obsessions with art, the theatre and a vagabond existence of experience through error; the *Lehrjahre* had extended the scope of his ambitions towards an ethical humanitarian goal in the company of élite spirits, an aristocracy of the mind in which art was subsumed under a broader educative purpose. Universal education, the fullest and highest exploitation of all one's potential talents, had been Wilhelm's personal ambition to which, by misfortune or negligence, wittingly or unwittingly, he had sacrificed those dearest to or most dependent on him: Mariane, Felix, Mignon and the Minstrel. No sooner is the narrative of the *Wanderjahre* under way than Wilhelm is informed by Montan (*quondam* Jarno) that this is now the age of specialism, of one-sided education or training, and that versatility or polymathy are only the basis on which a specialized skill is founded. Later, Montan even dismisses general or universal education ('eure allgemeine

Bildung') as foolishness; training and close guidance are of the utmost importance in a world that no longer allows the leisurely formative experience through error that the Abbé had advocated in the *Lehrjahre*. Or, as one of Makarie's aphorisms puts it, the modern world forces a general education on us willy-nilly; but general knowledge or learning does not advance us in a rapidly changing world, only a specific art or skill.

And yet this perspective is also relativized within the novel; for Jarno, even in his new persona as Montan, an expert mining engineer and geologist, is still the cynical commentator he had been in the *Lehrjahre*. His own solitary, even misanthropic, activity in the depths of the earth and the vast solitude of the mountains, isolates and marginalizes him; and his chthonic perspective is symbolically counterbalanced and complemented by Makarie's 'astral' mysticism. If the principal figures of the novel have a common purpose, it is, as the subtitle suggests, *Entsagung*, renunciation: an ideal of selfless service to the common good which, while it involves all manner of restriction, limitation and sacrifice of horizons, of personal ambitions and even of personal relationships, is its own reward and fulfilment. It has been suggested that the practical idealism of the novel is an attempt to salvage the battered certainties and humane values of the eighteenth century in the confused melting-pot of the early nineteenth, an ironic settling for less than absolute perfection, for less than Utopia, in the aftermath of the French Revolution, of the upheavals of the Napoleonic occupation and the subsequent liberation of Germany, of the abolition of the Holy Roman Empire, and above all in the rapidly accelerating pace of change, of agricultural, social and industrial revolution in post-Congress Europe.

The fiction of Wilhelm's 'journeyman' years is itself only sustained for part of the novel. At the outset, he is charged by the prescriptions of the *Turmgesellschaft* never to stay in one place for more than three days, or to return to any place within the space of a year; but these conditions are eventually abandoned, first by subterfuge (in Italy, Wilhelm decides that they shall hold for terra firma, but not on water), and later by formal dispensation (he is allowed a long period of training as a surgeon). In any case, his own personal story has from an early stage been interrupted, counterpointed and indeed swamped by a myriad encounters, anecdotes, characters and tales in which he is rarely the, or even a, central figure. The narrative is confused and obscured by a whimsical shifting of perspectives; the novellas interpolated into the story of Wilhelm are tales told to him, or read by him, and yet these 'fictive' tales also intrude into the framework. Wilhelm himself encounters on Lake Maggiore two of the women (Hersilie and the 'beautiful widow') from the story of *Der Mann von fünfzig Jahren*. He has gone to Italy to exorcise the phantom of Mignon, to visit the environment from which she had been tragically abducted; and as his companion he is given a young artist who, we are explicitly told, is himself the sort of figure common in novels and plays, and who has read of Mignon's fate in a novel – evidently *Wilhelm Meisters Lehrjahre*!

This shifting of fictional levels, though less sustained and whimsical than in, say, Brentano's *Godwi* or E. T. A. Hoffmann's *Kater Murr* (Tomcat Murr), has affinities with both Sterne's *Tristram Shandy* and with Romantic Irony in its deliberate disruption of the boundaries between fiction and life, imagination and reality; and Goethe himself described the novel as 'romantic' in a sense that may be close to that of Friedrich Schlegel.[27] The narrator frequently teases the reader by commenting on and drawing attention to the narrative idiom, as when he concedes that his own novel might have become 'more didactic than it should be', or when he promises to inform the reader further about a certain episode later in the novel – but does not; when he pretends to be anything but omniscient, or when the characters themselves profess that they talk about each other as if they were characters in a novel. In the third chapter of Book Three Wilhelm, relating the story of his medical studies, suddenly refers to himself in the third person – a disconcerting device that recurs in the anecdotal novella *Nicht zu weit* (Not too far), where Odoard's narrative switches from third to first person and back again, whereupon the narrator of the *novel* intervenes to admit to the reader that he has exploited the privilege of the epic poet, and promises to put the reader out of his confusion by means of a further narrative device. The novel also, in the manner of the *Lehrjahre* and *Die Wahlverwandtschaften*, breaks off the already complex narrative and interpolates long sections of aphorisms grouped under two headings: *Betrachtungen im Sinne der Wanderer* (Observations in the Spirit of the Travellers) and *Aus Makariens Archiv* (From Makarie's Archive). These maxims cover a multitude of subjects and disciplines: art, ethics, religion, literature, social and political issues, mathematics, philosophy, natural science. As one of the characters remarks, many of the sententious commonplaces in these sections contradict each other, are paradoxical, ambiguous and even self-contradictory – and yet they are often singly presented as, and legitimately taken as, profound expressions of Goethe's own Delphic wisdom.

The reader is often cast adrift on this fragmented, disrupted and subverted narrative which, like a shattered mosaic or stained-glass window haphazardly reassembled, can be grasped only through occasional glimpses, or by imaginative reconstruction, rather than followed coherently or systematically. At times, the novel appears to be based on sets of polarities or tensions – but polarities that do not always progress dialectically to a synthesis: travelling and settling, the new world of America and the old world of Europe, general and specialist education, the geological doctrines of vulcanism and neptunism, or other theories outlined by Montan to Wilhelm – a primitive version of plate tectonics, meteoric impaction and ice-age theory. Thought and action, Montan asserts, complement each other, like breathing in and breathing out, like question and answer. Whoever tests action against thought and thought against action will not go far wrong – a notion that appears to resolve one of the intractable dichotomies formulated in the *Lehrjahre*, that while thought extends the spirit, it lames the will; action animates the will, but limits the spirit (*der Sinn erweitert, aber lähmt; die Tat belebt, aber beschränkt*). Makarie and Montan appear to represent existential polarities, respectively the astral and the terrestrial, the cosmic order and the human spirit. The poem 'Vermächtnis' that concludes Book Two, and Makarie's mysticism, reiterate Kant's analogy of the starry heavens above us and the moral law within us, expressed as the relation between the Copernican solar system and the autonomous conscience as the central 'sun' of human morality.

The novellas around and between which the framework novel pursues its eccentric course are also intractable to systematic or consistent analysis. Many revolve around emotional confusion, inhibition or dissimulation: *Die gefährliche Wette* (The Perilous Wager), *Wer ist der Verräter?* (Who is the Traitor?), *Nicht zu weit* (Not too far) and *Der Mann von fünfzig Jahren* (The Man of Fifty) deal with the failure of the characters to order or control their personal destinies – not unlike *Die Wahlverwandtschaften*, though in less starkly tragic terms. Tactlessness, thoughtlessness, a lack of respect for the sensibilities of others, create emotional havoc; in the fairy-tale *Die neue Melusine* (The New Melusina), it is impatience and excessive curiosity that shatter the union between a tiny elemental creature and her clumsy mortal lover. Reverence or respect is the fundamental didactic principle of the 'Pedagogic Province' to which Wilhelm entrusts his son Felix, emblematized in the three formal gestures of reverence towards that which is above, that which is below, and those who are our equals: three forms of respect for others that culminate in the fourth, that of reverence for ourselves or self-respect. And yet Felix emerges from the exemplary disciplines of his intensive schooling as impetuous as ever, restlessly roaming the country in his rough wooing of Hersilie, and snapping the key to the casket in his impatience.

The key, it appears, is in two pieces, held together by a mysterious and powerful magnetism. Anyone who attempts wilfully or impatiently to open the casket will find that the key snaps in his hand, and only the 'initiate' can use it; but in any case, we are told, the casket is best left unopened. The symbolism is inscrutable, yet tantalizingly familiar – Pandora's Box comes irresistibly to mind, both in its original mythical version and in the many examples of casket or chest motifs in Goethe's works: Ottilie's secret repository, Eugenie's gift-chest of clothes, the treasure-chest of Plutus, the casket in which the child of Tamino and Pamina is immured, even the cosmetic box of tricks in *Der Mann von fünfzig Jahren*. The sexual or phallic connotations of the 'barbed' key can scarcely be overlooked; but the casket itself has the form of a book, suggesting that it might be a repository of wisdom or enlightenment. Felix had at the very beginning used force to open the chest that contained the casket; again, premature curiosity, precipitate impatience seems to be the original sin that blights personal relationships and separates people instead of joining them – the casket springs open only when the jeweller steps away from it. The casket is possibly the enigmatic symbol of the ground-bass of the novel – renunciation; and yet Felix, for all his immature exuberance, surely personifies a more vital and dynamic response to life than the solemn nostrums of the *Turmgesellschaft*, than the Delphic principles of the 'Pedagogic Province', than the earnest proselytizing of the fellowship of travelling craftsmen, or than the emotional confusions and ambivalences of the characters in the various novellas.

For his description of the 'Pedagogic Province', Goethe was drawing on his first-hand and vicarious knowledge of the educational theories of his age: Rousseau, Basedow, Pestalozzi, Fellenberg, even on the 'monitor' system of Andrew Bell and Joseph Lancaster. No doubt his own scepticism, or at least his ambivalence, towards all utopian schemes colours his description of the project; but it bears distinct traces of contemporary Swiss educational reforms. It was to

Switzerland, too, that Goethe turned for the extensive descriptions of cotton manufacture and linen weaving that are communicated through Lenardo's journal – an exhaustive and indeed exhausting account, derived often verbatim from material supplied by his close Swiss friend Johann Heinrich Meyer, of the technical and mercantile organization involved in the preparation of Egyptian cotton. The ostensible narrative motive for Lenardo's journey to Switzerland – his quest for his 'nut-brown maid' – becomes obscured as we read his account of an organic and settled industrial community, a traditional cottage industry perfectly harmonized with the geographical, social and domestic structures of the country, but threatened by the introduction of new technology with social and economic disruption in the accelerating (*veloziferisch*, as one of the maxims puts it) pace of change in the early nineteenth century. The threat of mechanization, and therefore of unemployment, gathers like a storm – it will come, and it will strike; the alternatives are to accept the new developments, thereby contributing to them and hastening change, or to seek a new life overseas. America haunts the fringes of the novel as a refuge from the changing and decaying structures of the old world, as an area of opportunity to be developed – or exploited – even if this apparently limitless possibility is in turn counterpointed by the alternative of reform in the old world with its cultural and historical traditions and continuities.

Also haunting the interstices of the novel is the eccentric and egregious figure of Makarie, who is rarely encountered directly, but rather in correspondence, report, recollection, and even in dream. At times she seems central to the book, a focal point to whom the figures refer and defer, and she, or the maxims from her archive, are given the privilege of concluding the novel. On one level, Makarie is a sharply percipient but kindly maiden aunt, invalid but energetic, introverted and reclusive, but fully informed about the character and the behaviour of those in her circle, to whom they turn for advice in all their trials. On another level she is a mystic sibyl, a clairvoyant seer whose entelechy or spirituality removes her from all mundanity into a cosmic orbit; the cosmic order, we are told, is innate in her, and she herself is an integral part of it. If physical beings display a centripetal tendency, such spiritual beings as Makarie are centrifugal; her mystical vision is not simply a rapt contemplation of the solar system, but she is also *as it were* ('gleichsam') one with it. She replicates within herself the rhythms and structures of the heavens like a kind of 'living armillary sphere'; she anticipates in her mind the undiscovered minor planets as she traverses the solar system in the eccentric orbit of a comet, in a dizzying track that is taking her from Mars past Jupiter and on towards Saturn.

Much of what we are told about Makarie matches Goethe's own more mystical pronouncements on entelechy (see above, pp. 48, 104 and 201), the term he uses as synonymous with the Leibnitzian monad, or that irreducible part of the personality that precedes life and survives death, that wanders the infinite spaces and might also become reincorporated in future existences. And yet for all her sibylline mystery, Makarie is also the philosopher-guide, the moral and spiritual counsellor, the shrewd and well-informed agony-aunt of those around her; and the novel (if this bizarre compendium of narrative and reflection, sobriety and fantasy, practical description and discursive theory, can be thus generically classified) concludes with a collection of her wisdom in the form of aphorisms covering all manner of experience and thought, from capital punishment to press freedom, from Shakespeare to Calderón, from geometry to crystallography, from Socrates to Kant. The book concludes with Makarie's archive – or, to be more precise, it concludes with selections from Makarie's archive, followed enigmatically by Goethe's poem on Schiller's skull, followed even more enigmatically by the words 'to be continued'. But it is less certain whether the book *ends* there, whether it has already ended with the departure of the throng of emigrants who will use their skills in the (as it then perhaps seemed) virgin territories of the world; whether it ended with the unresolved mystery of the casket that had been opened and immediately closed again; or whether it ended with the symbolic revival and rebirth of Felix who, having been saved by Wilhelm's medical skills, greets his father, we are told, as Castor greeted Pollux on their alternating journeys between the darkness of Hades and the light of day.

Wilhelm Meister has travelled a vast distance in time, in place and in spirit since he left home, as it were, to seek his father's asses; he has no doubt travelled as far as his creator had done in the years since his late twenties when he embarked on Wilhelm's story. The *Wanderjahre* is not so much the completion of the story of Wilhelm's mission or of his progress towards the status of master – mastery of his chosen skill as a surgeon, of human relationships, of life, of the harmonization of external and internal, or of perception and judgement; it is rather the author's attempt to give an account of and come to terms with the bewildering complexity of modern times, with the pace of change in a rapidly accelerating civilization – with the 'veloziferish' pace of human affairs. There was no simple or unequivocal response to these affairs on the part of the ageing Goethe; but it is scarcely accidental that *veloziferisch* is so close to *luziferisch*. Only a multiform, compendious and fragmented pattern of narrative and discursive material, of elliptical and tangential structures, could do anything like justice to his consciousness of their complexity.

THE SHORTER PROSE NARRATIVES AND NOVELLAS

Unterhaltungen deutscher Ausgewanderten
(Conversations of German Emigrants)

This oddly titled collection of tales (the flexional endings are consistent with eighteenth-century usage, but not with modern German grammar; *Unterhaltungen* can be read as conversations, or alternatively as entertainment or diversions) dates from the very beginnings of Goethe's literary collaboration and personal friendship with Schiller. Written between the autumn of 1794 and September 1795, the stories were published sporadically during 1795 in Schiller's periodical *Die Horen*, a monthly literary journal founded by him from both pragmatic and high-minded motives: not only to bring its editor fame and some fortune, not only to rival, and possibly supplant, Wieland's *Teutscher Merkur* in prestige and influence, but also to educate the German public in aesthetic and humanitarian values – the *haute vulgarisation*, as it were, of Schiller's *Briefe über die ästhetische Erziehung des Menschen* (Letters on the Aesthetic Education of Mankind). Schiller not only saw Goethe as a valuable ally in his educative mission; he evidently also believed that contributions from his celebrated new acquaintance would not only help to sell the journal, but would also serve to leaven the more ponderous philosophical material with an imaginative and poetic dimension. Schiller explicitly discouraged any direct religious or political debate in the journal; if it was intended as a reaction to the French Revolution and its descent into chaos and terror, or as a response to potential or actual Jacobin tendencies in Germany, it was a response based on a counter-culture of idealism. And though Goethe's contribution is set in a clearly recognizable historical context, although it contains, in the bitter dispute between the conservative *Geheimrat* and the fiery young armchair revolutionary Karl, or in the reports of skirmishes and sackings of property in the neighbourhood, direct references to the upheavals of the Revolutionary Wars, it does not take overt issue with the Revolution as such. Indeed, after this first partisan exchange, the Baroness expressly declares a ban on political or topical discussion – if not at all times, then at least within the family circle. As Boccaccio's *Decamerone* was set in the context of a secluded refuge from chaotic social conditions – that is, from the plague – the tales told in the *Unterhaltungen* are also the product of a flight from social and political turmoil; only the shadow of the Revolution falls, as it were, over these stories.

An aristocratic family has been forced to seek refuge from the German left bank of the Rhine, invaded by revolutionary forces in 1792, in one of their properties to the east of the river; and in this relatively comfortable exile the family of the widowed Baroness – her son Friedrich, her daughter Luise, their cousin Karl, a Catholic chaplain and a house tutor – pass the time over two days telling and listening to anecdotes and tales, most of which (with the exception of the imaginative *Märchen*) purport to be true, or at least based on real events or reports. While the tales themselves do not apparently relate to the social or political reality of the framework narrative – indeed, most of them are from a period well before the Revolution – they do constitute in certain ways an oblique commentary on the present political confusion by invoking values that appear to have been lost or violated in that confusion.

Seven tales are told in all, of varying length, interest and complexity. The Chaplain relates the opening story of Madame Antonelli, the singer who is haunted by the spirit of her rejected lover, two of the lengthier tales (the so-called *Prokurator-Novelle* of the merchant's wife and the lawyer, and the tale of Ferdinand and Ottilie) and the concluding *Märchen*. Friedrich tells the poltergeist anecdote that follows the story of the haunting of Madame Antonelli, and Karl tells the two anecdotes from the memoirs of Marshal Bassompierre. The connections between the tales, and their relationship to the framework narrative, are tenuous. The two Bassompierre anecdotes (one of which was later elaborated by Hofmannsthal) are tales of sexual encounters or adultery that end in voluntary or involuntary frustration or abnegation; the Antonelli story is a tale of retribution for heartlessness; the

poltergeist story is ambiguous, and has no very clear function other than as a
sensational or inexplicable happening. Only the stories of the lawyer and the
merchant's wife, of Ferdinand and Ottilie, and the *Märchen* appear to revolve
around distinct ethical or humane values, notably those of temptation and duty,
of crime and penance, of mutual support, self-sacrifice and co-operation in times
of severe personal or public trial. In particular, the theme of renunciation,
Entsagung – the sub-theme of *Wilhelm Meisters Wanderjahre* – is fundamental to these
three tales. The story of the merchant's wife, reminiscent of Boccaccio but in fact
from a French source, concerns a young woman who is encouraged by her
husband to seek sexual gratification during his long absence. Whereas in the
original source her adultery is averted by the chance return of her husband, in
Goethe's version the young lawyer she chooses imposes on her a bizarre form of
shared penance through starvation, as a result of which she voluntarily returns to
her marital duty and fidelity: an innocent woman is virtually forced into temptation, which she resists with the help of internal and external imperatives. In the
story of Ferdinand and Ottilie, Ferdinand, in attempting to make good the money
he has stolen from his father, represents the case of the sinner who repents and
atones for his deception, but who must also give up his fiancée, albeit half
willingly, for a less brilliant but ultimately satisfactory match.

   These tales leave the reader entertained perhaps, but puzzled; it is by no means
clear how, or whether, they relate either to the group of listeners or to the
turbulent historical events swirling around them. The other striking event in the
framework narrative, the dramatic splitting of a valuable desk at the very moment
that an identical piece made by the same craftsman is destroyed by fire in the
house of an aunt nearby, is similarly puzzling and inconclusive – a 'real-life'
anecdote of inexplicable causes. The framework narrative itself also ends incon-
clusively; we do not know how the family or its ancillaries fare, how or whether
they are to return to their home on the left bank. The collection concludes instead
with the enigmatic fairy-tale (*Märchen*), which is not so much an articulation of
Goethe's responses to the confusions of the times, but rather the vision of a
fantastic alternative to those confusions, a form of utopian redemption myth in
which the world is saved by a fortunate coincidence of values: co-operation,
generosity, self-sacrifice and love working together at a propitious moment.

   No conclusive interpretation of this luxuriant work of imagination has been
given; Goethe himself tabulated some of the efforts of his contemporaries, and
even promised jocularly to supply his own when ninety-nine had been
attempted.[28] The figures of the framework narrative, Karl and the Chaplain who
relates the story, themselves suggest that a fairy-tale should bear no relation to
truth or reality; it should not be allegorical, but its airy forms should follow only
the dictates of the imagination, it should play on our senses like music and
fascinate us without any conceptual reference. This could, however, be a disin-
genuous false clue: the Baroness, for example, had earlier expressed a preference
for a kind of straightforward narrative that is precisely not met by the tales told by
her companions.

   The *Märchen* draws on all manner of sources for its symbolism and its structure;
on elemental, alchemical and folkloric myths, gold, silver, light, precious stones,

giants and will-o'-the-wisps, a green snake and a beautiful lily, the 'old man archetypes' of the ferryman and the miner with his lamp – even on the *orouboros* of the snake biting its tail. We should, however, beware of reading these motifs in terms of traditional alchemical (or Jungian) meanings; Goethe specifically stated that he saw this last motif not as a symbol of eternity, but of 'a propitious temporality' (*eine glückliche Zeitlichkeit*).[29] The *Märchen* exploits magical effects, dreamlike transformations and resurrections, enchanted underground caverns and temples, questions and cryptic answers, tasks, quests and guiding mentors at times strongly reminiscent of the *Arabian Nights*; it also indulges in some quirky humour – the fee due to the ferryman to cross the river amounts to three onions, three cabbages and three artichokes. Like many other fairy-tales, whether traditional folkloric or contrived literary versions, Goethe's *Märchen* is based on the triadic myth of a lost state of harmony or innocence, on a state of fall symbolized in the spell cast on the lily-princess; the world is in a stage of chaotic or fragmented imperfection from which only a coming together of propitious circumstances, heroic effort and co-operative will can redeem it.

It is tempting to discern in some of the images of the story the broad outlines of a political or historical allegory. In particular, the river, which we are told at the beginning has burst its banks and rendered communication between its two sides difficult, if not impossible, invites identification as the Rhine, the geographical and symbolic, indeed in 1795 the effective political frontier between France and Germany; after all, the tale is being told to the émigré audience on the east bank of the Rhine, and within sight of the river itself.[30] The three subterranean kings of gold, silver and bronze are explicitly identified in the text as representing respectively wisdom, light (though *Schein* has connotations of appearance, of aesthetic form or of illusion) and power – together with a fourth composite monarch, made up of unstable alloys of the other metals; this might suggest an old order, once legitimate but now crumbling and ineffectual, which will be superseded by the new order of the young prince and the lily-princess when the temple is raised to stand by the river, and the bridge spans the two sides in reconciliation. The earthquake that forces the buried temple to the surface recalls Goethe's frequent allusions, in his imaginative work and his correspondence, to the French Revolution as an earthquake or volcano. And yet these few tantalizing threads are swamped by a mass of more diffuse and general references that suggest a broader, less historically specific allegory – if indeed the story has any such meaning at all.

The fundamental themes of the *Märchen* appear to revolve around ethical and humanitarian concepts such as selflessness, co-operation, self-sacrifice and transformation. The green snake sacrifices itself and is transformed into gemstones, forming the foundations of the magnificent new bridge that brings communication and prosperity to the people and countries on both sides of the river; the will-o'-the-wisps prove to be sociable, helpful and companionable, if volatile, creatures. The old man with the lamp acts as a wise guide and mentor of the new age; but the rays of the rising sun, caught in the mirror held by a hawk hovering high above the dome, flood the temple of the new order with light and render the old man's lamp superfluous. The restrictive or disruptive forces of the old order, the giant whose shadow allowed only occasional and limited passage across the river, are rendered harmless as the giant is turned into a huge obelisk whose shadow now only measures the hours. The *Märchen* represents an enigmatic myth of redemption, the return of light and harmony, the birth of a new age; but it is unclear whether this redemption is conceived in political, literary or philosophic terms. Precisely because of its cryptic and universalized idiom, it came to be regarded as the primal model of a *Kunstmärchen*, of the sophisticated literary fairy-tale into which later Romantic writers would encode their own poetic redemption myths, from Novalis's portentous *Klingsohr-Märchen* to E. T. A. Hoffman's tongue-in-cheek *Atlantis-Märchen* in *Der goldne Topf*.

PROSE FRAGMENTS

The remainder of Goethe's output of prose fiction is a rather uneven assortment of tales, fragments and a single exemplary novella. *Die guten Weiber* was commissioned by Johann Friedrich Cotta, later Goethe's own publisher, for his 1801 *Damenalmanach* (Ladies' Almanac) as an antidote to a series of scurrilous engravings in the same issue that caricatured feminine wiles and foibles. In a mixture of narrative and dialogue – a device used in the *Unterhaltungen* and again later in the *Wanderjahre* – Goethe constructs a debate between the sexes that resumes some contemporary attitudes to femininity, and reflects the often bitter exchanges between Schiller and the early Romantic school, between Schiller's views on graceful and gracious femininity and the more robust emancipatory ideology of the Schlegel circle in Jena. *Der Hausball* of 1781 is a fragmentary adaptation of an anonymous Viennese anecdote charting the fraught preparations of a would-be host whose plans for a *bal masqué* lurch from one crisis to another. Its cryptic subtitle (*Eine deutsche Nationalgeschichte*: A National German Tale) has been taken to indicate that it might be a satire on the frantic but hapless efforts of the Viennese to celebrate the reign of Emperor Joseph II – or, more strictly, his reforming efforts after the death of his mother Maria Theresa in 1780.

The *Reise der Söhne Megaprazons* (Journey of the Sons of Megaprazon) of 1792, though never completed, is an altogether more interesting fragment; it belongs with the *Unterhaltungen, Hermann und Dorothea, Die natürliche Tochter* and the 'Revolution Dramas' of the 1790s as a record of Goethe's long preoccupation with the French Revolution. As he himself reported, this strange work was conceived both as a distraction from the savagery of the events in France and as an allegorical caution on the state of affairs in Germany at a time when Goethe, together with many of his contemporaries across the whole political spectrum, more than half expected the flames, the fever or the earthquake of the Revolution to spread beyond the frontiers of France. Always an enthusiastic reader of Rabelais, he cast his story in pseudo-Rabelaisian mode, using Pantagruel's quest for the *dive bouteille*, the sacred bottle, and in particular his adventures among the islands in the Fourth Book, as the basis for his version. Megaprazon, purportedly Pantagruel's great-grandson, sends his sons on a voyage to the islands of the *Papimanen* and the

Papefiguen (pope-worshippers and pope-haters), which their ancestor had visited some generations earlier. In the meantime, however, historical changes have made their charts invalid; the papal and anti-papal islands have shifted their positions in the post-Reformation era, and, more significantly for the political present, a new island has been discovered – the island of the Monarchomanes. This once famed and flourishing island comprised three regions – the royal residence, the territories of the aristocracy and those of the lower orders; but in the course of a single night the three parts of the island had been split by a volcanic eruption, and the sundered fragments had drifted apart at the mercy of the storms.

The allegory of the Revolution is here clear enough; but in a further episode the brothers quarrel violently among themselves about these recent events, which are allegorized (as they were to be much later by Goethe in the Seismos episode in the second act of *Faust* Part Two) in terms of the mythical battle between the cranes and the pygmies, evidently representing respectively the aristocracy and the revolutionaries. A stranger assures the brothers that they are in the grip of the 'fever of the age', which he also characterizes as 'press fever' – a Goethean comment on the role of the press in the political upheavals in France and Germany. This fever, they are told, is a malign and infectious disease that is transmitted through the air; it leads people to sacrifice themselves, their families and their own interests to a passionate and partisan commitment, and ends in madness. The allegory of the 'floating islands' clearly reflects events in France – revolution, class warfare, social and political frenzy; but in so far as the message of this striking but fragmentary story is discernible, Goethe's principal concern appears to be that the revolutionary 'fever' might spread beyond France to infect neighbouring countries with the bacillus of Jacobinism.

NOVELLE

Goethe's most celebrated contribution to shorter prose narrative is his generically titled *Novelle* of 1826–7. Indeed this tale has, in the work of successive theoreticians of this purportedly 'native' German genre (Boccaccio and Cervantes notwithstanding), become the exemplary model of the *Novelle* form, and Goethe's own definition of the *Novelle* as 'eine sich ereignete, unerhörte Begebenheit'[31] has, for better or for worse and for all its inherent unclarities, been cited as the essential criterion of the form: a single striking or unique happening. And yet this work was originally conceived not as a prose narrative or anecdote at all, but as an epic poem in hexameters, or alternatively as a ballad, in 1797. In its final form it assumed, along with its exemplary character, the stamp of Goethe's later prose style: a restrained formality and reticence, a densely symbolic mode of expression in which specific or allegorical features and stylistic realism are overlaid, and indeed obscured, by a lyrical, emotive and quasi-mystical extravagance. References to topical or recent social and political reality – to the French Revolution and the lessons learned from it, or to America as a new frontier of activity and opportunity – merge into an ethical parable that is elaborated with fairy-tale motifs drawn from various cultural traditions: from Orphic and biblical myth and from the tales of the Arabian Nights.

Written in the political stability and quietism of Restoration Germany, but only a few years before the alarming upheaval of the July Revolution, the story concerns the sudden eruption of destructive, or potentially destructive, forces into a deceptively ordered and peaceful situation. The pivotal crux of the tale is a fire that breaks out in a small town on a busy market-day – a fire that is witnessed, vicariously and from a distance, by means of a telescope, by the young Princess and her companions, her uncle and the young squire Honorio. The Princess's imagination has already been sensationally primed by the uncle's lurid account of a fire he had once experienced; but her alarm appears justified when as a result of the fire a tiger escapes from its booth in a menagerie and pursues the Princess, who is now alone with Honorio. The young man kills the tiger without any great difficulty; but in the emotionally charged aftermath of the encounter he makes a veiled and ambiguous confession to his mistress in which his submissive request for permission to leave the court masks a barely concealed declaration of passion – a passion evidently unleashed, and indeed symbolized, by the dramatic course of events, as the tiger had been released by the fire in the town.

This potentially dangerous development is checked by restraint and decorum on the part of Honorio and the Princess; and the subsequent action of the story appears to mirror the emotional self-conquest of the two subliminal lovers. The travelling family of showpeople who own the menagerie arrive in pursuit of a lion that has also escaped in the fire, and with the permission of the Prince, who is now also present, they undertake to recapture the lion by non-violent means: their child will, like Orpheus or Tamino, charm the wild beast with his flute and lead it gently back into captivity. This is duly done; the lion is frightened rather than savage, wounded rather than aggressive. And yet the point is explicitly made that it still retains its strength and its potential bestiality; for all its docility, it has not been subjugated, but restored 'to its own peaceful will'. The passionate beast in Honorio, it seems, was also tamed – not so much by decorum, etiquette or convention, but by his own spiritual strength: the traveller-woman tells him he might go far away from here, to America even – but if he wishes to succeed there, he must first succeed in self-control. The oddly related themes of renunciation or self-conquest and westward emigration are twinned here as they are in the *Wanderjahre*: America, the cultural and historical *tabula rasa*, unencumbered, as Goethe fancifully perceived it, by the detritus and debris of European civilizations,[32] is a mythical archetype of enlightened adventurism.

The theme and purpose of his *Novelle*, Goethe declared, was to demonstrate how the untamed and indomitable is often better conquered by love and piety than by violence.[33] As the boy's devout song and natural 'Orphic' melody tames the submissive but still feral lion, so Honorio's passionate self must be curbed by devotion and respect – and, it might be inferred, so might the furious convulsions of nations or peoples be controlled; here too, the shadow of civil insurrection, war or revolution falls across the deceptively urbane and formal surface of the narrative. *Frömmigkeit* – a profound respect for God's creation in man or beast, in busy ant or impetuous horse, in running water or in mute stones – is, according to the fervent sermon delivered by the father of the exotic travelling family, the first virtue of princes and the strongest bulwark against anarchy. Even when nature is at its most hushed and serene, the narrator reminds us, panic fear and chaos are not far away; for at noon all creatures hold their breath for fear Pan should awake. The *Novelle* adumbrates the two polar forces in nature and man: elemental violence and sovereign will, passion and restraint, the anarchic frenzy of Pan and the pious devotion of Orpheus. It also exemplifies the ideal resolution of conflict in Isaiah's imagery of chiliastic harmony (Isaiah 11. 6ff.), where a little child shall lead the beasts, and there shall be no hurt or destruction in the holy mountain. This lyrical vision of mythic harmony is, as Goethe insisted, the ideal 'flowering' of the narrative of his *Novelle* – unexpected and startling, but as natural and as inevitable as the emergence of a flower from the structure of a plant;[34] and it is on the 'holy mountain' of the *Stammburg*, the abandoned ancestral home of the Prince's family, where nature and the work of men's hands have merged to create a remote and secluded idyll, that this dramatic miracle of reconciliation is enacted.

Verse Narratives and Epics

Goethe's interest in epic poetry no doubt dates from rather earlier than his years in Strasbourg, when Herder fired his enthusiasm for folk song and ballad, for epic and heroic traditions, for the perceived naivety and spontaneity of the oral traditions of bards and minstrels, from the Norse scaldic sagas to the Old Testament as the epic record of the Israelite nation. Goethe's perceptions of the 'naive' or 'patriarchal' biblical and Homeric traditions later became more sophisticated, but no less enthusiastic; in 1797 his correspondence and collaboration with Schiller produced an extended theoretical discussion on epic and dramatic poetry, including a collaborative essay on the genres, and in this so-called *Balladenjahr*, which also saw the resumption of work on *Faust*, the epic genre was in the forefront of Goethe's consciousness. Since the Strasbourg days, perceptions of Homer had changed: by 1798 the father of modern classical philology, Friedrich August Wolf, had developed the theory of the multiple authorship of the Homeric epics, and Goethe had begun to experiment with his own informal, but not entirely untutored, style of epic hexameter. Klopstock's mighty religious epic *Der Messias* (The Messiah) had appeared over three decades between 1748 and 1773; more recently Johann Heinrich Voß had been translating Homer into scholarly and accomplished hexameters, and in 1793 had published his three-part rural idyll in classical hexameters, *Luise*.

As early as 1774 Goethe had composed a brief and fragmentary epic poem in *Knittelvers* on the subject of the Wandering Jew (*Der ewige Jude*), possibly in part as an irreverent *Sturm und Drang* parody of Klopstock's *Messias*, in which Christ returns to find the political and religious institutions of the world in an even worse state than in his previous experience. Of the 291 lines surviving, only a brief section deals with the cobbler Ahasuerus, a figure from the popular narratives of post-Reformation Germany whose wanderings gave great scope for satirical commentary; the rest is devoted to Christ's experiences at the hands of the Catholic and Protestant clergy, described in exuberant doggerel. How Christ was to be reunited with the figure of Ahasuerus is unclear; the sardonic message is that if Christ were to come among men again, he would surely be misunderstood and crucified a second time.

A decade later, in *Die Geheimnisse* (The Mysteries) Goethe began, but again left unfinished, an altogether more high-minded and sententious narrative poem in solemn stanzas of *ottava rima*. A wandering friar, Marcus, is led to a mysterious religious community that operates under the device of the Rosy Cross; its founder and leader, Humanus, is about to depart the Order – and, we infer from Goethe's own commentary on the fragment, Marcus is to be his successor. Inside the chapel of the Order are twelve seats for the twelve elders, who represent the world's religions which, in the ethos of eighteenth-century enlightened deism, have at some stage in their evolution transcended the specific ethnic, cultural and theological differences of their respective creeds and have achieved a common level of enlightenment and truth – at which point the guidance and authority of Humanus become superfluous. It is not clear why Goethe should use the iconography of Rosicrucianism for this ideal deistic order, even if at this stage he was still relatively well-disposed towards the secret orders of Freemasonry; it was a decade or so later, in the aftermath of the French Revolution and the suspicion of Jacobin infiltration of the Masonic societies that he was to develop a deep mistrust of their activities – for all that he was, at one time and another, an active if warily sceptical member of Masonic and Illuminati groups in Weimar. Certainly, by 1790 Goethe had ceased to play any active part in the societies, though as always he retained a keen sense of the symbolic ritual that, for all the admixture of credulity, self-interest and mumbo-jumbo, preserved the vestiges of the high-minded ethical and humanitarian ideals of the early Freemasons. Humanus is himself a Sarastro-like figure who, like the magus of Goethe's sequel to *The Magic Flute*, voluntarily abdicates his position and authority to a younger successor who will take the Order into a new era. *Die Geheimnisse* continues, in an altogether less robust form, the drastic critique of orthodox religion in *Der ewige Jude*, in the spirit not of *Sturm und Drang* iconoclasm but of Weimar idealism; a more radical critique of religious orthodoxy and of clericalism was to emerge in Goethe's next, and his first completed, attempt at epic poetry.

REINEKE FUCHS (REYNARD THE FOX)

In spite of his interest in hexameter and the epic genre, it is still not entirely clear why Goethe was impelled in 1793 to adapt the medieval tales of Reynard the Fox, a corpus that has its roots in French and German traditions of monastic satire, the *Roman de Renart* and *Reynke de vos*, and to render Gottsched's prose translation of a Low German version into twelve cantos comprising an astonishing 4,312 lines of (by his own admission) rough-and-ready epic hexameter: *Reineke Fuchs*. Writing some thirty years later in the *Campagne in Frankreich*, he explains his satirical epic in terms of the political chaos of the time, and relates it in particular to his vision of the frivolity and corruption of the French court during the last days of the *ancien régime*.[35] His famous diagnosis of the necklace scandal of 1785 as the dire prefiguration of revolution and of the end of monarchy in France is associated with the epic, which he confesses was written as an attempt to come to terms with the upheavals he was witnessing in France in 1792–3 by means of parody and satire.

The satire of *Reineke Fuchs* is both general and specific: on the human condition conventionally allegorized in bestial terms (the genre of the satirical fable had enjoyed a revival in the didactic literature of the early German Enlightenment), and on the rivalries, vanities and jealousies of the ruling classes, in particular of the absolutist courts. This example of greed, venality, mendacity and cynicism, Goethe suggests, is what prompted him to throw off a few thousand lines of technically flawed hexameter – an exercise in classicizing verse which, he hoped, might not be entirely without contemporary interest, and possibly even of some lasting value.[36] Even so, the investment seems scarcely proportionate to the effect; the political comment is rarely as sharp or specific as in Goethe's other writings on the Revolution or its causes, with the exception of the digression in the eighth canto – a departure by Goethe from Gottsched and from the early narrative – in which Grimbart the badger and Reineke characterize the abuse of power by church and state in terms of bestial savagery.

The character and position of Reineke, the cunning and clever, but utterly unscrupulous survivor in the social, political and religious jungle, is ambivalent; a deplorable figure whose greed lands him in dreadful trouble and whose inventive wit allows him to extricate himself from it, he is a popular anti-hero not unlike Till Eulenspiegel. Whether there is also an allusive reference here to the egregious figure of Cagliostro, who also bamboozled those in political or religious authority, is not clear – for Reineke, however deplorable his gifts and his tactics, is presented very much more sympathetically than Cagliostro is elsewhere by Goethe; moreover, unlike Cagliostro, the fox does not so much infiltrate the establishment for his own ends, but rather derides it and confronts it head-on in his battle for survival. The parodic element, as distinct from the social and political satire, is literary; this is tongue-in-cheek Homeric stuff, with a parodic epic breadth and occasional specific echoes that travesty some well-known tableaux. The Judgement of Paris is aped in the tenth canto, and the savage battle between Reineke and Isegrim the wolf in the final canto is a bestial version of medieval single combat and of Achilles' mauling of Hector in the *Iliad*.

Reineke Fuchs has been seen as a satire on Rousseauistic optimism, on the idea of a natural human innocence corrupted by social culture; but since the fable is so transparently an allegory of brutal human behaviour and stupidity, this theory is unconvincing. The tale is, rather, Brechtian in its oblique value-systems and its candid pragmatism (not to mention its 'alienating' hexameter form). Indeed, it is more than likely that Brecht had the fable of Reynard in mind when creating his own ethically ambiguous protagonists: cunning, subterfuge, even savagery are justified instruments of personal survival in corrupt times. For all his treachery, for all his unscrupulous and amoral deviousness, Reineke elicits sympathy, if not admiration, for the way he fights greed, hypocrisy and sophistry with their own weapons, for the way he turns stupidity and cruelty against itself. Like Brecht's 'good bad judge' Azdak, Reineke also proves himself capable of something like the Judgement of Solomon when in the ninth canto he settles the case of a conflict between honour and survival: a man rescues a snake from a snare on its oath that it will not harm him, but on its release the snake invokes the imperative of hunger to violate its oath and devour the man. Appeals to conventional justice go against the man; but Reineke's judgement, based on an equal measure of trickery and justice, is that the snake should be returned to the snare, and the man then given the choice whether or not to repeat his generous gesture in releasing it.

HERMANN UND DOROTHEA

Goethe's best-known and most widely admired work in epic hexameter is the domestic idyll *Hermann und Dorothea*. In May 1796, the idyllic poem 'Alexis und Dora' served as a test-run for the genre; but the idea for an extended mock-heroic epic adumbrating the political turmoil of the time within the microcosm of a small German town to the east of the Rhine seems to have been with Goethe for some two years before he wrote the nine cantos of his epic between September 1796 and March 1797. Like *Reineke Fuchs*, it was the literary precipitation and sublimation of the harrowing experiences of war, persecution, disease and famine, of the real or imagined fears of the civilian victims of invasion and counter-invasion that he had experienced at first hand during the French Campaign of 1792 and the Siege of Mainz in the following year. For while Goethe had little enough sympathy for the querulousness and arrogance of the French aristocratic refugees who accompanied the Duke of Brunswick's army as far as Valmy, he was keenly sympathetic to the plight of the countless refugees driven by the shifting and arbitrary misfortunes of the revolutionary wars, whether the minor aristocratic family of the *Unterhaltungen* or the artisan refugee population of *Hermann und Dorothea*. The magistrate's account in Canto VI of the aftermath of revolution, of the rapid souring of high humane ideals in the terror of factional power-struggles, of the subsequent crimes committed in the name of liberty and military intervention, is a brief summary of Goethe's own views and experiences of events beyond the Rhine as he was to record them much later in his account of the French Campaign.

In literary terms, *Hermann und Dorothea* is also the precipitation of Goethe's close personal and intellectual collaboration with Schiller, of their reciprocal debate on epic and dramatic poetry. It also owes something to the Homeric scholarship of Wolf, and much to the example of Voß's *Luise* – for all that Goethe's hexameter here, though more consciously correct than the rough-and-ready prosody of *Reineke Fuchs*, does not remotely approach the formal, if pedantic, rigour prescribed by Voß, Wolf or August Wilhelm Schlegel. A line like 'In der Verwirrung des Kriegs und im traurigen Hin- und Herziehn' (In the confusion of war and the sorrowful toing and froing – Canto IV, line 214) strikes even the inexpert ear as a clumsy effort to observe the final two feet of hexameter; and the parenthetic device in Canto IX, line 175, 'Nicht der rollende Donner (ich hör' ihn) soll mich verhindern' (Not the rumbling thunder – I hear it – shall hinder my leaving) can hardly fail to make the reader blink, or at the very least smile. But the 'alienation effect' of discrete style and content is often deliberate; and the charm of Goethe's domestic epic depends on the reader's perception and tolerance of the humorous discrepancy between the mock-heroic sublimity of form and the modest scope and stature of the characters and their environment. When Hermann harnesses the dray-horses to the cart in the courtyard of his father's inn to go on his quest for Dorothea in the next village, there are echoes of Achilles harnessing his steeds to his chariot before going out to do battle with Hector; as he waits impatiently for the Parson and the Apothecary to bring him news of Dorothea, his nags snort and stamp the ground like war-horses before the fray; the Parson, driving the fearful Apothecary back to the inn, grasps the reins like a less than confident Phaeton as he struggles to control his foam-flecked steeds; and the Apothecary's proud description of his exquisitely petty-bourgeois *rocaille* garden, resplendent with gnomes and shells, with extravaganzas in lead and stone, is a delightful piece of gentle irony. The parodic dimension extends to the use of Homeric epithet, to set-piece similes and invocations of the Muse, or the reiterations of Dorothea's appearance and costume in Cantos V and VI – but there are also traces of Goethe's earlier perceptions of Homer: Hermann's encounter with Dorothea at the well in Canto VII is an extended enactment of Werther's idyllic vision of the well as the centre of a Homeric or biblical 'patriarchal' community.

Side by side with the gentle persiflage of the philistine or *spießbürger* are also figures of genuine, if modest, heroic stature whose experiences reflect in microcosm the historical convulsions of the time: the magistrate who is indeed the patriarch of the refugee community; Dorothea herself, her selfless altruism and her very real physical courage; the revolutionary idealism of her former fiancé who went to Paris to fight for the new ideals, only to fall victim to the Revolution as it devoured its own children. The refugees are given heroic moral stature, while those untouched by the disasters of war are treated with mild satirical irony: the blustering father, the cautious Apothecary, the didactic Parson, the shrewd but submissive mother, the awkwardly immature Hermann. The idyll of rustic wooing is threatened from within and from without; the ruse to entice Dorothea to Hermann's family threatens to destroy the course of their growing love as the thunderstorm gathers over the landscape, and the threat of renewed civil and military disorder is never far from the minds of the characters. The fire recollected by Hermann's parents, although it was that that brought them together, is, like the uncle's recollection of a fire in the *Novelle*, a background motif of elemental chaos and danger that erupts violently and arbitrarily into the peaceful rhythm of local or national life.

For all the contemporary success of *Hermann und Dorothea*, for all its subsequent affectionate popularity with the German public, for all that it arguably represents the one most consistently classical of Goethe's completed works and his single most substantial contribution to Weimar Classicism, it is striking, though scarcely surprising, that it marks the virtual end of his experiments with the epic form, at least in its classicizing hexameter versions. Voß's *Luise* of 1795 had been an erratic creative monument to the revival of Hellenic studies in the last decade of the century; but no significant epic or idyllic tradition had been inspired by it, or indeed by Goethe's own efforts. Into the nineteenth century, Goethe was to turn from this antiquarian idiom to the prose narrative that was more attuned to the post-classical era; the time for classicizing pastiche, however topical its reference, had passed, and Goethe's final experiment with epic hexameter, the *Achilleis*, remained fragmentary and did not sustain his interest beyond the turn of the century.

ACHILLEIS

The *Achilleis* grew directly out of Goethe's and Schiller's prolonged correspondence on the theory and practice of epic poetry. It was Goethe's project for an epic that would exploit the gap left by Homer between the death of Hector that closes the *Iliad* and the departure of the Greeks from Troy that provides the context for the *Odyssey*: that is, an epic treatment of the death of Achilles, of his raising of a mausoleum for himself and Patroclus, his love for Priam's daughter Polyxena, the debate among the Olympians on the respective destinies of Greeks and Trojans, the prospect of a peaceful end to the Trojan War, frustrated by the murder of Achilles at his own wedding-feast, and the struggle between Odysseus and Ajax for his armour. As far as we can tell from the planned course of the story, Goethe's introduction of an emotional dimension was to bring him close to a Racinian treatment of the twin themes of passion and fate; and it may well have been his theoretical reservations about such a hybrid mixture of the dramatic and the epic, of private and public affairs, that led him to abandon the project in 1799, which had not progressed beyond the first of eight planned cantos – though he had also toyed with the bizarre idea of completing the *Achilleis* in the form of a prose novel.

As a Homeric pastiche, the fragment is impressive enough, with its dense texture of mythical and historical reference, its epithets and metaphors, the measured flow of its hexameters, and in particular its portentous debates and quarrels among the Olympians concerning the relationship between ineluctable fate and human independence; for Zeus himself protests that even the highest gods cannot know the future fate of the Greek or Trojan heroes – to the dismay and indignation of his consort Hera, who insists that Achilles must die and Troy must fall as predestined. But the *Achilleis* remains only an unfinished monument, indeed a mausoleum, to the high-minded purism of Goethe's and Schiller's classical mission of the 1790s, as much a monument to its failures as to its successes. Goethe's experiment with the epic scope of hexameter narrative survives in the public mind not in terms of gods and heroes, not in the great mythical sweep of the Homeric legends, but in the more homely idioms: in the comic satires of his animal fable *Reineke Fuchs,* and in the juxtaposition of international tension and provincial quietism in his domestic idyll of *Hermann und Dorothea.*

5

The Scientist

A human being, as long as he uses his own healthy senses, is the greatest and most accurate physical apparatus there can be. And it is the greatest bane of modern physics that experimentation has, as it were, been segregated from human experience, that we seek a knowledge of nature only in what artificial instruments reveal to us, indeed, that we seek thus to confine nature and to prove what she can achieve. So it is also with calculation. Much that cannot be calculated is true, as is very much that cannot be demonstrated by experiment. Indeed, that is why humanity stands so high, because it represents what cannot be represented. For what is the string [of a musical instrument], and all the mechanical calibrations of it, compared with the ear of a musician?[1]

This extract from a letter to Goethe's close friend and musical adviser Zelter is on the subject of a theory of musical sound (*Tonlehre*), a project that did not progress beyond its preliminary stage; but it could stand as a revealing insight into Goethe's scientific method generally, and into his theory of colours (*Farbenlehre*) in particular. It is not difficult to see from this and similar declarations of faith how Goethe, in his almost lifelong preoccupation with science and scientists, often found himself at odds with much of the scientific orthodoxy of his day, and more especially with what he disparagingly called the 'physico-mathematical guild' of professional scientists.[2] Mathematics was Goethe's greatest blind spot; he lacked any real mathematical expertise, and though he once attempted to master algebra, he was forced to admit that it was incompatible with his nature. He honoured mathematics as 'the most sublime and useful science' – with the proviso that it is used where it is appropriate. Where it is misapplied, this noble science is reduced to nonsense: 'as if everything can only exist once it is mathematically proved. It would be foolish indeed if one were not to believe in a woman's love because she was unable to prove it mathematically!'[3]

In his treatise *On Mathematics and its Misuse* of 1826, Goethe's bafflement with and mistrust of mathematics is clearly displayed: calculation is a process of abstraction that removes the natural world from the reality perceived by our senses and strips it of its richness, its diversity and its individuality. A system of quantitative signs cannot adequately represent what we know qualitatively through experience; at best, mathematics is a self-contained system of logic, at worst a manipulation of unreal cyphers within a self-justifying system that bears no true relation to essential reality. Like the discipline of rhetoric, it is concerned only with form and is indifferent to content: 'whether mathematics counts pennies or guineas, whether rhetoric defends truth or falsehood, is of no concern whatever to either.'[4] For the same reasons, Goethe never took to astronomy, a science that was almost exclusively concerned with 'instruments, calculations and mechanics', an area where the human senses were no longer involved.

It is no surprise, then, that Goethe's innocence of mathematics and his insistence on the primacy of observation by sense perceptions should have set him at odds, not only with much of the scientific establishment of his own time, but also in so many ways with the whole development of post-Renaissance natural science, in so far as modern experimental science appears to contradict or correct the primary evidence of our senses. The sun appears to revolve around the earth, but does not; matter appears solid to the senses, but is engaged in an intricate and complex dance of sub-atomic particles; 'fixed' stars appear static, but are moving though space at very high speeds; 'white' light appears homogeneous, but is in fact composite.

Goethe's science is part of his attempt, as he put it, to describe the natural world through a limited number of general principles, to explain the bewildering diversity of nature in terms of coherent and universal laws, of 'a few great formulae' – in this respect at least, he was not so very far from the physicists and mathematicians he so mistrusted.[5] Among the guiding principles of his scientific assumptions was the belief in the universal validity of polarity (a notion almost as old as scientific enquiry itself) and of the 'primal phenomenon', the *Urphänomen*. Goethe speaks of certain 'higher laws which do not reveal themselves through words and hypotheses to the understanding, but through phenomena to the perception. We call them primal phenomena, because we can perceive nothing higher than them.'[6] The *Urphänomen* is an observable phenomenon that demonstrates a universal law, it is at once an abstract principle and an empirical fact.

Polarität und Steigerung, polarity and intensification or enhancement, were for Goethe the twin motive forces in creation, the 'two great wheels driving all nature', a dynamic dialectic of complementary opposites observable in general and in the particular.[7] Attraction and repulsion, plus and minus, inhalation and exhalation, expansion and contraction, light and dark, male and female, up and down, to and fro, north and south, *zona torrida* and *zona frigida* – or, in the emotional sphere, love and hate, hope and fear, joy and grief: in polarities Goethe saw the rhythm of the universe, the heart-beat of creation that produced the dynamic *Steigerung* of existence. One of his most resonant poetic metaphors is the to and fro of the weaver's shuttle as it speeds across the sheds, creating the texture that integrates *Zettel und Einschlag*, the warp and weft of the whole – a metaphor of creativity and of creation expressed most splendidly in the words of the Earth Spirit (*Erdgeist*) as it tells Faust how it works the living garment of God on the whirring loom of time (*Faust*, lines 501–9). Polarity and intensification Goethe also saw represented, not as idea or abstraction, but as manifest reality and experience, as *Urphänomen*, in the magnet, where attraction and repulsion, north pole and south pole, together – and only together – produce the phenomenon of magnetism.[8] This was for Goethe a self-evident truth requiring no further explanation and beyond which there was no further analysis, an indivisible and irreducible case that is at once theory and fact, idea and experience. The *Urphänomen*, Goethe's attempt to discern a unifying law in the confusion of diversity, ironically also limited his scientific vision because it was by definition the point at which scientific enquiry ceased.

COLOUR THEORY

It was his stubborn reliance on visual observation and his mistrust of abstraction or calculation that led Goethe into the greatest scientific adventure of his life, his protracted and ill-fated crusade to refute Newton's theory of optics. The anecdotal origins of his campaign against Newton, his uninformed experiments with Büttner's prisms, have been sketched above (p. 32). In fact, his interest in colour theory had been stimulated before 1790 by his discussions on pigments with his fellow-artists in Rome; but it was in the 1790s that he devoted himself obsessively to his attack on the Newtonian heresy – a campaign that had all the conviction and zealotry of theological dogmatics. Newton's doctrine was the original sin of modern science, Newton had attempted to split white light into seven, as the Church attempted to split God into three – 'a priests' notion', as Goethe put it in a polemical epigram:

> Das ist ein pfäffischer Einfall! denn lange spaltet die Kirche
> Ihren Gott sich in drei, wie ihr in sieben das Licht.[9]

> That is a notion for priests! for long the Church has divided
> God into three, just as you split into seven his light.

Light was for Goethe, as a matter of faith and of scientific conviction, an *Urphänomen*, a quasi-sacred unity, simple, not composite. Newton's heresy was to deny the integrity of light and to suggest that white light was composed of, and could be split into, the colours of the spectrum; Newton's classic experiment in the camera obscura of the laboratory was to submit light to prismatic torture, to pinch and twist it by means of 'artificial instruments' (Goethe's professed aversion to physical apparatus did not stop him using those very instruments of torture in his attempts to combat scientific heresy). Unable to reconcile the composite nature of light with his deepest convictions and the evidence of his senses, Goethe revived the Aristotelian notion that colours arise from a combination of light and darkness, in the intermediate zone where these polarities overlap and blend, and where the eye perceives the different colours according to the conditions under which they are perceived: colour is not inherent in light, the perceived colour does not depend on the absorption of certain colours (or particles or wavelengths) by an object, which then reflects or 'scatters' back to the eye those wavelengths not absorbed by the pigment to produce the sensation of colour. Colour for Goethe was a darkening of light; it was the blending of light and dark in or through a 'turbid' or 'opaque medium' (*trübes Mittel*), and the lightness or darkness of the background, that determined our perception of colour. Thus, light combined with little darkness gives the brightest colour, yellow; a greater degree of darkness will produce blue. Further colours are produced by the intensification or by the mixing of these primary colours: yellow intensifies into red, blue into violet, green is a blending of yellow and blue.

Goethe's theory of colour was of course based on visual perception. The many sets of experiments he provided for readers of his *Farbenlehre* invited the direct observation of phenomena in nature, rather than 'laboratory' experimentation; and he cited examples of the everyday application of his theories. We perceive the sky as blue because we see the darkness of space through the 'opaque medium' of the earth's atmosphere illuminated by the sun – here, darkness predominates. Light predominates when we see the sun through the clearer atmosphere at midday, when the sun appears white or yellow; at dawn or dusk it reaches us through a more opaque atmosphere, and appears orange or red. Other 'opaque media' are smoke, glass, lenses or prisms – smoke rising from a chimney appears blue against a dark background. And yet in view of his insistence on the primacy of observation in nature, it is ironic, but not entirely surprising, that Goethe was never to come to terms with the colour phenomenon that not only spectacularly demonstrates Newton's theory of refraction, but also does this in a perfectly natural environment: the rainbow. Although he frequently uses the rainbow as an important symbolic image in his poetic expression, Goethe could find no empirical or theoretical explanation for it. In the last weeks of his life he wrote an account of his correspondence on the rainbow with Sulpiz Boisserée, as it were in lieu of a definitive study of the phenomenon; but while he conceded that the rainbow was 'a case of refraction', he could only surmise that it was 'the most complicated case of all', one that brought him to the limits of his scientific abilities – and he never completed any explanation of it on the principles of his own colour theory.[10]

Goethe's central work on optics, *Zur Farbenlehre* (On Colour Theory), comprises several sections, didactic, polemical and historical. He had published several studies, including *Beiträge zur Optik* (Contributions to Optics), *Der Versuch als Vermittler von Objekt und Subjekt* (The Experiment as Mediator between Object and Subject) and *Von den farbigen Schatten* (On Coloured Shadows) in the 1790s; these were received with indifference by the scientific community, for whom Newton had explained virtually all there was to be explained about light. In 1794, Goethe developed the notion of 'physiological colours', in which his central principle is that the eye plays a crucial role in the perception of colour: the eye is not merely a passive lens, but an organ actively involved in registering colour sensation. His debates with Schiller and his correspondence with Philipp Otto Runge from 1806 until Runge's death in 1810 also contributed to the formulation of his ideas, and from 1800 to 1810 he worked intensively on the *Farbenlehre*. The Didactic Section was finished by December 1807, and the Polemical and Historical Sections by

1810, when he declared 16 May as a 'happy day of liberation' as he stepped into the coach taking him to Karlsbad.[11]

To take the sections in reverse order, the Historical Section is a vast if selective survey, not simply of physics or optics, but of science itself, from Pythagoras and Aristotle to Lucretius and Pliny, to Roger Bacon and Francis Bacon, Galileo, Kepler, Descartes, Newton, Franklin and Priestley (to name only some of the best known). The Polemical Section is a critique of Newton's *Opticks* of 1704, a scathing and immoderate attack not only on Newton's theories but also on his character and his integrity as a scientist; Goethe not only declares that Newton was wrong, but also implies that he might have been fraudulent and even unstable of mind. The violence of Goethe's polemic was no doubt partly a result of the indifference of the latter-day Newtonians to his own ideas; but he also felt passionately that Newton's method – practically the cornerstone of the exact method in modern science – drove a wedge between man and the world around him. It destroyed the harmonious relationship between man and nature by abstracting the object from the subject, whereas for Goethe the phenomenon under investigation was inseparable from the investigator.

The Didactic Section presents Goethe's own contribution to colour theory, and is itself divided into several sections: Physiological Colours, Physical Colours, and Chemical Colours, as well as further sections of which the least contentious, because it is the least concerned with physical optics, is the section entitled 'Sensuous and Moral Effect of Colours' – what we might now call the psychological, emotional or subjective response to particular colours. Chemical colours are for Goethe 'objective' colours, those inherent in minerals, plants or animals. It is in his sections on physiological and physical colours that Goethe presents his 'scientific' theory, based on the principles of the polarity of light and darkness and on the blending of these polarities in the intermediate zone of colour – which is also, symbolically, for Goethe the zone of human experience between the metaphysical polarities of light and dark, good and evil, God and devil. Colours are produced by the effects of light on objects, they are 'acts and sufferings of light'. The eye is an active organ in colour perception, because the eye seeks wholeness – in perceiving any given colour, it will 'demand' the opposite, complementary colour: yellow demands blue-red or violet, blue demands red-yellow or orange, purple demands green, and vice versa. These colours are diagrammatically arranged in a segmented circle in Goethe's illustration, with colours arranged anti-clockwise from purple at twelve o'clock, orange, yellow, green (at six o'clock), blue, violet and back to purple, the complementary colours appearing diametrically opposite each other.[12] Yellow and orange are active or 'plus' colours, blue and violet are passive or 'minus' colours, because they are respectively closer to light or dark. Yellow and blue are *Mutterfarben*, primary colours; the active or plus colours excite lively and energetic feelings, the passive or minus colours excite restless or nostalgic feelings. Green, being a restful synthesis of the two primary colours, is 'a true satisfaction to the eye'; if they are in perfect balance, our senses wish for nothing further (green is recommended as the ideal colour for domestic furnishings).[13]

Goethe's theory of colour appears from a modern standpoint (and indeed appeared to many at the time) disastrously wrong-headed from a scientific perspective, and from an aesthetic perspective subjective and even fanciful. He stubbornly refused to accept much contemporary research that sustained Newton's theories. Not only could he not account for the rainbow in his own terms, but he would not, for all his affirmation of *Polarität*, acknowledge the discovery of the polarization of light by Etienne Louis Malus, and instead developed his own theory of 'entoptic colours', which he proudly presented as 'the dot on the i' of his *Farbenlehre*, while gloomily predicting that such 'phantoms' as polarization would continue to haunt science into the second half of the (nineteenth) century.[14] He would not – could not, consistently enough by his own principles – accept the discovery by Herschel of infra-red rays beyond the visible spectrum; but neither would he accept the existence of Fraunhofer lines – a more disturbing form of obstinacy, since they are clearly visible to the 'healthy senses' as dark lines within the spectrum itself.

To be sure, efforts have been made to justify Goethe's ideas on colour, not only in the field of philosophy or aesthetics, but even, more dubiously, in the scientific field; distinguished physicists like Max Planck and Werner Heisenberg have seen in Goethe's methodology an ethical or human dimension, a respect for the natural world, as a corrective to the ethical indifference of analytical science. With the revolution in physics under Planck and Einstein, the whole positivistic and mechanistic tradition in science was relativized, and with it also Newton's physics; Goethe's optics were also subjected to revisionism, and his science enlisted by various anti-scientific or anti-materialistic causes such as Rudolf Steiner's anthroposophical school. While these developments might demonstrate the limitations of Newtonian physics, they do nothing to prove Goethe right. Modern physiological and psychological optical theory allows some function to the retina or to 'retina fatigue' in the perception of colour, as did Goethe; but neither does this validate Goethe's ideas in any substantive way.

Where speculation has concerned more philosophical or aesthetic aspects of colour theory, Goethe's work has had more resonance, in his reception by Hegel, and in particular by Schopenhauer, who actually collaborated with Goethe for a while on colour theory until intractable divergencies of thought (and, it must be said, Schopenhauer's overweening conviction of his own worth) drove them apart. Aestheticians and practising painters have responded more favourably to, and even drawn some inspiration from, Goethe's explanation of the emotional effects of colours: Runge, Klotz, Roux, Delacroix and, most notably, Turner, whose two paintings of 1843, *Shade and Darkness. The Evening of the Deluge* and *Light and Colour. The Morning after the Deluge* were expressly based on a translation of parts of Goethe's *Farbenlehre* by Sir Charles Eastlake in 1840. But efforts to make Goethe's optical theory relevant to modern science or to the science of his day involve much special pleading; as Albrecht Schöne has argued convincingly, Goethe's optics rest on assumptions that do not, other than very broadly and fortuitously, anticipate modern science, but on the contrary they look backwards to medieval or even ancient traditions. His crusade against Newton was a deeply personal, metaphysical issue that touched on his most cherished beliefs: his was not so much a theory as a theology of colour.[15] In no other area of knowledge or experience was Goethe so dogmatic, so insistently convinced that he was right; that is why he attacked Newton so immoderately, why he devoted so much time and energy to his project, and why he attached more importance to it than to his literary work.

MORPHOLOGY

If Goethe's relations with his scientific contemporaries in the fields of physics and optics were at best uneasy and at worst violently hostile, in other, less mathematically based fields he was more at ease. This is particularly true of his studies in what are now called the life sciences, and which around 1800 were only just beginning to develop as distinct disciplines from medicine: biology, anatomy, zoology, botany – in a word, what Goethe termed morphology. This he understood in general terms as the study of, and the search for, wholeness and unity in the natural world, of the 'formation and transformation of organic natural forms', the comparative study of organisms by form and structure through which he sought to explain the bewildering diversity of forms by means of universal laws or principles.

Goethe never provided, as he did in his *Farbenlehre*, a systematic explanation of his morphological credo, but from his many writings on plant and animal forms certain principles can be inferred. He believed as an article of faith that there is an ordered harmony and unity in the natural world comprising humankind, the animal kingdom and the rest of organic nature, a harmony that allows the systematic description, categorization and comparison of natural forms – though he also believed that there was more to the study of nature than the Linnaean taxonomy, which for him emphasized the separation of forms and species rather than seeking their fundamental harmony through similarities. Natural phenomena, Goethe believed, can be compared; plants and animals are related within their species, and there is a steady progression or hierarchy of species from lower to higher. *Natura non fecit saltus*; the chain or ladder of creation, of which humanity is the highest form that we know, is unbroken. For all the confusing variety of animal forms, they are fundamentally related in structure, even if the forms differ drastically; the arm of humans and primates, the fin of a whale or the flipper of a seal, the wing of a bird and the foreleg of a horse show a common structure, but differing proportions. The various limbs and organs of animals are determined by a law of equilibrium or compensation, by a natural budget or economy; one part can be developed or refined within a species, but only at the cost of another, nothing can be added to any part without being subtracted from another. If an animal has horns, it cannot have a full set of incisor teeth in the upper jaw; a horned lion is an impossibility, a rhinoceros, a cow or a stag cannot have a full complement of teeth. Darwin was later to acknowledge Goethe's thinking when he explained this 'balancement of growth' in terms of natural selection,[16] agreeing with Goethe in its effects but not in its causes, and showing that nature is continually trying to economize in every part of its organization – though this does not, as we shall argue below, therefore make Goethe a proto-Darwinian.

Goethe's fundamental belief in an archetypal form or *Urtyp* led him to formulate the principle of metamorphosis (touched on in the discussion of his 'Metamorphose' poems above, pp. 98–9). All plant forms and animal skeletons are metamorphoses of a primal form: plants are developments of the leaf, the skull is a modification of the vertebra, or a number of vertebrae. This does not mean that all parts of a plant – leaves, calyx, stamens, pistils – develop from leaves as a plant grows, nor that these parts have evolved from the leaf in the course of time, but rather that the leaf is the essential scheme that underlies these parts, and that they are all modifications of this basic pattern. Just where the root system fits into this scheme is not at all clear, and Goethe's study of roots and nodes is rudimentary to say the least.

Goethe's botanical studies began in the period following his arrival in Weimar, initially as a result of his official duties to do with the forestry of the Duchy, but also fostered by his interests in horticulture and landscape gardening. His anatomical studies began in 1781, and he was soon attending dissection classes at Jena University under the instruction of the anatomy professor, Justus Christian Loder. By 1784 his indefatigable curiosity and his instinct for observing analogies (or 'homologies', as they were later called) between diverse forms led to his excited 'discovery' of the intermaxillary bone in humans; his treatise on comparative osteology, purportedly showing that the *os intermaxillare* (Zwischenkieferknochen) was common to both humans and animals was written in 1784, but was only published in 1820 in the second volume of his *Zur Morphologie* (On Morphology). In 1786 he was studying micro-organisms under the microscope, and in Italy he botanized assiduously – especially in the rich 'garden' of Sicily, an exotic botanical paradise. In Venice in 1790 the chance finding of a sheep's skull in the Jewish cemetery brought the insight that the skull was an extension of the vertebrae. The years 1790 and 1791 saw the publication of works on the metamorphosis of plants and animals, and the first recorded mention of the concept of morphology is a diary entry for 25 September 1796. In 1796–8 he was concerned with entomology, weighing and measuring grubs and pupae, and devoting his attention to the mystery of the metamorphosis of larva to chrysalis to imago. At the same time he was contemplating a vast study of natural philosophy to be written in classical metres on the model of Lucretius's *De rerum natura* – a plan of which only vestigial fragments and the two 'Metamorphose' poems were written. *Zur Morphologie* was published in a series of fascicles between 1817 and 1824; in 1829–31 appeared his essays on the spiral tendencies of plants, and in 1830 and 1832 his two-part review of the dispute in the Paris *Académie des sciences* between Cuvier and Geoffroy Saint-Hilaire on comparative anatomy, which he followed with keen interest, the *Principes de philosophie zoologique*.

Goethe's biological study is a curious mixture, though not quite a synthesis, of painstaking realistic observation and general laws and principles. His concept of the primal plant (*Urpflanze*) is a fanciful notion similar to his vision of other archetypal natural forms (the leaf, the vertebra, even granite as the 'primal rock'); but he insisted that his method was empirical, realistic, based on analysis and observation, not on speculation or theory. In his scientific work he was forced, against his instincts, to adopt at least a quasi-theoretical method; and in this he was greatly encouraged and assisted by his friendship with Schiller. It seems that Goethe, perhaps only half-seriously, believed that he might find his *Urpflanze* in Sicily; and a much-quoted anecdote from 1794, from the uneasy beginnings of their relationship, relates how Goethe, eagerly expounding his theory with the help of a quick sketch of a 'symbolic plant', was severely put out at Schiller's reservation that it was a fine idea, but an idea, not an experience – whereupon Goethe riposted tartly that he was gratified that he could have ideas without being aware of it, and could even see them with his own eyes.[17] And yet by 1798 Goethe had accepted and acknowledged that he should combine observation and experience with a theoretical scheme by means of what Schiller defined as 'rational empiricism' – even if Goethe never abandoned his conviction that any idea must be tested against and confirmed by experience, by what he termed *sinnliches Anschauen* or 'seeing with the mind's eye'.[18]

One of the most gratifying and indeed exciting episodes in Goethe's scientific career was his purported 'discovery' in 1784 of the intermaxillary bone in humans. But though he excitedly announced his discovery of the 'keystone of humankind' in letters to Herder and Frau von Stein (swearing them both to the strictest secrecy) in March of that year,[19] he was unable to secure publication of his find, which was then delayed for some thirty-six years. But in any case, Goethe's 'first' was, for several reasons, less sensational than he imagined at the time; not only had a French anatomist, Félix Vicq d'Azyr, identified the intermaxillary bone in humans in 1780 (though his findings were not published until 1784, the year of Goethe's own observation), but also Goethe's 'discovery' was not as conclusive as he had initially – and understandably – believed.

The orthodoxy of the day was that the intermaxillary bone was distinct from the jawbone in animals, but not in humans; this was consistent with the theological conviction that humankind was physically, as well as spiritually, morally and intellectually quite distinct from the animal kingdom. While the intermaxillary bone is observably distinct in animals, in the adult human skull it is not, because the sutures between it and the jawbone have closed to render the two indistinguishable; in children and, more strikingly, in the human foetus, the divisions are clearer. Goethe looked for evidence of the intermaxillary in humans, and having found it to his own satisfaction he was able to suggest that the great unity of nature therefore applied to the anatomy of both humans and the animals; humanity was physically related to the animal kingdom, though (in the terms of his poem 'Das Göttliche', written the year before his discovery) distinct from it in moral, spiritual and intellectual faculties. However, as George A. Wells has cautioned, to say that humans 'have' an intermaxillary bone because it is quite distinct in the human foetus is tantamount to saying that humans 'have' gills or a tail because they are discernible at certain stages of embryonic development.[20]

Goethe's 'discovery' of the intermaxillary bone has often been extravagantly cited to suggest that he was a forerunner of Darwin, even that his purported find was an important early step in evolution theory. This is scarcely sustainable; for while Goethe, in common with many comparative anatomists of his day, was aware of the affinities between differently functioning limbs and organs of different species (between hands, wings and fins, between the lungs of animals and air-sacs in fish), while it is true that Darwin himself mentioned Goethe's work in a footnote to *The Origin of Species* in the same breath as that of his grandfather Erasmus Darwin, Geoffroy Saint-Hilaire and Lamarck,[21] there are fundamental gulfs between the analogies discerned by the comparative anatomy of Goethe's day and the systematic development and selection of species in evolution theory. The 'presence' of the intermaxillary in humans was for Goethe proof that there is a fundamental harmony of design, an overall law of unity – not that all creatures or species have a common ancestry. It is true that some anatomists of the time allowed a form a development or evolution within clearly related types – the jaguar and the leopard, for example. It is also true that Goethe, discussing the discovery of the fossil bones of an aurochs near Stuttgart in 1819–20, does talk of this extinct *Urstier* as the ancestor of the modern ox, and quotes with approval the suggestion of a fellow-anatomist that in the thousands of years of development from generation to generation, an ever stronger impulse (*Verlangen*) for better vision and hearing had led to the modification of the position and structure of the animal's eye-sockets and ear channels – a process of evolution over time as the wild ox became domesticated.[22]

Yet any claims to hail Goethe as a proto-Darwinist are surely the false attributions of hindsight, and this is as close as Goethe came to evolution theory – indeed, for his time, close enough perhaps. To be sure, natural philosophy in the eighteenth century had moved away from biblical creationism towards a more diachronic understanding of the origins of life, and Goethe believed that organic life had originated in water (citing the formation of coral reefs as evidence that this was a continuing process), in the primeval ocean (*Urozean*) in which, for him, rocks also had their first origins: plant and animal life had subsequently colonized the mountain slopes as the ocean slowly receded. It is true that the bizarre figure of Homunculus in the second act of *Faust* Part Two, who has an urgent impulse to come into physical being, is advised to begin his journey through the scale of creation in the ocean, where he will rehearse the process of creation from its origins and will progress by 'eternal laws' through a myriad forms – perhaps in time even achieving the dubious status of a human being; and it is tempting to infer that in the burlesque extravaganza of the Classical Walpurgisnight, Goethe might have poetically intuited a whimsical form of evolution theory, or that he might even perhaps have touched distantly on the hypothesis that the embryo passes through the scale of evolution within the womb.

But as a scientist Goethe could have had no conception, any more than his contemporaries could have done, of the principles of genetic mutation or of natural selection. He, and they, had only the most exiguous knowledge of the fossil records; and, most crucially, he and they had no notion of the then unimaginable time-scale of the evolution of species from a common ancestry. In 1779 Buffon had tentatively estimated the age of the earth at some 75,000 years (though he speculated privately with much larger figures); this was a bold departure from biblical calculations of some 4,000 years from Genesis to the birth of Christ, but utterly remote from present-day estimates of the 3,500 million years of evolutionary time, let alone the 4,600 million years of geological time – though by the end of his life Goethe would have had some grasp of the vast time-scale of geological eras from the speculations of geologists like James Hutton and Henry de la Beche. The great scale of being with which Goethe operated was part of a backward-looking neo-Platonic tradition; it was not an evolutionary scale, but rather a hierarchy of natural forms as nature's great design, from the most rudimentary to the most complex, that informed his biological thought and work, a design in which he laboured to discern a coherent, harmonious and meaningful totality and unity.

GEOLOGY AND MINERALOGY

The origins of Goethe's geological interests lie in his observations of the Swiss landscape during his 1779 journey, and in his activities as minister responsible for the revival of the silver and copper mines in Ilmenau. In 1777 Duke Karl August created a commission to investigate the possibility of reopening the workings that had been closed down in 1739, in order to swell his exchequer and to provide employment in an impoverished, and indeed in 1768 rebellious, area of the Duchy. The mines succeeded for a while in providing work, but they were never to be profitable, and the whole venture was abandoned in 1812. Goethe, who had already taken great delight in the landscape of Ilmenau (see above, pp. 73–4), now devoted himself to serious study of its configuration, and very soon accumulated a body of geological knowledge and a selection of rock and mineral specimens that grew over the years into an impressive collection. By 1780 he was in a position to provide Johann Karl Wilhelm Voigt, the brother of his close friend Christian Gottlob von Voigt, with detailed instructions for a geological survey of the area: Voigt had been sent to the celebrated mining academy at Freiberg (Saxony), where he had studied under Abraham Gottlob Werner, the leading 'neptunist' of his day, whose ideas were to have decisive influence on Goethe's own thinking.

Goethe's geological and mineralogical studies were among his most painstaking and constant scientific preoccupations, taking up about as much time and attention as his work on optics and morphology. To be sure, geology was a less obsessive concern than his campaign against the Newtonian heresy; but while he could boast no such spectacular 'first' as his purported discovery of the intermaxillary bone, this was the field in which Goethe arguably acquired his highest level of scientific expertise, to the extent that he was able to hold his own with the leading experts of his day such as Abraham Werner or Alexander von Humboldt – even if, in holding to Werner's neptunist doctrines, he once again, in the hindsight of subsequent developments, backed the wrong scientific horse. In the last half of the eighteenth century, neptunism or diluvianism was the prevailing theory on the origins of rocks and mountains, having superseded earlier vulcanist or plutonist ideas of such as Descartes or Leibnitz. Neptunist theory took some account of diluvian myths of a great flood in biblical, Egyptian and Indian cultures, but was based primarily on the conviction that rocks originated not in igneous or volcanic processes, but had first formed by chemical crystallization as granite in the primeval ocean (*Urozean*), by the erosion of this primary rock and the layering of debris around the more ancient formations, and subsequently by the gradual sedimentation of conglomerates like sandstone or limestone under the force of gravity as the ocean receded. To the neptunists, volcanic activity was a very late and superficial factor in the configuration of the earth's surface; lava forms were attributed by Werner to the 'pseudo-volcanic' liquefaction and eruption of rock masses such as basalt that had originally been crystallized in the ocean, and had then been melted by the combustion of vast underground coal deposits – a theory to which Goethe also broadly subscribed.

Goethe was as attracted by the neptunist account as he was repelled by the vulcanist school. A gradualist or evolutionist by instinct and temperament, he always professed a profound aversion to the doctrine of 'lifting, squeezing, hurling and heaving' – indeed, he frequently used the geological metaphor of vulcanism to express his fearful intuition of violence in the social and political sphere, of war and revolution. His resistance to vulcanist theory was the greatest blind spot in Goethe's geological thinking; but it was a more venial error than his obstinate misunderstanding of Newton, than his whimsical notions of barometric pressure, than his fanciful vision of the *Urpflanze* or of the skull as a modification of the vertebrae. Largely, though not totally discredited or corrected by modern discoveries, neptunism was a respectable and widely held theory at the time, and the rival doctrine of vulcanism was then at least as one-sidedly and as dogmatically upheld by its adherents as was monocausal neptunism.

The controversy flared throughout Goethe's lifetime; his own assistant Voigt in the late 1780s challenged the doctrines of his former teacher Werner when he identified lava as the origin of basalt, rather than the reverse. Basalt, indeed, posed a particular problem for Werner and the neptunists, who could not believe it was cooled lava, but held that it had formed by crystallization in the ocean, as granite had much earlier – in defiance of the sheer disbelief of many contemporaries that granite or basalt had been dissolved in water in order to be precipitated as crystallized rock. However, since basalt formations appeared to be younger than the sedimentary rocks which they covered, the neptunists were forced to conclude that the ocean had receded to form the layered or sedimentary (*Flöz*) rocks, and had then risen again to form the basalts by crystallization.

The neptunist–vulcanist controversy erupted again in the 1820s after the death of Werner in 1817, and the researches of Christian Leopold von Buch and Alexander von Humboldt into volcanoes, and Humboldt's discoveries in South America, began seriously to undermine the neptunist doctrine. Indeed Goethe, who enjoyed mutually respectful and friendly relations with Humboldt, came close on occasion to acknowledging the vulcanist theory, conceding that he could almost imagine that one day he might be able to accept it, and that had his own geological researches taken place in, say, the Massif central of France or in the Andes, then he too might have seen things differently. He would ideally have forged a compromise between the two dogmas; but to the end of his life he could not bring himself to accept a theory of cataclysm that was 'abhorrent' to him, or that the Himalayas had been raised with unimaginable violence 25,000 feet above the earth, 'and yet stand so fast and rise so proud to the heavens, as if nothing had happened'.[23] This, he insisted, was a notion beyond his comprehension; he could not accept it any more than he could accept the theory of the cooling and shrinkage of the earth to account for the 'wrinkling' of the earth's crust – a theory, proposed independently in 1829 by de Beaumont and von Klöden, that remained in favour until the plate tectonics of the mid-twentieth century.

Among Goethe's earliest writings on geology was a two-part essay on granite (*Über den Granit*) of 1784–5, a rhapsodic hymn in quasi-*Sturm und Drang* style written as a result of successive visits to the Harz mountains, and in which granite is celebrated as the *Urgestein*, the primal rock whose mysterious origins lay (as he then believed) neither in fire nor in water. Standing on these granite peaks, he proclaims, we stand on the bedrock of our earth, a rock that reaches to its innermost depths. No younger layers, no accumulated detritus comes between us and the very foundations of the world, here we do not walk over a continuous graveyard of eroded debris, of animal and vegetable organisms as we do in the fertile valleys below; these peaks have engendered nothing living, devoured nothing living, they are before all life and above all life. Here on this ancient and eternal altar, founded on the depths of creation, the soul is elevated to a sublime closeness to the Being of all Beings; this rock rose higher and steeper into the clouds when, as a sea-girt island, it stood in the ancient waters, and around it wheeled the spirit that brooded over the waves.[24]

This mystical invocation recalls the third stanza of the exuberant ode 'An Schwager Kronos' of ten years earlier; but such poetic outbursts were to give way to more sober and painstaking geological research, above all in and around the Bohemian spa towns of Karlsbad, Eger and Teplitz, and later Marienbad, where the mineral springs and their origins attracted his scientific interest, and in the mineral-rich mountains of the *Erzgebirge* on the borders of Saxony and Bohemia. He disagreed with Werner on the origins of hot springs, attributing them to chemical processes rather than to the heat from burning coal deposits – in which he was closer to modern explanations; he conducted one of the earliest geological experiments when with the help of a Jena chemist, J. W. Döbereiner, he had some rocks collected in Bohemia heated in a potter's kiln. He speculated on the transport of huge boulders over great distances by glaciers, and assumed at least one era of widespread glaciation; he did not accept the eccentric theories of Johann Ludwig Heim that whole mountain ranges had fallen from outer space. He was wrong to extrapolate from the geology of Central Europe conclusions he believed to be valid worldwide – but information from South America that similar or identical formations were found there fuelled his conviction. He acquired specimens of tin ore from Cornwall and Malaya, and studied all manner of minerals and gemstones. He received reports from the explorer von Eschwege who drew up the first geological map of Brazil, and was consulted by Christian Keferstein in 1821, when Keferstein was compiling the first geological map of Germany: Goethe's suggestions on the colour coding for rock formations (based on the principles of his colour theory) are still in use in some German maps today. Alexander von Humboldt sent him a dedicated copy of his treatise on volcanoes in 1823. While Goethe's stubborn neptunism and his ignorance of the then unimaginable time-scale of geological processes severely limited his perceptions by modern-day standards, these were limitations shared by many of his distinguished contemporaries. His great strengths in the field of geology were his characteristic gifts of acute observation, of collecting, comparing and assimilating, and his unflagging search for a consistent and coherent account of the natural world he saw around him.

METEOROLOGY

Goethe's meteorological studies are a late development in his scientific interests. Although he had shown some earlier interest in cloud forms and in readings of temperature and barometric pressure, it was only in 1815 that he turned his attention seriously to meteorology. Karl August, who saw the economic advantages of weather forecasting, had drawn to his notice a German account of a treatise by the English Quaker Luke Howard, *On the Modifications of Clouds, and on the Principles of their Production, Suspension and Destruction*, which had first appeared in *Tilloch's Philosophical Magazine* in 1803. Goethe, who was very doubtful of the feasibility of accurate weather forecasting, nevertheless found Howard's study and classification of cloud formations so instructive that he threw himself with characteristic energy into the study of meteorology. Apart from the poem 'Howards Ehrengedächtnis' (see above, pp. 118–19), he wrote in 1820 a series of meteorological notes, *Wolkengestalt nach Howard* (Cloud forms after Howard), and in 1825 an essay, the *Versuch einer Witterungslehre* (Towards a Theory of Weather), which he did not publish. He requested a brief biography of the English meteorologist; he was delighted when Howard himself sent one, and returned the compliment by reviewing Howard's *The Climate of London* in 1823. In his account to Goethe, Howard had admitted his own inexpertise in the mathematical sciences (he was a chemist), and stressed that his gifts were those of observation – which can only have commended him all the more to Goethe.

In spite of his scepticism towards weather forecasting, which to him smacked more of astrology than of natural philosophy (he allowed only that variations in air pressure could give a reasonable prediction of weather conditions over a period of some twenty-four hours), Goethe was active in establishing weather stations in the Duchy of Weimar. By 1824 there were several such stations, staffed by volunteers taking careful recordings of rainfall, wind direction and speed, cloud cover and formation, temperature, humidity and air pressure – even, with the help of a 'cyanometer', measuring the intensity of blue in the sky; these stations were closed not long after Goethe's death. He began to record barometric readings himself with obsessive regularity; it became for him 'the instrument that reveals nature's greatest mysteries to us',[25] and was given the status of *Urphänomen* – or, more accurately, the rise and fall of air pressure recorded by the barometer was thus defined. The Grand-Duchess Luise satirically dubbed him 'the Guardian of the Barometer', and it was mischievously believed that his moods rose and fell with the recorded air pressure – or at least that his morale for the day would be set by his early morning readings.

'I seized Howard's terminology joyfully because it offered me a thread I had previously found lacking.'[26] Goethe was clearly attracted to Howard's classifications because they systematized and confirmed his own uninformed visual observations of cloud forms; and indeed, for all the unimaginable advances in meteorological knowledge and the refinement of Howard's terms, his basic descriptions of clouds as stratus, cumulus, cirrus and nimbus are still fundamental categories today. But Goethe also sought to justify his observations with a theoretical hypothesis – and this is where he left science behind for speculation. His first efforts attempt to explain the metamorphosis of cloud forms as if they were, like the subjects of his morphological studies, independent organic phenomena, and not the products of temperature and condensation: for Goethe, the formation of clouds was a rising and falling process, a metamorphosis from lower to higher, indeed it was the result of a conflict between higher and lower regions, or between dry and moist conditions. As water vapour rises from lakes, rivers and oceans, it condenses into stratus or layered cloud, which then modifies or 'gathers' into cumulus; at this stage, cumulus will under dry conditions disperse into the upper atmosphere as cirrus, or under moist conditions will descend as nimbus, the rain-bearing form. Goethe added to Howard's terminology a further form, *Paries* or 'wall' cloud – an observation of distant cloud layered on the horizon that was later shown to be based on optical illusion; but it is an intriguing, if wholly accidental, historical footnote that recent research into thunderstorms and tornadoes in North America has identified 'wall cloud' as a phenomenon produced when an area of rotating cloud lowers to form a swirling funnel extending to the ground, and one that is increasingly adduced in the prediction of tornadoes.

In his early essay on granite Goethe had already talked, in the lofty style of that essay, of his intuition of 'the inner attractive and motive forces of the earth.'[27] In his meteorology he also ascribes variations in barometric pressure to a quasi-Aristotelian notion of the pulsation of 'tellurian' forces – as it were, to the inhalation and exhalation of the earth. Cloud formation, and therefore the weather, was governed neither by cosmic nor by atmospheric forces; Goethe ruled out any influence of the moon, stars or planets on the weather – though such ideas were still current at the time. He did concede that the drying of the atmosphere in summer was to some extent due to the influence of the sun; but he did not ascribe any major role to temperature in the creation of weather conditions – a fundamental error in the light of modern meteorology.

Principally for Goethe, it was the alternating pulsation of the earth, governed by the twin factors of gravitation and the regular rotation about its axis, that determined barometric pressure, and therefore the weather: as the earth 'breathes in', so to speak, it attracts the *Dunstkreis* (the atmospheric 'sphere of vapour'), and as a result clouds and moisture gather near the surface. This process of *Wasserbildung* or *Wasserbejahung* (water formation or 'affirmation') results in an accumulation of moisture that would cause catastrophic floods if the earth did not breathe out again to create a reverse process of 'water denial' (*Wasserverneinung*), whereby moisture rises and disperses into the atmosphere. Confusingly, however, even this somewhat fanciful process is not consistently described by Goethe. He appears to suggest that the 'inhalation' of the earth is a metaphor for increased gravitational pull, and that conversely its 'exhalation' corresponds to a decrease in gravity; yet in the *Versuch einer Witterungslehre* he states that greater gravitational pull resists the build-up of excessive atmospheric moisture, while in a less technical account of his theory to Eckermann, he is reported as correlating the earth's 'inhalation' with high rainfall, and its 'exhalation' with fine weather.[28]

Goethe's fundamental conviction of *Polarität* and *Steigerung* governed his theories both of barometric pressure and of cloud metamorphosis – and indeed also the metaphorical application of his cloud lore in his literary work, most strikingly illustrated in the cloud-symbolism of *Faust* Part Two: in the opening monologue of Act Four and in the final scene of Act Five. Cumulus and nimbus are the forms of greatest contraction or density of cloud, stratus and cirrus those of greatest expansion or dispersal; *Steigerung* is the upward movement of cloud towards its thinnest, driest and highest form of cirrus – or, in terms of the spiritual symbolism, of the soul towards a state of *Erlösung*, of release or redemption – as the *Cirrus* stanza of 'Howards Ehrengedächtnis' has it.

To be sure, weather forecasting is still today scarcely an exact science, even if the meteorological and physical methodology on which it is based is. But for all his enthusiastic reception of Howard's classifications, for all his energetic, indeed obsessive preoccupation with barometric pressures, his organization of weather records and his own close observation of sky and weather patterns, Goethe's meteorology was deeply flawed even by the standards of his own day. One of his most fundamental errors was to assume that barometric pressure was everywhere constant, at least in relative terms. Pascal had already long since demonstrated that air pressure decreases with altitude; but Goethe believed, rather as he had believed he could draw universal conclusions from the geology of Central Germany, that barometric changes were, allowing for altitude, consistent over wide areas, even universally so – because they were governed by the regular variations of the 'tellurian' forces of rotation and gravitation. This was a misunderstanding that the readings of the local weather stations in the Duchy of Weimar might not have corrected, but one which comparisons with wider records would have demonstrated clearly enough; combined with his refusal to attribute any fundamental significance to the effect of temperatures on climate, it vitiated the scientific basis of Goethe's meteorology.

It is perhaps too easy to point out from a present-day perspective where, and how seriously, Goethe's scientific observations and principles were flawed; it is also easy to patronize his endeavours by allowing that he did more than well enough for someone who was not in the first instance a scientist. But neither is it sufficient to suggest that the state or scope of scientific knowledge in that more leisured age of pre-specialization was such that an informed amateur could master several disciplines well enough, and even contribute significantly to them. Rather, it is that late eighteenth and early nineteenth-century science was, even in the mathematically based disciplines, still widely considered part of an integral philosophy, allied to thought, religion and even poetry. Indeed, the terms science and scientist, as we now understand them, only emerged in contradistinction to other intellectual disciplines in the course of the nineteenth century.

When thinkers of the age of Goethe (or of the period broadly known as 'Romanticism') spoke of nature, their understanding of that term went far beyond a simple emotional or visual response to landscape or scenery; it included much that we would now, with all due historical reservation, call a scientific interest in the physical world. Any number of seventeenth, eighteenth and nineteenth-century polymaths demonstrate, to our modern envy, that it was possible to combine great achievement in the literary, philosophical or theological fields with high expertise in other disciplines: Descartes, Pascal, Leibnitz, Haller the poet and physiologist, Spinoza the lens-grinder, Schiller the trained doctor and academic historian. Newton himself, the epitome of modern scientific rigour and discipline, devoted much of his time to the study of alchemy and to biblical exegesis. Rousseau and Diderot were informed in science and technology, and scientists like Humphry Davy were not only the close collaborators of men of letters, but frequently turned to poetry themselves. Goethe's English biographer, G. H. Lewes, was a biologist and physiologist.

The Romantic poets had a particular affinity, not simply with nature as a scenic source of inspiration, but as an object of serious scientific and philosophical study. Friedrich Schlegel urged his followers to study physics; the physicist Johann Wilhelm Ritter was a close member of the Jena Romantic circle. Wordsworth, an admirer of Newton, was captivated by geometry's 'independent world, / Created out of pure intelligence' (*The Prelude*, VI, lines 166–7). Novalis (Friedrich von Hardenberg), the consummate German Romantic poet, was a professional mining engineer, a graduate of the Freiberg Mining Academy, whose mysticism frequently reverts to the imagery and terminology of mathematics and physics; John Keats trained as a surgeon.

To be sure, many poets deplored the mechanistic reductions of Newton's physics as violently as Goethe did. As early as 1712, Addison had feared that Newtonian science had jeopardized the 'secret spell' that allows us to delight in nature, and insisted that the mind responds to nature in such a way as 'to add supernumerary ornaments to the universe, and make it more agreeable to the imagination'[29] – words that recall Goethe's vision of the 'living treasures / That adorn the universe' (see above, p. 120). Charles Lamb and Keats notoriously proposed a facetious toast to Newton, combined with 'confusion to mathematics', and Keats deplored the 'dull catalogue of common things' that could 'conquer all mysteries by rule and line' or 'unweave a rainbow' (*Lamia*, II, lines 231–8).

It was Coleridge who came as close as any contemporary poet to Goethe's holistic study of nature, even if the English poet's chaotic working methods prevented any final or systematic working out of his *Naturphilosophie* – a concept he was more than familiar with from his study of German thinkers like Schelling. For Coleridge, science was a source of imaginative insight; his ideas may have put him, like Goethe, at odds with the scientific establishment in so far as it was dominated by Newtonian mechanism, but he explored scientific method and was personally close to Humphry Davy and Thomas Beddoes, and he knew Erasmus Darwin. His studies with Davy even brought him close to a Goethean notion of *Polarität und Steigerung*, no doubt fortuitously: the polar opposition of oxygen and hydrogen found its synthesis in water. He wrote to Ludwig Tieck on 4 July 1817:

'To me, I confess, Newton's assumptions . . . have always, and years before I ever heard of Goethe, appeared monstrous *Fictions!*', and to Thomas Poole on 23 March 1801: 'Newton's . . . whole theory is, I am persuaded, so exceedingly superficial as without impropriety to be deemed false. Newton was a mere materialist – *mind*, in his system, is always passive, – a lazy Looker-on on an external World. If the mind be not *passive*, if it be indeed made in God's Image, & that too in the sublimest sense – the Image of the *Creator* – there is ground for suspicion, that any system built on the passiveness of the mind must be false, as a system.' If we substitute 'eye' for 'mind' here, we are very close to Goethe, as we are in a further comment by Coleridge: 'from the age of Des Cartes to that of Hartley and Le Sage, not only all external nature, but the subtlest mysteries of organisation, life nay, of the intellect and moral being, were conjured within the magic circle of mechanical forces, and controlled by mathematical formula.'[30]

But in spite of his broad affinities with the German Romantics in their reaction against the mechanistic physics of Newton, Goethe could not and would not make common cause with them or their scientific colleagues in their investigation of mysterious paranormal phenomena beyond conventional scientific analysis – the interface of physiology and psychology, or of chemistry, electricity and 'animal magnetism', somnambulism and states of trance (though there is an ambivalent reference to natural sympathy or animal magnetism in the 'pendulum experiments' of the English lord's companion in *Die Wahlverwandtschaften*, and Goethe did work on electrical experiments under the guidance of J. W. Ritter, who lectured on galvanism at Jena University). He also demarcated himself from his Romantic counterparts in his conviction that he was not one who studied nature with the eye of a poet, but on the contrary a student of nature whose scientific vision informed his poetry.

Goethe was wrong, and indeed wrong-headed, in much of his scientific work – not least in his judgement of Newton. And yet no one who takes the trouble to look more than cursorily into the *Leopoldina Ausgabe* of Goethe's scientific writing, or into the selections of it in other editions of his collected works, can doubt the seriousness, the scope or the detail of his scientific knowledge, which far exceeds that of the informed amateur, and is positively awesome to the non-scientist, indeed to many scientists, today.

He studied in painstaking detail crabs, snails, moths, micro-organisms, the anatomy of sloths and elephants, humans and reptiles, and he had a wide knowledge of plant species, rocks and minerals. He had some knowledge, within the limitations of his time, of electricity and magnetism; he knew the work of Galvani, Volta and Benjamin Franklin. He helped his friend, the Weimar apothecary W. H. S. Buchholz, with experiments into hot-air balloons. After his colour theory, he planned a theory of acoustics along similar principles. He knew of glaciation and hydraulics and the workings of the steam-engine. He preserved until his last days an acute interest in the most recent developments in science, technology and civil engineering, for all his ambivalence towards the ever-increasing pace of technical and industrial progress. He was a serious historian of science, and was well-informed in the history and theory of alchemy. He was abreast of much of the scientific research of his day, not only through his vast reading, but also because scientists and scholars would send him reports of their most recent work, and would even report personally to him their findings and conclusions; he corresponded with leading scientists like Carus, Döbereiner, Alexander von Humboldt, Iken, Loder, d'Alton and Cuvier. A suture in the bony palate of the upper jaw was named the *sutura Goethei*; an iron oxide mineral formation is known as Goethite; and a Brazilian genus of the family *Malvaceae*, comprising three plant species, was named the genus *Goethea* by the botanist C. G. D. Nees von Esenbeck. Goethe was a founder and president of the Jena Mineralogical Society, which very quickly established an international reputation; he would also, in his *Mittwochsgesellschaft*, hold Wednesday afternoon lectures in his own house at which he explained and illustrated, often with spectacular electrical or chemical demonstrations, his scientific ideas to the ladies of the Weimar court.

Goethe, no doubt because he is Goethe, has been accorded more respect for his science, and indeed for other aspects of his thought, than someone with a less formidable literary and intellectual reputation might have been. The efforts of historians, and indeed of some scientists, to justify his contributions to science in modern terms, or even to argue the superiority of his scientific ideas to those of modern science, whether on ethical, ecological, aesthetic or mystical grounds, are perhaps misguided; as H. B. Nisbet has argued, it is futile to clamour for the reinstatement of ideas that have been conclusively refuted by subsequent research, many of which were in any case not original to Goethe.[31] On the other hand, Goethe would surely have endorsed Richard Dawkins's recent contention that science offers far more scope for wonder, mystery and fascination than does superstition, as well as his plea that 'science needs to be released from the lab into the culture'.[32]

Goethe's science is an integral part of his life and work, its flaws are those both of the man and of the age, of his personality and of the then current state of knowledge. What remains is an informed, unremitting and urgent curiosity, a will to explain the world around him in comprehensive and comprehensible ways, a profound delight in and respect for the natural world and our place in it, and the search for an integrity, wholeness and harmony that is no longer possible in anything like the same terms, but which is not therefore a wholly futile quest, in literature, philosophy or science.

Conclusion

'Wer liest noch Goethe?': Who still reads Goethe? This fatuous commonplace has been modish for many years in Germany, and is understandable, if not excusable, in the light of Goethe's function as a national monument, forced on resistant schoolchildren and exploited by official ideologies, and therefore a target of abuse or derision from those whose ideological commitment or instincts of cultural iconoclasm resist the imposition of Goethe as a cultural exemplar. His merits as a writer are often obscured in the clamour.

In the English-speaking world, Goethe's reputation has suffered for different reasons. Occasionally quoted, more or less accurately, for pretentious effect, and often enough with guarded awe, his work has seemed inaccessible to a broad public, if only because of the intractable barrier of language; though translations of great merit have appeared in recent years, Goethe's greatest gift, that of poetic expression, is available only in attenuated form to those who do not read German, and it is unlikely that his work will ever be as widely known, as accessible or as appreciated as that of German musicians or visual artists. But the language barrier is not insurmountable, and exhilarating productions of *Faust* in Glasgow, Hammersmith, Stratford and London in recent years, as well as other productions of Goethe's and Schiller's dramas in this country, have shown that this area of German classical literature, at least, is not necessarily doomed to neglect.

Other reasons for the widespread indifference to or diffidence towards Goethe, in Germany and elsewhere, are his apparent remoteness in time and his assumed irrelevance to the twentieth century, let alone to the twenty first. This notion, if sustained, would apply to any form of art created much before yesterday. Ideologically or methodologically inspired attacks on the accepted canon of classical works have also contributed to the revision and devaluation of perceived 'great' works of literature. As we approach the 250th anniversary of Goethe's birth, his historical remoteness may well be emphasized – though no doubt many attempts will be made to demonstrate his 'relevance', too.

To be sure, some historical empathy, some effort and some learning are required to bridge the social, cultural and philosophical gulf between this age and

Goethe's, a gulf that cannot be ignored or dismissed: Goethe was a man of his age, indeed for many *the* man of his age. For that very reason, however, he should still be meaningful, and therefore relevant, to us. The seemingly remote and lofty constructs of German Idealism, expressed in Schiller's 'Ode to Joy' and Beethoven's setting of it – which even as I write is being optimistically proposed as the theme for the European Football Championship, and which was given an emotional performance in Berlin as an Ode to Freedom shortly after the *de facto* reunification of Germany in 1989 – evidently still have sufficient resonance to be exploited for commercial, cultural or political purposes. Frequently dismissed as a pompous and unreal sham, they are arguably more urgently relevant than ever in the bleak beggar-my-neighbour ethos informing the 'economic realism' of Thatcherite and post-Thatcherite Britain.

Goethe's remoteness is indisputable in many respects. His political and social attitudes, for all his purported striving for a poetic perspective of non-partisan mediation or ironic balance, are those of more or less enlightened eighteenth-century absolutism. His aesthetic and philosophical assumptions are similarly conditioned by the age of Winckelmann and Kant, of German Classicism and Idealism. His scientific thinking, when it was not misdirected, was constricted by the limitations of the knowledge and technology of his age. And yet from a different perspective of generations, he is not so very remote: the present writer's father might have known someone who had known Goethe. Many of Goethe's literary works require special knowledge or imaginative adjustment – but this was also required of many of his contemporary readers, as it is required by much serious literature of any age. His official style of correspondence to persons of distinction or rank is alien in its ponderous formality; but many of his letters to his close friends, his intimates in love, and other correspondents are unmatched in their exuberance, their relaxed informality and their warm affection. Above all, his lyric poetry and his dramatic writing, pre-eminently much of his *Faust*, the quality of his poetic expression and the vitality of his humour, whether high irony or low farce, are as accessible and as fresh on the page (or on the stage) as if they had been written yesterday.

For many and complex reasons to do with his literary stature, his personal and political subtlety (or ambivalence), and with Germany's problematic history, Goethe has been used for some 200 years as an ideological or cultural football, as national alibi or as national Aunt Sally, as exemplar or whipping-boy, as hero or villain, as a touchstone of German pride or German shame.[1] Indeed, from an early stage in his own lifetime, from the sensational and controversial reception of his novel *Werther*, he was the focus of passionate approval and disapproval, praise and censure from his contemporaries.

After the high public profile he enjoyed as a result of early success with *Götz von Berlichingen* and *Werther*, Goethe faded from contemporary public consciousness for some fifteen years after his removal to Weimar in 1775, to be revived with the publication of *Egmont*, *Iphigenie*, *Tasso* and the *Faust* fragment – works that presented a quite new image of Goethe to the reading public. With the publication of *Wilhelm Meisters Lehrjahre*, he was initially hailed by the younger Romantic generation as the supreme modern poet, and specifically by Novalis as 'the true representative of the poetic spirit on earth';[2] but within two years Novalis had bitterly condemned the *Lehrjahre* as a satire on religion and poetry, and the Romantics' worship of Goethe rapidly turned to a profound disapproval of his and Schiller's Weimar Classicism. The paganism, cosmopolitanism and political indifference of the Weimar partnership became increasingly alien to the national and religious tendencies of the younger generation during the years of Napoleonic dominance in Germany.

To be sure, during the high-minded years of Weimar Classicism, Goethe and Schiller did little to woo their public or to court popular success; on the contrary, they aimed expressly to educate the German public to *their* standards, and their own propaganda, above all the satirical *Xenien*, did little to correct their image as writers who were indifferent to public reaction. The elevation of Goethe and Schiller to unquestioned exemplary status was fostered by contemporaries such as Wilhelm von Humboldt, by Goethe's personal entourage (Eckermann, Riemer, Soret, Coudray and others), and was continued by such as Varnhagen von Ense and his wife Rahel. These were the foundations of a national cult of Goethe that has continued, in one form or another, with its inevitable counter-current of more or less violently hostile reaction, to the present day. It is not difficult to see how well-intentioned remarks like Varnhagen von Ense's of 1834, designed to present Weimar culture as a bulwark against unstable or revolutionary times, served as a provocation to those less liberally or conservatively minded: 'The spirit of Goethe is the spirit of order, of moderation, of self-possession and of reverence.'[3]

After his death, Goethe came under serious attack from quite different ends of the political spectrum. The radical writers of *Junges Deutschland* (Young Germany), the literary–political opposition to Metternich's repressive hegemony after 1830, and the revolutionary writers of the so-called *Vormärz* of the eve of the 1848 revolutions, while admiring Goethe's early literary radicalism, deplored his conversion to an aristocratic and exclusive classicism that for them inevitably followed on his move to the Weimar court in 1775. Ludwig Börne in particular, a radical journalist associated with Young Germany, who like Heine went into voluntary exile in Paris after 1830, saw Goethe as the figurehead of political reaction during the Restoration period, and expressed his resentment of the Goethe cult in many violent polemics, the most notorious of which was his declaration in 1830 (two years before Goethe's death) that with Goethe the old Germany would be buried, for on that day freedom must surely be born.

Conversely, Wolfgang Menzel, a nationalist quite at odds with the libertarian radicals of his generation, deplored Goethe's unpatriotic internationalism, exemplified in his worship of Napoleon and his sceptical reaction to German liberation in 1813, and also attacked Goethe immoderately. But whereas the left-wing radicals had lumped Goethe and Schiller together as writers of apolitical reaction, or at least quietism, Menzel was not alone in championing Schiller at the cost of Goethe – an invidious rivalry that has been perpetuated at various times and in various forms to the present day. Goethe was perceived as labile, chameleon-like, opportunistic, élitist and egotistic, Schiller as the poet of the people who sang of the fatherland, of honour, freedom and justice; even Schiller's family life was held up as an exemplary model against Goethe's philandering and his irregular domestic arrangements. Indeed, such comparisons had already been made during Goethe's lifetime, and Goethe's own impatient reaction, expressed to Eckermann in 1825, has not endeared him to critics of his élitist arrogance: 'They have been quarrelling for twenty years about who was the greater, Schiller or I; they ought to be glad to have two fellows like that to quarrel about.'[4]

Between the adulation of Goethe by liberals, conservatives or Hegelians, and the resentment of him by radicals or nationalists, between those who championed Goethe or Schiller, it was Heine who mediated between the extremes, who took up an ambivalent stance to Goethe's personality and achievements, who both deplored and admired, mocked and praised Goethe and who, in his own quicksilver mind, had the keenest sense of Goethe's complex, elusive and protean talents. While having no time for Menzel's bigotry or Börne's resentment, Heine also saw Goethe's death as the end of an unregretted era, that of the Holy Roman Empire. While admitting his own 'unfortunate passion' for Goethe, Heine also characterized him as a great oak tree whose spread had inhibited young growth – a tree resented by religious orthodoxy because there were no niches to be found for holy images, indeed a tree in whose branches the naked dryads of ancient pagan culture had disported themselves; a tree, he goes on, resented equally by the orthodoxy of political radicalism because it would not serve as a tree of liberty, let alone as a revolutionary barricade. Goethe's great works are like marble statues: they are beautiful but barren, and Goethe's fine words have left no children.

For Heine, Goethe was a dual figure, servile and liberal, great and petty, a remote genius and a man of the world. Heine was also one of the first to cultivate the ambivalent image of the 'Olympian' Goethe – an image that has dogged Goethe like a nemesis through the years. Heine facetiously dubbed him 'Wolfgang Apollo', and the description of his own visit to Goethe as a diffident (or so he would have us believe) young writer is memorable both for its sly exuberance and as a pointer to future perceptions of the Sage of Weimar:

> His outward appearance was as momentous as the word that lived in his writings; his figure was harmonious, serene, beatific, nobly proportioned, and one could study Greek art from him as from an ancient statue, . . . his eyes were as calm as those of a god. . . . I am convinced that he was a god. Goethe's eye remained in old age just as godlike as in his youth. Though time covered his head with snow, it was not able to bow it. He always carried himself proudly upright, and when he spoke, he grew in stature, and when he held out his hand, it was as if with his finger he could ordain the paths the stars in heaven should follow. Some claim to have detected a trace of cold arrogance about his mouth; but this is also a feature proper to the eternal deities, indeed to the father of the gods, great Jupiter, with whom I have already compared Goethe. Truly, when I visited him in Weimar and stood before him, I glanced involuntarily to one side, half-expecting to see beside him the eagle with the thunderbolts in its beak. I was on the point of addressing him in Greek; but as I found that he understood German, I spoke to him in that language.[5]

For all his irrepressible satire and ideological ambivalence, Heine could not share the resentment of those politically closer to him, indeed he was subsequently to despair of the abysmal literary quality of contemporary *engagé* poets, and to proclaim that Goethe's thought was a flower that would bloom all the more brightly 'on the dunghill of our age'.

Perceptions of Goethe varied wildly between his death and the foundation of the Second Reich in 1871. With certain exceptions, his poetic and literary talent was unquestioned, though much of his late work (the *West-östliche Divan*, *Wilhelm Meisters Wanderjahre*, the second part of *Faust*) was met with incomprehension, derision or satire. It was what he represented, or was perceived to represent, that came under attack: reaction or absolutism, élitism or political neutrality, classical isolationism or quietistic self-absorption. For early socialists, he was the lackey of princes who nevertheless adumbrated in *Wilhelm Meister* and in Faust's final vision the beginnings of a future utopia; for Friedrich Engels, Goethe was torn between his sympathy for common humanity and his petty philistine self-interest, between his understanding of the political and social misery of eighteenth-century Germany and his compromises with the ruling powers. For the realist writers of the mid-nineteenth century, he was both the prophet of an unworldly classical idealism and the poetic realist who had written *Hermann und Dorothea*, a patriotic, humane and real-life German idyll.

For the Church, Goethe was immoral, irreligious and pagan, responsible for elevating classical German culture to the status and function of a surrogate faith. Since the appearance of *Werther*, Goethe had been savaged from the pulpits of both Christian denominations; *Die Wahlverwandtschaften* and *Faust*, above all the issue of Faust's redemption, were anathema to religious orthodoxy; the ending of *Faust* was a heresy of salvation without the intervention of a Saviour, a way into heaven on purely human terms. But after 1871, the Lutheran Church, at least, made its accommodation with Goethe, and specifically Christian elements in his life and works were emphasized: his mother's piety, the ministrations of Fräulein von Klettenberg, his early relations with Lavater. A pastor in Bremen around the turn of the century even took to citing passages from Goethe or Schiller as texts for his sermons – an admittedly exceptional case.

With all the caveats of generalization, it is broadly true to say that with the foundation of the Second Reich, Goethe was officially installed in the national German pantheon, assimilated to the triumphalism of the new Germany and, together with Schiller as the other of the twin stars, the *Dioscuri*, in the cultural firmament, became a seriously pompous icon, a monumental national emblem. Germans pointed with pride to Goethe as a name to be placed alongside Homer, Dante and Shakespeare – or alongside Luther, Frederick the Great and Bismarck. *Faust* did indeed become, in the realization of a caustic remark by Heine, a secular Bible for Germans, and the figure of Faust himself the embodiment of the spirit of the new empire, ruthless and single-minded, titanic and exemplary. The Olympian image of Goethe projected so irreverently by Heine became the accepted perception as the poet was harnessed to the political ideology of Wilhelmine Germany.

This was also a Golden Age of Goethe scholarship, a period of positivistic study of Goethe, of careful textual criticism, of biographical and genetic studies of the works, together with an intensive preoccupation with the minutiae of Goethe's daily life, correspondence and conversations. The comprehensive, and still not wholly superseded, edition of the poetic and scientific works, the diaries and letters, the *Weimar* or *Sophienausgabe*, was started under the patronage of the Grand Duchess Sophia of Saxony in 1887, and completed in 1919; Goethe's conversations were collected and edited by Woldemar Freiherr von Biedermann from 1889–96, and later revised by his son Flodoard. In 1885 Goethe's last surviving grandchild Walther died, and the house on the *Frauenplan* and its contents were released for public scrutiny. The home became the national Goethe Museum, and in the same year the Goethe-Gesellschaft (Goethe Society) was founded in Weimar. Karl Goedecke's *Goethes Leben und Schriften* had been published in 1874, and Herman Grimm's lectures on Goethe in 1877; but astonishingly, the first truly standard German biography of Goethe, by Albert Bielschowsky, did not appear until 1896–1904 – almost fifty years after George Henry Lewes's English study of the life and works. Friedrich Spielhagen had no greater praise for Bielschowsky's scholarly and, within the expectations of the time, readable work than to hail him as 'the German Lewes'.

Bielschowsky's biography was followed by the less positivistic studies of Houston Stewart Chamberlain (1912), Georg Simmel (1913) and Friedrich Gundolf (1916). Gundolf in particular was concerned more with Goethe's ahistorical status; indeed, as a disciple of Nietzsche and Stefan George, Gundolf was careful to elevate Goethe's image above its exploitation by a banal and bureaucratic age. His fastidiously aesthetic and subjective perception of Goethe substituted for the public philistinism of the Wilhelmine Goethe worship a new, esoteric cult of Goethe as a vatic literary hero in the name of culture as opposed to a prosaic, soulless and materialistic 'civilization'.

While the unprecedented mechanical mass slaughter of the First World War did not totally obliterate the unquestioned status of Goethe and Weimar Classicism, it delivered a severe blow to such perceptions. The jagged and dislocated visions of Expressionism, the tragic aura of poets like Lenz or Hölderlin, the bitterly hostile universe of Kleist, or the visionary pathos of Büchner, were seen as a literature more appropriate to the present day than the received harmonious, unproblematic or effortlessly superior image of the Weimar Olympian. If German soldiers had set out for the front with Goethe's *Faust* in their packs, Brecht remarked in a 1929 radio programme, they had returned without it: the German classics were among the casualties of the war.

And yet in terms of official state culture, it was no accident that the Weimar Republic was constituted in, and named after, the cultural capital of Germany; and Friedrich Ebert invoked the 'progressive' Goethe and the humane ideals of Weimar Classicism in his speech to the new parliament in 1919. Goethe was derided by left-wing intellectuals of the inter-war years as the poet of the 'juste milieu', while traditional academic Goethe scholarship went about its business largely unaffected by the political turbulence: the first three volumes of Hermann August Korff's *Geist der Goethezeit* appeared between 1923 and 1930. Even here, however, there were revisions of the Olympian image and of the Faustian gospel of the Wilhelmine era in the work of such as Ernst Cassirer, Wilhelm Böhm, Walter Benjamin and Georg Lukács. Not only political or literary revisionism, but also Freudian analysis gave the impetus to a dismantling of the serene facade as the problematic and even pathological aspects of Goethe's personality were explored and brought to the surface: his sexuality, his neuroses, his relationship with his father, and above all with his sister. Goethe's violent attack on Newton was his struggle to come to terms with a dominant father-figure who stood in his way; his unfulfilled relationship with Friederike Brion was symptomatic of a castration phobia.

The Goethe year of 1932 was another turning-point in the turbulent perceptions of Goethe in the inter-war years. As the democratic experiment of the Weimar Republic faltered and collapsed, Goethe was rehabilitated in some quarters as a figure to whom Germans could rally in a time of threatening chaos. While both National Socialists and Communists despised the appeal of official German culture to the 'spirit of Weimar' as the last gasp of a moribund order, they also claimed Goethe as their own. Nationalists in particular adopted him as an icon in which Germans could take pride at a time of national humiliation and resentment, as one to whom the youth of Germany, alienated from the classical heritage in the 1920s, could turn as a leader figure. Disturbingly, though Julius Petersen was no Nazi, his 1935 speech as President of the Goethe-Gesellschaft invoked Goethe's imagined approval of 'our companions in black and our comrades in brown' in the struggle for the 'inner liberation' of a resurrected Germany.

Goethe was, however, an uncomfortable model for National Socialist ideology, which found his elusive irony too subtle to be pressed readily into service, his non-partisan stance, his cosmopolitanism and his humanism dangerously liberal, and above all his admiration for Napoleon subversively unpatriotic. Schiller's lofty idealism, albeit at the cost of some violence to the letter and the spirit of his work, could be tailored more easily to the Nazi vision of national freedom and the dynamic energy of the new state – as could, equally perversely, Kleist or Hölderlin. Nevertheless, Goethe could not be ignored – whatever else he might have been, he was decidedly not in the category of the *entartete Kunst* (degenerate art) of modernism so feared and reviled by Hitler. Adolf Bartels (*Goethe der Deutsche*, 1932) and Baldur von Schirach devoted themselves to claiming Goethe for their own purposes. Faust in particular, in a perverted echo of his Wilhelmine glorification, was dressed in a brown shirt and harnessed to the new ruthlessness of expansionism; the 'pedagogic province' of *Wilhelm Meisters Wanderjahre*, where clean-uniformed and well-behaved young people learned the disciplines of duty and obedience, was assimilated to the youth training of the *Hitlerjugend* and the *Bund deutscher Mädel*.

The traditional preoccupation of *Germanistik* with Goethe was continued in Germany during the war years by conservative, though not fascist, specialists – Kurt May, Ernst Beutler and Wilhelm Emrich – who, while not entirely immune to the style and vocabulary of the age, pursued politically inexplicit and more formalist critical methods. This tradition was continued after 1945, when *werkimmanent* or 'intrinsic' methodologies, avoiding the pitfalls of political commitment, became the norm, in the western sphere at least, with the work of Wolfgang Kayser, Emil Staiger and Erich Trunz as well as Emrich and Beutler.

In the immediate post-war era, Goethe was perceived as more valuable than ever to Germans as the reassurance of a civilized past, as a reminder of a humane tradition after twelve years of darkness. But scholars like Richard Alewyn were also moved to point out sharply that Goethe should not and could not be used as a national alibi; his dire warning that 'between us and Weimar lies Buchenwald' (the concentration camp was situated a few miles north-west of Weimar) was an equivalent to the despairing conclusion that there could be no poetry after Auschwitz. The total destruction of Goethe's family house in Frankfurt on the night of 22 March 1944 (Goethe himself had died on 22 March 1832) held a sober symbolism for many, and much controversy surrounded the question of how, or even whether, the house should be restored after the war.

The year 1949 saw not only the bicentenary of Goethe's birth, but also the foundation of the German Democratic Republic. The socialist state was quick to claim the inheritance of Weimar, both geographical and cultural; once again, Goethe was to be a prestigious and representative figure of a new Germany. While Georg Lukács and Hans Mayer perpetuated, in Marxist terms, the image of the classical Goethe, more conformist Marxist scholars revised the image and presented Goethe as the forerunner of socialist realism, even as an ally of the French Revolution and precursor of the 1848 revolutions. In 1956 Walter Ulbricht sanctioned *Faust* as the national poem of the GDR: the future history of socialist Germany was to constitute 'the Third Part of Goethe's *Faust*'. GDR critics have indeed tended to interpret the fifth act of *Faust* Part Two in a positive or 'perfectibilist' light as the anticipation (though not the realization) of a socialist utopia – in sharp contrast to scholars in the Federal Republic, where the negative, tragic or satirical dimensions of Faust's utopian vision have been emphasized.

Nevertheless, the perception of Goethe in both parts of Germany after 1945, for all the ideological divergences, was predominantly positive; as in the post-1918 period, Goethe and the classical tradition were revered as a corrective to the traumas of the Hitler years. It was during the 1960s that this reassuring image was mercilessly torn down, initially from literary sources (Martin Walser and Peter Weiß) as a new and virulent *querelle des anciens et des modernes* was unleashed, then more spectacularly as a sociopolitical movement in the universities undermined the cultural consensus. 'Goethe's Weimar did not prevent Buchenwald' – once again, the dire association of the two sites was invoked. One of the slogans thrown up by the student revolution of 1968: 'Schmeißt die Germanistik tot! Färbt die blaue Blume rot!' (Batter German Studies dead! Colour the Blue Flower red!) was based on the perception that *Germanistik* stood for all forms of authority, cultural, political and pedagogic.

Once again, new literary models were proposed to replace the Weimar classics: Lenz, Herder, Lessing, Kleist, Jean Paul, Heine – indeed, anyone but Goethe (and, to a lesser extent, Schiller). More radically, revolutionary protest movements and figures from German literary and political history were brought onto the agenda of German studies: Jacobins like Georg Forster, *Junges Deutschland* and

Vormärz literature. The short-lived Republic of Mainz, whose swift collapse Goethe had witnessed at first hand, was dubiously hailed as the first German republic, as authentic predecessor of the inter-war and post-war republics. Popular literature (*Trivialliteratur*) was held to be more revealing of the realities of a historical period than the much-derided 'timelessness' or universality of the classics. Much of the hostility to Goethe was based on a hostility to authority of any kind, or to 'greatness' as such, whether out of an egalitarian resentment of greatness, or out of a contempt for the uncritical acceptance of traditionally or officially sanctioned exemplars.

In the German Democratic Republic, there was also a revision of the classics; but official GDR ideology was generally suspicious of the new iconoclastic ideologies of the west. After all, the socialist state saw itself as the true heir to Weimar Classicism, and the western cultural revolution was perceived, over-hopefully, as a stage in the endgame of capitalism or, alternatively, as a belated attempt by the western state at coming to terms with the past (*Vergangenheitsbewältigung*). In the GDR, ideologues continued their painstaking task of constructing a perception of Goethe relevant to present socialist realities, and scholars their valuable editorial work in the classical archives in Weimar.

The fifteen years or so of *Klassikerfeindlichkeit*, of radical hostility to classical authors, and to Goethe in particular, spent itself, though not without leaving its mark, around 1980. The anti-authoritarian stance of the 1960s and 1970s survived in the new (or rather revived) methodology of *Rezeptionsgeschichte*. The history of the reception of the classics was an antidote to the individual authority of critical pundits, it was a more objective or 'value-free' discipline; tracing the reception of literary works and authors through history was held to be less futile than seeking their present relevance or their value as such. The highly politicized, indeed often abusive, critique of classical or canonical literature also introduced a renewed awareness of the sociological context in which all literature, whether 'classical' or not, is rooted; W. H. Bruford's scrupulous studies of the social background to the German literary revival, of the theatre audiences and reading public of Goethe's day, which had been unfashionable when they first appeared in the 1930s and 1950s, became required reading for students of new-wave German studies, especially in Germany itself.

More recently, the whole purpose of strenuously drawing present-day relevance or perspectives from literary texts has been challenged, explicitly or implicitly, by the notion that we should not be alienated or embarrassed by the historicity of authors or their works, but should acknowledge their status as part of a historical heritage worthy of study in its own right. Walter Müller-Seidel's collection of essays published in 1983, though most were written previously, is pointedly entitled *Die Geschichtlichkeit der deutschen Klassik*. Katharina Mommsen, Dieter Borchmeyer, Hans Rudolf Vaget, Wolfgang Wittkowski and others have, in their different ways, also situated Goethe and German classical writers against the cultural, political and social traditions and currents of the age of Goethe, exemplifying a pluralistic and undogmatic scholarship that respects author, text and context. Karl Otto Conrady and Albrecht Schöne have answered the anti-authoritarian impulses of the 1960s and 1970s, and have given their own –

authoritative – judgements of Goethe's work. The renewed turbulence created by the reunification of Germany is still too close to assess, though it appears to have left West German Marxists as the official, indeed almost the sole, representatives of that tradition. It might be feared that much of value in GDR criticism is in danger of being discarded, just as many scholars were dismissed from their posts in the 'New Bundesländer'.

The reception of Goethe in Britain has been very much less fraught with political ideologies; indeed, in extreme contrast to his fate in Germany, he has been threatened rather with cultural neglect or indifference. Nevertheless, his contemporary reception in Britain was vibrant, at least on either side of the Napoleonic Wars and the resultant blockades, and Goethe in turn was appreciative of his British audience and grateful to his 'English friends' for information both on his own standing and on the state of literature in this country. Many Britons travelled to Weimar and enjoyed warm relations with Goethe: Henry Crabb Robinson, Joseph Charles Mellish, James Henry Lawrence, Charles Gore and his two daughters, Charles des Voeux (who translated *Tasso* in 1827), and, latterly, Thackeray. Young Englishmen flocked to Weimar, drawn at least as much to Goethe's engaging daughter-in-law Ottilie as to the Sage of Weimar himself.

   Werther had of course appeared in many translations from 1779, provoking the same mixed reactions as it had in Germany. The *London Magazine* opined that suicide 'was placed in a too favourable point of view', while another reviewer considered that 'an excellent moral may be deduced from it – if the reader pleases'. Walter Scott's reception of *Götz von Berlichingen* was rapturous; he translated it in 1798–9, and it informed the romantic medievalism of his own historical novels and balladry – a literary debt Scott was to repay more than fully to Europe over the following years. Matthew Gregory Lewis was introduced to Goethe in 1792, translated 'Erlkönig', 'Der Fischer' and other early poems, and shortly after reading the *Faust* fragment of 1790 published his novel *The Monk* in 1795. *Iphigenie* was translated by William Taylor in 1793, *Clavigo* and *Stella* were translated in 1798, and *Hermann und Dorothea* by Thomas Holcroft in 1801. The first full translation of *Faust* Part One was by Francis Leveson Gower in 1823 – a much criticized version, and one of which Goethe himself did not approve. *Die Wahlverwandtschaften* was not translated into English until 1854.

   The impetus for a renewed interest in Goethe and Germany was provided by Madame de Staël's *De l'Allemagne*, which was reissued in London in 1813. Shelley and Byron received the first part of *Faust* more enthusiastically than their contemporaries. Shelley translated the 'Prologue in Heaven' and the 'Walpurgisnacht' in 1822; Byron, who had little German, declared he 'would give the world to read *Faust* in the original', and dedicated his dramas *Werner* and *Sardanapalus* to 'the Illustrious Goethe . . . the first of existing writers, who has created the literature of his own country, and illustrated that of Europe'. Coleridge, who translated Schiller's *Wallenstein*, was also drawn to Goethe, but, wavering between interest and disapproval, resisted the temptation to translate *Faust*, fearing accusations of immorality or even blasphemy; the general public reception of the first part of *Faust* in Britain in the years following its publication is characterized by a reviewer in the *Monthly Review* in 1810, who described it as 'impure trash' from 'this wanton competitor of Aristophanes'. Wordsworth and Southey were also cautious towards Goethe, but both signed the birthday greeting organized by Carlyle in 1831 from 'fifteen English friends'.

After Crabb Robinson, it was Carlyle who, for all the wide divergences of temperament, culture and taste separating him from Goethe, did most to establish Goethe's reputation in Britain, translating *Wilhelm Meisters Lehrjahre* in 1824, and the first version of the *Wanderjahre* in 1827. He corresponded with Goethe between 1827 and 1832, sending him his version of the *Lehrjahre*, which was politely received, and his *Life of Schiller*, which was more warmly acknowledged. After Goethe's death, Carlyle continued to correspond with Eckermann and Varnhagen von Ense, and to foster interest in Goethe with essays that tended to shift the attention of the British public away from Goethe the poet – whom the Romantics had acknowledged in spite of their reservations – towards Goethe the sage, the thinker and exemplary teacher: for Carlyle, he was 'the wisest of our time', and for Matthew Arnold 'Europe's sagest head'.

It was to Carlyle that George Henry Lewes dedicated his *Life and Works of Goethe* in 1855, a biographical study that remained authoritative, in Germany and here, until well into the present century; it was only because it was rumoured that an Englishman was working on a biography of Goethe that the first German study was completed by a schoolmaster, Heinrich Viehoff, in 1854. G. H. Calvert published a biography in New York in 1872, and in the same year Alfred Mézières' study appeared in Paris. Lewes and George Eliot did much to introduce and explain Goethe to an English readership; she even defended *Die Wahlverwandtschaften* from its critics in Germany, and wrote a perceptive essay on *Wilhelm Meister*. Sarah Austin had translated biographical sketches and memoirs of Goethe since 1833, and kept him in the public mind – though in her 1857 review of Lewes she voiced stern disapproval of Goethe's 'moral indifference' and of his attitude to Napoleon. Matthew Arnold had been introduced to Goethe's writings by Carlyle, and Goethe became a constant standard of reference for Arnold, whose notion of culture drew heavily on Goethe. But even Arnold, like most of his contemporaries, rated the thinker ahead of the poet: 'It is by no means as the greatest of poets that Goethe deserved the pride and praise of his German countrymen. It is as the clearest, the largest, most helpful thinker of modern times' (*A French Critic of Goethe*).

No doubt in part as a reverse effect of the national celebration of Goethe in Wilhelmine Germany, Goethe's reputation in Britain waned, save among a small number of literati and expatriate Germans, in the last part of the century – though the English Goethe Society was founded in London by Max Müller in 1886 (his inaugural address was on Goethe and Carlyle), and branches spread to Oxford, Cambridge, Birmingham, Edinburgh, Glasgow and Manchester. Two world wars did little to enhance Goethe's standing except in academic and literary circles, though it would be crude to attribute the twentieth-century neglect of Goethe in Britain entirely to jingoism, insularity or philistinism; such factors have after all not affected the appreciation of German classical music or of German *Lieder*, many of which are indeed settings of Goethe's poems. It must be concluded that the language problem is the principal barrier to Goethe abroad, together with the fact that there has been no classic translation of his collected works comparable to that of Shakespeare into German by August Wilhelm Schlegel and his collaborators. An additional factor is no doubt the stuffy or ponderous image of Goethe deriving from his Victorian associations – or, more accurately (for Goethe was no 'Victorian' in any sense of the term) from the Victorian associations of those like Carlyle, Lewes, Arnold or Walter Pater, through whom Goethe was mediated to the British public, and who themselves fell drastically out of fashion in the 1920s and 1930s.

This was particularly true for the generation of Aldous Huxley and D. H. Lawrence, who detested the 'perversity of intellectualized sex' and the didactic pieties of *Wilhelm Meister*. T. S. Eliot's notorious judgement that 'of Goethe perhaps it is truer to say that he dabbled in both philosophy and poetry and made no great success of either' is, as Eliot himself concedes, based on 'an unfortunate limitation and prejudice' and on an inability on his part to 'enjoy' Goethe; but it is not untypical of the wary approach of much of the English-speaking world to Goethe.[6] Stephen Spender and W. H. Auden were more positive in their judgement of Goethe, at least as a poet – for Spender he was 'the most European modern genius'; but he has remained a distant, if imposing, figure for most in this country outside the academic and literary world. Certainly, he has enjoyed nothing like the appreciation of Shakespeare by readers and audiences in Germany – which has at times been at least equal to Shakespeare's popularity in his own country.

In 1936 an article in the *Evening Standard* summarized a common perception of Goethe:

> Goethe is no longer automatically included, as he once was, among the little group of world geniuses. The spirit of the age is against his heavy romanticism; and, as Robert Louis Stevenson pointed out, his life counts against him heavily. He was a snob of the most obvious sort, who treasured a handkerchief into which Napoleon had blown his nose and kept his mistress in the kitchen because of her bad table manners.[7]

The bicentenary of Goethe's birth in 1949 saw more positive public judgements in the British press, with articles entitled 'A Great European', 'The German Giant', 'Goethe the World Citizen', perhaps reflecting a certain European idealism in the post-war years; but several writers also stressed his 'egotism'. He was hailed as 'an inspiration to all those who, today, are painfully laying the foundations of a united Europe' (the *Socialist Leader*), but also guyed as 'a kind of Pooh-Bah to the hobbledehoy Duke of Weimar' (*The Listener*). In *John O' London's Weekly*, B. Ifor Jones mused: 'I would have liked to see Goethe faced with this more tragic age in which we find ourselves. . . . Would he have been so confident?'[8]

If Goethe's reputation in this country has been threatened by indifference or neglect, he has been largely unburdened with the weight of his own country's triumphs and traumas, hopes and despairs. But that does not mean that he has escaped the shifting fashions of literary methodologies and ideologies, and Goethe is not the most popular figure in the university syllabus today in the aftermath of the revulsion from 'great' or 'classical' literature touched on above. Nevertheless, the academic Goethe industry can be said to be flourishing in many British and American universities as a vast scholarly and critical encrustation builds up around his work. In North America especially, much work is done on Goethe by anglophone and German–American scholars, to swell the mass of material from Europe, Japan and other parts of the world. The present-day scholar is faced with an ocean of primary and secondary material that no individual, however narrow his specialism, can cope with adequately: the number of entries in the 1995 *Goethe-Jahrbuch* for the previous year alone amounted to 838 items.

We have so much documentation on Goethe that we know more about his moods, his meals, his daily routine and his views on this and that than we can remember about our own. Not only has Goethe criticism become almost immeasurable, it has tended in recent years to become more technical, more jargonized and more polemical, to the extent that it often presents as *Forschungsbericht* or *état présent*, as criticism of criticism – or of critics. But Goethe must be reinterpreted and re-presented to each generation, just as he must be retranslated for readers without German; it would be absurd if we were to be confined, say, to Anna Swanwick's or Bayard Taylor's nineteenth-century *Faust* translations, or to early twentieth-century versions of Goethe in English. Indeed, one of the most encouraging signs for the anglophone reader or interpreter of Goethe is the number of new translations of his writings that have appeared recently, as collected or as individual works.

Goethe was, for those who did not know him or of whom he did not approve, an intimidating figure; and yet many eyewitness accounts testify to his personal warmth and magnetism and, above all in his younger days, his infectious sociability and easy companionship. He had many personal foibles of conduct and outlook: a disciplined routine verging on pedantry, a formality verging on cold aloofness, a sense of propriety verging on the sanctimonious, a sense of deference verging on the obsequious, and prejudices verging on the cranky – he detested coffee, tobacco, dogs and people who wore spectacles in public. He is not easily categorized in any terms. The poet who wrote the enthralling platonic love-poem 'Warum gabst du uns die tiefen Blicke' also wrote the coarsely anatomical vulgarities of *Hanswursts Hochzeit*; the profoundly moving tribute to Schiller in the 'Epilog zu Schillers "Glocke"' came from the same pen as the brutal character assassinations of the *Xenien*; the scathing, indeed scabrous critic of church ritual and dogma also wrote majestic hymns to the glory of God's creation; the mind that created Faust also created Mephistopheles; the writer who deferred to, and was lionized by, the highest social and political circles could empathize with the whores of Venice, the stocking-weavers of Apolda and the 'poor moles' who worked the mines of Ilmenau; the man who as Privy Councillor of the Duchy of Weimar supported (or at least did not oppose) the retention of the death penalty for infanticides also gave us the harrowing account of the fate of the infanticide Gretchen.

It is not always easy to penetrate the aura of reverence, or to dismantle the barriers of resistance and hostility, that surround Goethe's reputation. It is hoped that this volume might help to make Goethe's life and work more accessible to the non-specialist as well as to the conscripted student; it would be sad indeed if Goethe's gifts were available only to the student of German literature.

Notes

The main source of reference for Goethe's works is the *Frankfurter Ausgabe*. Since this edition is not yet quite complete, reference has also been made where necessary to the *Weimarer Ausgabe* and the Artemis *Gedenkausgabe*. In the notes, these editions are abbreviated respectively to FA, WA and GA. Correspondence to or from Goethe is identified by names and dates only; correspondence between others about Goethe is cited from *Goethe in vertraulichen Briefen seiner Zeitgenossen, zusammengestellt von Wilhelm Bode* (abbreviated: Bode). Conversations are identified by names and dates, and by reference to the 1909–11 edition of *Goethes Gespräche*, ed. F. von Biedermann (abbreviated: Biedermann); although more modern editions are available, this is still the most comprehensive edition of Goethe's conversations. References to poems are given to the *Frankfurter Ausgabe* and, where appropriate, to *Goethe: Gedichte*, ed. Erich Trunz (= Vol. 1, *Hamburger Ausgabe*, abbreviated: Trunz). Titles of critical books and articles are given in the notes in shortened form throughout; full publication details of all the above sources are given in the bibliography. Certain editions of authors other than Goethe, which are not included in the bibliography, are cited in full in the notes.

Notes to Chapter 1

1 Letter to Knebel, 12 September 1830.
2 See *Campagne in Frankreich* (FA. 16, 436) and letter to Knebel, 27 September 1792.
3 See Eric A. Blackall, *The Emergence of German as a Literary Language*.
4 *Campagne in Frankreich* (FA. 16, 571).
5 *Dichtung und Wahrheit*, Book 5 (FA. 14, 198–227).
6 'Vom Vater hab ich die Statur' (FA. 2, 682 and Trunz, 320).
7 *Dichtung und Wahrheit*, Book 1 (FA. 14, 36–7).
8 *Dichtung und Wahrheit*, Book 7 (FA. 14, 293–4).
9 *Dichtung und Wahrheit*, Book 8 (FA. 14, 369–73).
10 *Von deutscher Art und Kunst*, in Johann Gottfried Herder, *Werke in zwei Bänden*, ed. Karl-Gustav Gerold (Munich, 1953), Vol. 1, p. 885.
11 *Dichtung und Wahrheit*, Book 19 (FA. 14, 811).
12 *Dichtung und Wahrheit*, Book 20 (FA. 14, 852).

13   'Auf Miedings Tod' (FA. 1, 1064 and Trunz, 115).

14   Letter to Charlotte von Stein, 19 January 1778.

15   Letter to Karl August, 3 November 1786.

16   *Italienische Reise*, Naples, 23 March 1787 (FA. 15/1, 236–7).

17   See W. Daniel Wilson, *Geheimräte gegen Geheimbünde*, p. 138 and *passim*.

18   *Italienische Reise*, Palermo, 13–14 April 1787 (FA. 15/1, 272–83 and 15/2, 1110–18).

19   *Italienische Reise*, Rome, October 1787 (FA. 15/1, 452).

20   See K. R. Eissler, *Goethe: A Psychoanalytic Study*. In his recent 'outing' of Goethe, Karl
     H. Pruys (*Die Liebkosungen des Tigers: Eine erotische Goethe-Biographie*, Berlin, 1997) claims
     to have proved conclusively that Goethe was homosexual, or at least bisexual. Pruys's
     sensationalized claim is by no means new; it has been suggested that Goethe's
     relations with Christoph Heinrich Kniep in Sicily, with Charlotte von Stein's son
     Fritz, or even with Karl August, might have been, covertly or overtly, homosexual.
     Pruys firmly identifies Goethe's Düsseldorf friend Friedrich Heinrich Jacobi as his
     sexual partner. In the absence of proof either way, and given the complexity of the
     phenomenon, such speculations cannot finally be ruled out; but the evidence in all
     cases is exiguous and quite inconclusive, and Pruys appears to misinterpret, or to over-
     interpret, the extravagantly emotional language of much eighteenth-century corre-
     spondence. To be sure, Goethe was perfectly aware of the pederastic connotations of
     the Ganymede myth – though his poem exploits these only allusively; there are
     distinct pederastic overtones in the assault on the boy in 'Erlkönig'; the tensions
     between Clavigo and Carlos can be perceived as potentially or actually homosexual;
     and bisexuality appears to be a feature of Hatem's relations with Suleika and Saki in
     the 'Schenkenbuch' of the *West-östliche Divan*. Mephistopheles' pederastic lust for the
     young angel in *Faust*, lines 11759ff. is presumably an acknowledgement of the Devil's
     eclectic sexuality. All these instances are of course within the fictitious context of the
     imaginative works. Goethe's only recorded comment on homosexuality (or 'Greek
     love') is that it is an 'aberration' of aesthetic perceptions into the 'coarsely physical';
     pederasty is as old as humanity itself, so it can be said to be within nature, though
     it is also 'against nature' (conversation with Friedrich von Müller, 7 April 1830;
     Biedermann 4, 261).

21   Conversation with Friedrich von Müller, 30 May 1814 (Biedermann 2, 228).

22   *Italienische Reise*, Rome, April 1788 (FA. 15/1, 596–7). Translation is based on the
     German text.

23   Letter from Schiller to Körner, 9 March 1789 (Bode 1, 392).

24   For an informative account of the French Campaign, Goethe's report of it, and the
     political context of the time, see Thomas P. Saine, *Black Bread – White Bread: German
     Intellectuals and the French Revolution*.

25   *Die romantische Schule*, Book 1, in Heinrich Heine, *Werke. Säkularausgabe*, Vol. 8 (Berlin
     and Paris, 1972), p. 31.

26   Letter to Zelter, 1 June 1805.

27   *Unterredung mit Napoleon* (FA. 17, 376–84).

28   Conversation with Eckermann, 10 February 1830 (Biedermann 4, 207).

29   Conversation with Eckermann, 17 February 1830 (Biedermann 4, 215).

30   'Jedem Alter des Menschen . . . ' (FA. 13, 237).

31   Letter of 26 October 1813 (Bode 2, 592–3). See also conversation with Luden, 13
     December 1813 (Biedermann 2, 214–16).

32   As note 4.

33   See 'An Lord Byron' (FA. 2, 583–4 and Trunz, 348), and 'Stark von Faust, gewandt
     im Rat' (FA. 2, 703–4 and Trunz, 349); conversations with Friedrich von Müller, 20

November 1824 (Biedermann 3, 141–2) and with Eckermann, 24 February 1825 (Biedermann 3, 161–5); *Manfred* (GA. 14, 785–8); *Byrons Don Juan* (GA. 14, 789–92); and *Goethes Beitrag zum Andenken Lord Byrons* (GA. 14, 796–9).

34   Letter to Wilhelm von Humboldt, 17 March 1832.
35   Letter to Zelter, 11 May 1820.
36   Letter to Zelter, 19 March 1827.
37   'Prooemion' (FA. 2, 489 and Trunz, 357). See below, pp. 119–20.
38   Undispatched letter to Zelter, 21 June 1827 (see WA. IV, 42, 376).
39   See John R. Williams, 'Die Rache der Kraniche. Goethe, *Faust II* und die Julirevolution'.

Notes to Chapter 2

1   For a brief discussion, see John R. Williams, 'Goethe: the Crisis of the Lyric Poet?'
2   See the section *Lyrisches* in FA. 2, 447–81.
3   Quoted in *Publications of the English Goethe Society*, New Series 20 (1951), p. 164.
4   *Dichtung und Wahrheit*, Book 13 (FA. 14, 630–3).
5   *Dichtung und Wahrheit*, Book 11 (FA. 14, 544–5).
6   These obscure lines might be glossed by reference to a similar intuition invoked in Goethe's later essay *Granit* (see below, p. 270 and FA. 25, 315).
7   *Zum Schäkespears Tag* (GA. 4, 125).
8   FA. 1, 1035–9 and Trunz, 392–400.
9   See Albrecht Schöne, *Götterzeichen, Liebeszauber, Satanskult*, pp. 26ff.
10   *Ballade, Betrachtung und Auslegung* (GA. 2, 612–15 and Trunz, 400–2).
11   *Von deutscher Art und Kunst*, ed. cit. (as note 10 to Chapter 1), p. 852.
12   Ibid., pp. 847, 851–3, 864–5 and *passim*.
13   Ibid., pp. 862–3.
14   *Dichtung und Wahrheit*, Book 19 (FA. 14, 811).
15   Conversation of 23 October 1828 (Biedermann 4, 41–5).
16   Letter to Wieland, April 1776.
17   *Nordlicht* (FA. 25, 197).
18   Printed in FA. 1, 965 and Trunz, 525.
19   See John R. Williams, 'Goethe's "An den Mond": Controversy and Criticism'.
20   See Osman Durrani, 'The Fortunes of Goethe's Nocturnal Traveller. "Über allen Gipfeln ist Ruh"'.
21   *Iphigenie auf Tauris*, lines 317–18.
22   See FA. 1, 1046 and Trunz, 147 and 536.
23   *Iphigenie auf Tauris*, lines 1726–66.
24   Conversation of 3 November 1823 (Biedermann 3, 35).
25   Letter to Charlotte von Stein, 19 January 1778.
26   See *Volkslieder* in Herder, ed. cit. (as note 10 to Chapter 1), Vol. 1, pp. 320–2.
27   With the exception of 'Der Sänger', the songs of the Harfenspieler and Mignon are not printed by Trunz in Volume One of the *Hamburger Ausgabe*, but in their context in the Wilhelm Meister novel. Most editions also print them separately among the poems – see for example *Frankfurter Ausgabe*, 2, 103 and 321–3.
28   *Wilhelm Meisters theatralische Sendung*, Book 2, Chapter 3 (FA. 9, 81–2).
29   None of the four 'apocryphal' elegies are printed by Trunz. They can be found in most modern standard editions of Goethe's works (see *Frankfurter Ausgabe*, 1, 392–4,

420–2 and 440–1). They are also translated in *Goethe: Roman Elegies and The Diary*, trans. David Luke, introd. Hans Rudolf Vaget, and in *Goethe: Erotic Poems*, trans. David Luke, introd. Hans Rudolf Vaget.

30 See *Goethe: Roman Elegies and The Diary*, ed. cit., pp. 15–16, and *Goethes erotische Gedichte*, ed. Andreas Ammer (Frankfurt am Main and Leipzig, 1991), pp. 186 and 197.

31 Not all the published *Venetian Epigrams* are printed by Trunz. They are cited by number here as in the full collections (see for example *Frankfurter Ausgabe*, 1, 443–64), not as numbered by Trunz. Trunz prints none of Goethe's unpublished epigrams, and they are unnumbered in most editions. They are cited here by first lines; see for example *Frankfurter Ausgabe*, 1, 465–78. A selection from the published and unpublished epigrams is translated in *Goethe: Erotic Poems*, trans. David Luke, introd. Hans Rudolf Vaget, pp. 65–97.

32 Martial, *Epigrams*, Book 9, 67 ('Lascivam tota possedi nocte puellam').

33 See Albrecht Schöne, *Götterzeichen, Liebeszauber, Satanskult*, pp. 55–63.

34 Ibid., pp. 74–97.

35 'Compensation and Economy of Growth', in Chapter 5 of Charles Darwin, *The Origin of Species* (London, 1900), pp. 182–3. See also below, p. 264.

36 The *Xenien* referred to here are numbered as in Trunz.

37 See FA. 2, 1082–3.

38 Letter to Schiller, 22 June 1797.

39 Conversation with Eckermann, 29 January 1827 (Biedermann 3, 335), and *Ballade, Betrachtung und Auslegung* (GA. 2, 612–13 and Trunz, 400).

40 See FA. 3/1, 549–51.

41 *Noten und Abhandlungen zu besserem Verständnis des West-östlichen Divans* (FA. 3/1, 223).

42 The *Sprüche* are numbered here as in Trunz.

43 Conversation with Friedrich von Müller, 20 November 1824 (Biedermann 3, 142).

44 FA. 2, 1099–100 and 25, 242 and Trunz, 408. Both the poem and Goethe's commentary were translated into English and first published bilingually in *Gold's London Magazine* in July 1821.

45 See Trunz, 403–7.

46 FA. 13, 237.

47 In the conclusion to the *Critique of Practical Reason*; see *Immanuel Kants Werke*, ed. Ernst Cassirer et al. (Berlin, 1912–22), Vol. 5, p. 174.

48 See FA. 2, 1061–3.

49 Letter to Zelter, 31 October 1831.

50 *Schriften zur Kunst. Wilhelm Tischbeins Idyllen IX* (GA. 13, 898).

51 See conversation with Eckermann, 3 May 1827 (Biedermann 3, 384).

52 See Eckermann's report dated July/August 1828 (Biedermann 4, 11–12).

Notes to Chapter 3

1 Letter to Cornelia Goethe, 7 December 1765.

2 *Dichtung und Wahrheit*, Book 7 (FA. 14, 311).

3 Ibid., p. 312.

4 *Dichtung und Wahrheit*, Book 13 (FA. 14, 621).

5 *Von deutscher Art und Kunst*, ed. cit. (as note 10 to Chapter 1), p. 895.

6 *Zum Schäkespears Tag* (GA. 4, 125).

7 *Geschichte Gottfriedens von Berlichingen* (FA. 4, 247).

8 Letter to Zelter, 11 May 1820.
9 *Dichtung und Wahrheit*, Book 12 (FA. 14, 568).
10 Letter to Karl Friedrich Graf von Brühl, 1 October 1818.
11 Conversation with Eckermann, 12 February 1829 (Biedermann 4, 67).
12 Letter from Paul Wranitzky to Goethe, 6 February 1796.
13 *Dichtung und Wahrheit*, Book 20 (FA. 14, 840).
14 *Über Egmont, Trauerspiel von Goethe*, in *Schillers Werke, Nationalausgabe* (Weimar, 1943–84), Vol. 22, p. 203.
15 See for example M. W. Swales, 'A Questionable Politician: On the Ending of Goethe's *Egmont*'; T. J. Reed, *The Classical Centre*, pp. 51–3; G. A. Wells, 'Critical Issues concerning Goethe's *Egmont*'.
16 Notably E. M. Wilkinson, 'The Relation of Form and Meaning in Goethe's *Egmont*', and J. M. Ellis, 'The Vexed Question of Egmont's Political Judgement'.
17 *Über Egmont* (as note 14), p. 208.
18 See Erich Heller, 'Goethe and the Avoidance of Tragedy'.
19 *Dichtung und Wahrheit*, Book 20 (FA. 14, 840–1).
20 Letter to Charlotte von Stein, 6 March 1779.
21 *Italienische Reise*, Ferrara bis Rom, 19 October 1786 (FA. 15/1, 115).
22 Erich Heller, 'Goethe and the Avoidance of Tragedy', p. 32.
23 *Beantwortung der Frage: Was ist Aufklärung?*, in *Immanuel Kants Werke*, ed. cit. (as note 47 to Chapter 2), Vol. 4, p. 169.
24 Letter from Schiller to Körner, 21 January 1802 (Bode 2, 205).
25 Conversation with Eckermann, 6 May 1827 (Biedermann 3, 393–4).
26 Letter to F. J. Bertuch, 5 April 1788.
27 Letter from Karoline Herder to her husband, 20 March 1789 (Bode 1, 393).
28 *Italienische Reise*, Ferrara, 16 October 1786 (FA. 15/1, 107).
29 'Das Klassische nenne ich das Gesunde, und das Romantische das Kranke': conversation with Eckermann, 2 April 1829 (Biedermann 4, 81). See also conversation with Riemer, 28 August 1808 (Biedermann 1, 534–5).
30 Conversation with Eckermann, 4 January 1824 (Biedermann 3, 62).
31 Letter to Kayser, 14 August 1787.
32 See *Campagne in Frankreich* (FA. 16, 473 and 565–7); conversation with Eckermann, 15 February 1831 (Biedermann 4, 327); and conversation with Friedrich von Müller, 5 January 1831 (Biedermann 4, 317).
33 *Campagne in Frankreich* (FA. 16, 566).
34 Conversation with Eckermann, 4 January 1824 (Biedermann 3, 61).
35 In the political language of the time, 'democrat' was practically the equivalent of 'republican', even of 'revolutionary'. Nevertheless, Goethe affirmed to Eckermann many years later that the 'entirely respectable' views of the Countess were, and still are, his own (conversation with Eckermann, 4 January 1824; Biedermann 3, 61).
36 Ibid.
37 *Bedeutende Fördernis durch ein einziges geistreiches Wort* (FA. 6, 1122).
38 Letter to Schiller, 9 March 1802. See also *Die natürliche Tochter*, lines 2783–808.
39 Goethe alluded to this incident, but forbore to detail Herder's remark (see *Verhältnis zu Herder*, FA. 17, 364–5). Accounts of Herder's remark differ; according to one source, his words were 'After all, I still prefer your natural son to your "Natural Daughter"' (see *Goethes Gespräche*, ed. Wolfgang Herwig, Vol. 1, pp. 887–8 and Vol. 4, p. 163). Either way, the comment, if authentic, was characteristically malicious, even allowing for Herder's poor health, and the two never met again: Herder died at the end of that year (1803).

40   FA. 6, 251.
41   *Italienische Reise: Das römische Carneval* (FA. 15/1, 518ff.).
42   'Was haben wir nicht für Kränze gewunden!' (FA. 2, 743).
43   Letter from Iffland to Goethe, 28 May 1814.
44   See Albrecht Schöne, *Götterzeichen, Liebeszauber, Satanskult*, pp. 210ff.
45   Letter to Schiller, 5 May 1798.
46   See FA. 7/1, 593–6.
47   Letters to Wilhelm von Humboldt and Sulpiz Boisserée, 22 October 1826.
48   See conversation with Riemer (date uncertain: Biedermann 4, 414) and conversation
     with Eckermann, 17 February 1831 (Biedermann 4, 329).
49   *Über epische und dramatische Dichtung* (GA. 14, 367–70).
50   Conversation with Eckermann, date uncertain (Biedermann 4, 305–6).
51   See Katharina Mommsen, *Natur- und Fabelreich in Faust II*, pp. 183ff.
52   See John R. Williams, *Goethe's 'Faust'*, pp. 155–7.
53   As Goethe put it, Helen was to appear in Sparta 'on the cothurnus of ancient tragedy'
     (*auf antik-tragischem Kothurn*): see *Helena. Zwischenspiel zu Faust*, WA. I, 41/2, 292 and GA.
     5, 574).
54   FA. 7/1, 706.
55   *Dichtung und Wahrheit*, Book 4 (FA. 14, 174).
56   Conversation with Eckermann, 6 June 1831 (Biedermann 4, 374).
57   Ibid.
58   See FA. 7/1, 723 and 724.
59   See FA. 7/1, 733.
60   Conversation with Eckermann, 6 June 1831 (Biedermann 4, 375).
61   Ibid. (Biedermann 4, 374).
62   Conversation with Eckermann, 6 May 1827 (Biedermann 3, 394).

Notes to Chapter 4

1   Conversation with Eckermann, 10 February 1829 (Biedermann 4, 65).
2   Letter to Kestner, 2 May 1783.
3   Letter to Charlotte von Stein, 25 June 1786.
4   Conversation of 2 August 1829 (Biedermann 4, 135).
5   The rendering of *Wanderjahre* (strictly, years of travelling) by 'journeyman's years'
    exploits a fortuitous, but secondary, connotation. The English term journeyman refers
    primarily not to travel, but to a qualified craftsman who hires out his skills by the day
    (*journée*); the German term *Geselle* has no connotation of travel. Since, however, it
    was traditional, in Germany and elsewhere, for journeyman craftsmen to travel in
    search of work experience after the completion of their apprenticeship, the term
    'journeyman' seems appropriate to describe Wilhelm Meister's years of travel as a
    journeyman.
6   Letter from Schiller to Goethe, 2 July 1796.
7   For an account of the contemporary reception of the novel, see Klaus F. Gille,
    'Wilhelm Meister' im Urteil der Zeitgenossen.
8   Novalis, *Schriften*, ed. Richard Samuel et al. (Stuttgart, 1960–88), Vol. 3, pp. 638–9
    and 646–7.
9   *Über Goethes Meister*, in *Kritische Friedrich-Schlegel-Ausgabe*, ed. Ernst Behler (Munich,
    1958–), Vol. 2, p. 146.

10 *Wilhelm Meisters Lehrjahre*, Book 8, Chapter 5 (FA. 9, 927–35) and Book 5, Chapter 3 (FA. 9, 659).
11 Conversations with Heinrich Laube, 1809 (Biedermann 2, 62) and with Eckermann, 17 February 1830 (Biedermann 4, 215).
12 *Die Wahlverwandtschaften*, Part 2, Chapter 11 (FA. 8, 479).
13 *Tag- und Jahreshefte 1809* (FA. 17, 226).
14 Conversation with Riemer, 28 August 1808 (Biedermann 1, 534).
15 Goethe, *Elective Affinities*, trans. David Constantine, p. xx.
16 Letter from F. H. Jacobi to Friedrich Köppen, 12 January 1810 (Bode 2, 453).
17 Conversation with Eckermann, 21 January 1827 (Biedermann 3, 330) and letter to C. F. Reinhard, 21 February 1810.
18 See FA. 8, 974.
19 Ibid.
20 *Dichtung und Wahrheit*, Book 20 (FA. 14, 839ff.).
21 See Norbert Bolz (ed.), *Goethes Wahlverwandtschaften. Kritische Modelle und Diskursanalysen zum Mythos Literatur*, pp. 214ff., 326ff., 338ff. and *passim*; and Waltraud Wiethölter in FA. 8, 984–1017.
22 See FA. 8, 1017ff.
23 See H. B. Nisbet, '*Die Wahlverwandtschaften*: Explanation and its Limits'.
24 See Hans Rudolf Vaget, *Goethe – Der Mann von 60 Jahren*, pp. 123ff.
25 Letter to Schiller, 12 July 1796.
26 Quoted by Emil Staiger, *Goethe*, Vol. 3, p. 135.
27 See *Tag- und Jahreshefte 1807* (FA. 17, 204).
28 See WA. I, 42/2, 444–6, and letter to Prince August von Gotha, 21 December 1795.
29 Letter to Friedrich von Trebra, 5 January 1814.
30 I refer to the suggestion by Thomas P. Saine in the course of a discussion of *Hermann und Dorothea* (*Black Bread – White Bread: German Intellectuals and the French Revolution*, pp. 385–7) that in 1795 Goethe, though himself a Rhinelander, appeared willing to accept Prussian neutrality under the Treaty of Basel, conceding French possession of the left bank for the sake of peace, and in order to safeguard the German territories east of the Rhine – for the time being, at least – from invasion.
31 Conversation with Eckermann, 29 January 1827 (Biedermann 3, 335).
32 'Amerika, du hast es besser' (FA. 2, 739 and Trunz, 333). See *Wilhelm Meisters Lehrjahre*, Book 8, Chapter 7 (FA. 9, 944–5) and *Wilhelm Meisters Wanderjahre*, FA. 10, 342–5, 686ff., 723 and *passim*. See also Wynfried Kriegleder, 'Wilhelm Meisters Amerika. Das Bild der vereinigten Staaten in den *Wanderjahren*'.
33 Conversation with Eckermann, 18 January 1827 (Biedermann 3, 325).
34 Ibid.
35 FA. 16, 569.
36 FA. 16, 570.

Notes to Chapter 5

1 Letter to Zelter, 22 June 1808. See also *Aus Makariens Archiv*, FA. 10, 760.
2 *Ferneres über Mathematik und Mathematiker* (FA. 25, 90).
3 Conversation with Eckermann, 20 December 1826 (Biedermann 3, 304).
4 FA. 13, 153 and FA. 25, 119.
5 See letter to Georg Sartorius, 19 July 1810.

6   *Zur Farbenlehre. Didaktischer Teil*, § 175 (FA. 23/1, 81).
7   *Erläuterungen zu dem aphoristischen Aufsatz 'Die Natur'* (FA. 25, 81).
8   *Älteres, beinahe Veraltetes* (FA. 25, 62).
9   In letter to Schiller, 10 October 1795. See WA. IV, 10, 312.
10 *Verhandlungen mit Herrn Boisserée den Regenbogen betreffend* (FA. 25, 839–46).
11 *Tag- und Jahreshefte 1810* (FA. 17, 234).
12 See FA. 23/2, plate 36.
13 *Zur Farbenlehre. Didaktischer Teil*, § 802 (FA. 23/1, 256).
14 FA. 25, 97–8.
15 See Albrecht Schöne, *Goethes Farbentheologie*.
16 Charles Darwin, *The Origin of Species* (London, 1900), pp. 182–3.
17 *Glückliches Ereignis* (FA. 24, 436–7).
18 See letters from Schiller to Goethe, 12 and 19 January 1798; letter to Wilhelm von
    Humboldt, 3 December 1795; and *Erster Entwurf einer allgemeinen Einleitung in die
    vergleichende Anatomie* (FA. 24, 248).
19 Letters to Herder and to Charlotte von Stein, 27 March 1784.
20 George A. Wells, *Goethe and the Development of Science*, pp. 16–17.
21 Charles Darwin, *The Origin of Species* (London, 1900), p. xx.
22 *Fossiler Stier* (FA. 24, 553–60, esp. 555).
23 Letter to Zelter, 5 October 1831.
24 *Granit II* (FA. 25, 312–16).
25 See FA. 25, 1025 and WA. II, 12, 233.
26 *Wolkengestalt nach Howard* (FA. 25, 215).
27 FA. 25, 314.
28 Compare FA. 25, 259; FA. 25, 296; and conversation with Eckermann, 11 April 1827
    (Biedermann 3, 368).
29 Quoted by Stephen Prickett, *Coleridge and Wordsworth: The Poetry of Growth*, Cambridge,
    1970, pp. 7–8.
30 These quotations from: *Coleridge on the Seventeenth Century*, ed. Roberta F. Brinkley,
    Durham, NC, 1955, pp. 403, 401 and 397–8.
31 H. B. Nisbet, *Goethe and the Scientific Tradition*, p. 74.
32 Richard Dawkins, 'Science, Delusion and the Appetite for Wonder', Twenty-first
    Richard Dimbleby Lecture (BBC 1, 12 November 1996).

Notes to Conclusion

1   For a comprehensive survey and documentation of the reception of Goethe in
    Germany, see Karl Robert Mandelkow, *Goethe in Deutschland* and *Goethe im Urteil seiner
    Kritiker*. The present summary is much indebted to both works.
2   'Der wahre Statthalter des poetischen Geistes auf Erden' (*Blüthenstaub*, 106). See
    Novalis, *Schriften*, ed. cit. (as note 8 to Chapter 4), Vol. 2, p. 459.
3   Quoted by Mandelkow, *Goethe in Deutschland*, Vol. 1, p. 75.
4   Conversation with Eckermann, 12 May 1825 (Biedermann 3, 205).
5   *Die romantische Schule*, Book 1, in Heine, *Werke*, ed. cit. (as note 25 to Chapter 1), Vol. 8,
    pp. 43–4.
6   T. S. Eliot, 'Introduction to Goethe', *The Nation and Athenaeum*, 12 January 1929, and
    The Use of Poetry and the Use of Criticism, London, 1933, p. 99.

7   *Evening Standard*, 25 February 1936. Quoted by Ann C. Weaver in *Publications of the English Goethe Society: Index to the Publications, 1886–1986*, Leeds, 1987, p. 6.
8   These remarks quoted in A. J. Dickson, 'Goethe in England 1909–1949: A Bibliography', *Publications of the English Goethe Society*, 19 (1951), pp. 1–46.

Bibliography

The bibliography aims to include the relevant works of reference, the principal modern standard editions of Goethe's works, correspondence and conversations in German and English, and the major works of criticism in German and English. I have listed a broad, but by no means comprehensive, selection of Goethe's works available in English translation, but have generally restricted this list to not more than two or three translations of the same work. In order to keep the bibliography within reasonable bounds, scholarly articles are cited very sparingly, and where collections of essays and articles are included, contributions have not been listed individually. With certain exceptions, *Festschriften* have not been included, nor have critical editions of individual texts.

Detailed bibliographies of critical literature on Goethe's works, individual and general, are included in the relevant volumes of the *Frankfurter Ausgabe* and the recent *Goethe-Handbuch*; the bibliography in the most recent edition of Peter Boerner's Rowohlt monograph on Goethe (1996) is also a valuable guide to works of reference, editions, collections and the major critical literature. Annual listings of work on Goethe can be found in *The Year's Work in Modern Language Studies*, in *Germanistik* and in the *Goethe-Jahrbuch*. Mention should also be made of the yearbooks devoted principally to Goethe studies: the Weimar *Goethe-Jahrbuch* (under various titles since 1880), the *Publications of the English Goethe Society* (since 1886), the *Chronik/Jahrbuch des Wiener Goethe-Vereins* (since 1887), the *Jahrbuch des Freien Deutschen Hochstifts* (since 1902), the *Jahrbuch der Sammlung Kippenberg* (since 1921) and the *Goethe Yearbook: Publications of the Goethe Society of North America* (since 1982).

Among the most notable recent projects in Goethe scholarship are, in German, the appearance of the Deutscher Klassiker Verlag *Frankfurter Ausgabe* and the Hanser *Münchner Ausgabe* of the collected works, and the Metzler *Goethe-Handbuch*; all are currently in progress, and should be completed shortly. In English, major landmarks are the Suhrkamp edition of the *Collected Works* in translation, David Luke's verse translation of both parts of *Faust* in the Oxford World's Classics, John Whaley's verse translations of a wide selection of Goethe's poems, and Nicholas Boyle's OUP study of Goethe, of which one volume has appeared so far (two further volumes are in preparation). The 1995 CD-ROM edition of Goethe's works comprises the text of the *Weimarer Ausgabe* and *Goethes Gespräche*, ed. W. von Biedermann (1889–96).

1   Reference

Goethe-Bibliographie, Vol. 1 (–1954), ed. Hans Pyritz and Paul Raabe, Heidelberg, 1965; Vol. 2 (1955–64), ed. Heinz Nicolai and Gerhard Burkhardt, Heidelberg, 1968. Updated annually in *Goethe-Jahrbuch*.

Goethe-Bibliographie, ed. Helmut G. Hermann, Stuttgart, 1991.

Goethe-Handbuch, ed. Bernd Witte et al., Stuttgart and Weimar. Vol. 1: *Gedichte*, ed. Regine Otto and Bernd Witte, 1996; Vol. 2: *Dramen*, ed. Theo Buck, 1997; Vol. 3: *Prosaschriften*, ed. Bernd Witte, Peter Schmidt and Gernot Böhme, 1997. One further vol. in preparation.

Goethe-Wörterbuch, hg. von der Berlin-Brandenburgischen Akademie der Wissenschaften, der Akademie der Wissenschaften in Göttingen und der Heidelberger Akademie der Wissenschaften, Stuttgart, Berlin, Cologne, Mainz, 1978–. To date: A–F.

Goethe über seine Dichtungen. Versuch einer Sammlung aller Äußerungen des Dichters über seine poetischen Werke, ed. Hans Gerhard Gräf, 9 vols, Frankfurt am Main, 1901–14.

Der junge Goethe, ed. Hanna Fischer-Lamberg, 6 vols, Berlin, 1963–74.

Goethes Leben von Tag zu Tag. Eine dokumentarische Chronik, ed. Robert Steiger, 8 vols, Zürich and Munich, 1982–96.

Dobel, Richard (ed.), *Lexikon der Goethe-Zitate*, Zürich, 1968.

Hansen, Volkmar (ed.), *Goethe in seiner Zeit. Goethe-Museum Düsseldorf. Katalog der ständigen Ausstellung*, Düsseldorf, 1993.

Holtzhauer, Helmut (ed.), *Goethe-Museum. Werk, Leben und Zeit Goethes in Dokumenten*, Berlin and Weimar, 1969.

2   Goethe's Works, Correspondence and Conversations (German)

Goethes Werke. Hg. im Auftrage der Großherzogin Sophie von Sachsen, IV sections, 143 vols, Weimar, 1887–1919 (*Weimarer Ausgabe*). Reprinted with supplementary vols, Munich, 1987–90.

Goethes Werke auf CD-ROM. Weimarer Ausgabe, Cambridge (Chadwyck-Healcy), 1995.

Goethe. Gedenkausgabe der Werke, Briefe und Gespräche, ed. Ernst Beutler, 24 vols +3, Zürich, 1948–71 (*Gedenkausgabe*).

Goethes Werke, ed. Erich Trunz, 14 vols, Hamburg, 1948–64 (*Hamburger Ausgabe*). Paperback edn, Munich, 1982.

Goethe, *Gedichte*, ed. and comm. Erich Trunz, 15th edn, Munich, 1994 (=*Hamburger Ausgabe*, Vol. 1).

Goethe, *Sämtliche Werke nach Epochen seines Schaffens*, ed. Karl Richter et al., Munich, 1985– (*Münchner Ausgabe*).

Goethe, *Sämtliche Werke, Briefe, Tagebücher und Gespräche*, ed. Hendrik Birus et al., 40 vols, Frankfurt am Main, 1987– (*Frankfurter Ausgabe*).

Goethe, *Die Schriften zur Naturwissenschaft. Hg. im Auftrage der Deutschen Akademie der Naturforscher Leopoldina*, 20+ vols, ed. Günther Schmid, Dorothea Kuhn et al., Weimar, 1947– (*Leopoldina Ausgabe*).

Corpus der Goethezeichnungen, ed. Gerhard Femmel et al., 7 vols (in 10), Leipzig, 1958–73.

Goethes Briefe, ed. Karl Robert Mandelkow, 4 vols, Hamburg, 1962–7.

Briefe an Goethe, ed. Karl Robert Mandelkow, 2 vols. Hamburg, 1965–9.

Briefe an Goethe. Gesamtausgabe in Regestform, ed. Karl-Heinz Hahn et al., *c.*14 vols, 5 to date, Weimar, 1980–.

Goethe in vertraulichen Briefen seiner Zeitgenossen. Zusammengestellt von Wilhelm Bode, ed. Regine Otto and Paul-Gerhard Wenzlaff, 3 vols, Berlin and Weimar, 1979.

Goethes Gespräche. Gesamtausgabe, ed. Flodoard Freiherr von Biedermann, 5 vols, Leipzig, 1909–11.

Goethes Gespräche. Eine Sammlung zeitgenössischer Berichte aus seinem Umgang, ed. Wolfgang Herwig, 5 vols (in 6), Zürich, 1965–87.

Eckermann, Johann Peter, *Gespräche mit Goethe in den letzten Jahren seines Lebens*, ed. Ernst Beutler, Zürich, 1948 (=Vol. 24 of *Gedenkausgabe*).
Goethe. Begegnungen und Gespräche, ed. Ernst Grumach and Renate Grumach, 5 vols to date, Berlin, 1965–.

3   Goethe's Works, Correspondence and Conversations (English)

Collected Works. Suhrkamp Edition in 12 Volumes, ed. Victor Lange et al., Cambridge, Mass., 1983–9. Paperback edn, Princeton, 1994.
Selected Verse, with prose trans. and introd. by David Luke, Harmondsworth, 1964. New edn 1986.
Selected Poems, ed. Christopher Middleton, trans. Michael Hamburger, David Luke, Christopher Middleton et al., London, 1983 (=Vol. 1 of Suhrkamp edn).
Poems and Epigrams, trans. Michael Hamburger, 2nd revd edn, London, 1996.
Selected Poems, trans. John Whaley, London, 1998.
Roman Elegies and The Diary, trans. David Luke, introd. Hans Rudolf Vaget, London, 1988.
Erotic Poems, trans. David Luke, introd. Hans Rudolf Vaget, Oxford, 1997.
West-Eastern Divan, trans. John Whaley, London, 1974. New edn, introd. Katharina Mommsen, Berne, 1998.
Ironhand (*Götz von Berlichingen*), adapted and trans. John Arden, London, 1965.
Egmont, trans. Michael Hamburger, in Eric Bentley (ed.), *The Classic Theater*, New York, 1958–, Vol. 2, pp. 1–91.
Egmont, in *Five German Tragedies*, trans. F. J. Lamport, Harmondsworth, 1969, pp. 105–90.
Faust: A Tragedy, trans. Walter Arndt, ed. Cyrus Hamlin, New York, 1976.
Faust: Part One, trans. and introd. David Luke, Oxford, 1991.
Faust: Part Two, trans. and introd. David Luke, Oxford, 1994.
Iphigenia in Tauris, trans. John Prudhoe, Manchester, 1966.
Torquato Tasso, trans. John Prudhoe, Manchester, 1979.
Torquato Tasso, trans. Alan Brownjohn, introd. T. J. Reed, London, 1985.
The Sorrows of Young Werther and Novella, trans. Elizabeth Mayer and Louise Bogan, foreword by W. H. Auden, New York, 1971. New edn 1984.
The Sufferings of Young Werther, trans. and introd. Michael Hulse, Harmondsworth, 1989.
Fairy Tale of the Green Snake and the Beautiful Lily, trans. D. Maclean, ed. A. McLean, Grand Rapids, Mich., 1993.
Elective Affinities, trans. and introd. R. J. Hollingdale, Harmondsworth, 1971.
Elective Affinities, trans. and introd. David Constantine, Oxford, 1994.
Wilhelm Meister's Theatrical Calling, trans. and introd. John R. Russell, Columbia, SC, 1995.
Wilhelm Meister, Apprenticeship and Travels, trans. R. O. Moon, London, 1947.
Wilhelm Meister, trans. H. M. Waidson, 6 vols, London, 1978–82.
Wilhelm Meister's Travels: Translation of the First Edition by Thomas Carlyle, introd. James Hardin, Columbia, SC, 1991.
The Autobiography of Johann Wolfgang von Goethe, trans. John Oxenford, introd. Gregor Sebba, 2 vols, London, 1971. Reprint of 1848 edn.
The Italian Journey, trans. W. H. Auden and Elizabeth Mayer, New York and London, 1962. New edn, Harmondsworth, 1970.
Goethe's Theory of Colours, trans. C. L. Eastlake, London, 1840. Reprinted London, 1967.
Goethe's Colour Theory, arranged and ed. Rupprecht Matthaei, trans. Herb Aach, London, 1971.

Early and Miscellaneous Letters of J. W. Goethe, including Letters to his Mother, ed. Christoph E. Schweitzer, Columbia, SC, 1993. Facsimile of 1884 edn.
Letters from Goethe, trans. Marianne von Herzfeld and C. M. Sym, introd. W. H. Bruford, Edinburgh, 1957.
Selections from Goethe's Letters to Frau von Stein 1776–1789, ed. and trans. Robert Browning, Columbia, SC, 1990.
Johann Peter Eckermann, *Conversations with Goethe in the Last Years of his Life*, trans. John Oxenford, ed. J. K. Moorhead, London and New York, 1971. Reprint of 1850 edn. Also reprinted London, 1930.
Eckermann's Conversations with Goethe, trans. R. O. Moon, London, 1951.
Goethe, Conversations and Encounters, ed. and trans. David Luke and Robert Pick, London, 1966.
The Sayings of Goethe, ed. and trans. D. J. Enright, London, 1996.
Goethe on Art, ed. and trans. John Gage, Berkeley and Los Angeles, 1980.
German Aesthetic and Literary Criticism: Winckelmann, Lessing, Hamann, Herder, Schiller and Goethe, ed. H. B. Nisbet, Cambridge, 1985.

4   Secondary Literature

Adler, Jeremy, *'Eine fast magische Anziehungskraft'. Goethes 'Wahlverwandtschaften' und die Chemie seiner Zeit*, Munich, 1987.
Amrine, Frederick et al. (eds), *Goethe and the Sciences: A Reappraisal*, Dordrecht and Boston, Mass., 1987.
Arens, Hans, *Kommentar zu Goethes 'Faust I'*, Heidelberg, 1982.
Arens, Hans, *Kommentar zu Goethes 'Faust II'*, Heidelberg, 1989.
Arnold, Heinz L. (ed.), *Johann Wolfgang von Goethe* (= *text + kritik Sonderband*), Munich, 1982.
Atkins, Stuart, *The Testament of Werther in Poetry and Drama*, Cambridge, Mass., 1949.
Atkins, Stuart, *Goethe's 'Faust': A Literary Analysis*, Cambridge, Mass. and London, 1958.
Atkins, Stuart, *Essays on Goethe*, ed. Jane K. Brown and Thomas P. Saine, Columbia, SC, 1995.
Bahr, Ehrhard, *Die Ironie im Spätwerk Goethes . . . Studien zum 'West-östlichen Divan', zu den 'Wanderjahren' und zu 'Faust II'*, Berlin, 1972.
Barner, Wilfried et al. (eds), *'Unser Commercium'. Goethes und Schillers Literaturpolitik*, Stuttgart, 1984.
Barnes, H. G., *Goethe's 'Die Wahlverwandtschaften': A Literary Interpretation*, Oxford, 1967.
Baumgart, Hermann, *Goethes lyrische Dichtung in ihrer Entwicklung und Bedeutung*, 3 vols, Heidelberg, 1931–9.
Beddow, Michael, *Goethe: 'Faust I'*, London, 1986.
Bell, Matthew, *Goethe's Naturalistic Anthropology: Man and Other Plants*, Oxford, 1994.
Benjamin, Walter, *Goethes 'Wahlverwandtschaften'*, in Walter Benjamin, *Gesammelte Schriften*, ed. R. Tiedemann and H. Schweppenhäuser, Vol. 1/1, Frankfurt am Main, 1974, pp. 123–201.
Bernd, Clifford et al. (eds), *Goethe Proceedings: Essays Commemorating the Goethe Sesquicentennial*, Columbia, SC, 1983.
Besch, Werner and Steinecke, Hartmut (eds), *Goethe. Neue Studien zu seinem Werk*, *Zeitschrift für deutsche Philologie. Sonderheft*, 103 (1984).
Beutler, Ernst, *Essays um Goethe*, 2 vols, Bremen, 1957. New edn in 1 vol., Frankfurt am Main, 1995.

Blackall, Eric A., *The Emergence of German as a Literary Language, 1770–1775*, Cambridge, 1959. 2nd edn, Ithaca and London, 1978.

Blackall, Eric A., *Goethe and the Novel*, Ithaca and London, 1976.

Blessin, Stefan, *Die Romane Goethes*, Königstein (Taunus), 1979.

Bode, Wilhelm, *Charlotte von Stein*, Berlin, 1910.

Boerner, Peter, *Johann Wolfgang von Goethe mit Selbstzeugnissen und Bilddokumenten*, Reinbek bei Hamburg, 1964. 30th edn, 1996.

Boerner, Peter and Johnson, Sidney (eds), *Faust through Four Centuries: Retrospect and Analysis*, Tübingen, 1989.

Bolz, Norbert (ed.), *Goethes Wahlverwandtschaften. Kritische Modelle und Diskursanalysen zum Mythos Literatur*, Hildesheim, 1981.

Borchmeyer, Dieter, *Höfische Gesellschaft und französische Revolution bei Goethe. Adliges und bürgerliches Wertsystem im Urteil der Weimarer Klassik*, Kronberg (Taunus), 1977.

Borchmeyer, Dieter, *Weimarer Klassik. Portrait einer Epoche*, Weinheim, 1994.

Borchmeyer, Dieter, *Goethe, Mozart und die 'Zauberflöte'*, Göttingen, 1994.

Borchmeyer, Dieter, ' "Götterwert der Töne". Goethes Theorie der Musik', *Freiburger Universitätsblätter*, Heft 133 (September 1996), pp. 109–34.

Bowman, Derek, *Life into Autobiography: A Study of Goethe's 'Dichtung und Wahrheit'*, Berne, 1971.

Boyd, James, *Goethe's Knowledge of English Literature*, Oxford, 1932.

Boyd, James, *Notes to Goethe's Poems*, 2 vols, Oxford, 1944 and 1949.

Boyle, Nicholas, *Goethe: Faust. Part One*, Cambridge, 1987.

Boyle, Nicholas, *Goethe: The Poet and the Age*. Vol. 1: *The Poetry of Desire*, Oxford, 1991.

Brandmeyer, Rudolf, *Goethes klassische Dramen*, Frankfurt am Main, 1987.

Brown, Jane K., *Goethe's Cyclical Narratives: 'Unterhaltungen deutscher Ausgewanderten' and 'Wilhelm Meisters Wanderjahre'*, Chapel Hill, NC, 1975.

Brown, Jane K., *Goethe's Faust: The German Tragedy*, Ithaca and London, 1986.

Brown, Jane K., Lee, Meredith and Saine, Thomas P. (eds), *Interpreting Goethe's 'Faust' Today*, Columbia, SC, 1994.

Bruford, W. H., *Germany in the Eighteenth Century: The Social Background of the Literary Revival*, Cambridge, 1935. Reprinted 1965.

Bruford, W. H., *Theatre, Drama and Audience in Goethe's Germany*, London, 1950.

Bruford, W. H., *Culture and Society in Classical Weimar 1775–1806*, Cambridge, 1962. Reprinted 1975.

Burwick, Frederick, *The Damnation of Newton: Goethe's Color Theory and Romantic Perception*, Berlin and New York, 1986.

Butler, E. M., *Byron and Goethe: Analysis of a Passion*, London, 1956.

Butler, G. P. G. et al. (eds), *German Life and Letters: Special Goethe Number*, 36 (1982/3), pp. 1–155. Essays on aspects of Goethe, esp. lyric poetry.

Butler, G. P. G. et al. (eds), *German Life and Letters*, 47 (1994), pp. 385–476. Essays on aspects of *Die Wahlverwandtschaften*.

Cape, Ruth I., *Das französische Ungewitter. Goethes Bildersprache zur französischen Revolution*, Heidelberg, 1991.

Carlson, Marvin, *Goethe and the Weimar Theater*, Ithaca and London, 1978.

Conrady, Karl O. (ed.), *Deutsche Literatur zur Zeit der Klassik*, Stuttgart, 1977.

Conrady, Karl O., *Goethe. Leben und Werk*, 2 vols, Königstein (Taunus), 1982–5.

Cunningham, Andrew and Jardine, Nicholas (eds), *Romanticism and the Sciences*, Cambridge, 1990.

David, Claude, 'Goethe und die französische Revolution', in *Deutsche Literatur und französische Revolution. Sieben Studien von Richard Brinkmann, etc.*, Göttingen, 1974, pp. 63–86.

Degering, Thomas, *Das Elend der Entsagung. Goethes 'Wilhelm Meisters Wanderjahre'*, Bonn, 1982.

Dieckmann, Liselotte, *Johann Wolfgang Goethe*, New York, 1974.

Diener, Gottfried, *'Pandora'. Zu Goethes Metaphorik. Entstehung, Epoche, Interpretation des Festspiels*, Bad Homburg, 1968.

Diener, Gottfried, *Goethes 'Lila'* . . . *Vergleichende Interpretation der drei Fassungen*, Frankfurt am Main, 1971.

Dietze, Walter, *Poesie der Humanität. Anspruch und Leistung im lyrischen Werk Johann Wolfgang Goethes*, Berlin, 1985.

Durrani, Osman, 'The Fortunes of Goethe's Nocturnal Traveller. "Über allen Gipfeln ist Ruh": The Silent Birds and the Not-so-silent Critics', *Publications of the English Goethe Society*, New Series, 53 (1984), pp. 20–40.

Ehrlich, Lothar, 'Goethes Revolutionskomödien', *Goethe-Jahrbuch*, 107 (1990), pp. 179–99.

Eissler, K. R. *Goethe: A Psychoanalytic Study 1775–1786*, 2 vols, Detroit, 1963.

Ellis, J. M., 'The Vexed Question of Egmont's Political Judgement' in *Tradition and Creation: Essays in Honour of E. M. Wilkinson*, ed. C. P. Magill et al., Leeds, 1978, pp. 116–30.

Ellis, J. M., 'Once again, Egmont's Political Judgement: A Reply', *German Life and Letters*, 34 (1980/1), pp. 344–9.

Emrich, Wilhelm, *Die Symbolik von Faust II. Sinn und Vorformen*, 3rd edn, Frankfurt am Main, 1964.

Fairley, Barker, *A Study of Goethe*, Oxford, 1947.

Fick, Monika, *Das Scheitern des Genius. Mignon und die Symbolik der Liebesgeschichten in 'Wilhelm Meisters Lehrjahren'*, Würzburg, 1987.

Fink, Karl J., *Goethe's History of Science*, Cambridge, 1991.

Flaschka, Horst, *Goethes 'Werther'. Werkkontextuelle Deskription und Analyse*, Munich, 1987.

Flemming, Willi, *Goethe und das Theater seiner Zeit*, Stuttgart, 1968.

Friedenthal, Richard, *Goethe. Sein Leben und seine Zeit*, Munich, 1963. English: *Goethe: His Life and Times*, London, 1965.

Gaier, Ulrich, *Goethes Faust-Dichtungen. Ein Kommentar. Vol. 1: Urfaust*, Stuttgart, 1989.

Ganz, P. F. (ed.), *Johann Wolfgang von Goethe.* Special number of *Oxford German Studies*, 15 (1984).

Gearey, John, *Goethe's 'Faust': The Making of Part One*, New Haven and London, 1981.

Gearey, John, *Goethe's Other Faust: The Drama, Part II*, Toronto, 1992.

Geerdts, Hans Jürgen, *Goethes Wahlverwandtschaften*, Weimar, 1958.

Gille, Klaus F., *'Wilhelm Meister' im Urteil der Zeitgenossen. Ein Beitrag zur Wirkungsgeschichte Goethes*, Assen, 1971.

Göres, Jörn (ed.), *Goethe in Italien* (Catalogue of exhibition in Goethe-Museum, Düsseldorf), Mainz, 1986.

Graham, Ilse, *Goethe: Portrait of the Artist*, Berlin and New York, 1977.

Gray, R. D., *Goethe the Alchemist: A Study of Alchemical Symbolism in Goethe's Literary and Scientific Works*, Cambridge, 1951.

Gray, R. D., *Goethe: A Critical Introduction*, Cambridge, 1967.

Grimm, Reinhold and Hermand, Jost (eds), *Our Faust? Roots and Ramifications of a German Myth*, Madison, Wis., 1987.

Grumach, Ernst, *Goethe und die Antike*, 2 vols, Berlin, 1949.

Gundolf, Friedrich, *Goethe*, Berlin, 1916.

Haas, Rosemarie, *Die Turmgesellschaft in 'Wilhelm Meisters Lehrjahren'. Zur Geschichte des Geheimbundromans und der Romantheorie im 18. Jahrhundert*, Berne and Frankfurt am Main, 1975.

Hahn, Karl-Heinz (ed.), *Goethe in Weimar. Ein Kapitel deutscher Kulturgeschichte*, Leipzig, 1986.

Haile, H. G., *Artist in Chrysalis: A Biographical Study of Goethe in Italy*, Urbana, Ill., 1973.

Hamm, Heinz, *Der Theoretiker Goethe. Grundpositionen seiner Weltanschauung, Philosophie und Kunsttheorie*, Kronberg (Taunus), 1976.

Hamm, Heinz, *Goethes 'Faust'. Werkgeschichte und Textanalyse*, Berlin, 1981.

Hartmann, Horst, *Egmont. Geschichte und Dichtung*, Berlin, 1972.

Hatfield, Henry, *Goethe: A Critical Introduction*, Cambridge, Mass., 1964.

Hecht, Wolfgang, *Goethe als Zeichner*, Leipzig, 1982.

Heller, Erich, 'Goethe and the Avoidance of Tragedy', in Heller, *The Disinherited Mind: Essays in Modern German Literature and Thought*, Cambridge, 1952, pp. 27–49.

Henkel, Arthur, *Entsagung. Eine Studie zu Goethes Altersroman*, Tübingen, 1954.

Henkel, Arthur, *Goethe-Erfahrungen. Studien und Vorträge*, Stuttgart, 1982.

Herrmann, Hans Peter, *Goethes 'Werther'. Kritik und Forschung*, Darmstadt, 1994.

Hibberd, J. L. and Nisbet, H. B. (eds), *Texte, Motive und Gestalten der Goethezeit. Festschrift für Hans Reiss*, Tübingen, 1989.

Hill, David, 'The Portrait of Lenz in *Dichtung und Wahrheit*: A Literary Perspective', in *Jakob Michael Reinhold Lenz. Studien zum Gesamtwerk*, ed. D. Hill, Opladen, 1994, pp. 222–31.

Hinderer, Walter (ed.), *Goethes Dramen. Neue Interpretationen*, Stuttgart, 1980. New edn, 1992.

Hoffmeister, Gerhart (ed.), *Goethe in Italy, 1786–1986: A Bicentennial Symposium*, Amsterdam, 1988.

Hofmann, Frank, *Goethes 'Römische Elegien'*, Stuttgart, 1993.

Hohoff, Curt, *Johann Wolfgang von Goethe. Dichtung und Leben*, Munich, 1989.

Hölscher-Lohmeyer, Dorothea, *Johann Wolfgang Goethe*, Munich, 1991.

Höpfner, Felix, *Wissenschaft wider die Zeit. Goethes Farbenlehre aus rezeptionsgeschichtlicher Sicht*, Heidelberg, 1990.

Jenkins, Ian and Sloan, Kim (eds), *Vases and Volcanoes: Sir William Hamilton and his Collection*, London, 1996.

Jeßing, Benedict, *Johann Wolfgang Goethe*, Stuttgart, 1995.

Jost, Dominik, *Deutsche Klassik: Goethes 'Römische Elegien'*, Pullach, 1974.

Kahn-Wallerstein, Carmen, *Marianne von Willemer. Goethes Suleika und ihre Welt*, Berne, 1961.

Kaiser, Gerhard, *Geschichte der deutschen Lyrik von Goethe bis Heine. Ein Grundriß in Interpretationen*, 3 vols, Frankfurt am Main, 1988.

Kaus, Rainer J., *Der Fall Goethe – ein deutscher Fall. Eine psychoanalytische Studie*, Heidelberg, 1994.

Keller, Werner, *Goethes dichterische Bildlichkeit. Eine Grundlegung*, Munich, 1972.

Keller, Werner (ed.), *Aufsätze zu Goethes 'Faust I'*, Darmstadt, 1974.

Keller, Werner (ed.), *Aufsätze zu Goethes 'Faust II'*, Darmstadt, 1991.

Kommerell, Max, *Gedanken über Gedichte*, 2nd edn, Frankfurt am Main, 1956.

Korff, H. A., *Goethe im Bildwandel seiner Lyrik*, 2 vols, Leipzig, 1958.

Krauß, Werner, 'Goethe und die französische Revolution', *Goethe-Jahrbuch*, 94 (1977), pp. 127–36.

Kriegleder, Wynfried, 'Wilhelm Meisters Amerika. Das Bild der vereinigten Staaten in den *Wanderjahren*', *Jahrbuch des Wiener Goethe-Vereins*, 95 (1991), pp. 15–31.

Kuhn, Dorothea, *Empirische und ideelle Wirklichkeit. Studien über Goethes Kritik des französischen Akademiestreites*, Cologne, 1967.

Lamport, F. J., *A Student's Guide to Goethe*, London, 1971.

Lamport, F. J., *German Classical Drama*, Cambridge, 1990.

Lange, Victor (ed.), *Goethe: A Collection of Critical Essays*, Englewood Cliffs, NJ, 1968.

Larkin, Edward T., *War in Goethe's Writings: Representation and Assessment*, Lewiston, NY, 1992.

Lee, Meredith, *Studies in Goethe's Lyric Cycles*, Chapel Hill, NC, 1978.

Lemmel, Monika, *Poetologie in Goethes West-östlichem Divan*, Heidelberg, 1987.

Leppmann, Wolfgang, *The German Image of Goethe*, Oxford, 1961.

Lewes, G. H., *The Life and Works of Goethe*, 2 vols, London, 1855. New edn, London, 1949.

Lillyman, W. J. (ed.), *Goethe's Narrative Fiction: The Irvine Goethe Symposium*, Berlin, 1983.

Lohmeyer, Dorothea, *Faust und die Welt. Der zweite Teil der Dichtung*, Munich, 1975.

Lohner, Edgar (ed.), *Studien zum West-östlichen Divan Goethes*, Darmstadt, 1971.

Lohner, Edgar (ed.), *Interpretationen zum West-östlichen Divan Goethes*, Darmstadt, 1973.

Lukács, Georg, *Goethe und seine Zeit*, Berne, 1947. English: *Goethe and his Age*, London, 1968.

Lützeler, Paul M. and McLeod, James E. (eds), *Goethes Erzählwerk. Interpretationen*, Stuttgart, 1985.

Mandelkow, Karl Robert (ed.), *Goethe im Urteil seiner Kritiker. Dokumente zur Wirkungsgeschichte Goethes in Deutschland*, 4 vols, Munich, 1975–84.

Mandelkow, Karl Robert, *Goethe in Deutschland. Rezeptionsgeschichte eines Klassikers*, 2 vols, Munich, 1980–9.

Mason, Eudo C., *Goethe's 'Faust': Its Genesis and Purport*, Berkeley and Los Angeles, 1967.

Mayer, Hans (ed.), *Goethe im zwanzigsten Jahrhundert. Spiegelungen und Deutungen*, Hamburg, 1967.

Mommsen, Katharina, *Goethe und 1001 Nacht*, Berlin, 1960.

Mommsen, Katharina, *Natur- und Fabelreich in Faust II*, Berlin, 1968.

Mommsen, Katharina, *Goethe und die arabische Welt*, Frankfurt am Main, 1988.

Mommsen, Wilhelm, *Die politischen Anschauungen Goethes*, Stuttgart, 1948.

Morgan, Peter, *The Critical Idyll: Traditional Values and the French Revolution in Goethe's 'Hermann und Dorothea'*, Columbia, SC, 1990.

Müller-Blattau, Joseph, *Goethe und die Meister der Musik*, Stuttgart, 1969.

Müller-Seidel, Walter, *Die Geschichtlichkeit der deutschen Klassik. Literatur und Denkformen um 1800*, Stuttgart, 1983.

Nettl, Paul, *Goethe und Mozart*, Esslingen, 1949.

Nisbet, H. B., *'Die Wahlverwandtschaften*: Explanation and its Limits', *Deutsche Vierteljahrsschrift für Literaturwissenschaft und Geistesgeschichte*, 43 (1969), pp. 458–86.

Nisbet, H. B., *Goethe and the Scientific Tradition*, London, 1972.

Oppenheimer, Ernst, *Goethe's Poetry for Occasions*, Toronto, 1974.

Palencia-Roth, Michael (ed.), *Perspectives on Faust*, Chalfont St Giles, 1983 (=*Journal of European Studies*, 13, 1983, pp. 1–180).

Pascal, Roy, *The German Sturm und Drang*, Manchester, 1953.

Peacock, Ronald, *Goethe's Major Plays*, Manchester, 1959.

Rasch, Wolfdietrich, *'Torquato Tasso'. Die Tragödie des Dichters*, Stuttgart, 1954.

Rasch, Wolfdietrich, *Goethes 'Iphigenie auf Tauris' als Drama der Autonomie*, Munich, 1979.

Reed, T. J., *The Classical Centre: Goethe and Weimar, 1775–1832*, London and New York, 1980. New edn, Oxford, 1986.

Reed, T. J., *Goethe*, Oxford, 1984. New edn, Oxford, 1998.

Reich-Ranicki, Marcel (ed.), *Johann Wolfgang Goethe. Verweile doch. 111 Gedichte mit Interpretationen*, Frankfurt am Main and Leipzig, 1992.

Reiss, Hans S., *Goethes Romane*, Berne, 1963. English: *Goethe's Novels*, London, 1969.

Reiss, Hans S. (ed.), *Goethe und die Tradition*, Frankfurt am Main, 1972.

Robertson, J. G., *The Life and Works of Goethe*, London, 1932.

Robson-Scott, W. D., *The Younger Goethe and the Visual Arts*, Cambridge, 1981.

Rösch, Ewald (ed.), *Goethes Roman 'Die Wahlverwandtschaften'*, Darmstadt, 1975.

Saine, Thomas P., *Black Bread – White Bread: German Intellectuals and the French Revolution*, Columbia, SC, 1988.

Sauder, Gerhard, *Empfindsamkeit*, 2 vols, Stuttgart, 1974–80.

Schadewaldt, Wolfgang, *Goethestudien*, Zürich and Stuttgart, 1963.
Scherpe, Klaus, *Werther und Wertherwirkung. Zum Syndrom bürgerlicher Gesellschaftsordnung im 18. Jahrhundert*, Bad Homburg, 1970.
Schlaffer, Hannelore, *'Wilhelm Meister'. Das Ende der Kunst und die Wiederkehr des Mythos*, Stuttgart, 1980.
Schlaffer, Heinz, *Faust, Zweiter Teil. Die Allegorie des 19. Jahrhunderts*, Stuttgart, 1981.
Schlechta, Karl, *Goethes Wilhelm Meister*, Frankfurt am Main, 1953. 2nd edn, 1985.
Schlütter, Hans Jürgen, *Goethes Sonette. Anregung, Entstehung, Intention*, Bad Homburg, 1969.
Schöne, Albrecht, *Götterzeichen, Liebeszauber, Satanskult. Neue Einblicke in alte Goethetexte*, Munich, 1982.
Schöne, Albrecht, *Goethes Farbentheologie*, Munich, 1987.
Schönherr, Hartmut, *Einheit und Werden. Goethes Newton-Polemik als systematische Konsequenz seiner Naturkonzeption*, Würzburg, 1993.
Schrimpf, Hans-Joachim, *Das Weltbild des späten Goethe*, Stuttgart, 1956.
Schrimpf, Hans-Joachim, *Goethes Begriff der Weltliteratur*, Stuttgart, 1968.
Schwan, Werner, *Goethes 'Wahlverwandtschaften'. Das nicht erreichte Soziale*, Munich, 1983.
Schwarzbauer, Franz, *Die Xenien. Studien zur Vorgeschichte der deutschen Klassik*, Stuttgart, 1993.
Schwerte, Hans, *Faust und das Faustische. Ein Kapitel deutscher Ideologie*, Stuttgart, 1962.
Sengle, Friedrich, *Neues zu Goethe. Essays und Vorträge*, Stuttgart, 1989.
Sengle, Friedrich, *Das Genie und sein Fürst. Die Geschichte der Lebensgemeinschaft Goethes mit dem Herzog Carl August von Sachsen-Weimar-Eisenach*, Stuttgart and Weimar, 1993.
Sepper, Dennis L., *Goethe contra Newton: Polemics and the New Project for a Science of Color*, Cambridge, 1988.
Spaethling, Robert, *Music and Mozart in the Life of Goethe*, Columbia, SC, 1987.
Stahl, E. L., *Goethe: Iphigenie auf Tauris*, London, 1961.
Staiger, Emil, *Goethe*, 3 vols, Zürich, 1952–9.
Stammen, Theo, *Goethe und die französische Revolution. Eine Interpretation der 'natürlichen Tochter'*, Munich, 1966.
Stephenson, R. H., *Goethe's Wisdom Literature: A Study in Aesthetic Transmutation*, Berne, 1983.
Stephenson, R. H., *Goethe's Conception of Knowledge and Science*, Edinburgh, 1995.
Stern, J. P., 'On Goethe's "Pandora"', *London German Studies*, 2 (1983), pp. 31–49.
Stöcklein, Paul, *Wege zum späten Goethe*, 2nd edn, Hamburg, 1960.
Strich, Fritz, *Goethe and World Literature*, London, 1949.
Swales, M. W., 'A Questionable Politician: On the Ending of Goethe's *Egmont*', *Modern Language Review*, 66 (1971), pp. 832–40.
Swales, M. W., *The Sorrows of Young Werther*, Cambridge, 1987.
Thielicke, Helmut, *Goethe und das Christentum*, Munich, 1982.
Trevelyan, Humphry, *Goethe and the Greeks*, Cambridge, 1941. New edn, 1981.
Tümmler, Hans, *Goethe als Staatsmann*, Göttingen, 1976.
Vaget, Hans Rudolf, *Goethe – Der Mann von 60 Jahren*, Königstein (Taunus), 1982.
Vietor, Karl, *Goethe. Dichtung – Wissenschaft – Weltbild*, Berne, 1949. English: *Goethe the Poet*, Cambridge, MA, 1949; *Goethe the Thinker*, Cambridge, Mass., 1950.
Vincent, Deirdre, *Werther's Goethe and the Game of Literary Creativity*, Toronto, 1992.
Weimar, Klaus, *Goethes Gedichte 1769–1775. Interpretationen zu einem Anfang*, Paderborn, 1984.
Wellbery, David E., *The Specular Moment: Goethe's Early Lyric and the Beginnings of Romanticism*, Stanford, CA, 1996.
Wells, George A., *Goethe and the Development of Science, 1750–1900*, Alphen aan den Rijn, 1978.
Wells, George A., 'Critical Issues concerning Goethe's *Egmont*', *German Life and Letters*, 32 (1978–9), pp. 301–7.

Wilkinson, E. M., 'The Relation of Form and Meaning in Goethe's *Egmont*', in Wilkinson and Willoughby, *Goethe: Poet and Thinker*, London, 1962, pp. 55–74.

Wilkinson, E. M. (ed.), *Goethe Revisited: A Collection of Essays*, London and New York, 1984.

Wilkinson, E. M. and Willoughby, L. A., *Goethe: Poet and Thinker*, London, 1962.

Williams, John R., 'Goethe's "An den Mond": Controversy and Criticism', *German Life and Letters*, 28 (1975), pp. 348–60.

Williams, John R., 'Goethe: The Crisis of the Lyric Poet?', *Modern Language Review*, 78 (1983), pp. 91–102.

Williams, John R., 'Die Rache der Kraniche. Goethe, *Faust II* und die Julirevolution', *Zeitschrift für deutsche Philologie*, 103 (1984), pp. 105–27.

Williams, John R., *Goethe's 'Faust'*, London, 1987.

Wilson, W. Daniel, *Geheimräte gegen Geheimbünde. Ein unbekanntes Kapitel der klassisch-romantischen Geschichte Weimars*, Stuttgart, 1991.

Wittkowski, Wolfgang (ed.), *Goethe im Kontext. Kunst und Humanität, Naturwissenschaft und Politik von der Aufklärung bis zur Restauration. Ein Symposium*, Tübingen, 1984.

Wittkowski, Wolfgang (ed.), *Verlorene Klassik? Ein Symposium*, Tübingen, 1986.

Wittkowski, Wolfgang (ed.), *Revolution und Autonomie. Deutsche Autonomieästhetik im Zeitalter der französischen Revolution. Ein Symposium*, Tübingen, 1990.

Wünsch, Marianne, *Der Strukturwandel in der Lyrik Goethes*, Stuttgart, 1975.

Zabka, Thomas, *Faust II – Das Klassische und das Romantische. Goethes 'Eingriff in die neueste Literatur'*, Tübingen, 1993.

Zimmermann, R. C., *Das Weltbild des jungen Goethe. Studien zur hermetischen Tradition des deutschen 18. Jahrhunderts*, 2 vols, Munich, 1969–79.

General Index

Index to Goethe's Works